KU-329-936

WITHDRAWN

EASTLEIGH COLLEGE LIBRARY

Telephone: 0703 326326 Ext. 227

PLEASE RETURN OR RENEW THIS LOAN ON OR
BEFORE THE LATEST DATE STAMPED BELOW

FOR LIBRARY
USE ONLY

EASTLEIGH COLLEGE OF F E

03138

Author	Shelf Number
HALL, H Duncan	940 ·531

E.58A.

WITHDRAWN FROM
THE LIBRARY

UNIVERSITY OF
WINCHESTER

KA 0198768 2

HISTORY OF
THE SECOND WORLD WAR
UNITED KINGDOM CIVIL SERIES
Edited by Sir Keith Hancock

WAR PRODUCTION SERIES
Directed by M. M. Postan

The authors of the Civil Histories have been given
free access to official documents. They and the editor
are alone responsible for the statements made
and the views expressed.

NORTH AMERICAN SUPPLY

BY

H. DUNCAN HALL

Author of *The British Commonwealth of Nations*;
Mandates, Dependencies and Trusteeship; etc.

EASTLEIGH TECHNICAL COLLEGE
LIBRARY

LONDON: 1955

HER MAJESTY'S STATIONERY OFFICE

AND

LONGMANS, GREEN AND CO

03138

First published 1955

Crown Copyright Reserved

HER MAJESTY'S STATIONERY OFFICE

London: York House, Kingsway, W.C.2 & 423 Oxford Street, W.1
Edinburgh: 13a Castle Street   Cardiff: 109 St. Mary Street
Manchester: 39 King Street   Bristol: Tower Lane
Birmingham: 2 Edmund Street   Belfast: 80 Chichester Street

LONGMANS, GREEN AND CO LTD
6 and 7 Clifford Street, London, W.1
Boston House, Strand Street, Cape Town
531 Little Collins Street, Melbourne

LONGMANS, GREEN AND CO INC
55 Fifth Avenue, New York, 3

LONGMANS, GREEN AND CO
20 Cranfield Road, Toronto, 16

ORIENT LONGMANS, LTD
Calcutta, Bombay, Madras
Delhi, Vijayawada, Dacca

Price £1 15s. od. net

KING ALFRED'S COLLEGE
WINCHESTER

940.
5342
HIS

0198768 2

Printed in Great Britain under the authority of H.M. Stationery Office
by Sanders Phillips & Co. Ltd., London, S.W.9

CONTENTS

CONTENTS

APPENDICES

LIST OF TABLES

LIST OF ABBREVIATIONS

B.P.C.	British Purchasing Commission.
B.S.C.	British Supply Council.
C.M.A.B.	Combined Munitions Assignments Board
C.M.P.	Controlled Materials Plan.
C.O.S.S.A.C.	Chief of Staff to the Supreme Allied Commander.
C.P.R.B.	Combined Production and Resources Board.
C.R.M.B.	Combined Raw Materials Board.
F.E.A.	Foreign Economic Administration.
J.A.C.	Joint Aircraft Committee.
L.C.I.	Landing Craft Infantry.
L.C.T.	Landing Craft Tank.
L.S.T.	Landing Ship Tank.
M.A.C.	Munitions Assignments Committee.
M.A.P.	Ministry of Aircraft Production.
N.D.A.C.	National Defence Advisory Committee.
O.P.M.	Office of Production Management.
P.M.	Prime Minister.
R.A.A.F.	Royal Australian Air Force.
R.A.F.	Royal Air Force.
R.C.A.F.	Royal Canadian Air Force.
R.F.C.	Reconstruction Finance Corporation.
R.N.Z.A.F.	Royal New Zealand Air Force.
S.A.A.	Small arms ammunition.
S.H.A.E.F.	Supreme Headquarters Allied Expeditionary Force.
S.P.A.B.	Supply Priorities and Allocation Board.
U.N.R.R.A.	United Nations Relief and Rehabilitation Administration.
W.P.B.	War Production Board.

PREFACE

THIS book is a unit in a series within a series. It falls within the series of the history of war production, the scope of which is explained in the preface to Professor M. M. Postan's *British War Production*. The scope and conditions governing the writing of the British Civil Histories are explained by the General Editor, Sir Keith Hancock, in his preface to *British War Economy*.

This history of North American Supply is based on the British official records preserved in London, Washington and Ottawa. It gives an account, from the British records only, of a section of the story of American-British-Canadian combination during the war. Thus it is in no sense a combined history. Such a history cannot yet be written, since any complete history of British supply from North America will have to wait on the publication of accounts based on the official war records of Canada and the United States. Use has been made—with the consent of the Canadian and American Governments—of combined documents, i.e. those common to the three countries.

Some use has been made of publications dealing with the war years, which have appeared so far in the United States and Canada[1], where they seemed to throw additional light on the material in the British records. In the case of books by American or Canadian authors citations are made from the American or Canadian editions; and from the English editions in the case of books by British authors.

A history of North American supply was called for in the series on British war production. This was not only because in this war, more than at any previous time, British war industry was dependent upon imported raw materials; but also because of the greater degree of dependence of the United Kingdom on finished weapons and war-stores manufactured across the Atlantic. The rate and volume of production in the United Kingdom, even the kind and types of weapons manufactured, were affected in an important measure by the import of machine tools from the United States and later by the procurement—first by cash purchase and then by lend-lease and mutual aid—of substantial quantities of finished munitions from North America. When measured statistically the degree of dependence of the United Kingdom on munitions from across the Atlantic was less than perhaps the public in Canada and the United States imagined. In Chapter I figures are given which show that for the entire period of the war the United Kingdom supplied about seventy per cent. of the munitions required by the British Commonwealth of Nations, as

---

[1] i.e. up to the end of 1951.

against about ten per cent. supplied by Canada and seventeen per cent. supplied by the United States. But no general percentages of this kind could measure the great importance to British war production of particular supplies, such as the machine tools purchased from the United States in 1939 and 1940, or the merchant ships obtained late in the war under lend-lease.

A part only of the very wide field of North American supply is covered in this volume. It excludes, for example, such important aspects as petroleum and food supplies, and the shipment of supplies by sea to the United Kingdom. Its field of concentration is supply from North America which directly affected British war production. Thus it deals with the problems and policies governing the supply of machine tools, raw materials, ground army supply, aircraft, naval supply and ships. Since the emphasis is upon problems and policies, no attempt is made to give any detailed review of the actual import of each of these kinds of supply. Nor is the space given to each necessarily in proportion to its importance. Thus the space given to raw materials—of which North America was a large supplier—is kept at a minimum, since this forms the subject of a separate history in the Civil Series.[1] It has to be remembered also that a work of this kind is a vast act of compression, and in the process many things that seemed to bulk very large at the time were inevitably omitted; others that could easily be summarised tended to receive less space than more recalcitrant subjects which could not be compressed beyond a certain point save at the expense of clarity. Some of the themes touched on lightly in this book—such as the Combined Boards, scientific collaboration, supply from the Eastern Hemisphere—are treated in a later volume in this series, entitled *Studies of Overseas Supply*.

Although, both in subject and area, the book covers only a part of the field of overseas supply its scope nevertheless is very wide. Its theme touched a number of departments and its writing involved the risk of trespass upon the ground of other historians. Apart from the direct interest of the Supply and Service Ministries, supply from North America raised issues which affected the foreign policy of the United Kingdom, its relations with the other members of the British Commonwealth of Nations, its financial policy, its export trade and its sea transport. Thus the book made some use of portions of the records of ten Government Departments; and it has had the benefit of being read and commented upon in each of them.

The problem of the design and construction of a book covering such a wide field, and dealing with so many particular kinds of supply, was not easy to solve. One extreme to be avoided was the writing of a dry statistical chronicle focused upon the actual movement of supplies across the Atlantic in the different stages of the war.

---

[1] J. Hurstfield, *The Control of Raw Materials* (London: H.M.S.O., 1953).

Such a volume would not have been a real history, but, in Lord Acton's phrase, merely a 'rope of sand'. Thus it would have had little to say of the period up to Pearl Harbour, since until late in 1941 the flow of munitions from the United States and Canada had hardly become more than a trickle. Yet this period, though poor in supplies, was rich in problems; and it occupies well over half the pages of the present book.

Equally to be avoided was any attempt to use as a central theme the development of British overseas administration. The instructions which I received when the book was commissioned were to 'concentrate on the economic and political aspects of supply problems and deal as briefly as possible with the organisation of the Supply Missions'. The emphasis was to be therefore on problems. This meant the more important longer-term problems, and not their attendant multitude of small problems, which are the everyday business of the government official. At each stage of the war supply from overseas was beset by certain general problems, which from the high level of the policy-makers stood out as major features of the war's landscape. These were matters which preoccupied the minds of the higher officials of a number of departments at particular points of time. It was thus not possible to write the history on any sectional departmental basis. From the point of view of the Government, and therefore of the historian, what mattered was how such problems originally took shape; and how they were solved, or brushed aside by the course of events. The later stages of the detailed application of a solution were of minor historical interest.

These instructions emphasised the need of a broad treatment of the theme. Rather more space is given to the wider backgrounds of the war than might have been expected in a book dealing with a special theme. The justification for this must be not merely the scope of the volume but also its special interest to North America.

The difficulty of writing a book was increased by the late date at which it was begun. It was not commissioned finally until the end of 1947. Thus I did not have the advantage, possessed by some of the writers in the Civil Series, of being able to begin work on the subject at an early date and of keeping it under continuous observation throughout the later stages of the war. The book would have benefited greatly if it could have been rooted in an earlier study of the British supply organisation in Washington, undertaken when that organisation was still in full swing. In no section of war history did the jungle take over more swiftly than in the case of overseas supply. The British and Combined organisations overseas were already being demobilised when the first step towards a war history was taken. Each of the Missions in Washington (and later in Ottawa) was asked to appoint an official to prepare, under my general direction, a detailed history of the Mission. We were in general familiar only with our particular area of one of the many sides of the mountain. In nearly all cases during the war we had been working well down the slopes, shut off from general views by the thickets of detail that crowded these lower levels. Meanwhile the Missions were rapidly dispersing their staffs and winding up their business. By the time these primary departmental narratives were under way most of the higher officials with a wide view of the past had already returned to the United Kingdom. Archives, left without staffs, were falling into disorder and drifting into dead storage. The instructions of the writers of the primary narratives were to work from the departmental records in Washington. They did not have the advantage of access to the files of their London departments, nor even to the central files of the British Embassy in Washington; nor in practice could they make use of the files of the British Supply Council in Washington.

All these files, both in London and Washington, were thrown open to me freely when I took over finally the task of writing this book after the primary narratives had been finished. I had the advantage of being able to work for several months of each year, from 1945 to 1951, on the departmental records in London, especially on the central records of the Cabinet Office. In the main, however, the book was written in Washington. There were both advantages and disadvantages in this arrangement. One advantage was that the greater bulk of the records was available in Washington and in a somewhat more convenient and concentrated form. Another advantage was that in this war the factors governing supply from North America were less under the direct control of the United Kingdom than in 1914–18. The disadvantage was that a book written in Washington tended inevitably to look at problems from the standpoint of the man on the spot in Washington and not enough from that of the departments in London. On the other hand this loss of central perspective was compensated by the greater prominence that could be given to the experience of the man on the spot whose judgement was often a decisive factor in the development of British supply policies. This itself was indirectly a factor in determining where the book should be written. For the traditional British policy of trusting the man on the spot, combined with the traditional American reluctance to devolve power on its representatives abroad, made it inevitable that decisions on North American supply, as well as the combined British-American machinery of the second half of the war, should be centred more in Washington than in London.

The vantage ground from which the book was written tended thus to become the archives of the British Supply Council in North America. This body met weekly, from the beginning of 1941 to the end of the war, in the Willard Hotel in Washington. Though its importance fluctuated somewhat from time to time, it remained the principal forum in which the heads of all the British Missions (and a representative of the Canadian Government) met to co-ordinate their work, to look at the general problems of interest to more than one Mission, and to restore the sense of perspective which was in constant danger of being disturbed by the daily pressures within the separate Missions.

The shortcomings of the book are mine; so also are the judgements, which are made on my own responsibility. The shortcomings are not due to any lack of access to data, for that was without restriction; they are due rather to the enormous mass of the documentation and the maze of problems through which some sort of way had to be found. The defects of the book would have been greater but for the extremely valuable help which was given to me, both before and during the stage of official comment, by many officials whom I wish to thank though I cannot mention them by name. Since the writing of a history from the primary jungles of government records was a new experience, may I be permitted to pay a personal tribute, from the historian's point of view, to the value of the methods used in the writing of the Civil Series—the unfettered responsibility placed upon the author, his free access to sources, and perhaps most of all the objective and helpful criticism offered to him by experienced and disinterested officials who played their parts in the events described.

Since this is a book centred largely on the United States where officials are freely named in public, it should be explained that the author has observed the British principle of the responsibility to Parliament of the Ministers of the Crown in charge of the Departments of Government and the anonymity of the officials serving under those Ministers. In most cases officials, whether permanent or temporary civil servants, have been indicated by their offices. Departures from this rule have been made only in the case of a few officials who were well known by name to the public in the United States and Canada, where they were serving in a representative capacity, in the position, as it were, of ambassadors of supply.

I would like to express my indebtedness to the various authors of the histories of the British Missions in Washington, in particular to Mr. Victor Bates, Mr. L. G. Chance, Mr. Douglas Campbell, Mr. G. R. Ffennell, Mr. H. D. Hodgkinson, Mr. Eugene Melville, Mr. N. M. Munro and Mr. Henry Tetlow. Without their work, and that of many other officials who contributed important memoranda or narratives on the areas of their special experience, or who gave me data and guidance orally, this book would have been far more difficult to write.

I am indebted to my assistant in London, Mr. Christopher C. Wrigley. Though he came late upon the scene, when the book was far advanced, he showed himself at once as a gifted historian. He has had an important hand in more than one of the chapters of this book and became co-author with me of *Studies of Overseas Supply* which follows it in this series. The book was fortunate in passing through the skilled hands of Miss Irene Bains before it reached the printers. My thanks are due also to my secretary, Miss Helen Harrison, whose conscientiousness and devotion have left their mark on the book. The author's thanks are due also to the Bureau of International Research of Harvard University and Radcliffe College which, by a research grant made in 1940, helped him to begin a study of the early phases of British-American war-time collaboration. I am indebted also to Mr Hubert Penson, C.M.G., for suggestions regarding the structure of this book.

H. DUNCAN HALL

Washington, D.C.

CHAPTER I

MUNITIONS SUPPLY FROM CANADA: THE FIRST PHASE

(i)

Defence Supply within the British Commonwealth

For the British Commonwealth at war, as in peace, overseas supply is a two-way traffic. For the Island, raw materials and food from many parts of the world, supplemented by machine tools and some munitions from North America, have been a condition of survival and victory in the world wars of the twentieth century; for the members of the Commonwealth overseas Britain has been the principal source of armaments with local contributions of increasing importance in war-time. This volume is concerned with the first rather than the second of these two themes. The second belongs rather to the war histories of the overseas members of the Commonwealth.

The supply relations of the members of the British Commonwealth during the war had a long historical background. Since the beginning of the century—certainly after the Imperial Defence Conference of 1909—the defence chiefs of the different countries had pursued steadily the goal of full co-ordination in defence matters. Unity was sought in methods of training, in tactics, in military and naval doctrine, and in the use, as far as possible, throughout the Commonwealth of standardised equipment and weapons. What this meant in practice was illustrated when the forces of many parts of the Commonwealth—the United Kingdom, India, Australia, New Zealand and South Africa—intermeshed in North Africa in 1940 to form a single armed force. They used weapons and equipment of the same calibre and design. For two generations it had been a cardinal principle of Commonwealth defence that, throughout the Commonwealth, arms, ammunition and important equipment should be standardised and interchangeable. In accordance with that principle all orders placed by the United Kingdom in other Commonwealth countries were for the standardised British types. If London opposed as long as possible the adoption of American types, it was not merely because of the supply difficulties which a multiplicity of types would cause in the armed forces of the United Kingdom, but also because of the inroads which might be made into a long-standing principle of Commonwealth defence.

Co-operation in defence matters was at least as much in the interest of the overseas members of the Commonwealth as it was in the interest of Britain. For Britain, as the industrial heart of the Commonwealth, was its arsenal. It was to Britain that the overseas members of the Commonwealth looked for their main supplies of armaments for defence by land, sea and air. In the thirties there were only two Dominions that had reached a level of industrial development which would enable them to supplement to any appreciable degree the armaments produced in the United Kingdom. These were Canada and to a lesser extent Australia.[1] Neither country had a munitions industry apart from one or two government arsenals. Neither had the necessary specialised machine tools, nor the 'know-how', nor enough skilled labour. But they had potential enough to count if steps could be taken to develop it in time. The steps included the furnishing from Britain of blueprints, technicians, manufacturing data, machine tools, special equipment, components, even in some cases materials such as aluminium.

Not less important were the orders, backed often by capital assistance, necessary to get production under way in the outer parts of the Commonwealth. The political situation was such that if these technical and financial motive forces were to be applied in time, it was Britain that had to apply them in one form or another. In the dollar area its power to finance development was subject to strict limitations.

No steps towards exploring overseas war potential could be expected before the launching of the British rearmament programme. Until munitions capacity in the United Kingdom itself began to be used to an appreciable degree, there could be no question of placing large-scale orders abroad since there were in fact insufficient orders available even for educational purposes in the United Kingdom. In none of the Dominions was the capacity of its own government arsenals enough to supply more than a limited part of its local requirements. Thus, before the war, far from being a source of additional war supplies, the Dominions were dependent on the United Kingdom production for the bulk of their own military requirements. (Further reference is made to this point in the next chapter.) Canada was no exception, for the capacity of her one government arsenal was very limited. Moreover since the First World War Canada's defence relations with the United Kingdom were less close than those of Australia and New Zealand. Canada had only indirect contact with the Principal Supply Officers' Committee in London and no com-

---

[1] Reference is made in *Studies of Overseas Supply* to munitions production in Australia.

parable organisation of her own, so that no study had been made of her resources for war production.

At the outset of this account attention must be called to the matter of scale. In the first fifteen months of the war the United Kingdom supplied 90·7 per cent. (in terms of value) of British Commonwealth supplies of munitions from all sources. Canada supplied 2·6 per cent., the rest of the Commonwealth 1·1 per cent., and purchases in the United States 5·6 per cent. The proportions for the entire period of the war were United Kingdom 69·5 per cent., Canada 7·9 per cent., the rest of the Commonwealth 1·6 per cent., whilst 3·7 per cent. was purchased from the United States and 17·3 per cent. was supplied by them under lend-lease.[1]

With the beginning of serious rearmament, however, the British Government devoted some attention to the possibility that the overseas members of the Commonwealth, particularly Canada and Australia, might develop their industrial potential as a supplementary source of munitions supply, and in April 1936 the Chief of the Imperial General Staff, in a letter to his colleagues in Canada and Australia, referred to the investigation then proceeding into the munitions capacity of United Kingdom industry and asked if they would initiate some enquiries into the possibility of supplementing this by the production of certain items in their respective countries. This approach was made through ordinary service channels and not directly to the Dominion Governments. It was purely exploratory and was intended to provide data for the discussion of defence problems at the forthcoming Imperial Conference in May 1937.

Meanwhile the news of British rearmament had aroused the interest of Canadian industrialists, several of whom offered their services to the War Office and the Air Ministry during the course of 1936. While the War Office would have liked to see munitions factories developed in Canada as a reserve in case of war, it was not in a position to place orders there during the initial rearmament period. As far as immediate requirements were concerned, quicker and cheaper production could in nearly every case be obtained from firms in the United Kingdom. Thus, although all the offers were carefully considered and the position explained to the Canadians, only one offer was accepted: the National Steel Car Corporation, of Hamilton, Ontario, under the direction of Mr. Robert J. Magor, secured an order for 50,000 3·7-inch anti-aircraft shells, which incidentally was carried out in good time according to the terms of the contract. This shell plant was later expanded and became the first of several major and highly efficient units in Canada.

---

[1] Table by Professor R. G. D. Allen quoted in W. K. Hancock and M. M. Gowing, *British War Economy* (London: His Majesty's Stationery Office, 1949), p. 373. See below, Chapter X, The Mutual Aid Sector.

There was, however, an important exception to the general statement that immediate requirements could best be met by industry at home. At this stage of war preparation the most urgent requirements were related to air defence, and the virtual non-existence of modern anti-aircraft guns was regarded as the most serious weakness in Britain's war equipment. The possibility of reducing the deficit by overseas purchase was therefore considered; even a few guns would help if they could be got immediately without waiting on production. There was of course no question of getting such articles 'off the shelf' in Canada or of the production of these highly complicated equipments there within the near future. The War Office turned perforce to the United States as the only country that might be able to spare some guns. The United States War Department, however, was unable to help, partly for political reasons and partly because it had no guns to spare. Anti-aircraft guns were being manufactured only in small numbers and in Government arsenals. The War Department, however, was itself beginning to turn to commercial firms and it was ready to permit such firms to produce for the British Government American models, though it was not encouraging as regards equipments of British design. But this meant waiting. Large orders would have to be placed and no guns would result for at least eighteen months. At the end of January 1937 the idea of ordering anti-aircraft guns in the United States was abandoned on the recommendation of the Committee of Imperial Defence. It was hoped that orders might soon be placed in Canada, as a result of the discussions which were about to take place in the Imperial Conference. But the Conference, as indicated below, did not open up any immediate prospect of munitions supply from Canada, and in any case orders there could only have produced long-term benefits. Meanwhile the lack of anti-aircraft guns was becoming steadily more serious; the British 3·7-inch gun would not come into production until January 1938 and the 4·5-inch not until March. The War Office was instructed to give anti-aircraft defence absolute priority over all other forms of war material, and in November 1937 the question was again raised whether a few guns could not be obtained 'off the shelf' from the United States—even if this meant a direct approach to the President himself. The War Department, however, still had no guns to spare and the Embassy advised that there was little chance of any result from an appeal to the President.

(ii)

The Imperial Conference of 1937 and the Sequel

The assembly of the Dominion Ministers in London for the Imperial Conference in May 1937 marks the beginning of a new stage in the history of the supply relations between Great Britain and the rest of the Commonwealth. The practical results of the Conference in this sphere were meagre, yet the mere fact that the Conference was to meet with defence high on its agenda forced departments to look again more closely at possibilities in the Dominions. There were, as the Principal Supply Officers' Committee pointed out, two separate questions to be considered. First, could Canada contribute towards the short-term re-equipment and expansion of the British armed forces which was then being undertaken in what was spoken of as the peace-time Deficiency Programme? The deficiency programme was planned within narrow limits both of time and of finance. There was no Canadian munitions industry in being outside the small Dominion arsenal; and if new capacity had to be created it was better to do it in Britain than in Canada, where industry as a whole was undeveloped and costs were high. The munitions organisation in the United Kingdom, in fact, was the only 'sure basis for the carrying through of the programme in the time proposed'.

There remained, however, the larger question of establishing a war potential in Canada. The British Government felt that there were strong reasons for encouraging any step which the Canadian Government might feel able to take to this end. Assuming that the first shock of battle brought no decisive result, victory would ultimately be with the side possessing the larger war potential. It was certain that Service requirements would greatly exceed, at the outset at least, the capacity of the war industries in the United Kingdom, and these industries were liable to dislocation by air attack, from which industries in Canada and other Dominions would be immune. With these considerations in mind the British Government recommended to the Conference that the Dominions should take steps to build up capacity for munitions production, with the immediate object of reducing their dependence on the United Kingdom for the supply of munitions for their own forces. If this were done the Home Government would hope to assist development by considering the allocation of a part of its own programme to the new plant thus created.

This proposal was submitted to the Committee on Munitions and

Food Supplies set up by the Conference on 25th May 1937. But before discussing its reception a word may be said about the political background of the Conference as a whole. At the outset the attitude of the Dominions seemed reserved and there were some notes of criticism; but in the course of the meetings the atmosphere markedly improved. In particular the Canadian Prime Minister made it clear that on his forthcoming visit to Berlin he would warn the German Government that in the event of an attack on the United Kingdom all the Dominions would come to her aid. Thus, although the British Government was not given an explicit assurance that any facilities for munitions production set up in Canada would certainly be available to Britain in time of war, there was really no longer any room for hesitation on this score. Moreover, Canada indicated her increasing concern with the problems of joint defence by setting up, in belated fulfilment of a recommendation of a conference held in 1930, a 'Naval, Army and Air Supply Committee' on the lines of the supply organisations in Britain and other Dominions and by attaching a liaison officer for supply questions to the High Commissioner's Office in London.

None the less the Canadian Government did not feel able to commit itself to the full co-operation desired by the United Kingdom, still less to the acceptance of a prior responsibility for the creation of a war potential. The main difficulty was that a war industry could be established in Canada only by enlisting the co-operation of private firms, and this would not be forthcoming without a guarantee of large and continuous orders. Canada's own slender requirements could not provide an economical basis for the erection of such an industry and the tentative offers of assistance put forward by the United Kingdom Government were insufficient to justify the Canadians going ahead on their own.

In the circumstances, with neither party willing to shoulder the heavy burden involved in the creation of a large munitions industry, it was not surprising that little progress was made. The final conclusions of the Committee in relation to munitions production were tentative and non-committal in the extreme. They recommended 'that in view of the uncertainty of the international situation H.M. Government in the United Kingdom should at an early date give intensive consideration to the problems of placing orders for such armaments and munitions of war as can be manufactured in the Dominions and India' and more particularly that 'the United Kingdom and Canadian Governments might be invited to consider whether special means could be arranged for a further inquiry in Canada as to the possibility of establishing the production of armament and munitions stores'.

For various reasons the suggestion of a special inquiry into Canada's potentialities was not followed up. The Dominion Government played no active part in the direct negotiations on individual requirements which took place later between the War Office and Canadian industrialists.

There was, however, one important exception. For some time the Canadian firm of John Inglis Company had been negotiating with the Canadian Government, and through it with the United Kingdom Government, over a scheme for the erection of a Bren gun factory. The Canadian defence authorities were prepared to place an order with the firm for 7,000 guns; and the one concrete proposal brought by the Canadian delegation to the Imperial Conference was that the United Kingdom should support this project by placing an order for another 5,000 guns; the capital cost would then be shared by the two Governments. The Munitions Committee, while not pronouncing on the particular merits of the scheme, urged that it was the kind of offer which should be followed up. It was, in fact, very attractive to the authorities in London for reasons both general and particular. In the first place they naturally desired to take advantage of this first practical offer from Canada. Secondly, rearmament in Britain was already disclosing serious weaknesses in the supply of skilled labour and machine tools; whilst Canada had a good reserve of the one and could secure the other from the United States. Moreover British supply of this key weapon depended at the time on a single plant in a very vulnerable location; and alternative sources of supply in the United Kingdom (the only practicable suggestion being an expansion of the Birmingham Small Arms factory) could be developed only at the expense of the production of machine guns for fighter aircraft. Bren guns made in Canada would cost, it was estimated, £108 per gun as against £90 from the Birmingham Small Arms Company; but it was agreed in the autumn of 1937 to accept the proposal and to order 5,000 guns from John Inglis Company. Owing to domestic controversy in Canada further protracted negotiations were needed before the contract was finally settled in March 1938.

In the meantime no other action was taken to develop munitions production in Canada. On 31st March, however, the Minister for the Co-ordination of Defence, acting partly in response to external pressure, notably from Mr. L. S. Amery and Mr. R. H. Brand, reopened the whole question in a memorandum to the Committee of Imperial Defence. It had just been decided to send a mission to explore the possibilities of aircraft purchases in the United States and Canada, and the moment was thought opportune for a complete review of North America as a source of war supplies.[1] The creation of war potential in the United States, however, had been ruled out on the

---

[1] See below, Chapter II.

advice of the Foreign Office because of the barrier of neutrality; and as regards Canada the elements of the problem were still the same as in 1937. The desirability of a large munitions capacity in the safe seclusion of the west was not in dispute. In the War Office there was first-hand knowledge of the capacity of Canadian industry, and from September 1936 onwards a clear recognition of the importance of developing and employing the potential in Canada. But the creation of a large munitions capacity involved 'the establishment of large new industries in the Dominions, continuing in operation for an indefinite time under peace-time conditions'. By now it was certain that the Canadians would not undertake this venture on their own account. If war factories were to be set up at all the United Kingdom Government would have to pay for them. But the Government was not yet prepared to place a heavy new burden on the fiscal system, already badly overloaded by the standards of peace, on the chance of a war it still hoped to avoid. An inconclusive discussion followed in the Committee of Imperial Defence, the only result being that the Secretary of State for War was asked to prepare a list of 'stores and equipments which were a bottleneck in production and which might possibly be obtained from the U.S.A. or Canada'.

During the remainder of 1938, while far-reaching schemes were set in motion for the construction of aircraft in Canada, no comparable development took place in regard to munitions in the narrower sense. Indeed, the only further step taken was the provision by the War Office of an order of 800,000 lb. of T.N.T. in support of a Canadian Government project. In the spring of 1939, however, the question of munitions supply was again revived. Canadian manufacturers were now informed that the United Kingdom would consider placing orders for a wide range of armaments, including anti-aircraft, anti-tank and field artillery, machine-gun carriers, shells and machine tools. The plan was to create capacity with the aid of small 'educational' orders which would give private firms a chance to overcome the initial difficulties of manufacture and acquire the necessary experience for large-scale production in the event of war. As a first step a Mission, consisting of delegates of the Canadian Manufacturers' Association, visited the United Kingdom, headed by General McNaughton as a government representative.

The Mission sailed in the summer of 1939 with the objects of finding out British defence requirements, investigating British methods of armaments production and securing British orders. On the last question it was in the main disappointed since the United Kingdom Government could no longer afford to entertain large-scale projects overseas if the whole cost had to be borne by it from its slender dollar resources. Moreover, orders were not available on the scale of requirements then approved. Only two further steps were taken before the outbreak of war. First, the War Office undertook to place an order in Canada for 100 machine-gun carriers. In this isolated instance, as in the case of the earlier Bren gun scheme, the initiative came from the Canadian Government which was itself proposing to order 25 carriers from the same plant. This project did not mature until a much later date, Treasury approval being withheld after the outbreak of war. Secondly, a contract was signed in August 1939 with the firm of Marine Industries Limited, shipbuilders and salvage contractors of Sorel, a town some 50 miles east of Montreal, for 100 25-pounder field artillery equipments and 200 additional gun carriages. This was a revolutionary development; no artillery had ever been manufactured in Canada before. The contract was placed on the understanding that the full backing of the Canadian Government should be obtained together with assurances of the co-operation of appropriate allied Canadian firms and on the condition that the firm should engage technicians from the great French firm of Schneider-Creusot to supervise production in the early stages of development. The whole project depended on the enterprise of Messrs. Simard, the firm's directors, who were prepared to put up capital of £1 million on their own account; the British Government undertook to pay £100,000 on the delivery of the first gun. As might be expected, progress was slow at the outset, but in spite of many vicissitudes—including the loss of French technicians after the fall of France—great results were ultimately achieved. The firm had distinguished assistance from the Chrysler Corporation and technical advice from the British Purchasing Commission.[1]

Thus, at the outbreak of war, the Canadian munitions industry, outside the Dominion arsenal, still consisted of only one firm in actual production on British orders. This was the National Steel Car Corporation, which was turning out 3·7-inch shells at the rate of 3,000 rounds per week. Even the plants in preparation could be numbered on the fingers of one hand. There was the Inglis Bren gun factory then nearing completion; the Defence Industries T.N.T. factory, which was due to begin production in December at the rate of 150 tons per month; a second plant for 25-pounder shells being set up by the National Steel Car Corporation; and the Marine Industries factory on which work had just begun. The total value of the capital provided and projected did not exceed £1 million. Although each of these schemes was of great importance as a nucleus for the future development of munitions production, the capacity actually in preparation, even including aircraft, was negligible in comparison with the total resources of Canadian industry.

---

[1] For the sequel see *Studies of Overseas Supply*, Chapter I.

(iii)

Canada at the Outbreak of the War

The events leading to the sending of a British Purchasing Mission, headed by Colonel J. H. M. Greenly, to Ottawa in September and October 1939 are dealt with in Chapter III. Here it may be mentioned that the decision to send the Mission to North America was taken towards the end of August after a 'scout', Lord Riverdale, had made a swift visit at the beginning of that month to Washington and Ottawa and reported that all was clear. Ottawa was chosen as the headquarters of the Mission for two reasons: first, the attitude of the Government and industry of Canada was more favourable; secondly, there was no point in embarrassing the Administration in Washington by setting up a purchasing mission in the United States in the midst of the debate on the amendment of the Neutrality Act. The Mission did not arrive in Ottawa until well after the outbreak of war. On the very day on which its main party landed it became clear that the principal function for which it was designed—that of purchasing—would in fact be undertaken by the Canadian Government. The Prime Minister, in welcoming the Mission on 29th September, informed it that the newly created Canadian War Supply Board would be at its disposal to purchase supplies required by the British Government without any charge for the administrative costs involved.

At the same time the Canadian Government told London that in its view the main tasks for British officials in North America were likely to be the co-ordination of technical measures arising mainly out of the blockade. As regards war supplies the Canadian Government would prefer to handle matters directly with London. As for British supply organisation in Canada, preference was expressed for an arrangement whereby British officials in Canada, dealing with the special aspects of supply and economic warfare, would be under the general supervision of the United Kingdom High Commissioner. The Canadian Government, London was told, was about to attach a senior officer to the staff of the Canadian High Commissioner in London to deal with matters relating to economic defence, the blockade, export control and shipping.

From the point of view of the British Government there was much to be said for such an arrangement. War supplies did not come only from Canada. Raw materials and food were being purchased from all over the Commonwealth and from many other countries. It was therefore regarded as essential that the administrative co-ordination of supply should be centred in London. Direct sales in the United Kingdom of some Canadian products (e.g. timber) had for long been a trade custom. Nevertheless, there was some advantage to Britain, and probably more advantage to Canada than was realised at the time, in having a strong British mission at Ottawa in the opening months of the war.

In sending the Mission to Ottawa London recognised that three major factors had to be related: first, total British purchases—private and public—in Canada; second, the problem of financing British war-time expenditure in Canada, a dollar area; third, the readjustment of the Canadian economy to meet its war needs.

The Mission was directly concerned only with the supply of munitions; but it could not carry out its task without knowing what was going on in the matter of purchases of raw materials and food, which involved far greater expenditures. On 3rd October 1939 it was given a provisional outline of British requirements as regards armaments and raw materials. Next day the head of the Mission asked London for a complete statement of purchases of all kinds, including food. Without a clear view of total dollar expenditure it was not able to discuss intelligently with the Canadian Government how best to use Canadian capacity for the production of munitions.

To ensure the co-ordination of all the interests involved in the supply of armaments, it was agreed that the Board must have on it representatives of the British Treasury, Admiralty, Air Ministry, Ministry of Supply, and the Chairman of the Canadian War Supply Board (Mr. Wallace Campbell). Since its task of co-ordination was to extend also to purchases in the United States, the Head of the British Purchasing Commission (soon to be established in New York) must also be a member. This plan was put forward on 19th October and approved by the British Government a week later. France was brought into the arrangement by an agreement (suggested by the British to the French Government) that any war purchases France might desire to make in Canada should be handled by the British Supply Board in conjunction with the Canadian War Supply Board.

The organisation was hardly down on paper before it became clear that it could not work without agreement between the British and Canadian Governments on certain major issues of policy. At the end of October three such issues had become sufficiently acute to force the two Governments to consider at a high level the intermeshing of their war economies. In the first place it was necessary to come to some decision on the question of the opening of a Canadian credit to Britain. A sum of some $200 million was discussed; it was to be met by the sale to Canada of an equivalent amount of Canadian securities held in London. The second issue was how much Britain would buy of the bumper Canadian wheat harvest. A third issue was the financial implications for Canada of the British Commonwealth Air Training Plan whereby large numbers of airmen, British, Australian and New Zealand, together with Canadians, were to be trained in Canada out of the reach of bombing attacks.[1] The detailed discussions on the latter plan were begun in Ottawa by Lord Riverdale in the second half of October.

The initial impression of the Canadian Government was that the Air Training Plan involved, as Mr. Mackenzie King put it to Mr. Neville Chamberlain, 'costs of a huge magnitude' going beyond the financial resources of Canada. Canada's ability to expand her capacity and to finance the war, Mr. Mackenzie King pointed out, depended on her being able to keep up her sales of foodstuffs and raw materials to Britain. The disposal of the very large wheat crop was therefore a matter of some concern to the Government. The Canadian Government was thereupon informed in confidence of the purchasing plans of the Ministry of Food. Whilst British purchases of wheat up to the end of October had been only 100,000 tons, the Food Ministry was being authorised to purchase $1\frac{3}{4}$ million tons and hoped to raise this to a maximum of 3 million tons in the next twelve months.

To clarify the situation as a whole, the British Treasury drew up and sent to the Treasury representative at Ottawa on 6th November a tentative estimate of total British expenditure in Canada in the first year of the war.

	£ million
Raw materials[2]	52
Food	29–42
Private purchases of Canadian goods .	5
Air Training Plan	10
Munitions supplies (for the three Supply Ministries)	13–15

As will be indicated below this was an underestimate. By the end of May 1940 British expenditures in Canada were already over £150 million.

At this point, 5th November 1939, the two Governments exchanged very tentative figures of their war expenditures in relation to total national income. Total British expenditure, both national and municipal, was put at about £2,933 million out of a national income of some £5,750 million or a proportion of 51 per cent. If an allowance were made for the sale of British-held Canadian securities and gold, totalling, say, $200 million, the British proportion would

---

[1] It was known as the Empire Air Training Scheme up to May 1942, when it became officially the British Commonwealth Air Training Plan.

[2] British contracts already made or under negotiation covered Canada's exportable surplus of copper, zinc and aluminium, most of her lead and ferro alloys, and large quantities of nickel, timber and paper. Timber and cereals were the largest imports from Canada in terms of value and tonnage.

stand at 47½ per cent. The comparable figure for Canada was put at 36·3 per cent. (National income, $4,111 million; total Government expenditure, federal, provincial and municipal, $1,490 million.)

(iv)

Munitions Production in Canada up to the Fall of France

These differences of opinion on administrative and financial questions had not, however, interfered directly with the practical work of the Purchasing Mission. It had met with a warm welcome on the arrival of the first members at Ottawa in mid-September 1939, and had set to work at once with the full co-operation of the Canadian authorities on the initiation of a number of new projects for munitions production on British account. The ground had been well prepared during the recent visit to Britain of the delegation of Canadian manufacturers. For although no immediate results were obtained, the discussions had given the authorities in London a fairly clear idea of what Canadian industry might be expected to produce; it proved its value when the time came at a later stage to draw up a list of stores for which requirements could not be met in full from production in the United Kingdom and which were suitable for rapid development in the Dominions. Thus the Ministry of Supply representatives on the Mission brought with them detailed instructions as to the capacity for munitions production which they were to endeavour to create. Their concern at this stage was not so much with actual deliveries as with the rate of potential output desired; but small 'educational' orders, in most cases amounting only to a few weeks' production at maximum rate of output, were authorised in order to assist development.

The initial programme was not an ambitious one, either in quantity or in the range of munitions which it covered. It consisted in great part of gun ammunition, a relatively simple item which did not call for elaborate plant, lengthy preparation or very advanced industrial technique, and which had been successfully handled by the undeveloped Canadian industry of the First World War. For this type of work, moreover, Canada already possessed a nucleus capacity in the National Steel Car Corporation's plant at Hamilton, Ontario, and also, in the works of John T. Hepburn Limited, a valuable source of machine tools upon which British ordnance factories had already drawn. Thus out of the thirteen new unit plants authorised in the Mission's preliminary instructions, nine were to be for shell and cartridge-case production. The total potential output of shells, apart from that of the plants already existing or in preparation, was planned at 27,000 empty rounds per week or 1,350,000 rounds in a full year;[1] the bulk of these would be for anti-aircraft guns, but some provision was also to be made for heavier shells up to a calibre of 9·2 inch. In the matter of artillery the only new requirements notified were for modest outputs of anti-tank gun carriages and of anti-aircraft gun barrels and liners; the Marine Industries project was still the only one which involved the production of complete equipments. Finally, it was proposed to create capacity for the construction of infantry tanks at the rate of two per week.

The Admiralty representative on the Purchasing Mission had also been furnished with a list of requirements. This was at first sight more impressive than that carried by his Supply colleague, since it comprised, besides warships of the escort vessel class in considerable numbers, a wide range of ordnance including complete 4-inch and 4·7-inch guns. But whereas the Ministry of Supply instructions were intended as real requisitions, to be translated into actual contracts so soon as suitable firms could be located, it soon turned out that the Admiralty was merely making tentative inquiries; and, in fact, nothing more was heard of naval requirements, apart from ships and degaussing cable, until after the fall of France.

The advance party of the Purchasing Mission had sailed from England on the 2nd September 1939, and the instructions which it received from the Ministry of Supply had been conceived and formulated in an atmosphere which, by the standards soon to be accepted, was still essentially one of leisurely peace-time preparation. With the outbreak of war, and Canada's formal entry on 10th September, the situation was radically changed. The way was clear, and the need was apparent for a much more rapid development. If Canadian industry were to make any appreciable contribution to the war effort there was no room for the stage of gradual education in munitions work. Accordingly at the end of September the small initial orders were supplemented by a full production order assessed on the basis of a year's output of the plant which was to be set up. The programme remained, however, substantially the same; the weekly rates of output aimed at were not enlarged and no important additions were made in the first instance to the range of manufactures previously envisaged.

The main limiting factor in the planning at the beginning of the war was, of course, finance.[2] Even in normal times the direct balance

---

[1] To put this figure into perspective, it may be noted that the actual output of shells in the United Kingdom was 13 million rounds in 1940 and 29 million in 1941.

[2] On this factor see below, Chapter VII; also Hancock and Gowing, *op. cit.*, Chapter IV, ii.

of trade between Canada and the United Kingdom was extremely unfavourable to the United Kingdom. The limited dollar resources of the United Kingdom had now to be husbanded carefully in order to provide for supplies of essential foodstuffs during the whole course of the war, and for the raw material imports necessitated by the home munitions programme. The Ministry of Supply estimated that it would have to buy some £47 million worth of Canadian materials in the first year alone. Moreover, there was part of the cost of the Air Training Plan to be met; and a War Cabinet ruling gave this absolute priority over all other dollar expenditure. Further, the outcome of the negotiations described above, namely the acceptance of a higher price for wheat purchases and the deductions of Canada's own expenditure on the air training scheme from the amount of the loan to be raised there, meant that even more stringent economy had to be applied to other purchases in Canadian dollars. The opinion expressed by the Treasury before the outbreak of war, that expenditure on munitions of war, in Canada as in the United States, would have to proceed with the strictest caution, remained unmodified. (The warning sounded by the Bank of England in February 1940 that reserves were on the point of exhaustion shows that there was ample justification for a policy of prudence.) Moreover, provision had also to be made for Admiralty and Air Ministry requirements; and £5 million was allotted at the outset to the latter for the purchase of aircraft, raw materials and miscellaneous stores. This figure was quite separate from the heavy expenses incurred in connection with the joint Air Training Plan, and the Air Ministry made it clear that given a free hand it would gladly have raised the figure to over £20 million. All this left only a small margin for expenditure on munitions in the narrower sense. Such expenditure had in fact to be contained within the limits of the Ministry of Supply's original commitments, which it was calculated would entail the disbursement of £3¾ million, including £1 million for capital assistance in the first year of war, and of £9 million annually thereafter, when the new plant had come into full production. In addition it was proposed to spend £1½ million on machine tools.

But quite apart from the restrictions imposed by financial prudence, the development of munitions production in Canada during this first period of the war was limited also by considerations of time. On the ruling hypothesis of a three-years war, little was to be gained from very long-term projects; the expansion of the British Army to a force of fifty-five divisions was scheduled for completion in two stages before the end of the second year. But, seeing that capacity would have to be created and personnel trained practically from scratch, Canadian projects could not be other than long term. Two full years elapsed between the decision to set up a Bren gun factory and the delivery of the first gun in March 1940; perhaps under emergency conditions progress might be rather more rapid; but it was impossible to assume that heavy munitions such as tanks or guns could be shipped in quantities sufficient to warrant a heavy expenditure of scarce currency on capital development before the summer of 1941. It was not clear that such heavy munitions could in fact be produced in Canada in time to be used at all—for there was still at the end of 1939 some scepticism as to the ability of Canadian industry to undertake specialised production of this nature. Requisitions from Canada were confined in the main therefore to such minor projects as could be expected to bear fruit within the first year or so of war. Indeed, it was at first laid down that expenditure should be incurred only where production could begin within six months. This stipulation, as the administrative head of the British Supply Board at Ottawa pointed out, would have stifled munitions production altogether, and it was not strictly enforced. Nonetheless, just as in 1937 and 1938 the participation of Canada in the rearmament programme had been ruled out by her inability to make a substantial contribution before the zero year 1940, so now she was debarred from a real share in the building-up of munitions supplies because, as a result of the failure to create a war potential in time of peace, her co-operation could not become effective until a time when it was supposed the climax of the war would have been passed. It is not at all certain that orders would have been augmented much at this stage even if dollars had been plentiful.

In short, owing to the combination of a long view on finance and a short view on the value of a munitions potential, Canada continued to be treated during the whole period of 'the twilight war' as a purely marginal source of armaments supply, though in the case of aircraft the margin was bigger. The initial list of requirements for munitions was supplemented from time to time by individual orders for miscellaneous items, as new Service needs emerged which could not quickly or conveniently be met from home production. But practically the whole of the munitions programme was still allotted to United Kingdom firms and there was no real attempt to exploit the latent resources of Canadian industry on a coherent plan. Even the insurance value of a munitions capacity immune from air attack, though never far from the minds of the planners in London, only occasionally influenced a decision when the advantages of placing new orders in Britain or in Canada were otherwise nicely balanced. Moreover, such new munitions requirements as were notified to Canada during this period were all in the restricted field of ammunition and explosives; no additions were made to the original orders for guns and components, and the very modest proposal with regard to tanks did not mature at all until a later date. It has to be remembered that the United Kingdom was providing the major equipment of the

Canadian troops which were now arriving in England. By early February 1940 23,000 Canadians had arrived.[1]

Nonetheless in the first nine months of the war, in regard to munitions proper, as distinct from aircraft and machine tools, Canada was given, on the basis of express instructions from London, precedence over the United States as Britain's main supplementary arsenal. Covetous glances might be cast on the immense unused resources of the fully mature American heavy industries but financial reasons, and the obvious advantages of supply from a Commonwealth country fully at war, were decisive.[2] Generally speaking, even after the partial removal of the neutrality barriers, finished munitions at this stage of the war were ordered from the United States only if they were specialised articles not obtainable elsewhere (e.g. Sperry anti-aircraft predictors or Thompson sub-machine guns), or if sufficient capacity could not readily be created for the purpose in Canada. Thus there were a few overflow orders to the United States for shells, small arms ammunition, explosives and propellants, all of which were purchased from Canada in much larger quantities. In all, the value of Ministry of Supply orders placed or pending in Canada at the end of April 1940, excluding orders for machinery and raw materials, was approximately $81 million; the corresponding figure for the United States was only $33 million.

Details of the contracts placed in this early period will be given in *Studies of Overseas Supply*. Here it may be noted that up to the fall of France, Great Britain had done little more than scrape the surface of the Canadian potential for munitions production. Actual shipments were negligible. The production of Bren guns and of certain types of shells had started, but initial deliveries were taken by the Canadians for their own use. Actual shipments of munitions as such to Britain up to the 15th May 1940 consisted of 25 million rounds of small arms ammunition, 800 tons of toluol and 225 tons of T.N.T. and the first-fruits of the shell contracts mentioned above—appreciable and very welcome quantities of 3·7-inch, 25-pounder and 4·5-inch empty shell for British filling factories. For the immediate future only a few deliveries on a small scale were in prospect. The projects relating to tanks and anti-tank gun carriages still hung fire. Active preparations for army equipment were confined to the restricted range of 25-pounder guns, anti-aircraft gun barrels, Bren guns, carriers, ammunition and explosives. Apart from explosives, for which orders totalled nearly $29 million, the pre-war schemes for Bren guns and field

---

[1] The First Division arrived in December 1939; the Second on Christmas Day 1940; the Third in late summer of 1941. *The Canadian Army at War. The Canadians in Britain 1939–1944* (No. 1, Second Edition, 1946, The King's Printer, Ottawa), pp. 14–17.

[2] In reporting to the Treasury in October 1939 its plans for purchases in the United States, the Ministry of Supply commented that 'if restrictions were eased we could of course go ahead with very much larger orders'.

C

artillery equipment were still the most important, though even they were on a fairly small scale. The gun barrel projects were quantitatively unimportant, and even the planned output of shell, at some 450,000 rounds per month, was far below the potential output, estimated by the Canadians at two or even three million rounds. The vast resources of the automobile industry were virtually untapped, and there was a large unused reserve of heavy engineering capacity, especially in the railway workshops. Nonetheless the period was not wholly wasted. Much experience was gained in the method of converting peace-time industries for war purposes, and the small orders given provided the foundations on which the great structure of Canada's munitions production was subsequently erected. The large expansion in the production and shipment of aluminium, and of some other raw materials, must not be forgotten. The delivery of some aircraft had begun. There were some important first steps also in the matter of shipbuilding.

(v)

British Supply Arrangements in Canada after Dunkirk

The sudden grave turn of the war in May 1940 produced sharp reactions. Widespread anxiety about the fate of Canada's two mother countries, Britain and France, was reflected in pressure on the Government from all sides, including Parliament, to 'do something'. Charges and counter-charges centred on three main issues: that the Government was not moving fast enough with its own orders to Canadian factories; that it was not pushing output fast enough on British orders; that the British Government itself had failed to make proper use of the Canadian potential. The British Government, it was said, had not given enough orders; its officials were not sufficiently co-operative; and there had been some holding back by British industrialists on technical data and designs needed by Canadian producers.

The Canadian Government's main preoccupation was that of maximum possible aid to Britain and France. Already on 19th May the Prime Minister telegraphed a comprehensive offer of assistance to the United Kingdom in the production of munitions, aircraft and other war supplies. This message was in part the result of a recent visit to the United Kingdom by the Minister of National Defence, who had gained the impression that Departments in London were out of touch with the situation in Canada and did not fully appreciate the potentialities of Canadian industry. One outcome of the message was the completely-equipped squadron of Canadian Hurricanes that arrived, with air crews, ground personnel, and transport, on the day before the French surrender.[1] Offers of assistance were pouring in from all parts of the Commonwealth and Empire. Thus Australia diverted to the United Kingdom 49 Hudson aircraft on order in the United States for the Royal Australian Air Force.

At the same time, the Canadian Government, like all the Governments of the Commonwealth, was concerned about the interruption of essential supplies from Britain for the use of Canadian armed forces. The matter of trainers for the British Commonwealth Air Training Plan is referred to below. Another example was the interruption of supplies from Britain for the Canadian Navy. 'As you know', the Canadian Minister of Munitions and Supply (Mr. C. D. Howe), wrote to Purvis on 12th June, 'the Royal Canadian Navy have for many years depended entirely on the British Admiralty for supplies of arms and ammunition'. Purvis was asked to arrange through Secretary Morgenthau for an officer of the Royal Canadian Navy to discuss with the United States authorities the possibility of obtaining such supplies from the United States.

As regards Canadian war production there was no denial that it was lagging. But this was judged to be almost as much a British as a Canadian problem. If the responsibility for production rested with the Canadians, the responsibility for placing the orders, which alone could result in production, rested with the United Kingdom. The need for some simplification in the administrative machinery for placing orders was represented by the Canadian to the United Kingdom Government. At the same time the great increase in British demands on the United States convinced the Chairman and Vice-Chairman of the Anglo-French Purchasing Board in New York, Purvis and Bloch-Lainé, that some changes in the supply machinery, particularly as regards the subordination of the Board in New York to the British Supply Organisation in Ottawa, had become a matter of urgency. In the result two fundamental changes were made. In the first place the British Commission in New York became independent of the Board in Ottawa. Secondly, the functions of the Board in Ottawa, as intermediaries between the United Kingdom and Canadian Governments for placing orders in Canada, were abolished. Henceforward orders were handled direct between the Ministry of Supply in London and the Department of Munitions and Supply in Ottawa. The British Supply Board was wound up formally on 31st August after transferring its existing commitments to the Canadian authorities.

During the life of the British Supply Board its technical personnel

---

[1] *The Times* (London), 29th July 1940. A squadron of Canadian-built Lysanders had arrived in the United Kingdom in the spring.

helped in the laying of the foundations on which the Canadian munitions output was later to be built. Moreover, some elements of the British organisation continued to operate in a changed form on Canadian soil. Amongst these were the United Kingdom Payments Office and the United Kingdom Technical Mission (the latter a handful of experts working under the ægis of the United Kingdom High Commissioner). Most important, perhaps, was the strong and efficient British inspection service which, under a British general as Inspector-General, had been built up in Canada from September 1939. This reinforced the very small existing Canadian inspection department and became the nucleus of a strong team which carried out later the inspection of British-type munitions produced under British contracts in the United States. Late in 1940, as a result of a Memorandum of Agreement between the British and Canadian Governments and a Canadian Order-in-Council, the 'Joint Inspection Board of the United Kingdom and Canada' was created with the task of inspection both in Canada and the United States.

So ended the not very well conceived plan to unify British supply from North America by means of the British Supply Board at Ottawa. The Mission at Ottawa failed because the Canadian Government, already purchasing for the British Government, preferred to have direct relations with the Departments on whose behalf it was operating. The Mission at New York and Washington succeeded because it had to buy. The United States had reached the point of pre-belligerency rather than of neutrality, but it was still not possible for an American Government to purchase supplies for belligerent Britain, especially not with British funds. Part of this success, as the next chapters show, was due to the personality of Arthur Purvis. But the major factors were past history and the present danger that forced the British and American peoples willy-nilly to pull together in the same boat.

The Canadian Government now proceeded to supplement direct relations with London by direct relations with Washington. The first great visible step was the Ogdensburg Agreement of 17th August 1940, setting up the Permanent Joint Defence Board of the United States and Canada. On the British side the flanking approach to Washington through Ottawa was abandoned in favour of the direct route to the American Government which the British and French Governments, using Purvis as one of their main instruments, had built. The dropping out of France made it possible for the British Government to advance still faster to that intermeshing of British, American and Canadian supply organisations which Purvis seemed to have sensed as a possibility from the very moment that he found the doors opening to him in Washington in December 1939. The final outcome was the Combined Boards of 1942 which he did not live to see.

CHAPTER II

THE CREATION OF AIRCRAFT CAPACITY IN THE COMMONWEALTH OVERSEAS

(i)

The Unity of Air Supply in the Commonwealth

THE scope of a study of overseas supply is the supply from overseas that reached the United Kingdom or other areas for which it had strategic responsibility. Thus only the early, not the late, phases of aircraft production in Canada and Australia belong to it. The story in this volume begins with the placing in Australia and Canada by the British Air Ministry of important orders for aircraft to be manufactured for the use of the Royal Air Force. But the aircraft capacity resulting from such orders served later for the production of planes for the use, at home or abroad, of the Royal Australian or Royal Canadian Air Forces. This second phase belongs to the Australian and Canadian official war histories rather than the British. This is only one example of the many matters dealt with in this volume and in *Studies of Overseas Supply* which belong to wider unities. One such unity is the war effort of the British Commonwealth as a whole. Another is the history of the British Commonwealth-American combination, of which this study is only a section.

In the air the unity of the Commonwealth was even more marked than in the matter of military supplies. Unity in matters of air supply was merely one aspect of the wider unity in training and in Service operations in the principal Commonwealth air services, the Royal Air Force, the Royal Canadian Air Force, the Royal Australian Air Force and the Royal New Zealand Air Force. Unity in air training was demonstrated in one of the most important developments in the history of the Commonwealth, the Empire Air Training Scheme (later the British Commonwealth Air Training Plan). The scheme emerged from a conference of the British, Canadian, Australian and New Zealand Governments, over which the Canadian Prime Minister presided in Ottawa in the early winter of 1939.[1] The

---

[1] As a reply by the Prime Minister to a question in the Canadian Parliament indicated, 'informative exploratory negotiations in regard to the training of British air pilots in Canada' had taken place in 1938, but without result. H. of C. Deb. (Canada), 1st July 1938. See *Journal of the Parliaments of the Empire*, Vol. XIX, No. 4, p. 824.

agreement setting out the scheme was signed on 17th December. The scheme was administered by a joint board made up of the Air Missions of the three Governments, together with the Royal Canadian Air Force. It was extended as a result of a conference held in May 1942 for a further period of two years until 31st March 1945.

The bulk of the training was carried out in Canada where the scheme at its peak operated 359 establishments including schools and depots. A certain number of pupils from the United Kingdom were trained there as part of the Canadian quota of trainees and, in addition, pupils from Australia and New Zealand were sent to Canada to complete their training. In the summer of 1940 some R.A.F. schools were transferred from the United Kingdom in order to continue training unhampered by bombing attacks. Subsequently, further R.A.F. schools were opened in Canada for the training of pupils from the United Kingdom. For a time these schools operated outside the Empire Air Training Scheme and it was not until May 1942, when the revised agreement was signed, that they were incorporated into the scheme. From that time onwards the training organisation was usually referred to as the British Commonwealth Air Training Plan. By the end of the war 137,739 R.A.F., R.C.A.F., R.A.A.F. and R.N.Z.A.F. pupils had been trained in Canada.

Pilots and aircrewmen were also trained in schools in Australia and New Zealand under the British Commonwealth Air Training Plan; some completed their training in Canada; others went direct to the United Kingdom.[1] The training of British pilots in the United States is referred to in Chapter VI. Here it may be noted that one outcome of the British Commonwealth Air Conference in May 1942 was to set up a North American Combined Training Committee composed of air representatives of the United States, the United Kingdom and Canada. Through this important Combined Committee information on air training problems was exchanged and visits arranged. The Combined Committee met every two months alternately in the United States and Canada under the chairmanship of the Director of Flying Training, United States Army Air Force. These close bonds in training arrangements had their counterpart in the arrangements for the supply of training aircraft which are referred to in this chapter and in Chapter VI.

There was somewhat the same kind of fluidity in Service operations. Thus Royal Canadian Air Force crews, trained in the schools of the British Commonwealth Air Training Plan in Canada, mingled —as they had done in the schools in Canada—with Royal Air Force crews in all branches and operations of the Royal Air Force during

---

[1] Air Training Schools were also established under separate agreements in South Africa and Southern Rhodesia.

the war. There were also separate Royal Canadian Air Force squadrons. One of them—a day fighter squadron—destroyed thirty-one enemy aircraft in the Battle of Britain. In 1941 there were six more Canadian day fighter squadrons in the United Kingdom and three night fighter squadrons.[1]

These squadrons used impartially British aircraft produced in the United Kingdom or British-type aircraft produced in Canada under British or Canadian contracts. Similarly, Australian air squadrons in the various theatres used British aircraft, British types produced in Australia under British and Australian contracts, American lend-lease machines, even Canadian-manufactured aircraft. So also there were American squadrons flying British Spitfires in North Africa and elsewhere.

In placing orders in the Dominions (as in the United States) for war equipment the British Government aimed from the beginning at developing their war potential by creating new munitions capacity. The securing of the specific aircraft covered by the orders was a second, though still important, objective. It was assumed that the new overseas factories thus called into being would be available for the double purpose of supplying further British orders, if necessary, and of meeting the defence needs of the country concerned. The struggle against the Axis powers was regarded as a common enterprise in which by an iron necessity all the countries concerned in supply must participate—directly or indirectly, later if not sooner. From the outset, and increasingly as the war developed, supply from all was conceived of as a common pool, from which all must be able to draw in accordance with their need.

It followed that as time went on, as the air forces trained together and fought together, the shares which the different partners contributed to the pool became more and more difficult to disentangle. In the air—perhaps even more than on the ground and at sea—supply arrangements became so fluid, transfers and diversions so frequent, that it was not possible to isolate with any high degree of precision the contributions made in the matter of aircraft and air supplies by one Commonwealth country to another, or as between the United States and their allies.[2] For aircraft, as for munitions generally, it became increasingly difficult as the war went on to foresee where munitions manufactured in one country would finally be used in the

---

[1] *Canada at War, Recapitulation Issue* (No. 45, 1945, Wartime Information Board, Ottawa), pp. 44–45, 81.

[2] Thus in the statistics of aircraft and equipment received from North America, as compiled by the Ministry of Aircraft Production, there is a small margin of error. The monthly tables prepared by the Ministry could not differentiate always between aircraft received from the United States and those supplied from Canada. An early example of diversion from a British contract in the United States to the Royal Canadian Air Force, was the transfer in mid-November 1940 of eighteen Hudsons from a British order of 1938.

field, in which campaign and by what Forces. This fluidity increased from 1941 onwards, as supplies from the United States began to form an appreciable element in the equipment of the armed forces of Britain and of other parts of the Commonwealth.

In accordance with the principle throughout the British Commonwealth that arms and ammunition should be standardised and interchangeable, any aircraft orders placed in other Commonwealth countries by Britain were for British types. Thus Canadian and Australian aircraft production throughout the war was predominantly of British types made to British engineering standards. These types accounted for most of the production in terms of total structure weight. British types produced in Canada were: Hampden (Handley Page) ; Bolingbroke (Bristol Aeroplane Company) ; Hurricane (Hawker Aircraft); Stranraer (Supermarine Aviation); Anson (A. V. Roe & Company); Lancaster (A. V. Roe & Company); Mosquito (de Havilland Aircraft Company); Lysander (Westland Aircraft Company). A large number of the aircraft manufactured in Canada were of American or Canadian types, but except for Catalinas, these were largely for use in Canada as trainers in connection with the British Commonwealth Air Training Plan. The prevalence of British, rather than of American engineering standards, in the Canadian aircraft industry, was some indication perhaps of its limited scale of operations, since normally in peace-time Canadian mass production industry is geared to American engineering standards. Thus in the manufacture of trucks, armoured vehicles, tanks and other important war supplies, it was only possible for Canada to pull her full weight as a manufacturer of armaments by producing American types.

(ii)

Aircraft Production Overseas—Quantity and Time

Before turning to the more detailed history of the early British aircraft contracts in Canada it is necessary to give some idea of scale by citing certain figures.[1]

Canada produced altogether during the war (to June 1945) 16,431 aircraft on British and Canadian account as shown in Table 1.

---

[1] For the other Dominions see *Studies of Overseas Supply.* Up to 30th June 1945 Australia produced 3,393 aircraft and over 1,000 engines of different types. The initial scheme provided for the creation of capacity for the manufacture of aircraft for the joint use of the Royal Air Force and the Royal Australian Air Force. The aircraft produced were used for the most part in the Southern Hemisphere. There was no production of Service aircraft in India, South Africa or New Zealand. The idea of a de Havilland factory in New Zealand to start production with an order for 100 Tiger Moths was mooted in 1939.

Production of aircraft in Canada, September 1939 to June 1945[1]

TABLE I   Number

	On British account	On Canadian account
Hampden	160	—
Bolingbroke	—	626
Hurricane	1,051	400
Stranraer	—	41
Harvard (trainer) . . .	1,031	1,710
Anson (trainer)	—	2,882
Catalina	307	424
Lancaster	395	—
Mosquito	961	—
S.B.W.I. and S.B.F.I. . .	—	1,068
Cornell (trainer) . .	335	1,400
Others (mostly elementary trainers)	350	3,290
Total	4,590	11,841

In all 5,000 Service aircraft were delivered to the United Kingdom and other countries. Canada also assembled 3,200 aircraft received from the United Kingdom. The production of Canadian Hampdens ended in 1942, of Hurricanes in 1943. The production of Lancasters and Mosquitos began in 1943. All save nine of the Catalinas were also produced from 1943 to 1945. British aircraft contracts were mostly taken over in 1941 by the Canadian Department of Munitions and Supplies. After April 1943 aircraft produced in Canada on British account were furnished under Mutual Aid. In the first two years of Mutual Aid, April 1943 to March 1945, the value of aircraft supplied to the United Kingdom was put at $135½ million.[2]

The scale of the initial British orders in Canada and the size of the potential which it was estimated they would create, indicated a shrewd guess as to Canada's capacity to produce within a given time. The general public, which tended to judge industrial capacity by the number of automobiles the country could turn out in a day, was inclined to underestimate the difficulties of aircraft production—

---

[1] Aircraft (mostly Cornell, Catalina and Harvard) produced by War Supplies Limited for American orders under the Hyde Park Agreement are included in the figures. Such orders were financed from lend-lease until mid-1943 and then by Canadian Mutual Aid. Some Mosquitos produced in Canada on United Kingdom account were diverted to the United States Army Air Force.

[2] *Canadian Mutual Aid Board* (Second Annual Report to 31st March 1945), p. 14, gives the following figures of aircraft supplied to the United Kingdom:

Fiscal years (April to March)

	1943–44	1944–45
Lancaster . .	42	43
Mosquito (bomber) . .	102	89
Harvard	271	429
Cornell	254	149
P.B.—2B1 Boeing . .	98	21

See also Canada at War, Recapitulation Issue, op. cit., p. 81.

especially of the newer types of machines. Most of the total of over 16,000 aircraft for Canada mentioned above were trainers—advanced or primary. The achievement of Canada in building so many of these aircraft was a contribution of vital importance to the whole Common-wealth, for they were used in the training of aircrews needed for an important part of the great number of aircraft built in British factories or acquired by purchase or lend-lease from the United States. But the substantial output in Canada of Service planes—Hampdens, Hurri-canes, Mosquitos, Lancasters—largely on British Government ac-count, represented a still greater industrial achievement.[1] The achievement is better expressed in terms of airframe weight[2] than in numbers of aircraft. The total airframe weight of all military aircraft produced in Canada in 1941 was about 3·3 million lbs. compared with 26·4 million lbs. for the aircraft produced in 1944; the total air-frame weight of combat types alone increased more than threefold between 1942 and 1944 (from 5·9 million lbs. to 19·6 million lbs.) although the numerical output only doubled.[3]

It is difficult to find any scale by which to measure the size of British orders in Canada at the outbreak of the war. In the years before British rearmament began, e.g. from 1928–33, the orders placed by the Royal Air Force with the well established British air-craft industry ranged between about 500 and 800 aircraft a year. These orders were for planes which by the standards of 1939 were of low structure weight. Judged by this or any other scale, the order for eighty Hampdens placed in Canada in 1939 and the plan to produce Stirlings in Canada to a total of 500 in case of war or 200 if peace continued, could not be dismissed as unimportant. The size of the

---

[1] The proportion between trainers and combat aircraft in the period 1940 to 1944 is shown in the following table:

	Total military types	Combat types	Trainers	Communica-tion and transport types
1940	844	116	728	
1941	1,741	711	1,030	
1942	4,762	1,045	2,550	167(a)
1943	4,104	745	3,150	209(b)
1944	4,052	1,781	1,816	455(b)

(a) 17 transports and 150 communication-type aircraft.
(b) All transports.

[2] i.e. the weight of the bare structure together with such items as armour plate, wiring, oxygen equipment and instruments.

[3] The industrial effort involved cannot, however, be accurately measured either by the numerical output or by airframe weight figures. For a discussion of a more accurate index of measurement, i.e. airframe structure weight corrected by man-hour equivalents see M. M. Postan, *British War Production* (London: H.M.S.O. and Longmans, Green & Co., 1952), pp. 169–172.

orders was limited more by estimates of what Canada was likely to produce, and in time to count, than by consideration of cost. The best evidence of this was to be found in the fact that when dollar caution was thrown to the winds in the summer of 1940, it was to the United States rather than Canada that practically all the new British orders for aircraft were directed. The Air Ministry's view as set out in a minute of 19th July 1940 was that for a variety of reasons there was no point in any great expansion of British aircraft orders in Canada. These orders then exceeded $45 million for an industry which still had only 8,500 employees. In view of the specialised nature of the manufacture, the difficulty of adapting existing engineering plants and lack of skilled mechanics, it was best to concentrate on the production of a few types. This view was to govern subsequent British policy in placing orders. In mid-September 1940 when the United Kingdom had on order from the United States 7,239 aircraft and engines to correspond, its orders in Canada totalled only 850 airframes—600 Hurricanes (including a further order of 440 placed in July), 100 Hampdens and 150 Lysanders. In May 1941 the Ministry of Aircraft Production cabled that it would have no further major requirements from Canada for delivery before mid-1942. The reason was that it had placed all the orders it thought Canada could handle.

This did not mean that the factor of cost could be ignored. It was one thing to put it aside so far as sterling expenditure was concerned; but dollars were another matter. The April 1938 programme of 12,000 planes to be produced in the United Kingdom within two years (boosted to 17,500—including 12,000 of the newest types—at the outbreak of war) marked the end of finance as a limiting factor within the United Kingdom, and the substitution of another criterion —that of production to the very limit of the capacity of the industry. So far as dollars were concerned, however, cost still continued to be a limiting factor up to the fall of France. The cost of placing orders abroad had greatly increased with the progress in the late thirties towards high-speed, heavily-armed monoplanes of all metal construction driven by new engines of far greater horse-power. Such planes not only cost much more but also demanded a more advanced engineering technique. In any case costs of production in North America were normally higher than in the United Kingdom.[1] So long as British capacity was still not stretched to the full there was a good case, therefore, against placing very large orders overseas. Aircraft were not the only British purchases in Canada. It is important to bear in mind the total kind and scale of the various British dollar

---

[1] Thus it was estimated just before the war that fifteen Beauforts would cost in the United Kingdom $564,000 as compared with $790,000 in Australia and as much as $1,823,400 in Vancouver where it had been suggested production might be located.

requirements from Canada. They were indicated well enough in a conjectural balance of payments made late in 1940 for the second year of war. Total British purchases were estimated at £261 million (or $1,044 million U.S.). Air requirements were put at £16 million; naval at £10½ million; food at £55 million; raw materials at £71 million; munitions at £103 million.

More important, however, than the factor of cost was the quite separate factor of time. What mattered was not how many bombers and fighters Canada, or the United States, might produce in a war of unlimited duration, but how many they could produce within two or three years. The table above[1] shows that for Canadian production the accent was on trainers until late in the war; it was not till 1944 that larger planes such as Lancasters, Mosquitos and Catalinas were produced in appreciable numbers. Production rates for most types ordered by Britain fell far short of the rates hoped for in 1939; but the same was true of production rates in Australia and even in the United States in the first half of the war.

(iii)

Development of Overseas Air Potential—
First Steps

Following discussions at the Imperial Conference of 1937 the Canadian Government—as an Air Ministry official commented a little later—'embarked on a very ambitious programme of local construction of airframes of British Service types in quantities confined for the moment to R.C.A.F. requirements'. By August orders had been given, or were pending, for some fifty-two machines of three types, Sharks, Stranraers and Lysanders. To these were added a little later Bolingbrokes and other types. These developments were watched carefully from London as a clue to the capacity of Canadian industry in airframe construction, in case the United Kingdom might decide to place orders in Canada as part of its long-term production plans. In the autumn of 1937 the Air Ministry discussed the matter further. Whilst importance was attached to aircraft production in Canada the United Kingdom could not place large enough orders there to warrant the necessary expenditure on factories and plant. British requirements so far as could be foreseen had already been placed with British factories. But future orders might be diverted to Canada, if manufacturing plans there were successful; since the

---

[1] See p. 26, footnote (1).

British Government was committed to help as much as it could in the development of local armament schemes within the Commonwealth.

The question of testing out the war potential of North America came to a head in the spring of 1938. At this time the full extent of the war potential and of the war needs of Britain herself was still largely unknown. Rearmament was now getting under way but her economy was still on a peace-time footing and in March only 210 aircraft were produced in the United Kingdom.[1] In May an Air Ministry Mission visited the United States and Canada. Its first task was to make special purchases of aircraft, including trainers, from the United States. These were needed to fill the gap expected from war wastage in the first year of war. The second task of the Mission, as defined in its report, was to explore 'the possibilities of creating a war potential in Canada'. It was not interested in the immediate supply of special types of aircraft.

In Ottawa the Mission learned from the Canadian Prime Minister that it was expected to deal directly with the Canadian industry rather than with the Canadian Government. The place of meeting with the ten recognised Canadian aircraft firms was therefore shifted from Ottawa to Montreal, but the Canadian Ministry of Defence was kept closely informed on all the discussions. The Canadian Government hoped for British aircraft contracts large enough to provide the financial basis for the development of a Canadian aircraft industry. The aircraft firms were told at this meeting that the United Kingdom aimed at the manufacture of 'British types under licence' for the purpose of creating 'a genuine war potential' and especially 'a war potential for the production of heavy long-range bombers which could be delivered if necessary by flight across the Atlantic'. There was a hint, but no promise, of 'small peace-time orders to keep such a potential in existence', and under pressure the Mission mentioned a figure of '500 airframes' a year.

The meeting led to the taking of the first step to link together the different Canadian aircraft firms—a move which was much welcomed by the Canadian Defence Department. The firms agreed to set up a Central Contracting Company which would make contracts with the United Kingdom Government, and assemble airframes from parts made by sub-contractors. The United Kingdom was looked to for engines and instruments. The munitions industry in Canada, the Mission reported, had as yet 'no design or development organisation as we know it'. There had to be a Canadian aircraft industry, with a trained labour force and an adequate supply of raw materials, before there could be a war potential. The existing labour force was only

---

[1] Nevertheless production was rising steadily and by June 1939 the output was three times as high.

1,500. Even if orders were placed it would take two years to get the organisation set up and production started, and two more years before 200 Wellington aircraft (or an equivalent type) could be produced. Thus, if production began in May 1940 200 aircraft should be produced by May 1942. The sharing of orders by British firms with branches in Canada, which the Mission proposed, was permitted by the Air Ministry in 1938 but the higher costs in Canada were a barrier. Early in 1939 the de Havilland firm sub-let to its Canadian branch part of an Air Ministry order for 400 Tiger Moths at a cost thirty to forty per cent. higher than in the United Kingdom. The depreciation of sterling at the outbreak of war raised the cost and the Air Ministry hesitated about sub-letting part of a second contract.

The main proposal of the Mission was to place an order for bombers in Canada. It was put by the Air Council in June 1938 as 'a matter of vital importance and pressing urgency' and was to cost £3½ million. In effect capacity was to be subsidised by means of a large order but without capital assistance. The contracting firms were to undertake to maintain the capacity for ten years.

A special Mission was sent in July 1938 with instructions to arrange for a central factory linking firms which were to develop a capacity in peace of 200 large bombers, or of 500 in the first year of a war. Delivery was to be by air across the Atlantic for which the Halifax or Stirling would be suitable. The initial order was to be for 100 bombers (airframes) of the Hampden class. (The Hampdens produced in Canada were not apparently flown across the Atlantic.) The aim of the Government was to get the scheme into operation in the early autumn of 1938 so that delivery could begin in two years' time. It approved on 19th October the agreement reached by the Mission. The arrangement was one between the United Kingdom Government and Canadian industry and the announcement made it clear that the Canadian Government was not directly involved.

Meanwhile there had been a clearer definition of the policy of the Canadian Government towards British aircraft and munitions orders in Canada. The policy was defined in letters in July 1938 and May 1939, by the Canadian Prime Minister and the Head of the External Affairs Department to the United Kingdom High Commissioner at Ottawa. The Canadian Government would continue to furnish, as in the past, all information available concerning the production and also the capacity of firms or plants in Canada. It would welcome enquiries made by the British authorities and continue to render every facility. Such help would be subject to three conditions. First, the negotiation of contracts should proceed directly between the British authorities and the Canadian firms concerned. Secondly, British orders should not conflict with any specific requirements for the Canadian Defence

Programme. Thirdly, as far as practicable the arms and equipment to be made in Canada should be such as might eventually be required and suitable for Canadian defence purposes.[1]

(iv)

The First British Air Contracts in Canada

The Hampden and Stirling bomber contract, between the Secretary of State for Air and the Canadian Associated Aircraft Company, as the new central contracting company was called, was signed in November 1938. An initial order for eighty Hampdens was placed simultaneously with a promise of a follow-on order for 100 large bombers. The twenty-five per cent. higher cost of production in Canada was regarded by the Air Ministry as a reasonable price for the additional capacity thus created. An order for forty Hurricanes was placed at the same time with the Canadian Car and Foundry Company Limited. No other contracts for aircraft were placed by the Air Ministry up to the outbreak of war. The decision by the Air Council on technical grounds (and on the advice of the Air Mission) against the manufacture of aircraft engines for the R.A.F. in Canada was announced by the Air Minister in reply to a question in the House of Commons on 15th February 1939. Although the matter was brought up a number of times later, no aircraft engines were in fact produced by Canada during the war.

A full statement of Air Ministry requirements in the first year of the war was given early in October 1939 to the British Supply Board at Ottawa. The aim now was to create airframe capacity in Canada for more than 250 aircraft a month. The number consisted of upwards of 200 trainers monthly for the British Commonwealth Air Training Plan; also twenty Stirling bombers a month by the spring of 1942 (to be produced by the Canadian Associated Aircraft Company following on its order for Hampdens), twenty Hurricanes monthly from the Canadian Car and Foundry Company, and thirty-five Lysanders monthly from the National Steel Car Corporation. These aircraft requirements and a large order already given for 48,000 tons of aluminium ingots (with a further 12,000 tons pending) were to have priority over everything else. Gun turrets and aero engines were not hoped for from Canada; but the Ministry was ready to place large orders for a wide variety of other accessories —such as small arms ammunition, bombs, instruments, etc.

---

[1] The Prime Minister, however, rejected a suggestion that the Canadian Defence Department should inspect aircraft produced on United Kingdom orders. Inspection was undertaken by an Air Ministry Inspection Directorate until the R.C.A.F. took over the inspection of British contracts in December 1942.

The Air Ministry would take all the spruce and three-ply veneers which Canada could supply. Altogether, apart from the heavy expenditures involved in the Air Training Plan, the Air Ministry estimated its expenditure in the first years of the war at some $22 million (mostly for aircraft and aluminium). Its full needs would rise to far higher figures as the war progressed. But it was assumed in London from the outset that the Canadian Government would be willing to finance war production in Canada.

(v)

Supply for the British Commonwealth Air Training Plan

The British Commonwealth Air Training Plan demanded large supplies of aircraft and equipment for the training schools operating under it in Canada, Australia and New Zealand. It was estimated that upwards of 5,000 aircraft of different types would be required under the Plan for initial equipment and immediate reserve.[1] The Dominions were to do all their own elementary training whilst Canada provided the advanced training for her own airmen as well as for limited numbers sent from the United Kingdom, Australia and New Zealand. The need of elementary trainers called for the stepping up of the production of Moth and Fleet aircraft in Canada, which used British engines. As regards advanced trainers, such as Harvard, it was estimated that there would be a wastage rate of sixty-two per month. As a matter of extreme urgency, to safeguard the supplies on which the Plan depended, a further 600 Harvards with 750 engines were ordered from the North American Company the moment the arms embargo was lifted on 4th November. The initial estimate for twin-engined advanced trainers was 200 per month; these were to come from the United Kingdom. Then there were target-towing and attack aircraft, supply of which would have to come initially from the United Kingdom, but eventually, it was hoped, from Canada. The need for general reconnaissance aircraft was to be met by an initial contribution of 396 Ansons by the United Kingdom, which would increase its output for this purpose from 200 to 220 per month.

The working out of the Plan lies outside the scope of this volume; but some reference is needed to the division of responsibility for supply. Agreement on the allocation of cost for the joint scheme in

---

[1] Elementary trainers (Moth and Fleet)   .   .   648
Advanced trainers (Harvard or Master)   .   .   1,125
Advanced trainers twin engine (Anson or Oxford)   1,575
Target towing and attack (Battles)   .   .   .   1,125
General Reconnaissance (Anson)   .   .   .   396

Canada and on responsibilities for supply was achieved only after long and difficult negotiations. The conference was hastily prepared. The Canadian Government began by assuming that Britain would bear most of the cost. The agreement as initialled at the end of November 1939 provided for a United Kingdom contribution of $185 million to the scheme in Canada. It was to take the form of aircraft and equipment. There was to be a further British contribution, valued at £23 million, towards the cost of training in Australia and New Zealand. Canada undertook sole responsibility for the cost of initial ground and elementary flying training, estimated at $68 million. The balance of the cost, $354 million, was to be met as follows:

			Per cent.
Canada	.	.	80·64
Australia	.	.	11·28
New Zealand	.	.	8·08

The British contribution in kind was to take the form of the supply of the following: Battles, Ansons (without wings which Canada was to produce), Harvards (from the British cash contracts in the United States), and engines for the Tiger Moth airframes to be made in Canada. These arrangements worked smoothly enough for the next six months until the interruption of supplies from the United Kingdom in the summer crisis of 1940 forced Canada to take a heavier responsibility for the supply side of the Plan.[1]

(vi)

The Output of Trainers in Canada

After Dunkirk Canada was forced to concentrate on building trainer aircraft since neither the United Kingdom nor the United States could furnish the supplies required for the Air Training Plan. The decision was made easier by the difficulties which Canadian manufacturers had found in their attempts to build the more complex Service types.

The interruption of supplies of training aircraft from Britain was a severe setback for Australia as well as Canada. In neither country was local production as yet capable of supplying more than a fraction of the trainers needed for the Air Training Plan. 'The success we have with the Empire scheme', a British Air Force officer in Australia wrote in May, 'will depend almost entirely upon deliveries of aircraft

---

[1] The British responsibility was re-defined in financial terms, rather than in contributions in kind, by a revised agreement which came into effect on 1st July 1942. For the financial settlement at the end of the war, see Chapter XI.

and instructional equipment from the United Kingdom'. When Canada learned at the end of May that the supply of Battles and Ansons for the Air Training Plan must be suspended for at least two months, the Minister for Munitions and Supply sought the help of Purvis to secure trainers from the United States. But there were none to be had.

The upshot was a hurried decision to produce Ansons (fuselage as well as wings) in Canada. But it was a year before the first Ansons could be delivered. Meanwhile to engine the Ansons 2,000 Jacob engines were found in the United States through Purvis. There were discussions in May and August on the building of aircraft engines in Canada, but the idea was dropped as uneconomical.

In June 1940 Lord Beaverbrook suggested the diversion to the United Kingdom of a large part of the early deliveries from the 600 Harvard trainers ordered in November 1939 which had been ear-marked for Canada. This was followed in July by a clear warning that Canada could not look to Britain for further aircraft supplies, at least for a long time to come. In order to speed up the Air Training Plan the Canadian Government had urged the diversion to Canada of various aircraft including some fighters and light bombers from British orders in the United States. The Air Ministry, whilst agreeing to some diversion, informed the Canadian Government on 11th July, that 'the scale of the present and impending air attacks on this country against which we must provide by every means in our power, renders it imperative for us to scrutinise with the utmost care any suggestion for releasing or foregoing the delivery of aircraft of operational value which we have or can get immediately into this country. . . .'

For a while Ottawa toyed with the idea of manufacturing American types in Canada using American-made engines, but after various American designs had been obtained through Purvis the idea was abandoned and Canada continued to produce mainly British types. For some time to come the main emphasis had to be upon trainers. A press release in Ottawa indicated that in mid-September 1940 there were only 895 trainers (409 of them elementary) in Canada for use in the British Commonwealth Air Training Plan, against the total of 5,000 which would be needed. Deliveries would bring the number up to some 3,000 by mid-1941 leaving 2,000 still to be produced. By the end of September 1940 the release stated, thirty-two training schools were in operation and the rest of the total of eighty-three schools for which the Plan provided would be ready by the end of 1941.

To provide the necessary number of trainers still more contracts had to be let in Canada. The production of Ansons was greatly expanded in the next two years. The first Canadian order for Har-vards, to be built under licence in Canada, had been placed in

January 1940; other Canadian orders followed. In 1941 the still growing needs of the Air Training Plan led to the placing of a first order for Harvards by the United States War Department under lend-lease with War Supplies Limited, Canada. By mid-1941 the allocation of the supply of aircraft was governed by the concept of pooling supplies to meet the common needs of the British Commonwealth and the United States. The machinery for allocating the aircraft as they were produced was already operating in the form of the Joint Aircraft Committee. Financial responsibility for particular contracts was no longer any clear index as to the country or countries which would use the planes when produced. Lend-lease played a part henceforth in the financing of supply under the Air Training Plan.

(vii)

Combat Aircraft—The Main British Contracts in Canada

In conclusion a word may be said on the results of the main British contracts for Service aircraft placed in Canada during the war. The numbers of each type produced have been given above. A press notice in February 1940 indicated that the first war plane built in Canada for the United Kingdom had left 'for the Motherland'; it arrived on 29th February. It was a Hurricane built, only a little behind schedule, by the Canadian Car and Foundry Company. At the end of May, nearly half of the original order of forty had been delivered by the firm—enough for the Canadian Hurricane squadron that arrived in England in mid-June. The order was increased to a total of 160 in May, with the admonition by Lord Beaverbrook, 'so find your material quickly and go all the way out'. Eight weeks later another order for 420 machines brought the total up to 600.

By this time to 'find your material' was possible because of the progress made in the fabrication of aluminium in North America. In January 1940 the Director of Aircraft Production had noted that 'every bit of material' for the first forty Hurricanes had been shipped from the United Kingdom. Shipment of materials for the second batch of forty, he pointed out, could only be made at the expense of an equal number of Hurricanes in the United Kingdom. Some weeks earlier, in a letter to the British Air Representative at Ottawa, he had referred to 'the really desperate situation we are in as regards material'.[1]

---

[1] In a minute in April 1939 the Director had made the point that 'it would be a mistake to be cheeseparing on the matter of supplies' to Canada and Australia, since this would only lessen the potential value of the aircraft production capacity which the United Kingdom was trying to secure. See below, Chapter IX, Section iv on aluminium.

The plan to build a heavy bomber in Canada went less smoothly. The 'educational' order for Hampdens was to be followed by the Stirling. The Air Ministry thought that Canadian Associated Aircraft could produce three Stirlings a week by the middle of 1941 and with double shift and overtime could work up to an output of twelve a week. By bringing in the two great railroad companies of Canada, capacity could be raised to eighteen a week. To raise production up to this level an order for 150 aircraft would be needed. As a first step the Air Council Committee on Supply decided on 1st September 1939 to recommend expenditure of $2 million for the jigs and tools required to produce three planes a week. The parent firm (Short Brothers) was instructed to provide the Canadian firm with all possible technical aid in the manufacture of jigs and tools, as well as five complete sets of extrusions, forgings, sheet and strip, and other materials.

The Stirling contract was to pass through many vicissitudes before it was finally abandoned in January 1941. The contract was made in January 1940 for 150 machines. In March the order was reduced to 140. In June it was cancelled by the Ministry of Aircraft Production to release materials for the new Hurricane order. It was reinstated in August; but the delays meant that production could not be expected for another two years.

The contract illustrated what was involved in the manufacture overseas of a complex British type. The blueprints and practically all the necessary jigs and tools had been shipped to Canada by July 1940. The nine Canadian firms involved in the manufacture of the Stirling in Canada sent a total of sixty-seven technicians to British factories for training in the manufacture of each part of the Stirling—some for a period as long as eight months. It was expected that the bulk of the actual materials to be used in manufacture could be obtained from Canada or the United States. The plan was to deliver the completed machines by air, which meant that the United Kingdom was expected to provide and send to Canada all the embodiment loan equipment, such as turrets and armament.

Meanwhile, the production of Hampdens, of which there were 160 on order by the autumn of 1940, was lagging far behind schedule. By the end of the year only nine had been produced; the order was not completed in fact until the summer of 1942, by which time the Hampden was largely obsolete. The group scheme involved the training and co-ordination of six firms then relatively inexperienced in modern aircraft production. The supply of materials was irregular and there were other difficulties. The first machines could not pass inspection until certain faults had been corrected. In December a survey was made of Canadian aircraft production by private and independent experts of British and American industry. The review was for the use of the Minister (Mr. C. D. Howe) then on a visit to England. The conclusion was that 'in the absence of a production team from England', Canadian Associated Aircraft was 'not strong enough to carry through a large programme for the production of new type heavy bombers such as the Stirling or Halifax'. It was, therefore, recommended that the firm should carry on with the production of Hampdens. In January 1941, following consultations between the two Ministers, the scheme for the production of Stirlings was abandoned; and the Canadian Government decided to take over the productive capacity of the company on the conclusion of the Hampden contract.

Late in 1941 when the shortage in heavy bombers for the R.A.F. began to loom ahead, the British Government turned again to North America for the manufacture of a heavy bomber—the Lancaster. The order was placed in Canada because of the unwillingness of the United States to undertake a British type. Capacity which was being reserved for the R.C.A.F. was diverted to the Lancaster. In compensation a British allotment of 218 B.26 American bombers (Marauders) was transferred to Canada. The first contract was for 300 Lancasters, later increased by 430. By June 1945 nearly 400 Lancasters had been produced on United Kingdom account. The contracting firms were the National Steel Car Corporation Limited and, from November 1942, Victory Aircraft Limited, a Crown Company.

About the same time—towards the end of 1941—an order for 400 Mosquito aircraft was placed with de Havilland, Canada, by the Department of Munitions and Supply, acting on behalf of the United Kingdom Government. In May 1942 the order was increased to 1,500. By June 1945, 961 Mosquito aircraft (bombers, fighter-bombers and a few trainers) had been produced in Canada on United Kingdom account.

For both Lancasters and Mosquitos the arrangement called for the delivery of complete aircraft; all possible equipment and accessories were to be produced in North America. The equipment was to come from Canada when practicable, otherwise from the United States by cash purchase or by lend-lease. The British Air Commission at Washington made the arrangements and supervised any design changes needed because of the use of American components. The engines were Rolls-Royce Merlins produced in the United States by the Packard Company.

For all such aircraft built in Canada on British designs, there was a constant exchange of technical information and technical staff between the Canadian manufacturers and the designing firm in the United Kingdom. For the early British contract technical supervision was exercised by resident inspectors at each factory, acting under the

R.A.F.'s Canadian inspection unit. For Lancasters United Kingdom-based resident technical officers were stationed in 1944 in the factory (Victory Aircraft). The same arrangement was made for the Mosquitos (Canadian de Havilland), but in this case the early models were less satisfactory and some changes had to be made in the aircraft when they reached England. Rolls-Royce and Packard also had representatives in residence at the factories to supervise the installation of the Merlin engines.

Thus in the end the expectations of the Air Ministry in 1938 were found to be justified, although the time was longer than it had hoped. The three main Service aircraft contracts—for Hurricanes, Mosquitos and Lancasters—were carried out with skill and efficiency. They were an outstanding example of the degree to which 'combined production' became possible in the later stages of the war. They involved technical co-ordination on an international scale between the various Air Forces and factories concerned with the contracts. They required the adaptation of British designs to Canadian conditions of production, the adjustment of the supply of Canadian-built airframes to American mass-produced engines of British design, and the fitting of a large variety of American and Canadian components. By the end of the war Canada had built up an important military aircraft industry.

CHAPTER III

THE AMERICAN POTENTIAL: THE COMING OF WAR IN EUROPE

(i)

The Friendly Neutrality

As preface to the history of war supply from the United States it is well to mention the scale given in the first and last chapters of this volume. Over the whole period of the war the United Kingdom itself produced 69½ per cent. of all the munitions used by the whole of the armed forces of the British Commonwealth and Empire—some 8¾ million men. The other 30½ per cent. came from the United States, Canada and the other members of the Commonwealth.

Still more significant for the chapters up to Pearl Harbour are the figures for the successive phases of that period. In the first four months of war Britain furnished ninety-seven per cent. (in value) of the munitions supply of the whole Commonwealth and Empire. In the early months of 1940 the proportion remained more or less the same; for the whole year it was still eighty-three per cent., despite the using up of the British gold and dollar reserves after Dunkirk to purchase supplies from the United States and the efforts of the other Commonwealth countries. The United States supplied for cash twelve per cent., Canada four per cent., and the rest of the Commonwealth one per cent. The rapidity with which Britain geared up for war production is shown by the figures for 1941. In that year (which included the first nine months of American lend-lease), British industry furnished eighty-four per cent. of the British Commonwealth's war supplies, Canada six per cent., the rest of the Commonwealth two per cent., and the United States eight per cent. Of that eight per cent., seven were bought by Britain for cash and one was furnished by the United States under lend-lease.

The lesson of these figures is far reaching. There is no important part of the picture of British supply from the United States that is fully intelligible by itself without reference to the canvas as a whole. For the most part lend-lease supply, as well as British buying in the United States, was geared closely to the rate and scale of production in British factories. Sudden emergencies, calling for some special purchase in the United States or Canada, occurred from time to time, the most famous example being United States surplus arms shipments after Dunkirk. But in the main procurement was a regular and systematic element in long-term production plans. It therefore reflected to some extent British production priorities. Thus production plans were reflected in the early emphasis on machine tool purchases. The priorities assigned in the first years of the war to British production of field guns, anti-aircraft guns, shells and small arms ammunition[1] meant less emphasis on the buying of such munitions in the United States. The large orders placed in the United States in 1940 for small arms ammunition and certain types of shells were supplementary to larger British supply programmes.

The origins of most of the main problems and difficulties of the later periods in the history of overseas supply can be traced back to the first twelve months of the war. 'Important problems', the Australian war historian, Dr. C. E. W. Bean, has well said, 'are often met in their simplest form in the original stage of any undertaking. Often at that stage the object of the undertaking is most clear, and the difficulties most apparent.'[2] This truth justifies the amount of space devoted in this volume to the period before lend-lease. In terms of actual supplies moved across the Atlantic, the period is unimportant, but it is rich in history.

The North American potential was alluring. It was immense. It was secure from attack. It was probably open to the Allies and closed to Germany. But access to it was beset by many difficulties. It had to be explored, developed over a long period of time and paid for in hard cash. It could be paid for only in gold and dollars. The potential itself was unlimited in the sense that it could be measured by no known standard. The limits within which Britain could use the potential—after the revision of the Neutrality Act—were neatly summarised in the President's phrase 'Cash and Carry'. To that had to be added 'Time'. Britain could use only the minute part of the potential that was available for purchase, and then only within the limits of her cash and the amounts she could carry in ships across the Atlantic through the U-boat packs.

From the viewpoint of those who were planning supply in 1939, time mattered most. The dates at which actual guns, tanks and planes from the United States could reach the battlefields were distant and uncertain. They depended on a number of elements.

---

[1] Peak production rates were reached as follows: field guns, first quarter 1942; heavy anti-aircraft guns, fourth quarter 1942; light anti-aircraft guns, first quarter 1943; shells and bombs, fourth quarter 1942; light anti-aircraft and small arms ammunition, fourth quarter 1943. See *Statistical Digest of the War* (London: His Majesty's Stationery Office, 1951), Tables 117, 118, 123.

[2] 'Australia's Federal Archives' in *Historical Studies*, Melbourne University Press November 1947.

First, on American policy, since that might exclude any access to the potential; second, the date at which Britain would decide to commit her limited financial reserves; third, the months or years required by American industry to retool for munitions production; fourth, the point at which the slowly rising crescendo of production would begin to fill the ships for the Atlantic passage; fifth, the availability of enough ships to carry the large tonnages and of escorts to protect them.

The governing factors from 1939 to the end of 1941 were American neutrality and British finance. American neutrality dominated the first period up to the fall of France. The expenditure of the British financial reserves dominated the second period up to—and in the months after—the passage of the Lend-Lease Act. In the first period the Treasury held a tight rein on all buying in North America. Procurement in the United States was slowed down more or less to a snail's pace by the decision of the Government to treat the American potential as marginal and not to commit for the time being the main part of the financial reserves.

In the nine months before the war and the nine months after it began, it was American neutrality that occupied the centre of the stage and held the spotlight. No supply of arms or munitions was possible at all until the repeal of the arms embargo by the revised Neutrality Act of 4th November 1939. Both before repeal and in the early months of 1940 the main attention of the British Embassy and of the British Purchasing Commission was centred on the political significance, the legal interpretation and the practical effect of the Neutrality Act and the many proclamations and regulations applying it. No important step in the field of supply could be taken without reference to neutrality legislation and policy; they must therefore form the central themes of this chapter.

American neutrality must be looked at in its context. Its context was support for the Allies 'short of war', but with war always possible, later or sooner. How far-reaching the support was, and how deep the sympathy, has been made more clear in recent years by the Roosevelt papers, the memoirs of Mr. Cordell Hull and Mr. Stimson and the papers of Mr. Harry Hopkins. In public the support was tempered by public opinion; but in private it was made very clear, not only to the British Government, but also, as Mr. Cordell Hull's papers show, to the Axis Governments. Policy thus looked one thing at the high level of the President, who could see both before and after. It looked different at the lower level of the general public, which, preoccupied with the tasks of its daily life, tended to take refuge in traditional views and attitudes. In an election year like 1940 the confusion was heightened. British dispatches from Washington from January 1940 onwards contain many references to the 'election year'. Thus Purvis, in March, noting the anxiety of the Secretary of the Treasury to help, added 'The degree of help will vary very considerably from time to time as this is election year'.[1]

The President never forgot the lesson of the failure of the Wilson Administration in 1919–20. He said to a friend in 1937, 'Wilson made just one mistake: he failed to do the things that were required to bring the Senate along'.[2] It was not enough for a President to look forward to the future. He had to look backwards to be sure that he was not drawing too far away from the people who elected him; and sideways to see that he kept close to the elected Congress through which alone he could secure the laws and money needed to carry out that policy. This was above all true in the field of foreign affairs. For the vague words of the Constitution on this field, an American authority has said, are 'an invitation to struggle for the privilege of directing American foreign policy'.[3]

The British dispatches from Washington dwelt much in the years from 1937 to 1941 on the state of public opinion. This was a phenomenon which British Ministers and officials found difficult to understand. For government in the British system is not as it is in the United States. The American system, as a British authority has observed, makes 'the individual citizen the starting-point and motive power of the political process, the creator both of the President as the embodiment of the citizen's executive authority and of Congress as the embodiment of his power over legislation'.[4] It was to the individual citizen who had elected him, whose support he needed in securing legislation in Congress, and output in the factory, that President Roosevelt went back frequently in his famous fireside talks to the nation and in his press conferences. How painful it was for the President to mark time, inert and 'deedless', whilst he waited on the slow processes of public opinion is told vividly by Mr. Sherwood.[5] Mr. Churchill, waiting on the other side of the Atlantic, understood

---

[1] Departments in London were influenced strongly by this factor, e.g. London's rejection on this ground of Purvis's scheme for capital assistance for expanding aircraft production. See Chapter IV, Section iv.

[2] Dr. Luther Gulick, *Administrative Reflections from World War II* (Alabama: University of Alabama Press, 1948), p. 42.

[3] Edward S. Corwin, *The President* (New York: New York University Press, 1940), p. 200.

[4] L. S. Amery, *Thoughts on the Constitution* (London: Oxford University Press, 1947), pp. 12–13. In the British system, Mr. Amery observed, 'Government and Parliament, however closely intertwined and harmonized, are still separate and independent entities, fulfilling the two distinct functions of leadership, direction and command, on the one hand, and of critical discussion and examination on the other. They start from separate historical origins, and each is perpetuated in accordance with its own methods and has its own continuity'. Ibid., p. 28.

[5] Robert E. Sherwood, *Roosevelt and Hopkins* (New York: Harper & Bros., 1948), Chapters V–VI. This work was published in two volumes in the United Kingdom (London: Eyre & Spottiswoode, 1948) under the title of *The White House Papers of Harry L. Hopkins*.

the process. In the last week of June 1940, when faced with warnings passed on by the Ambassador and others in Washington about the waves of pessimism that were sweeping over America, he replied: 'Too much attention should not be paid to the eddies of United States opinion. Only the force of events can govern them. . . . No one is downhearted here.'

Before the outbreak of war whilst the debate on the Neutrality Act held the front of the stage, the President showed that he could act where action did not come into public discussion. The best example is the setting up of the Atlantic Patrol. As a foil to it was his failure to act over the Norden bombsight because it was one of the best advertised pieces of apparatus which the American War Department possessed. These two examples will be discussed in some detail.

It is easier to understand the discussions in London in the six months before the war on the possibilities of supply from the United States, if it is remembered that discussions were also going on at the same time between the defence authorities of the two countries. The British Government proposed in March 1939 the opening of conversations on the possible effect of a war in Europe on British and therefore American naval dispositions in the Pacific.[1] It was now clear that Britain might have to face war simultaneously with three naval powers, for which the British fleet was not sufficient. Singapore and Australia had to be defended, but how? An answer might be indicated by the dispositions of the American fleet, which had been temporarily in the Atlantic since January. The President moved the fleet back to the Pacific but was non-committal on policy, except for the expression of a personal opinion to an Australian statesman that an attack by a Japanese fleet on Australia might create a situation 'intolerable to America'. At the beginning of July 1939, however, the President, accompanied by the Chief of Naval Operations, the Secretary of State (Mr. Cordell Hull) and Mr. Sumner Welles, indicated to the Ambassador that in case of war the United States would want to establish a patrol over the waters of the western Atlantic, in order to deny those waters to belligerents. For the purpose of the patrol, permission was desired by the United States Navy whereby American ships and aircraft could make use of the ports and waters of the colonies of Trinidad, Santa Lucia and Bermuda. Permission to lease premises and to land stores was also desired. All this, he thought, could be accomplished by the sending of instructions to the Governors of the colonies concerned. The arrangement was to be terminable on due notice. Canada would have to be approached separately in connection with the possible use of the port of Halifax. He explained

---

[1] *The Memoirs of Cordell Hull*, Vol. 1 (New York: The Macmillan Company, 1948), pp. 630–31. This work was also published in the United Kingdom under the same title (London: Hodder & Stoughton, 1948).

some days later (on 8th July) that the proposal applied to the operation of submarines in the patrolled area and to any kind of attack against belligerent territory situated in the area. He could move, he pointed out, only as fast as public opinion would permit him. The only step he could take now was to request facilities in the three ports. No commitment in regard to the patrol could be made until some event had prepared public opinion to that extent, e.g. enemy submarine action near the American coast.

On 17th July the State Department was informed that instructions had been issued by the British Government to the Governors of the colonies concerned. The point was made clear in the discussions that no exclusive use of the ports either in peace or war was intended. It was essential that the Royal Navy should be able to use them for the purpose of safeguarding British possessions and commerce. On 25th August the Ambassador informed the Governors of Bermuda and of the Windward Islands of the desire of the American authorities to take immediate advantage of the arrangements. The necessary facilities were given forthwith by the Governors. All arrangements had been completed by the end of August and the American patrol began to operate with a force of destroyers, coast-guard patrol vessels and flying-boats over an area up to 300 miles out to sea, from the Newfoundland Banks down to the West Indian islands. Mr. Cordell Hull informed the press on 4th October that patrolling would be confined to gathering information on belligerent activities within the zone. On 2nd October the neutrality zone formed the subject of the first of the many war-time exchanges between the 'Naval Person' (Mr. Churchill) and the President.[1]

Exchanges at the highest level (involving, *inter alia*, the Prime Minister and the President, the Foreign Secretary and the First Lord of the Admiralty (Mr. Churchill)) had begun even earlier on one highly important item of supply, the Norden bombsight. On 25th August 1939 the Prime Minister wrote to President Roosevelt asking him to authorise the release to Britain of details of the Norden bombsight, and received a non-committal answer. The Norden sight was reported to be one of the 'most jealously guarded secrets' of the American Services. Attempts made from May 1938 onwards through the Air Attaché at the British Embassy to obtain the information, in exchange for data about the British automatic bombsight and aircraft

---

[1] 'The Naval Person' said: 'We should have great difficulty in accepting a zone which was only policed by some weak neutral. But of course if the American Navy takes care of it, that is all right.'
　　The Declaration of Panama (3rd October 1939) defined a hemisphere neutrality zone which 'the American Republics would patrol'. (*Memoirs of Cordell Hull*, Vol. I, op.cit., p. 690.) Mr. Cordell Hull's idea of a more 'flexible' zone, in which the United States would 'patrol out to sea whatever distance might be necessary to protect our shore line and territorial waters' was put into effect late in 1940.

turrets, had been unsuccessful. The United States Navy, the Air Attaché reported, believed it had 'the best equipment in the world in every line'. It was after he was allowed to witness the remarkable accuracy of the bombsight that it had been decided to take up the matter at the highest level. In mid-October 1939 Mr. Churchill told the President of the success of the Asdic apparatus in the anti-submarine warfare: 'We should be quite ready to tell you about our Asdic methods whenever you feel they would be of use to the United States Navy and are sure the secret will go no further'. A formal request for information about the Asdic device was made early in December by the United States Naval Attaché in London with the offer in exchange of information about an American submarine detection device. At the suggestion of Lord Halifax the idea of Asdic for Norden (the latter to be used with a self-destroying device) was put personally by Lord Lothian to the President in mid-December. The President, he reported, was 'not sure that Great Britain . . . would not be better without it (Norden) if it was not absolutely certain that Germany, with few ships of her own to worry about, could not gain possession of it'. Further personal approaches by the Ambassador to the President on 1st February and 12th May 1940 showed the continued importance attached by the British Government to the bombsight. The Air Ministry, on 19th June, put it at the head of the list of things on which it desired data from the United States. Earlier in that month, however, the Deputy Chief of the British Air Staff had informed the Air Attaché that British scientists had now succeeded in stabilising a British automatic bombsight. This was claimed to be as good as, if not better than, the Norden, but production was disappointingly slow and the release of a number of the Norden sights was still desired. By the end of June the efficiency of new German tactics of high-altitude bombing seemed to show they had a sight similar to the Norden. Even without the Norden sight, the release of its stabilising element would be helpful. The Ambassador put these points to the President on 1st July and was told that the moment the British sight, or a captured German sight, could be shown to be of practically equal efficiency, the release of the Norden sight would be possible. Finally Purvis in a 'Memorandum for Mr. Morgenthau' on the 9th asked outright, but again in vain, for as many actual bombsights as the American Army could spare. The release of the Norden sight, which was actually installed in some PBY5 flying-boats allocated to the United Kingdom in October, was refused because of an outbreak of press publicity. The Nordens were replaced by the Sperry bombsight, said to be equal to or better than the Norden. The Sperry sight was released at the end of September and the British Air Commission asked for 500 a month. From that point British interest in the Norden dwindled. The British gyroscopic sight was more accurate; and in 1941 the Air Ministry found in British radar a far more effective solution. A few days before Pearl Harbour the American Navy was still considering the question of the release of the Norden sight and 'still unwilling to do so for military reasons'.[1]

(ii)

The Neutrality Act and Supply

The great American debate on the revision of the Neutrality Act began, as Mr. Cordell Hull records in his Memoirs, with a decision of the President and the State Department at the end of 1938. They decided that the Act was an incitement to war, since it made it impossible for Britain and France, if at war, to purchase arms or aircraft from the United States.[2] In fact the Proclamations issued by the President under the Act, after the outbreak of war in September 1939, placed the Allies under the same prohibitions as regards the export of arms as Bolivia and Paraguay had been placed by the Proclamation of 28th May 1934, Ethiopia and Italy by the Proclamation of 29th February 1936, and Spain by the Proclamation of 1st May 1937.[3] Behind the Neutrality Act lay the Johnson Act of 1934 which prohibited loans, except renewals or refundings, to any government which was in default either wholly or in part on the payment of its obligations to the American Government.[4] This prohibition of loans to debt defaulters was independent of the Neutrality Act and continued in effect after America came into the

---

[1] *Minutes of the Council of the Office of Production Management* (21st December 1940 to 14th January 1942, Historical Reports on War Administration: War Production Board, Documentary Publication No. 2, Washington, 1946), p. 79, Minutes of Meeting, 2nd December 1941. In September 1941 the British Embassy had reported a statement made during a trial of German agents that drawings of the Norden bombsight had been sold to the German Government in 1938.

[2] See *Memoirs of Cordell Hull*, Vol. I, op. cit., p. 586, for the President's words spoken in Canada in August 1938.

[3] National Munitions Control Board, First and Second Annual Reports, 75th Congress, 1st Session House Document No. 10; 3rd Session House Document No. 465.

[4] The matter of the unpaid British war debts of the First World War to the United States figured much in the controversies of 1938 to 1941. Lord Riverdale found strong feeling on them when he came as a scout on war supply in August 1939. But the feelings only obstructed the facts. British purchases of war supplies from the United States from August 1914 to June 1919 amounted to about $12,000 million. The United Kingdom paid $8,000 million in cash and borrowed $4,000 million from the United States Government after the entry of the United States into the war in 1917. On the debt of $4,000 million, Britain paid $2,000 million (interest and principal) from 1919 up to the cessation of payment on transfer grounds in 1933. War debts of European countries to the United Kingdom amounted to $7,800 million on which the United Kingdom received $346 million.

war. The Neutrality Act merely doubled the prohibition by making belligerency also a ground for denial of loans.[1]

A British Foreign Office memorandum in the spring of 1937 dealt with the effects of the Neutrality Act of that year, analysed the beliefs on which neutrality was based, its legal aspects, and its effect on supply. The First World War, it was pointed out, strengthened rather than weakened the tradition of avoiding European entanglements. 'It is impossible', the British Ambassador in Washington had recently told London, 'to find anyone who is not determined that when the next war breaks out, come what may, America shall remain aloof.' There was a general belief, the memorandum pointed out, that 'but for the friction caused between America and Germany over the German interference with American lives and property at sea, the United States would not have come in'.[2]

The neutrality legislation was based thus on the idea of removing the frictions that were blamed for getting America into the last war. Once these were removed the 'natural impregnability' of the United States would come into play and they would regain their freedom of action. There were four such frictions, the memorandum pointed out:

   (i) The carriage by neutral vessels of goods which are, or are alleged to be, contraband.

   (ii) The carriage by neutrals of goods, whether contraband or not, to blockaded enemy territory or to a place in enemy territory which is blockaded.

   (iii) The carriage in neutral vessels of goods which, whether contraband or not, and whether destined for enemy blockaded territory or not, are goods owned by the enemy government or by enemy private subjects.

   (iv) The loss of neutral lives owing to belligerent action at sea.

As regards (i), the most dangerous forms of contraband, namely arms and implements of war, were forbidden to be exported at all to belligerent countries. But several possible loopholes were left. First, other forms of contraband were permitted; second, goods—whether American or owned by belligerents—might still be carried in American vessels. Third, United States citizens could still travel—and so be open to attack—in American ships, though they were denied travel in belligerent vessels.

The series of Neutrality Acts from 1935 to 1939 tried to close all these loopholes. Every breakdown of peace in Europe—the Italian

---

[1] Under the ordinary rules of neutrality loans to belligerents by private persons or firms in a neutral country are not prohibited, although the neutral government may be precluded from lending money to belligerents.

[2] Thus the *New York Herald Tribune* on 7th July 1939 referred to the 'widespread belief during the last two decades that it was the insistence on defending American traditional neutral rights that got the country into the World War'.

invasion of Abyssinia, the Spanish Civil War, and German expansion into Czechoslovakia—produced another American Neutrality Act.[1]

A further memorandum dated 9th May 1938, circulated by the Foreign Office to departments in London, concluded that the Neutrality Act in its existing form would hardly be workable in a major war. It would have 'depressing effects on the American economy', due to the loss of export markets and the forced liquidation by foreign governments of their American securities, and the laying up of American ships.

The revision of the Neutrality Act was a hard-fought political battle in the United States, in and out of Congress, from January 1939 to the signing of the revised Act on 4th November 1939. Mr. Cordell Hull devotes two chapters of his Memoirs to it. The battle was watched closely by Britain, indeed by all Europe. Every new development was reported by the Embassy in dispatches to London. The point of the battle was not the abandonment of American traditional neutrality, since this was a fixed concept agreed on all sides. The issue was the conditions under which neutrality should be exercised. The debate was conducted under a double pressure, that of events abroad (the invasions of Czechoslovakia in March and of Albania in April) and the deadline created by the expiring of one part of the Neutrality Act of 1937 on 1st May 1939. This was the 'cash and carry' provision which required belligerents to pay cash for goods they bought and to carry them away in their own ships.

It was mid-March 1939 before the Administration's Bill was presented in the Senate. When it was blocked there in April the Administration turned to the House. By then public opinion had hardened in support of 'cash and carry'. Then, in June and July, came what Mr. Cordell Hull called the 'Neutrality Disaster': a vote in the House for a partial arms embargo and the decision by a majority of one in the Senate Foreign Relations Committee on 12th July to shelve the Bill until January 1940. The Administration now published its proposals as they had been defined in letters of 27th May and 14th July to the Chairman of the two Foreign Affairs Committees.[2] Negotiations between the President, the Secretary of State and the party leaders in Congress finally broke down at the famous meeting on 18th July in which Senator Borah announced from his private information that no war would occur at least in the

---

[1] The main legislation was (*a*) the Neutrality Resolution passed by Congress and signed by the President on 31st August 1935 on the eve of the Italian invasion of Ethiopia which provided for an embargo on the export of arms. (A resolution modifying it was signed by the President on 29th February 1936); (*b*) A Joint Resolution by Congress on 8th January 1937 prohibiting the export of arms to either party in Spain; (*c*) Neutrality Act, 1st May 1937; (*d*) Neutrality Act, 4th November 1939.

[2] State Department release, 14th July 1939. The letters of 27th May are in the House Committee Report, House Doc. No. 856, 17th June 1939.

near future.[1] 'Congress as a group of individuals', the *New York Times* had reported on 13th July, was 'in an irritable mood and wants to quit. As a legislative body it is made up now of wilful and shifting blocs whose attitude on any major question can hardly be told in advance of the vote.' The breakdown occurred at a moment when the cables pouring into the State Department from the capitals of Europe all pointed to war breaking out in August or September. The cables reported that the failure of the United States to remove the arms embargo was regarded abroad as encouraging the dictators and discouraging the democracies.[2] From the British point of view the situation was highly delicate. The Embassy avoided direct contact with the State Department as far as possible and the British Government refrained from all actions or statements likely to increase the difficulties of the Administration.

The Arms Embargo. The situation which now had to be faced was analysed in papers prepared at the Embassy and in interdepartmental meetings in London in July 1939. It was foreseen that war would be followed by a proclamation of a state of war by the President under the law of 1st May 1937. The arms embargo would follow automatically, since Section 1 (*a*) of the Act provided 'it shall thereafter be unlawful to export, or attempt to export, or cause to be exported arms, ammunition or implements of war from any place in the United States to any belligerent state named in such proclamation, or to any neutral state for trans-shipment to, or for the use of, any such belligerent state'. There was not even a provision, it was noted, to exempt munitions already ordered or paid for by belligerents. Mr. Churchill pointed out to the American Ambassador on 8th September that material already ordered in the United States was being held up under the Act. Pending orders, such as an Air Ministry order for 1,200 Wright Cyclone aero engines, were frozen.[3]

Materials and goods other than arms, e.g. trucks, could still be purchased and as the Act then stood might even be carried in American vessels. But cash would be required and no loans or credit would be given.

Interdepartmental discussions took place in London from May to July 1939 on 'United States neutrality legislation and its effect on supply in War'. As a background to these discussions a word or two must be said about the state of British rearmament on the eve of the war.[4] The account given in *British War Production* shows the extreme poverty of the armed Services—at least of the Army and the Air

---

[1] *Memoirs of Cordell Hull*, Vol. I, op. cit., pp. 649–51. Sherwood, op. cit., pp. 132–33.

[2] *Memoirs of Cordell Hull*, Vol. I, op. cit., pp. 651–53.

[3] 'When the Neutrality Act was proclaimed on September 5', Mr. Cordell Hull notes, 'the large armaments orders that Britain and France had placed in the United States, especially for airplanes, were frozen.' See *Memoirs of Cordell Hull*, Vol. I, op. cit., p. 693.

[4] See M. M. Postan, *British War Production*, op. cit., Chapter III.

E

Force—in the matter of new equipment. The Air Force had pulled up somewhat since Munich (September 1938) when out of thirty operational fighter squadrons only one was equipped with Spitfires and five were in process of being equipped with Hurricanes. The Army side at the time of Munich had hardly enough equipment to put two divisions on the Continent. Until early in 1939 munitions production, apart from the air, had gone little beyond the scale of peace. It is pointed out below that before Dunkirk there was virtually no munitions industry in the United States outside the seven Government arsenals. The same could have been said of the United Kingdom a year or two earlier. In 1934 there was only one full-scale armaments firm that had survived in England from the First World War. Until 1939 the emphasis of British defence expenditure was still on the Air Force and the Navy. Little more than a defensive role was reserved for the Army and the funds available to it left little margin for purchases abroad. The Navy was better off since it began with a much higher level of peace-time equipment. Its requirements from North America during the war were therefore much less than those of the other Services. But it faced already a serious shortage of destroyers, escort vessels and minesweepers, a shortage which was not remedied until late in the war.

The interdepartmental discussions in July 1939 reached the conclusion that 'In the event of war, the question of the purchase of supplies of all kinds in the United States would at once assume importance; and, though the extent and range of these purchases may be limited by exchange considerations and (at any rate at the outset) by the question of neutrality legislation, there seems no doubt that we shall be obliged to rely upon the United States of America for supplies of a large range of raw materials and manufactured articles. It is therefore desirable that arrangements should be made in advance to enable such supplies to be obtained with the maximum of economy and the minimum of delay'. Both the general strategy of supply under American neutrality and the effect of neutrality on particular requirements were considered. The discussions proceeded on the basis of a strategic conception as to the changed conditions of warfare brought about by the development of air power. The belligerent with an outside position less vulnerable to air attack, and having superior sea power, could draw on the world for supply; and this might in the long run prove the decisive factor. On the other hand the belligerent in a more central position tended to be in a less advantageous position than when warfare was confined to land and sea operations. Being now open to air attack, his industries could be destroyed; the more he had attempted to make himself self-sufficient the more air attack and sea blockade might damage decisively his offensive power. Thus from a strategic point of view every effort should be made to place the least possible restriction on supplies reaching Britain from the United States.

Large-scale air operations over Britain, however, might vitiate in the very first days of the operations any lists of probable requirements from North America. If the destruction were sufficiently widespread the United Kingdom might find itself in the position of needing not a particular list but practically anything and everything which could be got from the United States. But lists of requirements of the various Services were examined. It was agreed that the field of possible supply from the United States which would be useful in time of war would be so great that it would affect most of the materials and stores required by the various Services. It was therefore desirable to keep open the door as widely as possible for supplies of all kinds.

The discussion on particular supplies from the United States was dominated throughout by the question as to the effect of the Neutrality Act and possible modifications of it. Other factors discussed were dollar costs, and the time American factories would require before there could be any appreciable output of munitions. As for raw materials, it was assumed that supply was not likely to be restricted or cut off. Particular emphasis was placed on molybdenum, essential for the making of high-grade steel for armament purposes; supply was limited and came almost wholly from the United States. If the latter could prohibit the export of molybdenum to the enemy this would leave more for the Allies and the United States. As regards Admiralty supplies, for some of them, such as rosin, turpentine, ash oars, pitch pine and American white oak scantlings, the United States was the only normal source of supply. The same applied to manila hemp from the Philippines, a territory to which American neutrality legislation was applicable. The greatly increased quantities of fuel oil and other petroleum products needed by the Admiralty would have to be drawn in part from the United States. The latter might also fabricate for assembly in Canada small ships, such as escort vessels and minesweepers. American supplies of copper and raw cotton would be much more important in war. Steel forgings and castings would also be required from the United States. The same applied to tobacco and foodstuffs. As regards manufactured goods, all sorts of machine tools, instruments of various kinds, aircraft accessories and so forth, would also be required from American production. Given time these could be manufactured in Britain. But in many cases time was not available for the preparation of the necessary designs. It was not thought likely that most of the articles mentioned would be subject to an embargo on arms and implements of war. Nor were requirements, as actually foreseen at that moment, so great as to make their cost seem entirely prohibitive when measured by the existing financial reserves.

The Neutrality Proclamations. The President's broadcast to the nation on 3rd September 1939 after the outbreak of war showed his preoccupation with the state of public opinion. A poll in mid-August had shown that three out of four people questioned expected the United States to be drawn into the war. The President declared that as long as it remained within his power 'there will be no blackout of peace in the United States'. Neutrality proclamations would be issued forthwith.

The early American neutrality policy after the outbreak of war in Europe went through three stages. First, a proclamation of neutrality under the general rules of international law was issued on 5th September; this continued in effect as long as America was at peace. Second, there were proclamations and regulations under the Neutrality Act of May 1937, which were issued on 5th September and later dates as different countries came into the war. These in turn were superseded by proclamations and regulations issued under the Neutrality Act as amended on 4th November 1939.[1]

On 8th September 1939 the President proclaimed a national emergency of a limited character. Measures were also taken to increase the strength of the armed forces. It had already been agreed on 1st September at a meeting at the State Department that a special session of Congress should be summoned shortly for the purpose of revising the Neutrality Act. The date set was 21st September. The President delayed the issuing of the summons in order to give public opinion an opportunity to demand repeal of the Act.[2] Lord Lothian —who had presented his credentials on 30th August—summed up on 8th September the state of opinion as one of 'overwhelming sympathy for the Allies'; but the unanimous and passionate desire of all Americans was to keep out of war. It was already clear, he thought, that the arms embargo would be repealed. The Ambassador noted, six weeks later, a slackening of tension, as the delay in active hostilities began to work in the minds of the American people. The neutrality debate was still dragging on in the Senate. Nine out of ten Americans wanted the Allies to win, he reported, but nine out of ten wanted America to stay out. The unspectacular nature of the war was strengthening the idea that this war was of concern to Europe alone; it was an 'imperialistic' rather than an 'ideological' war.

The President referred to the supply situation on 17th September 1939 in a discussion with the Ambassador on blockade and other

---

[1] The texts of the various proclamations and of the Neutrality Acts of 1937 and 1939 are given in *Documents on American Foreign Relations*, Vol. I, 1938–39 (Boston: World Peace Foundation), p. 629 ff. The State Department pointed out that the general neutrality proclamation was issued 'according to customary usage' and would have been issued regardless of the Neutrality Act of 1937. The other neutrality proclamations, on the other hand, were based solely on the Neutrality Act and therefore had to be revised when the Act was revised. See *Memoirs of Cordell Hull*, Vol. I, op. cit., p. 679.

[2] Ibid., p. 673.

matters. Given tact by all those concerned and avoidance of 'note writing about legal points' the President thought that trouble could be avoided over the blockade. He expressed his confidence that the arms embargo would be repealed and went on to say that he thought some seventy per cent. of the British requirements were not affected by the embargo provisions. Of the remaining thirty per cent. he asked which were regarded by the British as the most important. The answer was given to the Administration a fortnight later. The Ministry of Supply had so far assumed that steel and other raw materials, machine tools and instruments, were not on the prohibited list. It would like to see the position cleared up as regards gun liners, shell bodies, cartridge cases, and chemicals not made up finally into explosives, etc., and also aeroplanes and aeroplane engines. Semi-finished materials, it was agreed, were not on the prohibited list.

Cash and Carry. It was significant of the state of public opinion that although the repeal of the arms embargo definitely implied aid to Britain and France this fact was not mentioned by the President in his message to Congress asking for amendment of the Act. 'Nowhere in his message', Mr. Cordell Hull wrote, 'did the President mention the thought that had been in the minds of all of us, that lifting the arms embargo would assist Britain and France.'[1] In fact the President, in his statement to the press on 4th November explaining the Bill which had just been signed, completely ignored the lifting of the arms embargo. He laid all the emphasis on the exclusion of American shipping from all areas 'in which the actual operations of the war appear to make navigation of American ships dangerous'. But it was to the embargo that the British Prime Minister, Mr. Chamberlain, referred when on 8th November he wrote a personal letter to the President. 'The repeal of the arms embargo, which has been so anxiously awaited in this country', he wrote, 'is not only an assurance that we and our French allies may draw on the great reservoir of American resources; it is also a profound moral encouragement to us in the struggle upon which we are engaged.'

The general effect of the new Act is summed up by Mr. Cordell Hull in his *Memoirs* as follows:[2]

> Britain and France now had access to our war goods, but on a cash-and-carry basis. Our own ships could not go to France, Britain, Germany, Ireland, Sweden, Denmark, the Netherlands, Belgium, Baltic ports, or Norway south of Bergen; but the Mediterranean and Black Seas, the Pacific and Indian Oceans, and all ports in Africa south of the Canaries were still open. The shipment of arms, ammunition and implements of war on American ships to belligerent ports in the Pacific was prohibited. Most of the other provisions of the Act

[1] Ibid., p. 683.
[2] Ibid., p. 697.

were virtual continuations of provisions in the Act of 1937. . . .
The Act prohibited travel by Americans on belligerent vessels, the
arming of American merchant vessels, and loans to belligerents. It
regulated the solicitation and collection of contributions for the
belligerents, continued the National Munitions Control Board in
operation, and gave the President discretion to close our ports to
submarine and armed merchant vessels. . . .

The complex shipping provisions of the Neutrality Act were of
particular importance. The high seas were split up into a series of
five zones. 'American rights now differ', Mr. Walter Lippmann
wrote, 'from one patch of salt water to another.'[1] American ships
were withdrawn from the Atlantic routes and laid up in large
numbers. A legal interpretation in March 1940 and the entry of
Italy into the war forced the withdrawal of over fifty American ships
from the Mediterranean.[2] American ships were also forbidden to
carry paper pulp—not American goods—from Newfoundland which
was outside the combat zone. It became necessary for the British
Ministry of Shipping to spend dollars on the purchase of American
ships—privately owned vessels, since the legality of sale by the
Government to a belligerent was doubtful. The Exchange Requirements Committee in January 1940 authorised expenditure for this
purpose. By June $18 million had been spent on the purchase of
forty-two ships and in July it was indicated to Mr. Morgenthau that
another $8 million would be spent in the next twelve months.

Such purchases could replace only a fraction of the American
shipping lost to the Allies by the Neutrality Act. The possibility of
amendment of the Act to permit American ships to enter the combat
zone was raised in vain in June and again in November 1940, and
once again by the Prime Minister in his famous letter of 8th December to the President. 'Carry' was not eliminated until the revision of
the Act of 17th November 1941—twenty days before Pearl Harbour.
The Red Sea had been opened to American ships on 10th April 1940.
'Cash' had gone out with the Lend-Lease Act in March for ships as
well as everything else; it permitted the transfer to the Allies of
American ships owned by the Government. The real remedy for
shipping losses, however, was the supplementing of British building
by the vast American shipbuilding programme which British contracts had helped to start even before lend-lease.

---

[1] *New York Herald Tribune*, 27th January 1940. The complexities were set out in a
release issued by the State Department (No. 597) of 16th November 1939.

[2] Informal opinion by the Attorney-General released by the State Department on
14th March. As early as November 1939 the number of vessels withdrawn from routes
in the combat zone was estimated at 130. *Business Week*, 11th November 1939.

(iii)

Finance in the Transition

The financial aspect of Britain's problem of using the American potential was simple enough in itself. Only two forces could keep moving the stream of trade that brought imports to Britain from America. One was British exports, the other American credits. Without these the stream must cease to flow. There were three elements in the problem:

1. A heavy adverse trade balance with the United States and a general decline in dollar-earning exports from the sterling area.
2. A limited war chest (dollar securities and gold).
3. A double statutory denial of credit to the British Government— as defaulter under the Johnson Act, as belligerent under the Neutrality Act.

The vicious circle was complete. Heavy imports of war materials must increase the adverse trade balance. As the war chest was depleted to pay for these imports there was no way of refilling it. Credits were not available. From exports little if anything more could be squeezed; even the unfettered peace-time British export trade could hardly surmount the barrier of the American tariff. As men and materials were absorbed by the British war industries it would become impossible to maintain exports. There was left the strict rationing of dollars for purchases abroad and the cutting out of unessential imports such as American tobacco and films. But this last step was certain to create political friction with the United States.

The barring of credit under the Johnson Act applied only to purchases by the British Government itself. In theory the purely private importer could still get normal commercial credits. But these were only short-term, and they made little or no difference to the balance of payments.

The United States Attorney-General had given an opinion on 5th May 1934 that the Johnson Act exempted normal short-term commercial credits. Whether this applied to British Government purchases remained a theoretical point until the British Government itself began to order materials in the United States. A few such orders began to be made in 1938. In June 1939 the first case occurred of refusal of short-term commercial credits on a purchase made on behalf of the British Government. The Office of Works had placed contracts to buy rubber hose from two American companies and had asked the Bank of England to open documentary credits with a New

York bank. The latter replied that 'the Johnson Act prohibited extensions of credits to foreign governments or others acting on their behalf'; it therefore charged the purchases to the account of the London bank, which was acting for the Bank of England. From this the Governor of the Bank of England concluded, and the Treasury concurred, that 'Government purchases in the U.S.A. must be arranged in such a way as does not involve the opening of credits'. The correspondence indicated that contracts placed or pending by the Air Ministry came to over $33 million, whilst those for the War Office were $3¼ million. About $17 million had been provided on these contracts. There was also an Office of Works contract for the purchase of 250,000 feet of rubber fire hose with another in the offing for 1,000,000 feet. (Altogether 5½ million feet of fire hose were ordered in the United States in 1939—a piece of foresight that saved much of London from burning.)[1]

The fact that loans by the Reconstruction Finance Corporation and the Export Import Bank might be legally possible did not make them politically feasible.[2] There was still too much feeling about the 'war debts'. In any case this loophole was then of small importance from the point of view of war financing, since it covered short-term credits and not long-term loans. There was some toying with the idea that the loophole might enable the United States Government to make a loan against British dollar securities as collateral. The securities could then be sold when conditions were most favourable in such a way as to realise their full value without disturbing the market. The point was to become important in 1941 when an R.F.C. loan of this kind was arranged.[3]

The Neutrality Act denied credits to a belligerent government, but permitted it to the nationals of that government (for goods other

---

[1] From 1938 to October 1939 British orders for arms and munitions (as reported in November 1939 to the State Department by the Service Attachés at the Embassy) were:

	Contracted for		Actually exported
Aircraft . .	Lockheed	$22 million	Two-thirds
	North American	$15 million	
Military material .	Universal Directors (Sperry Gyroscope Company) . . .	$4½ million	Two-fifths
Naval material .	Nil		Nil

[2] *New York Herald Tribune*, 27th June 1939, statement by Mr. Jesse Jones, Head of R.F.C., *The New York Times*, 1st September 1939. The functions of the Export Import Bank, Mr. Jesse Jones explained, were to underwrite, in part, the shipments of private exporters, through recourse loans, after the foreign importer had received the approval of his own government for the import. This last condition assured the availability of the necessary dollar exchange when the bank loans fell due.

[3] See below, Chapter VII.

than arms) when not buying on government account.[1] But transfer of title was required on all goods, irrespective of kind or buyer, before they left American ports. Transfer of title before the goods left the United States meant in practice that ordinary commercial credits given by private American firms, though legally still possible, were not available to the private British firm purchasing on its own account. Thus the Act interfered with ordinary commercial practice. Normally American exports to the United Kingdom were financed by the American exporter through his own bank, which controlled the documents and released them to the British buyer against cash or in some cases against the latter's acceptance. The Bank of England pointed out in a letter on 1st December 1939 that since title passed before the goods were exported, they ceased to be available as security to the American bank financing the transaction. The many complexities of the Act continued to trouble exporters for many months. As a Department of Commerce publication[2] noted, it was not easy in time of war to decide whether private persons or firms in belligerent countries which purchased in the United States were acting for themselves or for their governments. Where government boards such as the British Timber Control . . .

> have been made the sole importing agency, the shipments of that commodity to the United Kingdom must be considered for or on behalf of the government and therefore not eligible for credit terms. Where the control boards exercise the power of licensing imports by private individuals or concerns, credit may be extended where the imports are definitely for private account. . . .

Legal complexities were not the only difficulty. From this time almost up to Pearl Harbour, British officials, when planning any important move involving supplies from the United States, had to ask two questions. The first was: Is it lawful under the Neutrality Act and its many proclamations? The second was: Is it politically wise? And each time it was necessary to confer with officials in the Administration before risking an answer to either question.

On the basis of the experience of the last war it was assumed generally before the war that the liquidation of British dollar securities would play an important part in war financing. The existence before the war of British plans to mobilise British dollar securities for this purpose was known to the American Treasury. The policy of the American Treasury was to prevent a strain on the

---

[1] By a regulation (issued by the President under the Neutrality Act) of 6th September, 'ordinary commercial credits' were exempted. State Department release No. 405, 6th September. But an American Treasury official warned the Embassy that this applied only to credit of a kind customary in normal peace-time commercial transactions. It would not cover, for example, a hypothetical purchase of millions of tons of steel.

[2] Articles from Commerce Reports reprinted by the Department of Commerce in *Comparative Law Series*, Vol. III, May 1940.

securities market in the United States by the flooding of the market with British and French dollar securities. From the outbreak of the war up to the eve of the Lend-Lease Act both the President and the Secretary of the Treasury continued to take a keen interest in the question of the disposal of British securities.[1] Discussions on the procedure to be adopted began in September 1939 in London and in October in Washington. The matter was mentioned by the American Ambassador in London at the beginning of October. Mr. Morgenthau on 19th October indicated that when London was ready to take up the matter of the disposal of dollar securities he would like the British Government to discuss it in Washington with the Treasury and the Securities and Exchange Commission.

A week later a discussion on the matter took place in London between the American Ambassador and the Chancellor of the Exchequer, assisted by a representative of the British Treasury and the Governor of the Bank of England. The American Ambassador was given a classified list of securities marketable in New York which he was understood to have sent to Washington. In these conversations the British Government indicated that it preferred to sell securities rather than ship gold in order to meet the adverse balance that would occur with the United States during the first year of the war. (The adverse balance was then estimated as likely to be about £100 million.) The possibility of a loan, against securities as collateral, to permit the gradual liquidation of securities was examined on both sides. The idea was dropped when enquiries in Washington showed that there was no likelihood of such a loan being arranged.

The British Government meanwhile accepted the suggestion that the question of dollar securities should be examined with the United States Treasury and the Securities and Exchange Commission. The Embassy was informed that a special representative, Mr. Walter Whigham, would be sent for this purpose and would bring with him a list of securities. But London was somewhat disturbed at the way in which the position had been developing. The sale of securities was a highly technical question which involved expert knowledge of markets possessed neither by the Federal Reserve Bank nor by the United States Treasury and the Securities and Exchange Commission. The British Treasury had therefore been hoping that some means might be found of securing a loan against the pledge of securities as had been done in the last war; otherwise the market was likely to be adverse whenever securities were shipped across the Atlantic for sale.

The discussions between the Treasuries and the actual process of liquidating securities became important after the fall of France when

---

[1] As they did also in British Government banking arrangements in the United States, a matter which is referred to in *Studies of Overseas Supply*.

the period of heavy purchasing of war supplies began. This aspect is therefore dealt with later.[1] Here it may be noted that already by November 1939 the two Governments had begun to raise some of the larger problems involved in the use of the British financial reserves for war purchases. At the end of October 1939 warning had been given that war supply and finance would involve a drastic change in the pattern of trade with the United States. The American Ambassador in London was told by the Chancellor of the Exchequer that the British Government was anxious to give advance information regarding any restrictions on imports from the United States which it proposed to make to conserve dollar exchange. A memorandum handed to the American Ambassador on that occasion indicated that British Government expenditure in the United States for war supplies in the first year of the war would be at least £100 million; the adverse balance with Canada would be not much under another £100 million. Against this the amount of readily marketable British dollar securities was estimated at $600 million American and $150 million Canadian.[2] British exports would inevitably be restricted seriously by the war and could not be counted on to fill the large gap in the balance of payments. It was thus clear that British dollar resources had to be concentrated on the purchase of essential war supplies at the expense of less essential imports from America. Dollars could not be refused to the fighting services for the purchase of munitions when apples and pears, films and tobacco, were being imported freely. This did not mean discrimination against the United States, it was explained. Total purchasing would not be less but the money would be spent for war supplies. But it was no comfort to the tobacco-growers in the Southern States or the fruit-growers of the Pacific Coast to learn that, instead of being spent on their crops, the buying power of the Allies was enriching the munitions plants and steel mills of the East. Their discontent came to a head in January 1940.[3]

(iv)

The Purchasing of War Supplies

The revised Neutrality Act of 4th November 1939 'opened the arsenal of the United States to Britain and France' in the words of Mr. Cordell Hull.[4] It was not till then that it became possible to take

---

[1] In Chapter VII.

[2] The 'war chest' contained also gold and other securities not readily marketable. See below, p. 245.

[3] See below, Chapter IV, Section ii.

[4] *Memoirs of Cordell Hull*, Vol. I, op. cit., p. 700.

the very important step of setting up the British Purchasing Commission which had been under discussion since the beginning of the year. It was opened formally on 7th November by Purvis in the Cunard Building, No. 25 Broadway, New York.

More than one British Ambassador in the United States has quoted the story of the successful Foreign Office candidate who gave to the question: What three things matter most in the world? the reply 'God, Love and Anglo-American relations'. In overseas supply it was the last that came first. Not only did American munitions, food and raw materials give the margin for victory in war; they also united politically the two halves of the Anglo-Saxon world. There could be no close supply relations without the closest political relations with the American Government. Supply from the United States involved continuous high-level negotiations in which economics and politics were as the two faces of one coin. Whoever handled British supply had the chance of becoming a second Ambassador of Britain or even of the British Commonwealth of Nations. Supply from other parts of the world might perhaps be left to private trade or be handled directly by the supply ministries in London with the aid of visiting experts or missions. But British supply from the United States was so much more important and complex that it demanded the setting up of a British overseas administration. This was recognised early. But it could hardly be foreseen that within three years of the outbreak of the war the overseas administration would have assumed such proportions as almost to suggest that the British Government was functioning in duplicate on both sides of the Atlantic.[1]

The discussions from January to October 1939, on the setting up of a Purchasing Agency, were influenced by impressions, not always accurate, of the British supply arrangements in the First World War. Unregulated purchasing by the Allied Governments at the outbreak of that war had rapidly created a chaotic situation. Governments competed with their own private traders; and even departments of the same government bid against each other for the same stores. An arrangement was therefore concluded early in 1915 by the British and French Governments with J. P. Morgan and Company to act as their agents to purchase most of their war supplies on a commission basis, and to act as clearing and paying agents, and to arrange loans and sell securities. This agency arrangement terminated, so far as supplies were concerned, when the United States entered the war. It was then no longer practicable for a private American firm to compete in the market for supplies which the United States Government was also purchasing. A British War Mission (known later as the

---

[1] See *Studies of Overseas Supply.*

Department of War Supplies) was then put in charge of purchases on behalf of the Ministry of Munitions. It worked with the United States War Industries Board.

Twenty-five years later there was a different set of economic and political conditions. For one thing British loans were not possible as they had been in 1914. Moreover American foreign trade had greatly expanded since 1919. Large American firms (e.g. The United States Steel Corporation) preferred to sell direct to the British Government rather than to deal through an intermediary. J. P. Morgan and Company took the view that the Allied Governments would find it better to establish expert government purchasing commissions than to revert to the arrangements of the last war; but it was ready if needed to perform any of the other services it had performed at that time. But both Governments took the view that in this war neither purchases, nor banking arrangements, nor securities should be handled through private firms.[1] Fear of a serious rise in prices was an important factor in the decision in favour of centralised government purchasing. A sharp rise in the prices of non-ferrous metals had taken place in the United States in September 1939 partly in anticipation of heavy Allied buying and partly because stocks were low. Thus tin rose to £390 per ton in New York against £250 in London, and lead from £25 per ton as against £16 10s. in London.

The discussion on the setting up of a Purchasing Agency began early in 1939. The British Embassy noted in January 1939 that it had not been informed of the plans which the British Government had under consideration for the organisation of purchases and the mobilisation of gold and securities in the next war. It was agreed in the Embassy that a purchasing agency would be needed and that for several reasons the duty should not be entrusted to an American firm as in the last war. The Embassy recognised however that "the uncertainty as to the eventual position under the Neutrality Act must greatly complicate the making of any definite plans'.

London's reply on 18th March indicated that the Departments in London were 'concentrating more on the supply end than on the actual mechanism of purchases', but that it could be taken as certain that a centralised purchasing agency of some sort would be needed in the United States. The Embassy pointed out that the need of such an agency was already being felt in connection with scattered Government purchases, such as petroleum by the Air Ministry and fire hose by the Office of Works.[2] Meanwhile the Embassy in

---

[1] Some American newspapers, however, described the Administration's known preference as due in part to 'New Deal antipathy to certain large banking groups'.—*The New York Times*, 13th and 15th September 1939.

[2] This was part of large orders for fire-fighting equipment, including hose, pumps, etc., most of which were met in the United Kingdom. Requirements against the air blitz were foreseen with remarkable accuracy.

Washington was doing what it could to get information on production capacity. On the side of aircraft production and of raw materials for aircraft, particularly aluminium sheet and extrusions, the ground had already been explored in some detail by the Air Attaché. He had made a survey of all the reputable aircraft and engine manufacturing and aluminium companies. These had given him their production figures and capacity which he had checked by his own estimates based on the amount of floor space, number of employees, shifts worked, etc.

Meanwhile France was acting. Already there had been a special French Air Mission led by M. Jean Monnet in the winter of 1938–39 which had placed important French aircraft contracts. The arrival of a second French Mission was announced on 3rd May 1939 by the Assistant Secretary of War, Mr. Louis Johnson. The purpose of the Mission was to report on the purchase of munitions in the event of war.[1] Instead of staying on as a Purchasing Mission, as first planned, it returned to France, without placing any orders, after the breakdown of the effort to amend the Neutrality Act. But it had made a very thorough survey of the American munitions industry which bore results in large French orders after the outbreak of war.

On 9th May 1939 the British Embassy reported to London the result of a discussion on a Supply Mission. The point was made that the 'technique of purchasing' in the United States had advanced 'so far beyond the stage that it had reached twenty years ago, or indeed has now reached in England, that individuals or firms who are not experts in the matter can no longer hope to make purchases on a large scale with economy and efficiency'. What was required was a properly qualified government purchasing agency staffed by specialists used to making large-scale purchases in the United States. The importance of intimate knowledge of the United States pointed to the need to use Americans who could be reinforced by experts from England sent out *ad hoc* in connection with particular transactions. The intimate local knowledge required by the staff of the agency must cover such points as ability to understand and do business with Americans; knowledge of local market conditions as affected by geographical factors and communications; the commercial standing and productive capacity, actual and potential, of individual firms; the effect of labour conditions on the fulfilment of individual contracts; and especially ability to ensure that delivery schedules would in fact be kept—a point that had caused great difficulty in the last war. From the moment of the outbreak of

---

[1] *The New York Times*, 12th July 1939, stated that twelve or thirteen missions from foreign countries, including Eire, had either purchased or explored the possibility of purchasing war equipment in the United States in recent months. The munitions export business had exceeded $10 million a month.

another war the American Government would be in the market with heavy military orders, placed no doubt with the very firms from which the British Government itself would want to buy. Allied governments would also be in the market. The unanimous conclusion was that no time should be lost in setting up a British Purchasing Agency. If action were postponed until an actual emergency had occurred there would be grave danger that all the available munitions capacity would already be bought up by the American or Allied Governments. The letter ended with the suggestion that the whole matter should be explored at once by the sending over of some fairly senior representative of the government department most intimately concerned, perhaps the new Ministry of Supply.[1]

The Foreign Office replied on 16th June that the matter was under urgent discussion between the interested departments; it sought answers to three questions: first, would the American Government welcome a purchasing agency and assist its work? Second, was it likely that an embargo would be placed immediately on a large range of exports from the United States in case of war? Third, would greatly increased American Government orders be placed for the equipment of the American armed forces in case of war? These three questions were the outcome of an interdepartmental discussion on 9th June reported by letter to Washington. All departments agreed at the meeting that a purchasing agency was essential. Separate purchasing machinery would be needed, however, for petroleum products and foodstuffs. The view was taken that American Government orders sufficient to provide in *stage one* for an initial American 'protecting force' had already filled a very large proportion of the immediately visible capacity. The moment war occurred in Europe American Army orders would be placed to complete the equipment for stage one. The protecting force would not be 'the great American Nation in arms'. This would only appear at *stage two* when the United States were either actually at war or virtually certain to be involved. Only a complete mobilisation of the American national economy could produce arms for this much greater force. At the meeting a 'sensation' had been caused by the view that in an emergency the American Government planned to place an embargo on the export of a number of raw materials and semi-manufactures which might include semi-manufactures of iron and steel. But even if American orders left very little capacity to supply Allied orders Britain must obtain her share of it.

A few days later a preview of the vast requirements which might be involved in American plans was given in a speech by Mr. Louis Johnson, the Assistant Secretary of War, delivered on 20th June 1939

---

[1] In actual fact this Ministry was not established until August 1939. See *British War Production*, op. cit., p. 78.

in New York.[1] The new programme of the War Department, Mr. Johnson was reported to have stated, would require 5,500 to 6,000 planes a year. In connection with supplies for the Army, representatives of the War Department had visited 20,000 American plants. On the basis of this survey the Department had selected 10,000 firms and had given them definite schedules of production. The plants could thus begin production the moment they received orders on M-Day (i.e. mobilisation day).

In considering its reply to London's questions, the Embassy took these ambitious plans into account. The Air Attaché noted that the construction during the next two years of over 5,000 aeroplanes a year for the United States Army and Navy would be a severe tax on the American aircraft industry. Approximately 1,800 military aircraft were constructed on United States and foreign account in 1938. To produce the 5,000 planes a year eighty per cent. of the capacity of the aircraft industry and ninety per cent. of the aero engine capacity would have to be used and manpower would have to be increased from about 49,000 to approximately 80,000. This would nevertheless leave a small margin for foreign orders. In the first year, he estimated that the British and French between them might get about 2,000 aeroplanes; in later years they could get as many as they wanted. In the matter of accessories, bombs and guns for aircraft would present difficulties, since supplies of these products were at the moment hardly adequate to meet the day-to-day needs of the Air Services of the United States Army and Navy. The Naval Attaché considered it was unlikely that any naval armament stores could be provided for some months after the declaration of war. United States shipyards and armament firms were working to capacity on the vessels and armament stores required for the American rearmament programme. They were behind schedule as regards gun mountings. There was an acute shortage of skilled labour in the United States as in Britain.

The outcome of the Embassy discussions and of its consultations with the American Government was given in an important telegram to London on 29th June 1939. A British Purchasing Agency would be welcomed by the State and War Departments. In the case of a grave national emergency (which would not be considered to have arisen unless the United States themselves appeared to be on the very edge of war), the American Government would insist on priority for its own requirements; otherwise it would give sympathetic treatment to orders placed in peace-time with American manufacturers. Moreover, it would allow the proportion of orders previously placed by the United States Government and foreign governments to be maintained, even in the event of war breaking out. A similar assur-

---

[1] *The Journal of Commerce*, 21st June 1939, and *The New York Times*.

ance had been given to the French Government. The Ambassador therefore urged the immediate sending over of a 'scout' familiar with the supply plans of the British Government and authorised to act as its spokesman. His task would be to establish relations with high government circles and to lay the foundations for the setting up as soon as possible of a purchasing agency. Preferably one man should be sent without any publicity. London replied on 11th July that Lord Riverdale of Sheffield had undertaken the mission and that he would come out as if on one of his regular business journeys. He arrived in Washington at the beginning of August on the day fixed by the State and War Departments. Seventeen days later he was back in London having spent five days in Washington, four in New York and two in Canada.

The Riverdale Mission. Accompanied by officials of the Embassy Lord Riverdale began immediate discussions with high Service and State Department officials. He saw the Assistant Secretary of War (Mr. Louis Johnson) and two other high War Department officials. He discussed with the heads or deputy heads of the Supply Departments of War, Navy and Treasury, as well as the State Department official in charge of munitions control. He was greatly impressed by the 'immense amount of good will' which he found and the assurance on all sides that Britain could depend on the close co-operation of the agencies visited. 'Utmost co-operation', 'we can depend on their entire co-operation', 'anxious to help us in every possible way' were samples of the phrases scattered through the report which he submitted to the Ministry of Supply. A detailed report of the discussions with the War Department officials was submitted by Mr. Johnson to President Roosevelt who expressed himself as '100 per cent. in favour' of the line taken. The President approved the setting up of a British Purchasing Commission with a liaison officer who could go direct to the heads of the Government Departments in Washington. It was urged in all quarters, Lord Riverdale reported, that a Purchasing Commission should be set up without any further loss of time.

He was assured that the War Department would be prepared for American production to be shared between the United States and Britain. Britain's share (which she would purchase) would be somewhere near 'three out of eight units'. In the talks with Treasury officials also it was agreed that 'some kind of a quota arrangement' would be necessary to apportion supplies between Britain and France and any other allies. Preliminary statements of British requirements of munitions, machine tools, aircraft, which Lord Riverdale brought with him, were examined and compared with American requirements. With War Department officials, he reported, 'we went into great detail as to our requirements, as to how they conflicted at the moment with theirs, as to the United States future programme'. The

F

amount of unused capacity, after allowing for United States defence orders, in the matter of aircraft and machine tools was indicated to him to facilitate the placing of British orders. He was offered invaluable 'know how' about procurement. The War, Navy and Treasury Departments were prepared to give all necessary information as to 'where to buy specific articles and how the buying can be done to the best possible advantage'. As for the War Department, he reported, 'They are prepared to discuss with us at any time the best contractors with whom to place orders for war material, to place at our disposal their contract forms, conditions and specifications (except a few secret specifications) and to assist us in every way possible to ensure quick deliveries and reasonable prices'. The importance of the contract forms and specifications, as was explained in the Navy Department, was that 'if we could adopt American phraseology and style, it would help considerably in the manufacturers here understanding our specifications'.

The lists of British requirements from the United States in the event of war which Lord Riverdale brought with him had been drawn up in July by the various Departments at interdepartmental meetings attended by representatives of all Supply and Service Departments and by the Treasury. Together the lists constituted the first general, though still very elementary, programme for supply from North America to cross the Atlantic. The lists were shown to, but not left with, the American departments concerned.[1] It was significant that even at this very early stage there should have emerged the idea of a general ratio of 3 : 5 for British and American shares of the United States munitions output.

The detailed comparisons of British with American requirements made during Lord Riverdale's visit showed that there was still much latent capacity for machine tools and that British War Office requirements could be met by spreading them over a number of machine-tool firms. As for aircraft, American orders about to be placed (most of them were actually placed before Lord Riverdale got back to London) would account for about $175 million out of the total capacity of $225 million to $240 million of the industry at that time. There was a little slack capacity for aero engines (in particular Pratt and Whitney, about which Lord Riverdale sent an immediate cable

---

[1] An example is the following Board of Trade list of requirements of raw materials from the United States in the first year of war:

	Tons			Tons
Bismuth	200	Rosin	.	20,000
Boron minerals	7,250	Phosphate rock	.	50,000
Cotton (1·2 m. bales)	300,000	Iron and steel scrap	.	500,000
Molybdenum concentrates	3,000	Abrasives	.	3,000
Sulphur	150,000	Magnesium	.	1,000
Turpentine	20,000	Aluminium	.	10,000

Timber: Hardwoods, six million cubic feet; softwoods, 100,000 standards

to the Air Ministry on 2nd August). Naval mines and mooring tackle could be supplied quickly in large quantities, but the filling of explosives would have to be done in Britain. The question of unused capacity for munitions, such as tanks, guns, etc., was the subject of a memorandum which was supplied later. There was also unused capacity for light armour plate. Lord Riverdale also ascertained that whilst 'educational orders' to a value of $48 million had been placed by the United States War Department for munitions with firms which had not previously manufactured munitions, progress was slow and real production had not yet resulted.

Generally speaking Lord Riverdale's conclusion was that British requirements for the next two years could be met in the main, provided America was not at war and Britain could find the dollars to pay. He mentioned that despite vast expenditures since 1933 America still had nearly eleven million unemployed. On the other hand the British trade balance with the United States was persistently adverse. Britain in 1938 had purchased $521 million from the United States and the latter only $118 million from the United Kingdom, and the balance was rapidly growing more adverse as quantities of aircraft, engines and machine tools were being purchased. The mobilisation of American securities, the pruning of unessential imports from the United States in the event of war and an increase in British exports could be only partial remedies. The Johnson Act made loans impossible. The Administration, he thought, but not yet the public, realised that it could not escape being involved economically in the war; it was faced with the bleak alternatives of either lending Britain considerable sums of money or of being drawn in as a belligerent.

He sensed a certain impatience that the British should do something quickly to take advantage of the American offer to share with them American war production. He urged the setting up at once of a nucleus purchasing mission. 'A few orders placed promptly through our nucleus purchasing commission after consultation with the department in Washington concerned could clinch the whole situation in the eyes of Americans and convince them that we had taken their offer seriously.' There was a general sense, he reported, that war was very close. But whose war would it be—America's or Britain's? He reported 'a strong feeling in Washington that it is quite possible that America will be at war with Japan before we are at war with Germany, and that in this case America would need our help in regard to blockading Japan'.

It was the future, rather than the immediate significance, of Lord Riverdale's visit that mattered.

The executive departments of the American Government had welcomed over their thresholds the representative of the British Government. They showed him, through the double barred gates of the

Neutrality and Johnson Acts, the promised land of the American industrial war potential. As officials they were powerless to open those gates. The assault on them had been waged already for months on Capitol Hill and the proposals of the Administration had so far been brushed aside. He found a general expectation in official Washington that if war came Congress would quickly repeal or amend both these Acts. But until this was done it was not thought wise to set up any purchasing mission.

The British Supply Board (Ottawa). The scene now shifted to London. Following the discussion of Lord Riverdale's report on 23rd August 1939 at an interdepartmental meeting, the Cabinet approved on the 28th the setting up of a purchasing mission for North America to be located in Canada. On both occasions emphasis was laid on the grave exchange difficulties involved in extensive purchases from North America. The Treasury, it was pointed out, was making an estimate of requirements which might form the basis of 'a system of rationing and priorities'. The Minister of Supply pointed out in a memorandum that a first instalment of expenditure, to be rationed between the Ministries, was necessary pending clarification of the problem as a whole. It was agreed that an advance party consisting of a small number of officials should be sent over as quickly as possible to Canada. Its functions, as set out in the interdepartmental meeting, were to prepare the ground for the main purchasing mission. The advance party would be informed of contracts already placed and would be empowered to place new contracts for the Ministry of Supply, the Air Ministry and the Admiralty. The nucleus of the mission would be an administrative officer with the rank of a director of contracts, a financial adviser and an adviser on contract practice. There would also be three technical officers, one representing each of the three Service Departments. For the purchase of raw materials, petroleum products and foodstuffs other arrangements had been made by the respective departments. Raw materials involved so many different commodities that in the view of the Board of Trade as expressed at the meeting, no one person in the United States could deal effectively with them. It was felt therefore that purchases of raw materials should be conducted from London.

The Embassy at first felt it was unnecessary to start the mission in Canada. Cabinet authority to establish a branch of it in New York was given on the recommendation of the Ministry of Supply. But action as regards the United States was held up for two reasons. The first was the need to follow up immediately the relations established with the representatives of Canadian firms, since Canada was still regarded as the chief source of supply in North America. The second reason was the wish of the President that the decision of the special session of Congress, called for 21st September to revise the Neutrality Act, should not be prejudiced. The first part of the special mission to Canada, headed by Sir James Rae of the Treasury, who was to act as Deputy Controller-General and administrative head of the mission, arrived in Canada via New York in mid-September. The second part, consisting of Col. J. H. M. Greenly, Controller-General, and six other officers, arrived in Ottawa on 1st October.

First called the British Purchasing Mission in Canada, its name was changed in November 1939 to the 'British Supply Board in Canada and the United States'. The change of title from 'Purchasing Mission' to 'Supply Board' was due to a narrowing of the real functions of the Board. It ceased to be a direct purchasing agency because the Canadian War Supply Board (later Department of Munitions and Supply), took over the task of purchasing in Canada on behalf of the United Kingdom. From 7th November the task of purchasing in the United States was *de facto* given to the British Purchasing Commission in New York. Thus the British Supply Board was left with the function of providing general and technical liaison. This proved inadequate as a basis for its survival.

The British Purchasing Commission. The administrative arrangements for purchasing in the United States were affected by misgivings about American neutrality. This resulted in the fixed idea that any mission in the United States must be controlled from Ottawa. The mission in New York was therefore planned as a Branch of the 'British Supply Board in Canada and the United States'. An informal visit to Washington to discuss arrangements was made from 10th to 13th October 1939 by Col. Greenly and other members of the Board. Discussions took place with Mr. Morgenthau, Mr. Louis Johnson and most of the other officials who had been seen previously by Lord Riverdale. Some days before both the President and the Secretary of the Treasury had shown their close interest in British supply in a message conveyed informally to the Embassy. They wished to receive for their exclusive use a weekly summary of orders placed by the British Government and of deliveries; also of orders placed in normal trade channels for foodstuffs, raw materials and other goods including manufactures. In the discussions the Secretary of the Treasury raised three main points: the weekly summary, the opening of a British purchasing account at the Federal Reserve Bank, and the sale of securities. He informed the British representatives that he had become the channel of communication with the President in the matter of priorities for war supplies.

The conversations during this visit made it still more clear that the American Government intended to give all possible help the moment the arms embargo was repealed. In separate messages the Ambassador and Col. Greenly impressed on London the need for action the moment the arms embargo was lifted. First, the Administration must be given a clear idea of the general nature of British requirements; second, this must be followed immediately by definite orders, particularly for aircraft and engines. Press estimates of Allied orders ranged 'from 3 to 11 billion dollars'. The French Mission, without waiting for the repeal of the arms embargo, was already placing large provisional orders, especially for aircraft and engines, and so eating up the small margin of surplus capacity. More important was the fact that the Administration itself appeared to expect large orders on the basis of its own estimates of British dollar securities available for payment. The Ambassador urged the importance of not discouraging either the Administration or American industry by giving the impression that Britain did not know what she wanted or was not able to place at once substantial orders.

One reason for not knowing what was wanted was given in a London telegram some days later: 'The difficulty of forming anything like an estimate in peace was the complete uncertainty as to damage likely to be done to production here by enemy action; and that still holds good'.

Proposals by Col. Greenly on 19th October 1939 to reorganise the Ottawa Mission, to define its relation to the Purchasing Commission in New York and to appoint Mr. Arthur Purvis as head of the latter, were accepted by the Departments concerned in London on 27th October. The terms of a simultaneous public announcement in London, Washington and Ottawa were then agreed on at a meeting with Mr. Morgenthau in Washington which Mr. Purvis attended. As given to the press on 7th November and published next day the announcement read as follows:[1]

> The United Kingdom Government have decided to set up a central organisation to be known as the British Supply Board in Canada and the United States, for the purpose of co-ordinating purchases in the two countries.
>
> Colonel J. H. M. Greenly has been appointed Controller-General and Chairman, with Sir James Rae as Deputy Controller-General and Vice-Chairman.
>
> The Board will place orders in Canada through the Canadian War Supply Board recently set up by the Canadian Government under the chairmanship of Mr. Wallace Campbell. Orders in the United States will be placed through a British Purchasing Commission under the charge of Mr. Arthur B. Purvis, who has been appointed Director-General of Purchases (United States). . . . Mr. Wallace Campbell and Mr. Purvis will be members of the central organisation which will also include representatives of the United Kingdom Service Departments and His Majesty's Treasury.

---

[1] On 10th November a notice was sent to British Consulates in the United States instructing them to channel through the B.P.C. all matters touching supply.

A later announcement will be made regarding the necessary arrangements to secure close co-ordination of British and French purchases in the United States.

The last paragraph referred to Anglo-French discussions then proceeding in London. From the outset the British Purchasing Commission had been conceived of as a joint body with the French. The head of the French Purchasing Commission, M. Bloch-Lainé, arrived simultaneously in Washington with Purvis. It was agreed in London on 31st October 1939 that in principle a unified purchasing organisation would be set up to avoid competition between British and French purchases in the United States. There was some hesitation at first between the idea of a two-headed mission, with joint French and British heads, and two separate missions. The British Government preferred the latter. The American Government, it turned out, was ready to accept either plan. The precise organisation was of less importance to the President and Mr. Morgenthau, the Embassy was told, than the fundamental objective of keeping prices steady, restricting profits to a reasonable level and avoiding competition between the three Governments—British, French and American—for the limited supplies which American industry could then produce.

The Ambassador in reporting this discussion to London added that Mr. Morgenthau evidently expected that he would have 'regular consultations with Mr. Purvis'. These 'regular consultations', which began forthwith, set in motion a famous combination of two personalities which was the mainspring of British supply from America in the most critical period of the war.

CHAPTER IV

THE AMERICAN POTENTIAL
BEFORE DUNKIRK

(i)

The Morgenthau-Purvis Channel

THE Morgenthau-Purvis combination lasted till Purvis was killed in an aeroplane accident at Prestwick, Scotland, on 14th August 1941. Informal though it remained, it was the forerunner of the Anglo-American Combined Boards, and ranks in importance with them. The problem of a central channel, by which the Administration could be approached on supply matters, was one of the perpetual problems of the British supply organisation during the war. Obviously the President could not be the channel. Nor could the head of one department speak for another department. The solution which the President adopted up to lend-lease was to name the head of the Treasury as the channel. After that the main channel was Mr. Harry Hopkins. How these solutions worked will be seen in this and the following chapters.

The Secretary of the Treasury began to act for the President in the matter of Allied purchases at the beginning of 1939. There was a grateful reference to this early aid by the French Prime Minister in a personal letter of 25th November 1939, in which he informed President Roosevelt of the setting up of the Anglo-French Purchasing Board with Purvis as chairman. The reference was to 'the French Mission headed by M. Jean Monnet last spring in connection with the purchase of aircraft'. Mr. Morgenthau has given his own account of that episode.[1] The Mission, in December 1938, was directed by the President to the Treasury because that agency could be depended on, in Mr. Morgenthau's words, 'to take a less parochial view of national policy in the sale of aircraft than either War or Navy'. It acted through its Procurement Division, 'the chief purchasing agency of the government.' There was as yet no specialised machinery in the United States to handle economic problems arising out of Allied

---

[1] See articles by Mr. Morgenthau in *Collier's* Magazine beginning 18th October 1947, and hearings on the Mission by the Senate Military Affairs Committee, 27th January 1939.

war purchasing.[1] The Treasury Department, moreover, was directly interested in the financial repercussions of a large-scale war and its effects on the American economy. It was natural, therefore, that when the President's Liaison Committee was set up on 6th December 1939 to handle supply relations with the Allies that the Secretary of the Treasury should head it.

Yet neither this general interest, nor the Department's normal procurement activities, was sufficient to account for its great activity in matters relating to Allied supply and economic warfare. Mr. Morgenthau was profoundly and passionately interested in the issues of the war. The President turned to him as the man on whom he could depend to do the job that had to be done and to throw himself heart and soul into the work. British supply officials were soon to find that when it became necessary no one could defend American interests more obstinately than Mr. Morgenthau. Relations were thus not always plain sailing. But they soon learned they could look to him for steady support in all vital matters. However much he might defend American interests he could always be counted on to take the broad view and to push the supply of arms and other essential war supplies. He was sometimes referred to in the early correspondence as 'our friend'. He was prepared to move heaven and earth when approached with a reasonable request. A British official who was associated with him during the war spoke of him as always ready 'to work far into the night, every day, for us'. The verdict of history may well be that given by two American columnists in 1941 on the eve of lend-lease. 'The Treasury, under Secretary Henry Morgenthau, Jr., has always thought first of the broader aspects of the President's foreign policy. Morgenthau hates to be taken in, and has never been soft with the British, but his strongest emphasis is on quick aid to Britain.'[2]

From November 1939 till March 1941 Morgenthau and Purvis worked almost as closely together as two Ministers in the same Cabinet. Their relationship was of primary importance in the supply machinery of the war until early in 1941 when the war organisation on both sides, British and American, began to broaden out into a more intricate system. On the British side the British Purchasing Commission expanded then into a whole group of missions linked by the British Supply Council, of which Purvis was

---

[1] The Procurement Division was responsible for facilitating supply to China under the various Export-Import Bank loans to that country. The first loan of $25 million was concluded on 15th December 1938. See Edward R. Stettinius, Jr., *Lend-Lease, Weapon for Victory* (New York: The Macmillan Company and Pocket Books Inc., 1944), p. 17. This work was published in the United Kingdom under the same title (London: The Macmillan Company and Penguin Books, 1944). Citations are given throughout from the United States Pocket Book edition.

[2] Joseph Alsop and Robert Kintner in *The Washington Post*.

chairman until his death in August. On the American side the President's Liaison Committee disappeared with the setting up of new machinery under the Lend-Lease Act.[1]

This history can deal only in a fragmentary way with the part played by the Scots-Canadian Arthur B. Purvis in his two last years which marked the peak of his career. He had already appeared in British supply history at the outbreak of the First World War in 1914. He had been sent from London to the United States as a representative of Imperial Chemical Industries, to make a deal for the purchase of $25 million worth of acetone, of which there was a shortage which threatened to cripple the Navy through lack of cordite.[2] He was sent by his firm to Canada at the end of 1924 to take over Canadian Explosives Limited.

At the time of his appointment as director of the British Purchasing Commission he had become the leading Canadian industrialist. He was head of Canadian Industries Limited (a Canadian affiliate of Imperial Chemical Industries Limited), vice-chairman of Dunlop's, Canada, and a director in eleven Canadian concerns, including the Bell Telephone Company. He had an intimate knowledge of the United States and the leaders of American industry, and had broadened his horizon by working for his firm in Latin America and South Africa. His qualities of mind and experience enabled him to deal with a vast multiplicity of supply problems without losing his sense of proportion. He had vast energy and powers of work. He liked people and they liked him, and liked to work with him, even though this meant working intensely for exceedingly long hours. He drew no salary, nor in the first phase did some of his American colleagues on the British Purchasing Commission.

His first appearance in the history of British supply in the Second World War seems to have occurred early in 1939 in connection with the manufacture in Canada of aircraft for Britain and the supply of aluminium. He was a member of the three-man committee appointed to advise in connection with the corporation established for this purpose, the Canadian Associated Aircraft Company. Colonel Greenly, on his arrival in Ottawa on 3rd October, made it his first business to see Purvis. Next day he suggested to the Governor-General that Purvis should be made British Director-General of Purchasing in the United States. The Governor-General replied that Purvis had performed very valuable services for the Canadian Government in

---

[1] Its termination was indicated by an exchange of letters (released on 15th April 1941) between Mr. Morgenthau and the President. Since July 1940 the Committee had handled, Mr. Morgenthau's letter revealed, some 2,000 requests, over 1,000 of which were British. As the record kept by Purvis showed, the requests covered not only purchases but many other matters.

[2] *The New York Times* of 24th January 1940 and article by Paul Farrington, *The Toronto Star Weekly*, 10th February 1940. *Fortune* Magazine, April 1940.

the past; in his view Purvis was the 'leading Canadian industrialist, a man of the highest integrity, with no enemies and indeed no critics'.

British supply relations with the United States, particularly in their opening phase, called for a rare combination of diplomacy and personal initiative. The diplomacy of supply was always important throughout the war, not least in the period after cash purchase ended and lend-lease began. The head of the British Purchasing Commission had to be more than a good Civil Servant or a business man with drive and initiative. He had to possess qualities of character and diplomatic skill of a high order. He needed the ability to weigh imponderables and feel intangibles. He needed above all the power to inspire trust. The combination of these qualities in Purvis made him a second British ambassador, with a more powerful influence in some ways on the American Administration than Lord Lothian himself possessed. 'He and the Ambassador are now the two outstanding British personalities in the U.S.A. . . .', Sir Arthur Salter noted in October 1940. He described Purvis as a

kind of Economic Ambassador, handling the major policy as well as the details of all questions except those which are definitely political in character. . . . His appointment (was) one of our definite bits of good fortune in this war.

His character and diplomatic skill was such that he never once drew political fire upon himself, although he was called upon by the British Government to ask so much of the United States and was known to exercise considerable influence on the Administration. Policy clashes were avoided by close liaison with the Embassy. Unhampered in his career by departmental traditions, the Director of the British Purchasing Commission cared little for artificial boundaries. He never thought of himself as merely a purchaser of supplies from the United States. From the outset he recognised that the purchasing with which he was charged could be used as a lever for wider purposes, in particular to expand the American war potential and to deny supplies to the enemy. It was in fact in this latter field that he was to win, in December 1939, his first great success which established his position with Morgenthau and the President.[1]

It was a decision of the British and American Governments that made the two men opposite numbers and laid the basis for a natural alliance between them. But it was their ability to get on together as personalities that clinched the alliance.

Morgenthau took an immediate liking to Purvis and after the war paid him the following tribute:

---

[1] See below, section on Strategic Materials.

From the first Purvis impressed me tremendously. He was not only the ablest British representative in Washington, but one of the rarest persons I have ever known. His death in an airplane accident in 1941 was an almost irreplaceable loss. He had a pleasant Scotch burr and a whole chain of anecdotes about the Scot triumphing over the Englishman. 'It always takes a Scotsman to pull England out of a hole', he used to say. I trusted Purvis more than any other British representative. We took every opportunity to make it clear in London, which occasionally tried to undercut him, that he was the man we proposed to deal with.[1]

This passage said much. Purvis had an advantage in being a Scot to whom American warmth for Britain goes more easily than to someone who 'talks like an Englishman'. He escaped the initial suspicion which tends to bar the path of the English official on his arrival in the United States until he can prove it is ill-founded. The remark about defending him from London showed the closeness of the personal relationship. Purvis no doubt welcomed such support. It was evidence of the strength of his position. But he did not need it. He was given a free hand in a rare degree. As a Minister of the Crown put it in the House of Lords on 18th July 1940, 'Never have wider powers to commit this country been delegated to any Mission, and indeed it is true also to say that no Mission has ever carried so grave a responsibility'.[2] In the account that follows it has to be remembered that Purvis was carrying out policies that had been worked out in London by Ministers and the high officials of their Departments.

Mr. Morgenthau's remark about undercutting was perhaps a reflection of American rather than British war experience in the matter of maintaining American supply missions abroad. For their authority and influence tended during the war to be in inverse proportion to the length of their absence from Washington. A British mission abroad could count usually on steady support from home and on being able to maintain a fairly constant degree of effective authority. The British tradition, born of long experience on the world's frontiers, of trusting the man on the spot, and keeping him informed, worked well in the case of the British Purchasing Commission. Differences of opinion, inevitable where action has to be swift and neither side has all the facts, were easily resolved. What was not always realised in London was that failure to use the recognised Purvis-Morgenthau channel could undermine the position of the latter, and diminish his usefulness to the President. Thus the attempts made on several occasions in July and August by the Minister of Aircraft Production (Lord Beaverbrook) to go direct to the President in order to get special priority for urgent requirements of his Ministry

---

[1] Article by Mr. Morgenthau in *Collier's* Magazine, October 1947.
[2] H. of L. Deb., Vol. 116, Col. 1056, 18th July 1940.

were regarded as endangering the British position in Washington. Examples, in August 1940, were the Ministry's steel requirements and its machine tool deliveries. In the latter case Lord Beaverbrook's own representative in Washington, Mr. Morris Wilson, warned him that the proposal to go direct to the President would cause considerable damage since, as he put it, this would mean side-stepping Morgenthau. There had been an earlier incident in July, when Lord Beaverbrook tried to get the Ambassador to use the State Department as a channel to secure the diversion to the United Kingdom of the first 100 Stinson planes then on order for the United States Army. The Ambassador replied that both he and Purvis agreed that the 'Morgenthau channel', which had worked so well in the past, should be used.

One of the strongest references in the British war papers to Morgenthau's special role, and the importance attached to it on the British side, occurred at the height of the Battle of Britain. The occasion was the report (referred to in Chapter VI below) by an American military mission. This was regarded as endangering Morgenthau's efforts, on the one hand to secure the release of aircraft to the United Kingdom, and on the other hand to prevent the diversion by the Army of aircraft engines and machine tools taken over by Britain from the French contracts. The report, based on data obtained by the mission in England, seemed to show that the British need was for pilots rather than planes. A joint message from Purvis, Sir Walter Layton and Morris Wilson at the beginning of October, marked expressly for the Prime Minister and the Ministers of Air and Aircraft Production, conveyed Morgenthau's request for a full disclosure of the figures of production, losses and replacement rates of planes and pilots. This vital strategical information was immediately supplied by Lord Beaverbrook 'to be disclosed only to the President, Stimson, Knox and Morgenthau'. The message from Purvis and his colleagues began with the remark that since December Morgenthau

> under direction from the President . . . has taken charge of our various demands. He is the one whose responsibility it has been to surmount resistance to our demands from various U.S. Departments, Army or others.

He was regarded by the President and the other Departments not only as

> responsible for the presentation of British needs but also for presenting the British supply position.

An incident towards the end of the month showed the President's preference for the Morgenthau-Purvis channel for an important personal message from the Prime Minister to himself. Mr. Churchill's message emphasised the urgency of British aircraft and munitions requirements from the United States which had 'already been laid before you by Layton and Purvis'. Purvis had himself thought the message should go direct from the Prime Minister to the President; but he had been asked specifically, he told London, that it should be 'addressed to me for Secretary Morgenthau for communication to the President . . . in order to conform with the procedure established over the past year by the President himself'.

The confidence which he inspired and his ease of access to Morgenthau and the President brought Purvis a constant succession of difficult and delicate tasks. They came both from the American and the British side. The Governments of other members of the Commonwealth, especially Canada and Australia, made frequent use of him. Thus in July 1940 both Canada and Australia, faced with a breakdown of aircraft building and training programmes through stoppage of supplies and materials from Britain, turned urgently to him. In passing on to Morgenthau on 6th July a request from the Canadian Minister of Munitions and Supply Purvis remarked: 'Mr. Howe is making this request of you through me, and will await your reactions before any official request is made through other channels'.

The requests put to Purvis sometimes involved matters that hardly belonged to his function even in his 'allied role'. They came his way not only because he had the connections but also because he could act without attracting too much attention. Examples could be quoted indefinitely. In the crisis of the summer of 1940, government departments on both sides of the Atlantic turned often to him. On 11th May he reported urgently to London information that had come to him regarding $600 million worth of American dollar securities held by investment houses in Holland, which, if saved from the German invader, could be used for the purchase of Allied supplies in the United States. He was asked in reply to suggest through Morgenthau that the United States Minister at the Hague should do everything possible to ensure the denial of the securities to the Germans.

His close relations with the President and with Morgenthau were shown by the messages which passed backwards and forwards during the next few days. On 14th May, in reply to a very urgent appeal from London for more planes, he emphasised the extreme good will —'higher than ever'—of the President and Morgenthau. The messages to London for the next week or two were full of references to 'Sylvia'—the code name of the President at the height of the summer crisis. Next day (15th May) Purvis sent a series of messages to London: 'Sylvia advises me that the Prime Minister has enquired as to the possibilities of arranging further aircraft priorities. . . .

Sylvia suggested this afternoon the possibility of utilising reserve civil transport planes and private owner planes for transport and for light bombing purposes'.[1] Another message began: 'Sylvia telephoned to me': 'Sylvia' said that it was not legally possible for a British aircraft carrier to enter a United States port to ship aircraft ready to fly; 'he suggests, however, that the carrier be sent to Botwood, Newfoundland. . . . We could then arrange to have the aircraft flown to the Canadian border, pushed across that border, and flown on to Botwood.' 'We already know', Purvis added, that 'this method is feasible and legal.'

Still on the same day Purvis talked with Morgenthau and suggested that the new Defence Bill about to be introduced in Congress should give the Administration authority to prohibit re-export of strategic materials such as alloying materials. He was told then that the Bill would authorise the Administration to build munitions plants complementary to existing Allied munitions factories in case the latter were destroyed by bombing. He asked London to send a list of classes of plants considered most important and most vulnerable, which could be handed to Morgenthau. The latter, Purvis told London, 'again assures me that Sylvia has agreed that any new defence plants will be over and above the existing capacity so that there will be no interference with supplies to the Allies'.

The Prime Minister, now in constant direct contact with the President, sometimes used Purvis as his channel; and the President's replies went back on occasion through Purvis.[2] It was in a message on 15th May that Mr. Churchill raised with the President the matter of 'the loan of forty or fifty of your older destroyers'. Monnet followed this up on 17th May with a statement of the most urgent supply needs, including the destroyers, which Purvis was to get to the President at once through Morgenthau. The President replied next day through Purvis that the time was not yet ripe for destroyers. Again on the 28th in a note to Morgenthau headed 'Naval Priorities' Purvis on instructions coupled the forty-eight destroyers with a new urgent request for motor torpedo-boats. The British Government returned again to destroyers on 5th June, having received confidential information that the President might now be willing to reconsider his refusal. Purvis was asked to keep up a steady pressure. The Admiralty turned to him next day to say that it wanted to be sure that any destroyers released to it could be put into service with the least possible delay. It asked him to secure information as to the types which might be available. The first consideration was to be 'maximum

---

[1] This suggestion proved impracticable as the planes, already in full use, were unsuitable—and the public not yet ready.

[2] For the role of Purvis in the summer crisis, see Chapter V.

possible readiness for service', and the second 'greatest steaming endurance'.

By now both navies had learned to use the Morgenthau-Purvis channel. Thus in May the United States Office of Naval Intelligence turned to Morgenthau for help in getting the Admiralty to change its adverse ruling about United States observers accompanying the British Fleet. Purvis in his plea to London that American observers should be welcomed emphasised the need to 'support Mr. Morgenthau's position in view of his valuable co-operation'. A fortnight later, at the end of May, Purvis was told that the 'British Admiralty have agreed to reverse their decision. You may inform Mr. Morgenthau.' It was Purvis also who sent an urgent message direct to the Admiralty on 16th June with the news of the sailing from Halifax at dawn that day of the two French carriers *Jeanne d'Arc* and *Béarn*, the latter with nearly a hundred American planes aboard. Again in July he was used by both sides for urgent messages about the leakage of oil through Spain.

(ii)

Strategic Materials:
Allied Supply and Denial to the Enemy

The general field of Economic Warfare is the subject of a separate study.[1] Two aspects that affected supply to Britain from North America must be mentioned here. In the early stages of the war there was no sharp administrative dividing line in the United States between supply and economic warfare. In theory America being still at peace could not engage directly in economic warfare; and the setting up of special machinery for this purpose would hardly have been appropriate. The Director of the British Purchasing Commission, however, was a purchaser of supplies rather than a diplomatic representative, and he could be used informally by both sides. Such use was facilitated by the fact that he was also Chairman of the Anglo-French Purchasing Board.[2] It was in the latter role that Morgenthau approached him on 8th December 1939 in the opening move in what was to become an important field of collaboration as regards strategic raw materials, especially ferro alloys.

Neutral America and belligerent Britain had a common interest on

---

[1] Professor W. N. Medlicott, *The Economic Blockade*, Vol. I (London: His Majesty's Stationery Office and Longmans, Green & Co., 1952), Chapter X, etc.

[2] The Board acted under the Anglo-French Co-ordinating Committee in London, one of whose Executive Committees had the task of co-ordinating Allied policy on economic warfare.

grounds of public policy in denying supplies to aggressor countries. They had also a second interest in common—that of securing for the United States and the Allies supplies of the scarcer strategic raw materials and strategic manufactures such as machine tools. The Allies were in a better bargaining position for raw materials than for munitions. They controlled the main sources of supply of some of the most important materials needed by the United States, such as nickel, rubber, tin, mica and jute. It was therefore an advantage for Purvis to have a wide authority to discuss strategic materials and not to be confined merely to the purchase of munitions. It was also useful for him to keep away from the more negative side of economic warfare, such as the blockade and interference with American rights at sea, which were handled by the Embassy. He was also fortunate in having nothing to do with the unpopular British import restrictions on un-essential supplies from the United States, such as tobacco and films. The restrictions in fact gave him more dollars to spend on munitions and aircraft. He stood out untrammelled before the public as the man who had large funds to spend on American goods.

The discussions on strategic materials have to be understood in their wider context. The main emphasis of economic warfare from September 1939 to May 1940 was on the regulation of supplies to adjacent neutrals rather than the direct blockade of enemy ports or frontiers. The control of exports from Germany, as a means of limiting her purchasing power abroad, began to be tightened after November 1939. Control over contraband entering Germany, which affected in some degree American exports and shipping, was exercised by a whole series of devices some of which did not apply to the United States. The devices included export licensing, war trade agreements, agreements with shipping companies, advance cargo information, hold-back undertakings, navicert system, the statutory and black lists, suspect lists, enemy export control, pre-emption, economic warfare intelligence. The system evolved slowly, with adaptations to meet different circumstances in different regions and adjustments to fit changes in the shape of the war. Thus when the invasion of Norway and Western Europe and the entry of Italy into the war in June destroyed most of the neutral zone, the number of neutral posts available to the enemy was reduced to very small proportions and contraband control by naval means diminished proportionately. Economic warfare policy began to shift its emphasis from control in European waters to control over exports at their source in overseas and colonial territories. This latter change was marked by the change-over—welcomed by the Administration in Washington—from voluntary to compulsory navicerts, and the issuing of ships' warrants which gave access to bunkering facilities, repairs, stores and insurance.

G

The beginnings of the close relations with Morgenthau on both supply and ferro-alloys in November and December 1939 took place against a background of State Department and Embassy discussions on the interference with American rights at sea and the cutting down of normal British imports from the United States. On 18th November the State Department issued a list of American ships which had been reported to it as having been detained by the belligerents since the outbreak of war for the examination of papers and cargoes. Several similar lists followed during the next two months. The State Department feared, Lord Lothian reported on 30th November, a 'tremendous explosion' in the United States, caused by some incident such as the sinking of an American ship in a contraband control port, especially if this were to happen in a port in the combat zone as distinguished from one in a restricted zone. But the notes exchanged between the two Governments in December and January, on belligerent search of American ships, delays at Gibraltar and interference with American mails, were studiously moderate in tone.[1]

A much more dangerous political issue for the Administration, and for Allied supply, arose from British import restrictions on American goods. The news of these restrictions broke without warning on the American public in mid-January. The blow was harder to bear because the vast Allied war orders that were to restore the sagging American economy were still not forthcoming. Farmers, well represented in Congress by the 'farm block', suddenly realised they might be forfeiting their only important foreign market. 'It seems clear', as a British official wrote in May 1940, 'that the necessary changes in the structure of the British import trade were made without enough attention to timing and presentation to the American public.' As mentioned above, advance warning of a sort had in fact been given in October by the British Government to the Administration. The object of the restrictions, the Chancellor of the Exchequer had explained in a memorandum given to the American Ambassador, was to save dollars for the purpose of war supplies. A saving of about $6 million would be made on apples and pears alone. The restrictions on imports would be accompanied, however, by large expenditures for war purposes in the United States. In the first year of war British expenditure in the United States would probably exceed American expenditure in Britain by about £100 million, and it was therefore highly important, the memorandum pointed out, to cut down on inessential imports such as films and tobacco. That the State Department

<hr />

[1] Medlicott, op. cit., Chapter X, iv. *Memoirs of Cordell Hull*, Vol. I, op. cit., pp. 679–80. Mr. Cordell Hull foresaw the danger of friction and suggested to Lord Lothian the setting up of a voluntary navicert system. See also *Documents on American Foreign Relations*, op. cit., Vol. II, 1939–40, for the text of Notes by the State Department on 14th and 27th December 1939, and 20th January 1940; also for text of Foreign Office Note of 17th January 1940.

understood the situation was shown by the explanation given by Mr. Cordell Hull to a Congressional Committee on 11th January 1940. The United Kingdom, he said, was fighting for its life, and if the United States were in the same position they would follow the same policy. Britain had to restrict imports of some commodities because she was increasing the imports of others. He went on to predict the resumption at no distant date of large-scale purchases of agricultural and other products.[1] For this explanation he was thanked by the Foreign Office through the Ambassador. But the explanation did not diminish the size of the headlines proclaiming that Britain had stopped importing tobacco from America and had made a twenty years' agreement to buy tobacco from Turkey.[2]

The setting up of the President's Liaison Committee was announced on 23rd January 1940 and the same day Purvis and Bloch-Lainé announced at a press conference the formation of the Anglo-French Purchasing Board. The British Purchasing Commission had spent so far $72·8 million, mostly on planes, machine tools and chemicals. French purchases had reached a higher figure.[3] The British figure was not impressive. It hardly balanced the cut in imports,[4] which had been the subject of a press outburst the day before. *The New York Times* Washington correspondent reported a feeling in official quarters of 'intense irritation with Britain' due to 'the adamant British attitude towards joint problems', such as restrictions on American exports, censorship of mails and diversion of American ships to contraband control ports. An Associated Press dispatch from Washington on the same day covered much the same ground, but added the point that British action was due to the desire to conserve foreign exchange for war purchases in the United States. Dispatches appeared simultaneously from American tobacco-, wheat-, cotton-, and fruit-growing areas protesting against import cuts.

The Ambassador reported that the State Department had inspired this publicity.[5] Mr. Cordell Hull summoned Lord Lothian to discuss the issues and asked for more consideration by Britain of American interests; otherwise American sympathies might be jeopardised. Further exchanges followed in the next ten days. The senators from

---

[1] House Committee on Ways and Means. Hearings on extension of Reciprocal Trade Agreements Act, 11th January 1940.

[2] Medlicott, op. cit., p. 352 ff.

[3] *The New York Times*, 24th January 1940.

[4] A State Department note of 4th May claimed that no import licences were being issued for American farm products representing an export worth $113 million in 1938. The note alleged virtual prohibition of practically all American agricultural products included in the Anglo-American Trade Agreement of 1938 except cotton. Moreover, it added, nearly seventy-five per cent. of non-agricultural goods included in the agreement were subject to prohibitions and restrictions.

[5] A minor State Department official held responsible for this leakage was later dismissed.

the tobacco states, Cordell Hull told the Ambassador, were crowding into his room with protests; and he feared a storm in Congress which might endanger the renewal of the Reciprocal Trade Agreements Act. Lothian in his replies followed more or less the line taken earlier in the month by Cordell Hull himself before a Congressional Committee. He referred to Britain's large requirements of war supplies from the United States, and her limited supplies of dollars, her inability to replenish them by credits because of the Johnson Act, and the inevitability therefore of stopping all inessential imports. Influential American newspapers had begun in fact to take the same line. Thus *The New York Times* pointed out on 23rd January that Britain could not make 'immense war purchases' to the tune of say a billion dollars and still keep unchanged her peace-time imports.[1]

Meanwhile these developments were not without their effect on feeling in Britain. 'The time may come', Monnet wrote to Purvis in a personal letter on 2nd February, 'when we shall have to ask you tactfully to let Mr. Morgenthau understand that he cannot expect us to make all the running.' But it took time for an understanding of the situation to seep down through the different strata of public opinion, from official Washington out into the agricultural areas of the Middle West, the South and the Pacific Coast. Meanwhile there was some risk that war supplies might be affected whilst these matters were being discussed in March and April. In the midst of the detailed discussions the Ambassador emphasised the importance of clearing up all obstacles to the free flow of munitions. The support of the agricultural senators, he told London, was of special importance to the Administration in an election year; the State Department was 'most anxious' to reach an agreement with Britain. 'But if they are to be able to do this and support effectively the Allied aeroplane-buying programme, they must be able to convince their supporters and powerful agricultural interests that Great Britain is still buying some of the key commodities.' In other words, as a British official in Washington put it at the time, 'The farmers worry the representatives, the representatives worry the State Department, then the State Department worries us'.

Fortunately during this period both sides were working towards a combined approach to strategic materials. The first emphasis in December 1939 was on denying American materials to 'dangerous destinations'. This was soon overshadowed by a second and even more important common objective, that of conserving supplies of vital raw materials for the munitions industries of the United States and allied countries. Up to the Lend-Lease Act, and even after it, there was an absence of clear-cut administrative dividing lines on the

[1] Compare also syndicated article by Joseph Alsop and Robert Kintner, 26th January. Here also Allied plans to spend a billion dollars on 12,000 aircraft were forecast.

American side. Thus Purvis on the same day could be dealing with Morgenthau on such a variety of matters as the pre-emptive buying by the United States of tungsten from China and on using British supply purchases of American molybdenum and copper as a lever to prevent leakages of these materials to the enemy. As American re-armament began and Britain's dependence on supplies from North America increased, such discussions began to be concerned increas-ingly with the question of total supply—whether there was enough of these and other materials to enable the combined armaments programmes to be completed.

The work of Purvis in these fields (though hardly foreseen when he was appointed) constituted one of the most important of his war services to the Allies.[1] Its influence radiated out over the whole field of Allied and Commonwealth supply from the United States. It was his ability to meet Morgenthau more than half-way in the latter's first approach on alloys, in December 1939, as well as the speedy, complete and steady support London and Paris gave him in this matter, that established once and for all his position with Morgen-thau and the President. His frequent, at times almost daily, talks with Morgenthau on ferro-alloys, and the good fellowship thus engendered, made it possible for him to talk more often and more intimately on aircraft and machine tools and by this means to get through more easily to the President and the Army and Navy. His letters and cables showed that he understood clearly from the outset how important his work on strategic materials was likely to be in facilitating his main task as purchaser of munitions. This was high ground giving a wide view over the American war potential. The more he could talk with American Departments on these wider issues the more he could influence the development of this potential. He was no man for papers; but one of the few complete and orderly personal files which he kept was devoted to 'Alloys'.

Before referring to the talks on strategic materials it is necessary to say a word on the administrative arrangements on the American side. The League of Nations sanctions against Italy in the Ethiopian war (1935–36) had brought strategic materials into the limelight. Subsequent studies in the United States, both official and unofficial, of the role played by non-ferrous metals in peace and war, emphasised their importance to American defence and the possibility of using control over them as a weapon against aggressors.[2] In June 1939 a stockpiling bill authorised the expenditure of $100 million between 1939 and 1943 in order to build up American Government stocks of

---

[1] See also Medlicott, op. cit., pp. 367–73.
[2] e.g. William Yandell Elliott, *International Control in the Non-Ferrous Metals* (New York: The Macmillan Company, 1937).

strategic materials, the supply of which from abroad might be
endangered in case of war.[1]

Two kinds of American embargoes, strategic and moral, both
essentially voluntary in character, were developed in 1938–39.[2] It was
the function of the Army and Navy Munitions Board in consultation
with the State, Treasury, Commerce and Interior Departments to
say what materials were 'strategic' or 'critical'.[3] The Treasury had an
important voice because it could initiate proposals for the purchase of
such materials for stockpiling and because it provided the funds. The
body responsible for preventing the leakage from the United States
of 'strategic' materials was the Division of Controls of the State
Department. The method was to advise the trade that a particular
material had been declared strategic and should not be exported or
re-exported to any other country—except in normal peace-time
quantities to old customers. The first strategic embargo (i.e. notification that certain strategic and critical raw materials should not be
exported in abnormal quantities) was issued by the Army and Navy
Munitions Board on 11th October 1939; it included antimony,
chromium, manganese (ferro grade), manila fibre, quartz crystals,
mercury, quinine, rubber, silk, tin and tungsten.[4] Mica and nickel
were added soon after. A strategic material was one that was essential
to national defence of which the main source of supply lay outside the
United States. Fifteen other materials (including aluminium, asbestos,
graphite, vanadium, hides and wool) were listed by the Board as
'critical', i.e. essential to defence and requiring controls in time of
war, but involving less procurement difficulties than a strategic
material.

The 'moral embargo' policy was also administered by the State
Department. A moral embargo was first applied by the State Department in the summer of 1938 to prevent the export of aircraft and
accessories to countries guilty of air attacks upon civilian populations.
The embargo was reinforced by a statement issued by the President
on 2nd December 1939 indicating that the embargo covered not only
'aeronautical equipment' but also 'materials essential to airplane
manufacture'. The State Department on 15th December sent the
President's statement to all manufacturers of molybdenum and alu-

---

[1] Herbert Feis, *Seen from E.A.* (New York: Alfred A. Knopf, 1947).

[2] Even in the case of licences for the export of arms the deterrent was moral rather
than legal. Export without licence was illegal, but in theory the issue of the licence by
the State Department was mandatory.

[3] This power was given to the Board under the revised Industrial Mobilisation Plan
of 1936.

[4] War and Navy Departments, Joint Release, 11th October 1939, on Strategic and
Critical Raw Materials. This was preceded by a statement by the President on 26th
September. The Board issued a further release on 19th January 1940 aimed against
abnormal exports of rubber and tin.

minium,[1] informing them that the word 'materials' must be taken as including these two metals. The supply to 'certain countries' (i.e. Japan and the U.S.S.R.) of 'technical information required for the manufacture of aviation gasoline' was subjected to the same ban on 19th December.[2]

The talks on ferro-alloys began with the summoning of Purvis to Washington for an informal discussion with Morgenthau on 8th December. The latter explained that this was a matter, distinct from supply, to be dealt with 'between himself and the President on which he needed Allied assistance'. The American Ambassador at Paris had raised the question of the possible use by the Allies of control over molybdenum and tungsten as a means of shortening the war. Since one American company (Climax) produced about seventy-five per cent. of the world's output of molybdenum, how could supplies of this metal, as well as substitutes for it, be prevented from reaching agressor countries? The Climax Company had voluntarily undertaken not to fill orders for such destinations. Purvis was asked, as chairman of the Anglo-French Purchasing Board, to obtain as full data as possible, first of the ferro-alloy supply position of Germany, and second of the world supply situation as regards molybdenum and its substitutes, as well as of other vital strategic materials required for war. He was asked whether the British Empire would take parallel action in relation to nickel if the United States did what they could to head off supplies of molybdenum from reaching Germany through Russia and Japan. This narrower issue led into one that was much wider. Purvis summed up this point as it was put to him in the discussion as follows:

> The possibilities for the Democracies in using their relatively favourable position in the production of vital alloys (or similar relatively easily controlled materials really essential to war), e.g. molybdenum, nickel, vanadium or even copper, as a more practical means of influencing and maintaining peace than was provided by the League of Nations with all its complex problems in co-operation.

Impressed by the intense interest shown by Morgenthau in the matter, an interest which he was told was fully shared by the President, Purvis went straight back to New York and spent the next few days collecting data on the whole ferro-alloy position from the best experts he could find. He then returned for a further talk on 12th December with Morgenthau and Treasury officials. The points raised were the withholding of molybdenum supplies by American firms, the amounts the Allies intended to buy from these firms in 1940, and parallel British-Canadian action on nickel exports. The talks ended

---

[1] State Department Release No. 692, 15th December 1939.

[2] The possibility that the embargo might be applied to machine tools was mentioned to Purvis at the end of January 1940.

with an invitation to Purvis to co-operate with Treasury officials and with the American firms supplying ferro-alloys in a comprehensive study of the whole question.

The official announcement on the 15th of the application of the moral embargo to exports of molybdenum and aluminium was followed by a two-column Associated Press account, published on the 18th, of facts 'officially disclosed' the day before in Washington. The dispatch outlined various steps taken under the leadership of Morgenthau between March and August 1939 to try to avert the oncoming war. In March, the dispatch said, a 'Morgenthau peace plan' had 'called for the buying by non-aggressive nations of such goods as copper, manganese, cotton, oil, rubber and nickel, so that aggressor nations, unable to get a sufficient supply for war purposes, would be stymied'. The plan broke down, it was stated, on 10th April when a report by Mr. Harry D. White of the Treasury concluded that it would cost about $100 million a month, and that the alternative of an embargo imposed jointly by the United States, Great Britain and the Soviet Union was impractical.[1]

A further talk on ferro-alloys took place at the Treasury on the 22nd December. Morgenthau explained that he had declined a suggestion, made by the Embassy, that he should discuss the question of alloys with Lord Riverdale. In the interest of orderly and efficient procedure, he said, Purvis must be the sole channel for his dealings with Britain and France in such matters. He then asked Purvis to get definite answers from the Allies to three questions: (1) whether they could increase their orders for American molybdenum; (2) what were the figures of British and French stocks of molybdenum and their estimates of consumption for 1940; (3) whether the British Government would be willing to place a moral embargo on exports of nickel both to Russia and to Japan. The possibility of a credit for the purchase from China by the American Government of tin and tungsten was also noted.

To these approaches the Anglo-French Co-ordinating Committee gave an enthusiastic welcome. Control by the American Government over export and re-export of essential ferro alloys would be of the greatest service to the democratic powers, particularly if the control were extended to other raw materials such as oil, copper and carbon black. An American and Allied policy on these lines, the Committee felt, might well shorten the war considerably. The utmost importance was therefore attached to any steps which the United States Administration might take to prevent the ferro-alloys from reaching the enemy directly or indirectly. The Committee forwarded figures to show the supply position of the various ferro-alloys and their inter-

---

[1] *New York Herald Tribune*, 18th December 1939.

relationship. All this information was handed to Morgenthau and was studied by American experts. Similar data were given on other substances on the Allied list of strategic raw materials. As regards molybdenum, London pointed out that British and French contracts called for the delivery by the Climax Company of £11 million worth of molybdenum. This was equivalent to about fifteen months' supply, and the Allies felt this was as much as they should be asked to purchase; but perhaps the United States could stockpile the rest? The British policy as regards nickel was to ration Russia and Japan very strictly so as to leave no surplus of supplies that might leak to Germany. The Committee enquired whether the United States were contemplating a complete embargo on ferro-alloys. It thought that a complete stoppage of nickel might be unwise because Russia might seize the Finnish mines. Canada, it pointed out, had adopted an export licensing system for nickel and was using this to restrict exports to both countries.[1] Reference was made also in the London message to the possibility that the Allies might buy up Turkish supplies of chrome. As for manganese the Allies could meet American needs if supplies from Russia were to be interrupted.

When Purvis conveyed this message to Morgenthau at a private meeting in New York on 27th December, the latter expressed 'considerable pleasure' at the reception given by the Allies to his suggestion. On the 29th when Purvis saw the President he found that the latter knew all about the discussions and warmly approved the joint studies looking towards co-ordination of policies on strategic materials. The next day at a meeting at the Treasury the discussion went beyond ferro-alloys and touched vaguely on oil, copper, rubber, tin and quartz crystals.[2] A suggestion which the Anglo-French Co-ordinating Committee had made on the 23rd that, if necessary, experts could be sent over for further discussions was taken up on the American side with the proviso that any such discussions should remain informal.

Three days later (2nd January) a message to London gave the line which the talks on ferro-alloys were to follow over the next four months. The 'present thought', the message said, was that the 'examination into control possibilities of various essential materials' should be made by 'an informal group, representing the governments'. It would work confidentially and utilise the help of various industrialists

---

[1] Purvis himself discussed the matter of nickel exports with the Canadian authorities some days later and again in April. Canada had suspended nickel exports to Russia in the spring of 1939. Exports to all destinations were made subject to licences from 20th September. Licences for particular materials were supplemented by Orders in Council prohibiting exports of all goods to certain neutral countries except under licence, e.g. P.C.286, 23rd January 1940, P.C.885, 29th February 1940, P.C.1471, 11th April.

[2] M. Pleven, a member of the French Air Mission which arrived in mid-December, was also present at the meeting.

from time to time as desired. The general position of the United States was that as a neutral nation it was politically much easier for it to adopt an 'all or nothing policy', expressing itself in the form of moral embargoes or 'inability to supply owing to other demands' than to adopt a policy of rationing. But the United States recognised, the message reported, that the situation of the Allies was different and was not inclined to question seriously their policy of strict rationing.

It was now clear that Purvis was being drawn into important issues of policy which closely concerned the Foreign Office and the Quai d'Orsay and their Embassies in Washington. The Anglo-French Co-ordinating Committee, Monnet told Purvis on 4th January, 'attach particular importance to your personal relations in your Allied capacity with the United States Administration in broader issues—e.g. your negotiations with Mr. Morgenthau in matters of economic warfare. . . .' Monnet followed this up on the 22nd with a further message that the Quai d'Orsay and the Foreign Office had confirmed the view that the channel for the discussions should be the Anglo-French Co-ordinating Committee and Purvis, and attached 'particular importance' to this arrangement. Such discussions on the technical level provided, it was felt, a channel through which 'the combined views of the French and British Governments could be obtained and transmitted to Mr. Morgenthau and the President'. The closest liaison was necessary, however, between the Anglo-French Co-ordinating Committee and the two Foreign Offices and between Purvis and the two Embassies in Washington.[1]

Immediately after the visiting experts had been nominated by London and Paris, Purvis received a message from Morgenthau that the Mission must be postponed. The postponement lasted well into February. Purvis explained that in getting Morgenthau rather than the State Department to initiate these talks on alloys the President had been 'using his famous "quarter-back" technique'. For the time being the quarter-back had carried the ball as far as he could without imperilling the valuable assistance he was giving to the Allies on the supply side. 'Mr. Morgenthau is as friendly as ever in his attitude', Purvis wrote, 'and I am sure the same condition applies elsewhere. Different types of men in different Departments have, however, different ideas as to how far they can go in translating into effective action their friendly feelings.' He added the further explanation, in a message at the end of January, that the Secretary of State had urged

[1] The Foreign Secretary, speaking for both the British and French Foreign Offices, drew the attention of the British Ambassador to the convenience of handling such matters from a technical angle. He thought that secret and unofficial exchanges of views between Purvis and members of the American Administration handled in this way were far more likely to lead to satisfactory results than those conducted through more official channels. The latter would have to be used if anything leading to a formal commitment had to be negotiated.

on the President the undesirability of imperilling the renewal by
Congress of the Reciprocal Trade Agreements Act by any premature
move towards an extension of the moral embargoes. Nevertheless,
Purvis indicated, the practice of routing discussions on ferro-alloys
through himself for Morgenthau was to continue at the wish of the
State Department itself. It was arranged that the British and French
Ambassadors should present the visiting experts to Morgenthau with
Purvis present. The State Department, however, would handle
questions other than ferro-alloys, such as export restrictions on
copper, oil, soya beans, etc.

Thus by March 1940 some of the earlier difficulties which had
interfered with Allied procurement had begun to be removed, in part
by 'a new and agreed upon allocation of responsibilities as between
the State Department and the Treasury' (in the words of Purvis) and
in part by closer co-operation between the Treasury and the War and
the Navy Departments. The initiatives taken by the Treasury under
the authority of the President had helped in producing a closer knit
team. It was the Treasury alone, in the view of those on the spot,
which in practice was able to render on strategic materials the kind
of help that the Allies needed and the President wanted to give. But
lack of certainty regarding administrative arrangements on the
American side embarrassed not only the British and French but also
Canada. The External Affairs Department, as Purvis learned in
January, found it difficult to 'cope with present American departmental methods' and felt it must deal with ferro-alloys through the
State Department.

The upshot was that Purvis remained primarily responsible for the
ferro-alloy discussions with Morgenthau. The instruction given to
the Allied experts (the Rist-Gwatkin Mission) for the unofficial part
of their mission was 'to assist the chairman of the Anglo-French Purchasing Board in its discussions with Mr. Morgenthau and United
States industrialists on questions of economic warfare policy and
particularly regarding the possibility of preventing certain essential
commodities from reaching dangerous destinations'. Their main
official role, which was to assist the French and British Ambassadors
in Washington in their discussions with the State Department on
matters relating to economic warfare in general, lies outside the scope
of this volume.[1] Only a brief reference to the later stages of the talks
on ferro-alloys is called for in this study. The important point to note
is that Purvis never lost sight of the close relationship between supply
and economic warfare. He soon learned that he could get nowhere
by discussing general policy with Morgenthau such as the possibility

---

[1] The matters discussed included, broadly, trade agreement questions, agricultural purchases, detention of ships, diversion of ships into combat zones, exports from Germany.
See Medlicott, op. cit., Chapter X, Section v, on the Rist-Gwatkin Mission.

of the United States adopting the system of rationing for which London and Paris still hankered. It was 'in the nature of things impossible', he advised at the end of March 'to make the United States authorities formally agree on a general line of policy'; the best line with Morgenthau was 'to avoid discussions on broad policy and to concentrate on specific points on which he can be of help'. Two messages on the same day (18th March) to the chairman of the Anglo-French Co-ordinating Committee showed how Purvis had to balance benefits to the Allies on the supply side against possible benefits in the matter of denial of supply to the enemy. In one message he spoke of Morgenthau as 'being extremely helpful in connection with the United States Administration releases required for the new aviation programme'. In the other he referred to the more cautious attitude being taken on ferro-alloys. Here there was continuing interest, and discussions were going on at the moment on molybdenum, nickel and tungsten. But 'the degree of help' Morgenthau would be able to give would 'vary considerably from time to time in view of the fact that it is an election year'. This was the dilemma that was continuously in the mind of the President and of the Secretary of the Treasury. The Anglo-French Co-ordinating Committee was thus made aware that in the then state of American public opinion the Administration could not give the Allies all the help it would wish to give. If the Administration were to give aid in facilitating purchases of aircraft and munitions this might have to be at the expense of its ability to co-operate more closely on questions of economic warfare.

The negotiations regarding molybdenum (where supply to the Allies and the denial of supply to the enemy were as mixed together as salt with sea-water) went on through the first half of 1940. In March, in accordance with the wish of Morgenthau, Purvis opened direct negotiations with the producers. London agreed reluctantly, since it did not want to create a precedent whereby the Allies would be committed to large-scale pre-emptive buying in the United States over and above their supply needs. The producers of molybdenum did not in fact ask for more than that the Allies should finalise (i.e. guarantee) their outstanding contracts for 1940 (10 million lb. with Climax and 3 million lb. with the independent producers). As Morgenthau advised this step, it was taken. But it was not possible to get the producers to agree in return to tie their hands with any pledge to shut off exports—even if the moral embargo were to be lifted —to Germany and Russia for the remainder of 1940. The objective was more or less assured, however, by the offer by Climax to advise Purvis unofficially of any suspicious orders from any European neutral.

An opportunity to tie in the supply of copper for Britain with denial of supply to the enemy was seized in May. At the outbreak of the war the central European market was lost to American copper exporters and Great Britain switched over to Commonwealth supplies—mostly Rhodesian and Canadian. The large surplus piling up in the United States, and the still considerable American exports of copper, were a matter of special concern to the Allies in view of known leakages into Germany through neutrals. Russia from September 1939 to March 1940 had imported from the United States 70,000 tons, compared with 12,000 tons in the first eight months of 1939. Copper in fact occupied, in the words of an official British report, 'the most disquieting position in the whole picture of the metal and alloy situation'. Copper was too important in the United States ('too large political interests were involved', a British official had been told in March) for it to be subjected to a moral embargo.

Talks early in May 1940 with American copper producers about the exports to Russia showed that they were sympathetic. They said that it would help if Allied orders for copper could be placed directly through the Allied missions and not through intermediaries. A fortnight later news of a British order for 17,500 tons of copper which the Non-Ferrous Metal Control was about to place directly on the American market, gave Purvis a chance to drive the point home. The British Purchasing Commission, he urged, should be 'entrusted with the lever this purchase would provide' both to 'mop up existing spot stocks' and as a means of getting 'informal personal undertakings' from the producers not to export to 'dangerous destinations'. He was instructed accordingly to negotiate the purchases.[1]

Various steps were tried to get the American strategic embargo strengthened. One step was the voluntary adoption by producers and exporters of a clause in contracts prohibiting re-export. The American Tin Trade Association had adopted such a clause for tin. It was also suggested to Morgenthau that further materials such as chrome, cobalt and industrial diamonds should be placed on the strategic or moral embargo lists.

Despite the good will of many American producers and exporters who put the cause of democracy above profit and the readiness of the Administration to do all in its power to aid the Allies, supply to the Allies could not be tied in closely with denial of supply to 'dangerous destinations' until the system of voluntary controls had been replaced by an export licensing system. Such a system was introduced under the National Defence Act of 2nd July (Section 6).[2]

---

[1] By the end of June 1940, contracts had been placed in the United States for 29,000 tons of copper. 'It is understood', Purvis noted, in giving instructions for the first purchase, that 'this purchase is to be distributed in such a way as to tie in with the desire to get personal assurances that copper will not be shipped to Russia and Italy.'

[2] At the same time the United States was moving slowly towards a policy of buying up for stockpiling purposes supplies of critical materials that might otherwise leak to Germany, such as the stock of tungsten in China on which Purvis had several talks with Morgenthau in the first half of the year. In July London was informed that the State Department favoured sharing with the British in the purchase of Turkish chrome.

Although all this activity on the part of Morgenthau and Purvis in the first half of 1940 seemed to produce few direct and concrete results, it helped in London and Washington to develop the habit of working together on matters of common concern. Gradually over the six months from December 1939 the two Governments, with France, reviewed together one by one the whole supply position of the more important strategic materials. April was a very active period in this process. On both sides of the Atlantic facts and figures were being assembled, assessed and co-ordinated. Thus already by June 1940 there had been assembled an appreciable part of the data needed for a combined view of the world supply requirements situation for many of the critical materials which from 1942 onwards were to be dealt with by the Combined Raw Materials Board. The next phase opened in July 1940 with a shifting of the accent from denial to the enemy to supply for the United Kingdom and the United States. For the new American rearmament programme now threatened acute competition between British and American demands for several strategic materials.

(iii)

Co-ordinating Supply and Expanding Capacity

That this anticipation of combined methods of solving supply problems was no mere isolated event was shown by what was happening in several parallel fields, notably machine tools and steel, in the first half of 1940.[1] Thus, in the case of machine tools, the exchanges between the two sides foreshadowed in their language and ideas the Anglo-American 'combined boards' of 1942. Already, at the beginning of 1940 there were passages in the papers of Purvis which showed that he envisaged the possibility of using the machine-tool shortage as an instrument for co-ordinating the aircraft production of Britain, France and the United States. In a message to London on 2nd February 1940 he asked for data on all machine-tool orders already placed in the United States with an indication as to their priority ratings and the dates of delivery. The information was to include also the machine-tool consequences of aircraft programmes still under consideration. The object, he explained, was to correlate British orders with French requirements and then to fit them in with the 'United States preparedness programme orders before they are placed'. This would permit, he added, 'the visualisation of the com-

---

[1] On the co-ordination of the supply of steel see *Studies of Overseas Supply*, Chapter I. The growing volume of Allied orders for steel began to cause concern to the Administration in the months before Dunkirk. Steel shipments to Britain in the second half of 1940 became by far the heaviest single charge on Atlantic shipping.

bined necessities'. The objects were 'so to arrange the productive output from existing machine-tool plants as to give the optimum deliveries, . . . to expand that output as fast as possible where combined necessities demand, . . . to enable us to avoid the unnecessarily costly prices and terms which have been inherent in the unco-ordinated method of purchasing'.

The special importance of machine tools in British purchasing policy in the first phase of the war is indicated in the next section of this chapter. In February 1940 it was estimated that more United States dollars would be spent on machine tools in the first year of war than on aircraft and ground munitions combined. Even in the first nine months of war the strain of filling these British machine-tool orders, the still heavier French purchases, the rapidly growing domestic requirements of the United States themselves, and the orders beginning to come in from other overseas countries, had begun to make machine tools the first really serious supply 'bottleneck' of the war. It was for this reason that the American, British and French Governments were being forced, even at this early period, into what they were already beginning to call 'combined' action. This combined approach began with the recognition of the need for programmes of requirements and supply. The programmes when made had to be fitted together and kept in adjustment by frequent consultations. This process was in full swing by the late summer of 1940.[1]

Each of the problems referred to above—the denial of strategic materials to the Axis powers and the assuring of supplies of scarce materials and machine tools to Britain and the United States—involved close co-ordination between British and American policies and action. In fact, in the six months before Dunkirk North American supply presented a whole series of problems of co-ordination. Most, if not all of them, were handled through the Morgenthau–Purvis channel. Some of the problems arose from the impact of Allied purchasing on the American economy. Others were due to the extreme difficulty of securing scarce war supplies by purchasing them on the open market, since manufacturers were engaged almost exclusively in the production of the normal civilian requirements of a still-neutral country. Other difficulties arose from the need for British capital expenditure to erect new factories in the United States as a means of speeding up war production, for American manufacturers were still reluctant to incur the risks and possible odium of engaging in the manufacture of war supplies. They were labouring, Purvis reported, under 'a combination of fears'. One was 'distrust of the New Deal régime, which made manufacturers anxious to avoid extending themselves financially'. Others were the uncertainties of an election year

---

[1] On the co-ordination of machine-tool orders see *Studies of Overseas Supply*, Chapter I.

and fear of a fresh war debts problem with an Allied default on payments. The net result, he noted, was that whilst the banks were 'bursting with money' and anxious to lend, manufacturers feared to assume further obligations.

In their initial policies both the United Kingdom and the United States were acting in the light of past experience. Thus the common experience of the First World War in the matter of war debts played a part in shaping both the American policy of 'cash and carry' and the United Kingdom policy of conserving its dollar reserves. British policy, as we shall see below, was not to order munitions in bulk from the United States, but to concentrate purchases mainly on machine tools to equip British factories, treating American manufacturing capacity as a reserve in case of need.

The Allies soon learned, however, that the American Government was not going to sit passively behind its neutral shop-front waiting for the Allies to pay cash and carry their goods away. The Administration's policy was one of active supervision over Allied buying in order to prevent disruption of the American economy and interference with its own rearmament. The Allies were told plainly from the outset that if they wanted to purchase supplies on a large scale from the United States they must fulfil two conditions: (1) co-ordinate their purchasing in order to avoid competing with each other and with the United States Government; (2) disclose to the Administration their purchasing plans and their financial assets. All cards, both of supply and finance, must be on the table. The Allies must not only say what they were buying, but must tell Washington well in advance what they intended to buy and how much money they had to spend. The Administration decided from the outset that it could only judge the long-range effects of Allied purchasing plans on the American economy and on American defence if it had full knowledge of Allied plans for financing their purchases. This applied especially to the unloading of dollar securities on to the American market.

These were the points on which the Secretary of the Treasury, speaking always for the President, hammered with great persistence from the beginning of October 1939. The President had told the Monnet Mission in January 1939 that Allied purchasing of munitions must be joint and co-ordinated. The Secretary of the Treasury made the same point with the French Mission in mid-September. He passed on to the British Embassy on 4th October 1939 the strong desire of the President that the British Government should give regular weekly data on its purchases and deliveries, including not only munitions but also raw materials, manufactured goods and foodstuffs. Orders placed through normal trade channels, as well as those placed through Government agencies, were to be included in the return. By this means the President hoped to facilitate deliveries to the Allies.[1]

Throughout these early discussions Morgenthau pressed the view of the President and himself that close contact between the Allied missions and the Procurement Division of the Treasury was essential if economic stability was to be preserved and wasteful competition prevented as between the Allies and the American Government. The Administration's policy in this matter was also pressed by the War Department. Thus on 8th November 1939, on the day after the British Purchasing Commission was set up, Purvis was told at a meeting in the War Department that the President was 'deeply concerned' over the lack of co-ordination between the Allied Governments and had intimated, Purvis reported, that 'if the two governments were unable to arrange matters amongst themselves he would have to step in.'[2]

The Administration insisted that prices must be kept steady and profits held down to a reasonable level. One consequence was that it became essential to the British Government to know what prices the American Army was paying for particular types of equipment. The first of many inquiries on this point was made informally by the Embassy on 3rd November. It asked the price which was being paid by the American Army for Wright aero engines, since the United Kingdom wished to place an order for 1,200 of these engines the moment the arms embargo was repealed.

The request for a weekly return was followed a month later by the suggestion by Morgenthau that he should meet each week the heads of the British and French missions to discuss the orders they desired to place and examine the technical aspects of supply, manufacturing capacity, shipment, and so forth. This would ensure Allied co-ordination and the avoidance of competitive buying.[3] Three days later in a formal note the State Department drew attention to the role of the Army and Navy Munitions Board in 'co-ordinating governmental action' in connection with foreign purchases in order to safeguard American munitions supplies. The Allies were asked for a second weekly return which more or less duplicated the one made to the Treasury. They continued to supply these two weekly returns for many months.[4] The next day (7th November) the Secretary of the

---

[1] Searchlights, of which the French Government, without assistance, could not get delivery before June 1940, were mentioned as a typical case.

[2] The French were regarded as having tried to beat the gun by placing many orders before the repeal of the Neutrality Act.

[3] Mr. Morgenthau pressed also the urgent need for Allied experts to serve on joint standardisation committees on the design and production of munitions required by both the Allies and the American Government.

[4] The latter was sent regularly each week from 27th September 1939 up to March 1941 when it was discontinued at the request of the State Department. Data for Allied and Commonwealth countries were included in many of these returns. The weekly returns by the Anglo-French Purchasing Board to the President's Liaison Committee continued till April 1940. It was then put on a monthly basis for the month of May onwards.

H

Treasury saw the President and asked him to set up a standing informal committee of liaison with the Allies. Unless the President gave
him positive instructions, he told Purvis, the Treasury could not act
in such a matter. This seemed a setback.[1] The British and French
Ambassadors then submitted a joint formal note to the State Department indicating the machinery of Allied co-ordination (the setting up
of the Anglo-French Co-ordinating Committee in London under
Monnet, and of the Anglo-French Purchasing Board under Purvis),
and asking how it was to work with the United States Government.
They were informed by a State Department note that a committee
was being set up with the task of discussing with the Anglo-French
Purchasing Board 'any questions which involve interference with
the purchases to be made by the Government of the United States in
connection with its preparedness programme . . . priorities . . .
and fair prices and which thus affect the internal economy of the
United States'. The committee, which was referred to as the President's Liaison Committee (or Synchronizing Committee, as it was
often called at first), began to function informally from 8th December
under the chairmanship of Captain H. E. Collins of the Treasury
Procurement Division.[2] The appointment of a Treasury chairman,
Purvis told Monnet, was at first objected to by the Army and Navy,
which were not represented at the earlier meetings, but the objections
were withdrawn at the end of December. The general purpose of the
Committee, as put by its chairman in a letter to Purvis, was 'to provide a channel through which all contacts with the United States
Government should be made by the British and French purchasing
organisation, such contacts to be made through the Committee and
no other medium'.

Meanwhile the machinery on the Allied side was being completed.
The Anglo-French Co-ordinating Committee in London held its first
meeting on 6th December 1939 and two days later its chairman,
Monnet, sent Purvis the text of the letters exchanged between the
British and French Prime Ministers, giving the terms of reference of
the Committee and of its Permanent Executive Committees.[3] 'The
French as well as the British Government', Monnet wrote, 'regard
you as charged with negotiations with the United States Government

---

[1] When next day at a meeting with the Assistant Secretary of War and his staff Purvis
mentioned his parting question to Morgenthau, 'Where do we go from here?', he was
told: 'You come here to us'.

[2] The membership and functions of the Committee were formally notified to the Allies
on 3rd January and given to the Press on 23rd January, with news of the setting up of
the Anglo-French Purchasing Board. Priorities between the American armed services
were dealt with by a priorities clearance committee of the Army and Navy Munitions
Board, set up in the summer of 1939, consisting of War, Navy, State, Treasury and
Justice Departments.

[3] The Permanent Executive Committees were to deal in the first instance with food,
shipping, munitions and raw materials, oil, economic warfare.

on their behalf, with a high degree of effective authority, in other words . . . in your capacity of Chairman of the Anglo-French Purchasing Committee in the U.S.A., you have the status of an Allied representative in the same way as myself as Chairman of the Anglo-French Co-ordinating Committee'. The phrase 'high degree of effective authority' expressed the desire of the two Governments, Monnet explained, that Purvis as chairman should take charge on their behalf of negotiations with the United States Administration. The joint action of the Anglo-French Purchasing Board was to cover (*a*) contacts and negotiations with the American Government, (*b*) the formulation of policy on important problems interesting both Governments and the submission of reports thereon, (*c*) negotiations wherever practicable of actual purchases of common products with American industry. It was arranged that the two missions would live under one roof in New York so that there would be daily informal meeting. 'We propose', the chairman wrote, 'to proceed jointly on negotiations for buying of common products, leaving for independent action after buying negotiations are completed only such matters as minor contract clauses; technical control where necessary during manufacture; inspection when necessary, and actual payment.' This organisation had begun to operate by mid-January. The Board held its first formal meeting on 18th January 1940. A joint announcement of the setting up of the Allied machinery in the United States was made in the press on 24th January and received wide publicity in the United States and Canada.[1]

The press announcement dwelt on co-ordination. Now, it said, 'the two nations can deal in this country authoritatively as one and competition and overlapping will thereby be avoided'. The words slid over the very real difficulties of achieving anything like complete co-ordination in the development and sharing of the American potential. For full co-ordination involved the smooth intermeshing of the main gear-wheels within each nation, of department with department, of government with government, and of governments with private traders. Trouble at the latter point was usually the reason for any slowness of response on London's part to the incessant proddings of Purvis and behind him of Morgenthau and the President.

The policy of the United States Government on the matter of co-ordination between the Allied Governments was clear and consistent. There was no evidence of any serious attempt by the American Government to play off Allies against each other, nor to interfere with the arrangements which existed between the members of the British

---

[1] e.g. *The New York Times, The Wall Street Journal, Montreal Gazette,* 24th January 1940. The statement indicated that on 23rd January the British Purchasing Commission numbered eighty-five people, including some forty-five Americans. The French Purchasing Commission was much larger, with a total of about 170, mostly French.

Commonwealth. The Administration set its face steadily against separate approaches to it on supply matters by foreign governments, Allied or Commonwealth. The Administration insisted that the Allies should co-ordinate their demands through the Anglo-French Purchasing Board, and that the Commonwealth countries should first co-ordinate their needs with the British Government and should use a common channel for their approach to the American Government. Even Canada came under this arrangement until special Canadian-American joint defence machinery was set up. The British Commonwealth channel was the British Purchasing Commission up to January 1941 and then the British Supply Council. This was an independent and unchanging American policy, although it happened to coincide with the policy preferred by London and its fellow members of the Commonwealth.[1]

Already in January 1940 leaders of American industry also had begun to press the same point with the Allied Purchasing Commissions. It was being pressed by the machine-tool manufacturers. A representative of the Aluminium Corporation stated 'most emphatically', at a meeting between Purvis and Bloch-Lainé and Captain Collins on 26th January, that 'all Allied orders and inquiries should be channelled through one agency'.

It has to be remembered that the first few months of the war were still a period of transition from normal peace-time channels to government controls. Direct government procurement was confined mainly to military and naval supplies. Here control presented few large obstacles. Since war supplies had not been imported in peace-time from the United States there was no private trade in them. All the governments from the outbreak of the war realised the importance of keeping each other informed of their orders for war supplies.[2] They were able also to bring their own departments fairly quickly into line to prevent overlapping or duplication in supply orders. Co-ordination between government departments was important not merely for the major arms programmes but also for sudden new requirements produced by some action of the enemy. Thus the Ger-

---

[1] For reference to the practice of the American Government during the war of referring in public statements, including those made in a legal context, to 'The British Commonwealth of Nations', see H. Duncan Hall, 'The British Commonwealth as a Great Power', *Foreign Affairs* (New York), July 1945.

[2] The difficulty of securing returns from all the supply ministries was shown by the fact that whilst the American Government's request for a weekly return of munitions orders placed or intended was made on 4th October, the first return (data up to 15th December) was not actually lodged until 27th December. It covered 'orders placed', 'being negotiated' and 'enquiries being made', on behalf of the Admiralty, Ministry of Supply and the Air Ministry. The total value of the orders placed by the three Ministries was put at approximately $115 million (Admiralty, $2 million; Supply, $22 million; and Air, $91 million. The latter figure included completed aircraft contracts for $33 million). Four contracts for raw materials (acetone, timber, wood pulp and silk noils) were mentioned as being under negotiation by the Ministry of Supply.

man use of the magnetic mine brought a flood of Admiralty orders
for many thousands of miles of electric cables to be dispatched to
ports all over the British Commonwealth.[1] The torpedoing of the
Royal Oak in Scapa Flow early in the war brought a sudden flood of
competing demands for large tonnages of chain cable for harbour
defences. The orders for chain cables came in from several governments as well as from different departments of the same government.
A few cases of this kind were enough to bring about better co-
ordination in the matter of purchases by governments of war supplies.
To secure effective co-ordination over the wide field of private trade
in commodities with both civilian and military uses was a much more
difficult operation. The Administration insisted on being told in
advance of all large purchases of supplies through private trade
channels as well as by the Allied missions. The only effective remedy
proved to be to concentrate all purchasing through the Allied missions. This difficult task was perhaps the main preoccupation of
Purvis during the period up to the fall of France when he was acting
in his dual role of director of the British Purchasing Commission and
Chairman of the Anglo-French Purchasing Board. He began to press
the point steadily from December 1939. But it was not until the eve
of Dunkirk that purchases of major supplies (such as machine tools,
steel and some other vital strategic materials) were concentrated
through the British Purchasing Commission.[2]

THE USE OF BRITISH CAPITAL TO EXPAND AMERICAN CAPACITY

So far the narrative has been following, roughly in order of time,
the main problems that arose on the spot in attempting to make use
of existing American capacity for the production of war supplies. The
American potential, which is the title of this chapter, had as yet
hardly been touched. Its full development waited on the expenditure
by the United States themselves of vast sums of capital. But the Allies
could not afford to wait on the slow processes of American policies.
They had to begin the process of expansion themselves by giving
capital assistance at certain key points such as explosives and aircraft
production.[3]

---

[1] American mills were working at high speed on these orders through the first half of
1940. An order for 5,250 miles of electric cable was received by the British Purchasing
Commission on 14th May for delivery in six weeks and was fully covered by contracts
three days later.

[2] For a detailed discussion of this problem, with particular reference to the case of
machine tools and steel, see *Studies of Overseas Supply*, Chapter I. On the importance of
machine tools in British purchasing policy see below, Section iv.

[3] On explosives see *Studies of Overseas Supply*, Chapter I. Assistance was less needed in
the case of machine tools where the conditions of the industry and the large volume of
Allied and American orders were a sufficient stimulus to secure a rapid expansion of
the industry.

The first problem, however, was to find even the dollars needed to cover the deficit caused by abnormal imports from the United States. The British Government's policy was to cover the deficit by the sale of securities, eked out by gold whenever the supply of dollars was too low to meet current payments. A vesting order covering sixty securities valued at $200 million was prepared in November 1939, but then postponed. This postponement was first criticised but later welcomed by Mr. Morgenthau on the ground that too rapid sales might disturb the market. Vesting orders were finally issued on 8th February and 15th April. They covered 177 securities with a total value of approximately $310 million.[1] By late February sales of securities had brought in $107 million and gold had been sold to the value of $228 million. (The vesting orders represented the winding up of the historical process whereby British capital had helped to settle the Great West and build American industry and railways. Two billions' worth of the securities sold from 1914–18 represented railroad stock.)

The deficit had been increased by the abnormally heavy demands for dollars caused by 'cash and carry'. Even for pre-war contracts such as aircraft payment had to be made in full before the goods could leave American ports. But the dollars so far secured from all sources were few when compared with the estimate of total cost of war supplies in the United States in the first year of war. A revised forecast given by the Embassy to the United States Treasury late in February put this figure at $800 million.[2] (French purchases were to reach about the same figure.) Visible and invisible exports to the United States, including those of the rest of the sterling area, would bring in not much more than half of this amount leaving a net dollar deficit for the sterling area of about $470 million, and this did not count the $100 million for the British share of the Anglo-French air scheme.

Moreover, capital assistance by the Allies to American industry was needed if arms were to be obtained in time. Arms production for foreign countries in an uncertain war involved more than ordinary risk for the American manufacturer. Thus one initial difficulty was that the manufacturer had to pay the American Government a twenty per cent. income tax on capital sums spent on the expansion of plant. At first the Allies themselves had to provide the sum needed

---

[1] British-owned American securities were registered with the Bank of England at the outbreak of the war; this facilitated transfer to the Treasury by the issuing from time to time of a vesting order as had been done in the First World War. An official estimate, issued by the United States Department of Commerce on 29th August 1939, put British investments in the United States—only a limited part of which was readily marketable—at from $2,300 to $2,400 million. The total in 1914 was put at $4,140 million, of which $3,500 million had been liquidated.

[2] The main groups (in £ million) were: Raw materials, 49; Foodstuffs and tobacco, 23; Machine tools, 23; Merchant ships, 31; Munitions, 38.

to pay this tax as part of any capital assistance they gave to American firms.[1]

In the end capital assistance was a burden which the United States Government alone could shoulder. After the passing of the Lend-Lease Act the Administration relieved the United Kingdom of any responsibility for capital assistance. This was done partly in the interest of American preparedness and partly as a form of lend-lease aid to the Allied Governments. It is of interest to note that when the matter of capital assistance was first raised by Purvis in talks with Secretary Morgenthau and President Roosevelt at the end of December 1939, the President coupled it with the idea of a loan of surplus American materials. The question, which Purvis put first to Secretary Morgenthau and then to the President, was whether the United States, as part of their preparedness programme, would be willing to bear some of the capital costs involved in the expansion of plants of strategic value. Secretary Morgenthau told Purvis that this was a point for the President, but that any fruitful discussion of the general problem of finance was not possible as the Allies had still not put their financial cards on the table. A joint account of the interview with the President on the 29th recorded that Purvis

> discussed the general question where, in order to meet Allied requirements in certain materials, new plants would have to be built and financed by the Allies which would create assets of national strategic value for the defence of the United States. As an example, Mr. Purvis mentioned the case of explosives for which new plants had to be created. Mr. Purvis asked whether the United States would give consideration to taking back such plants at a fair value at the conclusion of the war.

The President replied that he did not see any objection to the Anglo-French Board taking up with Captain Collins such matters, which were obviously of interest. The President went on to make a suggestion that bore fruit later. 'Certain re-worked materials', he thought, might be made available to the Allies as surplus to American requirements. The particular material he had in mind was trinitrotoluol which (as Purvis noted) the President 'thought might possibly be diverted to the Allies promptly as coming from what is really a United States stock, leaving it to be replenished later from deliveries available from a new plant'. This was the germ of two later decisions of great historical importance. The first was the decision taken in the first days of June 1940, after the evacuation of Dunkirk, to hand over to the Allies the 'surplus' stocks of arms which the American Army had kept

---

[1] On capital assistance see below, Chapter VII, Part II, Section viii. For a discussion of problems involved in giving such assistance, including details of some of the programmes, and on the matter of taxation, see *Studies of Overseas Supply*, Chapter I.

in store since 1918; the second decision was the general policy of loaning supplies known as 'lend-lease'.

In April 1940, in connection with the Tennessee Powder Plant, Purvis again raised the question of the United States sharing in the capital cost of plants of strategic importance. Since the Administration seemed powerless to act without new legislation, he suggested to the British and French Governments a loan scheme which they promptly rejected on political grounds. The scheme was to create a United States corporation with a capital of, say, $40 million provided by American, British and French groups. The corporation would buy the aircraft from manufacturers and on delivery would resell them to the Allied Governments at a price which would cover interest on capital and a small profit. The lawyers of the Anglo-French Purchasing Board advised that the plan did not infringe the Neutrality or Johnson Acts. It had the great merit of avoiding the heavy initial down payment of forty to sixty per cent. on aircraft orders and would defer for upwards of a year payments running into hundreds of millions of dollars. Nothing came of the scheme, nor even of schemes for long-term agricultural credits to avoid drastic cuts in British imports of cotton and other commodities. These would have been popular with American farmers, but they worried the Administration. It was election year.

The proposal by the Dupont Company in April 1940 to build the Tennessee Powder Plant was coupled with the suggestion that title to the plant should be retained by the British Government. This marked the adoption of an important new policy which was applied not only in connection with contracts for explosives but also to the large aircraft contracts placed in the summer of 1940 as part of the $600 million Anglo-French air programme. The new policy paved the way for the adoption after the Lend-Lease Act of the suggestion made by Purvis to the President about the United States Government 'taking back plants at a fair value'. Thus the Tennessee plant, which cost $25 million (as against an original estimate of $17 million) was taken over at cost price by the American Government late in March 1941.[1]

The new programmes adopted in the spring of 1940 for explosives and aircraft were only a dim foreshadowing of the scale of expenditure necessary to expand American war production. Before June 1940 the British Government had already allotted to explosives and aircraft firms over $50 million for capital assistance in building new plant.[2]

---

[1] See below, Chapter VII, pp. 290–91.

[2] British capital assistance up to March 1941 was well over $200 million. See below, Chapter VII, Part II, Section viii, and *Studies of Overseas Supply*, Chapter I.

(iv)

British Purchasing Policy up to Dunkirk

A convenient point has now been reached in the narrative to summarise British purchasing policy and its results before Dunkirk. In
the interest of clarity the summary will refer to some points touched
upon in previous chapters; but these references will be made in
relation to a new theme, the all-important one of supplies of aircraft
from the United States to which little reference has been so far made.

In the years before the war munitions supply from the United
States had two aspects: first, the supplementing of British rearmament
by special short-term orders and, second, the creation of a reserve
capacity for use in the event of war. It was realised at an early date
that the assistance of the United States might ultimately be necessary
as regards both of these aspects, but while the possibilities were
explored and constantly borne in mind, very little definite action
was possible (other than in certain detailed respects already mentioned) owing to financial and other limitations. The chief exception
was in aircraft production. By the spring of 1938, having slipped the
financial leash which still held other Departments in check, the Air
Ministry was beginning to run up against actual shortages of plant
and skilled labour. At the same time the German invasion of
Austria increased public anxiety and led to questions in Parliament
as to the possibility of securing supplies of aircraft from the United
States. It was accordingly decided to send an Air Mission to America
to see what could be done. One result of this Mission was the beginning of aircraft production in Canada (described in Chapter II).
Another was the placing, on 22nd–23rd June 1938, of two large
contracts for reconnaissance aircraft and trainers in the United
States. The first was for 250 Lockheed Hudson aircraft[1] and the
second for 200 North American Harvard trainers.[2]

In addition to making these immediate purchases, the Mission was
instructed to make enquiries regarding existing productive capacity
in the United States for various types of military aircraft. Discussions
took place with other manufacturing firms besides Lockheed and
North American, but no contracts were let, either because types were
unsuitable or cost excessive. The Mission was impressed by the backwardness of the United States from the point of view of military aircraft as compared with the high quality of American civilian trans-

---

[1] It was significant of the distance still existing between Britain and America that
turrets were to be installed in Britain, since it was thought premature to disclose details
of the British turret.

[2] Each contract allowed for the normal twenty per cent. provision of spares.

port machines. American military aviation, it pointed out in its report, was held up by a complicated system of design and prototype competition and development of squadron orders—a system that had been given up in the United Kingdom in 1930. In the United States an interval of seven years might elapse, according to one manufacturer, between design and its realisation in use—a handicap which did not operate in civil aviation. The Government concluded, on the basis of the report, that American designs were so far behind the more advanced designs with which war in Europe would be fought that it would be unwise at that stage to place any large orders for military aircraft in the United States, apart from these two special purchases.

The Munich crisis in September 1938 for a moment changed the Government's outlook. It led to an Air Ministry telegram to the Air Attaché at Washington, on 27th September, asking him to give urgently his estimate of types and numbers of aircraft which could be bought in America for delivery in Great Britain within one month. He replied two days later after private discussion with American aircraft manufacturers that the Air Ministry could, if it chose, place further orders for Hudsons and training aircraft; but this would be a gamble, because 'in the event of war the United Kingdom could not count on the Neutrality Act being amended in its favour before the end of the year at the earliest, if even then'.[1]

At this point President Roosevelt was giving much time to the problems confronting the Democracies. He regarded the Munich Agreement as forced on them because of their inferiority in the air. He was determined that the United States must never find themselves in such a position; and he had given instructions for an enquiry to be made as to the capacity of American aircraft factories. The President, the Air Attaché reported, took the view that if Germany could build 30,000 aircraft America could build 40,000. He also talked at this time of the United States supplying enough partly finished basic material (such as fabricated aluminium, tubing, steel castings, magnetos and other accessories), to which the Neutrality Act did not apply, for the Allies to build aircraft far in excess of German production. But the Air Attaché gave a warning in mid-November that, owing to the vast air rearmament being planned, the best United States aircraft manufacturers would not be able to accept any orders for aircraft for Great Britain after the spring of 1939. The warning was premature, but it had the effect of deciding the Air Ministry to order an additional 200 Harvards which had been under discussion

---

[1] Another alternative he suggested might be to arrange for the establishment of factories in Canada by American aircraft constructors for the production of British or American types. One American firm was prepared to set up a shadow factory in Canada.

since October; the contract was actually placed on 30th January 1939. On the other hand, an offer of the Lockheed Company just before the war to build another 250 Hudsons, if given a follow-up order, was not taken up by the Air Ministry till December 1939.

Thus the sum total of American aircraft ordered by Britain before the war was 250 Hudsons and 400 Harvards. Nevertheless, the importance for the American aircraft industry of these early contracts should not be under estimated. Their cost (about $43 million) was not far short of the total appropriations available to the United States Army and Navy for the purchase of aircraft in the year ending 30th June 1938. One direct result was the birth of the Lockheed Hudson bomber; another was 'some of the biggest engine orders placed in many years' with the two principal American aircraft engine firms.[1]

A second serious deficiency in British equipment for which the Government turned to the United States before the war—anti-aircraft guns—was referred to in Chapter I. Enquiries were made for such guns in 1936, but the idea was put aside in 1937 on the ground that nothing could be obtained 'off the shelf'. Moreover, even if it had been possible to arrange for British designs to be manufactured in the United States orders could not result in deliveries from the United States for eighteen months. In general British firms could supply more advanced models more quickly and more cheaply. The one important exception was the Sperry Gyroscope Company's anti-aircraft predictor, for which substantial pre-war orders were placed with the American as well as with the British branch of the firm.[2]

Behind this question of immediate purchases to supplement home production in the years of peace, there lay the wider question of creating a reserve arsenal in the United States from which Great Britain might draw much larger supplies in time of war. This possibility was never far from the minds of planners in London in 1938–39, but its realisation was attended with the same difficulties that prevented large munitions orders being placed in aid of the rearmament programme—the factors of dollar shortage, production costs, time and American neutrality.

AMERICA AS A MARGINAL SOURCE—AIRCRAFT

Even apart from these considerations, the Government's plan did not envisage the United States as a major source of war supplies. In the First World War the British had spent some $1,500 million (out of total purchases in the United States amounting to $7,200 million) on American munitions, but they did not intend to repeat even this

---

[1] Stettinius, op. cit., pp. 14–15.

[2] There was also before the war an 'educational' order for 3·7-inch gun liners as well as an order for 6-inch shell bodies.

fairly limited expenditure. Up to the spring of 1939 they were still envisaging modest land forces. 'The view that we shall in the next war as in the last require gigantic supplies of steel and munitions for a huge land army', wrote the Chairman of the Supply Board in March 1939, '. . . rests on a policy which the Government determinedly refuse to accept as a basis for peace supply arrangements.' In fact, so far as the Army were concerned overseas purchasing policy, like all other war plans, was still governed by the concept of a war of limited liability. Even after the formal abandonment of this concept and the introduction of the Army Expansion Programme in the spring of 1939 there were still grave difficulties in, and objections to, depending to any major extent on supply from the United States. It was admitted on all hands that the situation might be transformed if British industry were crippled by air attack, and that it might be wise to have a war potential in reserve in the United States. But here the argument of American neutrality barred the way. As the Minister for the Co-ordination of Defence pointed out in March 1939, it was doubtful whether the United States would let the 'reserve potential' function in war, 'and if they did not we should have taken a false step'. There was also the difficulty that such a potential could be created only by large orders in time of peace, and the funds at the disposal of the War Office were hardly enough to build up adequate capacity in the United Kingdom, leaving very little to spare for overseas orders. Thus the only step taken in this direction was an 'educational' order placed with an American firm for fifty anti-aircraft gun liners.

The Air Ministry was rather less confident of the ability of United Kingdom and Commonwealth industry to do all that was needed. The Government might not want a huge land army, but it did want an air force capable of meeting the German Luftwaffe on at least equal terms. Even if British production could eventually be built up to an extent which would make this possible, there would still be the problem of the wastage, estimated for the sake of planning at 225 per cent. of the front-line strength of the R.A.F. (150 per cent. for the Fleet Air Arm), which was thought likely to begin from the very first days of a war. This would mean a gap far beyond the replacement possibilities of a peace-time aircraft industry which could only be converted slowly to full war production. The Air Ministry foresaw as early as 1937 the danger that peace-time output in the United Kingdom could not be boosted high enough to provide before war broke out a sufficient war reserve, either of airframes or of engines.

There was therefore an obvious case for orders in the United States which would both add to the reserve available at the outbreak of war and guarantee a continuous flow of aircraft thereafter. The Hudson and Harvard orders hardly went any way towards meeting this need. Such purchases of existing types strengthened the American aircraft firms but did not create the fresh potential that was needed. On the other hand the Air Ministry had to consider not only the uncertainties of American policy and the poor quality at that date of most American military aircraft, but also the decisive factor of time. Even if those planning aircraft supply for the years ahead could assume the ultimate lifting of the arms embargo, they could not guess how many months of administrative manœuvring and Congressional debate would be required to get it lifted. To this unknown they had to add the time that must elapse between placing an order and delivery. In the case of a small order for an existing type of aircraft the time could be calculated with some precision; but for newer designs, especially of complex new types, and for very large orders even of existing types, British production experience warned against any optimistic expectation as to delivery. The production experience of the United States themselves was to confirm that warning. Thus, in the case of the American B.29 (the Superfortress), the designs were drawn in 1939, the initial order let in 1940, and the first squadron was available in 1944—five years later. In May 1940 the President set the target of 50,000 aircraft a year: output in the year 1942 still fell short of that figure. Thus the Air Ministry was right in believing that the United States could not make a major contribution to British air power in the early part of the war, when it was assumed that help would be needed most; and it was right in depending in the main on United Kingdom production for the air fleets with which the war would be waged in the first two or three years.

The idea of creating a munitions potential in the United States in advance of war thus came to very little. All the same, it was clear that once war began supplies of materials, components and machinery, if not of armaments proper, would have to be procured on a considerable scale. As early as October 1937 the Admiralty began to feel alarmed at the possible effect of American neutrality on its essential supplies, and suggested that the implications of the Act ought to be closely examined. There was not much comfort for their Lordships in the memorandum[1] prepared by the Foreign Office earlier in the year, which surveyed the problem in general terms and concluded that Britain, possessing command of the seas and stronger finances than Germany, should be relatively immune from the consequences of the Act, provided that she entered the war with large initial stocks of war material and munitions industries capable of supplying all her needs. The crucial question was whether Britain would in fact have these assets at the outset of war, and this was not

[1] See Chapter III, p. 47.

considered in relation to possible American purchases until the month of Munich. It was then decided to ascertain, amongst other things, 'what the British Empire and her allies are likely to want from the U.S.A. in the way of supplies and services'. With Munich the urgency of the matter was assumed to have passed. Only the Admiralty pursued the enquiry in any detail and its studies were limited to raw materials, components and ancillary items; munitions of war were excluded from consideration because of the Neutrality Act. The Admiralty was in normal times wholly or mainly dependent on the United States for some important materials, notably molybdenum, rosin, turpentine, manila hemp and certain special timbers. In an emergency it might also need to purchase supplementary supplies of oil, machine tools, steel forgings and castings and perhaps fabricated parts of small warships for assembly in Canada. The question was debated at an interdepartmental meeting in December 1938; here it emerged that the Air Ministry, and probably the War Office also, would need large quantities of materials and components from the United States. The field of possible useful supply from America, it was concluded, was very large, and every effort should be made to keep the door wide open. Here for the time being the matter rested. Uncertainty about the future of American neutrality served as a reason, throughout the early part of 1939, for not attempting any more definite estimate of requirements.

The next step came in June 1939, in connection with the Riverdale Mission. The initiative which led to the sending of this Mission came from the Embassy in Washington rather than from those responsible for supply in Britain.[1] It was clearly necessary, however, that Lord Riverdale should be given some idea, however speculative, of the nature and volume of the purchases which the Government had in view. At an interdepartmental meeting on 9th June 1939, the Air Ministry submitted the first real estimate of requirements from the United States in the first year of war. This disclosed a notable change of outlook.

Since British rearmament began there had been eyes in the Ministry that looked beyond the double barriers of American neutrality and the present backwardness of the American aviation industry to its immensely rich potential. Thus, a minute on American co-operation in the event of war, written by a member of the Air Staff after Munich, made the point that 'to deny the value of American support merely on the grounds that they cannot at present supply us with aircraft in sufficient quantities or of adequate quality is obviously to take a ludicrously short view'. Some six months later a British survey concluded that the main 'bottleneck' in the American

---

[1] For a full account of the Riverdale Mission see Chapter III, pp. 65–68.

aviation industry was sheer lack of plant capacity for the production of military types; and that 'substantial advances by way of capital expenditure' could overcome this obstacle. The Air Ministry now stated its desire, in the event of war, to buy all that American industry could produce, and to embark on a 'comprehensive development of United States capacity' that might cost £100 to £150 million in the first year of war.

By now, however, a new and yet more formidable obstacle had arisen—the shortage of dollars. The dimensions of this problem have been described above. Its consequence was that, in order to conserve exchange for the purchase of food and raw materials over a long period of war, the Government placed the most rigorous limitations on the purchase of American munitions. The Air Ministry therefore put forward as its first priority a much more modest programme of expenditure: £2 million for machine tools and £3 million for materials, chiefly aluminium and magnesium. Its second priority was for airframes and engines to the value of £15–£17 million. The larger programme remained in the background as a sign of what the Ministry would like to do if given a free hand.

A word may be said here in passing about the aircraft materials problem. Very soon after the outbreak of war, light alloys were to take their place as one of the most important factors in the war combination of Britain, the United States and Canada. The pre-war expansion of the R.A.F. coincided approximately with a fundamental change in the type of aircraft. The change was from wooden types, mostly biplanes, to the metal, stressed-skin monoplane, built of light alloys. It involved not only an entirely new technique of manufacture but also a greatly increased demand for aluminium and magnesium—both virgin and fabricated. Despite considerable expansion of British aluminium production and fabricating capacity, both were still quite inadequate to cope with the demands of the aircraft industry. If the R.A.F. had not secured a single plane from North America the United Kingdom would still have been brought into a close combination with that continent to ensure supplies of aluminium. This story must be left, however, for a later chapter.[1]

The minimum expenditure seen in July 1939 for the army in the United States during the first year of war was £8·1 million (£5 million for machine tools, £1·1 million for predictors and other instruments, £1 million for anti-aircraft gun barrels and liners, £1 million for chemicals and other materials). Second-priority requirements would bring the total to £10–£15 million; and if there were no financial restrictions the Ministry would like to spend as much as £50 million. A shorter view was taken of army requirements, how-

---

[1] See Chapter IX, Section iv.

ever, than of aircraft; and the last estimate covered only the supplies which could actually be made available during the first year of war. Large-scale capital expansions bearing fruit after that period were not yet considered.[1] As foreseen also in July the Admiralty's essential requirements, mainly for oil, amounted to £6·6 million, but there was also suggested, dollars permitting, a programme of warship building that might cost about £11 million. Raw material purchases, then the responsibility of the Board of Trade, were reckoned at £25·7 million—more than the minimum requirements of all the Service Departments put together.

FINANCIAL PRUDENCE—ACCENT ON MACHINE TOOLS

By the outbreak of war, then, the main outlines of British overseas purchasing policy were fairly clearly defined. Its keynote was self-sufficiency in munitions production: given adequate supplies of essential raw materials, British industry could and must provide the great majority of the weapons and equipment of Britain's armed forces; the United States were to be treated as a limited marginal source of war supplies. This thesis was already being called in question by the Services and supply departments, as the above-quoted 'ideal' purchasing programme showed. But it rested on the unchallenged facts of dollar shortage and the need, even with maximum diversion of demand to other sources, for heavy purchases of Americal raw materials. On the ruling hypothesis of a thirty-two-division army, the Ministry of Supply estimated in September 1939 that £95 million would have to be spent on imported raw materials in the first year of war, and some £23½ million of this (or $94 million) in the United States. But if, as seemed likely, the Ministry were called on to provide equipment for an army of fifty-five divisions, raw materials would have to be imported to the annual value of £164 million, and the United States' share would leap to £82 million, or $328 million. It seemed clear that the foreign exchange resources of the United Kingdom could not support expenditure of this magnitude, as well as heavy spending on finished munitions. Raw material imports could not be cut beyond a certain point without paralysing the British industrial effort. Therefore other purchases from the United States must be kept to the barest minimum, even if this meant severe cuts or delays in plans for the expansion of the Forces. On 11th September the War Cabinet approved a memorandum in which the Chancellor of the Exchequer urged the 'restriction of payments by the Defence Services, especially in North America, to the absolute minimum of essential and speedily available services'.

To this policy of restraint one necessary exception was already

[1] On the explosives programme see *Studies of Overseas Supply*, Chapter I.

evident. Given raw materials, British industry could no doubt produce munitions on the scale that then seemed adequate. But it could
not do the job *in time* unless it were also given, in a literal sense, the
tools. Machine tools are the backbone of mass-production industry
and therefore of modern warfare. In the early stages of British war
production, as later for the United States, they were the main controlling factor. 'The machine-tool problem', Purvis wrote to Monnet
in May 1940, 'lies at the base of successful production whether in
Great Britain or in the United States.' In the preparations for war,
and in mobilisation plans, the supply of machine tools was recognised
as of paramount importance. This was a guiding principle of British
supply planning in the months preceding the war and in its first year.

An unprecedented number of machine tools were required to
equip British industry quickly for full war production. They were
required not only for the expansion of existing aircraft or munitions
factories, but also to equip new plants that were being built or
coming into production in various parts of the United Kingdom.
The extent of the sudden new demand became apparent when
requirements were greatly increased in the spring of 1939. Thus
when the Air Ministry, early in 1939, discussed the conversion of
automobile factories to aircraft and aero-engine production, it was
found that few of the existing machines could be used; in fact, some
sixty per cent. of new special plant would have to be provided before
a factory producing car engines could be used for the aircraft programme. For example, in order to make fifty sets of a 'shadow' component assigned to it, the Rover firm would require over 400 new
machine tools. The value in war potential of such a firm lay in its
skilled personnel rather than in its equipment. Clearly, if the automobile and other civilian industries earmarked for munitions work
were to begin effective production within, say, three months of the
outbreak of war, a very substantial outlay in machine tools would
be called for.

British machine-tool firms were playing their part by providing
the greater part of the equipment of British munitions factories; and
no doubt if given ample time they would have done most of the job
unaided. But this would have meant a fatal delay in gearing up
British industry to full war production. Even in the rearmament
period a large volume of machine-tool orders had been placed
abroad, in the United States, Sweden, Switzerland, Belgium, France,
and also in Germany. With the outbreak of war the demand was of
course much larger and more urgent than before; and at the same
time, with much of the European supply cut off or placed in
jeopardy, the United States market became relatively more important. Machine tools were not subject to the arms embargo under the
earlier or later Neutrality Act. At no time was there any legal

I

barrier, save the general provision of 'cash and carry', to their free export from the United States. The machine-tool industry of America thus lay open to the power which had command of the seas and the means of purchase. The sums involved were considerable, but far less than the cost of importing the finished munitions.

It will already have been observed that machine tools occupied a high place among the first-priority requirements worked out by the supply departments in the summer of 1939. Their importance became still more marked when, between September and November, the departments submitted to the Exchange Requirements Committee (set up by the Cabinet on 28th August) their forecasts of American purchases in the first twelve months of war. The Ministry of Supply, at the end of October, put its first-year expenditure in the United States at $20 million for machine tools and $51 million for army supplies; raw material purchases were now estimated at $147 million. The demands of the Air Ministry, as put forward on 8th November, were very much heavier. The Ministry was now committed to an ultimate home output of 2,300 aircraft a month, which could not be achieved without a vast increase in machine-tool imports. Its total U.S. dollar requirements were now $243 million —$40 million for aircraft and other purchases in the first year, and $203 million, spread over eighteen months, for capital equipment, mainly machine tools. The Admiralty had only a few miscellaneous requirements amounting to less than $11 million, including some $2½ million for machine tools. In January 1940 the scale and distribution of the purchases which the Government was planning to make from the United States in the first twelve months of war were set forth as follows:

Class of purchase		$ million		Percentage of total
Raw materials	. . .	196		27·3
Foodstuffs	. . .	52		7·2
Tobacco	. . . .	28		3·9
Petroleum	. . .	52		7·2
General manufactures	. .	92		12·8
Machine tools .	. .	124		17·2
Merchant ships	. . .	24		3·3
Munitions: Aircraft and engines .	78		10·8	
Army equipment	52		7·2	
Navy equipment	12		1·7	
Other . . .	10		1·4	
		— 152		— 21·1
		720		100·0

The strength and persistence of the policy of treating the United States as a marginal source in the matter of war supplies was shown in a statement by the Minister of Supply (Dr. Leslie Burgin) on 19th March 1940. The statement dealt with the expansion of British industrial production and decreasing British dependence on foreign supplies. As United Kingdom, Empire and Allied production increased, the Ministry of Supply, 'the largest trading concern in the world', would spend less and less abroad. But purchases in the next six months would be specially important because they would give a breathing space for production in the United Kingdom to come up to capacity. Already the number of ordnance factories in operation had been increased from nine at the outbreak of war to sixteen; in 1941 there would be fifty-three.[1] The Minister emphasised the need of machine tools to equip the factories and referred to the increased activity in the machine-tool industry at home.

The New York Times London correspondent in reporting the statement commented that once the British had obtained all the machine tools they needed, the tendency to cut down purchases in the United States would become even more evident. He added,

> Now that the first six months are gone and the worst fears of the Allies have not been realised it begins to look as if there was no need to keep up the burning pace of the first six months. They can, it is now believed, cut down foreign orders and so conserve precious supplies of foreign exchange without running into the danger of being overwhelmed by Germany. In fact, so far from maintaining their initial level of war purchases, the British plan not only to meet their own supply needs to an increasing extent but to push the drive for increased exports into markets where they are bound to run up against United States interests.[2]

Neither the Minister's hopes nor the correspondent's fears were borne out by events. The British Government, though so far it had spent more on machine tools than on aircraft and other munitions together, was still very far from having obtained all the machine tools it needed. Heavy purchases continued all through 1940, and were not to slacken until towards the end of 1942. Moreover, in March 1940 there were already signs that, quite apart from machine tools, British procurement of war supplies was about to increase rather than diminish.

THE BEGINNING OF EXTRAVAGANCE—THE ANGLO-FRENCH AIRCRAFT PROGRAMME

The heavy expenditure on capital equipment that was foreseen at the beginning of the war naturally underlined the need for economy in other dollar purchases, especially of finished munitions. Nevertheless, even before the beginning of active warfare in May 1940, the needs of the Services were setting up a steadily growing pressure

---

[1] In actual fact the total number of Royal Ordnance Factories never exceeded forty-five.

[2] *The New York Times*, 20th March 1940.

against the barrier of financial restraint. The restraint was never absolute, as the figures given above have sufficiently shown. The Ministry of Supply was from the outset allowed dollars for the purchase of special types of army weapons or equipment (the Buquor adaptor, a patent device for the mechanisation of artillery, the Sperry predictor, and, later, the Thompson sub-machine gun) that were not available from sources outside the United States; also for purchases designed to strengthen definite weak links in United Kingdom production, such as spare barrels for anti-aircraft guns and key components for British-built tanks. The large new explosives programme adopted in January has been mentioned above. From March 1940 onwards there was a steady flow of orders and enquiries for ammunition to supplement British production.

Even in the aggregate, however, these purchases of army supplies did not constitute a real breach in the policy of restraint in dollar expenditure on munitions. On the other hand, certain proposals put forward by the Admiralty at the outbreak of war would, if accepted, have driven a gaping hole through the Treasury's defences. Faced with a sudden demand for great numbers of anti-submarine vessels the Admiralty had worked out a considerable shipbuilding programme for the United States and Canada, comprising sixteen destroyers, seventy corvettes and 136 smaller warships. For the United States alone this would have cost $132 million, mostly to be spent in the first year of war. Though powerful arguments were brought forward in support of this scheme, the decisive argument—heavy current shipping losses—was lacking; and it was whittled down to ten corvettes to be built in Canada. Henceforth the Admiralty was to be the most conservative of all the supply departments in its attitude to American supply. Proposals for building warships (apart from certain small craft) in the United States were not to be revived until the summer of 1941.

The heaviest and most successful pressure came from the Air Ministry. In its estimate of dollar requirements in the first year of war the Ministry allowed only $40 million for all purchases other than capital equipment. The $13 million included in this figure for complete aircraft was merely for final payments on the pre-war Lockheed and Harvard orders, and the only important new purchases envisaged were 1,200 Wright Cyclone engines, to cost $21 million. The Ministry explained that its plan of expenditure was framed in accordance with its policy of giving first priority to the purchase of plant and machine tools needed for the expansion of home output. But it went on to say that it had

> always contemplated that if a greater allocation of dollars were practicable it should order complete aircraft in the U.S.A. Capacity for production already exists in that country, and by the use of that

capacity the expansion of the Air Force can be made considerably more rapid than would be the case if reliance is placed solely on building up new capacity in this country.

A commitment of the order of $100 million was suggested, of which about $30 million would mature in the calendar year 1940. Actually, between the outbreak of war and the end of February 1940 the United Kingdom had ordered 1,320 aircraft[1] and 1,200 engines, at a total cost of $120 million.

Up to December 1939, however, French Government orders for aircraft and engines had been far greater than those of the United Kingdom, and had done far more to put the aviation industry on its feet and to expand its capacity. These purchases were the result of various French aircraft-purchasing Missions, including the Mission led by Monnet in the second half of 1938.

After the outbreak of war the policy of the French Government was to concentrate Allied purchases in the United States on aircraft, as the only means of securing air supremacy. This was pressed by Monnet, when he visited London at the end of September 1939. The vigour of French purchasing, before the arms embargo was lifted on 4th November, caused even some concern in British circles lest no capacity should be left to meet possible British orders. By the end of the year French orders placed since 1938 totalled 2,000 planes, mostly Curtiss Wright P.36 and P.40 types and twin-engine Douglas bombers. French orders for Wright and Pratt and Whitney engines were over 6,000.[2] One consequence of these orders was a doubling of the capacity of Pratt and Whitney in the summer of 1939.

But all this was but a prelude to far bigger orders. On 29th December, the French representative, M. Pleven, and Purvis talked to President Roosevelt of the plans of the two Governments to purchase 10,000 aircraft and 20,000 engines.

By this time the British and French aircraft production programmes had absorbed the *existing* capacity of both countries. In June 1939 the total number of aircraft on order in the United Kingdom was raised from the figure of 12,000 (set under Scheme 'L' in March 1938) to 17,500. (The additional 5,500 aircraft were for delivery after 1st April 1940.) In October a new Scheme 'M' added 12,000 aircraft for delivery from 1941. This was for the newer types of both fighters and bombers. The ultimate aim was to bring British production up to a level of 2,550 planes a month in the thirty-fourth month of war.[3] Similarly, by December 1939 nearly all the existing capacity of American aircraft factories and all that of the American

---

[1] Including 600 trainers for use in Canada and New Zealand.
[2] Stettinius, op. cit., p. 20.
[3] M. M. Postan, *British War Production*, op. cit., p. 69.

aircraft-engine factories was absorbed by French, British and American orders. It followed, therefore, as the French Prime Minister wrote to the British Prime Minister on 11th December, that, 'if we desire to obtain additional supplies from the United States, the potential output of the American aircraft industries must be considerably increased'. With this in view, a secret French Air Mission was leaving at once for the United States, with instructions to report, if possible by 15th January, on the feasibility of securing 'a very considerable supply of air material from the United States, deliveries to begin in 1940 and to continue until the spring of 1941'.

When the matter was considered at the fourth meeting of the Supreme War Council, late in December 1939, Mr. Chamberlain expressed the fear that the French plan might impede British manufacturers, by slowing down their supply of American machine tools. The British view still was that for a long time more aircraft could be produced in the United Kingdom than it could buy in the United States; but this was only possible if British factories could count on steady supplies of American machine tools. In any case, existing Allied orders would absorb American capacity, it was felt, as far ahead as 1941. The Prime Minister also felt that the financial commitments of Great Britain had already reached the limit of the available foreign exchange. He agreed, however, to add a British representative to the Mission and this was done at the end of December.

The brief prepared by the Treasury and the Air Ministry for this meeting of the Supreme War Council threw further light on the problem. The aim, it noted, was to secure an early and decisive margin of superiority in the air. To this end, a vast expansion of capacity for the manufacture of aircraft, both in the United Kingdom and in the Dominions, was in progress when the war began; and since then very big additions to this production capacity were being pressed forward with all possible speed. The plan could only succeed if there was no delay in the provision of machine tools. The British machine-tool industry had reached saturation point, and orders for $150 million worth of machine tools were being placed in the United States; in addition, large British orders had been placed since the outbreak of war for aircraft and engines to the extent of $120 million. This added to the pressure on the American machine-tool industry which was thought to be flooded out with orders. British purchases of machine tools and aircraft had already stretched British dollar resources to the limit. An expansion of the American aircraft industry, financed by the United Kingdom, involved continuing orders for the resulting planes and engines which Britain could hardly afford. Moreover, even a large order for American aircraft, say 2,500 machines, would only be equal to a month's production at the rate the United Kingdom hoped to achieve. If such an order meant any corresponding reduction in the machine tools Britain was getting from America, then British aircraft production might be reduced by many times the number of planes thus bought. An Air Ministry official commented: 'The French proposal is really incompatible with our present programme'.

These points were repeated in the instructions given to the British representative on the Allied Air Mission. He was told to be most careful not to give the impression that His Majesty's Government might be prepared to commit itself to expenditure on the creation of new productive capacity to be followed up by orders.

The Mission reported[1] on 25th January 1940 that, thanks in great measure to the co-operation of the General Motors Corporation in the difficult matters of engines and machine tools, the American aircraft industry was ready to undertake the delivery to the Allied Governments during the year 1st October 1940 to 30th September 1941, of a total of 8,400 airframes (2,800 fighters and 5,600 bombers), 13,650 engines and 14,000 propellers. All this was over and above existing orders as well as the requirements of the American Government. The greater part of the delivery to the Allies would take place before June 1941. The cost would be roughly $1,500 million. The Mission had insisted in its discussion that if important capital expenditure had to be added to the normal price of the machines the Allied Governments would have to give up the plan, but the estimate given included $509 million under this head. Under normal conditions the element of capital cost in the production of aircraft was low, between two and seven per cent. of the total price. The higher costs quoted to the Allies were due to the necessity of producing machines in an extremely short period. The firms were willing to work for the Allies at a margin of profit which would not exceed that allowed by the American Army to its suppliers, namely twelve per cent.

The Mission's report paid a tribute to the cordial attitude of the Administration, particularly on the part of the President and the Secretary of the Treasury, despite the extreme prudence engendered by an election year. All the meetings with the industry took place in the Treasury, and the American Army and Navy were represented at most of them. The Mission reported that the Administration, with the full agreement of the Service chiefs, was ready to bring any necessary pressure to bear on the industry to secure co-ordination. The American Government was well aware of the enormous benefit to it of the large Allied aircraft programme. It counted on a very rapid decision by the Allies on the principle of the scheme. Options

---

[1] The report was made by the French representatives to their Government and was concurred in by the British representatives.

on the necessary machine tools could then be taken. The actual placing of contracts could follow later.

The scene now shifted back to London, where the scheme was examined by the Air Ministry in the last days of January. The Ministry regarded the main lines of the scheme as sound; but it was convinced that the American aircraft industry could not realise the goal it had set itself. Instead of 7,000 complete planes (with 1,400 more as spares) in the period set—the twelve months ending 30th September 1941—the Ministry's calculation, based on its own experience, seemed to show that in these twelve months, taking into account existing Allied orders, the industry was not capable of producing more than about 4,800 aircraft of the types proposed. Nevertheless, the Ministry concluded that the full scheme had to be accepted, if only to make sure of the actual anticipated output of 4,800 aircraft. Whilst the full 7,000 should be ordered, a break clause could be used to limit the effective commitment to the 4,800 expected to be produced; the cost of these was set at about $1,100 million, of which on a 50/50 basis the United Kingdom would pay $550 million.

Acceptance of the scheme was recommended by the Air Ministry to the War Cabinet on the following grounds: that the air strength of the Allies would be increased in the second year of the war and decisive air superiority over Germany attained much more rapidly; that valuable reinsurance would be obtained against the risk of air raids on aircraft factories; that the enemy and neutral countries would be shown in no uncertain fashion that the industry of the United States as well as their Government was behind the Allies. The dollar cost was noted, but was not emphasised. As for the effect of the scheme on the supply of machine tools for the British aircraft industry, the Ministry concluded that the British programme might be affected somewhat in the third year of war, but not in the first or second year.

The decision of the British and French Governments was given on 16th February 1940. The British Ambassador was informed that after 'anxious consideration' the 'Allied Governments have agreed to combine to establish an increased potentiality in the United States for the manufacture of airframes and engines'. They also agreed to the placing of substantial orders. But they left open the question of numbers and types of aircraft to be ordered, as well as of armaments, and other technical details, until further enquiries could be made on the spot by a second Allied Air Mission which was leaving at once. This Mission was composed of Colonel Jacquin, M. Pleven, and Sir Henry Self of the British Air Ministry.

The Ambassador was instructed to convey this information first to Mr. Morgenthau, and then, if he agreed, to the aircraft and engine firms. It was suggested that the firms should go ahead on any preparations which they were making, without waiting for the decision on the size of the orders. The Allied Governments wanted to be reassured that in view of the extremely heavy dollar drain they would be getting their supplies at the lowest possible cost, that their investment for plant expansion would not be subject to American income tax, that supplies of machine tools would not be diverted from existing British and French orders, and that the supply of aluminium would be adequate. Assurances were obtained by Purvis on these points in the weeks following. Finally, the Ambassador was asked to convey to Mr. Morgenthau the 'expression of keen appreciation of the two Governments' for his assistance.

The discussions on the final details began with the arrival of the representative of the British Air Ministry on 4th March. Less than three weeks were needed to reduce the original scheme to the more realistic scale envisaged in London. Even then, it meant at least doubling the current output of the American aircraft industry. The new total, as recommended on 21st and 22nd March, was set at 4,600 aircraft, complete with engines, to be produced between 1st October 1940 and 30th September 1941. The total was composed of 2,440 fighters and 2,160 bombers of ten different types, with spares. The total number of engines involved in the scheme was 8,000, of five different types. Over and above this the French Air Ministry, at the same time, authorised Purvis to purchase a further 4,050 engines over which it already had option. The revised scheme was approved by the Supreme War Council on 29th March 1940. It was agreed that France should receive 2,160 and the United Kingdom 2,440 aircraft.[1] The estimated expenditure on the whole programme was put at $614 million, to be shared on a basis to be agreed between the two Governments.

Purvis was authorised to enter into the initial commitments, including the capital outlay necessary to implement the scheme. To administer the programme a special organisation, the British Air Commission, was set up; and the Air Ministry signalised the importance which it now attached to American production by allowing its representative, Sir Henry Self, to remain permanently in the United States as head of the new Commission. It functioned, at first, within the British Purchasing Commission, but in November became a separate Mission. On 8th April a blanket requisition was given to the British Purchasing Commission for the sum of $310 million. All the contracts were placed by the British Air Commission from April to early June. It was hoped in London that commitments could be entered into by stages; this would permit improved types to be ordered as they became available and would spread the financial

---

[1] Later modifications reduced the British total to 2,003 aircraft.

obligations over a longer period. The Air Ministry, in a statement submitted to the Exchange Requirements Committee early in May, foresaw a British expenditure on the joint programme—taking the British share as 40 : 60 French—of $70 million in the first year of the war and of $210 million in the second year.

Early in May 1940 a request came through from the President and Morgenthau for information on Allied commitments in the form of capital assistance in connection with the joint aircraft programme. From this it emerged that practically no capital assistance was being given for airframe production, since all orders were being carried out from existing capacity. On the other hand, capital requirements for new engine capacity were nearly $29 million. The details were given in a note to Morgenthau on 10th May, which showed that nearly a third of the total was earmarked for the training of personnel in the three great engine firms. But the furnishing of capital by the Allies carried an important advantage—the securing of options over output for the period of the war; a minute of 16th May noted that the options obtained on engines and equipment 'will give us complete control of the situation'.[1]

The Allied programme depended on the release by the United States of certain new American types of aircraft and of improved engines. Instructions had been given by the President himself on 29th December 1939, in the presence of Purvis and Pleven, that the Allies should be given access to prototypes of newly developed aircraft. Purvis now put a specific request to Morgenthau in a memorandum on 7th March 1940 for the release of new types. Most of the engines and aircraft covered by the programme would not be delivered until 1941, he pointed out. They had to measure up to the higher speeds then likely; the present indications were that in 1941 the war would be fought at 'a speed for fighters of not less than 400 miles per hour'. The memorandum asked, therefore, for releases of certain planes and engines known to exist and for the 'results of service and manufacturers' trials of airplanes, with details of performance and handling qualities'. Purvis was assured by the Secretary of the Treasury that release would be given. A minor reason for delay was the difficulties raised by London over the supply of two Rolls-Royce engines, which the Administration was anxious to obtain for examination by American experts. The matter was pressed hard, through March, by the Administration, which made it a condition of the release of new American types. An attempt by London to secure a *quid pro quo*, in the shape of an American engine, leaked immediately into the American newspapers and created 'a lament-

---

[1] It was the capital assistance given to American engine firms in 1939 that was the source of the French option over the 4,050 engines referred to above.

able impression'. By telegram and telephone Purvis succeeded in getting release, which, he told Monnet, 'served to strengthen my position with Morgenthau, and also Morgenthau's position with the Army'.[1]

A more important difficulty arose from the press criticism of the Allied Air Programme that began on 13th March, and was taken up the same day in both Houses of Congress. Discussion centred on two points: release of the latest American designs to the Allies, and interference with American rearmament.[2] The Administration's policy was justified by the Majority Leader in the Senate (Senator Barkley) on 13th March. He gave the following figures to show the increased labour force and floor space in American aircraft factories caused by Allied orders. The labour force had been nearly trebled by Allied orders and would now be more than quadrupled. Orders prior to March 1940 had almost doubled the floor space. The new Allied programme would increase it from 3,103,000 to 4,150,000 square feet. Before Allied purchases began American aircraft-engine factories could produce only 7,290 engines a year; their capacity was now 19,280 and the new programme brought it to 29,280 engines a year. Interventions by the President and the Secretary of the Treasury, and support by Army leaders in Congressional hearings at the end of March, made two points clear: the conviction that American rearmament would benefit, and the determination of the Administration to facilitate Allied purchases and to release designs, except certain secret devices.[3] On 27th March, in the House Military Affairs Committee, General Marshall declared that adoption of the Administration's policy was of 'vital importance for national defence'.[4] Three days later, the War Department cleared the way for the placing of Allied orders by a circular letter to aircraft firms. It informed them that the Department was ready to discuss, forthwith, the deferring of deliveries on its own contracts, to permit the placing of the new Allied orders. The only condition was that the firms must assure to the American Army the supply at a later stage of still better aircraft.

An account of the taking over of the French air contracts in mid-June—1,794 aircraft from the Joint Allied scheme, and another 1,745 from undelivered portions of previous French orders—is given in the following chapter. This section may be concluded by referring to the estimates made by American leaders of the significance of the Allied aircraft orders.

---

[1] For the sequel see below, pp. 191, 209, etc.
[2] e.g., *The New York Times*, 13th March 1940.
[3] President's Press Conference, 19th March 1940.
[4] *The New York Times*, 23rd, 24th, 26th, 28th, 29th March and 2nd April. *New York Herald Tribune* 24th, 25th, 26th March 1940.

In the spring of 1940, as Mr. Stettinius noted some years later in his book on lend-lease, 'three times as many orders were placed for planes by the French and the British in the first half of 1940 as in all of 1939—over 8,000 planes and 13,000 engines. This brought the total of orders placed in the United States by the French and the British for military planes in the eighteen months between 1st January 1939 and 30th June 1940 to 10,800'. This, he commented, was well over twice the number which the American armed services had been able to order out of their appropriations in the same period. He noted the heavy capital expenditure by the Allies on aircraft engines, which he estimated at $84 million to June 1940; this did not buy any engines, he pointed out, but merely created capacity to make them. These vast orders, he concluded, proved of vital importance to the American defence programme when the President, in June 1940, set for the United States the goal of 50,000 planes.

American accounts have emphasised the importance of the margin of time gained by the United States from these Allied orders. The orders of 1938 and early 1939, in Mr. Morgenthau's view, put the American aviation industry six months ahead; and the massive orders of early 1940, he thought, put it a further twelve months ahead. The Secretary of State for War, Mr. Stimson, made the same point during the debate on the Lend-Lease Bill: 'Without the head-start given industry by these foreign orders we would at the present time be in a very grave situation as to the plants and facilities which we now need for the pending emergency'.[1]

ON THE EVE OF DUNKIRK

The April 1940 number of the American magazine *Fortune* recorded that

'the Allied purchasing to date, in the words of an army officer charged with keeping an eye on it, "doesn't amount to a hoot in hell". The little that has been bought has been bought mostly by the French. . . . The British, beyond an estimated $125,000,000 for aircraft and machine tools, have only dabbled on the U.S. market. . . . Although both the British and French agents are talking vaguely of huge potential requirements in shells, rifle ammunition, machine guns, and even field guns, there is little prospect of the orders materializing at least in the near future. . . .' In short, it concluded, except for aircraft, 'Mr. Purvis . . . will be window-shopping until economic war gives way to shooting'.

At the time it was written this account was not very wide of the mark. The total value of British munitions orders placed in the United States up to the end of April 1940 (including pre-war con-

---

[1] Letter to Senator George, February 1941, quoted by Stettinius, op. cit., p. 24. See also Mr. Morgenthau's articles in *Collier's* Magazine beginning 18th October 1947.

tracts) was $236,049,000. Of this, Air Ministry contracts accounted for nearly eighty-seven per cent.—$204,835,000—and this figure included only a small fraction of the new Allied programme, under which orders to the value of some $250 million were still to come. Ministry of Supply orders for munitions amounted to $28,691,000, with requisitions outstanding for a further sum of just under $4 million. It is an indication of the extreme narrowness of the margin which American supply was being called on to fill in the matter of Army equipment that one-third of the Ministry's total commitments in the United States consisted of a single order for heavy shells, which did not amount to a significant fraction of the total gun ammunition programme. Contracts let on behalf of the Admiralty, chiefly for motor-boat engines and degaussing cable, added up to a mere $2½ million.

The relatively heavy purchasing of aircraft after December 1939 detracted somewhat from the pre-eminence of machine tools, but still left them a very high place in the scheme of British procurement from the United States. The total value of orders is difficult to ascertain, since purchasing was carried on in this period through private commercial channels; but in mid-March a British Purchasing Commission estimate put British orders, placed and pending, at $108 million ($83 million for the Air Ministry and $25 million for the Ministry of Supply); French orders, placed and pending, then amounted to $105 million, with requisitions for a further $50 million expected later.

Meanwhile, despite every effort to find other sources of supply, dependence on American raw materials had been steadily increasing. Whereas in October 1939 expenditure under this head in the United States during the first year of war was put at $147 million, in October 1940 the estimate was $222 million. Actual imports in the first eight months of war cost $199 million.[1]

Thus, up to the moment when the shooting war began in earnest, the British Government had on the whole succeeded in avoiding heavy purchases in the United States, except in respect of the capital equipment of the British munitions industry and its essential raw materials. Even raw material import policy was still governed to a large extent by the desire to conserve dollars. With the major exception of aircraft and the relatively minor exception of explosives, orders for munitions of war had been on a trifling scale. And even for aircraft the United States remained a purely marginal source of supply: the R.A.F. did not expect more than 400 American aircraft a month at the peak, as against 2,550 from the United Kingdom and other British Commonwealth countries.

---

[1] This figure, derived from the Board of Trade's Trade and Navigation Accounts, includes a certain amount of semi-manufactured goods.

Within a few weeks all this was to be changed by the onrush of the German armies. The British Army was to lose at one blow the greater part of its modern equipment. Britain was to be cut off from all her Scandinavian and West European supplies of raw materials and was to be left alone, without the support of the French Army, to face the threat of invasion, devastating air attacks and the continuous attrition of her mercantile marine. In this new situation she would have to depend far more than ever before upon the North American continent for the raw materials without which her war industries could not function. Because of the perilous location of those industries and because of shipping losses, she would have to import supplies so far as possible in the form of finished goods—steel rather than iron ore and scrap, and munitions rather than steel. She would need immediate supplies of all kinds of weapons and equipment to replace the losses of Dunkirk, and continuing supplies for the much larger Army now essential. She would need ships to carry these supplies across the Atlantic in face of the most formidable air and undersea attacks. Since the Air Arm was now her only remaining offensive weapon, she would also need American aircraft on a far bigger scale than before. And at the same time her need for machine tools to accelerate production in the United Kingdom would be more urgent than ever.

The story of the main events in the great supply crisis of midsummer 1940—the decision on 24th May to throw financial prudence to the winds and buy all that America could produce until dollars failed, the 'breathless days of June' in Mr. Churchill's phrase, the dispatch of the American surplus arms across the Atlantic, and the taking over and sorting out of the French contracts in the United States—are best told in a separate short chapter. Meanwhile it may be noted—as this chapter should have sufficiently shown—that the importance of the first phase of war purchases in the United States was greater than the unimpressive totals themselves might suggest. This was due not only to the fact that they filled gaps in British production and began to lay the foundations of an American munitions industry, but also because of their indirect contribution towards the forging of close political and supply links between Britain and America.

CHAPTER V

THE GREAT SUPPLY CRISIS, SUMMER 1940

(i)

The Effect in the United States

THE launching of the German offensive in the Low Countries on 10th May 1940 and the series of disasters of the next few days had an immediate effect on the attitude of Government and Congress towards the war as a whole and towards war supplies for the Allies. The full gravity of the German attack became quite clear with the breach of the French line at Sedan on the 14th. Holland surrendered on the 16th and on the same day President Roosevelt, in a special message to Congress, asked for a greatly increased budget. Further important messages to Congress on the last day of May and on 10th July marked the increasing gravity of the crisis. The President's message of 16th May gave as the target for aircraft the then colossal figure of 'at least fifty thousand planes a year'. (The United States had produced only 2,100 military aircraft in 1939, and these were mostly trainers.) He noted that the doubling of the American aircraft capacity in the past year had been 'due in greater part to the placing of foreign orders here'.[1]

By now Congress had become deeply uneasy and was no longer in any mood for delay. It was now ready, as it had not been in January, to vote the money asked for by the President to increase the Army and Navy, to replace and modernise all old equipment, to put Army and Navy contracts on a twenty-four-hour basis and to increase production facilities to enable the country 'to turn out quickly infinitely greater supplies'. In another message on 31st May the President referred to the 'almost incredible events of the past two weeks' and the possibility of war spreading to all continents. Congress responded with three Acts in succession, on the 11th, 13th and 26th June, involving defence appropriations totalling some $3,000 million. After this rush there was a pause and the President's request on 10th July for another $5,000 million was not enacted till 9th September —a delay that set back the defence programme. Meanwhile steps

---

[1] Orders placed in 1939 had, of course, reached a much higher figure—roughly 7,000, including about 3,000 on Allied account.

were taken to set up new administrative machinery to direct defence production: the Office for Emergency Management (25th May), the National Defence Advisory Commission (28th May), the Board of National Defence Purchases and the National Defence Research Committee (28th June), and the Priorities Board (18th October). The powers of the Reconstruction Finance Corporation were extended to permit it to participate in defence production. Under its new powers it set up on 28th June the Rubber Reserve Company and the Metals Reserve Company, followed late in August by the Defence Plant Corporation and the Defence Supplies Corporation.[1]

For the Administration leaders the period from mid-May onwards was one of intense activity. Not only the Secretary of the Treasury, but also the President himself kept in close touch with Purvis as well as with the Ambassador. On the eve of the blitz in the west Purvis had reported to London that Allied supply prospects were not bright especially in the vital matter of aircraft. 'We do not think', he told London on 8th May, 'there is any possibility in the present mood of public opinion to obtain anything more in the way of release of deliveries of the U.S. Army.' From 10th May onwards the insistence of both London and Paris on more and more planes from the United States became daily more urgent. Bloch-Lainé, the head of the French Mission, was being bombarded daily from the 14th onwards by direct telegrams from Paris asking for all possible planes in the shortest space of time—if possible by carrier from Halifax. He asked Purvis, in a memorandum dated 17th May, to try to get through Morgenthau 'un envoi massif d'avions'. He mentioned in the memorandum that Morgenthau had told him personally on 16th May that the Army and Navy were opposed to any release of Curtiss P.36 fighters or Northrop dive-bombing planes.

In the frequent talks Purvis had been having with Morgenthau since the break-through at Sedan, urgent supply needs predominated; but long-term plans still had their place. He was being consulted about the new American Defence Programme and had been given the assurance, mentioned above, that it would in no way be allowed to interfere with British orders.[2] Next day, 15th May, was a high point in the history of British supply. It was marked not only by the President's direct telephone calls to Purvis, already mentioned, about pushing planes across the Canadian border and the possibility of using American civilian aircraft, but also by Mr. Churchill's first message as Prime Minister to the President. His message covered

---

[1] U.S. Bureau of the Budget, *The United States at War* (Washington: War Records Section, Bureau of the Budget), pp. 21–27. *Documents on American Foreign Relations*, op. cit., Vol. III, 1940–41, Chapter XI. The next important stage in the organisation of U.S. defence machinery came in the first half of 1941.

[2] See above, Chapter IV, p. 79.

'everything short of actually engaging armed forces'. It outlined the main Allied supply requirements as follows:

> Immediate needs are, first of all, the loan of forty or fifty of your older destroyers to bridge the gap between what we have now and the large new construction we put in hand at the beginning of the war. This time next year we shall have plenty. But if in the interval Italy comes in against us with another one hundred submarines we may be strained to breaking-point. Secondly, we want several hundred of the latest types of aircraft, of which you are now getting delivery. These can be repaid by those now being constructed in the United States for us. Thirdly, anti-aircraft equipment and ammunition, of which again there will be plenty next year, if we are alive to see it. Fourthly, the fact that our ore supply is being compromised from Sweden, from North Africa, and perhaps from Northern Spain, makes it necessary to purchase steel in the United States. This also applies to other materials. We shall go on paying dollars for as long as we can, but I should like to feel reasonably sure that when we can pay no more you will give us the stuff all the same.[1]

The message ended with the promise of a supplementary and more detailed statement of material needs. This followed in a cable on the 17th from Monnet to Purvis. On the 18th the Prime Minister telegraphed again: 'if American assistance is to play any part it must be available soon'. On the same day came the President's reply to the message of the 15th. The time was not opportune, he said, for any transfer of destroyers, but he would facilitate to the uttermost the Allied Governments obtaining the latest types of United States aircraft, anti-aircraft equipment, ammunition and steel; and he promised to give most favourable consideration to any request put forward.[2] The detailed statement of requirements sent on the 17th was prefaced by an instruction from the Anglo-French Co-ordinating Committee to convey the message direct to Morgenthau and to ask him to deliver it to the President personally, which was done forthwith. 'It is clear', the message began, 'that Germany is now determined to throw in all her resources in an attempt to force a decision over the next few weeks.' In particular, she was making the utmost use of her numerical preponderance in the air, and it was therefore essential to reinforce the Allied air forces. The Allies asked for as many United States planes as possible from existing United States stocks and current deliveries, repayment to be made from deliveries off Allied contracts in the United States. Reference was made in particular to the 200 Curtiss P.40 fighters which it was understood

---

[1] Winston S. Churchill, *The Second World War:* Vol. II, *Their Finest Hour* (London: Cassell & Company Limited, 1949), p. 23. This book was also published in the United States (Boston: Houghton Mifflin Company, 1949.)

[2] Ibid., pp. 23 and 50.

were in the course of delivery to the United States Army. Aircraft carriers could be sent for any Army planes released. London also asked for accelerated deliveries of raw materials and machine tools for the Allied air programme; for destroyers and for any assistance the United States could give in the form of anti-aircraft guns, 75-mm. field guns, machine guns, sub-machine guns, rifles and Colt automatics, with ammunition for all these weapons. Anti-aircraft guns were 'most urgent'. A further cable received next day pressed for accelerated deliveries on a list of existing British orders, some of long standing.

Purvis was advised on the 18th by his purchasing agents for munitions, after a rapid survey of each of the items contained in the London list, that for the rest of 1940 there was nothing to be got from American manufacturers save small arms ammunition and possibly a limited quantity of small arms. 'The only prospect for any important quantities of weapons and ammunition for delivery in time for service in the field for 1940 is from United States Government stocks—Army and Navy.'

The same day Purvis again saw the Secretary of the Treasury. His report on the talk was read out at the War Cabinet next day. The stocks of aircraft held by the United States Army, which had any combat value, were very limited, he reported, but some Curtiss P.36 fighters and Northrop bombers were offered by the Administration, although the United States Army in fact possessed only 150 of the first type and 144 of the second. As for trying to get priorities on other British orders, Purvis said that he did not know what they were since orders for machine tools, alloy steels and many steel and copper products had not been placed through the British Purchasing Commission. The 20th May was the day on which the Prime Minister ordered planning to begin for 'the emergency evacuation across the Channel of very large forces'. It was decided that he should make an appeal to the President for the best fighters the United States then possessed. He put as the most vital need 'delivery at the earliest possible date of the largest possible number of Curtiss P.40 fighters'.[1] The Americans had already earmarked over 300 for the United Kingdom; there were another 200 on order. But Washington replied regretfully that it was too desperately short itself to give any more. The answer was to come rather from British aircraft factories which by a spurt in production enabled the British Fighter Command to emerge from the Battle of Britain with more fighters than it had when the battle began.

---

[1] Ibid., p. 50.

(ii)
Dunkirk and the American Arms Shipments

Over the exact span of the next fortnight, 20th May to 4th June, there were parallel operations on both sides of the Atlantic, though of unequal magnitude. One led to the evacuation of 338,226 men from Dunkirk—with the loss of most of their arms and equipment; the other to the replacement in part of this loss from the stocks of the American Army and Navy. The first men were taken off the Dunkirk beaches on the night of 26th May and the movement ended on 4th June. The moves in the United States for the transfer of American arms began to take definite shape on 21st May and on 4th June Purvis cabled to London the list of supplies released by the United States Army and Navy, involving an immediate initial purchase of over $36 million. By this date the arms were in fact already moving down the railroads and beginning to arrive at the seaboard. Any financial obstacle to a purchase of such magnitude had been removed on 24th May by a cable from London. Its effect was to commit Britain's reserves of gold and dollars to the purchase of war supplies from across the Atlantic.

The first move in Washington towards the American arms surplus transfer was taken on the 21st, when Purvis and Bloch-Lainé handed to Morgenthau a six-page memorandum listing in detail the Allied requirements as received in the series of cables over the previous five days. It was this document that set the lines for the release of the Army and Navy World War I stocks. It asked for two things: first, 'supplies from stocks on hand with U.S. Army, *Specially urgent*'; second, priorities on existing British orders and diversion to the Allies from current American Army and Navy contracts. On the latter, which meant mostly aircraft, it got nowhere. It suggested the possible diversion from American Army deliveries of the following aircraft: Curtiss P.40, 200; Lockheed P.38, 30; Bell P.39, 40; Douglas A.20, 180; Glen Martin B.26, 200; Douglas D.C.3, 35; and 500 Harvard trainers for Canada. Against this list of aircraft Purvis pencilled in the margin of his copy, after he had seen Morgenthau on 11th June, 'Not a hope'. There were many references to 'surplus arms' in the document—in particular to stocks of rifles, machine guns, 75-mm. field guns and to ammunition. Thus under the heading of Rifles there was a note: 'We are informed that a large stock (said to be 1,500,000 of Lee-Enfield ·30-caliber rifles) is held by the United States Government which may be considered as surplus to their requirements.' The French mission, it was noted, had already applied for the release of part of those rifles and had been refused.

Action was swift on the American side. On 22nd May the United States Chiefs of Staff had in their hands a list showing the stocks of ordnance material which could be released without endangering national defence. The releases recommended were within hailing distance of those finally made. Next day Purvis noted down on the margin of this list when it was handed to him the words: 'Breaking our necks to try to do this'; this was followed by the words: 'Destroyers. No. Quite firm.'

That evening he reported to London the results of the day's discussions with the Secretary of the Treasury, General Marshall and the President. The President could hold out little or no hope of aircraft from stock or of fresh priorities over further deliveries.[1] But the possibilities regarding equipment where there were Army stocks was 'quite promising provided the United States Department of State can find a legal way to effect the transfer'. It was this question of a legal way that held up further action to the end of the month.

Just as the Dunkirk evacuation got fully under way on 29th May a further memorandum was given by Purvis to the Secretary of the Treasury. It submitted 'specific urgent cable requests' just received from London which asked not only for 500,000 Enfield rifles (with 500 million rounds of ammunition), but also for 25,000 Thompson ·45 machine guns (with 100 million rounds); and 20,000 revolvers (with 5 million rounds). 'These three items', the document added, 'are urgently required to meet parachute attacks expected in the early future.' In addition, London asked for 'as many 75-mm. guns as can possibly be spared with all ammunition available'.

Next day Purvis was asked to send an expert to go over the stocks of arms with General Marshall to see what could be sent at once to the Allies.

Here the narrative must pause to bring together three relevant sets of data: British purchases of new arms in the United States up to Dunkirk; the loss of equipment in France; and the amounts now purchased from United States stocks. As indicated above, British purchases so far except for aircraft had been extremely small. Machine tools rather than arms had been ordered. But no matter what arms orders had been placed when the arms embargo was lifted on 4th November, little or nothing could have been received by the time of Dunkirk. Thus by June 1940 the Allies had ordered 10,800 military aircraft, or about five times the number produced in the

---

The inroads which the Allies were already making on the air strength of the United States was shown in a tabulation Purvis made at the time. Out of 734 fighters of four types which the Army and Navy had on order, 405 had been released to the Allies when delivered and they had asked for all save forty of the remainder. Out of 605 bombers of various types on order for the United States, the Allies had asked for well over half, but none had been released. All existing Army and Navy aircraft Purvis dismissed with the words 'nothing suitable for European combat conditions. . . . No planes are armoured, no self sealing tanks, and insufficient fire power'.

United States in 1939.[1] But in the six months of January to June 1940 American factories had actually shipped to Britain only 104 planes (all ordered in 1938) and to France 557.[2] Apart from aircraft, orders for munitions had been trifling except for explosives and perhaps small arms ammunition. The rest of the orders as tabulated by the British Purchasing Commission on 23rd May looked like the odds and ends they in fact were—small deficits here and there in the British production programme. Up to 24th May there were on order no guns of any sort (save for the very small order for Thompson sub-machine guns), virtually no shells, no rifles, no tanks, no trucks. There was a small spurt of ordering in the next seven days, as shown in the British Purchasing Commission's next weekly return, but it amounted to very little. The big orders placed in that week were for more millions of dollars' worth of machine tools. There was little or nothing in the list which, in the months ahead when delivery was finally made, would help greatly in replacing the arms lost in France.

The arms and materials lost in France were modern equipment. They were not just arms on order, but arms that had been delivered and incorporated in formed divisions in the field. 'We had lost', Mr. Churchill wrote, 'the whole equipment of the Army to which all the first fruits of our factories had hitherto been given:

7,000 tons of ammunition
90,000 rifles
2,300 guns
120,000 vehicles
8,000 Bren guns
400 anti-tank rifles

. . . We had very little field artillery, even for the Regular Army. Nearly all the new 25-pounders had been lost in France. There remained about five hundred 18-pounders, 4·5-inch and 6-inch howitzers. There were only 103 cruiser, 132 infantry, and 252 light tanks. Fifty of the infantry tanks were at home in a battalion of the Royal Tank Regiment, and the remainder were in training-schools. Never has a great nation been so naked before her foes.'[3]

Losses on such scale could only be recovered from one source: the new production over many months of all British munitions factories working at full blast. A London message received by the Ambassador and Purvis on 25th May analysed the prospects very clearly. For immediate help Britain had to rely mainly on British production. This was being switched over from the previous long-term basis to

---

[1] See p. 127 above; also *Historical Statistics of the United States 1789–1945* (U.S. Department of Commerce, Bureau of the Census, 1949), series K.239–245.

[2] Stettinius, op. cit., p. 25.

[3] Churchill, op. cit., pp. 125 and 128. The loss of rifles was made up in part from stores retrieved later from south of the Seine (see below). An offer from Canada of 70,000 Ross rifles was gratefully welcomed by the British Government.

cover short-term needs. Priority was being given to the factories and types of arms that could be turned out most speedily. But with this was joined the plan discussed in the next chapter: 'To create in (the) United States a vastly increased productive capacity for those types of munitions and armaments which are most essential for active war', namely aircraft and tanks.

Any American contribution to immediate needs, it was recognised, must be strictly limited in scope, since American factories could deliver little or nothing in 1940. That applied as well to rifles. Even in November 1940 Purvis was still warning London not to expect rifles since none had been manufactured in quantity in the United States for twenty years. There was left only the lucky hoard of old arms, well preserved in grease since 1918, in the depots of the American Army and Navy. In terms of the supplies needed in modern war the amounts involved in the surplus arms transaction were small; but from a strategical and political point of view they were of the greatest importance. It is difficult to make any real comparison between them and the lost equipment. This would mean comparing old with new, and 'existing' with 'on order'. Neither in time nor in calibres could there be a comparison. Britain had on order in North America large quantities of ·303 ammunition to fit British rifles. But delivery was a long time ahead. Ammunition of the right calibre was needed now for the surplus weapons released from the United States.[1]

Table 2 shows the main supplies included in the American surplus arms transaction.

American surplus arms consigned to Great Britain, June to September 1940[2]

(Figures in brackets represent the final amounts as fixed in exchange of letters on 21st June, 2nd August and 23rd September)

TABLE 2	Number
Lee-Enfield rifles	500,000 (785,000)
Rifle ammunition, ·30 calibre (million rounds)	130
Machine-gun ammunition, ·30 calibre (million rounds)	— (6)
75-mm. field guns	900
75-mm. shells	1,075,000
3-inch Stokes mortars	500 (513)
3 inch Stokes mortar shells	97,680
Machine guns (various types)	80,000 (87,000)
Browning automatic rifles	25,000
Revolvers	20,000 (21,000)
Revolver cartridges	1,000,000

[1] At the time of the transfer in June Britain had on order in Canada and the United States 575 million rounds of small arms ammunition of ·303 and other calibres. Purvis calculated the minimum quantity of ·30 ammunition needed for the rifles and machine guns as ten times the amount released. As his attempts to secure further releases failed (he hoped for an additional 250 million rounds) the British Purchasing Commission had to place large orders for new ammunition of this calibre.

[2] In round numbers. See Stettinius, op. cit., p. 27. The consignments included also a large assortment of accessories and some 12,000 tons of propellants.

There was special need of the 75-mm. guns to stop tanks. The 4th June arrangement released only 400 and most of them Purvis was asked to 'rush with the utmost speed . . . to France . . . with absolute priority'. London pressed for still more and Purvis secured the release of another 500 at a meeting with Morgenthau on 11th June.

The transfer still left the United States Army with 'enough World War stocks to equip 1,800,000 men', though it had modern equipment for only 75,000.[1] The surplus material had cost originally about $300 million according to a report by the President of Congress. Great Britain paid for it ('as is' and 'where is') a total sum of $43 million.[2]

The release of aircraft was a separate and parallel transaction since these were not World War stocks. The Navy on 6th June released fifty Curtiss Wright dive-bombers and the Army on 8th June earmarked for trade in and transfer ninety-three Northrop light bombers. These were traded back to the manufacturers (as against later-type planes then in production) and resold to the Allies. Forty-four of the Curtiss planes and some military planes for Belgium were loaded on the French aircraft carrier *Béarn*, which sailed suddenly at dawn on 16th June and was diverted at sea by Admiral Darlan to Martinique. Here the planes remained useless for three years until taken over by the Free French National Committee.[3] The first batch of the Northrops, fifty-five in number, were flown to Halifax on 21st June and loaded on a British aircraft carrier.

It was one thing to decide what stocks could be spared and quite another to decide how to effect the transfer. On the 29th June Purvis reported that the President still saw no clear way out of the legal difficulty; he assumed that new legislation was needed and did not see how to get it from Congress. But, Purvis added, 'the possibilities of finding a solution within the existing law are still being actively explored by General Marshall, Chief of Staff, who is in complete control of these stocks and who is sympathetic to the Allied cause'. Three days later a way out was found without waiting on Congress.[4]

---

[1] Stettinius, op. cit., p. 27. The B.P.C. also arranged for the release by the U.S. Army for Canada in June of 80,000 Lee-Enfield rifles with four million rounds of ammunition. Canada paid $1,849,557 for the stocks released to it. In October there was a further release from U.S. stocks to Canada.

[2] *Operations Under Lend-Lease Act*, First Report from the President of the United States under Lend-Lease Act, 77th Congress, 1st Session, U.S. Senate Document No. 66 (Washington: 11th June 1941). The initial contract was for $37,619,556, but was increased by subsequent transfers. The total included $1,664,360 for the out-of-pocket expenses of the U.S. Steel Export Co., including freight charges.

[3] The *Béarn* had also on board seventeen Curtiss and six Brewster fighters, also twenty-five Stinson 105s.

[4] The Senate passed the Defence Appropriation Bill on 11th June with a clause authorising the trading in of surplus war stocks, against new replacements, as a means of aiding the Allies. The 'Act to Expedite the Strengthening of the National Defence' was approved on 2nd July 1940. *Documents on American Foreign Relations*, op. cit., Vol. II, 1939–40, pp. 793–95.

A legal opinion was given by the Attorney-General that under an Act of 11th July 1919 arms owned by the Government on that date could be sold, without advertisement and on such terms as might be deemed best, by the Secretary of War to any corporation or individual.[1] It meant that the War Department could legally sell the equipment to a private concern for replacement by new equipment and that the private purchaser could then resell to belligerent governments subject to 'cash and carry'. The President at once called for reports from the War and Navy Departments as to the arms they could spare for Britain and France. 'It took', Mr. Stettinius records, 'less than 48 hours to decide what the Army could turn over as a reasonable risk in view of the vital importance to America's defence that Britain hold out.' General Marshall set the wheels in motion by an instruction to his Chief of Ordnance and Assistant Chief of Staff. They were told to list the disposable surplus after examining all reserve stocks in Army depots. The list was ready and was approved by General Marshall on 3rd June.[2]

On the same day the list was handed to Purvis and his military adviser to Morgenthau's office, and they were asked to indicate on the spot what the Allies could use. They had to decide on a vast range of stores of various types from their own knowledge and within the space of two hours. Late that night Purvis read the list over the teletype to Monnet in London and Monnet at once informed the British and French Prime Ministers. Purvis confirmed by telegram next day the lists agreed upon, paying tribute to 'Mr. Morgenthau's strenuous efforts'. 'Orders have tonight been given', he reported, 'for the despatch of the material by railway express from the various arsenals throughout the country.' London's acceptance, with appreciation for Purvis, 'gratitude to Mr. Morgenthau', guidance as to the allocation of the stores between Britain and France and shipping instructions, was received in Washington on 7th June. The War Department's telegraphic instructions to its depots ordered all stocks to be moved to the Army docks at Raritan, New Jersey, for shipment overseas. Much of the material was already stored in Raritan and was carefully inspected on the spot by a party of British, French and American Army officers on 6th June. Material from other arsenals was already pouring into Raritan before the legal formalities for the transfer were completed. The movement had begun at the depots on 4th June and in the next forty-eight hours 600 freight cars were moving down the lines to Raritan. From Rock Island arsenal in Illinois half a million rifles left in freight cars on 6th June and were at the dock four days later. Purvis was reminded on the day the opera-

---

[1] The opinion was given in a letter to the Secretary of War and published on 7th June. Text in *Documents on American Foreign Relations*, op. cit., Vol. II, 1939–40, pp. 790–91.

[2] Stettinius, op. cit., pp. 26–31, and Churchill, op. cit., pp. 125–26.

tion began of the saying of a famous American Army officer that 'Regulations are meant for damned fools and second lieutenants'.

The United States Steel Corporation had been selected as the most suitable private concern for the purpose of the sale of the stocks and resale to the Allies. Its chiefs were summoned to Washington on 5th June to hear the War Department's proposal, which they accepted next day. At a press conference on 7th June the President himself announced the plan in general terms. He would not say how far he was prepared to go in supplying the Allies. He denied that he had any intention of releasing 'brand new' aircraft to them, but added characteristically that military aircraft now had a way of becoming obsolete very fast.[1]

On 11th June the Secretary of War and officials of the United States Steel Export Company signed the contract transferring title to the material for $37,619,556.60; the latter then took a taxi to the office of the British Purchasing Commission where Purvis and Bloch-Lainé were waiting and resold the material for the same price to the British and French Commissions. Under 'cash and carry' no material could be loaded until paid for; the payments were duly made when the contract was signed. Five days later when France capitulated the whole contract was taken over formally by Great Britain. The $16 million which France had paid was refunded to her by Great Britain on 25th July 1940.

The contract took the form of a letter signed by Purvis and Bloch-Lainé to which was attached a schedule of the material purchased.[2] The prices for the different items were fixed by the War Department on the basis of original cost less depreciation, and were roughly equivalent to ten per cent. of prices current at the date of the sale. Considerable quantities of spare parts were afterwards thrown in free of charge. The material was taken 'as is, where is' with no guarantee of condition. The United States Steel Export Company was to be reimbursed for out-of-pocket expenses, including handling charges and freight to seaboard, but made no charge to Britain for salaries, overhead expenses, commission or profit. Contracts had then to be made by the United States Steel Corporation with American producers to replace the material, but this belongs to the American history of the war.

The tonnage involved was estimated at 70,000 tons and special shipping arrangements had to be made. The cutting off of supplies from Western Europe and Scandinavia meant far heavier calls on

---

[1] *The New York Times*, 8th June, and Stettinius, op. cit., p. 28. The Anglo-French Purchasing Board issued on 10th June a press release referring to the transfer and another followed from the United States Steel Corporation on the 12th giving further details, including the sum paid.

[2] See text in Appendix I.

British and Allied shipping. The opportunity was seized by the Ambassador to raise the question of the entry of American ships into the combat zone. But the President replied (on 17th June) that the difficulty lay with Congress. Meanwhile British ships had moved into the bay at Raritan on 11th June; they began to load as the contract was signed in Washington. The first to sail two days later was the *Eastern Prince*. She arrived on 23rd June in a British port bringing 48 75-mm. guns, 12,000 rifles, 15,279 machine guns and over 37 million rounds of ·30 ammunition. Between 16th and 22nd June six ships were despatched with half of the arms. By the end of June a dozen ships had sailed. There were fifteen further sailings in July and shipments were completed by the last week of that month.

The work involved in moving such quantities at such short notice was enormous. The staffs engaged on it, British and American, civilian and military, worked far into the night week after week. It was very soon found that the facilities at Raritan could not possibly handle the quantities arriving from all over the country, and stores which did not require repackaging or co-ordination were diverted elsewhere to be called forward to ports by the Ministry of Shipping, as ships became available. The operation involved difficulties and maladjustments. The report of an inspection party which visited Raritan on 6th June showed they were alive to what might happen when the operation began. Would spares go with the guns to which they belonged? What about handbooks and range tables for field guns, manufacturing drawings and all sorts of accessories, including spanners to fit American bolts? The 75s needed horse poles and straps were missing. The Army in Washington undertook to look to this. It was necessary to reproduce manufacturing drawings of the French and British 75s. What handbooks still existed had to be collected. For reasons of security the precious 75s, and the rifles and ammunition to match, had to be distributed over a number of sailings. The material from all over the United States had been rushed forward to port without proper sorting out. Purvis warned the Ministry of Shipping that a large space and great numbers of workers would be required to match up guns and caissons; limbers and sights, standards, bayonets and rifle slings. An adequate and technically competent staff must be ready to ensure that the supplies being rushed to England were assembled quickly in their proper units. Shipment was further complicated by the fact that large quantities had been consigned to the French under the original allocation, and diversion to Britain sometimes involved reloading. In the end none of the material covered by this transaction was retained by France. The French ship *Pasteur* interrupted loading and sailed on 17th June on urgent orders from France, but was held at Halifax.

(iii)

The Fifty Destroyers and their Sequel

One item of the American surplus war material was to assume special importance. The question of 'forty or fifty of your older destroyers', first mentioned by Mr. Churchill to the President on 15th May, became a matter of the highest importance after the losses of ships and destroyers in the Dunkirk operation. There was a sharp rise in sinkings by U-boat attacks following the occupation of western European ports from the Arctic Circle to the Bay of Biscay; and the Italian entry into the war brought a fresh submarine fleet into the fray. Political difficulties in the United States made the problem of transfer insoluble on the ordinary supply level. It could only be solved by raising the transaction to the highest level of policy and strategy. Under American law the transfer of an organised part of the American naval forces could only be made against a *quid pro quo* which represented such an obvious increase in American security that the Administration could safely transfer to a foreign power part of its naval forces. Even so, the transaction on a narrow interpretation of international law might be taken as a breach of neutrality. Although transfer of the destroyers in return for bases in British Atlantic islands was in essence a simple enough transaction, getting it through required prolonged negotiations and the settlement (in Lord Lothian's words) of 'endless difficulties about a matter on which there is complete agreement of purpose on both sides'. Most of the difficulties he ascribed 'solely . . . to the consequences of a written constitution and a system of government in which legislature and executive are equal and co-ordinate powers'. It was these legal and constitutional difficulties which led to the dropping out of the scales of a series of other supply items which until the last moment Britain had counted on receiving as part of the arrangement.

Since this was a matter of the highest policy and of strategy, the most important part in the negotiations was played by the Ambassador. But Purvis also played his part; and it was he who took charge of negotiations on the other items in the deal (mainly rifles, motor torpedo-boats and aircraft) in the months after the agreement was signed. The Embassy remained until December 1940 the formal channel for all communications on the matter. The following account must concentrate on the more purely supply aspects of the main story.[1]

Perhaps nowhere else was shown more clearly the essential unity of things—of supply, high policy and strategy; of belligerency, active

---

[1] Churchill, op. cit., Chapter XX, 'United States Destroyers and West Indian Bases'.

and passive; of warships and bases; of the Atlantic and its shores; of Commonwealth and Empire. The President had shown both in action and in words how clear was his own sense of this unity. So far as the Commonwealth and Anglo-American relations were concerned this was revealed in various ways. One has been referred to above —the insistence by the Administration that the whole of the British Commonwealth should use a single supply channel. Another was the conception of Commonwealth and Empire as a political and strategic unity from the point of view of American defence. If the worst came to the worst, the President suggested to Lord Lothian just as the Dunkirk evacuation was beginning, that all movable war equipment —especially the British Navy, including partly-built ships, and merchant vessels and aircraft should be treated 'not as British but as Empire possessions and transferred before they could be captured or surrendered, to Canada or Australia. . . .' It was part of the same thinking that when the destroyers-bases agreement was signed on 2nd September, the American Government sought and obtained an assurance that if in the war, 'in which Great Britain and the British Commonwealth' were engaged, the waters surrounding the British islands should become untenable for British ships of war, the British fleet would in no event be surrendered or sunk 'but would be sent overseas for the defence of other parts of the Empire'. Mr. Cordell Hull was especially anxious that these last fourteen words should appear in the exchange of letters.[1]

When the President told Congress that the American bases in British territories was 'an epochal and far-reaching act of preparation for continental defence in the face of grave danger' he was saying what many thousands of Americans had been saying since June by their spontaneous gifts of sporting rifles, shotguns, pistols, binoculars and ammunition.[2] The destroyer-bases agreement, as Lord Lothian put it, meant American acceptance of the British fleet based on Britain as America's outer line of defence. To strengthen this outer line they contributed destroyers. The offer of bases in the British transatlantic islands was Britain's recognition that these islands were the inner line of American defence.

The President's answer on 17th May to the idea of a 'loan' or sale of destroyers was that this required an act of Congress for which the public was not yet ready. The many references in the correspondence of the next three months to legal difficulties in fact came back to this political obstacle of opinion in Congress and in the country. Ameri-

[1] Department of State release, 3rd September, No. 398, and Cmd. 6224. *Exchange of Notes regarding U.S. destroyers and Naval and Air facilities for the United States in British Transatlantic Territories,* 3rd September 1940.

[2] An American Committee for the Defence of British Homes was set up. British Consulates were instructed by an Embassy circular to channe all gifts through the British Purchasing Commission to a warehouse in New York.

cans were a naval-minded people. Historically the Navy was their front line; and in fact at that time it was their only serious defence —apart from the British Commonwealth. The public sensed (though it did not know the full facts) the complete inadequacy of the Army and Air Force. Thus giving destroyers meant giving a visible part of the American front line. It would only become practical politics when Congress and people were convinced that they were getting in return tangible defence assets which would more than offset the destroyers.

As the last section indicated, destroyers were the first item on the British list, all through the surplus arms discussions of May and June. They were pressed in turn by the Prime Minister, the Ambassador and Purvis. On 11th June, the moment the arms transaction was through and loading had begun, the Prime Minister took the matter up again in a direct message to the President. Without thirty or forty old destroyers, he urged, the ocean traffic by which Britain lived might be strangled. The same night the Ambassador and Purvis both cabled (Purvis also telephoned to Monnet) the news that the President was not convinced of the need of destroyers and was therefore concentrating on other Allied needs. In Morgenthau's view, Purvis said, the 'best way of breaking the deadlock with Sylvia' was to give frankly all the data regarding destroyers lost and in repair. Two days later Purvis was at work with the Secretary of the Treasury and the President trying to undo the adverse decisions on a number of items. These included the old destroyers ('from the existing United States naval stocks', as he put it in a note), new motor torpedo-boats, more aircraft, a further batch of rifles.[1] The figures of destroyer losses were given by the Prime Minister to the American Ambassador on the 15th. In home waters 133 destroyers were in commission of which 68 were fit for service; in 1918 433 were in service.

That night, the 17th, the President told the Ambassador that it would be impossible to get Congress to release destroyers. He was having the greatest difficulty in getting the Naval Affairs Committee of the Senate to agree to the release of the Navy's new motor torpedo-boats of which the Admiralty had been pressing the purchase since the matter was first raised through Morgenthau on 28th May. Next day (18th June) there was a premature public announcement by the Acting Secretary of the Navy that the Navy had released to Britain twenty motor torpedo-boats for replacement by later models. The President had to cancel the release on the 24th because of the opposition that had developed in Congress as well as of an adverse opinion

---

[1] The U.S. Navy had then on order twenty-three motor torpedo-boats, of Scott-Payne design, powered by 1,200-h.p. Packard motors. The Admiralty hoped to get priority over twenty, or all twenty-three, as delivery was made. Formal application was made for them by the B.P.C. on 13th June.

by the Attorney-General. The same opinion ruled out any transfer of destroyers. The agitation resulted in a clause in the Defence Act signed a week later which forbade such transfers unless the Service chiefs certified they were 'not essential to the national defence'. An Act of 15th June 1917 forbidding the transfer of war vessels to a belligerent was also reaffirmed in the Act.[1]

It was a month or more before things began to move again. The matter was kept before the public by a nation-wide broadcast which the Ambassador gave on his own initiative on 22nd July. Britain, he said, might be saved from invasion if she could get now 100 American destroyers and some seaplanes. On the last day of July the Prime Minister sent a personal message to the President on destroyer losses. This 'minor and easily remediable factor' might decide the whole fate of the war. The need of destroyers was more urgent than ever to cope with invasion, hold open the Atlantic approaches and deal with Italy. 'Mr. President, with great respect I must tell you that in the long history of the world this is a thing to do *now*.'[2] This message forced matters to a head in Washington. It brought together once and for all two things that had been separate up to that time— destroyers and bases. The idea of offering facilities and bases had been under study in London since 24th May when the matter was first raised by the Ambassador. Without the *quid pro quo* of bases for destroyers the President saw no way out, Lord Lothian reported on 1st August. On the same day he reported a talk with the President. To sell the destroyers would require legislation. There was opposition in Congress and the matter would become an election issue. But Congress might agree, the President thought, if the transaction could be presented as an exchange beneficial to the defence of the United States whilst not involving the risk of war. There was already active discussion in the Administration on exchanging destroyers for bases; and the Navy agreed.

The pre-war background of the matter has been mentioned in Chapter III in the reference to the Atlantic Patrol. The patrol was in operation, but the United States had made no move to use the lease-hold rights it had acquired in Trinidad, Bermuda and St. Lucia, since the Navy did not have enough long-range flying-boats for this purpose. All it had were watching Japan in the Pacific. The working of the patrol was mentioned by the President to the Ambassador on 17th May and this led to the latter's suggestion that the scope of the patrol arrangement should be extended by giving the United States still larger defence facilities in British Atlantic islands. Shortly afterwards, whilst the matter was under consideration in London, the United States War Department raised the question of giving various

---

[1] *Documents on American Foreign Relations*, op. cit., Vol. II, 1939–40, pp. 788–89.
[2] Churchill, op. cit., p. 356.

operating facilities in British territories to Pan-American Airways; the American Army in turn could use these for the defence of the Panama Canal.[1] The War Cabinet had already decided to grant these and other defence facilities when it received the Ambassador's cable on 2nd August reporting the joining up in Washington of destroyers with bases. The letter embodying the War Cabinet's offer was sent to the President on 5th August.

The broadening out of the idea to the full destroyer-bases arrangement, the addition of the declaration on the British fleet, and the events leading to the signing of the agreement on 2nd September, have been told by Mr. Churchill. It remains here to sum up the fate of the other supply items or 'desiderata' that had been linked constantly with the destroyers as part of the arrangement. On 8th and 9th August, in personal messages to the President, Mr. Sumner Welles, Colonel Knox and Mr. Stimson, the Ambassador listed the most important immediate supply needs as follows: 20 motor torpedo-boats, 50 Consolidated bombers, 5 P.B.Y. flying-boats, some dive-bombers, and 250,000 Lee-Enfield rifles.

The Prime Minister followed up with a personal message to the President on 15th August; the worth of every destroyer the President could spare was 'measured in rubies'. 'We also need', the Prime Minister added, 'the motor torpedo-boats which you mentioned, and as many flying-boats and rifles as you can let us have. We have a million men waiting for rifles.'[2] Two days later the President gave the first hint that the transfer of destroyers might have to be made as an independent transaction. He already hoped that it could be done by executive action without legislation by Congress, but the other supply items were in a 'different legal category and may take rather longer'. A revised list of the 'other desiderata', drawn up by Purvis on direct instructions from London, was sent on the 23rd to the State Department for the President. It asked for twenty-three motor torpedo-boats (Britain would take 100 if they could be obtained); more P.B.Y. flying-boats, up to 100; perhaps 200 Curtiss fighter planes; rifles; and priority on seventy of the M.2 A4 tanks for the campaign in the Middle East, and the making good of a priority already promised on 10 million rounds per month of .30 rifle ammunition for delivery from August to December.

In the drafts of the exchange of letters for the destroyer-bases arrangement, made in the days following, the motor torpedo-boats,

---

[1] At this time (July and August) there was newspaper talk, joined in by some Congressmen, of Britain giving bases, not for destroyers, but in return for cancellation of the war debts. In July a Pan-American Conference at Havana adopted a trusteeship agreement to cover the possibility of European territories in the Western Hemisphere being left derelict by the German conquest of their mother countries.

[2] Churchill, op. cit., p. 360.

rifles, and so forth still kept company with the destroyers. It was not until the 27th August that the Administration finally came to the conclusion that the fifty destroyers must stand alone in the balance against the bases; the other items, it was decided, came under a different law. There was not much that the British Government could do about this. Mr. Stimson refers to the omission of 'a part of the American obligation' as a 'sheer inadvertence', a 'simple error'. But it was hardly that.[1] The delicacy of the whole transaction from a political point of view was underlined by Mr. Cordell Hull in a talk with Lord Lothian on the 28th. The deal involved, he said, the political life of the President and the Administration; it was only with the utmost difficulty that some of those on the American side had made up their minds that the transfer was valid. For several days longer, however, London still hoped to obtain the other items. On 30th August the Ambassador told London that he and Purvis were meeting the Secretary of the Treasury to see how far they could get with them. Purvis was asked by the British Government to continue to follow the matter closely and to make a daily report on his negotiations on the different items. The President accepted the view held in London that there was an informal commitment to give the other things which he had agreed to as part of the offer of the bases.[2]

It was impossible at the moment, the President told the Ambassador on 6th September, to transfer the motor torpedo-boats because of the Attorney-General's adverse opinion. Sufficient time must elapse for them to be put into service and to be replaced by later models. He authorised the Ambassador, however, to ask the Secretary of the Treasury and Purvis to put forward alternatives, such as the delivery of additional flying-boats—the next in importance on the Admiralty's list of requirements. But it now seemed that the other items would not come like the destroyers as an exchange for the bases, but that payment would have to be made, with a possible refund later. For the understanding which had been reached with the President (as set out by the Ambassador) recorded that 'while it might be necessary for the British Government to pay for these items, for the time being, a way would be found for refunding the purchase price or of offsetting it before British dollar resources available for the purchase of munitions in the United States neared exhaustion'.

---

[1] Henry L. Stimson and McGeorge Bundy, *On Active Service in Peace and War* (New York: Harper & Brothers, 1948), p. 359. Also published in the United Kingdom under the same title (London: Hutchinson & Co. Ltd., 1949).

[2] The agreed text of the letter of the Ambassador to the Secretary of State as published on 3rd September refers expressly to 'naval and military equipment and material' to be transferred under the arrangement. Mr. Cordell Hull's reply accepting the offer of bases merely said that 'In consideration of the declaration above quoted: the Government of the United States will immediately transfer to His Majesty's Government fifty United States Navy destroyers....'

Throughout these weeks the emphasis from London was on urgency. Most of these supplies were needed immediately. Only the Lee-Enfield ·30 calibre rifles, however, were available in stock; and even they were badly needed for training purposes in the Philippines. The rifles were released on 22nd September a few hours after a further direct message from the Prime Minister to the President that their despatch would enable the Home Guard to hand back to the Regular Army an equivalent number of British standard army rifles.[1]

The rifles were all shipped during the next two weeks through the same machinery as was used for the original consignments of surplus arms in June. Of the 250,000 rifles, 20,000 were earmarked on arrival in the United Kingdom for the Government of Eire and were shipped immediately to Dublin.

Meanwhile Purvis was hard at work on the other items. He reported release of the Swedish aircraft and of five Flying Fortresses. The P.B.Y. flying-boats (Catalinas) were more difficult. All of the P.B.Y.4s, the older model, were out on the Pacific watching Japan. The first of the new model, P.B.Y.5s, had only just been delivered. But on 27th September he was able to report that the Navy had agreed to a very important acceleration on deliveries of P.B.Y.5s. Up to July 1941 deliveries would go alternately to the United States Navy and to the British Navy. This meant the release of four in November, five in December, ten in January and twelve in each of the next three months. In October he reported a promise of twenty in May and seventeen in June 1941. Other aircraft releases, also agreed in October, included B.24 bombers (Liberators). The cost was high —the giving in exchange of 274 British-held Wright aircraft engines— but the B.24s were needed for the Atlantic ferry service, to take mail and bring back ferry pilots.

The most difficult item of all, the motor torpedo-boats, dragged on into the lend-lease period. They were covered by the first lend-lease appropriation. Purvis took the view that any connection between them and the destroyer-bases arrangement was wiped out by the far greater fact of lend-lease. Twenty-eight motor torpedo-boats were transferred to the British Government on the day the President signed the Lend-Lease Act, 11th March 1941. The Navy Department followed this up in July with the release of twenty minesweepers and other vessels; and by the laying down of a programme for the construction of 100 convoy escort vessels on behalf of the British Government.

---

[1] On the need of rifles, see Churchill, op. cit., pp. 406–07.

(iv)

The Crisis of the French Contracts

The *Eastern Prince*, the first ship to sail with arms for Britain, had been at sea for less than forty-eight hours when Purvis received a secret telegram from London which marked the beginning of an even greater crisis in supply from the United States. The telegram warned him that France was on the point of surrender. Next day he was instructed to direct all supplies to Britain and was asked to secure if possible a complete list of all ships at sea carrying war materials to France; he had the list back in the hands of the Admiralty within a few hours. In between these events he had taken the most important step in his whole career. The story of the French contracts runs from the signing of the agreements on 16th June to the final financial settlement at the end of the war. It is convenient to treat the whole affair in this section.

When the warning telegram was received it was clear that the whole British supply programme in North America was in peril. The French war contracts were so closely geared in with the British that the dropping out of France as partner could have brought supply almost to a standstill. Most of the large contracts placed under the joint Anglo-French aircraft and explosives programmes had been signed by one only of the two Commissions. This was a matter both of policy and of convenience. It underlined Anglo-French unity and permitted the two Allies to allocate the material according to their needs at the moment when deliveries were made from the factory. Since the break-through at Sedan it had become difficult to persuade American manufacturers to accept new French contracts. It was obvious that any wholesale cancellation of the French contracts might deal a fatal blow to the already waning confidence of the American business-man in the will and ability of Britain to keep on fighting. It might then become almost impossible to re-establish the British supply programme on an independent basis. If, on the other hand, Britain took over the vast financial commitment involved in the French contracts, but without any of the dollars and gold of France to pay for them, a sudden and enormous burden would be thrown upon British dollar and gold reserves. The Secretary of the American Treasury, with whom Purvis and his French colleagues were in the closest touch during these difficult hours, gave Congress some time later a measure of the financial dangers involved in the transfer.

British liabilities were doubled. They were left to face Germany alone. The result was that the British began to lose gold and dollar assets twice as fast after June as before.[1]

---

[1] Lend-Lease Hearings, Senate, Part I, S.275, 27th January 1941.

Purvis was fully aware of the implications when with a steady hand he signed the transfer agreements at 3 a.m. on 17th June. So was Monnet (to whom Mr. Churchill paid tribute for his help) and the others who acted swiftly at the London end.[1] A telegram received from London on the afternoon of the 16th of June said: 'We are trying to clear immediately the issue of necessary French authorisation from this end . . .', but left it to Purvis 'to handle French at your end'. The French representatives in New York were swift and resolute in signing this last great act of the Anglo-French alliance.

On receipt of the warning telegram on Saturday, 15th June, Purvis, after a short consultation with two colleagues, cabled to London asking for full authority for 'instant action'. The reply came back the same night giving him full authority to act. A second message next day added that he might take whatever steps he deemed necessary including the securing of the assignment to Great Britain of French contracts for aircraft, machine tools, munitions, explosives, and raw materials for war production purposes. By nine o'clock that same Sunday morning it was clear from the radio news that the break was coming in Bordeaux. His two colleagues came to the office of the British Purchasing Commission just before noon and decided that negotiations for transfer of the contracts must begin at once with the French Air Commission. They broached the point with Colonel Jacquin, head of the Air Commission, who was in the office. He agreed without hesitation that the air contracts over which he had authority should be assigned. At two o'clock the news came that the French Government had resigned and a little later that Marshal Petain had decided to ask for an armistice. The legal advisers on the two sides began to prepare the necessary agreements for the transfer. By the early evening Bloch-Lainé, who alone had full authority over the ground contracts, was working together with Purvis in the latter's apartment on a complete assignments arrangement. Once the news of the armistice request had come through it was clear that the agreements must be rushed through with the utmost speed. At any moment the full powers possessed by Bloch-Lainé to dispose of the French contracts might be revoked, whether by the action of the new government or by the intervention of Germany. At any moment, also, the Treasury in Washington might freeze French assets in the United States—a decision which in fact was taken the moment the Treasury office opened on Monday morning, five hours after the agreements had been signed.[2]

---

[1] Churchill, op. cit., p. 189. Monnet gave the first hint of the possibility of the taking over of some of the French contracts in the United States in a letter to the Prime Minister early in June.

[2] Stettinius, op. cit., p. 34. In announcing the freezing order the Secretary of the Treasury, in agreement with Purvis, stated that the British Government would assume all French munitions contracts in the United States. Later Purvis issued a release confirming this.

Mr. Stettinius has described in his book what happened when the agreements were signed at 3 a.m. by Purvis and Bloch-Lainé.[1]

> Purvis hesitated for ten minutes before he signed, going over the whole transaction in his mind. With two signatures—one for air contracts and one for ground—he was accepting six hundred million dollars in obligations for the British Government. There was no time to consult London again. The whole deal might fall through at any moment. This was a complete reversal of the careful spending policy the British had followed in order to make their dollars last through the long war of attrition they had expected. But now it was all or nothing if Britain was to fight on. Purvis told his friends later it was the biggest decision of his life when he finally picked up a pen and signed the transfer papers.

In reply to a question some days later from the United Kingdom Treasury representative in Ottawa: 'What need was there for an assignment?' the following answer was given by the head of the British Air Commission in New York:

> There were many reasons. Although the Administration was friendly the Defence Department were anxious to take over some of the contracts. There were other competitors in the market, e.g. Sweden, Holland and China. Again had there been no assignment the contractors would have a legal right to pocket the $200,000,000 already advanced to them and we might have had to pay this twice over. In addition, the contractors would most probably have charged higher prices. There was an extreme urgency to obtain aeroplane engines and the British Treasury had agreed to the assignment. Finally it may be that the contractors were becoming alarmed about British credit. The Assignment Agreements were discussed with Morgenthau, who agreed to them, perhaps not knowing the attitude of his Defence Departments, who wanted machine tools, small arms, ammunition, etc., and had even attempted to make contracts themselves, which Mr. Purvis told me he got cancelled through Knudsen.

Any figures cited in the previous paragraphs were guesses. Purvis had to act without full knowledge of what was being taken over or how much it would cost. The French Purchasing Commission had been buying much more freely than Britain in the United States, and it had been much less particular about prices. Some at least of the contracts were known to be very onerous. Artillery and ammunition were in metric measure and followed French specifications; and there were other supplies that were not suitable for use by the United

---

[1] The documents signed (see texts in Appendix II) comprised: two principal agreements (one covering the main aircraft contracts and the other all other contracts) and two covering letters. The first letter dealt with payment and the second with French territories. The first letter, though dated the 16th, was apparently not signed until some days later. The half share in the Tennessee Powder Company was covered by a separate letter.

Kingdom. The exact number of the contracts, their status, and the total liability involved under them were not known with any degree of exactness until an exhaustive analysis had been made by the well-known firm of chartered accountants, Price, Waterhouse & Company. It was necessary for the firm to use a large staff and to spend much time in disentangling the French records. In the end the firm had to resort to individual application to all contractors in order to secure full data. Its detailed report was made at the end of September and was forwarded by the British Purchasing Commission to the North American Supply Committee in London by letter dated 8th October. The report put the total commitment, as at 30th September, at approximately $612 million.[1] Of this total, aircraft contracts accounted for approximately $425 million. Of the balance of about $187 million, commitments on contracts still active (other than for air) amounted to about $148 million. The other $39 million were accounted for mostly by three items: (1) $12 million on contracts already cancelled or in process of being cancelled at 30th September; (2) $16 million paid to France for United States surplus arms stocks; and (3) $8 million repaid to the French Commission for its half share of the Tennessee Powder Company. The total of $148 million for active contracts comprised the following main items: machine tools, $87 million; automotive equipment, etc., $26 million; gasoline, $18 million; brass and zinc, $9 million. The figure for armaments was only $5 million and was mostly for field cables and metal parts for fuses. It was part of the agreement that the French Commission should be repaid for advances which it had already made on contracts. The advances were calculated at nearly $227 million out of the total commitment of $612 million, and of this about $152 million were advances on air contracts. The total commitment, it was pointed out by the British Purchasing Commission in its letter to London, was still approximate. Some cancellations would still take place and part of the cost of cancellation would be borne by the French. How the commitment wasted away later is indicated below.

There was much cabling back and forth with London in the weeks after the making of the Assignment Agreements. It was not surprising that the vast and indefinite commitments which they involved should have caused much concern to the British Government. Whilst there was never any doubt that the final and overriding consideration was to make certain of supplies that were now more than ever vital to the defence of Britain, two main questions were raised with Purvis. The first was whether it was not still possible to vary the arrangement so that Britain would not be forced to take contracts she did not need. The second expressed the lingering hope that some means would be found to avoid payment in dollars.

---

[1] See document in Appendix II.

On the first point Purvis replied that from the very outset it was a matter of all or none for the French representatives. They insisted that the United Kingdom should not be free to pick and choose between the contracts. Moreover, after sounding out several of the leading aircraft firms, Purvis, on 24th June, had sent a circular letter to each holder of a French contract notifying him of the transfer of his contract and asking him whether he accepted it. Replies were coming in slowly. To reopen the whole question would endanger British credit, imperil supplies, and invite trouble from the French, whose attitude had become more difficult after the bombardment of the French fleet at Oran on 3rd July. Purvis feared that any attempt to revise the agreements would risk an injunction, entailing long and doubtful legal proceedings in the American courts and a holding up of supply under the contracts. Already the French Purchasing Commission took the view that the British were in default on certain payments. The pressure was such that to save the agreements Purvis felt it necessary to pay over in the next few weeks $27 million which were due under various headings.

It was the obligation, undertaken in the assignment, to pay in American dollars that was the main point questioned in London. Purvis pointed out in reply that Bloch-Lainé's instructions were incompatible with acceptance of payment in sterling. The arrangement whereby funds were paid to the account of France in the Bank of Canada was made, Purvis pointed out, with the idea that the funds could be blocked, as eventually they were, by the Canadian Government. Part of the arrangement between Purvis and Bloch-Lainé, made on the 16th, was that $500 million of French gold and dollars in the United States should be transferred to Great Britain for payment in the United States on the French contracts in return for a corresponding credit to be made available to France in Canada. The Secretary of the Treasury was prepared to unfreeze French funds to facilitate such a transfer. 'Mr. Morgenthau', Purvis told London on 18th June, 'gave his blessing both to the assignment agreements and to the arrangement which permits of the gold transfer. He strongly recommended the French representatives to act and to act quickly.' The plan for the gold transfer was blocked, however, by the French Ambassador. He approved of the transfer of the contracts, but regarded the transfer of gold as going beyond the authority of the French representatives.

The working out of the assignment agreements was complicated by an agreement for the transfer of French contracts in the United States made between Sir Ronald Campbell, British Ambassador in France, and General Weygand, who was then French Minister of National Defence. The Purvis–Bloch-Lainé and the Weygand agreements were actually signed on the same day, 17th June, but the latter came some hours later. Purvis learned of it on the 19th. It was embodied in letters exchanged between the British Ambassador and General Weygand at Bordeaux.[1] The terms of the letters were somewhat wider than the New York counterpart signed by Purvis and Bloch-Lainé. The intent of the Weygand agreement, though the wording was not precise on this point, was that Britain was to owe the sum due to France until a settlement could be made after the war. The agreement covered not only war materials but supplies of any nature whatsoever ('de quelque nature qu'ils soient'), and not only contracts entered into by the French State, but all contracts in the United States for the direct or indirect benefit of the French Government ('à son profit direct ou indirect'). The purpose of the Weygand letter was to enable the French Government to say that it had no contracts whatsoever in the United States. It was not until the end of July that the French Purchasing Commission showed much sign of interest in the Weygand agreement. It sent on the 29th a note to Purvis saying that the French Government regarded this agreement as covering contracts made by groups of French companies (called 'groupements d'importation') formed by directions of the French Government for procuring materials, such as aluminium, for the French defence programme. In the same communication it was suggested that as the Weygand agreement set no territorial limits, it must be taken to include cargoes on French ships in British ports, also French aircraft in Canada and any other French material capable of being delivered to the British Government outside the United States. All such material would have to be paid for on the conditions set by the agreement.

Up to that time Purvis had taken the view that the validity of the Weygand agreement in the United States was somewhat doubtful and that contractors would want evidence of its authenticity. London, however, took the view that it was valid, that contracts covered by it, but not covered by the Purvis–Bloch-Lainé agreement, had to be accepted, if the French representatives insisted, and had to be settled on the best terms obtainable. It was the financial implications of the Weygand agreement which made London anxious not to call its validity into question. Since the agreement in assigning the contracts specified no particular method of payment, reimbursement to the French Government could be left for a post-war settlement. This, it was hoped, might be used as a lever to reopen the whole question of repayment if this could be done without jeopardising supplies.

The British Purchasing Commission objected that in the long run any reliance on the Weygand agreement might prove both costly and dangerous. The French representative in the United States had

---

[1] See texts in Appendix II.

been unable to indicate what specific contracts would be covered by its wording. It could obviously be stretched to cover any contracts entered into by associations or individuals who could be represented as acting in any way for the benefit of the French State. If it were once accepted as the valid instrument of transfer, any American manufacturer could compel Britain to take over any contract which could be brought within its terms. But in fact all the contracts Britain wanted were already covered by the Purvis–Bloch-Lainé agreement, and any undermining of the method of repayment it set out could only lead to obstruction on the part of the French officials in the United States. For these reasons the Commission preferred to regard the Weygand agreement solely as an authorisation to the British and French authorities in the United States to carry out an assignment, the terms of which had already been agreed upon by Purvis and Bloch-Lainé. The Weygand agreement indeed implied some further document 'effecting and defining the limitations of the assignment', and that further document existed in the form of the Purvis–Bloch-Lainé agreement. This view, as submitted early in October in a memorandum prepared by the Commission's General Counsel, was accepted by London. Henceforth, the transfer of the French contracts was governed entirely by the Purvis–Bloch-Lainé agreement.

THE EARLY PAYMENTS AND THE FINAL SETTLEMENT

The history of the Purvis–Bloch-Lainé agreement on the financial side until the final settlement at the end of the war can be told briefly. By the terms of the agreement, for an interim period (which ended on 29th June), the French were to be reimbursed 'promptly' in New York (not Canada) for any payment, made by them as the agents of the United Kingdom, on current deliveries. Under this head they were paid $4,300,000 on 25th June. It had already been decided to send a representative of the British Treasury to Washington for general financial discussions; and Purvis was urged to hold up all further payments until his arrival. It proved impossible, however, to hold up important payments. Insistence by the French, after the events at Oran on 3rd July, on strict compliance with the terms of the agreement, forced Purvis to make the payments totalling $27 million referred to above. Already delay in making the down payments, necessary under 'cash and carry' before goods could be loaded, was causing congestion at the ports, which he relieved by authorising on 11th July the payment of $10 million. He had to pay over also the $16 million due to France for her advance on her share of the American surplus arms.

By 2nd August, the French had been reimbursed (in free dollars in New York) for all expenditure made by them in the interim periods as agents for Britain. Payments to the blocked account at the Bank of

Canada continued until May 1941, when they were suspended on instructions to the British Treasury representative in Washington. By that time the bulk of the supplies under the French contracts had been delivered and lend-lease had begun. Owing to the changed attitude of the French representatives in the United States, the British Purchasing Commission had adopted some time before this a policy of allowing to them only the amounts to which they were explicitly entitled by the letter of the Purvis–Bloch-Lainé agreement. At the time the agreement was made, it was intended that the many points not covered should be amicably discussed and settled as they arose. As France fell more and more under duress it became increasingly difficult to secure any agreement on points at issue and before the end of 1940 negotiations were discontinued. Thenceforth, the British Purchasing Commission interpreted the agreement unilaterally. Since the agreement made no specific reference to French payments for capital assistance no credit was allowed to France in respect of such amounts (except for the Tennessee Powder Company, which was governed by a separate letter). The British Purchasing Commission also retained French over-payments recovered from suppliers when contracts were cancelled without cost. By these means, and by cancellation charges to the French, the total commitment to them, as originally estimated, had been substantially reduced when payments were discontinued in May 1941.

As all these payments from the beginning had been made to the Bank of Canada under licence from the United States Treasury, it was hoped that the Secretary of the Treasury would see his way to revoking the licence and thus relieve Britain of responsibility for stopping further payments. The Treasury Department was reluctant to act, since the United States still recognised the Vichy Government. Britain was thus forced to suspend payment on her own responsibility. After some half-hearted requests for resumption of payments, the French representatives confined themselves to pressing in vain for information on the progress of the contracts. This also had been withheld after May 1941 because of the danger of possible leakage to the enemy of information on current deliveries of war supplies.

The total payments up to 31st May 1941 were approximately as follows:

Paid in free United States dollars:
For the period 17th–29th June, when the French were agents for

His Majesty's Government	$28,100,000
For advances to Tennessee Powder Company	4,300,000
TOTAL	$32,400,000
Paid to the Bank of Canada	158,000,000
GRAND TOTAL	$190,400,000

After 31st May, 1941, amounts which would have been paid to the Bank of Canada for French account were credited to a Suspense Account in the books of the British Purchasing Commission. But in November 1942 this too was discontinued on instructions from London, and the existing balance on the Suspense Account was wiped out. A report to the Ministry of Supply on 31st March 1944 estimated the still outstanding commitment to the French State in respect of advances at 16th June 1940 as approximately $56,300,000. This liability was finally cancelled in March 1945 when the British and French Governments signed an agreement in Paris settling all financial claims arising out of the war. The passages in this agreement relating to the transfer of the French contracts in June 1940 are as follows:

> The French Government shall waive their claim to all payments by the Government of the United Kingdom for . . . the transfer to the Government of the United Kingdom on 16th June 1940 of the munitions contracts in course of execution in the United States for the account of the French Government.
>
> . . .
>
> In application of the provisions of the above paragraph, the French Government shall refund to the Government of the United Kingdom the sums which the latter has paid in dollars to an account at the Bank of Canada in connection with the transfer of the said munitions contracts. This repayment shall be made by instalments *pari passu* with the implementation of the programme of deliveries referred to in paragraph 2 (iii) (*b*) above. [The latter paragraph deals with equipment and supplies to be furnished to the French Army and Navy by the British Government.]

The task of handling the French contracts imposed a heavy administrative burden on the already overworked British Purchasing Commission. When taken over the number of contracts was thought by Purvis to have been about 2,000. Some of these were virtually completed, and on others production had never begun. The air contracts on 16th June 1940, as listed by the French Air Commission, numbered 171. Out of some 600 active contracts, other than air, nearly 500 were for machine tools. The total number of contracts (including all the air contracts) placed in the life of the British Purchasing Commission up to September 1940 was only about 400. Thus the Accounting Division found its work more than doubled overnight. The position of the Machine Tool Division, already struggling with the first flood of agents' orders from London, was almost as bad. It had no complete list of the French contracts which it had taken over, nor did it have any reliable information on deliveries up to the time of the transfer.

Many questions arose with contractors as a result of the transfer.

All in time accepted the transfer notified to them by circular letter on 24th June, but some made difficulties and insisted on guarantees of various kinds. There were cases in which the British Government was asked for irrevocable letters of credit or down payments up to 100 per cent., on the theory that Britain, like France, would soon pass under German control. Complete or partial cancellations had to be negotiated in a number of cases. All machine-tool contracts had to be amended to eliminate metric standards, motors wound for French current and special French tooling. These and other difficulties continued to harass the Commission long after the summer of 1940.

CHAPTER VI

PACKING FOR THE JOURNEY, DUNKIRK TO LEND-LEASE

(i)

The New Situation after Dunkirk

SHORT-TERM AND LONG-TERM PLANS

DURING and immediately after the disasters sustained by the Allied armies in May and June 1940 the imminence of invasion for a time dominated supply policy in London. Long-term programmes, however vast, were little comfort to the Army and the Local Defence Volunteers who stood-to each summer dawn on the coasts and uplands of Britain, or to the Royal Air Force, waiting for the Luftwaffe with meagre first-line strength and inadequate reserves. What they needed were weapons of some sort in their hands at once. No wonder, then, that the Foreign Office should have informed the Ambassador on 24th May of a change in British production policy, namely, the 'switching over from . . . long-term . . . to short-term programmes . . ., with priority . . . to munitions which can be produced quickly . . . to resist the German onslaught', or that the Air Council, as Lord Beaverbrook told Purvis in mid-June, should have been 'concerned only with deliveries up to the end of 1940'.

The American response to this crisis, as we have seen, was prompt and generous. None the less, if these had been the British Government's last words on the subject, the history of overseas supply in the Second World War, and perhaps the war itself, would have been a short one. There was, in fact, little left to be got 'off the shelf' in the United States. The American Army, as Purvis had told Monnet at the end of May, were 'desperately short themselves of aircraft fit for combat service', and once the surplus stocks had been shipped the same was true of most munitions; nor could much be done to speed up deliveries within the current year. The United States could make a great contribution to British strength, but not yet.

Fortunately preoccupation with invasion needs was only a passing phase. The main emphasis of British supply policy continued to be on long- rather than short-term plans. While British factories worked round the clock to produce fighter aircraft and tanks to meet the immediate emergency, steps were being taken on both sides of the

Atlantic towards the production of the tanks which drove the Germans from Alamein to Tunis and from Normandy to the Baltic; of the ships which saved the day in 1942 and 1943; and of the bomber aircraft which ultimately brought the war home to Germany with such devastating effect. The surplus arms were hardly loaded on the ships before discussions on aircraft supply in 1941, 1942, even 1943 were in full swing in Washington between Purvis and the heads of the British Air Commission on the one side and Morgenthau with the American production and Service chiefs on the other. The short breathing space of high summer, before the Battle of Britain was fully joined, saw the launching of vast air programmes and the coming of British missions to arrange for tank and gun production which could not begin until long after that battle had been won or lost.

In fact, while the first result of Sedan and Dunkirk was a desperate appeal to the United States Government for all immediately available implements of war, these disasters led also to a profound and permanent change in the role assigned to North American munitions production. The Government, and in the first place the Ministry of Supply, went on ordering munitions and planning production on the assumption that British war industry would have to bear the main burden of military requirements. But the need of immediate American assistance was now felt more acutely and more urgently than ever before; and there was hope that it would be forthcoming. Day by day, as the battle in Belgium and Northern France continued on its calamitous course, it became more apparent that only with vast American aid could Britain hope to ward off from herself and finally avenge the fate that was rapidly overtaking her ally. On 16th June, the day of M. Reynaud's fall, the Minister without Portfolio, Mr. Arthur Greenwood, presented to the British War Cabinet a review of the economic consequences of Germany's conquest of Western Europe. His sombre conclusion was that 'however indomitable the spirit of the country, the task of maintaining a (prolonged) resistance . . . will be well-nigh insupportable unless we are able to draw assistance on a large scale from the New World'. There were, he considered, two main ways, apart from the immediate dispatch of such military equipment as lay ready to hand, in which the United States could render aid. First, they could help to reinforce the blockade by putting a complete stop to the export to the enemy of vital raw materials, especially oil, rubber, textile fibres and non-ferrous metals, and by inducing the other American states to do likewise. The value of such action lay not so much in the cessation of trade with Germany and Italy, which was in fact already inconsiderable, as in the relief afforded to the Royal Navy. Secondly, and this was much more important, the United States could constitute themselves the great reserve arsenal of the democratic cause. Pointing out that a nation's ability to wage modern war could be 'measured almost exclusively in terms of the manpower, plant and raw materials available in the engineering trades', the Minister dwelt with covetous admiration upon the immense industrial resources of America. The engineering workers of the United States outnumbered those of Great Britain by three or four to one; in particular there were in the railway workshops and the tractor plants eight times as many potential tank builders as were actually making armoured vehicles in the United Kingdom. The American output of machine tools was four times, and that of motor vehicles eight times, greater than the British. If they could be induced to convert their industries to war purposes the Americans would be able after about a year to turn out enormous quantities of aircraft and tanks—ultimately on a scale sufficient to make victory secure.

A few days later the Minister without Portfolio proposed, and the War Cabinet agreed, that a definite approach should be made to the United States Government on these matters. Accordingly, on 3rd July 1940, Lord Lothian handed an *aide-mémoire* to the State Department. In this he began by repeating what had been said before, 'that the immediate sale of destroyers and power boats, airplanes and sea-planes, guns, rifles and ammunition of all kinds is of the utmost importance if the impending attack on Great Britain is to be beaten off before winter sets in'. The great value of the material received from the United States was acknowledged, but it was emphasised that further releases, if promptly made, would be of immeasurable value. It was also necessary, however, the Ambassador went on, to look beyond these immediate reinforcements to a long-term increase of supplies from new production. Whilst the German successes had increased the resources available to the Axis powers, Britain had been cut off from many of her European supplies and was threatened with the destruction of her factories from the air. She thus stood in need of war material from America on an altogether larger scale than hitherto.

THE END OF FINANCIAL CAUTION

While the question was being thus debated in general terms at a high level, concrete plans were taking shape for transferring to America some part of the burden of production which Britain had hoped to shoulder practically alone. The first step was to unlock the dollar chest. Hitherto, as we have seen, purchasing policy had been dominated by considerations of finance; and financial policy had been based on two assumptions: namely, that it would be impossible to draw further supplies of any kind from America after the very meagre British assets had been exhausted, and that provision had to be made for the procurement of food, oil and raw materials over the whole period of a long war. Hence purchasing had been largely confined to the materials and machinery needed for the creation and maintenance of war industries in the United Kingdom. Plans for the procurement of finished munitions, other than aircraft, had been laid on very modest lines. By the third week of May, however, it was clear that neither assumption any longer held good. In the first place there had been a revulsion of feeling in the United States and the risk that credit would eventually be refused was now considered almost negligible. Secondly, there was every prospect that if the build-up of the Allied forces were not accelerated by every possible means the war would not be a long one after all, but disastrously short. It was therefore obvious that the long-sighted prudence of previous months must be cast aside, in order that the whole material resources of the American continent might be invoked in defence of the Allied cause.

A reversal of policy on these lines was of course implicit in the purchase of arms and ammunition from United States stocks, and even more in the acceptance of the French contracts. It was also visible in a steady acceleration during May and June of the trickle of orders for miscellaneous articles of military equipment to fill the growing hiatus between requirements and home production and to make good the losses of Dunkirk. In themselves these orders did not amount to very much. They still consisted of small quantities of 'easy' items which could be turned out in a short time and with relatively little capital expenditure—pistols and sub-machine guns, small arms ammunition and mechanical transport, gun forgings and tank components. Meanwhile, however, much further-reaching projects were maturing. On 17th May a new and larger theme had been introduced in a discussion between Morgenthau and Purvis. Morgenthau let it be known that the Administration was about to take wide defence powers which would include the power to build plants complementary to those of Britain and France, so as to insure against the latter's destruction. Purvis accordingly cabled to Monnet for a list of the most important and most vulnerable Allied plants. Monnet seized at once on the importance of this project. In a letter addressed to the Prime Ministers of France and Great Britain on 20th May he called for the abandonment of the policy of financial prudence which had restricted the purchase of munitions from abroad, urging that it was necessary above all to establish centres of production outside the shadow of the Luftwaffe. As an insurance against the imminent destruction of plant in France and Britain arrangements similar to those already in train with regard to aircraft should be made for the creation of capacity in the United States, immediately and on the largest possible scale, for the manufacture of all the more important munitions of war. With this object the Allies should spend freely.

This proposal was of course in tune with the character of the new British administration and with the spirit of 'reckless abandon' with which the war was henceforward to be waged. Mr. Churchill at once signified his agreement in principle. In his own later words: 'We followed a simpler plan, namely, to order everything we possibly could and leave future financial problems on the lap of the Eternal Gods.'[1] M. Reynaud likewise agreed; and on 24th May Purvis and Lord Lothian were informed of the decision to create a vastly increased productive capacity in the United States for the benefit of the Allies. Purvis was asked to report on the present scope of the American armaments industry and on the possibilities of development; tanks, ammunition, anti-tank and anti-aircraft guns were specifically referred to. It was suggested that he should explain the new situation in confidence to the President and Morgenthau and ask for their guidance.

THE ARMY INSURANCE PROGRAMME

From the fourth week of May 1940 onwards, then, there was hard work on both sides of the Atlantic on the task of translating the new spending policy into detailed programmes. On the one hand a steady flow of telegrams from the British Purchasing Commission during the month of June set forth, in respect of each of the main classes of munitions, the orders that had already been placed, the extent to which further orders could be placed for delivery in the near future and, finally, the longer-range possibilities on the assumption that a large-scale expansion of capacity was to follow. At the European end the Ministry of Supply, and the French for the little time left them, sought to estimate the scope of their requirements—no longer merely purchasing piecemeal as individual deficiencies were discovered but elaborating a comprehensive programme like that already worked out for aircraft. The task of the Ministry of Supply was very much more complex and difficult than the Air Ministry's had been, owing to the vastly greater number and variety of independent stores used by the Army. The concept of 'insurance', however, offered a rough formula: estimate the percentage loss of output at home likely to result from enemy bombing (or, on the French side of the Channel, from the overrunning of industrial areas) and order from America a corresponding percentage of the current indicated requirements of each major item. The percentage chosen was bound to be arbitrary and was for some time in doubt. The French were setting the pace at the outset. Before the collapse they had already forwarded a list of requirements to New York, sent out a special tank mission and started active negotiations with

---

[1] Churchill, op. cit., p. 492.

American firms. And their plans were based on the provision of capacity in the United States amounting to fifty per cent. of their home programme. For the time being the British prepared to follow suit, but with the French out of the picture the whole question was reopened.

The Ministry of Supply had always had doubts of the utility of such ambitious programmes as had been proposed. From the start there had been two great obstacles to large-scale purchase from the United States—the shortage of dollars and the time factor. The former was no longer allowed to count for much, but the latter was a more powerful deterrent than ever. Could the American potential possibly be developed 'within the time available'? And would not grandiose long-term schemes merely serve to impede the delivery of such kinds and quantities of munitions as could be produced in the immediate future? The time available was indeed at first sight very short. Invasion was expected during the present summer, and clearly the placing of fresh production orders in America could avail nothing in that immediate emergency. Suppose, however, that the impending invasion were not mounted or, being mounted, were repulsed. Then Germany, resting on her enormous stocks of army equipment and devoting the winter and the whole resources of Europe to the making of aircraft and invasion ships, could launch a more formidable offensive in the spring, preceded by an intense air and undersea attack on British shipping and by heavy bombing of British factories. To this remoter danger an overseas insurance programme, designed to offset the effects of the bombing, might indeed be relevant. But it could only be so if the production which it called into being could be in full swing by the early summer of 1941 at the very latest. And it was doubted, with reason, whether this was in fact possible. In the making of munitions, it was thought, the United States were no further advanced than Britain had been three or more years ago when rearmament was in its earliest phase. Existing capacity for armaments production, Purvis had pointed out, was 'trifling'. Nothing much could be achieved until new plant had been created, and this meant an interval of between twelve and eighteen months, according to the type of equipment concerned, before full production could be attained. A valuable reserve capacity could no doubt be established for the simpler kinds of army equipment—pistols and tommy-guns, wheeled vehicles, ammunition and explosives—for which a nucleus capacity was already in being or for which existing plant could be adapted without undue difficulty. But major items such as artillery and tanks were another matter. So long as the planning of overseas supply was dominated by the concept of insurance against loss of output at home in the near future, there was a tendency to argue against incurring vast commitments which could not bear any proportionate

M

fruit until a time when Britain would either have saved herself or have been defeated.

But Monnet himself, the originator of the insurance concept, had never intended that the planning of American supply should be thus restricted. In almost the last words that he wrote as Chairman of the disintegrating Anglo-French Co-ordinating Committee he asserted the need for a longer view. 'The enemy cannot obtain a rearmament reserve outside the range of bombers. You can. You cannot win by force of arms without great superiority in the air and at least mechanical equality. This cannot be obtained by United Kingdom production alone. Therefore it is not too much to say that not a day must be lost in the creation of this reserve which may mean the difference between defeat and victory.' Beyond the campaign of 1941 there lay the campaign of 1942. Beyond the fending-off of invasion and the endurance of air bombardment there lay, though it demanded an effort of will and imagination to plan for it at that time, the necessity of offensive action; and for this American aid, in armaments if not in men, was clearly the indispensable condition. To this far horizon the British Government had in fact lifted its eyes. On 19th June 1940 the Defence Committee of the War Cabinet decided not only that thirty-six divisions must be made ready by the end of June 1941 instead of September 1941 as previously planned, but also that equipment should be provided for a full fifty-five divisions by $Z + 27$, i.e. by the end of November 1941. In this longer perspective American supply took on a new importance, for by the end of 1941 much more than a trickle of munitions could be hoped for from this source. The Defence Committee accordingly authorised the Ministry of Supply to requisition from North America such supplies as were needed to complete the equipment of fifty-five divisions, and also to place large supplementary orders 'in view of the danger of interruption to output as a result of enemy action'.

Fortified by this authoritative sanction, the Ministry of Supply set to work to put the army 'insurance' programme into its final form. The scale of insurance was now fixed at twenty-five to thirty-five per cent, of current requirements, varying according to the importance of individual items and the vulnerability of the plants producing them. On this basis a formal request was put before the Treasury for the expenditure of £90 million in dollars on this scheme. Partly in order to satisfy the urgent desire of the Canadian Government and people to make a real contribution in munitions as well as in men to the safety of the Commonwealth, a third of the whole programme was allotted to Canada[1]; the expenditure envisaged in the United States thus amounted to some $240 million. The Treasury raising no

[1] See below, section vi.

demur, simultaneous telegrams were despatched on 5th July 1940 to New York and Ottawa giving details of new requirements. The main emphasis in these instructions was laid on the monthly rate of output for which capacity was to be created, but it was of course necessary to provide initial orders for definite quantities of material. These were calculated on the basis of the output which might be expected to accrue by the end of 1941, and it was stipulated that no commitments should be entered into beyond that date. The programme covered most of the standard army weapons and ammunition, with the important exceptions of field artillery and armoured fighting vehicles which, for special reasons which will appear later, were reserved for further consideration. A supplementary list of naval ordnance requirements, amounting to £13½ million, was cabled later in the month.

AMERICAN REARMAMENT AND ITS IMPLICATIONS

Taken in conjunction with the Allied aircraft programme launched a couple of months earlier, the army 'insurance' programme meant that Britain was now committed to planning the development of the American munitions potential on a considerable scale. The question was whether she would be able to carry her plans into effect. By midsummer 1940 conditions were in many respects much less favourable than they had been during the twilight war. Hitherto British purchasing had been treated as though American industry were a shop from which munitions could be bought—an expensive shop indeed, and one which might take a long time to deliver the goods, but still one in which the Allies were the only important customers. But now American rearmament was beginning, and in consequence the British could no longer carry on their purchasing in isolation on a purely commercial basis.

At the beginning of 1940 the United States disposed of a one-ocean navy, very limited air forces and modern equipment for an army of some 75,000 men; and only the first tentative steps had been taken towards rearmament. The Allied *débacle* in Europe abruptly brought home to government and people the extent of the peril which confronted them and the inadequacy of the preparations so far made to meet it. A new spirit of vigilance and resolve took hold of the nation. Arms were rushed across the Atlantic to stiffen what was now widely understood to be America's first line of defence. Two Republican statesmen, Mr. Henry L. Stimson and Colonel Frank Knox, took office under President Roosevelt as Secretaries of War and of the Navy. A National Defence Advisory Commission of industrialists, economists and labour leaders, headed by Mr. William S. Knudsen of General Motors, was set up to supervise the production of warlike stores. And Congress responded to Presidential messages and the people's mood by passing on 2nd July a National Defence Act providing for great increases in the land, sea and air forces of the United States, and by appropriating over $10 billion for the purpose during the next two months. At the end of July the Selective Service Bill was introduced—involving conscription in time of peace for the first time in American history.

In all this there was an obvious threat to British supply. There was now coming to pass, in fact, what the British had feared at the outset of the war. One of the main reasons for the Riverdale Mission had been a report that as soon as war broke out in Europe the Americans would begin to rearm on a scale which would leave little room for British orders and, further, would place an embargo on the export of war supplies, not merely of munitions but of machinery and critical materials, and not for reasons of neutrality but because they needed them themselves. These fears were not unfounded. Their realisation was delayed only because in American eyes war in Europe began on 10th May 1940, not in September 1939. Henceforward British buyers could no longer range freely over the whole field of American industry, negotiating with firms which were hardly less anxious to secure contracts than Britain was to secure the goods. They had now to face the formidable competition of large defence orders backed by the whole authority of the American Government and inevitably enjoying priority over the requirements of a foreign state.

Foreseeing this, Purvis had repeatedly warned London, while the United States Administration's plans were maturing, of the need for immediate action to secure a firm foothold before it was too late. On 29th May 1940 he had pressed for 'immediate authority to proceed with the placing of orders for such supplies as you know are vital', and for information as to the quantities required and the order of priority. Again, on 15th June, he told London that the Defence Advisory Commission would shortly be swinging into action and that munitions orders, if they were to be placed at all on a large scale, would have to be placed at once. To this Monnet added his own emphatic warning on the 23rd that if the Administration were not fully informed at once of British requirements, capacity would be filled up with American orders and progress retarded by shortages of machine tools, chemicals and other key materials.

But by the middle of July, when the new British army programme became known in New York, it was already too late to secure a safe position for British contracts. The United States Defence Programme was getting under way and the authorities were taking action to secure its progress against undue competition from foreign orders. An important factor in their attitude was, of course, the general fear that Britain was about to succumb. During the summer of 1940 the decisive air battle raging over Britain was never far from the minds of all those engaged in Washington on the forward planning of supply. It was a time of much public and official anxiety in the United States. Inability to render immediate help and lack of precise knowledge of the major factors that were deciding the issue only increased the anxiety.[1] Towards the end of June the Ambassador, and the Australian Minister in Washington, reported on the wave of pessimism that was sweeping the country (to which the Prime Minister replied that too much attention must not be paid to eddies of American opinion). The British Treasury's emissary noted on 17th July the 'terribly pessimistic' atmosphere. Thus it was widely felt that, while existing stocks of weapons might be depleted in a last attempt to stave off Britain's fall, new weapons and the means of making them should be reserved for the defence of the western hemisphere.

The Defence Act, which enabled the Administration to apply to materials and machinery the same licensing procedure as to actual military equipment, gave it the power to enforce this policy. On 20th July the National Defence Advisory Commission declared itself opposed to the export 'to vulnerable areas' of any further machine tools other than those required to 'round off' existing plant—a grievous threat to the expansion of war production in Britain. At the same time the British Purchasing Commission was obliged to report any enquiries regarding the purchase of munitions to the President's Liaison Committee and obtain the sanction of the Defence Advisory Commission before proceeding with any contracts involving more than $150,000. These 'Reports of Preliminary Negotiations' were not only a cause of delay in themselves, but enabled the authorities to exercise a suspensary or absolute veto over any British orders which were regarded as opposed to the interests of American defence. And it was soon clear that the creation of plant equipped to produce weapons of purely British type would be so regarded.

In these circumstances it was evident that the penetration of American industry on a wide front which was implied by the army 'insurance' programme was not going to be an easy operation. Nor was the outlook much better in those sectors where a substantial foothold had already been secured. The threat to deliveries of machine tools has been referred to above, and a similar situation was developing in regard to aircraft and aero engines. When the President, on 16th May, set the ultimate goal of 50,000 aircraft a year, he did not put this forward as a production programme. The reason for this figure, ten times the current annual production, Mr. Cordell Hull suggests in his Memoirs, was political—to impress the American

---

[1] When the Battle of Britain began, even the Administration had no exact knowledge of British aircraft production figures. Morgenthau estimated the total output of all types at 700–800. Purvis was authorised by the Embassy to tell him that the real figure was 'more than double' and 'rapidly increasing'. See p. 205.

people, encourage the Allies, and dismay the enemy.[1] None the less, the demands about to be made on the aircraft industry were formidable enough. The President asked Congress for appropriations for 7,000 aircraft, a figure raised on 10th July to 26,000. Actually, as Mr. Stettinius noted in his book, 21,401 aircraft were ordered by the United States Army and Navy in the second half of 1940, nearly half of them trainers. Total British Commonwealth and Allied aircraft orders to 20th July, as set forth in a British Air Commission return, were 9,720, of which 8,221 were still undelivered. A similar statement as to engines revealed much heavier total orders, namely 26,260, of which 21,340 were still undelivered. Moreover, there was a significant figure showing British options over an additional 20,589 engines running from April 1941 to December 1942. As indicated earlier, the major 'bottleneck' in expanding aircraft production was the supply of engines, which took more time and skill to produce than airframes; and the British and French Governments had sought to balance their home production by importing large quantities of engines from the United States. Thus Allied orders already absorbed a large part of the existing capacity, especially for engines, up to the autumn of 1941. The early orders, British and French (placed before the Allied programme of March), were for delivery, in part, by October 1940. This was supposed to clear the way for the main Allied programme of March, on which deliveries were to run from October 1940 to October 1941. So it looked as though for over a year the American Army and Navy would have to be content, in the main, with the output from new capacity created after mid-June 1940. Moreover, it was obvious that British aircraft needs from the United States would not come to a sudden end in October 1941. The danger was foreseen in a joint Anglo-French note given to Knudsen on 20th June. Headed 'without commitment', it noted that the Allied programme would result in a production of some 1,000 aircraft a month by June 1941; it went on to say that proposals were being worked out aiming at 'the continued employment of *at least* that capacity thereafter for the duration of the war'. Clearly the American Army and Navy could not be expected to acquiesce in the indefinite absorption of the greater part of the limited capacity for aircraft production by foreign orders. Before the end of July it was made evident that, while the formula, 'continued employment of capacity' was accepted—it was indeed to become the basic principle of successive aircraft programmes up to and after lend-lease[2]—Britain would be allowed no

---

[1] *Memoirs of Cordell Hull*, Vol. I, op. cit., p. 767. Sherwood, op. cit., p. 162, refers to the working out in June of a programme for the 50,000.

[2] Thus, at the Churchill–Roosevelt meeting after Pearl Harbour, a British Supply Council programme took as its principle 'continued employment of the capacity already allocated for the execution of direct British contracts, as well as British lend-lease requisitions'.

more than the continued yield from existing contracts; also that aero engines would not be released for export while there were airframes waiting for engines in the United States.

In short, the position in the summer of 1940 was that the American and British demands for munitions could no longer be fitted without collision into the margin of American industry which was not occupied in satisfying an undiminished civilian market. There were bound to be conflicts over factory capacity, machine tools and raw materials, and American needs were bound to receive priority. So long as British munitions orders appeared as something distinct from, and in competition with, the United States preparedness programme, only slow and fragmentary achievement could be looked for on new projects, and deliveries even from existing contracts would be in constant peril.

All this, however, was only one aspect of the picture. Those Americans who were directly responsible for remedying, out of existing resources, the deficiencies of United States defence, could not but take a restrictive view on British orders and shipments. But at the very highest level the authorities were prepared not merely to accept but to welcome and encourage a large programme of production on Britain's behalf. American rearmament plans were still on a relatively small scale. They were not enough to give the nation security and the Administration knew that they were not enough. But if British orders were added to its own defence programme the Administration could plan the development of the munitions potential on a really adequate scale without laying itself open in an election year to the charge that it was preparing, not for defence, but for war.

The obvious danger that the placing of vast American orders might interfere with deliveries on orders already placed by the Allies was foreseen by the Administration from the outset. Morgenthau, in whose sympathetic hands the general direction of rearmament was placed, had in May explained to Purvis, in giving him advance notice of the projected defence programme, that it was not intended to do anything which might damage the Allied cause. For example, the licensing of the export of 'critical' war materials would not be operated to the detriment of the Allies—would indeed assist them, since its object was to put teeth into the moral and strategic embargoes on exports to enemy and dubiously neutral countries. And United States armament needs would be provided for by the erection of new plant so that there would be no interference with orders already placed. The President repeated this point in public on 10th June, saying that the Government would 'superimpose on top of the munitions industry, created with foreign capital, a new munitions industry to fill our own orders and additional foreign orders'.

A few days later Morgenthau went further. He told Purvis on

14th June that the Administration had decided to advance to the Allies the full capital costs of factory expansions through the medium of the Reconstruction Finance Corporation (a New Deal government investment agency); the Allies would pay their share only on the completion of contracts in proportion to the amount of equipment actually supplied to them. For Britain the advantages of this offer were manifest, though in practice it was found to be applicable only in a few cases. Tax payments would be eliminated, the manufacturers' profits would be restricted (under the Vinson-Trammel Act) to twelve per cent., and above all her scanty stock of dollars could be devoted entirely to the actual purchase of supplies without current expenditure on long-term capital investments. But it was stipulated that the offer applied only to *joint* schemes, which would be of value to the United States as well as to Britain. In other words, the British were being asked to desist from simple purchase and embark with the United States Government on a co-operative effort to exploit the American industrial potential.

The rewards of such an undertaking, as Purvis repeatedly pointed out, would be immense. On a short view, American rearmament might be a handicap to Britain, but it was also her opportunity. It was now possible to get the whole drive and impetus of the United States Government behind her schemes and so to secure supplies on a scale otherwise impossible. For instance, there were tentative negotiations afoot to harness important parts of the American automobile industry to the production of aircraft and aero engines. The head of the British Air Commission noted on 8th June that this offered a possibility of 'quantity production on a scale, and within a time, transcending what has been practicable in the United Kingdom'. Quantity production could not indeed begin until the late summer of 1941, but it could then be 'almost unlimited if the whole industrial and financial resources of the United States are applied to the task'. Clearly, if Britain could share in the fruits of such an expansion, one of her most crucial problems, the attainment of air supremacy, would be immensely simplified. And this was only one example of what American industry might be made to do.

But if the rewards of full collaboration were immense, the problems thus raised were formidable. One of the most intractable was the problem of types. 'Complementary' programmes, Washington's objective at this time, meant the production of common Anglo-American types of weapon. The difficulties in the way of agreement in such matters were obvious and acute. Another problem was the shortage of key items, such as machine tools and aero engines, vital alike to American rearmament, and to production on British account in the United States and production in the United Kingdom. The answer to this was allocation in Washington and a general system of priority. But this meant that in seeking to build up a reserve capacity in the United States Britain might be forced to slacken the pace of expansion at home. Nor were all the departments in London yet ready to present a full statement of their requirements from the United States without which there could be no solid foundations for joint programmes. Co-operation with the United States Government, in fact, entailed in many ways an onerous readjustment of British plans and procedures.

One other general consideration must be mentioned. British supply leaders in the United States had to think on several different levels of time and reality. One represented ground level, the solid reality of actual deliveries from the factory. The others involved various degrees of speculation as to the future. Even when requirements reached the point of expression in a definite contract with a manufacturer, the contract was still in the nature of a promise rather than performance. In attempting to estimate or 'programme' requirements for a year, two years or even three years ahead, the British and American officials were climbing the misty uplands of prophecy. There were two great initial and obvious uncertainties, the ability of American industry to produce the goods and the ability of the United Kingdom to pay. Thus, the series of major air programmes up to lend-lease, each pushing a little further into the future, were all highly speculative. They did not reach the stage of contracts, much less of deliveries, until the Lend-Lease Act cleared the way in March. It was not until the lend-lease appropriation of March 1941 ($2,054 million for aircraft) and the filing of requisitions under it for 11,800 aircraft that these earlier air programmes began to come to earth. Even at this date the aircraft industry still had a heavy backlog of British orders placed in the spring and summer of 1940. The other munitions programmes of this period were chained nearer to the ground; and two, the tank and shipbuilding programmes, attained the reality of firm contracts before the year ended. But here too the British Government had to wait till 1942 to see its plans bear fruit in the form of large quantities of weapons crossing the Atlantic. In the main it was rather as an earnest of the will of the United States to defeat the Axis than as supply programmes in the ordinary sense that these earlier schemes had value and significance.

(ii)

The Framing of British Munitions Programmes

THREE THOUSAND AIRCRAFT A MONTH

It was in July 1940 that these issues began to take shape. The month was marked not only by the launching of the vast air programme about to be described but also by the arrival of the Dewar Tank Mission and the first exchanges in the 'battle of the types', and by the beginning of negotiations over machine tools and aero engines. It witnessed also, appropriately, the arrival of a British Treasury representative, Sir Frederick Phillips, to begin with the American Treasury the joint discussions of British financial resources.

The problem of the air programme came to a head in a series of joint discussions on 23rd–24th July. These discussions were at a high level and involved the leading figures on both sides. In preparation for them the British Purchasing Commission was asked, several days in advance, to supply detailed information as to the total numbers of aircraft, engines and propellers covered by all existing Allied orders. The 23rd was a particularly heavy day for Purvis, who took the lead at one important meeting after another. Two were devoted to aircraft, one being the critical meeting, referred to below, on the disposal of the French aircraft engine contracts which the United Kingdom had taken over and which the American Air Force now sought to obtain. There was also a further important meeting, called by Mr. Donald Nelson, in which Purvis had to fight hard to retain some hold by the United Kingdom over its French machine-tool contracts. He has left his own account of all the meetings that occupied the whole of this and the next day.

The first meeting, on the 23rd, took place with Mr. William Knudsen and American Service chiefs. Purvis records that 'Mr. Knudsen suggested that we table U.K. orders as against U.S. orders or orders expected to be placed. . . . Arising out of this discussion it transpired that during the period on which the U.S. was calculating, i.e. up to the end of March 1942, the allocation would be of the order of 14,375 aeroplanes for the U.K., 19,092 for the U.S. Army and Navy'. A short memorandum, given to Purvis at the meeting, showed that the figure of 14,375 was arrived at by adding to existing British unfilled orders, and orders pending for a further 1,300 planes, the continued yield from British contracts from October 1941 to March 1942. Against this part of the memorandum Purvis scribbled on his copy the words 'freezing very worrying'. Against another sentence of the memorandum which read: 'It is understood and agreed that all planes, American and British, get priority on engines and that optional and unallocated engines are distributed in accordance with the above understanding', Purvis wrote, 'engines are taken from us'. The difficulties caused by this vague formula are referred to below.

Next day (24th) in a discussion with Knudsen the British representatives objected to the aircraft formula used in the memorandum on the ground that 'it froze British supplies at the high point to be attained under existing orders, or some 700 planes per month'. At this point Purvis had to leave the meeting to see Morgenthau, at the latter's request, for a hurried consultation before he went into a larger and more formal meeting to discuss the whole issue. At the private interview Morgenthau showed that he was himself concerned at the freezing of the British position and put forward a proposal that dramatically altered the course of the negotiations. He suggested as a way out, according to Purvis's record, that the United Kingdom should order 'a further 3,000 planes *a month* from January 1941 onwards, if they could be produced'. 'After a hurried consultation', Purvis noted, 'I decided to take this line.' Mr. Stettinius, in his account of the episode, described Purvis as being startled at being confronted with what seemed an almost astronomical figure. But it was one which he had already been turning over in his own mind and had even hinted at in earlier talks. He had, in fact, been given a lead in this direction a fortnight before in a letter from the Defence Advisory Commission on 11th July which accepted the principle of 'continued employment' and asked whether the British did not wish to earmark still further capacity for their future needs over and above that absorbed by their existing contracts.

Purvis was perfectly aware of the magnitude of the figure now suggested. It meant in all roughly 4,000 aircraft a month for the United Kingdom which, added to the 2,000 a month needed by the United States, meant a total of 72,000 planes in a year. At the moment the United Kingdom was getting some 250 planes a month from its contracts, which was a high proportion of the American output of combat planes at that time.[1] It was characteristic of him that he should seize with both hands the opportunity thus offered. He went straight from this interview to a meeting of American Secretaries of State, Stimson, Knox, Morgenthau, Knudsen and General Arnold, and put before them the new proposition. According to his own account of what happened he asked Knudsen

to estimate for the United Kingdom the cost of building up U.S. output for an additional 3,000 planes per month . . . as from January

---

[1] A memorandum amongst Purvis's papers dated 12th November 1940 noted that 'current output for U.S.G. does not exceed 100 *combat* planes per month'.

1941 onwards. Mr. Knudsen's first reaction was negative, but it was obvious that the Army and Navy representatives were enthusiastic for this type of approach.

Purvis was told it was necessary to know what types the United Kingdom wanted, and the meeting evidently expected that the answer would take some time to prepare. But the head of the British Air Commission was able to give the breakdown on the spot, which, as Purvis recorded, 'further improved the atmosphere of the meeting'. Finally, as Stettinius notes, Knudsen thought it could be done, but not before the end of 1942. 'The meeting', Purvis records, 'closed with a general expression of satisfaction.' It had not only taken this important decision on aircraft, but also agreed to set up a committee for the allocation of aircraft engines on a monthly basis, which shelved for the moment that difficult question.[1]

In London, Lord Beaverbrook acted no less swiftly by giving out the news in a special broadcast the same night. The British Purchasing Commission confirmed it in a communiqué, issued next day in New York, which gave the public some inkling of the progress which was being made. It indicated that British aircraft output had doubled in the past twelve months, whilst 'hundreds of planes per month' were being delivered from American factories to the United Kingdom.

The estimates Purvis asked for reached him in a letter from Knudsen dated 31st July. It gave data on materials and delivery dates for the additional 3,000 planes a month, as well as for the necessary engines and accessories. The cost of capital construction, involving at least fifty new factories, was put at $880 million; no precise estimate was given of the cost of the 3,000 aircraft a month, but it would obviously run into several billions of dollars. Since Knudsen judged the full scheme to be impracticable for a considerable time, he gave a second estimate which was in the nature of a first instalment. This was for a new output of 1,250 (later raised to 1,500) aircraft a month, the capital cost of which he put at $415 million.

The '3,000 a month' scheme, a bold and far-sighted proposal boldly and far-sightedly accepted, has no real parallel in the story of overseas supply. Its nearest rivals were the tank and shipbuilding programmes about to be described. Neither of these, however, was conceived on quite the same imaginative scale; and in general those responsible for the land and sea supplies consciously declined to follow the lead given them by the Ministry of Aircraft Production. Part of the reason for the difference of approach can doubtless be found in the temperament of Lord Beaverbrook, but it followed also

---

[1] It was agreed also to add a total of 1,820 aircraft to the British programme for the needs of Canada, Australia, South Africa and India.

from the peculiar importance attached to aircraft in British strategic plans. 'The Navy can lose us the war', the Prime Minister wrote in September, 'but only the Air Force can win it.'[1] Despite its apparent extravagance the aircraft scheme was more than justified in the end. The Royal Air Force never got 4,000 American aircraft a month or anything like that figure. Instead, they were to enjoy the comradeship in arms of American airmen, who were flying aircraft which otherwise might not have existed. Eventually, though not till 1943, the United States aircraft industry reached and surpassed the goal of 72,000 aircraft a year now set before it. And it was this British initiative that laid the foundations of the expansion.

THE DEFICIENCIES OF THE ARMY

Purvis had urged in June 1940 that if full advantage were to be taken of the Administration's offer of capital assistance for Allied projects it was 'more than ever essential that Allied purchases should be made on a programme basis similar to that for aeroplane production', and no longer by a trickle of uncorrelated requirements which gave no sort of basis for joint planning. The 'insurance' programme of 5th July provided to some extent an answer to these representations. By itself, however, it was considered to be far from adequate. Not only were two of the most important items, tanks and field artillery, still excluded, but the quantities asked for were smaller than the communications from London in May had seemed to imply. For example, British supply representatives had been working on a 'theoretical programme' which included a monthly output of 2,000 anti-aircraft and 1,000 anti-tank guns for Britain alone. The monthly requirements now indicated by London were 140 of the former and 300 of the latter. Purvis had 'assumed that the ultimate British requirements of small arms ammunition would be in the region of 300 million rounds a month'. London asked for 125 million only, and for 2,000 revolvers a month instead of the 20,000 which Purvis had suggested.

Hence continued pressure was exerted on the Ministry of Supply to transcend the concept of insurance and work out a single comprehensive programme on a much more ambitious scale, providing not merely for a reserve against the effects of bombing and for immediate requirements but also for all future requirements based on the approved scale of the Army and for wastage during the period of expansion. It was the firmly held view of British representatives in the United States that British needs should be overstated at this stage rather than understated, since there would be no second chance of getting British requirements included in the American production

---

[1] Churchill, op. cit., p. 405.

plan once it had taken shape. The same view was pressed with great force by Sir Arthur Salter, the chairman of the new North American Supply Committee in London, which had taken over some of the functions previously exercised by Monnet's committee. In a letter of 24th July to the Ministry of Supply, and in a memorandum presented a few days later to the Minister without Portfolio, who had been charged with a general oversight of North American supply questions, Salter urged that if the British acted promptly and decisively they would be able to share in the benefits of the enormous expansion being prepared in the United States. If, on the other hand, they hesitated or underestimated their needs they would find themselves excluded. The '3,000 a month' scheme was held up as a model of what could be achieved by foresight and courage. Early in July, Salter explained, the Americans had shown a desire to lay hands on some of the French aero engines taken over by Britain; but 'the bold decision of Lord Beaverbrook . . . (had) changed the whole perspective of the negotiation'; the engines were saved and Britain had secured first claim on the huge new capacity now to be created. The Army side of the picture was far less promising. If the difficulties which so far held up the placing of orders for tanks and field guns could be overcome, present plans would no doubt cover all that could be obtained by the middle of 1941. But the capital development started now would determine the quantity, and also the type, of equipment available in the latter part of 1941 and afterwards. Salter urged that plans should be laid on a much further-reaching basis, with an eye not merely to immediate defensive needs but to the possibility of offensive action in 1942 or later, and without too much speculation as to how far such plans could be realised. Financial prudence should be wholly cast aside. Heavy spending now would merely compel the Americans to face the inescapable problem of credit a little sooner. In short, 'a bold, comprehensive and imaginative statement of the whole of what we think we may wish to obtain . . . is an urgent and imperative necessity'.

The Ministry of Supply, however, was reluctant to go ahead as fast or as far as Salter and Purvis were suggesting. The planning of supply is, after all, normally governed by three factors: requirements, i.e. definitely formulated requirements related to a definite programme of Army expansion, estimates of what can in fact be produced, and cost, in relation to the financial resources available. The whole idea of proceeding without reference to any of these factors was alien to the official mind, and indeed to the first principles of administration. The Ministry of Supply had been instructed to provide for the equipment of fifty-five divisions by the end of 1941, with a margin for interim wastage and for loss of output due to bombing, and thereafter for their maintenance. It could not go ahead on its own initiative with orders for more material than this programme called for. Nor would it be justified in ordering material, most of which could not possibly be delivered until 1942, when the equipment of the Army should have been already completed. Moreover it feared, with good reason, that, if the Americans were encouraged to embark on really large-scale munitions production, the first result would be to endanger the immediate deliveries of machine tools and raw materials vital to the expansion of British output; and British output, it was held, must in all circumstances come first. Again, as to finance, suggestions that the faster the reserves were spent the better did not win general acceptance. On the contrary, the Ministry's case was that 'whatever view may be taken of the dollar problem in the future, we must seek to obtain the maximum advantage from our remaining resources, i.e. suitable munitions actually delivered rather than long-term investments from which we shall receive no return until it is too late'. The fine abandon of May and June was in fact replaced before long by a mood of relative caution: on 22nd August the War Cabinet gave general approval to a memorandum by the Chancellor of the Exchequer in which it was urged that dollar expenditure must be 'limited to vital needs, including munitions of war for delivery not too far ahead'.

However, although the more far-reaching implications of the Purvis–Salter arguments were not accepted, the 'insurance' programme was by no means the end of the story as far as the Ministry of Supply was concerned. Even if home production were not seriously curtailed by enemy air action, it was obvious that there would be large deficiencies in many important items of military equipment at the end of 1941; and the more closely the problems were studied the less likely did it seem that Britain could by her own unaided efforts equip the armies which she was proposing to raise and which she must raise if she was to have a chance of victory.

The worst of all these deficits would be tanks. After Sedan there could be no serious argument about the supreme importance of the tank in modern warfare, and the General Staff were now asking for over 10,000 by the end of 1941. But production of efficient types was only just getting under way, and though granted very high priority could not possibly be stepped up to this extent. Moreover, greater emphasis was now being laid on the fast cruiser type of tank suitable for mobile warfare. Of these the War Office required some 3,000 by the *middle* of 1941, of which United Kingdom factories could hope to provide little more than a third. Provisional approval was accordingly granted early in July 1940 to the purchase of 2,000 tanks of this class from the United States, at a cost which was reckoned to be in the neighbourhood of $120 million; and a special mission was sent out to make the necessary arrangements.

Among other requirements field artillery, which was expected to be the key to the rate of formation of infantry divisions, ranked very high. At one time during the French collapse Purvis had been told that the eventual order would probably run into several thousand guns. Here, however, home production was making great strides and it was thought that under favourable conditions new output could just keep up with the planned expansion of the Army. But this calculation allowed nothing for wastage in the field and nothing for the probable destruction of plant at home. Reserve capacity was still needed, therefore, in the United States. Moreover, once it was assured of substantial deliveries of field guns from America, the Ministry of Supply would have greater freedom of action at home, that is, would be able to switch United Kingdom plant over to other types of artillery if need arose. And, when all was said, Germany already possessed something like four times as many guns as Britain was hoping to make during 1941. The Ministry of Supply therefore indicated a probable requirement of 1,800 guns per annum, together with a monthly output of a million shells. At least equally urgent in the eyes of the War Office was the supply of anti-tank and anti-aircraft guns. For the latter especially there was a demand of indefinite magnitude. The need for these weapons was not related to any particular programme of army expansion; they could with advantage be placed about the world at many points. The Ministry specified a requirement of 6,000 anti-aircraft guns (3,000 heavy and 3,000 light), but this was only in order to keep its demands within reasonable bounds. There were also likely to be considerable deficits of light machine-guns and anti-tank rifles.

It was more and more apparent, however, that, after tanks, the worst shortage in the Army's equipment would be its basic weapon, the ordinary rifle. Hardly any provision had been made in pre-war plans for rifle manufacture, existing stocks being more or less adequate for the small land force then contemplated. These stocks had been depleted at Dunkirk and now vast new requirements had emerged with very little capacity available to meet them. New plants were being built in Australia as well as in Britain, but Commonwealth production could not possibly keep pace with the rate of recruitment which was now intended. There was, in fact, a grave danger that the whole programme of Army expansion would be thrown out of gear for lack of rifles for primary training. Hence there had been included in the 'insurance' programme a request for 400,000 rifles, a figure greatly in excess of the ordinary insurance margin; and the Ministry of Supply now contemplated asking for half a million more.

Thus by the beginning of August 1940, at the prompting of Purvis and Salter, the Ministry responsible for army supply had formulated a tentative programme of 'deficiency' orders in the United States, the cost of which was estimated at about $183 million. When this was added to the $120 million tank programme and other orders previously authorised which, including the July 'insurance' programme, amounted to $330 million, the total demand for army munitions from the United States now totalled in value $633 million—a considerable sum, but less than the *capital* cost alone of the air programme. Moreover, the demand was still not firm. The deficiency list was an estimate of probable requirements, not a definite programme of orders. In practice, as will appear later, tanks were the only items of army equipment, with some minor exceptions, on which real progress was made in the summer of 1940. In fact the statement made earlier in this chapter that the United States ceased after Dunkirk to be treated as a merely marginal source of supply needs to be qualified so far as the needs of the Army were concerned. The margin was very much broader than before, but in some ways the principles of planning remained the same. British industry was still to be the mainstay of the British Army. The Ministry of Supply turned to America for help in supplementing its own efforts and to provide a reserve against contingencies, relating its stated requirements closely to the actual, fairly short-term needs of the Army. It was not willing to be committed to vast programmes framed, as one departmental minute put it, 'more on the basis of what the Americans want than what we want'. The main arguments in support of this view have been outlined and they were cogent. But they did not perhaps fully allow for the extent to which the ordinary principles of planning must be modified by the overriding need for full collaboration with a foreign government. If complementary programmes were to be established in the United States it was inevitable that large concessions would have to be made to the American Government as to their nature, scale and timing. And unless complementary programmes were established Britain could expect few supplies. Moreover, such collaboration was not merely a practical necessity for Britain, but could hardly fail to draw the United States in the direction of alliance. The whole theme and burden of the case presented by Purvis and Salter was the need for joint action to develop to the maximum extent the American potential for munitions production, regardless of the use to which the munitions might ultimately be put. In the latter's words:

> The products will be available for our war effort, if by us—good; if by the Americans themselves—better still.

SIXTY MERCHANT SHIPS

In regard to warships and naval supplies generally the attitude of the Admiralty towards American purchases was even more reserved in 1940 than that of the Ministry of Supply. Its policy was summed up in a memorandum approved by the Controller in September:

> Apart from the destroyers which are now being transferred to us by the U.S.A., the demands which it has been and still is necessary for the Admiralty to make upon the resources of the American continent for war supplies of various kinds are, in relation to the demands of the Ministry of Supply and the Ministry of Aircraft Production, of very small dimensions. . . . The most important factor is that, in the main, it has been possible to carry out in this country the necessary programmes of new construction . . . and in great measure to produce in this country the additional armaments, stores and equipment which the increasing Fleet requires.

There was, however, a major exception to this policy—merchant ships, for the construction of which the Admiralty had been responsible since February 1940. In the First World War the United States, despite a late but important contribution in shipbuilding, did not have enough ships to meet their own needs and had to be helped out by the United Kingdom. Despite this, in the years before 1939 no provision had been made for the building of merchant ships in the United States in any new emergency. In addition to the other factors which deterred British planners from relying on American supply, there were over-optimistic assumptions about war-time shipping needs. Nor did the outbreak of war bring any real change of plan, though during the first twelve months the Ministry of Shipping acquired some forty second-hand ships in the United States market. The German occupation of Europe brought under British control a large part of the French, Dutch, Norwegian and Danish merchant fleets. But with its sequel, the entry of Italy into the war, it meant the loss of near sources of supply, the diversion and lengthening of shipping routes, and military operations in distant theatres of war. The enemy, from his new air and U-boat bases on the Atlantic coast and in the Mediterranean, began to launch a very much more formidable attack on Britain's sea communications. In the three months June–August 1940 well over a million gross tons of British, Allied and neutral shipping were lost through enemy action. New construction at home could not possibly make good such enormous losses. The British shipbuilding industry, which had suffered severe and continuous depression throughout the inter-war years, was proving more difficult to expand than any other war industry. It had, moreover, to devote more than half of its resources to the construction of warships. The output of merchant ships from United Kingdom yards was then running at less than a million tons a year, and there was little chance that this rate could be more than fractionally improved upon. Thus in default of a large increment from overseas sources the tonnage available for the provisioning of the United Kingdom was likely to diminish at a catastrophic pace.

The Government therefore turned of necessity to North America. Further purchases of old ships were contemplated, but the market was already contracting, and this particular remedy could be no more than a temporary palliative. To redress the balance permanently it was clearly necessary to place large orders for new ships in Canada or the United States or both. Accordingly, on 22nd August 1940, the Admiralty asked the British Purchasing Commission to ascertain the prospects of building plain cargo ships of 10,000 tons deadweight in North America, if possible at a rate of sixty a year.

The reply was not encouraging, so far as the United States were concerned. Once again British would-be purchasers found themselves in competition with the United States defence programme, and this time with that part of it which was being most vigorously pressed. Under a recent Act of Congress a sum of $4 billion had been set aside to provide for a seventy per cent. expansion of the United States Navy. Plans had been laid for the construction of 138 warships and a large number of contracts had already been let. Meanwhile the Maritime Commission, a Government agency charged with the rehabilitation of the American shipping and shipbuilding industries, was pressing on with its 1938 programme, which called for the construction of fifty merchant ships a year. Building berths were therefore filling up fast and there was little or no room in established shipyards for the construction of ships to British order.

However, a parallel approach through the United States Embassy in London proved rather more fruitful. As a result of the Ambassador's intervention, the Maritime Commission agreed to 'hold off to let us in, provided we act quickly', and indicated certain American shipyards as probably available. The Admiralty therefore decided to send out a special mission, headed by a prominent British shipbuilder, Mr. R. C. Thompson, to see what could be done. Application was made to the Treasury for authority to order sixty ships at an estimated cost of $80 million. The War Cabinet approved an order of thirty ships with a possible thirty to follow. The full programme was confirmed early in November.

This was without doubt one of the most momentous supply decisions of the whole war. It led to the signature on 20th December 1940 of contracts with the Todd-Bath and Todd-California Shipbuilding Corporation for two brand-new shipyards and a total of sixty 10,000-ton cargo ships. There thus began, on British initiative and with British money, an enterprise—associated especially with the name of Mr. Henry J. Kaiser—which became perhaps the most remarkable feature of the American war effort. The quantity of shipping directly involved was comparatively small—no more than a third of the ton-

nage built in the United Kingdom during 1942. As usual the significance of the British contracts lay not so much in the amount of
material actually supplied as in the impetus which they gave to the
development of the American potential. They were in fact the first
and one of the most important steps in the process which raised the
output of merchant ships in the United States from little over half a
million deadweight tons in 1940 to the colossal figure of 19 million
tons in 1943. During 1942 and the early part of 1943 shipping losses
rose to alarming heights. But the United States had to make up
their own deficit in shipping before they could make a really significant addition to British shipping in the second half of 1943.

(iii)

British versus American Types

THE PROBLEM

The summer of 1940 thus saw the formulation of a vast British aircraft programme and of considerable programmes of ships, tanks and
other classes of army equipment. But before these programmes could
be well and truly launched there was one very thorny question to be
cleared up—the problem of types. Not much need be said about it
here since it is dealt with in detail in *Studies of Overseas Supply*. The
initial assumption was that munitions supplies obtained from the
United States would have to be American types. There were obvious
disadvantages, however, in equipping the British Army and Air Force
with mixed types. Thus the new British supply proposals in July—the
'insurance' requirements for ground forces, and the scheme for
3,000 additional aircraft per month—provided for British types of
arms. They were based on two assumptions, both of which proved to
be untenable. One was that American firms would be willing to
produce British types of tanks, aircraft and other arms; the other was
that the American Government would authorise and facilitate such
production. The more experienced American firms were already
working on, or hoping to obtain, American Army contracts for
American types. To undertake the production of British types they
would have to change over their production lines, to retool and to
forgo valuable American contracts, and perhaps strain the good will
of the American War Department. The latter had two strong objections against permitting American firms to produce foreign types.
One was the point of security. Some American firms were already
tied up with orders for French types which were not very useful either
to the British or the American Army. An even stronger objection was
the belief in American Army circles that American types were as

good as, perhaps even better than, British types. Both sides were in full agreement that standardisation was necessary if American mass-production techniques were to be used to full advantage. Each side stood to gain greatly if its own types could be chosen as the basis for standardisation.

The debate on types had hardly begun when it became clear that the War Department was already committed in most cases to standardisation of American types of the principal arms, notably tanks and aircraft. The belief in London that British types of tanks and aircraft, such as the Spitfire, which were fully proven in battle, were superior to any known American types was natural enough. But in order to convince the War Department British models had to be demonstrated in the United States and this proved very difficult to arrange. Moreover part of the argument for British types was based on designs which in certain cases were not yet fully tested, such as the Stirling bomber. Arrangements to produce the Stirling in Canada were already under way and it was hoped to fix on the Stirling, instead of the American B.24 (the Liberator), as the type of heavy bomber to be supplied from the United States. In October, however, it was decided that if a British-type heavy bomber was to be produced in the United States it must be the Halifax rather than the Stirling. For trials in that month had shown that the Halifax was 'immensely superior in performance' to the Stirling.

On the other hand some of the objections to American types were based on inadequate or out-of-date technical data. The United States War Department was testing out new models of tanks and aircraft of which details had not yet reached London. Thus a British Tank Mission, composed of experts in the field of tank production, design and use, which witnessed at the end of July the trials of the new American M.3 tank (known later as the General Lee), reported very favourably and urged its adoption. It reported also, as Purvis had done earlier, that the War Department was already committed to the manufacture of the M.3. Faced with the dilemma of either placing an order for the American model or of forgoing any early supply of tanks from the United States the British Government decided on 22nd August to place an initial order for 1,500 tanks. Once agreement was reached on the basic design it was easy for the British tank experts to secure the essential changes in the fighting compartment of the M.3 which British battle experience had shown to be necessary. From this point onwards tank design in the United States moved rapidly towards a common type involving both British and American features.[1]

Much the same formula—American types with British improve-

---

[1] See *Studies of Overseas Supply*, Chapter I.

ments—was applied to aircraft. The British improvements applied
particularly to armour and armament, to power-driven turrets and
to self-sealing tanks. Standardisation involved such a host of technical details that it could only be secured gradually and as a result
of much patient work on both sides. This process was helped greatly
by the setting up in September 1940 of the Joint Aircraft Committee
(of which more later) with standardisation as one of its main
objectives.[1]

In pressing for modifications British air experts were greatly helped
by two developments in August and September which made a profound impression in official circles in the United States. One was the
successful fight put up by the R.A.F. in the Battle of Britain. This, as
a British representative noted in September, 'has done more to convince them that at least some of our ideas are sound than all arguments, and the change of attitude during the last week or so is
noteworthy'. The second development was the disclosure of the
scientific and technical advances, particularly in radar and armament, that had done so much to win victory in the air over Dunkirk
and Britain. The disclosure was made at the end of August and early
in September 1940 by the members of a British Scientific Mission,
led by Sir Henry Tizard.[2] It was made in the most explicit terms,
with much technical detail; specimens of the apparatus in use, or
prototypes, were brought by the Mission. Until the arrival of this
body, London was told, the American side 'fully believed that they
had more to give than to receive'. London was urged to take advantage of this new attitude so that development of the standardised
programme should proceed jointly. British requirements should be
introduced in the design and development stage. 'If they are not
introduced at this point they never will be.' To ensure this, British
technical and Air Staff representatives should work closely and continuously with their American opposite numbers. The possibility of
such an arrangement had been broached by Purvis in a note to
Morgenthau on 5th August. It was mooted again in the technical
talks and was welcomed on the American side.

For the basic weapons of British armies in the field, such as rifles,
anti-tank guns and field artillery, there were very strong arguments
against the introduction of American types, since this involved too
many complications and risks. It would mean a whole series of
separate stocks and services: ammunition, accessories, spare parts,
tools and maintenance staffs. Moreover, British production of many
weapons was advancing fast and steps had been taken to secure production of a number of British types in Canada and Australia.

---

[1] On the Joint Aircraft Committee see pp. 195, 300–01.
[2] See *Studies of Overseas Supply*, Chapter VIII.

In the long run the argument which was decisive was not so much the virtues of particular types, but the fact that the production of the now very large British requirements required capital expenditure on such a scale that only the United States Government could provide the funds. And the American Government was not ready to provide them except for the production of types that would be used by the armed forces of the United States. At an important meeting on 24th August, Secretary Morgenthau offered to finance the production of British requirements if they were for 'common types', that is types which the United States Army had adopted or could adopt. To take full advantage of this offer it was necessary to undertake high-level negotiations between the two Governments. In reporting the offer to London, Purvis called for the despatch (1) of additional technical experts able to discuss the merits of various weapons and (2) of 'some person fully acquainted with . . . and able to discuss with competence the broad general outline of the United Kingdom programme'.

It had for some time been clear that British requirements from the United States were now on such a scale that they could no longer be dealt with on the commercial plane but only by direct negotiations between the British and American Governments. What seemed to be needed was a high-level mission, headed by some person having the full confidence of the War Cabinet and including financial advisers, high officers of the General and Air Staffs and a series of technical experts able to judge, from the producer and user points of view, the merits of each of the main types of weapons. Instead, there was a series of uncorrelated expedients. A production expert paid a brief visit in July. Then an *ad hoc* mission arrived to deal, very successfully, with the isolated question of tanks. In August a military mission appeared on the scene, but without any member with special knowledge either of the weapons whose merits it was to expound or of general operational requirements. This body was unfortunate in being the last straw which caused an outburst of American irritation at so many separate and overlapping missions. Meanwhile there had been the entirely separate financial discussion between Mr. Morgenthau and Sir Frederick Phillips.[1] And Purvis had been left to bear the brunt of a task which far exceeded in scope and importance anything imagined at the time of his appointment and for which he possessed neither the necessary fullness of authority nor the necessary expert advice.

Thus whilst progress had been made on tanks little or none had been made on army ordnance. There was deadlock on the question of types and the Americans were going ahead with their own programmes. By the end of August the 'insurance' programme was

---

[1] See Chapter VII.

nearly two months old, but few orders had been placed thereunder or were likely to be placed. Apart from the pistols and sub-machine guns already in production before Dunkirk, the only complete new army weapons ordered from the United States were 500 American-type anti-tank guns, accepted by the War Office as a stop-gap solution to one of its most pressing problems. Agreement on common types of ordnance was as far away as ever.

The request made by Purvis for 'some person' to negotiate was met promptly in London by the sending of Sir Walter Layton (afterwards Lord Layton), Director-General of Programmes in the Ministry of Supply. His task was defined as being

> to give to the United States Administration and the Defence Advisory Commission a general picture of our supply position and requirements and to supplement by way of explanation in detail the orders which have already been authorised; to consider and report on the general position of the manufacture of munitions in the United States and on the relation between the British Purchasing Commission and the Defence Advisory Commission; to make any general recommenda-tion which he thinks desirable as to our policy and procedure with regard to supplies from North America in future . . . and to take such current and urgent decisions as are necessary concerning negotia-tions which are at present in progress. . . .

He was not given plenary powers, for the War Office declined to allow a civilian to commit it to the acceptance of foreign weapons, even though he would have at his disposal the advice of the army officers already in the United States; weapons of American design could be ordered only with the explicit concurrence of the Army Council. Nor was he empowered to accept financial commitments, over and above those previously authorised, without reference back for Treasury approval.

The functions of the new emissary, who arrived in Washington on 22nd September 1940, were nevertheless wide. They covered war production, and also the British administrative arrangements in the United States. The greater part of the Mission's two and a half months' stay, however, was devoted to an effort to clear up the tangle which had arisen over army ordnance.

Conversations early in October led to the submission on the 11th of a full memorandum on army ordnance requirements. The memo-randum followed fairly closely the list of requirements which had been tentatively put forward by the Ministry of Supply in August, but they were now put forward as definite requests. The main emphasis was laid on field guns (1,800); tank guns (2,250) for tanks built in Britain, together with the 3,000 needed to match the British tank programme in the United States; anti-tank equipments (3,000, of which 1,000 should be the new 6-pounder); anti-aircraft guns (a minimum of 1,600 heavy and 1,800 light); and rifles (one million).

This considerable programme, backed as it was by a full statement of the reasons for the quantities mentioned, was a great improvement on the previous accumulation of uncorrelated, unexplained and largely tentative requisitions. The intractable problem of types, however, which had been in abeyance since the end of August, was not brought much nearer to solution. Apart from several British weapons which the United States Government was still considering[1] the British Government had now finally to make up its mind whether it would accept American-type weapons or continue to press for the manufacture of British types, even if it had thereby to forgo the advantage of standardisation.

The financial arguments in favour of the former course were very strong. The United Kingdom was now not far from the end of its financial tether as regards dollar expenditure and acceptance of the American offer of capital assistance for joint schemes would at least lengthen the tether until after the elections, when it hoped to be cut loose altogether. The Treasury had therefore impressed on Layton the very great importance of securing the extension of the Reconstruction Finance Corporation scheme, so far applied only to tank engines, on the widest possible front. The United States Government was willing and eager to help in this way, but not, as Secretary Morgenthau once again made clear, to the extent of paying for plants which it could not use itself.

On the other hand the military arguments against the acceptance of American-type field guns and rifles for the British Army were maintained. On 10th October Layton was instructed to order 25-pounder guns of British type—in preference to American 105-mm. guns—even if the United Kingdom had to pay the whole initial cost of development in the United States.[2] Even stronger was the case for the manufacture of the ·303-inch rifle. American-calibre ·30-inch rifles, if they could be obtained, were desired for issue to the Home Guard and other static units; but for the main field army rifles of the standard British calibre were essential. Layton confined his arguments for the production in the United States of British types to the quantities necessary to make good specific deficiencies in the British programme and insurance against a serious loss of output as a result of enemy action.

The nature of the response was for some weeks in doubt. Since the Battle of Britain the fear of a British collapse had lost much of its

---

[1] These were the Bofors and Oerlikon anti-aircraft guns, and the British 6-pounder tank guns and 4·5-inch medium guns, all of which the United States Services later adopted.

[2] Canada, however, was to remain the sole North American source for the supply of 25-pounder field guns. See pp. 187–8 and *Studies of Overseas Supply*, Chapter I.

force as a deterrent to the setting-up of plants for purely British weapons. The main argument now was that there simply was not room for separate British and American programmes. So long as the United States Government persisted in its attempt to superimpose rearmament upon a flourishing peace-time economy, there was only a small segment of American industry that could be used for munitions production; and the better part (in both senses) of this segment had already been earmarked for the American defence programme. If a large new programme of production were to be launched on British account, wholly new plants would have to be erected. But this meant complete new sets of machine tools, and machine tools were the 'bottleneck' of rearmament. Owing largely to the demands of British industry, the machine-tool situation was likely to remain critical for at least fifteen months. The War Department, therefore, while prepared to allow Britain to share in the output of its own plants, which would require relatively little additional tooling for the purpose, remained firmly opposed to the creation of plants for Britain's sole use. Layton had tried in vain to persuade the Americans that such plants, by 'broadening the base' of American armaments production, would be of real value to the United States as well as to Britain, despite the difference of types.

As a result the negotiations over the army ordnance programme submitted on 11th October followed a tortuous and inconsistent course. A few days later Purvis learnt unofficially that the Chief of Staff, General Marshall, was prepared to see it approved, practically intact. Yet within twenty-four hours, while Layton was away in Canada, Purvis was told by officers of the War Department that no orders would be allowed for British-type ordnance, except medium artillery. This was naturally not accepted as final, and on 22nd October Layton had an interview with Mr. Stimson and the army leaders, at which British claims were again pressed. The tone of this meeting was not particularly encouraging; with regard to field artillery, for example, it was made clear that, apart altogether from the problem of types, the provision of 1,800 guns in 1941 was quite out of the question—the Americans were expecting no more than 1,000 from their own orders. But on the following day the Americans put forward a new and startling proposal which was designed to cut through the whole tangle at a single stroke.

The main strands in the tangle were, to recapitulate, as follows. The Americans desired to help Britain. They desired also to see the war potential of the United States developed further and faster than their own plans allowed. Separate facilities for British-type weapons would not, in their view, contribute to this end, and would be exceedingly wasteful of machine tools. On the other hand, they had now nearly completed the placing of contracts under their own programme, and in so doing had provided for capacity considerably greater than was needed for the production orders which they could afford with existing appropriations. If the British could be induced to share in this expansion, the capacity could be more economically employed, and they could to a great extent be given priorities on deliveries. On the other hand again, they now understood, as a result of the Layton Mission, not only the real urgency of Britain's needs, but also the real difficulty of incorporating alien weapons into the equipment of her main forces. They therefore now proposed that the United States should provide Britain with United States type equipment for a complete force of ten divisions, which could be raised, trained and maintained in the field quite separately from the rest of the British Army.

This scheme was not entirely new. It was in fact a revival of a proposal tentatively submitted by Purvis in June, before the arrival of the 'insurance' programme. That proposal, however, had never been seriously considered by the British Government, if indeed it had ever been brought to its notice, and it was quite outside Layton's terms of reference. He therefore approached it with due caution. Having secured an interview with Mr. Stimson himself on 24th October, he asked for an assurance that it would be possible to produce the amounts of material required by the dates indicated, i.e. mostly before the end of 1941, and that, as the new force would be entirely dependent on American supplies, the United States would guarantee its maintenance, granting priority of allocation where necessary. Mr. Stimson asked his Chief of Staff, who was present, whether it would be possible to allocate to the British nearly the whole new output of United States defence plants, while American divisions were still equipped with old weapons. General Marshall said it would. Mr. Stimson then authorised Layton to submit the proposal to London. This was done on the following day, in an Embassy cable which was to be brought to the notice of the Prime Minister.

The new offer was regarded as supplementary to, not a substitute for, the original British programme of insurance and deficiency requirements related to the formation of fifty-five divisions at home (hereafter known as the Army 'A' programme to distinguish it from the 'B' or ten-division programme). On the contrary, having once secured Britain's assistance in the solution of their own difficulties in this way, the Americans let it be understood that they would be much more accommodating in their attitude to earlier British requests. The production of 25-pounder guns in the United States would still not be possible; no actual veto was applied, but machine tools could not be made available for this purpose until mid-summer 1941, so that no guns could be delivered before the autumn of 1942. The

British were therefore compelled to rely after all upon Canadian manufacture which promised an earlier start than this; the Americans offered to help by way of sub-contracting. Nor was there any chance of 3·7-inch anti-aircraft guns within two years. But orders were sanctioned for the 4·5-inch medium gun, which the Americans were probably going to adopt themselves; also for 2,250 2-pounder tank guns, and for 1,000 6-pounder anti-tank equipments. For ·303-inch rifles the British were to be allowed to take over and lease to the Remington Company certain disused plant in the United States Government arsenal at Rock Island. In short, the British Army had now a prospect of securing a fair proportion of its ordnance requirements from the United States, though it would have to resign itself to supplementing from Canada alone its supply of 25-pounders, Bren guns, anti-tank rifles and perhaps Bofors guns.

Although the ten-division offer was very far from satisfying what the British Government and its representatives in Washington considered their most important immediate needs, it was very welcome to them. Sir Walter Layton, with the full support of the authorities at home, did much to promote the ten-division plan as a means of educating and developing American munitions-making capacity. In its final form the plan proved wholly acceptable to the General Staff and the Ministry of Supply provided the Americans would guarantee to supply all the equipment required, including ammunition, accessories and equipment, and provided also that the new programme would not be allowed to interfere with the early delivery of equipment requisitioned under the 'A' programme, which was no less urgent than before. It was clearly understood that the new 'B' programme was one half of a compromise, and that acceptance was a condition precedent to the placing of orders for British-type weapons. But what chiefly influenced the British Government in favour of the offer were its wider political and military implications. The significant question was now posed—who was going to man the ten additional divisions? Not Great Britain, whose manpower resources would be fully extended by the formation of the divisions already planned. Perhaps, in part, the European allies, or the Dominions or the Colonies or the Dutch East Indies—or perhaps the United States themselves? From the United States Government's point of view the great merit of the plan was that it would prepare the ground for a much larger American army in case of need. And on a long view this was quite as much a British as an American interest. The Prime Minister therefore signified his enthusiastic assent in a personal telegram to Sir Walter Layton on 28th October: 'This is splendid. You should accept at once'.

In the much more auspicious atmosphere now prevailing, progress seemed at last to be possible. On 1st November Mr. Stimson confirmed that the British Purchasing Commission could now go ahead with the placing of orders under both the 'A' and the 'B' programmes. Though it would still be necessary to act through the existing procedure (reports of preliminary negotiations, etc.) this, it was thought, should be a mere formality, since the Defence Advisory Commission as well as the War Department had approved the concessions.

This, however, was not the end of controversy over types of weapons. For the new ten-division programme there was in most cases little difficulty; the 105-mm. field gun, the ·30-inch rifle, the 60-mm. and 81-mm. mortars, the 37-mm. anti-tank and anti-aircraft weapons were close enough equivalents of standard British Army equipments to be accepted without cavil. But the British 5·5-inch close-support gun, the Bren gun, the Universal carrier and the scout car had no real counterpart in the American Army; on some of these points, despite the view shared by Layton and the Ministry of Supply that Britain must take what she could get and for diplomatic reasons must at all costs 'avoid a rigid rejection of the types offered', the War Office remained adamant, insisting that equipment supplied from America 'must fulfil minimum military requirements'. The ensuing discussions, however, were largely academic, for, as will be seen later, the ten-division programme never took shape as a major contribution to British supply.

Nor did the approval given in principle to the 'A' programme imply an unqualified agreement to manufacture weapons of British design. On the contrary, 'it took the rather curious form of a categorical announcement that apart from items already clear, which include medium guns, orders will only be permitted henceforth for items of equipment identical with United States models, with three exceptions'. These were: one million ·303-inch rifles; 2,250 2-pounder tank guns, without ammunition (large amounts of armour-piercing shot were already on order); and 1,000 2-pounder anti-tank equipments, also without ammunition. In themselves, Layton felt that these reservations 'need not be taken too tragically'. They were in fact merely the negative aspect of the positive concessions previously reported. The British Government had already abandoned hope of 25-pounders, and the exceptions specified took care of most of their other really urgent needs. In point of fact, however, even these limited concessions were by no means firm. The efforts of the British Purchasing Commission to place actual contracts for British-type tank and anti-tank guns broke down early in the new year. In the event the ·303-inch rifle was the only complete 'non-common' weapon of any importance to be made for Britain in the United States; and even in this case negotiations dragged on for several more months before a conclusion was reached.

None the less, from the end of October 1940 the 'battle of the types' begins to fade out of the foreground of the picture. As a result of the compromise then adopted the high feeling which the controversy had engendered began to die down. Henceforward the British avoided raising the issue of general principle, and, as was forecast by Sir Walter Layton, a situation was gradually created in which individual weapons could be judged on their merits at the technical level. Negotiations over the 3·7-inch anti-aircraft gun continued throughout the early part of 1941, but ended in failure so far as the United States were concerned, in spite of an equipment with a gun's crew being sent over for demonstration purposes. British additional supplies were ultimately met instead from Canada. On the other hand the Oerlikon gun was adopted by the Americans in November, the Bofors somewhat later and a version of the 6-pounder later still.[1] But the course of the controversy had already determined the main lines of American munitions supply for the remainder of the war. Britain was to receive vast quantities of American-built aircraft and tanks, but not of guns, except for a number of American type more especially for tanks and self-propelled guns.

(iv)

The Beginnings of Combination

Meanwhile, despite delays in translating programmes into production, important advances were being made in other directions towards Anglo-American combination. One was the disclosure of secret information, particularly of strategic and operational data on the progress of the war in the air and of scientific and technical advances. A second was the launching of the scheme for the training of British pilots in the United States. Thirdly, there were the important first steps towards the sharing out by agreement, or assignment as it was later called, of scarce equipment.

DISCLOSURE OF INFORMATION

A brief reference to the Scientific and Technical Mission led by Sir Henry Tizard must be made here, because of its important immediate effect on Anglo-American supply relations.[2] The Tizard Mission, which arrived in Washington at the end of September 1940, covered the whole field of weapons, munitions, equipment and materials.

---

[1] For the remarkable history of Oerlikon production see *Studies of Overseas Supply* Chapter I.

[2] A fuller account is given in *Studies of Overseas Supply*, Chapter VIII.

Exchanges of relatively minor importance had been made before. They were involved, for example, in the release of American types of aircraft, in return for which valuable data were given on performance under combat conditions. On June 13th the complete designs and specifications of the British Rolls-Royce Merlin engine were handed over to the President, leaving the rights of the Rolls-Royce and Handley Page firms for 'subsequent determination and adjustment between the two countries'. A letter from the Ambassador to the Secretary of the Treasury confirmed the informal arrangements and licensed him on behalf of the United States Government, 'upon such future payments as it wishes and consents to make to His Majesty's Government', to use the patents and designs and to manufacture the engine and indemnified the American Government against any claim. Two of the Merlin engines had been sent over on loan in May for examination by American engineers, and a team of Rolls-Royce technicians was sent later to assist in the production of the engine by the Packard Company.

But the riches now brought by the Tizard Mission made anything that had gone before seem insignificant. They included not merely devices like the British power-driven turrets, which American observers had seen, but all the most secret British anti-aircraft and anti-submarine devices and methods. The Mission brought over the radar devices that were winning the Battle of Britain and were to play a decisive part in the air war over Germany. Most important of all was the magnetron valve, which became the basis for the manufacture of ten-centimetre radar sets in the United States, and later of the proximity fuse. On the American side valuable information on radar and other matters was given in exchange. At the end of September the Sperry bombsight was released, and forty sights provided from stock. At the same time, the Tizard Mission was given full reports on American tests of ·50-calibre aircraft guns. In return the full data on tests of British lower-calibre guns were despatched at once from London by flying-boat.

On the side of strategy, although American consent to full staff talks had not yet been given, discussions were held in London in August 1940, disguised as the meetings of a Committee on the Standardisation of Arms, between the British Chiefs of Staff and an American military mission consisting of Admiral Ghormley, the United States Naval Attaché in London, General Strong of the War Department and General Emmons of the Army Air Corps. The British Government had resolved on a degree of frankness with the American that was probably unprecedented in the relations between a belligerent and a neutral state; and the talks ranged over the whole field of war strategy. Unfortunately, however, the American Mission had no contact with the supply departments, and returned home with imperfect knowledge of the progress being made on the production side. On some points, indeed, it had formed definitely erroneous impressions which took some time and effort to dispel. The deficiency was largely made good by Layton. In order to fulfil his primary task of explaining the background to British requirements, he had been authorised to communicate British supply plans freely to a limited circle within the Administration; and a memorandum which he submitted to Morgenthau on 2nd October followed very closely the terms of a report presented by the Minister of Supply a few weeks earlier to the British War Cabinet itself.

About the same time a flare-up in Washington showed that it was not enough to share scientific secrets, to disclose the supply position and to discuss strategy in general terms. It had become necessary for the British Government to reveal, in the most explicit detail, strategic and operational secrets of the highest importance. There was anxiety in Washington as to the effect of air-raids on British aircraft production. Fear that the planes bought from the United States might be destroyed in air-raids was mingled with concern as to the fate of American machine tools housed in British factories. On an urgent message from Washington, London gave at once (26th September) highly secret data on the effect of the air-raids. The damage done to aircraft factories was less than the loss of time due to the raids; very few machine tools were damaged—only 1,200 out of a total of 'several hundred thousand', and all could be repaired.

On the same day, serious doubt was thrown from quite a different angle on the British need for aero engines and aircraft. The American Military Mission had just come back with a story, seemingly backed with figures, of a serious deficit in the supply of pilots. Mr. C. D. Howe, the Canadian Minister of Munitions and Supply, came to the office of Secretary Morgenthau on 26th September 'for a brief call' and was met with an unexpected barrage. The Secretary of the Treasury was just back from a meeting where the Army's bombshell had been exploded. Howe wrote, late that night, a long letter to Purvis:

> He surprised me very much by saying that U.S. observers in the United Kingdom have reported that the Canadian Air Training Plan is a failure, that it is short of aeroplanes, that its output is below schedule; that consequently Britain will be short of pilots; thus it is useless to ship more aeroplanes from the U.S.A.

Hurried talks followed between Purvis and Morgenthau; and between Layton and the President. But the story was already spreading. To kill it the Canadian Minister took what Lord Lothian called 'a gallant act'. He risked the anger of the Canadian Press, which had been refused the data, by revealing in a British Purchasing

Commission press release the monthly output of pilots from the British Commonwealth Air Training Plan. It still remained necessary to answer the requests of the President and Morgenthau for information as to the course of the Battle of Britain, including the output and losses of pilots and aircraft. Figures on output were requested for the next nine months. Lord Beaverbrook gave the answers next day, for the eye only of the President and the Secretaries of the Army and Navy and Treasury. On 27th September there were just over 500 more aircraft of the six principal operational types than when the air battles began on 10th May. More aircraft than pilots had been lost, since over Britain pilots often escaped by parachute. The output of pilots from the air schools of Britain and the Dominions was increasing very fast. It would be doubled in the first few months of 1941, and more than trebled in the next few months. On the other hand, the destruction of several aircraft factories meant a drop in production. Therefore, the message concluded, 'continuing and increasing flow of aircraft from the U.S.A. is completely essential to pilot programme in Great Britain'. In order to obtain a still clearer view of operations, the Administration then made an urgent request through Purvis and the Ambassador that the Chief of the British Air Staff should come in person so that the Administration could adjust its aid still more closely to British needs. At that moment (9th October) large new British aircraft orders were under negotiation and had to be fitted in with the programme of the American Army. There still seemed a chance for British types. In any case, the incorporation of British fighting experience into American types was a matter of great importance, and in this a visit by the Chief of the Air Staff might have a decisive effect. As he could not be spared from the air battle, it was finally arranged to send the Director of Plans at the Air Ministry. Transport difficulties delayed his arrival until after the election.[1]

TRAINING OF PILOTS IN THE UNITED STATES

Further important evidence of the growing Anglo-American combination on the air side was the scheme, broached in September 1940, but not under way until 1941, for the training of large numbers of British aircrews in the United States. The release issued on 27th September by Mr. C. D. Howe showed that the British Commonwealth Air Training Plan was well ahead of schedule in all respects—number of aerodromes, schools open, and output of pilots. The main trouble was trainer aircraft; of 5,000 called for by the

---

[1] He took part not only in aircraft supply discussions but also represented the United Kingdom in the staff talks in Washington in December on air defences in the Far East and remained for the General Staff discussion that began at the end of January 1941. See below, pp. 308–12.

plan at its peak only 895 had so far been obtained. Because of the situation in Europe the United Kingdom had been unable to furnish its full quota of trainers. The deficit had been made up, in part, by purchase in the United States and from Canada's own production. The large new scheme for pilot training in the United States accentuated this supply difficulty. But the scheme was considered to be even more important than the supply of combat aircraft. Acting for the Air Ministry, at its express request, Purvis outlined the scheme to Morgenthau on 24th September. The plans called for the training in the United States of 4,000 British or Dominion pilots a year. Flying training (without combat subjects) was to be done at civilian schools whose agreement had been obtained at an earlier meeting in New York.[1] The British Government was to find the capital cost, pay for the training, and provide the elementary trainers needed, 328 machines. But it could not provide the advanced trainers which the scheme would require. The hope of getting them from the United States was dashed by the discovery that the Army and Navy had only 700 of these machines, and were in the process of doubling their own yearly output of pilots from 600 to 1,200. The British, in fact, had just been approached by Morgenthau with the proposal that the United Kingdom should release 300 of the Harvard trainers about to be delivered from the British contracts in the United States. These, however, were earmarked for the Air Training Plan in Canada and New Zealand. As no progress at all was being made with the scheme, the Air Ministry decided, in mid-October, to make Purvis its 'sole official intermediary' on this matter with the President and Morgenthau. But he could make little headway, partly because of the nearness of the November election, but mainly because of the shortage of trainers.

The shortage of dollars also retarded the scheme. Even the Lend-Lease Act could not easily remove this difficulty. The President, in March 1941, gave instructions that help was to be given in providing training for British pilots in the United States.[2] Requisitions were submitted in April, at the suggestion of Harry Hopkins, covering the cost of six complete air schools to train 1,200 student pilots. It was ruled however in September, partly on legal but also on political grounds, that the direct costs of the students (food, pay, lodging and tuition) involving $10 million could not be met under lend-lease.

---

[1] The meeting was called on 28th August by the Under-Secretary of State for Air, Captain H. H. Balfour, who also made the preliminary approach to the President, Morgenthau and Hopkins.

[2] See below, p. 316. One of the proposals submitted in April 1941 was for the expansion of the Refresher Training Schools by doubling the size of the three existing schools and forming a fourth. These schools, which had been opened a few months earlier, trained American civilian pilots for service with the R.A.F. Subsequent offers of flying training facilities by the United States Army and Navy overtook the proposal.

The ruling was reversed in December, after Pearl Harbour, and from April 1942 funds were provided for the schools, which by then had been operating for some time.

FIRST STEPS TOWARDS ASSIGNMENT—AERO ENGINES

The basic problem confronting the British and American Governments in the latter part of 1940 was the insufficiency of current and prospective American production to meet at one and the same time the clamant needs of a hard-pressed belligerent and of a neutral busily engaged in repairing its defences. To this problem there were, in principle, two solutions. One was to expand supply, by an all-out mobilisation of America's industrial resources. The second and more immediately practicable solution was to ration the demand by means of allocation and a general system of priorities. These points were grasped at the outset by the British Government. In his *aide-mémoire* of 3rd July Lord Lothian suggested immediate discussions between Great Britain, Canada and the United States with a view to the allocation of scarce and vital supplies such as aluminium, steel and machine tools. This was looking far ahead; it was not until a year later that things began to move fast in this direction, and the full combined programme here suggested could not in fact be achieved until after Pearl Harbour. None the less the first hesitant advances towards assignment on a combined basis were made in 1940. The items chiefly in question were aero engines and machine tools. Both of these were vital to the development of output in the United States and Britain alike, and in both cases the negotiations posed, or at one time seemed to pose the question—how far was Britain prepared to forgo an expansion of production at home in order to secure a more rapid build-up in the United States?

The general shortage of aircraft engines and the occupation by British contracts of a large part of the American production capacity have already been mentioned. By July the United States had airframes waiting on engines. On the 18th Morgenthau indicated that there were fifty-four P.36s and P.40s waiting for Allison engines; and a wide survey, a little later, by the Defence Advisory Commission revealed a still more serious position. In these circumstances it was natural that the United States Army should scrutinise closely all exports of aero engines to the United Kingdom, and should seek to lay hands on deliveries off British and French contracts. On 24th July, the day on which the '3,000 a month' scheme took shape, it was agreed to set up a committee for the allocation of engines on a monthly basis. Soon afterwards, on 21st August, this was followed up by the establishment of a formal Joint Aircraft Committee, whose functions were to plan production programmes, to deal with matters relating to types and standardisation and to allocate airframes,

engines and other air supplies produced in the United States. British
members sat on this committee, together with representatives of the
United States Army and Navy. It became, thus, in fact though not in
name, the first of the Combined Boards. But combined machinery
for allocation was of little use without agreement on the principles and
methods by which allocations were to be made. The ruling formula
adopted for the Combined Munitions Assignments Board in 1942
was 'assignment according to strategic needs'. This was not too easy
to apply, even when the United States were at war, and it could
clearly have no relevance to the conditions of 1940. Instead, there
was the vague formula produced by Knudsen on 23rd July (see
above, p. 170) which only made the darkness darker. It embodied
the idea of an engine pool, which Purvis had already accepted in
principle some days earlier at the suggestion of Philip Young. This
implied that both sides would draw engines from the 'pool' as and
when they had airframes ready to match them. But it left unsettled
the real point at issue—what was to happen when both sides tried to
draw from the pool more than was in it.

At the end of July 1940 Lord Beaverbrook was warned by his
representative in America that the Administration would not release
engines for export so long as there were airframes waiting for engines
in the United States. The Minister's retort in mid-August was that
there were airframes waiting also in the United Kingdom, that these
engines were the 'property' of the British Government and that he
had in any case given 'justification for export'. He added that the
Ministry did not regard it as desirable that details of our airframe
and aero engine programme should be communicated to the United
States authorities. Once the Joint Aircraft Committee had begun to
function, however, the British representatives soon discovered that to
get engines they had to reveal the relevant part of the British airframe
production programme; this was done at a meeting on 10th September. By this time, a still graver view of the engine shortage was being
taken by the Army and the production authorities. On the same day
Morgenthau asked whether the United Kingdom really had airframes for all the engines it was receiving. On 20th September
Knudsen suggested as a basis for allocation in the next *six* months
the ratio in which each side was purchasing aircraft in the United
States over the next *eighteen* months. It was objected that six months
in both cases was a fairer basis. Otherwise, as Purvis pointed out in a
note for Morgenthau on 28th September, the scheme would mean
the diversion to the United States of 966 British engines. The need in
the United Kingdom was greater than ever, partly because of the
partial breakdown in the production of the Taurus and Hercules
engines.

For some days the alleged shortage of pilots, referred to above, seemed to threaten the whole aircraft supply position. But the sky cleared early in October with the success of the R.A.F. in the Battle of Britain and the full disclosure of the strategic position. A direct appeal made by Purvis and Morris Wilson led to the release of 2,300 badly needed engines.[1]

FIRST STEPS TOWARDS ASSIGNMENT—MACHINE TOOLS

To a great extent, the story of machine-tool supply during the latter part of 1940 followed, on a broader canvas, the pattern traced by the negotiations over aircraft engines; overall shortage, leading to a threat to British supplies; acceptance of the theory of allocation, but dispute over the governing formula; finally, marked easing of the American attitude when the British volunteered detailed information in support of their claim.

Machine tools were at this time so much the dominant factor in the production plan of the United States and Britain alike that their distribution largely determined the contribution which each country could make to the sum total of munitions output. Some account has been given in Chapter IV of the efforts of the British Purchasing Commission in the early part of the year to mobilise the American machine-tool industry and to secure a good share of its output for British war factories, in face of competing demands from France and from the United States itself. These efforts had borne belated fruit at the end of May when the first British 'float' orders were placed. Then a few weeks later the British Government fell heir to all the French orders during the period when the French had been much the more active of the two partners in the American market. These events led to a generalisation which was current in Washington during the summer, that the United Kingdom controlled sixty per cent. of capacity in the 'munitions' sector of the American machine-tool industry for the remainder of 1940. The figure itself was doubtful; the industry was expanding fast and its capacity was hard to measure; it was still not working three shifts. All the same, with the launching of American rearmament it was beyond doubt that a grave shortage was developing.

Even before this, the spectacular things that were happening in the machine-tool industry had become front-page news in the United States.[2] The demand had become so acute that speculators were buying up secondhand machines and offering them at greatly

---

[1] Engines were not, of course, the only 'bottleneck' in aircraft production in 1940–41. Another was raw materials and, still more difficult, aircraft guns. It was calculated in October 1940 that there was then a deficit of 4,000 machine guns needed for British aircraft for delivery from January to July 1941 and that the new 12,000-aircraft programme called for 100,000.

[2] e.g. *Fortune*, April 1940, and *Saturday Evening Post*, 18th May 1940. Article: 'Biggest War Baby—The Boom in Machine Tools'.

increased prices; and the help of Morgenthau had to be called in to safeguard British supplies. Purvis handed him a memorandum on 21st May asking for the utmost acceleration of deliveries of machine tools, amongst other supplies. The placing of new orders, it was noted, was becoming difficult because the suppliers expected machine-tool orders from the American Government. Even orders already in production were being seriously delayed by many suppliers. 'Apparently the only way in which our requirements could be met would be by the granting of priorities.' Ten days later Morgenthau was given a further statement listing seventeen types of machine tools on which priorities were desired. There was no immediate result from these representations. For a moment there even seemed some danger that exports to the Allies might cease. An embargo was imposed at the beginning of June on the export of machine tools from the United States. But assurances were given through Purvis to London and Paris that it would not be applied so as to interfere with the vital war orders of the Allies.

The prospect of big Allied orders for finished munitions added a new factor to the problem. Clearly, if orders for machine tools for export were not at the same time curtailed, the strain on the resources of the industry would be greatly aggravated. Purvis therefore suggested to the British Government on 15th June that some of the machine tools then on order for new factories in Europe should be retained and put to work in the New World instead.

A certain movement in this direction was already discernible, especially in connection with machinery for the manufacture of small arms ammunition. Up to March 1940 the policy of the War Office and the Ministry of Supply had been to depend mainly if not wholly on production of small arms ammunition in United Kingdom factories, and machinery for these factories occupied an important place among machine-tool orders in the United States. But from that time on there was a steadily rising stream of orders and enquiries for finished ammunition, and considerable sums were spent on capital assistance for American firms. Notably, in mid-June, the British Government agreed to capital assistance involving over $4½ million in connection with heavy orders for rifle ammunition—and this included the diversion of a large part of the machinery ordered for British factories earlier in the year. Another example occurred early in June when the British Purchasing Commission told London of an offer of some four million dollars' worth of heavy gun lathes. The reply came back that it would be better to keep the lathes in the United States for use in the production of British-type guns, say 12-inch howitzers.

In general, however, the Ministry of Supply (and still less the Ministry of Aircraft Production) was not prepared to accept the principle that it should refrain from shipping machine tools across the Atlantic in order to put them to work in American factories. The British Government wanted North America to become a reserve arsenal, but not its main arsenal. Efforts to step up the rate of production in the United Kingdom were to be intensified, not relaxed, whatever happened in the United States. Machine tools were therefore wanted more urgently and in greater quantities than ever. To have altered the destination of the machines already on order would not merely have amounted to a confession of weakness which London was in no mood to make; it would have been disastrous in practice, since machine tools could be used at once and with decisive effect in Britain, whereas, if retained in America they would lie idle for many months while war factories were built to house them.

The planners of American rearmament feared that machine tools shipped to Britain would be destroyed or perhaps captured as soon as they arrived. The Canadian Government, too, had an interest in the retention of machine tools in the western hemisphere, since it needed American tools to the value of $45 million to carry out its own new munitions programme. Covetous glances were cast in particular upon the tools due to be shipped under the French contracts; it was pointed out that Britain had never counted on this windfall and so could not really be in need of it. At a joint meeting on 23rd July some on the American side expressed the opinion that machine tools should not in future be shipped 'to vulnerable areas'. In response to the plea that if this attitude were adopted rigidly the British munitions effort would be largely paralysed, it was conceded that Britain should have the tools necessary to 'round off' existing plants. The American suggestion that the machine tools on order must be 'much in excess of United Kingdom necessities' was met by agreement that the two sides together should examine the lists of orders.

A month later, on 26th August, the British side reported to London that it was under heavy pressure to make concessions on the machine-tool front. British orders for delivery in the next six months would, it was estimated, take up about $120 million out of a total forecast production of $180 million, leaving the United States defence programme 'at the mercy of the remaining available output'. This, in the American view, was an untenable position. Already, some British applications for export licences were being refused, as 'contrary to the interests of national defence'. It was clear that the point had now been reached when not only some sort of joint programme but also monthly allocation of machine tools had become inevitable. The plan of allocation proposed by the National Defence Advisory Commission was as follows: special priority, ahead even of United States defence programme needs, would be given to machine tools required to *maintain* the existing United Kingdom output of critical munitions; after this all the tools produced would be kept in North America and divided *pro rata* between the production of munitions on British, American and Canadian account.

London was profoundly disturbed by the terms thus offered, which, if strictly interpreted, would strike a crippling blow at the expansion of British armaments production. Many factories which were all but complete would be rendered useless for lack of a few American machine tools. The British team was warned that suspension of deliveries would dislocate all existing plans and damage the whole British war effort, with 'consequences so grave that we need not elaborate them'. It was recognised, however, that it would be futile merely to stand firm on Britain's rights in this matter, at least in regard to the French machines. For example, London accepted the idea of making a gesture of co-operation by releasing some machine tools for the new joint tank programme, so long as there were no inroads on tools required for the production of aircraft, aircraft guns and anti-aircraft guns or of the related ammunition. On the general issue, the British Government insisted, however, that it 'must maintain its vital right to British orders placed and accepted over a long period', chiefly on the ground that 'whereas the expansion of American armaments production is largely in the planning stage, all tools which can be obtained for this country can be utilised immediately'. As for the French orders, it was pointed out that the fall of France had altered much else besides the ownership of certain machine-tool contracts. However, so long as British orders proper were safeguarded, the British side was authorised to agree that French tools scheduled for shipment after an agreed date, which must not be earlier than 1st November 1940, should be released to the United States. It was calculated that this would secure for Britain about 8,000 out of the 12,000 machine tools ordered by the French, some of which had already been diverted to Canada.

On 20th September Purvis reported that the United States Government was willing to release all tools from British or French orders delivered before 1st December 1940 on the understanding that considerations would be given to specially urgent American claims. After that date British orders would still be delivered as of right, but French orders would in general be released to the United States. The future output of the expanded industry would be allocated in the light of combined needs. Meanwhile the United States Army and Navy had renounced the use of the priority system which had been holding up shipments to Britain. This news was received with great relief in London, and the War Cabinet declared that 'Mr. Purvis was to be congratulated on arriving at so favourable a settlement'.

Satisfaction, however, was premature. Confronted with the actual allotment of tools which would have resulted from this arrangement, the American authorities felt compelled to reconsider it. The demands of the Services were becoming ever more pressing, and the British found themselves, Purvis reported on 27th September, 'in a steadily deteriorating situation in which our tools are being effectively detained through pressure on the manufacturers'. The Services were putting pressure on Morgenthau as well as on the manufacturers. Representatives of the United States Army had told him that, according to their private information, the British were building up stocks of machine tools indiscriminately in the United Kingdom, where they would be exposed to damage or destruction by enemy action. In countering such charges the British representatives were hampered by lack of information as to the specific purposes for which the machine tools on order were required; in response to repeated requests, the authorities in London had set about assembling the necessary data, but had let the matter drop on receipt of the reassuring cable of 20th September. There was little or no truth in the allegation about hoarding. But the British team agreed that, in view of the temper now prevailing on the American side, it was necessary to abandon the abortive settlement and accept allocation of machine tools before as well as after the end of November. Attempts to negotiate on the basis of a general formula were now given up. Instead, it was proposed to undertake, in conjunction with the Americans, a detailed survey of the machine tools on order and thus arrive at a final agreement as to which should be exported during the next two months and which retained.

A memorandum prepared in the course of the negotiations revealed that unfilled British orders—still valued at upwards of $100 million—were now less than forty per cent. of the total orders on the books of the American machine-tool industry, and that the percentage was declining as the industry expanded. It now had a capacity fifty per cent. greater than at the beginning of the year.[1] Because of their date of placement, however, British orders still had in October a 'dominant position'. Moreover, for many critical machines they were estimated at two-thirds or even three-quarters of the productive capacity.

On 9th October 1940 the British negotiator, Mr. J. G. Weir, was able to send to London the text of a new agreement which, a few days later, was finally approved by the American Chiefs of Staff. Here was the second major step along the road towards 'assignment' which was already envisaged by Purvis and Layton as the ultimate solution to

---

[1] Machine-tool production in the United Kingdom at this time was estimated at three and a half times the normal peace-time output.

most of the problems now being encountered. In one important respect, however, the precedent of the Joint Aircraft Committee was not followed. Though the Defence Advisory Commission was amenable to the idea of allocation by a joint committee, the Army and Navy authorities would not hear of this, insisting that the final arbiter must be an all-American tribunal. It was agreed, however, that this body should be helped in reaching its decision by the recommendations of a Working Committee which should include British and Canadian representatives. For the Working Committee's guidance certain basic principles were set forth. Although these consisted largely of an unreconciled reaffirmation of the opposing points of view, the British had thereby succeeded in getting formal recognition of the essential points in their case, namely, that machine tools should in general be sent wherever they would help to produce most munitions by the following spring; that this aim would usually be achieved, air-raid risks notwithstanding, by sending them to Britain; and that the objective should include the expansion, not merely the maintenance of United Kingdom output. With these points established it was not difficult to concede that the needs of American rearmament were increasing and that even during the next sixty days some machine tools would have to be diverted.

The precarious balance of agreement was nearly wrecked once more, this time from the British side. On 17th October the North American Supply Committee cabled its acquiescence, though with the proviso that if the new arrangements did not work out satisfactorily the whole issue might have to be raised 'in the highest quarters'. But the Ministry of Aircraft Production, which had all along maintained a stiff and uncompromising attitude on machine tools, emphatically dissented. The 'Weir Agreement' was 'regretted', and the Ministry reserved 'its separate and independent position'. It was evident that the realities of the situation had not been fully understood. In the words of a statement prepared by the British Purchasing Commission and endorsed by Lord Beaverbrook's own representative in the United States, 'it ought by this time to be recognised in England that the U.S. Army and Navy consider themselves the owners of these tools and our allotments are more or less on sufferance'. As matters stood, any United States armaments contractor could obtain machine tools off British orders simply by applying for priority. The system of review of competing claims now proposed, whatever its imperfections, offered a measure of protection against such depredations. The Ministry of Aircraft Production would gain nothing by withdrawing the tools ordered on its behalf from the consideration of the committee. On the contrary such action would probably mean the breakdown of negotiations and a cessation of shipments. The 'separate and independent position' was therefore abandoned after explanations had been made. The Working Committee—with two British representatives present—duly held its first meeting on 23rd October.

Having once established their right to assign deliveries off British orders, the Americans exercised it in a sense favourable to immediate British needs. On 2nd November machine-tool makers were told that they were not to divert or postpone deliveries for Britain or Canada on their own initiative, but were to follow the detailed directions of the Committee. In December the American machine-tool authorities decided to ration the key types of machine tools on the basis of a percentage of each month's output according to the relative importance of British, Canadian and United States needs. Since the existing supplies still fell far short of satisfying all requirements, this meant the United Kingdom would be called upon to release additional machines. Nevertheless a report to the British Supply Council (the new 'federal' organisation of missions in Washington) at the end of January 1941 showed that since the Weir Agreement had been in operation about 11,000 machines had been released for shipment to the United Kingdom and no more than 300 lost by diversion. Thus in the crucial winter of 1940–41 the British had in the end managed to secure the great majority of the machine tools so vital to their future war production. From time to time thereafter, as with most commodities, a crisis would threaten and then subside—as happened in February 1941 when the newly-formed Office of Production Management protested that manufacturers were still overloaded with British orders, and threatened to halve British allocations. But in the main British interests were well protected by the machinery of the Working Committee, which continued its weekly meetings until after Pearl Harbour; it was then merged into the larger scheme of the Combined Boards, for which it had helped to pave the way.[1]

(v)

Marking Time, October to March

THE BRITISH BACKGROUND — STRATEGY AND SUPPLY

Despite these evidences of growing co-operation, and despite the progress achieved in the matter of standardisation, the general outlook for United States supply, when October 1940 began, was dis-

---

[1] Like the Boards, the Working Committee was essentially a piece of machinery which enabled two men, one on the American side (Mr. Mason Britton, the machine-tool expert of N.D.A.C.) and one on the British side (Mr. A. J. M. Baker, head of the Machine-Tools Division of the B.P.C., himself American) to produce an agreed solution and to get it accepted by both countries.

couraging. Little progress had yet been made in translating the great programmes of the summer into the solid reality of contracts placed and factories building, still less of munitions shipped. Only in the tank sector had British negotiators reached the point of firm orders. The rest of the Army programme was still bogged down in the controversy over types. On the air side, the '3,000 a month' scheme had not advanced beyond the stage of paper planning. The merchant shipbuilding mission was still on the high seas, and when it did arrive in New York (on 3rd October 1940) it was to find its path far from smooth.

It was in a general attempt to get steam up and the wheels turning over, not merely to solve the specific problem of army ordnance described above, that the British Government had sent Sir Walter Layton to the United States. Layton was introduced by Lord Lothian on 27th September to the President, with whom he had half an hour's general discussion. The President showed a keen and sympathetic interest in Britain's problems. He was, he said, anxious that she should have everything she wanted, but explained that it would be easier to give help after the election, 'whichever way it goes'. A few days later, in order that the American Government might see for itself the scale and urgency of the effort which it must make, Layton presented to Morgenthau a long memorandum setting forth the strategic realities lying behind British requests for aid.

Since the disasters of May 1940 British industry had 'gone to it' with such good effect that, with the aid of the equipment released from America, the nakedness of the land was now covered with a thin garment of steel. At sea, the latent menace of the French fleet had been in great part removed, and with the advent of the American destroyers the Royal Navy's defensive and offensive powers were about to be greatly strengthened. The output of aircraft under the new dispensation had been much accelerated; there were more squadrons in operation and stronger reserves. But the biggest proportionate improvement was in the state of the land forces. When the British Expeditionary Force returned to England there were less than 800 field guns of all calibres available for issue to units; by the end of August there were about 2,500. Thanks to the shipment of American weapons, a Home Guard numbering one and a half million men would soon have been raised and armed on a scale of one rifle for every two men. Stocks of ·303-inch ammunition were sufficient for any foreseeable expenditure during the rest of the year. Thus the country had been enabled to face with confidence the threat of immediate invasion; and even while the Mission was on its way across the Atlantic the decisive air victories on 15th and 21st September, coupled with the approach of the season of storm and fog, had practically removed the danger.

Britain, in fact, had gained a breathing space, and for the first time since May could concentrate on planning for the future—first for defence against a renewal of the onslaught in the spring and then for the offensive action which must ultimately be mounted. For each of these purposes aircraft and more aircraft were the supreme require-ment. The enemy, Germany and Italy, could afford to devote a great part of their resources in the coming winter to the raising of more air fleets for the destruction of Great Britain. On the evidence then avail-able it was expected that by the summer of 1941 the enemy's output would reach a rate of 2,500–3,000 aircraft a month. The British, whose own current production of combat types was only about 800 a month, stood in danger of being overwhelmed if they did not receive early and substantial aid.[1] Beyond that, a large margin of superiority in the air was the only means whereby the crushing weight of Ger-many's land armies could be countered and the war ultimately carried to the enemy. Hence aircraft production had been given the highest priority in the United Kingdom, and aircraft were placed in the fore-front of the supplies needed from the United States. The first specific requests by the Layton Mission were for assistance 'in accelerating and treating as a matter of vital urgency the delivery of armaments which can be produced before the spring and early summer of 1941', with top priority for aircraft and aero engines ordered in the early part of 1940, and for permission to place orders as soon as possible for the new and larger aircraft programme.

Reliance upon the air arm as the main instrument of victory did not, however, exclude the need for a large and powerfully equipped army. Bombing and blockade might loosen the foundations of Ger-man power, but its final overthrow could hardly be accomplished without direct assault. It was indeed not easy to see whence the manpower for this undertaking was to be provided, failing large-scale rebellion in Europe or an American expeditionary force. But it was thought that there would be increasing scope for offensive action on the periphery of the Axis dominions—in Africa and the Near East and perhaps, when local air supremacy had been gained, in bridge-heads across the Channel. The production of land armaments was therefore to go vigorously ahead, and the Government saw no reason to reconsider its objective of equipping fifty-five divisions before the end of 1941, though this entailed an increase of more than fifty per cent. in the output planned before Dunkirk. Between 1st August 1940 and the end of 1941 the stock of field and medium artillery was to be almost trebled, that of anti-tank guns and of infantry and cruiser tanks multiplied about eleven times. In the same period over 5,000 anti-aircraft guns, 54,000 Bren guns and more than half a million

---

[1] It is now known from German documents that the average monthly output by Germany in the summer of 1940 was approximately 800 *operational* aircraft, i.e. almost exactly the same as the British output. See below, p. 165, footnote (1).

rifles were to be produced. It was hoped, in fact, that by the end of the second year of war, despite the vastly greater effort devoted to aircraft production, Britain would be turning out land armaments at a rate not achieved until the last year of the previous war.

Even so, there would still be some large gaps, notably tanks and rifles, in the desired scale of equipment at the end of 1941. Moreover, the above estimates took no account either of the probable loss of output through bombing or of the probable losses of equipment in fighting during the intervening period. Nor was provision made thereby for the supply of arms to possible future allies. Action was therefore asked to clear the way for large-scale orders for 'guns, small arms and various weapons included in the Army programme'.

More generally, the disparity between the war potential of Germany and Great Britain, as measured by the crude but significant index of steel output, was so great that Britain could never hope to match her enemy's strength out of her own resources alone. With the industries of most of Europe at her disposal, the enemy could turn out 42 million ingot tons of steel a year. Against this the British Commonwealth could provide only $18\frac{1}{2}$ million tons. Only by adding in a large part of America's 50 million tons could the gap be bridged. 'It is therefore clear', Layton concluded, 'that, while the situation must be maintained in the meantime by United Kingdom weapons, a final decision must be based on the great industrial potential of the United States.'

THE AMERICAN BACKGROUND AND BRITISH FINANCE

There was a long, long road to travel before the potential could become actual. Britain had now gone about as far as she could go. She had put forward her requirements and justified them by detailed explanation, had given way, or was about to give way, on most of the questions of type, had spent or committed most of her slender stock of dollars. The next move lay with the United States. The problem which now confronted the American Government was essentially the same as it had been since June—the problem of reconciling three things which in the last analysis were irreconcilable: the desire to sustain Great Britain in her mortal struggle (and this desire was deep and genuine); the need to repair with all speed the meagre defences of the western hemisphere; and the reluctance to disturb the peace-time economy with drastic measures of restriction and control.

In this autumn of 1940 sympathy with Britain was running high, and the sense of partnership in a common cause was rapidly spreading. The formula 'all aid short of war' was common ground between the parties to the election, and according to Lord Lothian[1] the policy

---

[1] In an address which he gave to the North American Supply Committee during his last visit to London.

of the William Allen White Committee was now for the first time really representative of public opinion at large. The dramatic victories of the Royal Air Force had stirred the imagination of the American people. Official and unofficial observers, testifying alike to the horrors of air bombardment and to the steadfastness with which the citizens of London were enduring it, had at once aroused eagerness to help and dispelled the feeling that help was bound to be in vain. In the summer it had been the common belief that Britain was doomed and therefore that any assistance given must be wasted. Soon there would be a reaction to the opposite view, that Britain was doing well enough on her own and so needed no assistance. But for the moment opinion was poised between these two poles, and to that extent the time was propitious.

On the other hand Britain's successful resistance had by no means relieved the prevailing anxiety about the security of the United States. The Administration was being subjected to steadily growing pressure from Congress and from public opinion generally to speed up the process of rearmament, which by common consent was conceived on too small a scale and was being executed at too slow a tempo, on the Army side at least. The War Department's ultimate objective was only twenty-seven divisions, and no more than nine of these were to be ready by midsummer 1941. There was already a great shortage of small arms ammunition for training purposes. Few orders had yet been placed for artillery, the provision of which was likely to lag behind the intake of recruits; except for light anti-tank and anti-aircraft guns, deliveries would only be just beginning at the end of 1941. Public anxiety was thus well-founded. Yet, as matters stood, more arms for America could only mean fewer arms for Britain since the total capacity available for munitions production was contained within narrow bounds by the continuing pressure of civilian demand. This dilemma could only be resolved by a real industrial mobilisation, and of this there was as yet little sign.

Administrative weaknesses helped to make matters more difficult. Judged by the standards of war-time Britain, the pace of discussion and action seemed very leisurely; echoing complaints by an earlier generation of European diplomats in London, British officials chafed against the long Washington week-end. Apart from this there were structural weaknesses on the side of the Administration, such as the responsibilities imposed on the Treasury in connection with the defence programme, for which it had neither the technical experience nor the staff. The industrialists of the National Defence Advisory Commission had little or no executive authority. Actual procurement rested with the War and Navy Departments, whose activities, Layton reported, were geared to no general strategic plan and subject to no single controlling authority.

Yet even if the organisation of rearmament had been flawless its progress must still have been slow and halting so long as the economy as a whole remained on a peace footing. That it should so remain was of course only to be expected. The United States was a pacific democracy absorbed in the controversies of an election year and lacking the sense of urgency and the single-mindedness which could only come with actual participation in the war. Much earlier, at the beginning of July, Lord Lothian, repeating a point made by the War Cabinet in London, had warned the United States Government that if American rearmament were to be carried out in time, and if Britain and the Dominions were to be given the means to hold back the enemy in the interval, far-reaching changes in the industrial organisation of the country were essential. British experience had shown that it was not possible to superimpose adequate defence pro- grammes upon an undisturbed civilian economy. This advice fell on deaf ears—or at least produced no positive response. No check had been placed on civilian consumption or investment; and meanwhile rearmament and Allied war orders had indirectly raised the level of effective demand. Sir Walter Layton estimated in January that if all the British and United States Government orders then pending were to materialise the war effort of the United States would amount at most to fifteen per cent. of the total national income. For all practical purposes the ability of American industry to deliver the goods was a political, not a physical, question. It involved the exercise of the sovereign powers of government in the control of the economy, in the interests of British and United States defence orders alike. Failing this, the British and United States Governments must continue to com- pete with one another and with the American consumer for labour, materials and above all for machine tools.

Meanwhile the question of Britain's ability to pay had been raised in an acute form. The 'Eternal Gods' (incarnate in the President and Congress of the United States), to whom in May the British Govern- ment had delegated the problem of payment, had as yet made no sign; and dollars were running out fast. The financial impasse became clearly enough defined in the second half of October when the total picture of British requirements, assembled for Layton's visit, was presented by him in Washington and discussed in a series of high- level joint meetings that lasted on into November. Aircraft and munitions requirements together showed totals which, when com- pared with the shrinking dollar reserve, were on an astronomical scale. At the maximum an expenditure was foreseen of $8,000– $9,000 million. This was only for two years' requirements and in fact the war was to last more than twice as long as that. For aircraft alone, a table drawn up by the British Purchasing Commission in mid- December showed that the 'present and immediately foreseeable' needs of the United Kingdom involving dollars would amount to $6,350 million up to the end of 1942. Of this amount $650 million had been paid. At least another $2,080 million was due by August 1941.

The preoccupation of the Ministry of Aircraft Production with the financial consequences of its programme was already evident in a series of telegrams from August 1940 onwards. Their burden was: 'We attach importance to the utmost limitation of dollar expenditure in the immediate future so long as production is not thereby postponed.' The following were some of the questions put by the Ministry at this time and the answers of its Washington representatives. Cash payments in advance of contracts: Could payments lower than those so far made be negotiated? (No, the manufacturers wanted more.) Ownership of assets and amortisation: ('We shall do our best to retain ownership'—but that would mean giving an option to purchase at a 'knock-out price'. The French had paid full capital cost and given ownership with it.) Capital costs: Would the manufacturers bear any part of them? (No.) Would the Administration bear any part of the capital expenditure? (Probably not.) Purvis, indeed, had worked hard to secure the extension to aircraft of the precedent whereby the Reconstruction Finance Corporation had financed the capital expenditure for the production of tank engines on British as well as American account—amortisation being in the form of higher prices for the product. Layton asked formally on 20th October that the principle should be extended. But the expedient had broken down over the manufacture of Rolls-Royce Merlin engines since the American share was to be only 3,000 out of 9,000 engines. The Reconstruction Finance Corporation found that it could not finance schemes unless the American share of the produce was at least fifty per cent. —a condition not likely to be satisfied in many contracts. Negotiations over capital assistance for machine-gun orders—a vital element both of the tank and aircraft programmes—also dragged on through the autumn without positive result.

But capital assistance for British contracts was in any case no real solution; at best it was a temporary expedient that might defer for a few weeks or months the final exhaustion of Britain's dollar supplies. A more radical answer was needed for the twin problems of American mobilisation and British finance, and this answer was not to be found in a day.

The six months from October to March were to be spent in marking time, at least as regards any serious expansion of supply from the United States. The six months were spent—as the preceding three months had more or less been spent—in piling programme on programme, with seemingly endless revisions, to cover aircraft and other supplies from the United States for the years ahead. Many important meetings of high officials were devoted to the matter month after month; their occasions were various—some variation in British requirements for particular types of aircraft such as the increasing emphasis on heavy bombers, some modification in American production plans or requirements, or some new angle to the basic problem of payment. Both sides were groping amongst many kinds of uncertainties, those of the war, those of production, design and finance, labour and materials, and not least those of American politics. Not even the President could see very far ahead. In retrospect all the activity looks like a great deal of packing for a journey that could never begin until the President had pioneered the unexplored country and opened up a road. Each important move forward was part of an American political process—the shaping of issues for the November election, the finding of a new political and economic formula for aid to Britain, the patient marshalling of forces to remove political obstacles one by one until the chosen formula was made law in the Lend-Lease Act. No doubt time was lost in the process—time that might have shortened the war by advancing American production schedules by many months. But such calculations are very theoretical. It was of the nature of American political processes that they should take time; and meanwhile the discussions served some purpose in defining more sharply the real supply needs of Britain and the United States, in creating the habit of working together and a better understanding between the leaders on both sides, in gearing together a little more closely the war production of Britain, America and Canada. It was a matter of no small importance that when lend-lease was finally enacted the packing was largely done and the teams ready to start.

ALL AID SHORT OF WAR

By the autumn any possibility of action had passed out of the hands of subordinates into those of the President himself. His public speech of 30th October 1940 was a sign that the British representatives, led by Purvis, and the heads and high officials of the chief American departments, including the General Staffs, had gone as far as they could go on the technical and Service levels. Five days before, Purvis had informed London that 'the critical moment had arrived for action from the highest quarters'. The discussion had reached the final obstacles of finance and the 'necessity for interfering with normal peace-time outputs'. Purvis warned that unless action were taken forthwith, 'lethargy will supervene' and 'in a few days' time'. That afternoon the President had discussed the matter with his Cabinet and had decided to intervene to sweep aside opposition to prompt action. But for this he needed, Purvis said, a message from the British Government, if possible couched in 'the Prime Minister's own language'. A message to the President from the Former Naval Person duly arrived through the Purvis–Morgenthau channel two days later. It discussed the 'defence of the Island against invasion', the strategic outlook, the coming campaign in the Middle East and the air attacks on 'our remaining life-line, the North-Western Approach'. It referred to

> the extreme urgency of accelerating delivery of the programme of aircraft and other munitions which has already been laid before you by Layton and Purvis. So far as aircraft are concerned, would it be possible to speed up deliveries of existing orders so that the number coming to our support next year will be considerably increased? Furthermore, can new orders for expanded programme also be placed so promptly that deliveries may come out in the middle of 1941?

Britain also depended on American deliveries to complete her existing programme for the equipment of her armies. The message was to be delivered by Purvis with a memorandum on the technical details.

The British side duly filed with the Prime Minister's message detailed lists of requirements for aircraft and land armaments which were immediately examined at a meeting of Secretaries of State and the Chiefs of Staff. They agreed that orders could be placed for all the requirements at once, in so far as they were for types which the Chiefs of Staff could certify as being of use to the United States. On 29th October Purvis was called to a meeting of the President's Liaison Committee, in Morgenthau's room, in which the passage for the President's speech next day calling for 'all aid for Britain short of war' was discussed. A number of modifications, suggested by him, were accepted. They were made (as his account of the meeting recorded) in order to 'mask such information as might be derived by the enemy'. It was agreed, Purvis noted, that the United Kingdom could now place at once without further negotiation orders for 4,250 aircraft (4,550 including spares). Formal applications were arranged with Knudsen on 31st October for fresh contracts to this amount to cost $673 million.[1] The President also directed the Priorities Board, as he noted in his speech, to consider the placing by the United Kingdom of additional orders for 12,000 planes. The Board gave its approval on 8th November. On the same day the President announced publicly an important 'rule of thumb' policy which he had suggested the day before to Purvis. This meant sharing American output with the United Kingdom on a fifty-fifty basis. Actually the United States was receiving at the time only about 100 planes a month—which was less than the United Kingdom was getting from its own contracts. But the rule meant that Britain might expect more heavy bombers. It had immediate political importance and would help supply once a

---

[1] The order included 1,200 B.24s (Liberators) which virtually marked the end of hopes of the manufacture in the United States of a British type of heavy bomber.

way was discovered by the President to finance British orders. A week earlier Mr. Stimson had given formal approval to the placing of orders under the Army 'B' programme and, in the limited sense described above, for the 'A' programme also.

Thus, at the beginning of November 1940, it seemed that the atmosphere was clearing, especially as in addition a prospect had opened up of securing the construction of the sixty merchant ships desired by Britain. It is worth while to pause at this point to summarise the progress made on British orders in the United States up to 1st November 1940 and the length of the road that lay ahead.

British munitions orders in the United States:
the position at 1st November 1940

TABLE 3 $ million

	Value of orders placed	Amount paid	Value of orders to be placed
Aircraft products	*1,261·6*	*437·2*	*2,525·9*
of which: Airframes . . .	721·8	241·7	
Aero engines . .	480·5	166·2	
Accessories . .	59·3	29·3	
Other munitions products . . .	*568·4*	*224·9*	*630·0*
of which: Tanks . . .	99·5	13·7	110·0
Motor vehicles . .	41·7	17·4	—
Ordnance . . .	114·5	56·1	290·0
Ammunition . .	124·8	43·7	120·0
Explosives . . .	39·9	15·1	20·0
Communication equipment . . .	7·1	1·8	—
Ships . . .	13·3	7·4	90·0
Machine tools . .	127·6	69·7	—
Capital	*154·8*	*122·6*	*50·0*
TOTAL	1,984·8	784·7	3,205·9

From Table 3 three points stand out for comment: first, the heavy financial burden facing the British Government in the mere completion of payments on its existing orders. Here may also be recorded a fact of which there has so far been little mention, namely, that with the loss of her European supplies in April–May 1940 Britain had been obliged to turn to the United States for vastly increased supplies of steel, timber and other vital raw materials as well as for munitions. Prospective payments for steel alone now amounted to $665 million. Secondly, the table shows the continuing predominance of aircraft over other munitions (even including machine tools) not only in orders placed but still more in future programmes. Admittedly the table does not include the ten-division programme. But even with this problematical addition to army orders the aircraft programme remained unique as the only real departure, in the words of Layton's report, from the treatment of the United States as 'a shop from which we can buy munitions'. All other British programmes up to lend-lease, he noted, 'only provided for filling the gaps in our own preparations; they do not represent, in any adequate manner, a plan for the full mobilisation of the industrial resources of the United States'. Thirdly, the table shows the huge accumulation of contracts still awaiting placement. A quantitative summary of the position may be found in *Studies of Overseas Supply*, but it may be noted here that the British had ordered 13,173 aircraft (only about 4,000 more than in July) and wanted 23,000 more; that they had ordered 1,000 out of 3,000 medium tanks; that all sixty merchant ships were still to order, and that ordnance contracts were still confined to a few anti-tank guns, sub-machine guns and revolvers (the figures in the table include the value of the weapons released from stock in the summer).

Moreover, the hopes of immediate progress raised by the President's speech and accompanying measures were mostly illusory. The President's intervention was not in fact the 'action' at the 'critical moment' as described to London. Its significance was primarily political: it committed the Administration (and Wendell Wilkie, the opposition candidate, who also adopted this slogan) to 'all aid to Britain short of war'. But it settled none of the immediate supply problems. As soon as the British representatives tried to push forward to actual contracts they found the way barred as before. Thus, it had been understood that the orders for 4,550 aircraft sanctioned on 29th October were to be 'without charge for plant cost', but it turned out that this point was still not settled.[1]

Difficulties also arose over the ten-division Army programme. The authorities in London had gone ahead at once to work out the programme in quantitative terms—initial equipment for seven infantry and three armoured divisions, plus six months' wastage and a small allowance for training. On 14th November Layton wrote to Stimson setting forth the quantities of material required by Britain under both the 'B' and the residual 'A' programme and asking for 'the benevolent support of the War Department and the National Defence Advisory Commission in expediting the placing of contracts and securing delivery of these items in our "A" programme'. Little more was heard from the American side until 27th November, when Layton was given advance notice of a letter which he was to receive from Stimson two days later. This revealed that the conditions attached to the ten-division offer were more onerous than had been supposed. The Secretary of War was unable to give an assurance that Britain

---

[1] A down payment of twenty-five per cent. was required, with another twenty-five per cent. by June 1941.

would not be involved in capital expenditure, though he thought that the Reconstruction Finance Corporation procedure might well be applied. This, Layton explained, was only to be expected; the onus of granting financial relief was merely being passed to the Treasury. More serious were the reservations regarding delivery dates and priorities. Mr. Stimson hoped that, with some obvious exceptions (such as medium and heavy artillery), the full equipment of ten divisions would be ready by April 1942; but he declined to give any firm undertaking. Moreover, he now stipulated that the United States Army must receive its initial training equipment before any deliveries could be made to Britain. In fact, the following conditions were now imposed. First, the British must place their 'B' programme orders at once and in such a way that the American munitions capacity would be increased to an extent which would offset any interference with the defence programme. This was understood and accepted in London from the outset. Secondly, orders for American-type equipment, i.e. the ten-division programme plus the whole of the American rearmament programme, must be recognised as taking precedence over all orders for British types. And thirdly, the British must admit, and explicitly confirm in their contracts, the right of the United States Government to take delivery at any time of the stores ordered by Britain.

These latter conditions put a very different complexion on the whole project, as it was viewed in London. To the War Office the ten-division programme was an 'extra' of doubtful value which in no way altered the status of its own fifty-five division programme. It had acquiesced in the 'B' programme, but only in order to clear the way for a general settlement which would give it what it really wanted, namely the 'A' programme. There was general dismay, and talk of a protest at the Prime Minister–President level, at the apparent relegation of the 'A' programme to the very last place in the American production scheme. Layton, however, was inclined to play down the significance of Stimson's *démarche*, pointing out that it was probably only a 'departmental' letter, that no government could give explicit priority to the needs of a foreign state, and that in practice negotiations with firms for 'A' programme orders were going ahead. The Ministry of Supply accepted this view and Layton was authorised to acquiesce formally in the terms proposed. This he did on 3rd December.

From this point on finance took charge. Early in December Sir Frederick Phillips of the British Treasury took Layton's place as the principal negotiator on the British side. By then the dollar position was desperate, and it had finally become obvious that in some form or other the United States must pay for British supplies. Also, as Layton noted in his report, 'all Washington had come to realise that our programmes must be handled in conjunction with their own by the machinery of the American Government'. It was more than a matter of handling the programmes together. Both sides were getting into the habit of planning them together as parts of a single whole. For example, the head of the British Air Commission had drawn up a table on 12th November setting out the 'combined prospective programmes' of the two Governments in terms of monthly capacity. Such joint planning of production was an essential feature of lend-lease—the instrument now being designed by the President on board the u.s.s. *Tuscaloosa*.[1]

THE GREAT WINTER FREEZE

Before that instrument could become law three more months of intense political preparation were needed. There were to be speeches and declarations by the President and a most important letter from the Prime Minister, that of 8th December 1940.[2] In this letter Mr. Churchill bluntly posed a request for immediate and unstinted financial aid. He also asked for 'the greatest production of aircraft which the United States of America is capable of sending us'. The output as then planned was not enough. He suggested 'an immediate order on joint account for a further 2,000 combat aircraft a month', as many as possible to be heavy bombers. This, he was aware, would be a heavy burden for American industry but not one beyond its powers to carry. 'We ask for an unexampled effort, believing that it can be made.' On land armaments the Prime Minister said little, believing that here the necessary arrangements were already practically completed. The major part of his letter was devoted to the problems of shipping, which had quite suddenly become Britain's acutest need; 'the decision for 1941 lies upon the seas'. He asked that 'the United States should make available to us every ton of merchant shipping' that was surplus to their own requirements and should provide also 'not less than three million tons of additional merchant shipbuilding capacity'.

This letter had its effect, and its place among historic documents of the war. But in the meantime procurement languished. The expansion of aircraft capacity still hung fire. The tank programme ground to a standstill after 2,085 medium tanks had been ordered, leaving certain important components still unprovided for. No progress was made with orders under the ten-division programme, and in the 'A' programme an order for ·303-inch rifles, the only item for which a definite contract was in sight, had to wait till March 1941 for final

---

[1] For an account of the origins and development of lend-lease—which becomes the main thread of the narrative from November 1940 to April 1941—see below, Chapter VII, Part II.

[2] Quoted in Churchill, *Their Finest Hour*, op. cit., pp. 494–501.

signature. Meanwhile other smaller but even more urgent orders were being held up. Outside the main programmes considerable progress had been made on subsidiary items that were none the less of great immediate significance. This now came almost to a halt. On 17th January 1941 Purvis cabled a long list of the orders thus awaiting finance. It included twenty Flying Fortresses, thirty-six light tanks, ammunition for Oerlikons and other naval guns, degaussing cable, agricultural machinery, sub-machine guns and key components for British-built aircraft, tanks, field guns and marine engines. The list was shown to Harry Hopkins, then in London, who agreed that this was 'no way to beat Hitler'.

From December to the passing of the Lend-Lease Act in March 1941 the attention of Purvis and the British Purchasing and Air Commissions was devoted, first, to the preparation of a full statement of British long-term requirements, which had been promised by the Prime Minister in his letter, and, secondly, to the placing of a limited number of very urgent contracts. The main sequence of events in this interim period belongs to the chapter on finance which follows. Here we may note briefly the principal steps forward. Most important among these was the final signature, on 24th December, of a contract for sixty merchant ships for which the British Treasury scraped the barrel to find $23 million by way of initial payment. Many and diverse expedients were proposed with a view to keeping British orders moving. The most fruitful was the use of certain unexpended War Department funds amounting to $60 million for ordnance and $230 million for aircraft. This was a partial solution to the problem of finding $160 million to complete the original programme of 14,000 aircraft. For the rest, to save time whilst waiting for lend-lease British officials were urged by Knudsen to enter into preliminary discussions with manufacturers so that contract documents could be ready for signature as soon as funds were available. Such negotiations were time lost, since under lend-lease it was the American Government which had to place orders and which alone was in a position to negotiate with the manufacturers.

LOOKING AHEAD — VAST PLANS AND SMALL DELIVERIES

Meanwhile vast plans were being drawn up for the use of the American war potential in the new situation which would be created by lend-lease. The Prime Minister's statement of British requirements for 1941 and 1942 was sent to Morgenthau on 5th January 1941 by Purvis, acting now in his capacity as Chairman of the British Supply Council. After further revisions he gave personally to the President a second and more elaborate version on 13th February. Both statements covered not only aircraft but all munitions, as well as ships, iron and steel, and machine tools. The January statement gave merely British requirements from the United States. That of 13th February gave the same figures (with minor variations), but in a novel and much more significant form. It was the first version of the kind of balance sheet on which lend-lease discussions were to be founded and which, when broadened to include the needs of the United States and other allies, was to supply the statistical basis from 1942 onwards of the Combined Boards. The statement began with figures giving strategic *requirements* by the end of 1941 and during 1942. It added figures for *stocks*; then gave those for *British and Canadian production*. Against this were set *deliveries from the United States in respect of British contracts*, and finally the answer to the sum, the *deficiencies* to be provided for from the United States.

The figures thus arrived at for United States supply were truly formidable. They included 50,000 aircraft in the next two years, of which only 11,500 might be forthcoming under existing contracts, and nearly six million gross tons of merchant shipping, against which only 400,000 tons had so far been provided for. By midsummer 1942, the limiting date for the first lend-lease appropriation, over 7,000 tanks, more than 5,000 anti-aircraft guns and nearly two million rifles, amongst other requirements, were to be provided.

The sequel belongs to the later chapter on lend-lease. But that, in the main, will have to move in the more rarefied atmosphere of planning and policy. This chapter may well end, therefore, by a descent to the ground level of actual deliveries during the whole of the year 1941.[1] At no point was there a greater contrast between the desires of the planners and the rate of delivery actually achieved by industry. It has to be remembered, of course, that those framing programmes on the British side were in a difficult position. In the United Kingdom longer experience of planning the war output of industry had curbed extravagant expectations. But planners in the United States still rode ahead with a loose rein. Purvis and his colleagues were under pressure from the Administration to pitch their claims high. It is very improbable that they expected to get anything like the figure of 19,500 aircraft they put down for delivery in 1941 (9,600 from British contracts and 9,900 to be provided by the United States Government). Actual deliveries to the United Kingdom in 1941 were about a quarter of this figure, namely, 5,012 (from British cash contracts 4,823, from lend-lease 189). Actual deliveries of tanks in 1941 were 1,032, but only 250 of these were medium tanks. No new anti-aircraft guns were shipped till 1942.

No programmes could anticipate that America would be at war in 1942. But it is of some interest that aircraft deliveries in the year 1942 were still about a quarter of the forecast: programmed figure—

---

[1] This subject is treated more fully in *Studies of Overseas Supply*.

30,500 (1,900 from British contracts and 28,600 from lend-lease); actual deliveries—7,775 (2,048 from British contracts and 5,727 from lend-lease). The total United States production of combat aircraft in 1942 was 24,876—less than half the target set by the President in May 1940.

The figures show the difficulty which the Imperial General Staff encountered in laying down long-term strategic plans for the various theatres of war in proper relation to the supply of munitions. The main part of its supplies, drawn from the United Kingdom, could be calculated ahead with some degree of accuracy, but not so the 'deficiency' element that could be counted on from the great neutral, undeclared ally, across the Atlantic.

(vi)
The Role of Canada

If the story of war supply from Canada here forms a relatively brief appendix to a long chapter devoted to the United States, this is not because there was nothing of importance to report from the Canadian sector of overseas supply during this period. It was, of course, inevitable, once the strings of Britain's dollar purse had been loosened and once the United States had advanced from benevolent neutrality to a most unneutral non-belligerency, that Canada should cease to play the leading role assigned to her before Dunkirk, since her potential capacity for war production was so much smaller than that of her neighbour. But while British negotiators in the United States moved slowly and at times imperceptibly forward towards a distant goal of vast deliveries through a thicket of present difficulties and uncertainties, progress in Canada, though more limited in its ultimate objectives, was solid and steady. The obstacles met with in the United States never impeded the build-up of Canadian munitions capacity or the flow of Canadian supplies.

The problem of organisation which had bulked so large in May and the early part of June disappeared in the middle of that month when the dissolution of the British Supply Board was decided on. Henceforward the Canadian Department of Munitions and Supply was to play a dual role. It provided much of the equipment needed by the Canadian armed forces; and it acted as the direct agent of the Ministry of Supply and the other departments in London in procuring supplies for the Imperial forces in general. By this arrangement the British Government lost the close control over contracts and deliveries which it had sought to establish before Dunkirk, but this was more than offset by the goodwill which it won by its withdrawal and by the freeing of Canadian energies that resulted. There was of course some competition between the two sets of orders, and there was justice in British complaints that the needs of the Canadian Government tended to take precedence over requisitions coming from London. But these were questions which could be discussed within the framework of a common war effort and bore no resemblance to the disputes over the allocation of capacity and output which bedevilled British procurement in the United States.

Nor was there any serious problem of types. Canadian forces had always been equipped with weapons of British design and the Canadian Services were still content to follow Britain's lead in these matters. Such departures as there were from common British-Canadian types were taken for manufacturing reasons. There were close links between the heavy industries of Canada and the United States and obvious advantages in assimilating the products of the two countries. The adoption of American types of aircraft for manufacture in Canada has been referred to above (Chapter II). In much the same way it was decided towards the end of 1940 that part of Canada's tank programme should consist of a tank similar in structure to, and using the same components as, the 'Anglo-American' M.3. The result was the 'Ram', which, though it did not go into action except as the chassis for a self-propelled gun, occupies an important place in the history of tank design as the intermediate stage between the Grant and the Sherman. In the field of ordnance, however, where the greatest difficulties were being met with in the United States, Canadian production remained entirely faithful to British models. This fact was of the greatest value to the British. It was, for example, largely because in the autumn of 1940 a Canadian factory was being tooled up for the production of 25-pounder guns that they were able to dispense with orders for the unwelcome American type.

Nor, again, was finance a serious impediment to supply from Canada. The problem of payment was, indeed, little less difficult in relation to Canada than to the United States, and even a partial solution to it was not found till some weeks after lend-lease. A comprehensive solution on the lines of lend-lease itself had to wait for the enactment of mutual aid in the spring of 1943. But meanwhile, by allowing sterling balances to pile up in London and later by the free gift of a billion dollars, the Canadian Government saw to it that United Kingdom supplies were not placed in jeopardy.[1]

Thus, after June 1940 there were few issues of major policy in the supply relations of Canada and the United Kingdom. The latter had, indeed, to wait till 1942 before really substantial quantities of Canadian, as of American, munitions began to move across the

---

[1] See Chapter VII, Part I.

Atlantic. But the reasons for the delay were purely practical, namely, the difficulties of erecting a great edifice of war production on a base of heavy industry much narrower than was available in the United States. The difficulties and the achievement belong partly to the domestic history of Canadian war production and partly to the more detailed account of procurement in *Studies of Overseas Supply*. Here it will be sufficient to describe the setting in motion of the process and to indicate the broad outlines of Canada's contribution to the industrial war effort of the Commonwealth.

As already related, the German attack in the West gave a sharp edge to the dissatisfaction of Canadian industry and the Canadian Government with the volume of war orders so far received from Britain. One result of this was the elimination of the British Supply Board and of the 'dilatory procedures' which, it was alleged, had been holding up the development of Canada's war potential.[1] The real reason for the paucity of British munitions orders in Canada, however, had been the policy of restraint in dollar expenditure. This policy had now been discarded, and the way was clear for a great expansion. None the less, attention was at first focused upon the United States rather than on Canada, which was not mentioned in Monnet's letter of 20th May to the Prime Ministers of France and Britain, nor in his subsequent cable to the head of the Anglo-French Purchasing Board.[2] Only later, and at the prompting of Purvis, was it expressly stated that the plan for an increased production of armaments overseas applied to Canada as well as to the United States. During the next few weeks evidence of mounting Canadian discontent accumulated in cables from the High Commissioner and British supply officials in Ottawa, from various independent observers and from Mr. Mackenzie King himself,[3] and with British sentiment in any case pointing that way, Canada was assured of the largest possible share of any new munitions orders to be placed in North America.[4]

This decision, however, was based in the first instance mainly on political considerations. London remained for a time somewhat doubtful of the utility of large munitions programmes in Canada, especially on account of the time factor. In early June planning was dominated by preparations for the current invasion season and the Ministry of Supply showed itself more concerned with the speeding

---

[1] See above, Chapter II.

[2] See above, p. 159.

[3] Also in a memorandum presented to the Canadian Prime Minister on 6th June by a delegation of manufacturers and passed on to the British Government through the High Commissioner in London. This called for a big programme 'to mobilise immediately the intelligence, skill, equipment and capacity of Canadian industry'.

[4] It has to be remembered that the organising of North American production was not the primary task of the United Kingdom supply departments. Their first and main task was the immense one of organising war production in the United Kingdom itself.

of deliveries from existing orders than with long-term projects. The first Canadian estimates of what could be produced in the near future if large new orders were sanctioned erred too much on the side of overstatement and did little to dispel British scepticism. Later, however, the Department of Munitions and Supply, with the aid of British Supply Board officials and after consultation with the manufacturers, worked out a more realistic forecast of the production possibilities. It was now admitted that deliveries from the new plants could not begin much before the autumn of 1941. Meanwhile London had begun to take a longer view of supply planning, based on the equipment of fifty-five divisions by December 1941 and on insurance against loss of output in the intervening period. Canadian projects thus began to acquire a real value.

Canadian planners had emphasised that a prompt start was absolutely essential, especially to avoid being forestalled in the purchase of machine tools on the American market. The Government had therefore encouraged the manufacturers to go ahead and buy or at least take a short option on the machines that they would need. A Crown company, Citadel Merchandising Limited, was set up to act as a central purchasing and distributing agency for machine tools. These developments caused some concern to British Supply Board officials who feared that capacity was about to be created, presumably at British expense, for types and quantities of munitions which Britain might not want. They therefore pressed London strongly on 18th June for a definite programme of orders, so that Canadian expansion could be guided into the most appropriate channels.

After this, action was not long delayed. The Ministry of Supply accepted the latest Canadian estimate, which reached London on 23rd June 1940, as 'on the whole a sound and reasonable estimate of the possibilities'. Using this as a basis the Ministry divided its 'insurance' programme into two sections and offered one list of guns and ammunition orders amounting in value to £30 million, or one-third of the total, to Ottawa. A little earlier, long-delayed approval had been given to an order for 300 Valentine tanks, which had been pending since the beginning of the war, and also to an order for 20,000 lorries.

So far as the United States were concerned the army 'insurance' programme of July 1940 ran into the obstacles of dollar payments and types. But the 'insurance' orders were nevertheless valuable. In the case of Canada the 'insurance' programme was the real turning-point. It marked the beginning of serious war production after which Canadian industry never looked back. As time went on Canada absorbed more and more of the original United States share of the programme. The two lists were discussed at a series of meetings in July and early August between the Department of Munitions and

Supply and the British Purchasing Commission, and a number of minor adjustments were made, which on balance left Canada with a larger proportion of the total orders. This was partly on the general principle that, other things being equal, orders should be allotted to a belligerent Dominion rather than to a neutral state; Purvis had repeatedly asserted his 'purpose and preference' that this course should be adopted. But it was also because there was in many cases a much better prospect of early delivery from Canada, especially in view of the deadlock which had arisen over ordnance. Thereafter every British setback in the 'battle of the types' was to add to the responsibilities which Canada shouldered for the equipment of the Commonwealth armies. She was soon to be recognised as the only possible alternative source of Bren guns, Boys anti-tank rifles, 25-pounders, 2-pounder anti-tank equipments and eventually of 3·7-inch anti-aircraft guns.

British orders were not the only stimulus which Canadian war industry received in the summer of 1940. Before Dunkirk the munitions orders placed by the Canadian Government on its own behalf were few and small. Now it sought to provide from its own resources the full complement of arms and equipment required by Canadian troops both in the field and during their period of training at home. Within a few months Canadian orders were playing a substantial, in some cases a predominant, part in the building-up of Canada's munitions potential. Generally these orders were placed as supplements to those stemming from the United Kingdom, the capital cost being shared between the two Governments. In some instances, e.g. in the production of universal carriers, the Canadians went ahead without the help of the United Kingdom to create facilities which the latter was afterwards glad to use.

Thus began the remarkable expansion which was to make Canada the fourth among the United Nations as a producer of munitions and to give her a permanent place among the major industrial powers of the modern world. As a proportion of the Commonwealth's total munitions supplies from all sources, Canada's contribution does not appear particularly striking; four per cent. in 1940, six per cent. in 1941, and in 1943 nine per cent. of a total which had of course enormously increased. Considering the complete previous inexperience of Canadian industry in the manufacture of armaments other than ammunition and small arms, however, it was a very considerable achievement. Moreover, it is of interest that in the crucial year 1941 the Canadian contribution was only slightly smaller than that of the United States (eight per cent.).

Canadian production was perhaps least significant in those fields in which the United States had most to contribute, namely, aircraft and tanks, though even here it was by no means negligible. Aircraft supply has been described in Chapter II. Tank production to the end of the war amounted to 3,556 vehicles (against the United Kingdom's 25,115 to 30th June 1944[1]), and the great majority were either retained in Canada for training and home defence or shipped to Russia as part of the British quota of supplies under the Russian Protocol. Relatively much more important was the Canadian output of minor armoured fighting vehicles, such as scout cars and carriers, and also of other military motor vehicles, i.e. 'B' vehicles. The bulk of the Eighth Army's transport was made in Canada, and in the medium groups (15 cwt. to 3 tons) the Canadian contribution to Commonwealth supplies was only slightly less than that of the United Kingdom itself. In artillery Canada's output was only a moderate supplement to supply from other sources, but in small arms it was much more: 952,000 rifles and 270,000 machine guns were turned out during the war; by 1943 Canada was making sixty per cent. of the aggregate world output of Bren guns. Seven entirely new Canadian filling factories, in part financed by British capital, were an important element in Canadian munitions production. They filled the ammunition and bombs produced in Canada and whatever empty ammunition could be obtained from the United States. The shipyards of the Dominion played a notable part in the Battle of the Atlantic. Besides making the Royal Canadian Navy a formidable force, they built for British account some 200 ships for use by the naval forces of the United Kingdom. These included twenty-seven corvettes, sixteen Landing Ship Tank III, and large numbers of minesweepers and other vessels. Moreover, by 1943 Canada was turning out merchant shipping at the rate of about a million gross tons a year, only fifteen per cent. less than the United Kingdom itself, which had been for generations the world's greatest builder of ships. Raw materials, however, remained a most valuable contribution to the Commonwealth war effort. Throughout the war, but especially after the cutting of European supplies, the Dominion was the most important single source of the materials, other than steel, which fed the United Kingdom's war industries. Her aid was invaluable not only in the traditional exports of timber and pulp, copper, lead, zinc, nickel and ferro-alloys, but also in the relatively new field of aluminium production.[2]

---

[1] See *Statistical Digest of the War*, op. cit., Table 126.

[2] These are a few selected indications of the magnitude of Canada's war effort: on aluminium, see below, Chapter IX, pp. 366–68. For a full analysis see *Studies of Overseas Supply*.

CHAPTER VII

THE BARRIER OF THE EXCHANGES:
1940–44

PART I—CANADA

TWICE, in two world wars, Finance—the difficulty of payment across the exchanges—has proved a formidable barrier to the combination of the English-speaking peoples. After the First World War the barrier projected far into the peace in the form of the war debts. The existence of separate economic and monetary systems has been a consequence of the freedom which the English-speaking peoples have granted to, and upheld against, each other. But in war against a common enemy these separate systems have delayed and restricted their combination and imperilled their survival. Even between the countries of the sterling area the difficulty of the exchanges existed. It was serious enough to leave an aftermath for Britain in the shape of the post-war sterling debts to India, Australia, and other countries; but during the war it did not impede supply seriously enough to warrant space in a study dealing primarily with supply rather than finance as such.

As between the sterling area and the dollar area of North America, however, the barrier of the exchanges was so serious in the first half of the war that a chapter must be devoted to its effects on supply. The finding of passes by which supplies could be got through the barrier was one of the chief anxieties of the British, American and Canadian Governments in the first years of the war. It was only in its later years that American lend-lease and Canadian mutual aid, supplemented by British mutual aid, opened the passes for the free passage of men, munitions and materials into the main theatres in which the war had to be fought—the British Isles, North Africa and the South Pacific.

It is not the purpose of this chapter to examine the philosophy of the Barrier of the Exchanges. Such an enquiry would show that the barrier was not part of the order of nature; it could have been levelled if the principle of pooling had really been carried to its logical conclusion. The exchanges need not have been barriers at all. They were not an inevitable result of separate monetary systems. If the dollar sign had been fully removed, as it was not, then there would have been no 'debts' or 'gifts', nor any 'lending' or 'leasing' after the

United States entered the war. Each country would have met its own expenditure on war supplies—Canada and the United States all their dollar expenditures, India all her rupee expenditures, and so forth. It was fundamentally absurd that a Canadian bullet fired by a Canadian pilot should be treated differently in the matter of payment from a Canadian bullet fired by a British pilot. It was illogical that when it was a British and not an American airman who was risking his life in an American plane the plane should be regarded as 'a loan'. In the case of Canada the point was obscured from the outset by the fact that Canada was short on American dollars and had to make up her deficit in dollars by using gold supplied by the United Kingdom. In a war that was common, and not solely Britain's war, there was not much logic in Britain sacrificing her dollar securities as a means of filling the gap in the balance of payments in the earlier part of the war. In its earlier phase, lend-lease did not meet the whole deficit in the balance of payments, and the last of the British reserves had to be thrown in to avoid default. Later lend-lease more than met the deficit, and the reserves grew again slowly. But the logic of pooling was still not applied. Because the rupee and other 'signs' still remained, colossal sterling debts were created. If the large transatlantic payments of the cash period could have been refunded by a kind of grant-in-aid—as the logic of pooling might have suggested—the disastrous post-war deficit in the British balance of payments might have been avoided. Such a 'pensioning of the past' was indeed suggested during the loan negotiations in the autumn of 1945, but it was then too late.[1]

CANADA

Already in the years between the wars, Canada was ranked by the International Labour Office as one of the eight chief industrial countries of the world. And it was from Canada that the main industrial centre of the British Commonwealth, the United Kingdom, drew much of the raw material for her own industry. Canada had the great advantage of being able to expand her war capacity in relative security from air attack. But the task of moving the raw materials and munitions of Canada across the exchanges into the United Kingdom (which was for Canada the main field from which battle had to be waged against the enemy) presented both countries with problems of great difficulty and complexity. Even in peace-time the United Kingdom had an adverse balance of payments with Canada, as well as with the United States. In 1938 the adverse

---

[1] See below, p. 478, and the Treasury study printed in Appendix IX. For a good summary of the British dollar position during the war, see D. F. McCurrach, 'Britain's U.S. Dollar Problems, 1939–1945' in *The Economic Journal*, No. 231, September 1948, pp. 356–72.

balance with Canada was $127 million.[1] During the war years British orders for munitions, raw materials and food far exceeded Canada's purchases in the United Kingdom; hence a continuous and mounting deficit in the British balance of payments with Canada. Both countries contributed as best they could towards the solution of this problem. At first the principle of elimination of the dollar sign was not adopted by the Canadian Government. But it began to act on that principle after the enactment of lend-lease by the United States. 'It has been, and will continue to be,' the Minister of Finance declared in the Canadian House of Commons on 20th March 1941, 'the policy of the Government to see that United Kingdom purchases in this country are not hampered by reason of any lack of Canadian dollars. We have seen, and will continue to see, that the problem of the deficit is solved.'

(i)

The Bridging of the Exchange Barrier: the Main Stages, 1939–45

At this time the Canadian Government was being criticised in some quarters in the United States on the ground that it too should adopt a policy of lend-lease to Britain. But such criticisms, as the Prime Minister pointed out in a speech in New York on 17th June 1941, ignored essential differences in the position of Canada as compared with the United States. One was that Canada needed no new legal machinery in order to give financial aid to Britain, and had in fact been giving it to the amount needed since the beginning of the war. Moreover, in addition to this aid, Canada, as a belligerent, had a direct war effort which was 'not leased or lent'.[2] He went on to say that Canada was carrying already a burden which for a country of the population and resources of the United States would amount to $35 billion. Such comparisons of national income and war effort could be misleading. The British and Canadian Treasuries in the autumn of 1939 had indulged for some weeks in this exercise, but

---

[1] The adverse balance of Great Britain with the United States in 1938 was $315 million. The year 1938 was not, however, typical. Thus, the normal substantial surplus of the sterling area as a whole with *North America* was changed to a deficit of $525 million, largely through a falling off of United States imports. The deficit was met by the sale of newly-mined gold, purchased by the United Kingdom out of its normal surplus with the rest of the sterling area. Britain's overall balance showed in 1938 a deficit, which was financed by drawing on her reserves which had increased during the preceding three years. *United Nations Economic Bulletin for Europe*, Second Quarter, 1949, Vol. 1, No. 2.

[2] *The New York Times*, 18th June 1941.

had then abandoned the attempt on the ground that such comparisons were 'full of pitfalls'. But about Canada's direct war effort there was nothing hypothetical. The first Canadian division that landed in Britain on 17th December 1939 had been followed by other divisions and air squadrons. By the time the United States entered the war, Canada had in the United Kingdom an armoured division, an army tank brigade and three infantry divisions. The Canadian Navy, which had begun the war with six destroyers and nine smaller vessels, was fighting in the Battle of the Atlantic with more than 300 vessels.

In the account that follows it is well to remember both the unity of the exchange problem and the differences within that unity. There was a British-Canadian problem linked with, but distinct from, the British-American problem; but there was also a Canadian-American problem arising from Canada's continuous deficit with the United States. Neither Britain nor Canada could solve her problem without the help of the United States, which was, therefore, in a position to see both sides of it. Just as on the supply side, Secretary Morgenthau as Chairman of the President's Liaison Committee always insisted that the members of the British Commonwealth of Nations must approach the Administration as a group, and not as individual states, so as Treasurer he preferred Britain and Canada to discuss with him their exchange problems together rather than separately.

This account of the British-Canadian aspect of the exchange problem may begin with a broad survey of the road travelled by the two Governments in solving the many problems of the deficit in the United Kingdom's balance of payments with Canada. With this must go the warning that though in retrospect the road may look easy, it was immensely difficult to survey and to build through the war years.

The deficit was the gap left after the sterling area had paid out all its Canadian dollar receipts for the supplies it was importing from Canada.[1] In the main these receipts came from Canadian payments of various kinds, e.g. payments for British exports to Canada, and for British freight services, and payments by way of interest and dividends on British loans or investments in Canada. An important new source of receipts in the later part of the war was payments in Canadian dollars for the maintenance and supply of Canadian forces stationed in the United Kingdom. A number of different methods were used to meet the deficit. They involved contributions from the British side to Canada; contributions from Canada to Britain; and contributions by Canada both to Britain and to other parts of the British Commonwealth in the sterling area as well as to Allied countries.

---

[1] The figures that follow are from *Canadian Mutual Aid Board* (Second Annual Report to 31st March 1945). On Mutual Aid see table below, p. 242.

Six methods or stages in the process of meeting the deficit can be distinguished.

1. *The British Gold Payments* (or payments of United States dollars) to Canada. (These Canada used in turn to pay for imports of war supplies from the United States—especially American materials and components needed for the manufacture in Canada of war supplies for the United Kingdom).

2. *The British Sale of Securities* back to Canada for dollars.[1]
   (*a*) Repatriation of British-held Canadian Government and Canadian National Railways securities. Such transactions totalled some $700 million during the war.
   (*b*) Sale by Britain in Canada of other British-held securities which yielded some $100 million.

3. *The Canadian interest-free Loan to the United Kingdom* of $700 million (January 1942, under War Appropriation [United Kingdom Financing] Act. Proceeds from any sales by Britain of her remaining Canadian securities were to be used to pay off the loan.)

4. *The Billion Dollar Gift* of Canadian war supplies to the United Kingdom, and other British Commonwealth and Allied nations, under the War Appropriation (United Kingdom Financing) Act, 1942 ($1,000 million).

5. *The Sale of British Capital Assets in Canada* (1943). Repayment by Canada of British contributions towards munitions plants in Canada to produce war supplies for the United Kingdom, approximately $200 million.

6. *Canadian Mutual Aid Appropriations* 1943–45 ($1,800 million) for supplies to the United Kingdom, other British Commonwealth countries, Allies and Relief, under the War Appropriation (United Nations Mutual Aid) Acts, May 1943 and June 1944.[2]

(ii)

The Financing of Supply from Canada to March 1941

At the beginning of the war British orders in Canada lagged for other reasons besides finance. The tempo on both sides of the Atlantic was still slow in matters of supply. On the British side, orders were retarded because of the conception of Canada as a marginal source,

---

[1] The total sales of United Kingdom owned investments in Canada during the war is given as $905 million in *Statistical Material Presented during the Washington Negotiations*, Cmd. 6707, December 1945.

[2] See table below, p. 242, and texts of Acts in Appendix VI.

as well as because of the shortage of dollars. On the Canadian side, war production had hardly begun in September 1939. Little had been done to work out systematically in advance, in terms of money, materials and organisation, the economic and industrial conse-quences of war. Enthusiasm ran first to recruitment. About 50,000 men were enlisted immediately, but without any immediate assurance of equipment. The initial plans of the Government on the supply side involved such a high financial programme that a drastic scaling down was necessary. The turning over to war production of a high proportion of the national income of Canada could only be achieved step by step over a fairly long period. The Canadian Government was anxious to obtain British defence orders as one means of expand-ing the Canadian economy, so that Canada could make a greater contribution in a later stage of the war.

The Bank of Canada estimated the probable British deficit in Canadian dollars in the first war-year as about $250 million. The British estimate (based on a first-year purchasing programme, figured in December 1939 at over $500 million) ranged as high as $320 million. The first step on the Canadian side towards meeting part of the deficit was a bankers' loan for $200 million, which the Government raised in October 1939.[1] Part of the loan—$100 million to $125 million—was earmarked for the buying back of Canadian Government securities held in Great Britain. It was planned to meet the second half of the deficit by a further sale of securities to the extent of $65 million, and by the sale of gold to Canada to the amount of $45 million. In the first Canadian National War Loan for $200 million which followed in January 1940, another $50 million was earmarked for the purchase of Canadian securities from the British Government.

Buying back by Canada of Canadian bonds held in England was obviously not a loan by Canada to the United Kingdom, as it was sometimes loosely called. An early British dispatch from Ottawa made the point clear. 'It is cash on the barrel head in all North America.' The securities thus purchased by the Canadian Govern-ment were cancelled, and not sold on the Canadian market. This process ultimately strengthened the economy of the country, but its immediate effect was that the Canadian people had to save the sum

---

[1] The detail of the purchasing programme as revised in March 1940 was:

	£ million
Admiralty and shipbuilding	$3\frac{1}{2}$
Air Ministry	3
Munitions (output)	$3\frac{1}{4}$
Munitions (plant)	$3\frac{1}{4}$
Aluminium (plant)	$3\frac{1}{2}$
Raw materials	$37\frac{1}{2}$
Food	50–53
General manufactures	5

equivalent to the amount of the securities purchased.[1] Moreover, it was preferable to at least one alternative which, in the first weeks of the war, was discussed between representatives of the British and Canadian Treasuries in Ottawa, and was rejected. This was the suggestion that important Canadian producers of metals, timber, and other products might be willing to accept payment in blocked sterling. Whilst Australia, which normally had an unfavourable balance in terms of sterling, might be able to hold large sterling balances, it was thought to be more difficult for Canada, where it might even be looked upon as in the nature of a 'forced loan'. Firms which accepted the arrangement ran the risk of immobilising their capital; since they might not be able to use the funds to purchase in the United Kingdom, they might be tempted to raise their prices.

But as the early months of 1940 passed by, the Bank of Canada showed itself more and more willing to increase its temporary holdings of sterling. Thus, in mid-May, it offered to accumulate a further $50 million worth of sterling. This factor, as an official of the Bank of England noted at the time, made it 'definitely much easier to raise Canadian dollars than United States dollars'.

A rough guess, made by the British Treasury in July 1940, as to the working of these arrangements in the first nine months of the war was that during the period an actual adverse balance of £49 million had been met as follows: by repatriation of loan and sale of securities, £18 million; by transfer of gold, £13½ million, by an increase in the sterling balances held by the Bank of Canada, £12½ million. The remaining £5 million had been met by depletion of the dollar balance of the Exchange Equalisation Account in London.

Late in July, the situation was reviewed again in a series of discussions at Ottawa between the British Treasury representative, Sir Frederick Phillips, and the Canadian authorities. The picture for the first year of the war was now more clear. When still more complete data were available in September, the revised estimate of the deficit with Canada for the first year of war was some $400 million; of this amount Canada had met by repatriation of securities about $195 million, and by holding sterling, $20 million. The sale of gold by the United Kingdom to Canada had produced $185 million.

A request made during the July talks, by Sir Frederick Phillips to the Treasury, for 'any useful guess' at the requirements for the second war-year produced figures which seemed to show that the adverse balance was likely to be almost double that for the first year; the figure suggested was $640 million. Even allowing for increased gold payments this would still mean that Canada must be asked to find as much as $400 million through purchase of securities and the

---

[1] Statement by Minister of Finance (Mr. Ilsley) in the Canadian House of Commons, 18th February 1941.

holding of sterling. As a first contribution towards this expected deficit it was agreed that Canada should provide against sterling for the first six months of the second war-year (from August 1940 to January 1941) $150 million; a further review would then be made at the end of the year. To facilitate the necessary transfer of securities to Canada, the British Treasury issued in October an order vesting in the Treasury a large number of Canadian securities, covering sixty different bond and stock issues.

Thus, for a further six months the Canadian Government continued to help as much as it could by repatriating securities and allowing its sterling balances to rise. Up to this point, it was providing dollars in amounts fixed by informal agreements made in advance by the two Treasuries. The amount of its help was limited only by the ability of Canada to raise funds internally without danger of inflation. A second National War Loan for $600 million was issued in October 1940 and was over-subscribed. The money was used, in part, to finance Canada's own war expenditures as well as for the purchase of securities. The total war expenditure of Canada for the calendar year 1940, as calculated by Canadian financial authorities early in 1941, was $902 million. Of this amount $549 million was for Canada's own war expenditure, $265 million was for assistance to Great Britain (in the form of repatriation of securities and accumulation of sterling) and $88 million was Canada's contribution to the British capital assistance programme in Canada.

In mid-January 1941 Secretary Morgenthau issued a statement (in a letter to Mr. Sol Bloom) which gave the following figures, showing Canadian financial relations with Britain and the rest of the sterling area for the sixteen months of the war down to the end of December 1940.[1]

U.S. $ million

A. Payments to Canada and Newfoundland by Empire countries:
1. For purchases from Canada and Newfoundland by the United Kingdom   795
2. For purchases from Canada by other Empire countries   125
3. Other payments to Canada by Empire countries   10
                                                    ——   930

B. Receipts from Canada and Newfoundland by Empire countries:
1. From merchandise exports to Canada and Newfoundland by United Kingdom   .   .   .   170
2. From merchandise exports to Canada by other Empire countries   100

---

[1] Letter to Mr. Sol Bloom, Chairman, House Committee on Foreign Relations, printed by the United States Congress in the Lend-Lease Hearings.

U.S. $ million

3. From interest and dividends paid by Canada to
   United Kingdom 85
4. Other United Kingdom receipts from Canada,
   principally Canadian Expeditionary Forces . 20

   ——

   375

British Empire deficit with Canada and Newfoundland
on merchandise, interest and dividends, etc. . . 555

Canadian assistance to United Kingdom—repatriation
of British-held Canadian securities and increase in
sterling balances held by Canada . . . 330

Gold payments by British Empire countries with
Canada and Newfoundland, 1st September 1939 to
31st December 1940 225

The figures, as the letter itself indicated, had been supplied (at very short notice) by the British Treasury representative. The letter failed to mention that Canada had already advanced for the period *after* 31st December 1940 a further $150 million. The omission was due to a misunderstanding, but its reason was to avoid, as far as possible, seeming to commit Canada to a higher rate of assistance than in 1940. The omission led, nevertheless, to public criticism that Canada was not doing enough.[1]

The $150 million referred to here was the amount which had been promised in July to finance the British deficit from August 1940 to January 1941: it had already been exhausted, however, in December, and a resumption of the gold payments had therefore become necessary. In view, however, of the critical position the British Treasury asked in January for a further sum of dollars and received another $50 million. Ottawa warned, however, that this meant drawing upon the aid due in the second half of the second war-year. By the end of the first fortnight in January the extra $50 million was also exhausted; a further appeal for dollars had to be made by London in order to avoid paying over the gold which was almost the last British asset left for continued purchase of arms from the United States until the passage of the Lend-Lease Act. The decision to make the appeal was accompanied by the warning on 12th January by the Financial Adviser at the British Embassy that 'we are straining the Canadian economy by asking them to help us at so rapid a pace'. His conclusion was that not all the need could be met by Canada in dollars, and that some gold would have to be paid in February.

Meanwhile, the 'rapid pace' had begun to perturb Canadian officials at Ottawa, who did not at first recognise the real gravity of

---

[1] The figure of $795 million for United Kingdom purchases in Canada was too high. The real figure was about $700 million.

the crisis. What could happen without continuous direct personal liaison between the two Treasuries was shown in a series of misunderstandings, which had arisen rather suddenly in December 1940, as to the extent of the assets remaining to the United Kingdom. It was known that the United Kingdom still had $865 million in gold in an account in the Bank of Canada, but it was not realised that this was not the property of the British Government but was held on behalf of foreign governments, such as Switzerland and Belgium. Another wrong assumption was that Britain had taken over French gold—a step not favoured at the time by either the Canadian Prime Minister or President Roosevelt. Because of these misunderstandings, recent Bank of England telegrams, as one of the Canadian financial authorities put it, had seemed 'unintelligible and almost hysterical'. These fogs were cleared up in a joint meeting in Ottawa on 10th January. It was made clear that British reserves of gold and dollars were down to a mere $360 million (U.S.), of which in practice about $80 million could not be used.[1] The estimated dollar needs (including those in the United States) were: for January, $340 million; and for February (including $100 million in gold for Canada), $670 million —figures which, as the British Treasury representative at Ottawa drily remarked, 'adequately showed the urgency of the position'.

A further $25 million, advanced by Canada after this talk, was practically exhausted before the end of the month. 'We are losing about $12 million Canadian weekly on the average at present', the British Treasury told its Washington representative on 27th January. By now, it pointed out, a new factor had begun to affect payments in gold to Canada; there might be an objection on the part of the United States against such payments, on the ground that all available British gold should be used for payments to the United States to cover urgent current orders before lend-lease was enacted. This remark was the outcome of discussions which had begun several days earlier on the relation of Canada to lend-lease, to which reference is made below (pp. 236–37).

By January 1941 it was clear that the second war-year programme of British requirements from Canada would reach a much higher figure than the guess in July 1940 of $640 million. A better guess now put the probable deficit for the sterling area as a whole at $960 million (£216 million)—a figure which showed that the weekly loss of $12 million referred to above was likely to continue indefinitely. Clearly, therefore, the Treasuries were already faced with a breakdown of the kind of arrangements by which they had hitherto dealt with the deficit. It would no longer be possible to fix in advance, from time to time, a sum to be met in part in dollars advanced by

---

[1] See pp. 231–32. Secretary Morgenthau's letter to Bloom, which was a week later than the Ottawa talk, showed that the $360 million had already dropped to $346 million.

Canada against cancellation of long-term Canadian debt to the United Kingdom, and in part by the United Kingdom in gold. From this point the Canadian Government would have to carry on from week to week with fresh allocations of Canadian dollars made against sterling. This stage was marked by a letter from the Canadian Prime Minister to the High Commissioner of the United Kingdom on 16th February. The Prime Minister noted that to meet the urgent need of the British Government, the Foreign Exchange Control Board had been authorised to accumulate, at intervals from 28th January, additional sterling (up to £5 million). To meet urgent British requirements for the remainder of February, the Foreign Exchange Board had been authorised to accept additional sterling up to $40 million Canadian. The Prime Minister noted that Canada had also made upwards of $200 million available since mid-December, against repatriation of the Canadian debt. Since very heavy increases in direct war expenditure in Canada were contemplated, it was difficult to forecast the extent of further assistance Canada might be able to give in the next six months, either by repatriation or by acquiring sterling. The best plan, therefore, he suggested, was to deal with the situation from time to time as it developed, taking into account Canada's expenditure and commitments and the state of the market for further loans.

Two days later the Canadian House of Commons was informed that Canada's war expenditure was now running at well over a billion dollars a year. For the new financial year expenditure was expected to run to $1,415 million; the appropriation asked for was $1,300 million. In addition, another $400 million would be needed for assistance to the United Kingdom by way of repatriation of loans. To all this had to be added several other large sums: for the Dominion Government's non-war estimates, $433 million; and for expenditures by the Provincial and Municipal governments, $575 million. In all, this made a total of $2,700 million, or over fifty per cent. of the national income.[1]

A month later the Prime Minister gave to the Canadian House of Commons figures indicating that the deficit in the balance of Great Britain with Canada for the first eighteen months of the war had been $737 million. This had been met by the United Kingdom as follows:

		$ *million*
1. In gold	. . . .	250
2. In sterling (equivalent to a Canadian loan)	.	155
3. By repatriation of securities	. . .	332
	Total . . .	737

[1] Statement by Minister of Finance (Mr. Ilsley), 18th February 1941.

He informed the House that for the next twelve months the deficit was expected to be $1,150 million.[1] Next day, in a message to London, he pledged Canada's 'best endeavours to continue meeting the United Kingdom's full deficit with Canada' by repatriating securities and accumulating sterling. He hoped for some gold payment, but that was bound up with the relation of Canada to the United States, to which Canada expected to be indebted on the next year's transactions to the amount of $478 million. The net debit in Canada's trade balance with the United States in the first eighteen months of the war he put at $471 million U.S., of which $227 million had been met by paying over practically all the gold received from the United Kingdom during the period.

By now it was becoming clear that if British and Canadian attempts at striking balances ahead were ever to agree, something must be done to put them on a more uniform basis. The estimates made in London and Ottawa were always divergent. It was obvious that such calculations would have to continue throughout the war. Discussions were begun, therefore, in the summer of 1941, to secure a more uniform basis for such figures. Finally, after negotiations lasting over a year, an agreement was worked out between the two Governments in August 1942 for the exchange of two regular forecasts, drawn up on a more or less uniform basis. These were: first, a monthly forecast of payments made to Canada by the United Kingdom and sterling-area countries; second, an estimated balance of payments between Canada and the sterling area.

(iii)

The Effect of Lend-Lease on Supply from Canada

As soon as lend-lease became a possibility, the part hitherto played by British gold as a factor in adjusting balances between Great Britain, Canada and the United States came to the forefront. The matter was brought up in mid-January 1941 by the British Treasury,

---

[1] The British purchasing programme in Canada for the second war-year as given at the beginning of March 1941 by the Treasury was approximately £305 million (Canadian $1,357 million). The main items were:

	£ million
Admiralty	11·5
M.A.P. and Air Ministry . .	26
Aluminium	20
Munitions (tanks, transport, explosives, guns and ammunition) .	110
Raw materials	51·5
Food	62

when it was faced with the fact that there was not nearly enough gold left, or coming in from South Africa, to pay its debits both with Canada and the United States. Canada, it pointed out, was bound to ask the United Kingdom to cover a large part of its payments in gold as long as the latter had to make 'large U.S. dollar payments for raw materials and components required to carry out our orders'.[1] About a quarter of Canada's war production for the United Kingdom was imported from the United States in this way. If this could be brought under lend-lease, Canada would not have to pay gold for it, with a corresponding drop in British payments of gold to Canada. Up to this stage, Canada—so far as could be judged in London—had not drawn much on her pre-war holdings of gold and United States securities; moreover, war loans had as yet drawn only to a limited degree on the national savings.

The Canadian authorities were at first doubtful whether it would be to Canada's advantage to make use of the Lend-Lease Bill. 'Rightly or wrongly', the United Kingdom Treasury representative reported to London, 'they feel that they are in a much weaker position than we are *vis-à-vis* the United States.' The Canadian Treasury leaned towards the policy of drawing first upon Canada's gold and American dollar securities. At a later and more favourable stage it might raise the question of American help under lend-lease. There were further discussions on the matter between the representatives of the two Treasuries in Washington at the end of February and early in March, from which it appeared that Canada was ready to begin to liquidate her gold and dollar securities in the hope that 'components' would soon be brought under lend-lease. Her gold and American dollar assets at this moment were, in millions of American dollars: gold 136, American dollars 115, marketable securities 378. In the next four months, March to June 1941, the British Treasury representative calculated that the United Kingdom would have to pay $385 million to Canada (in repatriated securities, gold or sterling). The amount of gold which the Treasury then had available was only $120 million. Moreover, it was still not clear whether the United States would object to the United Kingdom paying gold to Canada. This possibility had been prejudiced by a statement which, as was discovered a little later, Mr. Morgenthau had made in the Lend-Lease Hearings. In reply to a question he had said, 'I believe any amount of South African gold that the United Kingdom receives during this year they should use to pay for merchandise which they buy in this country'. Representatives of the two Treasuries discussed the matter on 18th and 19th March with Secretary Morgenthau.

---

[1] Examples were aircraft engines for installation in airframes manufactured in Canada. Another item was material bought for the British Commonwealth Air Training Plan, on British account, which cost some $60 million a year.

They gave him full data on the balances of the two countries and their bearing on the relation of lend-lease to Canada. He replied in the affirmative to a question whether Canada should start liquidating her United States securities. The question of bringing under lend-lease the British element in Canadian imports from the United States was a matter, he suggested, for Harry Hopkins.

The Canadian Prime Minister referred also to the matter in a statement in the House of Commons on 26th March. He put the total deficit of Canada with the United States in the first eighteen months of the war at $417 million. Over half of the deficit, or $227 million, had been met by the gold received in Canada from the United Kingdom. Any gold or United States dollars received by Canada from the United Kingdom, he told the House, was solely for the purpose of enabling Canada to make payments to the United States for war supplies. In a message to the British Government next day he indicated some of the preoccupations of the Canadian Government as to the indirect effects of lend-lease on Canada. He foresaw that lend-lease might conceivably result in the diversion of orders for munitions and foodstuffs from Canada to the United States, thus disorganising the Canadian war effort and undermining the Canadian economy. If this were to result in the setting up of duplicate plants in the United States there might be a falling off of war production in Canada. To win the war it was necessary to have the closest possible co-operation between the Governments of the United Kingdom, Canada and the United States in order to plan the most effective utilisation of the productive facilities of North America as a whole. The British Government had already reassured the Canadian Government that there would be no diminution of its orders to Canada because of lend-lease. It pointed out that the extent of its orders in Canada would depend solely on the amount of gold and dollars it possessed from time to time, as well as the amount of financial assistance Canada could render to the United Kingdom.

The agreement between the two Governments that emerged from these exchanges can be summarised as follows: there was to be no diversion of British orders from Canada to the United States, whether for munitions, raw materials or agricultural products. British orders would continue to ensure 'maximum possible use' of Canadian factories. There would be no duplication of plant in the United States to meet any orders which Canada could supply. The United Kingdom would make the maximum use of all types of foodstuffs produced in Canada; and there would be joint consideration between the two countries of any United States proposals for British purchases of agricultural products in the United States. On the food side, liaison between the two Governments was now closer as the result of the setting up of the British Food Mission in Washington, with instructions to maintain the closest possible relations with the Canadian Government representatives.

It was not possible to give any guarantee as to the future exchange rate of sterling. The Canadian Government acquiesced in the accumulation of sterling balances—in its case temporary—without pressing for any such guarantee, although the matter came into the discussions. All parts of the Commonwealth had already committed themselves to the accumulation of sterling balances without seeking any guarantee.

American components in British orders in Canada were brought under lend-lease by the Hyde Park Declaration, announced on 21st April, following discussions between the Canadian Prime Minister and President Roosevelt at the latter's home at Hyde Park, New York. 'Insofar', the announcement said, 'as Canada's defence purchases in the United States consist of component parts to be used in equipment and munitions which Canada is producing for Great Britain it is . . . agreed that Great Britain will obtain these parts under the Lease-Lend Act and forward them to Canada for inclusion in the finished articles.'[1] Under this arrangement the United States not only met the cost of components but placed contracts in Canada for certain war supplies for Britain and paid for them with lend-lease funds, e.g. contracts for Cornell, Harvard and Catalina aircraft. Under a procedure known as 'Canex' Canada was empowered to obtain components (which covered a very large range of commodities) within a ceiling of $350 million through the British Missions in the United States. The latter obtained the items under lend-lease and transferred them to Canada. The agreement not only reduced the deficit of Canada with the United States but also that of the United Kingdom with Canada, and therefore the amount of gold or American dollars which Britain had to pay to Canada.

From this point onwards the fact that Canada was freely meeting British requirements for Canadian dollars relieved the heavy pressures and anxieties of the preceding months. Adjustments were

---

[1] The reciprocal nature of the agreement emerges from two other paragraphs of the Declaration. 'While Canada has expanded its productive capacity manifold since the beginning of the war, there are still numerous defence articles which it must obtain in the United States and purchases of this character by Canada will be even greater in the coming year than in the past. On the other hand, there is existing and potential capacity in Canada for the speedy production of certain kinds of munitions, strategic materials, aluminium and ships, which are urgently required by the United States for its own purposes.

'While exact estimates cannot yet be made, it is hoped that during the next twelve months Canada can supply the United States with between $200 and $300 million worth of such defence articles. This sum is a small fraction of the total defence programme of the United States, but many of the articles to be provided are of vital importance. In addition, it is of great importance to the economic and financial relations between the two countries that payment by the United States for these supplies will materially assist Canada in meeting part of the cost of Canadian defence purchases in the United States.'

necessary from time to time, but they could be made without much difficulty. Early in May 1941 Purvis reported the point put to him by the Canadian Minister of Munitions and Supply that, since lend-lease, relatively minor orders had been placed in Canada. He asked whether continuation orders on previous contracts were being given. He was informed in reply that the United Kingdom was making every effort to make continued use of Canadian capacity. Continuation orders were being placed to keep fully employed all capacity which had been earmarked in Canada for the United Kingdom. The only exception was a few cases where full requirements had been met. Whilst it was the policy of the United Kingdom to make full use of Canadian capacity and to integrate American and Canadian facilities, it had a short- as well as a long-term interest to consider. The immediate aim was 'maximum production up to June 1942'— even if this meant some delay in creating capacity which would come into operation after that date. It was pointed out that the programmes arranged by Layton and Purvis in October and November 1940 had been allocated between Canada and the United States on the basis of their productive possibilities for different types. The orders which were being placed under lend-lease in the United States were not new but were in execution of these original programmes.

(iv)

The Billion-dollar Gift and Mutual Aid

Meanwhile, the repatriation of securities was continuing. Towards the end of June 1941 the Treasury arranged, in accordance with the wish of the Canadian Government, for the repatriation of further securities to the value of £30 million. On the other hand, in July and August, payments by Canada for the maintenance of Canadian troops and services in the United Kingdom began to assume a greater importance in the balance of payments between the two countries. In the last two years of the war, as indicated in the table at the end of this section, this was to become for the United Kingdom its most important source of Canadian dollars.

In the autumn of 1941 it had become clear that despite this new factor and the bringing under lend-lease of components from the United States, Canada was beginning to pile up formidable sterling balances. Early in October the balance was nearly £130 million and was increasing at the rate of £20 million a month. At this rate it might reach as much as $2,500 million by October 1943. Repatriation of the remaining securities held in the United Kingdom, which were calculated at £90 million (in addition to the £30 million covered by the agreement in June), would not go far to fill the gap. If the war went on indefinitely the indebtedness would pile up to the point where payment was no longer possible. The ideal solution from the British point of view would be for Canada to adopt some sort of lend-lease arrangement. This idea was mentioned on the British side in mid-August. In the view of the British Treasury representative such a development had the advantage of satisfying American opinion. A hint that the Canadian financial authorities had already come to some such conclusion was given at the end of August when the British High Commissioner in Ottawa was told that proposals of 'far-reaching importance' on the financial side were under consideration. There was no longer any suggestion of a British exchange guarantee to protect Canadian sterling holdings against possible inflation in the United Kingdom. (Such inflation, in the view of Lord Keynes, was more likely in Canada and the United States than in the United Kingdom.) The announcement of the proposals was delayed until January 1942, partly because of the preoccupation of the Canadian Government with the tightening of domestic controls and the entry of the United States into the war. The Canadian Government announced in January that sterling funds accumulated by Canada in London were being converted into an interest-free loan for the duration of the war to the amount of $700 million. It was further announced that as from December 1941 all munitions and war supplies, including food, produced in Canada for the United Kingdom would be an outright gift to the extent of one billion dollars. This sum, it was calculated, would see the United Kingdom through to March 1943. From the spring of 1943 to the end of the war the deficit in the British balance of payments with Canada was met mainly from Canadian mutual-aid appropriations under the War Appropriation (United Nations Mutual Aid) Acts of May 1943 and June 1944.[1] Mutual aid continued until 2nd September 1945.[2] Its history belongs rather to the Canadian history of the war than to that of the United Kingdom. Even under mutual aid, however, British cash payments[3] still continued to meet about two-thirds of the cost of the war supplies obtained from Canada:—

---

[1] For the texts of these Acts see Appendix VI.

[2] The post-war 'Financial Agreement and Agreement on the Settlement of War Claims between the Governments of the United Kingdom and Canada', Cmd. 6904, March 1946, and the settlement of the British debt of $425 million on the British Commonwealth Air Training Plan, are dealt with in Chapter XI.

[3] *Canadian Mutual Aid Board* (Second Annual Report to 31st March 1945).

Expenditure on war supplies from Canada to the United Kingdom
$ million

		1943–44	1944–45
Mutual aid	. .	723	719
Cash	. .	1,133	1,625
		1,856	2,344[1]

Table 4 (see next page) gives a general view of the financing of war supplies obtained from Canada by the United Kingdom from 1943 to 1945. Mutual aid was administered in Canada by the Canadian Mutual Aid Board as lend-lease was administered in the United States by the Office of Lend-Lease Administration. Under the $700 million loan and the billion-dollar gift the Department of Munitions and Supply acted as agent of the British Government in using Canadian funds to purchase supplies in Canada. The requirements of the British Government, as well as of other British Commonwealth countries and Allied Governments, were indicated to the Department by the British Ministries concerned. The administration of mutual aid, however, was wholly a Canadian affair. Under a mutual-aid agreement made by Canada with each nation, requests for supplies were made to the Canadian Mutual Aid Board. It was the Board that decided what supplies should be granted, and it was the Board that undertook procurement through the Canadian Ministry concerned. As under lend-lease, supplies were provided subject to such considerations as 'strategic essentiality', ability to pay for supplies, and 'the effect on the Canadian economy'. Military supplies produced in Canada and in relatively short supply 'were subject to a process of assignment each month' by the Canadian Munitions Assignment Committee operating under the general machinery of the Combined Munitions Assignments Board.[2]

This account has been too much preoccupied with bare figures and the dry bones of financial arrangements. It is important, however, that the spirit and the feeling which lay behind these large transactions should not be forgotten. Their nature was shown in the campaign by which the $600 million Third National War Loan was launched in Canada in June 1941. The central theme of the campaign was a torch. The torch, escorted by representatives of the three Services, was carried in stages across Canada by a bomber aircraft. Each landing and take-off was marked by ceremonies. When subscriptions to the loan passed the objective of $600 million (total subscriptions were $837 million) the torch was flown from Halifax to London and presented to Mr. Churchill. The inscription on its base read: 'Part of the tools—Canada's Victory Loan 1941'.

---

[1] In addition, mutual aid to the value of $258 million was given in the period 1943–45 by Canada to the U.S.S.R., Australia, New Zealand, India, China and France.

[2] *Canadian Mutual Aid Board* (Second Annual Report to 31st March 1945), pp. 9–11.

R

TABLE 4

Expenditure on war supplies from Canada to the United Kingdom 1943–45

$ million

Canadian mutual-aid expenditure on war supplies to United Kingdom	1943-44	1944-45
Munitions and military supplies, including raw materials, ships, etc.	554	586
Foodstuffs and farm products	169	133
Total Canadian mutual-aid expenditure	723	719

United Kingdom cash purchases in Canada	1943-44	1944-45
Munitions and military supplies	342	799
Foodstuffs	252	341
Raw materials (base metals, lumber and other wood products)	230	185
Other exports and services including shipping	309	300
Total United Kingdom cash expenditure	1,133	1,625

United Kingdom receipts of Canadian dollars	1943-44	1944-45
British exports to Canada	100	94
Receipts for freight services	38	32
Interest and dividends	59	60
Payments by Canadian forces abroad	530	1,282
Other receipts and adjustments	102	247
Sale of United Kingdom equity in Canadian war plants to Canadian Government	165	—
Repayment of United Kingdom advances to working-capital funds (D.M.S. and contractors)	190	—
Deduct United Kingdom dollar-pool advances to rest of sterling area—net balance	—61	—91
Apparent errors and omissions	10	1
Total receipts of Canadian dollars	1,133	1,625

Source: Second Annual Report of the Canadian Mutual Aid Board.

PART II—THE UNITED STATES

The new British spending policy, adopted on the eve of Dunkirk, put the accent, henceforward, on supply. The watchword was the utmost supply of arms from North America in the next six months, supply quickly and at all costs. Despite, or because of, the decision to use up the gold and dollars in the war chest, finance, present and future, continued to dominate supply policy. Finance present —because the amount in the war chest was small and even if spent fast had to be spent wisely. Finance future—because no one knew what would happen when the chest was empty. 'We shall go on paying dollars for as long as we can', the Former Naval Person had told the President on 15th May 1940, 'but I should like to feel reasonably sure that when we can pay no more you will give us the stuff all the same.' Certainty, however, there could not be. British wishes could not be father to American thoughts; and American action might have to wait long on the thoughts of the Administration and still longer on the thoughts of Congress. But to give thoughts time the Ambassador was instructed to present a formal note on supply to the State Department, which he did on 3rd July. The United Kingdom, the note said, would pay as long as it could, but His Majesty's Government felt that they should 'in all frankness inform the United States Government that it will be utterly impossible for them to continue to do this for any indefinite period in view of the scale on which they will need to obtain such resources from the United States. Their immediate anxiety arises from the necessity of entering into long-term contracts.' This was not a request for credit. The United States Ambassador in London had warned that such a request would be unwise. But Lord Lothian was told informally ten days later 'not to worry too much' on the score of dollars.

(i)

'We shall go on paying dollars for as long as we can . . .'

As the weeks flowed by from July to December a close watch was kept on two trends. The first was what was called in the official papers 'the drain'—the rate at which the level of the gold and dollars in the war chest was being lowered week by week. The second was the watch for signs as to what the Administration was thinking and what it was likely to do when British gold and dollars were exhausted.

Action by the United States was governed by certain definite legal provisions, as well as by political factors such as the policy of neutrality and the state of public opinion. In the war of 1914–18 the United Kingdom and France had borrowed freely from the American money market. When the United States came into the war, loans were made to the Allies by the American Government under the authority of Section 2 of the Liberty Loans Act of 1917. In the Second World War, as noted in an earlier chapter, the money market was closed by a double barrier—by the Johnson Act because the United Kingdom was in arrears on the war debt, and by the Neutrality Act because it was a belligerent. In any case, after Dunkirk and the fall of France, Great Britain was in a poor position to borrow on the open market in the United States.

The exchange difficulty might have been mitigated in some small degree if it had been the practice of the United States to accept and hold foreign currency. The holding of large sums in sterling had been a normal pre-war practice of the trading nations in the British Commonwealth and Europe. The practice was based on confidence in sterling. Sterling had never been held in the United States in this way, either as a matter of banking practice or of inter-governmental agreement. If foreign currency were acquired it was immediately exchanged for dollars.

American Government loans to Britain were hedged round by legal and political difficulties. The possibility that the Administration might use the Stabilisation Fund, set up by Section 10 of the Gold Reserve Act 1934 'for the purpose of stabilising the exchange value of the dollar', was closed by a promise given by the Secretary of the Treasury to Congress in March 1939 that he would never use the Stabilisation Fund to assist any country engaged in war. Purvis suggested in vain that the Fund might be used to purchase sterling as a means of tiding over the gap before lend-lease. As a matter of law, American Federal Agencies were specifically exempted from the Johnson Act, but not from the Neutrality Act, though it was not clear that the latter applied to them. Two agencies, namely the Reconstruction Finance Corporation and the Export/Import Bank, had small funds available which might have been loaned; but neither could operate on any scale without new appropriations by Congress. Thus, as a British Embassy memorandum concluded after the fall of France, 'the United States Government alone remains'. But this also led back to Congress. For the Government could not make a large foreign loan without the authority of a new law passed by Congress together with an Appropriation Act. In Mr. Stimson's words, 'the British were running out of dollar exchange and the hands of the Americans were tied by statute'.[1]

---

[1] Stimson and Bundy, op. cit., p. 359.

At the outbreak of war in September 1939 the British war chest amounted to some £700–£725 million ($2,800–$2,900 million) in gold and negotiable dollar securities.[1] This was regarded as extremely meagre for the financing of a long war. The Government had the advantage of the newly-acquired techniques of exchange control and was able to make more effective use of reserves than in any previous war. In the first months of the war, however, it was necessary to make larger imports than had been anticipated from North America of machine tools, oil, steel and other raw materials. Moreover, in the first phase, efforts made to slow down the rate at which the reserve was spent, by boosting exports and cutting down inessential imports, were not very successful. Imports of inessential goods, which drained cash, continued at too high a figure for too long. One sign of a new attitude was the warning of the Chancellor of the Exchequer in August 1940 against importing 'unfinished goods involving a much heavier burden for wages and profits to foreigners'. His advice to import instead raw materials had the disadvantage of a heavier burden on shipping. Thus it was steel, not iron ore and scrap, that had to be imported heavily from the United States. In the end it was the sudden grave shipping situation of autumn 1940 that did more than anything else to cut imports. Exports, on the other hand, were being starved by the growth of British war production as well as by the cutting off of markets and fell heavily in the second half of 1940.[2] Up to June 1940 the only really large purchases of American armaments had been the Allied aircraft orders, amounting to some $614 million. The fall of France brought a drastic change. In June alone American surplus arms were purchased for $43 million and the French contracts taken over at a cost of some $800 million. Just after these commitments were made the drain for the next twelve months was put at $1,640 million. But the commitments for munitions and aircraft towards the end of July foreshadowed a far larger figure. In August the Chancellor of the Exchequer foresaw a drain of $3,200 million for the next twelve months. Already December 1940 was being forecast as the fatal month when the reserve in the war chest would be empty and the Treasury would have to fall back entirely on its meagre current receipts of gold and dollars.

Incidentally, as a precaution, the gold and dollar securities were being moved in June to Canada and two-thirds of the gold was there

---

[1] See McCurrach, op. cit., p. 358, where a somewhat lower figure for liquid assets is given. Total dollar assets, liquid and potential, were put at some $4,385 million.

[2] Hancock and Gowing, op. cit., Chapter IV, pp. 79, 206, 354. Volume of exports: (1935 = 100) 1938, 98; 1939, last quarter, 82; 1940, first quarter, 89; second, 91; third, 63; fourth, 44; and in 1941, 55. By 1943, exports, excluding munitions, had fallen to 29. From October 1939 to June 1940 imports (under departmental programmes) were at the annual rate of 45·4 million tons (quarterly average 11·3); they fell to 10·3 million tons in the third quarter and 8·4 million tons in the fourth quarter. For 1941 imports were 30·5 million tons.

by the end of that month. A reply to a question in the House of Commons on 17th July stated that to ensure the orderly realisation of American securities the bulk of them were 'being held in Canada pending their realisation. . . .'[1] The process of realisation of securities (referred to in an earlier chapter) was going forward steadily.

In view of the growing strain on dollar exchange, important financial talks were held in Washington from 15th to 20th July between Sir Frederick Phillips, representing the British Treasury, and Secretary Morgenthau. The latter asked, through the British Ambassador and the American Ambassador in London, just after the invasion of the Low Countries in May, that such talks should be held. Lord Lothian took up the point again at the end of June in a message which emphasised the importance of the personal factor. The 'confidence and understanding' which had played such an important part in the relations between Purvis and Morgenthau existed between the latter and Phillips and dated from their discussions in the autumn of 1937. The talks opened with characteristic initial points by Secretary Morgenthau and Secretary Hull. The one began on the supply of arms and the other on the ultimate triumph of liberal ideas of trade —the latter in reference to the recent adoption of exchange control by the United Kingdom. The point on supply was the need to co-ordinate the supply demands which the various countries of the British Commonwealth, including Canada, were making on the limited resources of the United States. The Secretary of the Treasury asked for supply programmes from the Dominions on which, he said, both he and Purvis were still in the dark. The longer the Commonwealth waited to co-ordinate its programmes the more difficult it would be for it to get what it wanted from the United States.

The main topic of the discussion, however, was the position of sterling in relation to the dollar. On 17th July Phillips, accompanied by Secretary Morgenthau, talked with the President; he presented a financial balance sheet covering for the next twelve months not only the dollar expenditures and requirements of the United Kingdom but also those of the entire sterling area. He informed the President that the United Kingdom would want help, probably in six months' time, in disposing of British dollar securities. More important still, the United Kingdom would want 'massive assistance' in the form of credit not later than the middle of 1941.

---

[1] Another precautionary measure, taken early in June, to minimise the danger of a possible break in communications through enemy action, was to ensure that British representatives in overseas countries had authority (by means of letters lodged with the Ambassador in Washington) to operate on Government accounts. A form of notification was agreed with the United States Treasury and the Federal Reserve Bank. On receipt of it all accounts of the Bank of England were to be transferred into the name of His Majesty's Government, to be drawn on only by the Ambassador or representatives designated by him. In view of the normal large holding by the South African Reserve Bank of gold for the United Kingdom, the Bank of England letter to it was lodged, from April 1941, with the British High Commissioner in South Africa.

The dollar requirements of the United Kingdom Exchange Control from July 1940 to June 1941 were as yet very imperfectly known, and the real requirements turned out to be several times higher than the preliminary conjectures of the Treasury. But even the Treasury minimum showed that the drain on British gold and dollars would be at least $1,632 million. When the dollar-earning assets of the sterling area as a whole were taken into account the drain would be slightly less, namely $1,552 million. (*See* Table 5. July 1941 was, of course, an arbitrary date; the drain would continue to be formidable so long as the war lasted.) On a world basis, including Canada and foreign countries, the net drain on exchange resources was estimated at $1,632 million. (*See* Table 6.)

Conjectural balance of payments between the Sterling Area and the United States, July 1940 to June 1941

TABLE 5 $ million

United Kingdom imports from United States	1,892	United Kingdom exports, visible and invisible	180
Rest of sterling-area imports from United States, visible and invisible .	280	Rest of sterling-area exports	440
		Adverse balance	1,552
	2,172		2,172

Conjectural net drain on British exchange resources, July 1940 to June 1941

TABLE 6 $ million

Adverse balance between sterling area and United States, as shown in Table 5	1,552	Proceeds of sale of newly mined gold: sent direct to United States .	80
Adverse balance with Canada	560	sent to United Kingdom	400
Adverse balance with foreign countries	220	Loans and credits from Canada and other countries	220
		Net drain on exchange resources .	1,632
	2,332		2,332

United Kingdom imports from the United States (the main element in the adverse balance) comprised chiefly aircraft, munitions, raw materials, merchant ships and food. A figure of $400 million was included for the purchase of iron and steel; this was a large new element due to the loss of access to the Continent and the failure to stockpile ore. 'We should have preferred', the British representative pointed out, 'to buy scrap iron, etc., but in view of the possibility of blast furnaces being damaged or of port congestion we felt that it would be unsafe not to buy a substantial amount of manufactured steel....'[1]

---

[1] For the amounts imported see J. Hurstfield, *The Control of Raw Materials* (London: Her Majesty's Stationery Office, 1953), p. 160.

This is the first of a number of Treasury forecasts, for varying periods, which will be mentioned in this chapter. It has to be remembered that such forecasting was not an exact science.[1] The major uncertainties of war affected all the elements of expenditure and receipts. The rate and scale of production from contracts placed in the United States could not be forecast—and were underestimated. In addition there was the unpredictable element of the financial policies of overseas governments. This latter was especially important as regards Canada and the United States in the first half of 1941 when it was impossible to foresee the exact scope of lend-lease or its effect on the Canadian-American balance of payments. Even short-term forecasting of the British dollar 'deficit' for a month or two ahead was difficult since income and expenditure were of the order of two billion dollars a year.

On the side of British assets in gold and dollars the following data were supplied to the American Treasury:

1. Gold held in the United Kingdom Exchange
   Equalisation Fund . . . . . $1,444 million
   (Since the Fund was in the position of a bank it had to carry a substantial cash reserve. It acted for the whole sterling area, received the proceeds of sales from sterling to dollar countries, and provided the dollars needed by sterling countries for purchases from the dollar area. The minimum cash reserve the Fund required to carry out these functions was put at $600 million.)

2. Dollars held by the Fund . . . . $108 million
   (Only minimum amounts of dollars, needed as working capital, remained in private dollar deposits.)

3. Estimated present value of dollar securities remaining to be sold[2] . . . . . $700 million

In addition to these dollar securities two other kinds of assets on which it was not possible to give exact figures were mentioned in the July talks: direct investments in the United States; and sterling investments in other parts of the world. For neither sort was either the face or the 'liquidation' value known. The President suggested that by a process of mortgage, whilst retaining the right to repurchase, Great Britain might raise dollars from her direct investments in the United States. He was told that the necessary negotiations would take a long time and that a great many such transactions would be needed in

---

[1] Moreover there were 'huge gaps' during the war in the data needed to measure the various factors involved. See the British Treasury Memorandum prepared in February 1951 which is printed in Appendix IX.

[2] Sales from January to June 1940 had yielded $132 million. By the end of November another $288 million was obtained by sales—a rate of sale which Secretary Morgenthau found satisfactory. Meanwhile, values had risen and the securities still left were valued in November at $800 million.

order to make any impression on the deficit. But he kept the point in mind; and it was to cause trouble later.

On the second sort—'large British investments in the rest of the world in sterling'—it was pointed out to the American Treasury that they could not be turned into dollars unless willing purchasers or lenders could be found in the United States.

Earlier in the year the President had shown an interest in regard to British assets in Latin America, including the Argentine Railways. Secretary Morgenthau had warned Phillips on 16th July to be ready to discuss the matter next day with the President as it was very much on his mind.[1] It was necessary, Morgenthau pointed out, for the Administration to 'see both sides of the British ledger'; the British must show that they were examining every possible means of raising funds, just as they must show whether they could succeed in defending their shores. Only then would the United States be in a position to decide what action they could take. The fostering of the British export trade, as a source of dollar exchange for the purchase of supplies from the United States, was another matter in which both the President and the Secretary of the Treasury showed their interest. Both took the view that the two countries should co-operate in the matter of exports to South America in order to minimise American competition with British exports.

Here a slight diversion may be permitted to follow up this 'favourite topic' of the President—the mobilisation of British resources in South America. He came back to it again in mid-October in a talk with the British Ambassador. He thought that by this means the financial crisis might be postponed for a month or two. At this time the Secretary of the Treasury was exploring, on his own initiative, an arrangement whereby the Argentine might use surplus sterling accruing from her favourable balance with the United Kingdom to repurchase British investments. The issue was obscured by greatly exaggerated figures quoted in the press as to the value of British investments in Latin America. Many of them had not paid dividends for a long time and their real value was only a fraction of their face value. The idea was that the United States might make dollar loans to the Argentine Government to be secured on the credit of that Government, the British sterling securities being lodged as collateral. The British Government was agreeable to such an arrangement; but the technical and political difficulties proved too great for the realisation of such securities in the United States. Further discussions took place in Washington in November and December 1940,

---

[1] The President first raised the matter of Allied investments in Latin America in April, when he expressed the idea that the Allies might acquire the investments of their nationals in that area, and sell them to American investors or even to a Corporation created by the United States Government.

and a finance mission from the Argentine participated. A plan, originally put forward on the Argentine side in 1938, for the purchase of the British Argentine Railways was revised for the discussions, but without result; the plan was impracticable without a dollar loan and that was not forthcoming. American dollar credits were given at this time to enable the Argentine to balance her foreign payments; but collateral was not needed for this purpose. Once lend-lease was under way Anglo-American economic collaboration in Latin America began to take a new form—that of co-ordinated purchasing of essential supplies, and concerted action to deny them to the Axis powers.

(ii)

'When we can pay no more . . .'
The Stalemate on New Production

The financial talks in July 1940 ended with an invitation by Secretary Morgenthau to Sir Frederick Phillips to come again in the autumn—after the election. Meanwhile, the foundation was laid for a monthly return which would enable both sides to keep a close watch on the drain in the balance of payments. The study began with a table, presented at the last meeting on 19th July, showing, in millions of dollars, for the past six months the holdings of *gold* and *dollar* exchange and at the end of each month the 'change on the month'. Any purchase during the month of freshly-mined gold was reflected in the holdings of gold. To find the figure of the total drain for the month, the sales of securities had to be added.

Monthly drain in balance of payments between the United Kingdom and the United States, January to June 1940

TABLE 7 $ million

	1939 31 Dec.	1940 31 Jan.	29 Feb.	31 Mar.	30 April	31 May	29 June
U.K. holdings of gold and dollar exchange	2,100	2,002	1,954	1,883	1,772	1,694	1,572
Change on the month		98	48	71	111	78	122
Add sale of securities		16	26	30	30	18	7
Total drain in the month		114	74	101	141	96	129

This made a total loss on reserves of gold and dollars for the six months of $655 million. It was pointed out that earlier figures of gold and dollar exchange were of little value since the precise value of the assets, state and private, at the beginning of the war were not known; moreover, the first four months of the war were a period of transition marked by wholesale requisitioning of British-owned balances and vast changes in the method of financing trade due to large-scale Government purchases.

After the public announcement by Secretary Morgenthau on 25th July 1940 of the '3,000 a month' aircraft scheme, the newspapers figured the cost at $7,000 million, and asked him whether the United Kingdom could pay. He replied that he was not worried about lack of funds: 'they have plenty of money—plenty.' The British Embassy took this as implying ultimate financial assistance by the United States; no promise of any kind, however, had been given. It was now clear that British requirements for the next twelve months would be many millions of dollars more than the $1,892 million indicated to the President on 17th July. A week later the loss on gold and exchange for July was known; it was $210 million. The war chest was emptying faster than the Treasury had expected; it was now down to $1,280 million in gold and dollars (excluding securities).

To enable a still closer watch to be kept on the monthly expenditures in the United States, Purvis was instructed to send each month from August a statement of actual expenditure. The Chancellor of the Exchequer warned the Government on 22nd August that new expenditures looming in the United States would run the deficit up to £800 million ($3,200 million) by June 1941—an amount far beyond the resources of the Treasury. In the last six weeks the drain had been £88 million ($352 million); 'mere continuance of such losses . . . would run us out of gold by the end of December'. (For August, as a whole, the drain was $228 million.) There was still room, the Chancellor pointed out, for a little 'scraping of the pot' by way of requisitioning gold ornaments and works of art, pushing exports, and selling to the United States South American investments (whose equities, however, now stood at 'rubbish' prices). All these measures together could not raise more than a few million pounds. Small gold reserves in other parts of the Commonwealth were not likely to be available (e.g. in the Reserve Banks of South Africa and India); nor were the considerable amounts of gold held in London by the Belgian, Dutch and Norwegian Governments to the amount of about £370 million.[1] Finally, French gold to the value of £500 million, scattered about the world in Ottawa, New York, Dakar and Martinique, would be a real help if it could be secured 'for the

---

[1] A Belgian loan was held up until after the Lend-Lease Act, largely because the British Government was not able to accept one of the conditions set, namely, the inclusion of Belgium and the Congo within the Imperial Preference system. See below, p. 272.

prosecution of the war on which the future of the French nation depends'; the prospects, however, were not bright.

It was clear that only the United States Government was left; without its aid purchasing from the United States must cease. The Chancellor shared the view of Lord Lothian, that assistance 'by a country not at war to a country in default' would not be given unconditionally and without limit. Moreover, no aid could be given before the November presidential election. For several reasons Britain must keep some reserves even in 1941—to make payments to Canada, to continue some payments to the United States, and to command enough confidence, as the 'central safe-keeper of the Empire's gold', to be able to continue to buy the current gold output of South Africa, and to sustain the still considerable volume of trading credit transactions in international trade based on sterling. Everything, therefore, pointed to caution in expenditure over the next six months. It should be limited to vital needs and munitions 'for delivery not too far ahead'. Exports would still have to be fostered, especially to North America, and all possible supplies should be got from the sterling area.

New arrangements came into effect late in September 1940 as a means of keeping watch on the monthly drain and maintaining close touch with the American Treasury. Three regular returns were to be given to the American Treasury. One, to be sent after the 3rd of each month, was a statement showing the loss of gold and dollars and sales of vested and unvested securities during the previous month. The second, to be given after the 10th of each month, was a classified statement of the expenditure of the British Purchasing Commission during the previous month, together with an estimate of expenditure during the remainder of the year to the end of June 1941. The third, after the 16th of each month, gave complementary data showing the monthly dollar expenditure other than through the British Purchasing Commission. The latter figure proved very difficult to obtain.

The Administration thus had full data on the monthly drain; but it had as yet no clear indication of the monthly cost of the new British aircraft and munitions programmes. If the programmes were not to be delayed to the benefit of the Axis, expenditures in connection with them should begin to add to the drain before the end of the year—unless, meanwhile, the United States provided the capital required to finance the schemes. The Ambassador pressed this point on London at the end of September with the support of Purvis. In reply, the Treasury gave in October figures to be handed to Secretary Morgenthau. These showed estimated air purchases up by $1,694 million to a new total of $2,410 million and munitions up by $419 million to a new total of $759 million. Total British purchases for the second war-year were now calculated at $3,976 million as compared with the estimate of $1,892 million of 17th July. This gave an estimated deficit of $3,500 million by August 1941.

The rate of the monthly drain was a fitting commentary on the impossibility of bridging such a vast gap in the sterling-dollar balance. At the end of September 1940 the gold and dollar reserve was $897 million—or $297 million after deducting the minimum working capital of $600 million for the Exchange Equalisation Fund. To draw the balance lower than $600 million was not feasible, the Treasury pointed out, because of the charges—partly in gold—which had to be met in Canada. Moreover, Britain would be in an 'extraordinary uncomfortable hole' if she could not see her way even a week or two ahead to pay for essential imports. But by now the monthly drain was running at a rate which showed that the reserves would be below the $600 million minimum by the end of November. The growing sense of urgency in London was shown by a query from the Treasury on 11th October as to when the second Phillips Mission, suggested by Morgenthau in July, could take place. The Ambassador put the question to the President and Morgenthau on the 14th October and was told that the visit would have to be after November 20th. (Later the date was shifted to after 1st December; the Mission arrived on the 4th.) This talk on 14th October, and one which Purvis and the British Financial Attaché had next day with Secretary Morgenthau, was not encouraging. The President came back to his 'favourite topic' of British investments in Latin America; whilst Secretary Morgenthau seemed to be preoccupied mainly with the delay of the United Kingdom in beginning the liquidation of its direct investments in the United States.

THE RED LIGHT ON FINANCE AND THE FIVE-MONTHS STALEMATE

Next day, 15th October 1940, the Ambassador told Morgenthau that 'the red light had gone up about finance'. The date and the statement may be taken as the beginning of five months' stagnation in British supply from the United States. Or more precisely it meant five months' loss of new American war production on British account —the months of the winter lull before Germany uncoiled again in the spring. Supplies still continued to come forward under the old orders and there was even a continuation order for 4,550 aircraft—but the vast new orders involved in the air and munitions programmes could not be placed. It took some time before the full gravity of what was happening could become clear. The impasse was disguised by the desires and the explorations, of both sides, to find some way out of the maze. The Ambassador, on his return from London nine weeks later, reported that the Administration was 'still discussing ingenious ways of giving us assistance'.

Time after time the British side was told to go ahead with orders, only to find the way blocked by insuperable difficulties. On 20th October Purvis reported that in week-end talks with Secretary Morgenthau at the latter's home he had received 'a complete green light' for the immediate ordering of 9,000 aircraft. The green light was given again in public by the President on 30th October for the ordering of 12,000 aircraft. He spoke of 'large additional orders . . . being negotiated for artillery, machine guns, rifles and tanks'. In the next few days Purvis and Layton were told to go ahead with their orders on the assumption that the Reconstruction Finance Corporation would pay for the capital cost. An agreement to this effect was worked out with the War Department. The admonitions to go ahead continued at intervals through December. The complicated manœuvres to which both sides were reduced in trying to place orders were described by the two acting heads of the British Purchasing Commission in minutes written on 5th December. It was finally agreed, they noted, that each item of the programmes would be discussed separately with the War Department. The Department would indicate the particular firms to be approached for particular equipment; it would then itself make the initial approach to the firm. The British Purchasing Commission would then discuss details of the proposed contract with the War Department, and having done this would clear them with the firm. After these preliminaries the War Department would 'formally introduce' the British Purchasing Commission to the firm. This meant that in the end each contracting firm was left to decide for itself whether the B.P.C. could, in fact, pay for the order which it wanted to place. At that stage the firm—since it could not take the risk that Congress might not support the Administration—had to look behind the contract to see whether the British cupboard was indeed bare as the British Ambassador had already suggested in a public statement. Having looked, it would then either refuse the contract or ask for impossible advance payments. As for the financing of capital expenditure by the Reconstruction Finance Corporation, this had been shown in practice to be 'difficult if not impossible'. What was wanted, the officials concluded, was 'weapons not credits. . . . There appears only one solution to the difficulty of the British position and that is retiring from the American market as a contractor and passing to the United States the responsibility of purchasing American-type material required for the British, on the understanding that such materials when delivered will be released to the British to the extent of their requirements. . . . Furthermore, there appears no legal reason why at the time of such release, such releases might not be made simply on credit.'

(iii)

'You will give us the stuff all the same'

THE ORIGINS OF LEND-LEASE

On 15th November 1940, the day before he left for London, Purvis had noted that if a full statement of British requirements, in the framework of a 'general staff picture', could be put before the President it would reveal that the United States must have 'a budget on a full war scale, plus restrictions upon industry and the suspension of labour regulations, although she may not be officially at war'. In fact, since the presidential election, British representatives had deliberately concentrated their efforts on quantities and dates of delivery. Contracts and finance, they were convinced, had already become a problem which only the United States could solve. The Prime Minister in his letter of 8th December also subordinated finance to supply; he drew a strategic picture of 'the prospects for 1941' and the danger involved in the loss of shipping. The costs of the full British programmes, which he promised to send later, would 'many times exceed the total exchange resources remaining at the disposal of Great Britain'. He added that his letter was not 'an appeal for aid, but as a statement of the minimum action necessary to achieve our common purpose'.[1] When the Lend-Lease Act was passed, he described it in Parliament as 'the most unselfish and unsordid financial act of any country in all history'.

Lend-lease, however, was far more than a 'financial act'. Historically it was as much rooted in American necessity as in British need of dollar exchange. American Government spokesmen (especially Mr. Stimson) emphasised this point in the Lend-Lease Hearings.[2] It was recognised in the title of the Bill as an 'Act to Promote the Defense of the United States'. It was reiterated by the President in his reports to Congress and given prominence by Mr. Stettinius in his account of lend-lease. Yet it never fully succeeded in overtaking the popular view that lend-lease was merely an alternative to a loan— just another form of financial aid. Lend-lease was an American necessity in the sense that the United States had reached the point where their own defence requirements (together with those of Great Britain —which alone represented eight to nine billion dollars spread over only two years) could no longer be produced in time by ordinary commercial means. Lend-lease had two advantages: first, it enabled (in Mr. Stimson's words) the War Department to become 'a service of supply to Allied armies everywhere'; in the second place, it pro-

---

[1] Churchill, op. cit., p. 494 ff.

[2] Stimson and Bundy, op. cit., pp. 360–62.

vided the means for putting American munitions on a war footing. It armed the President with 'tremendous powers over the lives and fortunes of his countrymen'.[1] It made possible government direction of production and a network of government controls, and the switching over of industry from peace-time production to the manufacture of supplies for war.

Lend-lease was the President's own idea, 'another great Rooseveltian triumph', in the words of Mr. Stimson; a supreme example, as Mr. Sherwood has shown, of his political genius. It had already taken some shape in his mind before he left on his cruise on 2nd December. It was not due to any suggestion from the British side. It was not, indeed, for the British Treasury to try to foresee possible American methods of solving what was now an American problem. The Treasury was thinking on traditional lines, as was shown by the instructions Sir Frederick Phillips brought with him on 4th December. As he put it, two days after his arrival, he was to ask for 'a free gift of munitions and aircraft'—if that were possible; otherwise, he was to seek some kind of loan. But in the latter case he was to make it clear that 'repayment of a quasi-commercial loan can only, in our judgement, be effected after the war to the extent to which our exports to the U.S.A. exceed imports. . . .' It was with more homely phrases that the President, on his return, in his press interview on 17th December and his fireside chat on 29th, won the political fight for lease and lend—phrases such as 'eliminate the dollar sign'; 'Suppose my neighbour's home catches fire, and I have a length of garden hose. . . .'; 'Arsenal of Democracy'.

There had been a hint of lending materials, for subsequent replacement, in the President's talk with Purvis on 29th December 1939. This was six months before the Pitman Act of June 1940 which authorised Government manufacture or purchase of arms for sale to Latin American Governments. Purvis was told by Morgenthau on 2nd January 1941 when the President, in the presence of Purvis, charged him with the drafting of the Lend-Lease Bill, that the Pitman Act was being taken by the Treasury lawyers as the starting-point for the Bill. The Treasury lawyers had also unearthed an old statute of 1892, permitting the Secretary of War to lease army property for a limited period of time.[2]

A further ingredient was the practice of dividing up (on a sales basis) American arms production between the United States and the United Kingdom, a practice which was established soon after the outbreak of war. On 7th November 1940, two days after the election, the President suggested to Purvis a rule-of-thumb allocation, on a fifty-fifty basis, of military supplies between the United States on the

[1] Sherwood, op. cit., p. 228.
[2] See also Stettinius, op. cit., pp. 41–42; 68–69.

one hand and Britain and Canada on the other. Their talk then turned to ships, and in this context the President linked the idea of allocation with a second idea, that of leasing supplies to the Allies; and he said nothing about payment.[1] The Prime Minister already on 27th October had mentioned the vital need of ships. This had now become suddenly the most important British requirement from the United States. Loss of ships through sinkings and air raids on ports had caused a serious shrinkage in the rate of imports into the United Kingdom. In 1937 the total was 60 million tons. For the second war-year the planned minimum of imports was 40 to 43 million tons. At the then rate of sinkings not much more than 33 million tons would reach the island in a year. (The actual figure for 1941 was 30·5 million tons.)[2] This was the 'mortal danger' the Prime Minister dwelt on in his letter of 8th December. 'The convoy system,' he then wrote, 'the *détours*, the zigzags, the great distances from which we now have to bring our imports, and the congestion of our western harbours, have reduced by about one-third the fruitfulness of our existing tonnage.'[3] The situation could be met only by a drastic cut in imports and a large programme for new production of merchant shipping in North America.

The President, in the conversation of 7th November, was 'obviously anxious', Purvis reported. The President discussed the new Ministry of Shipping programme for building in the United States sixty cargo tramp vessels, totalling 400,000 gross tons. He referred to the possi-bility of reconditioning seventy of the old ships of the First World War and went on to suggest that the United States might build 300 new ships. He thought British dollar resources would be exhausted in six months' time and he suggested that the United States should build these 300 ships 'and rent them to the United Kingdom'; and that this system might be extended to cover certain other supplies. Three hundred ships meant 2 million tons gross and the British Government now put its needs at $4\frac{1}{2}$ million tons, of which it could build only $1\frac{1}{2}$ million tons. 'We should have to look to the United States for 3 million tons gross', the Minister of Shipping told Lord Lothian in London, and the Prime Minister a month later repeated the figure in his letter of 8th December to the President.[4] The latter's continued

---

[1] It appears from Mr. Stettinius' account that the President had made this suggestion —the building of ships by the United States and leasing them to the United Kingdom for the duration of the emergency—at a meeting with the Defence Advisory Commission 'in the later summer'. Ibid., pp. 68–69.

[2] See above, p. 245, footnote (2), and Hancock and Gowing, op. cit., Chapter X, for the general background.

[3] Churchill, op. cit., p. 499.

[4] It was of special importance, the Minister of Shipping pointed out to Lord Lothian, to obtain, as quickly as possible, a million tons of shipping in the form of fast vessels of 15 to 16 knots to provision troops in distant areas and cut down the time spent on long import voyages—a need which was met in part a year later.

S

concern about shipping was shown by an urgent request on 30th November, by an official in the Defence Commission to the British Embassy, for a memorandum on the whole British shipping position. Enquiries revealed that the request came from Mr. Harry Hopkins, and he was given the information in a letter which reached him on the President's yacht on 9th December, together with the Prime Minister's letter to the President.

In the weeks following 7th November this favourable spring in Washington seemed to disappear into the sands of American politics. On 2nd December, the day the President left on his cruise, the Prime Minister remarked to his colleagues in London that he had been rather chilled by the attitude of the United States since the election; but perhaps the President was waiting for the election atmosphere to disperse. What had happened, meanwhile, had been an apparent switch of interest by the President and Morgenthau to the question of British investments. There was an inspired Press outburst on this theme after the Ambassador's calculated indiscretion of 23rd November. As he stepped from the plane Lord Lothian was reported by the Associated Press as saying that Britain was 'beginning to come to the end of her financial resources'. The President promptly said in his Press conference that there had been no discussion in the Government of credit for the United Kingdom. The *Washington Post* next day (26th) attributed to the White House an 'Administration view . . . that the British request for financial aid is premature' and went on to mention a figure of $8,000 million unused British investments in the western hemisphere.[1] American public opinion, Lord Lothian reported to London, was still 'saturated with illusions . . . that we have vast resources available that we have not yet disclosed . . . and that we ought to empty this vast hypothetical barrel before we ask for assistance'. It was this fact, he explained, which had induced him to make his statement. It is clear that the exhaustion of funds could hardly have been concealed much longer. Moreover, the Administration reaped a possible advantage from the fact that the Press campaign led the public to believe that it was the United Kingdom and not the Administration that had opened the question of aid. In a cordial interview with the Ambassador and Sir Frederick Phillips, on the latter's arrival on 4th December, Secretary Morgenthau remarked that the Ambassador's statement had forced the President and himself to take up the question of finance immediately. Later he expressed the view that the Ambassador's public disclosure had made it more difficult for the Administration to give help to Britain in the period of transition.

---

[1] *The Washington Post*, 26th November 1940. *New York Herald Tribune*, 2nd December, article by Alsop and Kintner: 'British Anger Administration by Abruptness on Credit Issue'.

Under the constitutional system of the United States it is the President (rather than his Cabinet or his individual Secretaries of State) who must himself personally take all important decisions of policy. This is the consequence of what Mr. Sherwood has called his 'extraordinary and solitary constitutional powers'. Already, on 30th November, the momentous question of financing war supplies to the United Kingdom had finally been brought to the President for decision. On that day Sir Walter Layton presented Secretary Morgenthau with a document which the latter took at once to the President and asked for instructions. The document bore the headings 'Initial Orders to be placed for Output' with a figure of $2,062 million, and 'Capital Investment necessary for creating New Productive Capacity' amounting to $699 million.[1] For the first sum there was no possible solution without new legislation. For the second, there had been talk of a possible block grant of $700 million by the Reconstruction Finance Corporation; but that too probably needed legislation. And the legislation must be such that it would involve the most far-reaching changes in the whole tradition of American foreign policy. Here was the irrevocable act the President had so far avoided, lest defeat in attempting it should lose the war. He alone could solve the problem, and to solve it he took it with him to sea.

(iv)

The Problems of Transition and the Purvis Balance Sheet

The main story of lend-lease from this point belongs to the American history of the war. The interim period of three months between the announcement of the principle of lend-lease on 17th December and its enactment into law on 11th March 1941 was one of the most difficult and complex in the history of British supply relations with the United States. For the first time in its history the United Kingdom waited anxiously on the passage of an American law, knowing that its destiny might hang on the outcome. London waited with an imperfect knowledge of American legislative processes and little understanding of American public opinion. Its eyes were fastened not so much on the slow eddying of Congress towards the Act as on its own vast programmes for 1942 grounded month after month in the shallows. It searched for the dollars needed to pay for deliveries from existing orders as well as for the new continuation orders necessary to keep its contractors busy.

---

[1] These 'initial orders' were *additional* to orders, already placed or under active negotiation, amounting to some $2,600 million.

Purvis returned from London on 16th December.[1] He had just been made a member of His Majesty's Privy Council, and had also been appointed chairman of the newly-created British Supply Council in North America, which began its first meetings a month later. In the week before his return important issues had been raised by Secretary Morgenthau with Sir Frederick Phillips and the heads of the Purchasing and Air Commissions. The Secretary presented them with certain decisions by the Administration: first, that it had decided to ask Congress to legislate on the question of financing British supplies; and second, that the United Kingdom could place at once all orders needed to carry out the scheme to provide American equipment for ten divisions (the 'B' programme); for this, he said, capital expenditure of $100 million had been assured by the War Department and the Reconstruction Finance Corporation. Third, as a follow-up to the 'B' programme during the interim period the United Kingdom was offered a choice between its shipbuilding orders ($100 million) and repeat orders for aircraft ($250 million).

These proposals raised in an acute form the question of priority in the expenditure of the small remaining reserve of gold and dollars. The reserve, it was explained, was now down to $574 million. Payments of at least $1,005 million had to be faced before the end of February—the earliest date at which the Lend-Lease Act could pass. Of this sum, commitments or down payments on existing orders or orders under negotiation accounted for $580 million—that is, more than the immediately available dollars. Moreover, the 'B' programme was much less important than the British Army's 'A' programme covering deficiencies in, and insurance on, British production; any delay on 'A' would cause serious shortages which would deprive large numbers of Army units of essential equipment. Most urgent of all were the shipping orders. Even new capacity for aircraft was regarded as of greater urgency than the 'B' programme. These views were upheld by Ministers in London, who were even prepared to drop the 'B' programme altogether since, in any case, Britain could not pay for it. Phillips warned them this might mean to lose good will and create a deadlock.

These exchanges overlapped with the President's announcement on the 17th December 1940 of the principle of leasing and loaning to Britain. On the same day he instructed Secretary Morgenthau to authorise the placing of orders for all the main British requirements, including aircraft, the army programmes 'A' and 'B', steel, and merchant ships. A statement was handed to the Administration on the 19th by the Embassy outlining the orders which the United Kingdom wished to place at once in accordance with this invitation. Their value was set at five to six billion dollars. In effect the President was

---

[1] Lord Lothian had died suddenly on 12th December.

inviting London to enter into commitments far beyond its capacity to pay without any clue as to how it was to be done. By an ironical twist, Ministers were meeting in London that day (19th December) to discuss a question formulated as follows: 'how to meet bills maturing for payment on or after Tuesday, 24th December, when on present showing our dollar resources in the U.S.A. would be exhausted'.

All efforts to make Washington realise how serious had become the problem of interim payments seemed to have failed. The Treasury representative had interpreted the silence of the Administration on this matter as due to its feeling that Britain could easily find the necessary cash—by such measures as the further liquidation of securities, by sacrificing direct investments in the United States, by borrowing the Belgian gold, and by inducing the Canadian Government to agree to the release of the French gold in Canada. The President on the 17th, in his Press interview, had said, in answer to a question, that he believed the British Government had sufficient exchange left to pay for all the orders it had already placed. Broadly speaking this was true, but funds could be accumulated for this purpose only over a considerable period; meanwhile, there were not enough dollars actually on hand to meet payments a week ahead. The first thought of the meeting on the 19th was to use the United Kingdom gold reserve held in South Africa. But it was desired to keep this as a last nest-egg to maintain confidence in sterling and for other needs. Some gold was needed to sustain the Greeks and the Turks, who required some dollars for essential war supplies. Since the securing of Belgian and French gold was at best a slow and uncertain operation, it was judged better to try to secure an advance against the sale of further securities in the United States. At the meeting Ministers recalled the plea of the Prime Minister in his letter to the President on 8th December against stripping the United Kingdom to the bone by divesting it of all its saleable assets.

Meanwhile, further confusing pieces of information were coming in from Washington. One was a warning from Phillips that it was questionable whether lend-lease would cover the British-type material in the 'A' programme. Then followed an announcement which reversed the President's instruction of the 17th; no further British contracts could now be signed (except for ships for which $50 million had been 'earmarked') until Congress had been 'consulted'. The United Kingdom was invited, however, to negotiate contracts up to the point of signature. Ministers, not well versed in American constitutional procedures, were inclined to interpret this as meaning that the President expected the approval of Congress 'almost at once'. Long delay, they pointed out, would mean not only more losses of gold and dollars; it would also be 'disastrous as regards production'.

The British Government could not bring itself to believe that when the premium for time saved was so enormous, supply could stand still; yet it continued more or less to do so until mid-March.

Here we may pause for a moment to refer to a point which is expanded at the end of this volume under the heading: Reflection on two systems. This was not the first, nor by any means the last example during the war of the constitutional difficulties and consequent delays involved in the conduct of American foreign relations.[1] The war began with one such episode in the long-drawn-out process of amending the Neutrality Act. It ended with another, the breakdown of lend-lease. Each fresh episode showed how difficult it was for the British Government to learn to make allowance for the leisurely procedures of the United States, the American sense that life had ample margins—margins of security, of time, of resources. It was always difficult for London to understand the difficulties of synchronisation inherent in the American constitutional system, the time-gap between judgement and decisions of Government and judgement and legislation by Parliament, the inability of the President of the United States to bind Congress.

A talk with the President by Sir Frederick Phillips took place on 23rd December. The President gave one part of the answer to a direct question put some days earlier to the Secretary of the Treasury: How was the United Kingdom supposed to finance its immediate expenditure? The President stated that an American warship was being sent to South Africa to pick up all available gold and bring it back to the United States. The 'embarrassing effects' of the publicity that might follow were emphasised by the Prime Minister in his message to the President on New Year's Eve.[2] But the gold—$150 million—was duly loaded on the U.S.S. *Louisville* on 5th January, and an equivalent amount in dollars was made available to the British Government. A second consignment, $132 million, was taken by an American cruiser in the second half of March, and a third in April.

The second part of the answer, put strongly by Secretary Morgenthau, was that the British should sell part at least of their direct investments in the United States. This matter is referred to below. The third part of the answer was given in discussions between the British Purchasing Commission and the War Department. The War Department had some unexpended credits which it was prepared to use to finance the most urgent British orders: $60 million was available for aircraft and $30 million for ordnance. This was a

---

[1] See below, Chapter XI. The real point of the classical example—the failure of President Wilson in 1919 to carry through Congress what he had signed in Paris—had been lost because the failure came to be attributed more to the President's lack of political skill than to the difficulty inherent in the Constitution.

[2] Churchill, op. cit., pp. 507–08.

partial solution of the problem of urgent orders; but the money could be used only for American equipment and not for British types.

On 30th December Purvis put five points to the President on the British financial situation:

(a) Between 23rd December and the end of February the British Purchasing Commission would have to pay out $400 million on existing, and essential, continuation orders;

(b) It needed to spend also $250 million on new orders—this in addition to any funds the War Department might make available;

(c) The remaining cash reserves on the 28th December were $385 million. (Of this only some $295 million was available; the rest was locked up in various ways);

(d) Newly accruing resources from the sale of securities in the period could not amount to $100 million;

(e) These reserves, he pointed out, were the last balance of the Exchange Control and had to cover much else besides the purchase of arms from the U.S.A.

The position had been regarded as being on the danger line at the beginning of the month; it was now perilous in the extreme. The only remedies that could be seen on the British side were: to secure from the United States an advance on securities, to borrow Allied gold (which could only be repaid with United States help), to induce the United States stabilisation fund to buy sterling, to induce the United States Government to repay the $160 million capital assistance paid by Britain to American firms. Purvis went on to express 'great anxiety over the delays which would occur in the placing of new orders unless some way could be found of putting us in funds prior to Congressional action'. The President shared this anxiety, but saw possible ways out in using unexpended American balances and Reconstruction Finance Corporation funds. As for ships, he had already ordered the allocation of $36 million to the Maritime Commission to build seven additional shipyards.

Thus, the new year began for Britain with a fairer promise—brightened especially by the President's 'fireside talk' on 29th December.[1] But the old year ended with the Prime Minister's reminder on 31st December that a few weeks' delay could bring 'default in payments'. 'Remember Mr. President, we do not know what you have in mind, exactly what the United States is going to do, and we are fighting for our lives. . . . They burned a large part of the City of London last night . . .'[2]

---

[1] Brightened also by spontaneous gifts from workmen in American munitions factories, such as the Hudson bomber 'The Spirit of Lockheed Vega', which arrived in England on 30th December.

[2] Churchill, op. cit., pp. 507–08.

THE PURVIS BALANCE SHEET

What the President had in mind as his long-term solution became clearer on 3rd January, when he disclosed to Purvis and Phillips the main outlines of the Lend-Lease Bill. The text of the Bill was published a week later. What the United States was 'going to do' was then mainly a matter for Congress. But Purvis could now report that the signs were favourable for the realisation of the far-reaching conception which had formed in his mind early in November. It was, in short, the production by the United States of the additional munitions required to out-strip and to overwhelm Germany. This went far beyond any British programmes hitherto discussed for supply from North America. After discussing the idea with Monnet and Layton, Purvis had gone to London in mid-November.[1] He asked the British Ministries to furnish him with data of a new kind: first, the total requirements of the United Kingdom in the matter of the armaments needed to defeat the enemy; second, the amounts which British industry could produce towards that goal in the years 1941–42; third, the deficiency—i.e. the difference between these two sets of figures which would have to be obtained from the United States in order to win the war. The first two sets of figures were intended for the statement promised by the Prime Minister to the President in the former's letter of 8th December (paragraph 16). The Ministry of Supply officials were unwilling themselves to compute the third element—the deficit—on the ground that any such calculation would be very misleading. Purvis did the arithmetic himself and arrived at a figure which went far beyond any total that had ever been suggested by the British or the American Government. He then sought the first opportunity to try it out on the President. The opportunity came at their talk on 30th December. Purvis began by saying that the Prime Minister's statement of requirements would soon be ready. Preliminary calculations showed, he said, that the value was 'perhaps of the order of $15,000 million'. For a while, Secretary Morgenthau has recorded, 'Purvis talked round the subject. Then, in a quiet tone of voice, he said that the British requirements might go over fifteen billion dollars' or even more. The President 'took this figure in his stride'[2] and proceeded to give his ideas of the Lend-Lease Bill, and then asked Secretary Morgenthau to see that the Treasury was ready to draw up the Bill when he gave the word, which he did

---

[1] There were several hands in the balance sheet. Monnet, leader of the French Air Mission to the United States before the war, architect of the Anglo-French air purchasing programme in the spring of 1940, came in July to the United States as 'a British official' to assist Purvis, and to bring into the American scene the experience of the Anglo-French combination. The balance sheet bears the mark of his thought and methods. But the mind of Purvis worked on the same lines; in any case, it was he who was captain and carried it through.

[2] Article by Mr. Morgenthau, *Collier's* Magazine, 18th October 1947.

on 2nd January 1941. The Treasury lawyers had the draft ready by midnight.

On January 5th, the night before the President appeared before Congress to give his annual message on the 'State of the Union' in which he was to ask for the funds for lend-lease aid to the Allies, Purvis gave the President the preliminary statement of requirements which indicated how the deficiency figure of $15,000 million was calculated. The more detailed estimates that followed showed that on his own initiative, with the support of the British Supply Council, Purvis had added to the original 'A' (Army) and 'B' (ten divisions) programmes a new 'C' programme which covered the deficiency figures. The result was far higher totals than had ever before been indicated—so high in fact that officials in the Ministry of Supply were seriously perturbed. The experience of the Ministry was that of planning production in a country extending itself to the limit of its resources, where ordering more than was necessary of one item meant going short of another. In the United States, however, the situation was entirely different. For practical purposes the extent of American resources for armaments production was not so much a physical as a political question. The higher the British figures the higher became the American production rates; and American defence gained, since in effect the American War and Navy Departments controlled the allocations of all arms produced in the United States.

The British Government, true to its traditions, trusted the man on the spot. Purvis had acted not merely with the support of the British Supply Council in North America, but with the full encouragement and support of Secretary Morgenthau and the President. It was the former who asked Purvis, on 10th February 1941, for these more detailed estimates; he wanted them for the express purpose of their use as a basis for the appropriation under the Lend-Lease Bill, which was to be discussed at a meeting on the 13th of the Secretaries of the Treasury, War and Navy Departments and Office of Production Management. The estimates were drawn up by the British Supply Council, and Purvis, as Chairman, handed them personally to Secretary Morgenthau and the President. They showed estimates of total British General Staff requirements, United Kingdom stocks, production in 1941 and 1942, and 'the deficiencies which we look to the United States to fill'.[1] The grand total was $18,850 million, made up in the following stages: one, requirements for the fiscal year ending June 1941, $7,300 million; two, for the fiscal year ending June 1942, $1,550 million; three, for delivery after June 1942,

---

[1] The data (for the years 1941 and 1942) were under the following headings: Strategic requirements; Existing United Kingdom stocks; United Kingdom and Canadian production; United States deliveries against United Kingdom contracts; Deficiencies to be provided for from United States; Total United States effort.

$10,000 million. The President, Purvis reported, expressed himself as 'greatly interested' in the statement; and he immediately gave orders for United States requirements to be drawn up on similar lines to form 'combined U.S.-U.K. programmes'. This led on step by step in the months that followed to the Victory Programme or Anglo-American Consolidated Statement.[1]

(v)

The Dark Time of Interim Finance

Whilst long-term plans were going well, the immediate outlook for the unknown weeks or months up to lend-lease was dark. In the darkness the Treasury in London, and its representatives in Washington and Ottawa, were faced with a series of questions which they could neither answer themselves nor get the Administration to answer. Day by day from January to April 1941 a close watch was kept over commitments, payments and receipts, and the steady sinking of the last reserves of gold and dollars. The drain in January was $80 million. The question how to spend what was left depended on a series of unknowns. Would lend-lease, when it began to operate, cover the dollar needs of Dominions and Allies? To this there came, early in January, a clear and positive answer. But the effect of lend-lease on the triangular financial relations with Canada was not cleared up for over three months. Would gold still have to be paid to Canada because Canada was short on American dollars? Another important question was whether lend-lease would cover things other than munitions, such as food, raw materials and oil, which still had to be imported in quantity from the United States. By 29th January the legal advisers of the War Department and Treasury had given assurances that legally the Bill covered them all. But there was still the fear that the President might have to 'go slow'. In any case, all the hitherto private purchases like timber, paper and chemicals would have to be made by the British Purchasing Commission. No less important was another question: would lend-lease cover, as the Prime Minister had put it to the President on 31st December, the 'immense heavy payments still due to be made under existing orders before delivery is completed'?[2] That sum on 1st January was $1,300 million. There were two elements in the problem—American-type

---

[1] See below, Chapter VIII. By October, Purvis's figure of $15,000 million had been exceeded by the total of the first two main lend-lease appropriations, $7,000 million and $6,000 million, together with the amount of $1,300 million from existing appropriations authorised by the Lend-Lease Act itself, and a supplementary of $1,300 million provided in August for the Maritime Commission.

[2] Churchill, op. cit., p. 507.

arms and British types; and the answer might be different for each. Since the whole matter was one of policy rather than law, London hoped that the early negative indication given by the President on 17th December and repeated in January by Secretary Morgenthau before the Committee of Congress might be reversed when the Act was passed.

One difficulty in getting clear answers to such questions was the rapid expansion which was taking place within the American Administration. The setting up by the President of the Office of Production Management on 7th January 1941 was the beginning of a long transition towards the full war organisation of 1942. Although new machinery was being shaped and staff appointed, powers, functions and responsibilities remained ill-defined.[1]

No small part of the delays and uncertainties in getting answers to the difficult questions which were troubling the British Government sprang, of course, from the major uncertainty about the strength of the opposition in Congress, its effect on the shape of the Lend-Lease Bill and on the subsequent administration of the Act by the President. But there was also a serious lack of understanding of important aspects of the British financial position in high places in the Administration itself. By early January the President, with the Secretary of the Treasury and leading Treasury officials, understood well enough. But beyond this inner circle there was confusion not unmixed with suspicion. 'The situation in the interim period', Purvis wrote on 10th January, 'is difficult and complex. . . . It is quite evident that even the most friendly Cabinet elements do not find it easy to believe that our immediate position is as grave as we know it to be. . . .'

Purvis felt that, whilst there was little evidence of any intention or desire to strip Britain of all available assets, there was suspicion that not all these assets were being disclosed or used for payments. He was pressing at the time for swift action on the sale of such part of the direct investments as could be sold without serious harm to the fabric of British and American industrial and technical relations. The fixed notion of 'the richness of the British Empire', and the belief that somehow and somewhere the United Kingdom still had billions of available assets, were obstacles which Secretary Morgenthau had to overcome in the President's Cabinet before he

---

[1] An important administrative expansion was also taking place on the British side. Following the setting up of the British Supply Council in January 1941, separate British missions for Food and Shipping were arranged in March and began to function in May. The British Central (later Commonwealth) Scientific Office was set up in March. The British Admiralty Delegation began to operate in June. Other Service missions were set up in midsummer (Royal Air Force Delegation and British Army Delegation, later British Army Staff Mission). The British Colonies Supply Mission (first called Colonial Supply Liaison) was set up in July. Dominion Supply Missions were also established. A British Petroleum Mission set up in May 1941 was merged in January 1942 with the Shipping Mission. See *Studies of Overseas Supply*, Chapter VII.

moved on to encounter them in the Committees of Congress.[1] Until
the eve of the Lend-Lease Hearings the Cabinet was divided on the
question whether lend-lease should be given with or without
collateral. One suggestion, according to Mr. Morgenthau, was that
the United Kingdom should provide a further $2,000 million in
cash, or as collateral, before arms began to be supplied under lend-
lease.[2] He had difficulty in convincing his colleagues that all the
available funds which could be raised from securities and direct
investments—some $1,500 million—would only be sufficient to pay
for existing orders. To strengthen his hand with Congress, he sought
several concessions from London. One, which was agreed, was the
dispatch of an expert to discuss the sale of direct investments (see
below). A second was the issuing of a further vesting order for market
securities. The order was issued on 11th January, vesting securities to
the value of $100 million. There had already been Press comments
(e.g. in the *Wall Street Journal* of 3rd January) that the United
Kingdom was selling securities at a loss. At the same time, the
Treasury warned that the Administration was getting rather close to
giving the impression of British bankruptcy which the Administration
leaders wanted to avoid. The complete sacrifice of investments and
securities would not make sense unless the British Government could
count on its existing contracts being met under lend-lease and on the
refunding of the advance payments and capital assistance it had given
with the contracts. Unless this were done, the United Kingdom
would be left without any working balance to finance dollar purchases by itself and the sterling area and to pay Canada. (Dollars
were needed, for example, to buy Bolivian tin and Venezuelan oil.)
'With the whole of the responsibility for conducting the war upon
us', as the Treasury put it, the British Government was reluctant to
sacrifice its last reserves. For the same reason it was reluctant to pile
up debts to its Allies by borrowing their gold. It was ready to accept
a scheme whereby the United States paid in advance for strategic
materials imported from British Commonwealth countries, such as
rubber, tin, wool and jute. But since the United States would import
less at a later stage such advances would be at the expense of later
dollar receipts. Moreover, it was soon clear that purchases of this
sort were liable to antagonise support in Congress.

A third request by Secretary Morgenthau was for permission to
give to the Foreign Affairs Committee of Congress on 15th January
(repeated later in the Senate Committee on 27th) a full statement of

---

[1] The liquidation of British investments in India had already begun. See section vii
below on the extent of sale of British investments in the sterling area.

[2] Morgenthau, article in *Collier's*, 18th October 1947. He refers to the President as
meeting suggestions regarding the handing over of the British West Indies with the reply
that: 'If they offer us islands as security remember they had better pay us to take the
islands'.

British financial reserves and commitments. This was the kind of information no great Power had ever disclosed so completely in time of war. The disclosure covered also the British balance of payments with Canada. 'The British Government', Morgenthau wrote to the Chairman of the House Committee, 'owes American manufacturers $1,400 million on orders already placed. This sum will largely have to be met in the calendar year 1941. It has enough gold and dollar exchange assets to meet these outstanding commitments, but the British just haven't got the dollars to take care of their additional needs.'[1]

The gold and dollar exchange assets of the United Kingdom were given in the statement as follows:

	31st August 1939	31st December 1940
	(In millions of dollars)	
Gold	2,038	292
Official dollar balances	50	54
Private dollar balances	545	305
Marketable United States securities	950	616
Direct and miscellaneous investments in United States	900	900
Total gold and dollar exchange assets	4,483	2,167

A table of the estimated expenditures and receipts of the British Commonwealth (excluding Canada) for 1941 was then given. It foresaw total receipts as $1,555 million, and expenditures—dollar requirements—as $3,019 million. The deficit foreseen for the year was thus $1,464 million. The United Kingdom had begun the war with gold and dollar assets of $4,483 million and it had raised some $2,000 million more. But it had paid out nearly four and a half thousand million dollars on war supplies, so that gold and dollar assets were down to $2,167 million (of which only $1,811 million was in practice available). The drain was thus $2,316 million for the period of sixteen months. Table 8 shows where the payments had gone.

The receipts of the Commonwealth in the sixteen months totalled only $2,030 million (including exports visible and invisible, $1,015 million and sale of gold $965 million).

Secretary Morgenthau added a comparison of British and American taxation. He gave British war expenditure as approximately sixty per cent. of the national income. He gave also a tentative estimate of British investments in various parts of the world. He ended by emphasising that the problem was not whether the British had resources, but whether they had dollars to buy in the United States; they could pay for what they had bought, but they could buy no more.

---

[1] *Lend-Lease Bill, Hearings before the Committee on Foreign Affairs, House of Representatives.* U.S. Government Printing Office, Washington, 1941.

United Kingdom gold and dollar expenditure,
1st September 1939 to 31st December 1940

TABLE 8 $ million

	$ million
Payment by the United Kingdom to the United States on Government orders .	1,380
$ million	
for goods delivered 660	
advance payments 570	
capital assistance 150	
Other United Kingdom imports, services, etc., from United States .	902
Payments to United States by other Commonwealth countries, excluding Canada	483
Commonwealth payments (mostly by United Kingdom) outside the United States and Canada requiring gold and dollars	550
Commonwealth (mostly United Kingdom) gold payments to Canada . .	225
Withdrawal of capital[1]	735
Residual	71
	4,346

But failure to place any new orders for several months would mean the loss of the high momentum already given to American industry by British contracts. The President's instructions in December to stop new orders were holding up the placing of new British orders worth $1,200 million—many of them continuation orders. In effect this was like stopping dead a high-powered machine running at full speed. Factories left without orders would be turned over to other uses. Many of the orders balanced British production which would be thrown out of gear by their loss. 'Six weeks lost now may mean six months lost a year hence', according to a British Embassy minute. The ban was not absolute enough to prevent the placing of some orders of extreme urgency; and in fact new British orders worth $122 million were placed between December 19th and January 16th. From this last date no new orders could be placed without the approval of Morgenthau and the signature of Phillips. New orders 'often of the greatest interest and urgency, come forward every day', the latter noted on the 18th. But $300 million had to be found somehow to pay for existing orders up to the end of February. 'If', he said, 'we place no new contracts at all and get in no new cash, our balance by the end of February would be down to two or three days' expenditure.' There could be no new orders, he thought, unless new cash could be found. The Administration was 'certainly trying hard and we have some reason to think that progress will be made soon'. One idea that had been mooted was that the Reconstruction Finance Corporation should take over and pay for British capital assistance. On the basis of a twenty-five per cent. down payment the money would suffice to launch new contracts to a value of some $650 million. But reluctance to take over existing British contracts extended also to the capital investment that went with them.

---

[1] Foreign holders of balances in the United Kingdom had been permitted to withdraw their funds in sterling. The sterling was then sold in the free market, so that the dollars acquired escaped control.

Purvis furnished Morgenthau on 21st January with a list of orders which it was imperative to place in the interim period. The value (cost of product and capital assistance) was $1,259 million, $884 million for United States-type equipment and $375 million for British types. This figure did not include the contracts for American types, which the United States Army had already agreed to finance, to the amount of $290 million, out of its own appropriations. Next day, with other British representatives, Purvis discussed the whole situation with Secretary Morgenthau and with the Secretaries of War, Navy, Commerce and the head of the Office of Production Management (Mr. Knudsen). The result was an agreement (1) that the Reconstruction Finance Corporation 'could and would' finance the $884 million for contracts for United States types, (2) that it would take over British capital assistance. But, as usual, questions of legal powers and political expediency prevented action on these lines. The hard core of the problem was British-type orders. The Treasury representative warned London that it would probably have to pay for all contracts for British types, whether new or old, and that this might be the case for all such orders placed after the Act was passed. The North American Supply Committee expressed alarm at the news; to cancel British-type orders would have 'a disastrous effect on our ability to carry on the war'. It asked for some assurance as to the intentions of the Administration, since the Bill did not expressly exclude British types. The reply of Purvis was that to raise the question then 'would in all probability crystallise a degree of opposition against anything but strictly standard United States types which would bolt and bar the door against us'. The passage of the Lend-Lease Bill unamended was the first consideration. Moreover, friendly Cabinet Ministers were 'genuinely sceptical of the wisdom from the United States view of allowing United States production output to be allocated to ammunition for weapons they do not use or to weapons for which they do not manufacture suitable ammunition'. Their feeling was that the American interest was better served and the British interest sufficiently met by delivering to Britain complete and balanced quotas of weapons and ammunition of United States type. Nevertheless, the placing in the next six weeks of new contracts for British types to the value of $75 million for munitions and $285 million for aircraft was considered by London to be so important that it authorised them on 27th January, 'without waiting to know from what specific source the necessary finance will be met'. On the same day, Secretary Morgenthau testified before the Senate Foreign Relations Committee on the danger caused by delay in the placing of British-type orders for aircraft. On production grounds, in order to keep capacity occupied, Knudsen was pressing for the immediate placing of new orders for British types of aircraft to the value of $179 million, and the Secretaries of the Treasury and of the Commerce Department approved. As the Administration had no funds (since none of the expedients hitherto discussed had produced any money), Morgenthau suggested that the United Kingdom should use the French or Allied gold. The British Treasury representative put forward the idea of an American Government loan of $200 million against the Belgian gold, with the understanding that the Administration would contract for wool, tin, and rubber up to this amount after the Lend-Lease Act was passed; funds received from these sales could then be used to repay the Belgian Government. It was decided in London to authorise the placing of aircraft orders for $179 million, against a loan of Allied gold. As a result of these developments, and of the taking over by the United States Army and Navy of American-type orders, the problem of the more urgent new orders in the interim period was solved, except for British-type contracts valued at $90 million.

Secretary Morgenthau went on leave at this point to recuperate from the heavy strain he had been carrying. He left authority with the United States Treasury to approve new British orders up to $35 million weekly—a ration which lasted until the Act was passed on 11th March. The money was found by various expedients—the sale of more gold from South Africa, the purchase of sterling by Canada, and early in March a gold loan of $300 million from the Belgian Government.

(vi)

The British Contracts and the Reconstruction Finance Corporation Loan

Meanwhile, no progress had been possible on the financing of existing orders. On 12th February, as soon as Morgenthau returned from leave, Purvis gave him a note on the matter. It suggested that Congress should be asked not only to take over the orders (which he valued then at $1,352 million) but also to repay the $781 million advance payments made by the United Kingdom. But neither the permission given by the Lend-Lease Act to use for the Allies $1,300 million from prior appropriations, nor the passage of the Appropriation Bill[1] authorising a sum of $7,000 million for lend-lease supplies produced money to pay for existing British contracts. Indeed, during the passage of the latter Bill, Congress extracted a promise from the Director of the Budget that none of the $7,000 million

---

[1] Defence Aid Supplemental Appropriation Act, 27th March 1941.

would be used for this purpose. The occasion of the Bill was taken by the Administration to bring to a head the long-standing issue of the disposal of the direct British investments in the United States. This action in turn led four months later to a solution by way of a Reconstruction Finance Corporation loan against collateral in the form of direct investments, and most of the remaining securities which were saleable.

No accurate estimate of the value of the British direct investments in American industry was possible. The American Treasury made a guess of $900 million in the estimates of British assets given by Morgenthau to Congress in January. An estimate by the Financial Secretary of the British Treasury, in October 1940, put the value at $600 million. The investments were not quoted on the Stock Exchange. Many of the British-American firms involved had never published a balance sheet and there was no ready market for their assets. In many cases a forced sale would destroy the asset. A subsidiary existing by virtue of its connection with an old firm with world-wide interests and reputation would stand to lose much of its value. Severance would mean loss of goodwill, of technical assistance, of patent rights, trade names and other assets. In the view of the British Government these businesses were in a different category from market securities. They were going concerns, resulting from decades of healthy competitive effort. They were part of the living tissue uniting the British and American economies, which could only be cut at the risk of hurting both. Thus, the American Viscose Corporation, which was to be the main victim of the policy of forced liquidation, was closely interlocked with the parent controlling firm, Courtaulds Limited, in the matter of trade marks, patents, technical knowledge and development; fear of the effects of severance lowered the sale value of the assets in such cases. Amongst the scores of subsidiaries of British firms covered by the term 'direct investments' were many important British insurance companies, whose assets were peculiarly vulnerable. Credit built up in generations of successful business relations could be extinguished by sale, and once lost could not be replaced.

Secretary Morgenthau had hammered persistently, from July 1940 onwards, on the need to sell direct investments. He returned to the matter at the end of September 1940 with the suggestion that a 'liquidator' should be sent from London with the power to make sales. The Secretary of the Treasury would certainly want to be satisfied, the Ambassador reported, that the United Kingdom had taken every possible and reasonable step in this matter before any approach was made for financial assistance. In mid-October 1940 Morgenthau again pressed the point in a talk with Purvis, when the latter brought to him a statement regarding British assets and the

T

cost of existing and new British programmes. The day before, the Secretary had received a message from the British Treasury that a critical and frank study of direct investments would be placed before him, but that the Treasury was not very hopeful of raising many dollars since sales to American investors would be extremely difficult to make. Morgenthau was disturbed that the problem of direct investments had not been taken up earlier. The right time to sell securities, he suggested, was six months before financial pressure made it necessary to sell.

After the President's announcement of the principle of lend-lease on 17th December, the British Treasury representative asked the Treasury for lists of properties that could be sold or mortgaged. He reported that Secretary Morgenthau was pressing for some action to help with Congress. Complaints were appearing in the Press that British firms were refusing to sell their American businesses. The Embassy reported on an inspired article by two newspaper columnists on 26th December, dealing with the Phillips-Morgenthau discussions.[1] In it the President was reported to have given up hope of using British South American investments, especially the Argentine railways, which would be of little value to the United States. The only serious point at issue was now the British direct investments in the United States. The article asked for the sending of a British agent to discuss the sale of some of the investments. At the end of December the Treasury indicated that it was sending an expert (Sir Edward Peacock) and he arrived in January 1941.

By this time, however, Purvis and Phillips both felt that members of the Administration had begun to believe that the United Kingdom was resorting to delaying tactics. The passage of the Lend-Lease Bill was likely to be held up by Congress; they recommended, therefore, immediate sale of a substantial part of the direct investments. One of the danger signs was the suggestion that the United Kingdom should lodge collateral against lend-lease. Phillips was thereupon authorised to inform Secretary Morgenthau that negotiations were being opened immediately which should result in the sale of more than $100 million of direct investments. It was agreed that Morgenthau should refer to the matter at the Congressional Hearings on the 15th January. The British Government, he told the Committee, 'propose to sell as rapidly as they can find buyers the so-called direct investments in factories or businesses which are not listed on the exchange'.

In mid-February 1941 the pressure was renewed both from the side of the Administration and from Congress. The negotiations during the past month for the sale of American Viscose and two other important firms had not yet produced results. Secretary

---

[1] Alsop and Kintner in the *New York Herald Tribune*, 26th December 1940.

Morgenthau appealed on 14th and 15th February to both Purvis and Phillips to effect 'some immediate operation of magnitude'. On the 18th the Ambassador reported the atmosphere 'clouded' and 'bad trouble ahead', but it was not the Administration that was making the trouble. This convinced Ministers in London. The Prime Minister, who earlier had doubted the wisdom of selling the remaining British assets, now thought it was necessary. Great Britain, he pointed out, would receive from the United States far more than she could give; but the sales should not be at knock-down prices. The idea of an appeal to the President through Harry Hopkins was at first entertained, but was abandoned when the Ambassador pointed out that it was on Morgenthau, Britain's 'best friend, after the President', that the President relied in these matters. An Embassy plan, which in effect placed direct investments under the control of the United States Government, was agreed to with 'extreme reluctance' by the British Government. The idea was to give power of sale to a joint committee of the two Governments, the final decision resting with the United States. The price was to be agreed, if possible, with the vendor, but sale could be made without his consent. If the American Government were made responsible for action the Ambassador hoped that it would see that to strip Britain bare would be 'both bad business for them and morally unjustifiable, when we are doing the fighting for both'. In handing the plan to Secretary Morgenthau on 27th February, the Treasury representative explained that the cash reserve was now about $69 million, and that at least $100 million would be needed to carry on until the Lend-Lease Act was passed. Sales of direct investments could yield nothing during the critical next weeks. He was given to understand that the Administration expected the Belgian gold to be borrowed. At the same time, he was left with the impression that once lend-lease was out of the way the Administration would favour a loan against remaining British assets.

The signing of the Lend-Lease Act on 11th March in fact opened the way for new pressure. There was an urgent plea for a spectacular sale to placate Congress before Secretary Morgenthau testified on the $7,000 million Appropriation Bill. The result was an arrangement within a week for the sale of American Viscose to a syndicate, for a sum to be settled later.[1] A move towards further sales drew from the Prime Minister the remark that 'this is no time for us to be driven from pillar to post'.

[1] Attempts, in May, to save the Viscose investment by bringing it under the R.F.C. loan scheme, broke down because the success of the loan scheme with Congress was regarded as dependent on the sale of Viscose. The marketing of the Viscose shares by the banks was expected to produce for the United Kingdom $55 million to $62 million. The actual sum received by the United Kingdom was about $54 million. The compensation paid in sterling to the former British owners, Courtaulds, was twice as high, namely £27 million. See McCurrach, op. cit., p. 361.

The next step took the form of a Reconstruction Finance Corporation loan of $40 million to the British-controlled Brown and Williamson Tobacco Corporation. A loan, as Secretary Morgenthau explained to the Press on 17th April, served the same purpose as sale. By means of the loan, he explained, the United Kingdom raised money 'to pay its contractors in the United States on pre-lend-lease contracts'. It was not till July, however, that means were found for paying the whole amount involved in the pre-lend-lease contracts. For the period April to December 1941 the deficit which would be produced by the payments was estimated at $600 million. By April, some $200 million had been raised towards this amount, in part by the sale of American Viscose and the $40 million loan on Brown and Williamson.

A comprehensive settlement, covering all direct investments by an R.F.C. loan, was now sought. Mr. J. M. (later Lord) Keynes, who was on a mission in the United States in June, took part in the negotiations. The way was cleared by an Act of 10th June, empowering the Reconstruction Finance Corporation to make loans to belligerent governments against collateral in the form of American securities. Under this Act a loan agreement was made by the British Government with the Reconstruction Finance Corporation on 21st July. This was issued as a British White Paper and confirmed by Act of Parliament on 29th July.[1] The loan was for a sum up to $425 million to be advanced against collateral securities, valued at some $500 million, which were to be assigned to the Reconstruction Finance Corporation and lodged with the Federal Reserve Bank.[2] The interest was three per cent. and the loan ran for fifteen years, with the option of extending it to twenty years. The income from the collateral was reserved for interest and the repayment of the loan. The investments remained the property of the owners. Thus, the solution saved investments from forced sale, preserved trade channels and supplied funds as needed to pay off British contracts.

How matters looked after the loan was shown in statements, given early in October, by the United States Treasury to the House Appropriations Committee of Congress. They covered for the six months from 1st September 1941: (a) an estimate of the United Kingdom and sterling areas gold and dollar expenditure and receipts; and (b) the gold and dollar exchange assets of the United Kingdom as of 1st September 1941. The figures had been agreed

---

[1] *Financial Powers (U.S.A. Securities) Act*, Cmd. 6295, July 1941. Statement by Chancellor of the Exchequer in House of Commons, 25th July. H. of C. Deb., Vol. 373, Col. 1173 ff.

[2] The amount of the loan actually drawn by the United Kingdom during the war was $390 million. The value placed on the collateral by R.F.C. in March 1946 was stated by the Secretary of the United States Treasury to be $895 million. Statement before Senate Committee on Banking and Currency, 5th March 1946. The loan was paid off by the British Government in mid-1951.

with the British Treasury representatives. They indicated that by virtue of lend-lease and the Reconstruction Finance Corporation's loan (of which only an initial amount of $100 million had been drawn) the financial crisis was on the way towards solution. Between 1st January and 1st September 1941, $907 million had been paid off against total commitments for existing orders of $1,851 million ($1,393 million existing on 1st January and $458 million placed after that date). In a projected balance sheet for the sterling area for the next six months, expenditures were estimated at $1,035 million and receipts at $885 million, leaving a deficit of $150 million.

Liberal interpretations of lend-lease, mostly made in its first quarter (such as a wide interpretation of the non-military exports from the United States covered by the Act and the inclusion of some off-shore purchases) had alleviated somewhat the very heavy financial burden of 1941. With the entry of the United States into the war in December, further alleviations were possible, although the United Kingdom still continued to pay for the old contracts until their fulfilment. In the year 1941, however, the United Kingdom had paid the heaviest financial toll of the war. At home, capital equipment and stocks were run down by over £350 million; and abroad disinvestment and borrowing came to nearly £820 million.[1]

(vii)

The Last Phases of Cash Payments, 1942–44

Some words are called for, by way of summary and evaluation, on the last phases of cash payments and the part played by British finance in American war production.

The stages traced, so far, may be summarised as follows. In the first stage, roughly up to Dunkirk, buying was being done mainly 'over the counter'. But an immense stimulus was given, even in this

---

[1] Cmd. 6707, December 1945 (Appendix VI), gives the following figures of United Kingdom external disinvestment. (Capital loss through realisation of investments, through debt incurred in the form of sterling balances, and through running down of gold and dollar reserves.)

	£ million
1939 (September to December) .	212
1940	811
1941	820
1942	674
1943	689
1944	663
1945 (January to June) .	329
Total	4,198

early period, to the American aircraft industry. Some of the special contracts for aircraft and engines were the largest so far received in the history of the industry. The second stage was marked by the policy of creating new aircraft and munitions capacity by large capital investments and the placing of very large orders. The stage began with the Anglo-French aircraft programme in the spring of 1940. On the fall of France, the United Kingdom doubled overnight its dollar commitments in the United States by taking over the French war contracts, valued at $800 million, without benefit of the French gold and dollar resources on which the contracts had been based.[1] The rate of the drain on gold and dollars was now more than doubled, with payments on deliveries from orders, heavy down payments against future deliveries, and capital assistance to American firms. By December 1940 the war chest was almost empty and new contracting came virtually to an end. Barely enough gold and dollars were left, or expected to come in from new supply, to pay for the output on existing orders, and little or none for continuation orders necessary to maintain the momentum gained since Dunkirk.

By the free use of the last of the gold, by borrowing gold from Belgium, by the sale of securities, and by help from the unspent margins of the United States Army and Navy, default on payment was avoided. In the process $820 million of American securities and investments had been sold up to lend-lease. The lowest point reached by British gold and dollar reserves was in April 1941, when they fell to $12 million. From mid-March 1941 new contracts for munitions and defence articles were paid for by the United States Government and delivered under lend-lease. The United Kingdom continued to pay in cash (eked out by the R.F.C. loan) for existing British orders until the contracts ran out, mostly in 1942.

It was long before lend-lease supply caught up with and passed supply under the British cash contracts. Comparisons between the value of supply from British cash contracts in the United States and deliveries from lend-lease are difficult to make because of the different levels on which lend-lease figures were presented. One was the appropriation level; another what was known as 'lend-lease transfers'; a third—the closest to reality—was actual exports. A 'transfer' might be changed by later diversion.[2] It was not the same as a delivery or an export which took place usually at a later point of time. Figures compiled in London in the autumn of 1942 illustrate the difference between transfers and exports; they show the amount of exports to the United Kingdom under lend-lease, deliveries from

---

[1] The value of the French assets frozen in the United States (mostly gold and securities) were given in the Lend-Lease Hearings as $1,593 million.

[2] Lend-lease transfers to the United Kingdom contained a small element of inflation, due to unrecorded diversions to other countries that had taken place in the earlier period.

British cash contracts in the United States and Canadian deliveries to the United Kingdom.

> Lend-lease *transfers* (all commodities) for the first eighteen months of the Act were $3,616 million.[1] (Transfers of munitions alone from January to August 1942 were $927 million.)
>
> Lend-lease *exports* to the United Kingdom (all commodities) in the first twelve months of the Act were $765 million.
>
> Lend-lease *exports* to the United Kingdom in the first eighteen months of the Act for all commodities were $1,654 million, which was less than half of the total shown for transfers.

In addition to exports, lend-lease services, such as shipping and expenditure on plant, etc., have to be added. Up to August 1942 the cost of shipping and other services was put at $666 million, which with the export figure gave a total of $2,320 million for the first eighteen months. As regards Canadian deliveries and those from British contracts in the United States, exactly parallel figures cannot be given. Without being a comparison the following figures for the period January to August 1942 (for munitions alone) give some idea of the order of magnitude.

	U.S.$ million
Lend-lease transfer of munitions to the United Kingdom .	927
Canadian deliveries of munitions to the United Kingdom .	559[2]
Deliveries from British contracts in the United States .	710

It was in fact nearly two years before lend-lease transfers (for the same articles as were covered by the British contracts in the United States—mainly aircraft, munitions, machine tools, ships, iron and steel) exceeded the $3,200 million, including capital assistance, spent by the British Government on these articles up to the date of the Lend-Lease Act; and by that time cash expenditures had climbed to a higher total by reason of the expenditures made to complete the contracts. Total lend-lease 'transfers' including food and raw materials were, of course, much higher. Thus, foodstuffs had topped $1,000 million by January 1943.[3] (In addition to expenditure on munitions before lend-lease there was considerable British Government expenditure in the United States on purchases of food. Up to the end of 1940 many of the British raw material imports,

---

[1] There was a large food element in this figure. It included also some diversions to other countries.

[2] In addition, Canada supplied in the eight months trucks to the value of U.S.$170 million.

[3] Total lend-lease aid to the British Commonwealth and Empire was as follows: 1941 (March–December), $1,082 million; 1942, $4,757 million; 1943, $9,031 million; 1944, $10,766 million; 1945 (January–August), $4,437 million. Total $30,073 million. See below, Chapter X, for final totals of British cash expenditure and lend-lease aid.

including oil, were still in private trade channels, and these expenditures also would have to be counted in order to arrive at a total figure of United Kingdom expenditure in the United States.)

It is difficult, however, to make any real comparison in terms of economic effort between the cost of dollars to the United Kingdom and the cost to the United States. Quite apart from factors such as time, differences in total national incomes, and divergent price levels, a billion dollars raised painfully by the United Kingdom in the hardest of foreign currencies could hardly be compared with a billion dollars raised and spent by the United States in its own currency area.

By the late summer of 1943 total British cash expenditure in the United States for supplies of all kinds during the war had reached a figure of some $6,000 million. Total cash expenditure for munitions (including ships but not machine tools) was given by Professor R. G. D. Allen at the end of the war as $3,600 million.[1] Even at the height of lend-lease in 1943 and early 1944 there was still a 'hard core' of cash expenditure for goods and services outside lend-lease. At its lowest point it was still about $20 million each month for the sterling area as a whole. It was to rise again sharply soon after the United States Treasury and the Lend-Lease Administration began early in 1943 to note and criticise the rise in British reserves. The Lend-Lease Administration began to question the 'eligibility' for lend-lease of various supplies such as tobacco and 'off-shore purchases', i.e. articles supplied under lend-lease but produced outside the United States such as Cuban molasses, sugar and Mexican fibre. Tobacco was one of the first of the major items to revert to cash purchase. In September 1943 the Lend-Lease Administration raised with the British Supply Council the question of the removal from lend-lease of two categories of stores. The first was machine tools and other capital equipment; the second, maintenance and repair equipment for oil companies. Both were regarded as politically dangerous. Machine tools in particular were open to attack from Congress, on the ground that tools supplied at this stage of the war were likely to increase the competitive power of British Industry after the war to the detriment of United States exports. The British Supply Council came to the conclusion that this was a matter which the Lend-Lease Administration had to decide for itself—which it promptly did in November 1943 by removing the items from lend-lease.[2] Early in 1944 civilian supplies to British colonies not in actual war zones were removed from lend-lease, even though these colonies were the source of goods supplied by the United Kingdom under reciprocal aid.

---

[1] See below, Chapter X.
[2] See below, Chapter XI, p. 438.

There had been some increase in British gold and dollar reserves since 1942, due in large measure to the dollar expenditures of American troops in Europe and Australia. A suggestion had been received from the United States in January 1943 that lend-lease might be restricted if and when such reserves rose above a certain figure; the figure mentioned informally was $1,000 million. Explanations and figures were given in February by Sir Frederick Phillips to the United States Treasury to show that the improvement in cash reserves was more apparent than real. The issue was again raised, however, in a State Department *aide-mémoire* on reciprocal aid, presented to the British Embassy on 18th August 1943. The figures of the February statement were, therefore, brought up to date and presented to Secretary Morgenthau, with a long personal letter of 3rd September from the Chancellor of the Exchequer (Sir Kingsley Wood).

The particular proposal in the State Department's *aide-mémoire*, that raw materials should be brought under reciprocal aid as a makeweight to lend-lease, was accepted by the British Government. It involved the purchase for sterling of a number of raw materials and foods—such as rubber, sisal, hides and cocoa—produced in British colonies. (Raw materials from the Dominions and India were given as reciprocal aid by their own governments.) The Chancellor expressed the readiness of the British Government to bring under reciprocal aid 'all the procurements by the United States Government of essential requirements for war needs of foodstuffs and raw materials in so far as they can be supplied from the United Kingdom and the Colonies'.[1] He did not agree, however, with the proposal in the *aide-mémoire* to make this arrangement retrospective, i.e. that Britain should reimburse the United States for all such purchases of food and raw materials as from 1st July 1943. This suggestion, he pointed out, was based on the idea that the British gold and dollar balances, the 'quick reserves', were now large enough to justify such a course. The real position had been explained in his budget speech to Parliament on 12th April. The reserves, he pointed out in his letter, were held against much heavier liabilities; and the liabilities were growing inexorably at a much faster rate than the reserves. The financial problem had been largely solved in relation to the North American continent by the generosity of the Governments of the United States and Canada. But in other parts of the world the United Kingdom had been providing the finance for carrying on the war in the Middle East, India and elsewhere. 'We can only do this, in the main, by borrowing local currencies against a credit in sterling in the respective countries, and thus we are incurring unfunded indebtedness on a vast scale.' This necessitated the holding of enough reserves, in the form

---

[1] For this purpose a procedure, somewhat similar to that of lend-lease, was adopted with programmes and requisitions submitted by the United States Government.

of liquid assets, to meet—if called upon to do so—the more pressing part of the liquid indebtedness.

The gold and dollar reserves, although shown as United Kingdom balances, were, in fact, 'the pooled reserves of the sterling area'. The countries in that area turned over their surplus dollar earnings in exchange for sterling credit; and the United Kingdom was thus under an 'implied obligation' to turn back, as far as it was able, the sterling into dollars whenever other parts of the sterling area needed dollars.

A British Treasury memorandum accompanying the Chancellor's letter gave the facts and figures on which it was based. The quick reserves were not being built up out of net external earnings, because there were none; they were, in fact, in the nature of a debt rather than a reserve, since they had been acquired by borrowing—with an obligation to repay—the liquid assets of other parts of the sterling area. The memorandum gave figures, some of them provisional, to show the growth of liabilities in relation to assets. The excess of the financial burden overseas (beyond what could be met out of current income) in the three and a half years from January 1940 to June 1943 had been met in four ways as shown in Table 9.

Financing of the deficit in United Kingdom overseas payments, 1st January 1940 to 30th June 1943

TABLE 9 $ million

Method of financing	1st January 1940 to 31st December 1941	In 1942	First half 1943 (approx.)	1st January 1940 to 30th June 1943
(1) By overseas loans:				
R.F.C. loan	345	15	−10	350
Canadian secured loan .	—	635	−15	620
Sundry loans and advances	115	125	15	255
Total loans .	460	775	−10	1,225
(2) By sale of overseas investments, including sinking funds .	1,545	845	535	2,925
(3) By net increase of quick liabilities, excluding those carrying a gold or dollar liability	2,585	1,240	1,235	5,060
(4) By sale of gold and dollars (net, i.e. allowing for gold and dollar liabilities)	1,950	−305	−330	1,315
TOTAL .	6,540	2,555	1,430	10,525

Net gold and dollar reserves, which were $2,585 million at the beginning of 1940, were down by June 1943 to $1,020 million. As against this quick reserve there were quick liabilities seven times as high —namely $7,000 million.

It was true that there was an increase of several hundred million dollars in the reserve as compared with 1942, but this was due to dollars acquired from the rest of the sterling area—mostly from payments by American troops—and the repatriation of $182 million of South African securities. Apart from the troop payments there had been an unfavourable balance on current account between the United Kingdom and the United States; and the amount of the deficit with the United States forecast for the whole of 1943 was over $80 million. There had been a decline in commitments in the United States as the British contracts were paid off, but this would be offset by payments for reciprocal aid on raw materials and food. Capital transactions in the eighteen months January 1942 to June 1943 had made only a small contribution towards meeting deficits in the period.

	1942	1943 (1st half)
	(In millions of dollars)	
Sales of gold in United States .	8	4
Sales of securities in United States.	22	21
Instalment of R.F.C. loan . .	40	—
	70	25

The sources of the quick assets were summarised as shown in Table 10.

Sources of United Kingdom quick assets, January 1942 to 30th June 1943

TABLE 10 $ million

Source of quick assets	1942	1943 (1st half)
United Kingdom current account with United States .	−287	− 62
United States troops in United Kingdom	+ 50	+ 45
United Kingdom dollar payments outside United States .	− 2	−165
Sale of gold and securities and loans in United States .	+ 70	+ 25
Rest of sterling-area current account with United States .	+119	+115
United States troops in rest of sterling area . .	+194	+166
Special gold from South Africa for repatriation of South African Government sterling securities	+ 15	+167
Other gold and dollar movements (net)	+146	+ 39
Increase in United Kingdom's quick assets . .	+305	+330

The conclusion was that the quick reserves were seriously inadequate. Whilst it was the United Kingdom that had the liabilities —all of them—the reserves formed a pool for the sterling area as a whole. Whilst saddled with vastly increased liabilities, the United Kingdom had lost its second line of defence—its saleable capital assets. The total loss of assets and increase of liabilities already totalled $10½ billion.[1] 'In this respect', the memorandum concluded, 'our position is unique amongst the United Nations. In fact more than ninety per cent. of this loss has accrued to the advantage of other members of the United Nations, many of whom have improved their overseas position during the war. The United Kingdom alone has been expected to mortgage the future on a large scale by incurring overseas liabilities.' Against the gross gold and dollar reserves of the United Kingdom, about $1,000 million, there were sterling liabilities of $7,000 million; but if all the liabilities of the United States were deducted they would still be left with *net* gold reserves about eighteen times the *gross* reserves of the United Kingdom without counting the latter's liabilities.[2]

These explanations no doubt served a useful purpose. The cuts in eligibility referred to above and the supplying of raw materials under reciprocal aid slowed down the rise in British reserves. Nevertheless a slow rise in the reserves, which was essential to the stability of the sterling area, continued. At one point, in March 1944, the Prime Minister had to intervene with an important message to the President;[3] but a month later it was noted in an official paper in London that the policy of placing a limit on the reserves of the United Kingdom 'was never actually put into effect and is at present, at any rate, in abeyance'. Reserves were still increasing, due to the temporary factor of the American troop payments within the sterling area. But liabilities were increasing 'at least five times as fast as our reserves'. There was a clear foresight of what this would mean for the future when lend-lease and possibly mutual aid would be reduced or come to an end. The United Kingdom would then be faced with the greatest difficulty in finding 'means to pay for the minimum imports required to maintain a tolerable standard of living in this country'. Reserves had reached their peak at $1,748 million in the late summer of 1944 when the Stage II negotiations opened. The sequel must be left to Chapter XI.

---

[1] *A Report on Mutual Aid*, Cmd. 6483, November 1943, para. 37

[2] Chapter XI below on the winding up of lend-lease indicates the position at the end of the war. The following figures are from Cmd. 6707, December 1945. The total loss of assets and increase of liabilities stood, in June 1945, at some £4,198 million ($17,000 million). The total loss of overseas investments of all kinds in all countries was £1,118 million ($4,506 million). The net loss of American dollar securities and investments from 1939 to the end of the war was £203 million ($818 million) (excluding collateral for the R.F.C. loan). British loss of Canadian securities was £225 million ($907 million). The loss of British securities and investments in the rest of the sterling area was double that in the whole dollar area. The income of the United Kingdom from foreign investments had fallen from some $1,000 million in the year before the war to less than $400 million after it—a sum worth a third of what it would have been in 1938 in terms of 1938 prices.

[3] Winston S. Churchill, *The Second World War*: Vol. V, *Closing the Ring*. (London: Cassell & Company Limited, 1951), pp. 611–12. (Also published in the United States, Boston: Houghton Mifflin Company, 1951.)

(viii)
Reciprocal Aid

Reciprocal aid forms an essential element in the context of this chapter, and a brief reference must be made here to it.

The fundamental underlying principle was expressed as follows in the Reciprocal Aid Agreement between the United Kingdom and the United States of 3rd September 1942:[1] 'The war production and the war resources of both Nations should be used by the armed forces of each and of the other United Nations in ways which most effectively utilise the available materials, manpower, production facilities, and shipping space.' Section 2 of the Agreement declared that as to financing such aid, the general principle held that 'as large a portion as possible of the articles and services which each Government may authorise to be provided to the other shall be in the form of reciprocal aid so that the need of each Government for the currency of the other may be reduced to a minimum'. The British White Paper on Reciprocal Aid of November 1943 prefaced its figures of British reciprocal aid with a warning.[2] Mutual aid was not regarded, it noted, as resting on the principle of the creation of mutual indebtedness supported by detailed accounts. American price levels for labour and materials were substantially higher than the levels in the United Kingdom: 'American book costs probably exceed British costs by more than fifty per cent.' Lend-lease was centralised and came mostly from large contracts, which made book-keeping easier. Mutual aid was diffuse and scattered over a very large number of transactions in all theatres of the war and by its nature could not be recorded with any exactitude. The figures were, therefore, in the nature of rough estimates of cost to the British Exchequer:[3]

United Kingdom reciprocal aid to the United States (goods, services and capital facilities) to the end of June 1943	£216 million ($864 million)
Cumulative total to the end of June 1944	£604·7 million ($2,419 million)

The total value of British reciprocal aid to the United States throughout the war up to 1st September 1945 was estimated at £1,241,402,000 or just over five billion dollars. In addition, reciprocal aid estimated at £519 million ($2,092 million) was given to twelve foreign countries. The grand total of reciprocal aid to the United

---

[1] Cmd. 6389.

[2] Cmd. 6483, op. cit.

[3] White Papers on Mutual Aid: Cmd. 6483, November 1943; *Mutual Aid Second Report*, Cmd. 6570, November 1944; *Mutual Aid Third Report*, Cmd. 6931, October 1946; also see below, Chapter X, section iii, 'The Mutual Aid Sector'.

States during the war was classified under the headings given in Table 11.

United Kingdom Reciprocal Aid to the United States

TABLE 11	£ thousand
Supplies in the United Kingdom . .	453,955
Services in the United Kingdom . .	297,065
Capital facilities in the United Kingdom .	222,800
Exports of raw materials	31,351
Exports of bulk foodstuffs	22,556
Exports of military stores	45,676
Reciprocal overseas aid	167,999
TOTAL	1,241,402

Some idea of what these expenditures meant in terms of key supplies to the United States Army and Navy—such as the 2,100 British aircraft supplied to the United States forces, the million British spark plugs used throughout the United States bomber fleet, and the special air bases in the United Kingdom from which it operated, the Mulberry harbours and the Bailey bridges—was given in a graphic report by the President to Congress.[1]

The first British White Paper on Reciprocal Aid (11th November 1943) showed that at that stage the United Kingdom was devoting ten per cent. of its war expenditure to the mutual aid of the other United Nations, as compared with twelve per cent. of United States war expenditure applied in the form of lend-lease. Taking into account the raw materials supplied free by the United Kingdom to the United States and the lower British price levels, the White Paper concluded that the United Kingdom and the United States were giving much the same proportions of their national incomes in the form of reciprocal aid and lend-lease.[2]

(ix)

The Part of British Finance in American War Production

The United States had a great and unique advantage amongst the United Nations in that it was able to enter the war with a munitions industry greatly expanded and experienced, and an economy highly stimulated by the pouring in of billions of dollars of foreign funds.

---

[1] *Seventeenth Report to Congress on Lend-Lease Operations*, Reverse Lend-Lease Aid from the British Commonwealth of Nations, 77th Congress, 1st Session (Washington: November 1944). Also Stettinius, op. cit., Chapter XXV.

[2] See below, Chapter X (The Mutual Aid Sector) and Chapter XI (Settlement with the United States).

This note is concerned with the largest—but by no means the only—contribution, that of the United Kingdom. The total sum of British money poured into the American economy before and during the war is difficult to compute. The British White Paper on Reciprocal Aid of November 1943 gave a total of $6,000 million as spent by the United Kingdom since September 1939 on supplies of all kinds from the United States. Cash purchases were then running at over $20 million a month; and they increased as lend-lease began to taper off, e.g. for foodstuffs, raw materials and capital goods. The total, up to the termination of lend-lease, was probably at least $7,000 million. The larger part of the sum was spent on munitions and machine tools before the United States entered the war.

Administration leaders in the various Lend-Lease Hearings before Congress, the President's quarterly reports to Congress on lend-lease, and Mr. Stettinius in his book, have borne witness to the fact that the phenomenal American war production of the peak years, 1943 to 1944, owed a good deal to the initial impetus given by the British expenditures before Pearl Harbour. Up to lend-lease, as Secretary Morgenthau emphasised in the Lend-Lease Hearings, the American people had made no financial sacrifice, 'not one dollar', in assisting Great Britain to defend the United States against the totalitarian governments.[1] In the words of a British official paper of December 1942, the British assets used up in the United States were a 'main instrument in building up American war industry'.

The instrument was applied in a number of different ways. With the money went factors of considerable importance, although they could not be assessed accurately in monetary terms, such as British inventions, patents, designs, and technical data of many kinds. Specialised manufacturing experience is of particular importance in the production of arms, since it involves many techniques outside the range of normal peace-time industry. The main impetus came by the normal economic process of placing very large orders. But the effect of the orders was intensified by two factors that were abnormal. One was the heavy advance payments ranging up to sixty per cent. which accompanied most of the orders. Purvis calculated such advance payments up to early February 1941 at $781 million. The other factor was large-scale capital assistance to American production. Although the sum involved was only about a third of the amount spent on advance payments, its effect was much more important from the point of view of American defence.

---

[1] British expenditures were reflected in increased American exports before lend-lease. 'The total dollar value of all exports to the British Empire for the first quarter of 1941 was nearly two and one-half times the value for the first quarter of 1939 and over half again higher than the value for the same period of 1940.' *Operations Under Lend-Lease Act*, First Report from the President of the United States under Lend-Lease Act, 77th Congress, 1st Session, U.S. Senate Document No. 66 (Washington: June 11th 1941).

For the period before lend-lease, British Government expenditures in the United States on the main elements of supply for the armed forces (excluding food and most raw materials) and for capital assistance to American industry, amounted to approximately $3,200 million.[1] The greater part of this $3,200 million was spent on war supplies under the following heads:

		$ million
Aircraft, aircraft engines and materials	.	1,750
Iron and steel		264
Ordnance		220
Ammunition		213
Machine tools		196
Tanks		150
Ships and marine equipment . .		160
Non-ferrous metals		50
Motor vehicles		50
Explosives and propellants . . .		30

The list indicates the wide areas of American industry affected by the expenditure, the impact of which was accentuated by the short period of time in which it fell.

The expenditure of the United Kingdom on capital assistance to American firms was well over $200 million.[2] Capital assistance on a large scale had also formed part of British expenditure in the First World War. But in that war the cost of plant expansion was usually included in the price of the product on the basis of the initial orders. The usual practice followed in the Second World War, from the summer of 1940, was to pay separately for the plant which remained, in most cases, the property of the British Government. Thus, some two-thirds of the total capital expenditure on aircraft up to March 1942 was under arrangements of this kind. Contractors normally acted as agents for the British Government in providing the capital facilities, once the lump sum to be spent was agreed. One advantage was the preservation of valuable assets, from the sale of which part of the expenditure was recovered at a later stage in the war, through sales to contractors or to the United States Government, or by an allowance made in the final lend-lease settlement. Another advantage was the saving of a twenty per cent. United States income tax payment which the British Government would have had to meet in practice if capital cost had been included in the price of the commodity.

Some of the most serious 'bottlenecks' in American munitions production were broken by means of British capital expenditure. This

---

[1] Press release (OWIX 74931) by the U.S. Office of War Information, based on figures supplied by the British Supply Council. Of this amount at least $2,700 million were spent by December 31st 1940.

[2] British capital expenditure in Canada was on much the same scale. In 1943 the Canadian Government repurchased for about $200 million munitions plants which the United Kingdom had financed in Canada. See below, p. 484.

assured a much more rapid expansion of American aircraft and armaments after Pearl Harbour than would otherwise have been possible. Thus forty per cent. of American aircraft production before Pearl Harbour came from Allied air contracts. The principal expenditures were on facilities for the production of aircraft engines, airframes, and accessories, machine tools, tanks, shipping, explosives, small arms and small arms ammunition.

The general character of the expenditure, although by no means its total, was indicated in a British Supply Council return of 4th January 1941. It showed, up to that date, a figure of $198 million (three-quarters of which had been paid up) for capital and extraordinary charges undertaken by the United Kingdom since 1939 in financing American industry, under the following headings:

	$ *million*
Land	5
Buildings	59
Machine tools (including jigs and tools) .	101
Plant alterations	6
United States development costs . .	2½
Rental on leased equipment . .	7
Training of personnel (United States) .	6
Expediting charges	11
Income tax (United States) . . .	½
	198

The number of contracts involved in the payments was nearly 200, and the list of firms reads almost like a 'who's who' of the well-known names in the American aircraft, machine-tool, engineering and chemical industries. Information was given to Congress in March 1941 that up to that date the United Kingdom had spent some $171 million in financing the building and equipment of sixty-one munitions plants.[1]

On aircraft from the United States the total British cash expenditure during the war was $1,739 million.[2] Of this sum, capital assistance amounted to $122½ million. Of this latter amount, $11 million went with airframe contracts, $17 million with aircraft machine-gun contracts, $7½ million with light metal orders, and the bulk—over $80 million—with aircraft engine contracts.[3] As the supply of engines

[1] *Industrial Mobilisation for War*, Vol. I, Program and Administration, Historical Reports on War Administration, War Production Board (Washington: United States Government Printing Office, 1947), p. 51; Stettinius, op. cit., p. 25, indicates capital assistance as over $200 million.

[2] This included American aircraft furnished as a British Government contribution to the British Commonwealth Air Training Plan in various parts of the Commonwealth, and aircraft bought in the United States and supplied to Russia. In addition, British aircraft were supplied direct to Russia. British aircraft to the number of 2,100 were also supplied to the American Air Forces under reciprocal aid up to June 1944. (See *Seventeenth Report to Congress on Lend-Lease Operations*.)

[3] The Packard Company received in 1940 some $20 million to produce the Merlin engine; the Wright Company also received over $20 million for new facilities, Pratt & Whitney some $15 million, and Allison Division of General Motors over $6 million.

was the main 'bottleneck' in the aircraft industry, the expenditure, made largely in 1939 and 1940, was of incalculably greater importance than the same sum of dollars spent, say, in 1942. Over half of the total capital assistance was recovered or allowed for during and after the war. Some $51½ million was recovered by the sale of assets and credits, or in prices of production diverted to other governments.

The effect on the American machine-tool industry of British capital orders and assistance is referred to in an earlier chapter. Little direct assistance was given to the industry by the United States Government before the United States entered the war. The expenditure by the United Kingdom of over $100 million in equipping American munitions factories, together with very large orders for machine tools for British factories, was the main reason for the more than doubling of the output of the industry before Pearl Harbour. Again the factor of time was of the utmost importance, since it was on the output of the machine-tool industry that the rate of acceleration of American war production largely depended.

The factor of time was also important in the case of explosives. The limited output of explosives and propellants was a serious 'bottleneck' in American, as well as British, war production. At least six months were required to build a large new explosives plant and to get it into full production. By 1st September 1940 British capital assistance of over $60 million had been provided in North America for this purpose. The amount of capital assistance actually paid out for expenditure in the United States by the end of 1940 was $37 million. The expenditure went with fourteen contracts, most of the sums going to the DuPont Company (through the British Tennessee Powder Company) and the Hercules Powder Company (through the British New Jersey Powder Company).

An important part of the Ministry of Supply's explosives production programme was provided for by the erection of the Tennessee Powder Plant, at Memphis, on the Mississippi. The contract was signed on 10th June 1940 between E. I. DuPont de Nemours and the Tennessee Powder Company. The latter (like the New Jersey Powder Company) was an instrument of the British Government operating under the laws of the State of Tennessee. Its officers and directors were members of the British Purchasing Commission, and it was financed entirely by the British Government. It acted in effect as a financial channel through which funds passed to DuPont and the products of the explosives plant passed back to the British Government. The contract provided that DuPont should construct the plant and operate it. The construction of the plant was finished on 13th December 1940 and the first output was ready for delivery in January 1941. The total cost of the plant to the British Government was $25,460,379. After the Lend-Lease Act the plant was transferred for a little less than this sum to the United States Government.[1] Simultaneously the plant was leased to the DuPont Company which continued to produce directly for the British Government. The latter paid in cash for the explosives until its contract with DuPont ran out on 31st January 1942; total payments for products under the contracts were $27½ million. Thereafter DuPont continued to produce British requirements under lend-lease.

In the case of the Hercules Powder Company of Wilmington, Delaware, the company undertook the construction and the operation of two explosives plants in New Jersey under a contract which was to run to August 1945. The capital—over $10 million—was advanced by the British Government through the New Jersey Powder Company, which held the title to the land, the plant and facilities. Some $23 million was paid by the British Government for the explosives produced under the contract until it was taken over by the United States War Department on 7th September 1942. The sale of the two plants to the Defence Plant Corporation on 6th February 1943 returned a little over $9½ million to the British Government.

An account of how the vast American war output of shipping was started on its way by initial British orders and capital expenditure is given in the preceding chapter. The $17 million of British capital that went into the creation of new shipbuilding facilities produced the first Kaiser yard at Richmond, in California, on a site selected by British experts, and the expansion of the Todd-Bath works on the Atlantic seaboard. This money and the two contracts of thirty ships each, placed with these two companies in September 1940, were to have ultimate results out of all proportion to the sums involved.

This is also true of tanks, which are dealt with in the same chapter. The United Kingdom lodged orders from September to November 1940 for 2,086 tanks. The orders, together with British engineering assistance and $16½ million capital assistance for plant and machine tools, went to companies (Pullman Standard Car Manufacturing Company, Pressed Steel Car Corporation, Baldwin Locomotive Works and Lima Locomotive Works) which had never before made tanks. The effect of the British orders spread in wider circles as other orders were placed for tank engines, transmissions, armour-plate and armaments. These orders started some of the firms—such as Republic Steel and Lima Locomotive—on war production which was to be of considerable value to the United States after Pearl Harbour. A British estimate in December 1942 was that production facilities developed by British contracts would produce twenty-five per cent. of maximum United States medium-tank production, and an even

---

[1] The proposal for transfer was received on 19th March 1941 and the actual transfer to the Defence Plant Corporation, a subsidiary of the Reconstruction Finance Corporation, took place on 17th May.

larger proportion in the case of armour-plate. The total cost of the tank contracts was just under $150 million. Some $66 million of the cost of the materials produced under the contracts—in the form mainly of finished tanks, tank engines and guns, was recovered in 1942 from the United States War Department. The purchase arrangement was made under a contract known as Sale 555 of 19th May 1942. Of the capital expenditure, however, not much more than a million dollars was recovered from the companies.

Although emphasis has been placed in this section on the importance of all this expenditure—both by way of orders and capital assistance—from the point of view of American defence, it has to be remembered that the primary purpose of the expenditure was to provide aircraft and munitions for the United Kingdom. It served this purpose effectively. From it came the greater part of the aircraft and munitions actually received from the United States by the United Kingdom up to and even beyond the end of 1942.

CHAPTER VIII

LEND-LEASE TO PEARL HARBOUR: THE BEGINNINGS OF BRITISH-AMERICAN COMBINATION

THIS chapter is not much concerned with the things that were happening in 1941 on the well-lit stage of lend-lease. The setting up of the administrative machinery and the first-fruits of the first thin harvest of lend-lease—less by far than the yields from British cash contracts, but promising far bigger things to come—will be dealt with in the procurement chapters in *Studies of Overseas Supply*. This chapter is concerned in the main with matters of greater moment that were happening off-stage, largely out of sight of the public on both sides of the Atlantic. The first long-term combined plans were being laid for the joint strategy, and the joint war supply, necessary to defeat the Axis.

The year opened with lend-lease. Its midsummer witnessed the invasion of Russia. Its winter began with Pearl Harbour. Less spectacular, and spread over the year, was a fourth great development, the rough-forging of the Anglo-American combination, which 1942 was to hammer into shape. In the forging, a number of individuals and the Supply and Service Ministries in London and Washington played their parts. On the supply side in Washington leading roles fell to Purvis, as Chairman of the British Supply Council, and to Harry Hopkins, as *de facto* Lend-Lease Administrator, although he never had that title.[1]

For them, as for Monnet and other colleagues in London and Washington, the simple essentials of the problem, the assumptions of action, were the same. They might be stated as follows. The Axis could not be defeated without organising American production and supply to Britain and the Commonwealth on a far larger scale. The size of the scale depended, first, on the magnitude of the resources which the enemy could mobilise; second, on the plans of the General Staffs to defeat him; and third, on their estimates of the arms and supplies they would need for this purpose. The size of the production problem could not be settled until the combined requirements were

---

[1] Until the setting up of the Office of Lend-Lease Administration in October 1941, under Mr. Stettinius, lend-lease was merely the 'Division of Defence Aid Reports' in the Office of Emergency Management, with Hopkins in charge but without official status. The Executive Officer was Major-General James H. Burns.

better known. If only because of the ultimate limiting factors of raw materials, machine tools and manpower, production would suffer unless planned as a fully combined affair. As a first step to clear thinking, both countries must know with far greater precision how much of the main types of arms each country was already producing and was planning to produce over the next two or three years. But production in the United Kingdom would come to a standstill if there were not ships to bring in food and raw materials. Production in the United States, moreover, would be of little use unless it could be shipped to bases of operation in Europe and Africa. Combination in shipbuilding, in shipment by sea, in defending the sea lanes of supply, in convoying the ships and in securing bases necessary to control the convoying routes, as well as combination in ferrying aircraft across the Atlantic to Britain and to Africa—all these were essential conditions of success. Some of these things were the direct business of the British Supply Council; the rest concerned it indirectly.

(i)
Lend-Lease—Banker or Partner?

Lend-lease appropriations paid for only a fraction of total American production and covered short periods of six months to a year; they could influence, but they could not control, the planning of American production. Lend-lease was merely an agency to direct and to co-ordinate foreign aid. It procured nothing itself. Actual procurement was done by the powerful and long-established American departments—the War Department (munitions and aircraft); the Navy Department (naval vessels and naval aircraft and oil); the Maritime Commission (merchant shipping); the Department of Agriculture (food and agricultural products); the Treasury (metals, raw materials and miscellaneous manufactures). The planning of the national war production was mainly in the hands of the War and Navy Departments and the Office of Production Management. The latter co-ordinated and regulated war production; the Secretaries of War and the Navy sat on its policy-making council.[1] The influence of lend-lease funds on the expansion of production before Pearl Harbour was shown by such examples as the following: lend-lease funds helped to build the Ford bomber plant at Willow Run, the Chrysler tank plant, the Kaiser and other shipyards, and to expand all the big aircraft companies. It helped to build powder plants, anti-aircraft gun factories and many other capital facilities from which

---

[1] *The United States at War*, op. cit., pp. 53–56.

vital war supplies came at later stages of the war; lend-lease supplied the American funds for many joint British and American enterprises overseas.[1]

Yet for various reasons, which this account cannot discuss in detail, it was not easy for combined machinery to crystallise round lend-lease. One reason was its lack of flexibility due to the fact that it was based on an Act of Congress, and that its administration was constantly under the eye of Congress and subject to frequent review. Other reasons were to be found in lend-lease history and theory.

Because of the publicity that had to be given to lend-lease in order to secure its enactment and to safeguard it from attack, it had to make compromises with long-standing American traditions, such as neutrality, the avoidance of alliances, wariness about 'the British', and extreme caution about financial transactions with foreign governments. The Lend-Lease Administration was thus more vulnerable politically, more open to political pressure, than any of the older departments or new ones such as the Office of Production Management. Such pressures occurred in waves throughout the war. Emotionally they were rooted obscurely in traditional attitudes and ideas. Their secondary causes might take many shapes and a variety of combinations; such as some incident that aroused the basic colonial anti-British sentiment dating back to the Revolution, or garbled reports of British export of lend-lease goods or their equivalents, or unfair British competition with American exports and discrimination in favour of Empire imports, or misuse of lend-lease goods in the United Kingdom, and many others. The Administration did not create these pressures, but it had to anticipate them, to try to ward them off if possible, or to provide safety valves. Sometimes it met them head-on; at other times it deflected them to the British Government. The latter sometimes foresaw the danger, as in the case of the re-export problem; but more often than not it was caught by surprise.

One trouble was that the Lend-Lease Act (section 4) required an undertaking that the government in receipt of lend-lease would not permit the transfer of title or possession of defence articles to private persons.[2] Any rigid interpretation of this clause would have crippled internal distribution in the United Kingdom, particularly of food and raw materials. But in this case the Act was interpreted flexibly; the Administration was satisfied with the assurances given by the British Government, which were confirmed in the White Paper of 10th September 1941.

More difficult was the problem of lend-lease goods or materials in the export trade. Once lend-lease came into effect there was a tendency to assume that Britain's financial troubles were at an end. There was

---

[1] Stettinius, op. cit., Part III.

[2] For the text of the Lend-Lease Act, see Appendix III.

little understanding of the financial problems outlined in the previous chapter. Even before lend-lease supplies began to arrive in substantial quantities there was a flood of curious stories in the United States about the attitude of Britain to American supplies and about diversions into the export trade. Thus the slogan used in Latin America, 'Britain delivers the goods', provoked the question whether the British tools and machinery that were being exported were made out of lend-lease steel. In fact, as the British trade statistics revealed later, British exports to Latin America, in these and other goods, were being cut drastically in the second half of 1941. The British Government deemed it wise, however, to give the necessary assurances in a unilateral statement of British policy handed to the American Ambassador on 10th September 1941.[1] This was known as 'the White Paper'. It disposed of the main controversy, but it could not prevent a constant succession of minor difficulties. The Office of Lend-Lease Administration set up a section to police the observance of 'the White Paper', to draw attention to breaches and to go through the ritual of issuing waivers.

For a time the entry of the United States into the war and the setting up of fully combined British and American machinery seemed to promise an end to 'White Paper' difficulties. The hope that in the new partnership they would disappear was supported by a letter from the Lend-Lease Administrator, Mr. Stettinius, on the last day of 1941. He noted that as a general rule the United States authorities would wish to be consulted in advance about British exports coming under the restrictions of the 'White Paper'. But he added that 'to adopt such a procedure at once would greatly interfere with our joint war effort'. For the time being, therefore, he proposed that the United Kingdom should be free to export such goods without advance clearance. The letter went on to suggest that exports should be dealt with in future on a programme basis, rather than as currently on a case-by-case basis, and that the export programmes should be tied in with allocations by the United States to the United Kingdom of materials in short supply in the United States. Any decisions on exports, the letter concluded, should be taken in the light of 'the entire strategy of the joint economic and military war effort'. Such a broad approach was welcomed by the United Kingdom, but it proved difficult to apply in practice. An attempt was made from the summer of 1942 to draw up combined export programmes. But the system could be applied only to a few commodities; and exports and the 'White Paper' continued to provide a fairly steady flow of minor troubles to the end of the war.[2]

---

[1] Cmd. 6311. See Hancock and Gowing, op. cit., pp. 242–46.

[2] On the question of exports and the supply of essential civilian goods see *Studies of Overseas Supply*, Chapter V.

Such difficulties were inherent, indeed, in the theory of lend-lease. Lord Halifax, in a dispatch written in March 1941 a week after the Lend-Lease Act came into force, referred to a question asked by a columnist: 'whether America has become the banker or the partner of the British Commonwealth?' The Ambassador reported that 'the partnership theory is gaining ground'—despite the widespread desire that the United States should not be drawn into hostilities. 'As I see it', the Prime Minister observed in a message to Lord Halifax on 10th April 1941, 'we are confronted with the singular situation of two great Powers committing themselves to and actively entering upon an association before any attempt has been made by either to define the objectives or the articles of association. . . . So far all that has been agreed in effect is that the British Empire and her Allies shall be used as the agent to do the actual fighting, while America furnishes the means in the form of material and money. . . .'

In lend-lease theory, however, even the fact that Britain was doing the actual fighting did not end her obligation in the matter of 'benefit to the United States'. In the words of the Act (Article 3 (5) (b)), 'the benefit to the United States may be payment or repayment in kind or property, or any other direct or indirect benefit which the President deems satisfactory'. On 7th April 1941 the President gave general assent to the view put to him by the Ambassador that 'the true and only consideration he should ask for all the goods that are to be lease-lent to us is simply that we should go on fighting'. But this answer was too simple. The question of benefit (or 'consideration' as it was to be called) became the subject of long drawn-out discussions in the summer of 1941 in which Mr. J. M. Keynes took part. Although drafts of an agreement were submitted by him as early as July, it was not until 23rd February 1942, eight months later, that the Master Lend-Lease Agreement was signed.[1]

Before the Master Agreement was signed, but after the setting up of the Combined Boards, the British Government thought that a 'natural sequel' to them might be a new financial arrangement with the United States. This would replace the idea of agency contained in lend-lease by the concept of equal partnership expressed in the Combined Boards. 'The partnership into which our two countries have entered', the Treasury observed in a message to its representative in Washington, 'calls for some comprehensive financial arrangement between the United States and the United Kingdom parallel to agreements on munitions, shipping and raw materials.' Under such an arrangement it was hoped that the United States would take over responsibility for the British contracts in the United States. On the British Commonwealth side, no payment would be sought for any

---

[1] See Appendices III and V for texts of the Lend-Lease Act and the Master Agreement. Also Hancock and Gowing, op. cit., pp. 246–47.

munitions produced in the Empire (apart from Canada) whether they were eventually to be used by Britain, the United States, Russia or China. The idea sprang, in part, from increasing alarm at the rapid growth of British liabilities overseas, other than in the United States, which were then mounting at the rate of some £500 million a year.[1] But the past history and the theory of lend-lease and the difficulty in changing an Act of Congress proved too strong for any such arrangement. The mutual aid part of the idea was expressed, however, in the Master Lend-Lease Agreement and came fully into effect with the signing of the Mutual Aid Agreement of 3rd September 1942.

From 1942 to the end of the war lend-lease kept alive an obsolete theory of inequality which was incompatible with the principles of full partnership and equality of sacrifice that inspired the common war. President Roosevelt hinted at the theory of equality of sacrifice in a number of his quarterly reports on lend-lease and reciprocal aid. But the hints of a President could not change an Act of Congress —at least not without a large and successful campaign of public education. Some Americans, official and unofficial, suggested such a campaign in the favourable atmosphere before D-Day. But for this much fuller statistics of the British war effort were needed to show convincingly the degree of its war mobilisation in comparison with that of the United States. Pleas from the British side in Washington for the release of such detailed statistics were rejected on security grounds. Thus the obsolete notion of lend-lease, as merely a form of financial aid to the United Kingdom, survived after the war to the detriment of the post-war financial settlement.

(ii)

The Fraternal Association: Origins and Character of 'Combination'

The 'fraternal association', as the Prime Minister called it, of the British Commonwealth with the United States had begun to grow long before the Lend-Lease Act. That Act greatly helped its growth, but the growth itself continued outside the lend-lease machinery. In order to grow an idea needs a word-symbol which is both positive and of good omen. 'Cash and carry' had served its turn. 'Lend-lease' was limited and suggested inequality. 'Association' was too vague. 'Union' went too far. 'Alliance' was a word of ill omen in the American vocabulary. The word—adequate though without warmth—was

---

[1] See above, Chapter VII, Part II.

found in 'combined' or 'combination'. It began to be used on the British side early in the war. Thus Purvis began to use both adjective and noun freely in the first months of 1940. Use by American officials began a little later. Already in an American official document of 24th July 1940 there occurred the phrase 'combined British and American airplane programme'.[1] A detailed history of the use of the word in 1940 and 1941 would provide interesting clues to the growth of closer relationships between the English-speaking peoples. Here it is sufficient to note that there was combination in many fields before the Combined Boards, and that the word 'combined' was freely used, although it was not yet attached to any particular piece of joint machinery.

The essence of the Combined Boards was that the opposite numbers on the two sides—the men responsible for dealing with particular fields, such as aircraft or raw materials—were brought together, given some degree of authority to act or to advise, and that they learned to work together as a team. Already in 1940, and still more in 1941, something like this was happening at many points. At the higher level Purvis and Morgenthau were a combined team, and a little later Purvis and Hopkins. After December 1940 close and continuous liaison was maintained between the two Treasuries. There was also joint consideration in the matter of machine tools. The tank experts on both sides were brought together in the summer of 1940, and continued to work in a combined way on design, development and supply. There was close combination between the scientists of the United Kingdom, the United States, and Canada. A far-reaching pooling of inventions and technical knowledge followed the visit of the Tizard Mission in August 1940. Hopkins took back with him from London in February 1941 important technical secrets.[2] From the spring of 1941 combination in science, research and development was close and unbroken to the end of the war. From the summer of 1941 the statisticians worked together. In the matter of raw materials, combination began on an informal basis in the late summer of 1940. It followed the line where supply and economic warfare met. By the time of Pearl Harbour it had broadened out, though still on an informal basis, to cover most of the phases dealt with, from January 1942 and onward, by the Combined Raw Materials Board.[3] Com-

---

[1] *Minutes of the Advisory Commission to the Council of National Defence.* (Historical Reports on War Administration; War Production Board, Documentary Publication No. 1, Washington: 1946), p. 36. On the word 'combined' see below, p. 343.

[2] Sherwood, op. cit., p. 261.

[3] See *Studies of Overseas Supply*, Chapter VII. From April 1941 Canada and the United States had their own combined arrangement for raw materials in the shape of the Materials Coordinating Committee, United States and Canada, *Minutes of the Council of the Office of Production Management* (War Production Board, Washington: 1946), Minutes of meeting of 29th April 1941, p. 16; and *Industrial Mobilization for War*, op. cit., p. 125; also R. Warren James, *Wartime Economic Cooperation* (Canadian Institute of International Affairs: 1949).

bination in supply matters before Pearl Harbour was not confined, of course, to the United States. Already before Pearl Harbour it had extended out along the supply routes into far-flung joint enterprises in connection with the transport and maintenance of supply in Africa, the Middle East, Persia and Russia.

Aircraft, however, afforded the most impressive and clear-cut example of combination before the Combined Boards. Here were to be seen, as early as September 1940, all the elements of a typical Combined Board. In that month the Joint Aircraft Committee was set up on the basis of a letter from Secretary Stimson of 13th September 1940. The Committee consisted of two members each from the United States War and Navy Departments, two later from the Office of Production Management, and two from the British Air Commission, one of which was supplied later by the Royal Air Force Delegation. The Committee was appointed 'to consider and decide matters pertaining to aircraft standardisation and aircraft delivery schedules'. By the latter phrase was meant 'allocations of deliveries'. In words similar to those used later in the terms of reference of the Combined Raw Materials Board, the directive issued by Secretary Stimson stated that 'each group of members of this committee is authorised to act for and obligate the agency it represents'. The British members were given the right to participate in the consideration of applications for aircraft received from 'countries other than the British Empire'.[1] The powers of the Joint Aircraft Committee were as extensive as those of any of the Combined Boards. Its powers continued unchanged in form to the end of the war, although in practice some of its functions were taken over by other bodies. In January 1942 the War Production Board became responsible for all production for the United States forces. The Joint Aircraft Committee continued, however, to exercise part of its functions in relation to the aircraft industry. Its power to allocate the output of production facilities for *complete* aircraft and spares to particular governments lapsed, however, when these functions were taken over, early in 1942, by the Combined Munitions Assignments Board. From March 1943 the functions of the War Production Board, in regard to aircraft production, were exercised through its newly-formed Aircraft Production Board. Although the powers of the Joint Aircraft Committee remained unchanged, a directive was issued that these powers must be exercised with the concurrence of the Aircraft Production Board.

---

[1] Letters from Secretary Stimson, 13th September 1940 and 13th January 1941. A new directive issued on 22nd April 1941 by Secretary Stimson redefined the powers of the Committee as follows: 'This Committee is vested with the power to schedule the delivery of, and allocate the capacity for, aircraft and aircraft components in the official programme of all customers, Army, Navy, British, other Foreign and Commercial, and in addition thereto, will take under consideration and approval matters pertaining to the standardisation of aircraft and aircraft components between the United States Government and foreign customers.'

The setting up of the Joint Aircraft Committee, and the wide powers of control over production assigned to it, were necessary to prevent competition between the various authorities in the United States concerned with production of aircraft and components. These authorities had established their own production schedules. The result was unrelated demands on labour, materials, accessories and armaments. Concentration of authority was essential to make full use of the productive capacity of the aircraft industry. The Joint Aircraft Committee established a sub-committee on the allocation of deliveries. From this, an additional sub-committee to deal with engines and propellers branched off in September 1941. Finally, the sub-committee on the allocation of deliveries was functioning through four joint sub-committees dealing respectively with the allocation of aero engines, propellers, armaments and radio. A somewhat singular branching out took place in the Joint Aircraft Committee's sub-committee on standardisation. Since for radio and radar standardisation presented special difficulties, a new sub-committee known as the Joint Radio Board was set up in November 1941. This Board dealt not only with technical airborne radio problems and the standardisation of radio material between the United States Army and United States Navy and the British forces, but also with research and development.

The existence of the Joint Aircraft Committee made supply of aircraft to the United Kingdom, up to lend-lease, more stable than were supplies of munitions. On 8th April 1941 Secretary Stimson notified the British Supply Council of the setting up in the War Department of five Joint Defence Aid Committees. The British Supply Council appointed the British representatives (including Service officers) who sat as regular members. The function of the Committees was defined as the 'determination under the Defence Aid [Lend-Lease] programs of material requirements as to type, quantity and destination'.[1] They could review stocks, follow deliveries from American factories, ensure that capacity was kept occupied continuously with orders, and that new facilities were created where needed. Quite apart from these bodies, frequent informal joint meetings took place between British and American officials in connection with the administration of lend-lease.[2]

From the point of view of organisation, arrangements were shifting and informal. What mattered were the close and regular personal

---

[1] The set of directives dated 8th April by which this action was taken were communicated formally to the British Supply Council by Secretary Stimson. The Joint Aircraft Committee was regarded as part of the set-up. Later the five committees (Ordnance, Chemical, Signal, Engineer, Quartermaster) were amalgamated into a single body.

[2] For both food and petroleum, representatives sat regularly in American committees. See United States Department of the Interior, *History of the Petroleum Administration of War*, 1941-1945 (Washington: 1946), p. 22.

relations between individuals on both sides who were responsible for dealing with a particular part of the war effort. Combination of this kind, at many points down the line, was crowned by the combination at the top between the President and the Prime Minister. The great war conferences, from the Atlantic Conference in August 1941, in which the Prime Minister and the President conferred with their staffs on the general course of the war, and discussed their common problems and future action, set the course for all the combined machinery. The Prime Minister kept a watchful eye on any tendency for new machinery, such as the British Joint Staff Mission in Washington, to narrow or obstruct his direct channel with the President. Nothing must be permitted, he emphasised in a telegram to the Ambassador on 28th April, to discourage the President from posing questions direct to him.[1]

The importance of another informal and fluid element in combination, that of visiting missions from both sides of the Atlantic, will be referred to later in connection with the working of the machinery of the Combined Boards. Military and supply missions from both sides were important in the second half of 1940. In 1941 they became a factor of still greater importance with the first visit of Mr. Harry Hopkins to London in January. In Mr. Cordell Hull's words—this was the beginning of 'Hopkins's career on a world scale'; he was sent 'to establish a direct liaison between Mr. Roosevelt and Prime Minister Churchill and to make a firsthand survey of Britain's war needs . . .'[2] 'He was the most faithful and perfect channel of communication between the President and me', Mr. Churchill wrote later.[3] The mission had important consequences for supply. Some days after his return, Hopkins wrote to the Prime Minister: 'I have worked out a scheme with Purvis last night which will keep your orders moving. . . . I am in daily touch with your Purchasing Commission.'[4]

A series of notes had been given to Hopkins on 17th January by the different supply ministries, setting out their immediate needs and desires.[5] The Air Ministry put as the first consideration the supply of trained personnel technicians as well as pilots.[6] The Neutrality Act

---

[1] Winston S. Churchill, *The Second World War*, Vol. III, *The Grand Alliance* (London: Cassell & Co., Ltd., 1950), p. 677. (Also published in the United States, Boston: Houghton Mifflin Company, 1950.)

[2] *The Memoirs of Cordell Hull*, Vol. II (New York: The Macmillan Company, 1948), pp. 922–26.   (Also published in London: Hodder & Stoughton Ltd., 1948); Sherwood, op. cit., Chapter XI.

[3] Churchill, *The Grand Alliance*, op. cit., p. 21, and Sherwood, op. cit., p. 269.

[4] Sherwood, op. cit., p. 265.

[5] Air Ministry, Admiralty, Ministry of Aircraft Production, Ministry of Supply, Ministry of Shipping.

[6] It listed its immediate needs as: 800 to 1,000 pilots; 300 observers, navigators, etc.; 5,000 fitters; 1,500 electricians; 500 instrument makers; 1,000 fitter armourers; 1,000 ground wireless operators; 200 metal-workers; 150 machine-tool setters and operators.

for a time prevented action on this matter. An attempt was also being made by the United Kingdom to recruit urgently 8,000 radar mechanics from Canada and the United States. The release of pilots for service in the R.A.F. was already under consideration in Washington. Civilian pilots from the United States were needed, Hopkins was told, to replace the many R.A.F. pilots who had to be diverted from combat service to the ferrying of aircraft. Subsequent action by Hopkins on some of these matters was greatly helped by his visit to London.

The stationing in London, from the spring of 1941 onwards, of the Lend-Lease Mission led by W. Averell Harriman, added a further direct link between the Prime Minister, Hopkins and the President, as well as a direct channel between the supply authorities of the two countries.[1] Personal relations at the highest level were strengthened further by the arrival of Lord Halifax as Ambassador in January 1941. He received an unprecedented personal welcome from the President on board the *King George V*. He retained his seat in the War Cabinet and communicated directly and freely with the Prime Minister.

The war was thus a massive illustration of the truth taught by the history of diplomacy, that dispatches and formal communications are not enough. Perhaps in Anglo-American relations, more than between most peoples, the less said in writing the better—unless it be writing that is interpreted through a personal link.

Thus, it was not easy, though the attempt was made, to set down in writing the lessons of British war administration and economy. A lengthy report on this subject was sent to Mr. Stettinius, at his request, in August 1940. In November 1940, through the British Purchasing Commission, and in July 1941, through the Harriman Mission, extensive further data were sought by the Administration. A flood of requests for information poured into the Embassy after Pearl Harbour. This led to the suggestion by the Ambassador on 13th December 1941 that documents which for some months had been coming to the Embassy from London to provide background for the answering of questions put by American officials might be circulated on the American side. This was refused on the ground that such documents could not be understood without personal interpretation. They were drafted, London pointed out, to facilitate discussions in the United Kingdom of domestic administrative problems. Their writers could use short cuts in drafting because the limited circle of readers knew how to interpret their elisions and omissions. The terminology, as well as the statistics and facts found in such documents, could not be used out of context without much explana-

---

[1] Sherwood, op. cit., p. 269.

tion and clarification. A similar problem, it noted, had already been faced some months earlier in drawing up the Consolidated Statement of British and American production. The American experts had worked for many hours in the Central Statistical Office in London before they could reach an understanding as to the meaning and complications of the different statistical series in use. Moreover, the situation changed so rapidly that facts and figures in memoranda and documents could never be up to date.

Meanwhile, events were solving the problem in quite a different way. No formal reply to the Ambassador's telegram of 13th December, in fact, was sent. The real reply was to be the setting up of the Combined Boards as a result of the discussions between the President and the Prime Minister from the 22nd December to 14th January 1942. The method of the Boards was to direct enquiries, data and discussion, through a series of personal channels, at different levels, from the two men at the top, who constituted the Board, down the line through opposite numbers on their staffs. This intermeshing of the two Administrations made possible continuous personal interpretation, the smoothing out of misunderstandings, and the assembling and keeping up to date of the common body of fact on which the efficiency of combination depended.

During the war, and particularly from 1941 onwards, the British and American Governments were developing methods of working together which bore some resemblance to the intimate informality of the British Commonwealth of Nations. They worked on the Commonwealth principle of continuous consultation. They kept each other informed, through diplomatic and other channels, of important developments of common concern. They built up at many points the habit of regular and frequent meetings. Ministers and officials travelled back and forth on frequent missions. There was now a transatlantic telephone—as there had not been in the First World War—and it was freely used. In Washington itself thousands of British officials, who formed a sort of lesser Whitehall overseas, shared common telephone switchboards with American officials in a vast network of informal relations without parallel in past history.

(iii)

Combination: Production and Strategy

The elementary and formless combined machinery of 1941 could not work without some sort of combination in the planning of production, supply and strategy. Reference has already been made to the first attempts of Purvis and Monnet, from November 1940 to

January 1941, to launch the 'Purvis Balance Sheet'. Its purpose was to fill a gap noted by Sir Walter Layton, in December 1940, in his report on his mission to the United States: 'We have not asked the United States, nor has Congress authorised the Administration to produce munitions on the scale needed to overwhelm Germany and win the war.' Purvis's figure of 15 billion dollars' worth of war supplies, which he gave the President and Morgenthau on 30th December, was a shot in the dark.[1] The whole basis of such a programme was highly conjectural. No adequate measure of the strength of the enemy had yet been made by the United Kingdom, much less by the United States. Nor had there been any real pooling of production plans or comparison of rates of production or sharing of adequate production statistics by the two countries. Much of the attention of Purvis in 1941 (up to his death on 14th August) and that of Monnet, was given to the building up of what emerged in the late summer as the Anglo-American Consolidated Statement of Production, or 'Stimson Balance Sheet' (production statistics and estimates) and the Victory Programme (requirements for victory). The work continued with the active assistance of Secretary Stimson all through what he called the 'Valley of Doubt' from April up to Pearl Harbour. During this time, as Monnet put it in a letter to London in July 1941, the United States, still neutral, and with no present intention of entering the war, were pursuing immediate and limited supply objectives. These were to manufacture only enough arms to equip the army of two million men, authorised by Congress, and to give the limited defence aid to the Allies which Congress made possible by the lend-lease appropriations. The little the United States had done so far to rearm was determined by these objectives, and not by the strength of the Axis powers.[2] The civilian peace-time economy was booming and war production had merely taken up some of the slack. As Stimson noted later, 'it continued [up to Pearl Harbour] to be the general practice merely to add military production to the ordinary civilian business of the country'. This was, in part, the consequence of the original decision in June 1940 to rearm by using idle plants, machinery and men.[3]

In these circumstances, and in the absence as yet of any agreement on a combined strategy, Purvis and Monnet could make little progress with the 'Balance Sheet'. It was, however, one of the first

---

[1] American calculations based on Purvis's list of requirements put the figure of $16–20 billion for the two years 1941 and 1942. *Industrial Mobilization for War*, op. cit., p. 123

[2] See *Minutes of the Council of the Office of Production Management* (War Production Board, Washington: 1946), Minutes of meeting, 29th May 1941, p. 26.

[3] Stimson and Bundy, op. cit., p. 381. 'Only the partial attention of such great industries as those making automobiles and rubber and electric machines was given to military production.' See also *Industrial Mobilization for War*, op. cit., pp. 185, 196–97; for the automobile industry—a gradual cut, to reach 43·4 per cent. on the models for 1942, was agreed on 20th August.

W

subjects singled out by Halifax for a report to the Prime Minister. He had discussed the matter, he reported, on 6th February 1941 with Purvis and Monnet. They had gone over the steps to be taken to secure the production of the 'Balance Sheet' requirements immediately after the Lend-Lease Bill passed. The Ambassador suggested that the Prime Minister should mention the matter to Hopkins, but this was not possible before the latter left London. It was vital, Purvis, Monnet and the Ambassador felt, to get an instruction from the President that 'the stuff must be produced by the time required in the quantities shown in the list'. But meanwhile they had to be content with a lower goal. The estimates submitted a week later (February 13th) covered only a part of the 'Balance Sheet', namely, requirements up to June 1942, to the amount of nearly $9 billion. The Lend-Lease Appropriations, as voted in March, were well under even this figure.[1] The total appropriations made available amounted to $8,300 million ($7,000 million plus $1,300 million diverted from the Services); but the total included a considerable figure for food and other indirect war supplies. For munitions there was actually a cut of some twenty-four per cent. of the requirements submitted by Purvis on 13th February.

There was thus little sign, so far, of a 'Victory Programme' in the true sense. Little use was being made of the full United States capacity for war production. Until the second quarter of 1942 United Kingdom production would still outstrip that of the United States. This was, in fact, one of the reasons for the mixed reception given in London to the filing even of the figure of $9 billion, which has been mentioned above. The huge programme was 'accepted calmly', Purvis was told in a letter from the Central Office for North American Supplies, on 24th February. There was 'relief' at its 'good reception' in Washington. But apart from the question whether such large quantities could be shipped there were doubts on the side of production. An influential body of opinion in London felt that 'the army estimates in the "Balance Sheet" have little to do with reality in that the enormous totals given cannot be produced in the time, and that even if they could we would not know what to do with them. . . . They are obviously anxious lest the large size of the programme leads to restriction in shipments of machine tools, steel and non-ferrous metals to this country. . . .' If such diversions occurred and the American programme could still not be produced in the time allotted, there might be a net loss in war production. It was soon clear that the United States War Department's own programme was still much too nebulous to afford (with lend-lease requirements) a sound basis for any combined production programme. In May the

[1] *Industrial Mobilization for War*, op. cit., p. 123.

Office of Production Management had still 'not yet obtained from the Services an adequate outline of military requirements, projected over a fairly long period'. It had to wait another six months for them. The situation in May was indeed so obscure that in the judgement of the Office of Production Management no industry in the United States could yet be declared to be non-essential—for might not the Army discover a large need for such things as refrigerators?[1]

How little advance had been made towards a 'Victory Programme' was shown by production charts of bomber deliveries up to June 1943, circulated by the Office of Production Management in May 1941. The charts indicated that lend-lease orders had not, in fact, produced any additional bomber capacity. They were merely in the nature of follow-up orders after existing contracts had been completed. The bomber output in the United States in the first half of 1941 nearly all came from British, French and American contracts let at the beginning of the war; this flow would be increased by the output from the Anglo-French programme of the spring of 1940. The United States' own bomber programme of December 1940 would not yield medium bombers before the summer of 1942, and heavy bombers before the beginning of 1943, and then only in very small numbers.

The situation was particularly serious as regards heavy bombers. 'The Bombers alone provide the means of victory', the Prime Minister said in September 1940.[2] Energetic action had been taken by London, through Purvis, in January to bring forcibly to the attention of the American production authorities the importance of heavy bombers in the strategic programme of the United Kingdom. The need was pressed on Major-General H. H. Arnold during his visit to England in April, and his representations caused the President on 4th May to order production at the rate of 500 a month.[3] This was not enough, and the Prime Minister made an immediate and direct appeal to the President for a still greater increase in American production. The Prime Minister pointed out that the total striking force of Bomber Command was only half that of Germany. British production would give parity in the spring of 1942. To give air mastery, however, a front-line force of not less than 4,000 heavy bombers would be needed by the spring of 1943. To achieve this, 7,000 heavy bombers would be needed during 1941 and 12,000 in 1942. British production, however, would yield only 4,500 in 1941, and from 500 to 600 a month in 1942. The United Kingdom would need from the

[1] *Industrial Mobilization for War*, op. cit., p. 104.

[2] Churchill, *Their Finest Hour*, op. cit., p. 405.

[3] *Minutes of the Council of the Office of Production Management* (War Production Board, Washington: 1946), Minutes of meeting, 6th May 1941, p. 17; and *Industrial Mobilization for War*, op. cit., p. 126.

United States 500 heavy bombers a month in 1942 and still larger numbers in 1943.

A rate of production of even 500 a month in the United States, however, still belonged to a rather remote future. It would not be achieved much before the end of 1942 and as matters then stood Britain could not hope for much more than a third of the output. From a strategical point of view production on the two sides of the Atlantic was now out of balance—too many fighters and light bombers and not enough heavy bombers.

Figures which Purvis took with him to London on 1st August (based on an Office of Production Management return of 18th July) showed that the United Kingdom would receive only 594 heavy bombers by December 1942 (including 139 out of its own contracts). It would get nothing from any lend-lease contracts before August 1942.

STRATEGY AND SUPPLY— THE STAFF TALKS AND THE JOINT STAFF MISSION

The degree of emphasis that should be laid on the heavy bomber, the scale on which it should be produced in the United States and the percentage of American production that should be allocated to Great Britain, were all questions that led back to strategical considerations. The civilians in charge of negotiations on supply programmes in the United States soon realised that they could make little headway on such matters without further developments on the military side. These were: (1) joint staff talks between the two Governments; (2) continuous contact between the Staffs; and (3) the presence in Washington of Service representatives at the Staff level who could advise on the user side in the light of actual war experience.

The first Staff talks on joint strategy, in the event of the United States entering the war, began in Washington at the end of January 1941 and continued to the end of March.[1] In Mr. Sherwood's judgement they 'made for far greater efficiency in all planning of Army and Navy organization and training, of production and, most importantly, of administration of lend-lease'. This perhaps goes too far; but it is clear that the talks helped supply-planning in several ways —most of all by the basic agreement of the two sides that if the United States (and Japan) entered the war the strategic objective should be 'to concentrate on the defeat of Germany and Italy and subsequently to deal with Japan'. There was, however, a significant difference of opinion as regards the importance of South-East Asia and of Singapore as the 'card of re-entry' to the Far East. For the United Kingdom the primary consideration was the security of the

---

[1] Hancock and Gowing, op. cit., p. 380; Sherwood, op. cit., pp. 272–73. The purpose of the mission of American senior officers, led by Admiral Ghormley in August 1940, had been to gather information rather than to discuss joint plans.

British Commonwealth. The defence of Australia and New Zealand against invasion was judged to be more important even than the holding of the Middle East—if a choice had to be made. The primary American emphasis was on the interests of the United States in the western hemisphere. On the air side, the planning of supply was helped by the light thrown on the obscure question of German air strength as compared with that of the United Kingdom. The evidence produced by the British Staff representatives showed that German front-line strength as compared with that of the United Kingdom was about four to three. German productive capacity was estimated at 3,000 planes a month, but actual production at only 1,400.[1]

From the point of view of supply, the Staff talks had two important consequences. One affected the allocation of British requirements—particularly for aircraft—and the other led to the setting up of permanent Staff missions in London and Washington. On military materials there was merely an agreement in general terms to adopt a procedure which would ensure 'the allocation of military material, both prior to and after the entry of the United States into the war, in a manner best suited to meet the demands of the military situation'. On aircraft the agreement was much more precise. It was decided that 'the policy pertaining to supply and distribution of aircraft is an essential factor . . . of such immediate and vital importance as to deserve special treatment'. A sub-committee appointed to report to the two Chiefs of Staff submitted the following recommendations on 29th March 1941: Great Britain was to receive: (*a*) the output from production in the British Commonwealth; (*b*) the output of the approved British airplane programmes from United States industry; (*c*) the allocation of a continuing output from United States capacity, existing or approved, in such numbers as the military situation might require and circumstances permit; (*d*) the entire output from new United States industry. If the United States should enter the war, it was agreed that Great Britain could assume for planning purposes that new production in the United States would then be divided on a fifty-fifty basis. This was known as the Slessor Agreement. There was no procedure for the formal ratification of such an agreement by the United States. It served at first as the working basis for allocation, but by August it had broken down.[2]

On the side of organisation, the Joint Staffs proposed in a 'joint

---

[1] See pp. 205 and 338. The reason for the discrepancy was not then known. See Churchill, *The Grand Alliance*, op. cit., p. 35 ff and p. 694 ff: 'Note by Prime Minister and Minister of Defence, December 1940, on estimated British and German air strengths.'

[2] See below, Section (vi). The Material Division of the United States Air Corps produced a schedule of releases from American Army contracts which the United Kingdom might expect to receive on the basis of the Agreement; the total up to June 1942 was to be 5,817 aircraft.

letter of transmittal' that the British and the American Governments, in order to avoid duplication and wasted effort, should 'establish at the capital of the other a central agency to supervise and co-ordinate the activities of all its own non-military councils, missions or com-missions, which may function within the territory of the other power. Where these non-military bodies require military advice they should obtain it through the military missions rather than through other channels.' At the same time a recommendation was made that a British Joint Staff Mission should be set up in Washington, as soon as possible, with a corresponding American Mission in London. By this means it was hoped to keep in touch at the Staff level, so that if a change-over had to be made from peace to war it could be brought about 'rapidly and smoothly when the time comes'.

The proposal for a 'central agency' fell to the ground. The matter was discussed in the British Supply Council in Washington in May and June. Both Purvis and the Ambassador thought that a new central organisation in Washington, to supervise and co-ordinate all the British organisations, was not necessary. Freedom of action would be impeded, they felt, if the different British agencies, including the Embassy and the Supply Council, had to secure the approval or endorsement of some central body before taking any major step, such as an approach to the American authorities on an important issue. The purposes of co-ordination were achieved if the different missions and agencies kept each other fully informed. It was already the established practice to circulate papers and important telegrams between the Embassy, the Supply Council, the Supply Missions and the newly created Joint Staff Mission. It had become the practice of the Ambassador to call meetings from time to time between the heads of the different missions. These might perhaps be held more often and at regular intervals, but the Ambassador remarked that 'I am still inclined to let them develop naturally—and I am still afraid of them tempting those who attend to try to do one another's work'.

The nucleus of the British Joint Staff Mission was formed on 3rd April by Staff officers who remained on after the Staff talks. The nucleus was expanded in May and June into the full body. The British Joint Staff Mission had a corporate responsibility to the British Chiefs of Staff. It consisted of three sections each representing one of the three Services; the British Army Staff (which amalgamated several British Service groups already in Washington), the British Admiralty Delegation, and the Royal Air Force Delegation.

Its link at the London end, in the Department of the Chief of the Imperial General Staff, was called the North American Bureau. The corresponding United States Military Mission, representing the United States Chiefs of Staff, was set up in London in May.

Purvis had learned in connection with his 'Balance Sheet', and the lend-lease programme, how important it was for the British Supply Council to have proper advice on war experience and the strategical background. He felt the need for 'representatives of the Chiefs of Staff who could translate cold lists of materials into terms of military operations'. Part of the difficulty that had arisen in London about the 'Balance Sheet' figures was due to the fact that the figures had to be submitted at a time when strategical plans were being reconsidered in London in the light of war experience. Some of the preliminary results of this reconsideration—still far from complete—were given to Purvis in a personal letter of 20th March from London. He was told that the changes involved in the British programme in the light of experience were substantial. Ammunition requirements of all kinds would be severely cut. There was a trend—subject to the limitations of shipping and manpower—towards more armoured divisions and fewer infantry divisions.[1] But there would be a limit to British demands for tanks and guns until the supply of ships (and men) was increased. Ships, therefore, ranked with or even ahead of aircraft and the fact that they took a long while to build postponed the stage when the United Kingdom could effectively use more guns and tanks. Since production took time American capacity for guns and tanks should be developed on a large scale.

The virtual doubling in the early summer, on the insistence of the Prime Minister, of the projected front-line strength of heavy and medium bombers was a further result of the continuing review of supply in the light of war experience.

Thus, whilst supply problems continued to be the responsibility of the British Supply Council and of the Supply Missions represented on it, the Joint Staff Mission played an essential part in advising the Supply Council on the strategical background of supply and in preparing the ground with the United States Army and Navy Chiefs of Staff.[2] Its representatives attended meetings of the Supply Council. They presented there the point of view of the 'users' of war supplies. A member of the R.A.F. Delegation attended the Joint Aircraft Committee. It became a rule that before any requisition for military equipment was submitted to the Lend-Lease Administration the approval of the Service representatives concerned in its use had to be obtained. To function effectively, however, the Joint Staff Mission had to receive regular information on war plans and experience. Harry Hopkins emphasised, in April, the need felt by the Lend-Lease

---

[1] Churchill, *The Grand Alliance*, op. cit., p. 656. There was, however, a scaling down of the proportion of armoured divisions in the Army and the fixing of a definite limit to its numerical strength.

[2] Such preparation, for example, played a useful part, in the summer of 1941, in smoothing the way for the new arrangements for the routing of lend-lease supplies direct to the Middle East theatre of the war.

Administration of advice and information on the political and strategical implications of the British lend-lease programmes. But channels were of little value unless the right kind of information flowed regularly through them. A daily operations telegram was being received at this time by British Service representatives in Washington. It was arranged by the end of May that this should be supplemented by periodical summaries of the strategical situation. The information thus furnished was transmitted by the British Staff Mission to the United States Chiefs of Staff. At the same time information was given at the London end to the United States Service representatives at the American Embassy. Transmission of information was facilitated by the regular flights of bombers going to England, and of the B.24s (Liberators) which brought back the ferry pilots.

In order not to embarrass the Administration, the British Joint Staff Mission remained 'under cover' in Washington until after Pearl Harbour. The existence of its constituent bodies, however, was known. They were described officially as technical advisers to the British Supply Council. The wise rule expressed in an Embassy minute at the beginning of November that 'the nearer the United States get to war the less we ought to act as though we took it for granted that they are coming in . . .' was followed to the end. Uniforms were not put on until four days after the attack on Pearl Harbour. An American press release announced on 20th December, that 'for some time, as has been hitherto intimated by the President, the United States Military Mission in London and the British Joint Staff Mission in Washington, have been in close contact with their opposite numbers in both places'.

(iv)

All Action Short of War

Both the scale and rapidity of lend-lease aid and the forward planning of war production were hindered by the unwillingness of public opinion in the United States to face the issue of war. From April to December 1941 the country lay in what Mr. Stimson has called the 'Valley of Doubt'; 'national indecision', he concluded, produced not only a 'serious problem of morale in the Army' but also seriously disorganised and retarded production.[1] Uncertainty whether the United States would enter the war meant that all planning for the future, whether national or combined, had to be built

---

[1] Stimson and Bundy, op. cit., Chapter XV, p. 380.

round a core of doubt. By March it was clear that without controls, which were possible only for a country at war, the production targets undertaken for Britain and the United States themselves could not be achieved in time. An example of the effect of uncertainty mentioned by Mr. Sherwood was that of landing craft. The Army knew that it must have landing craft, but how could it approach Congress with a demand which it knew would immediately produce the charge that it was planning an American expeditionary force?

The official attitude of the United Kingdom was that expressed by the Prime Minister on 9th February: 'Give us the tools and we will finish the job.' The emphasis was upon 'us' and 'we'. But lend-lease by its unprecedented nature seemed to promise more than the giving of tools. Logically it seemed to imply a guarantee of their delivery across the Atlantic, which in turn seemed to imply that the United States would soon enter the war. Mr. Sherwood refers to a 'strange misapprehension' discovered by Harry Hopkins on his mission in January and February. This was the 'belief in London that Roosevelt would have the United States in the war by the 1st May'.[1] Belief perhaps goes too far; some expectation there was, and it was not without foundation. There is evidence enough in the reports to London in the British dispatches to show that some of the leading members of the Administration, if not the President himself, had some such anticipation. On 16th December 1940 Secretary Stimson noted in his diary after a meeting with Secretary Knox, General Marshall and Admiral Stark, that 'all four agreed that this emergency could hardly be passed over without this country being drawn into the war eventually'.[2] The President and his Cabinet agreed that supplies must be got through to the United Kingdom if it was to hold out. The then rate of sinkings by the U-boats, as Mr. Stimson recorded in his diary, made it 'seem clear to Stimson, Marshall and Knox, even in December, that the Royal Navy must have the assistance of Americal naval units in defending the Atlantic highway. No halfway measures would do'.[3] This was on the 19th December 1940. Knox, in January 1941, thought America would be in the war by April. The Battle of the Atlantic was launched in March after deadly shipping losses. At the end of the month, Stimson recorded the belief in the need of convoys, held by his own military advisers and those of the Navy Department, and his agreement with Secretary Knox that 'the crisis is coming very soon and that convoying is the only solution and that it must come practically at once'.

The strong words of President Roosevelt after signing the Lend-

[1] Sherwood, op. cit., p. 263.
[2] Ibid., pp. 263, 271, 276; Stimson and Bundy, op. cit., p. 366.
[3] Stimson and Bundy, op. cit., p. 367.

Lease Act—words expressly encouraged by Secretary Hull—seemed
to point to speedy action.[1] Lend-lease, he said, was the answer of the
people of the United States to the challenge of dictatorship. The
United States had 'gone into action' in a 'total effort'; supplies were
moving from the 'assembly lines of our factories to the battle lines of
democracy'. The British people would get what they wanted:
'. . . they need tanks and guns and ammunition and supplies of all
kinds. From America they will get tanks and guns and ammunition
and supplies of all kinds. . . .'

The very fact that at that moment the Staff talks were still going
on—they continued to 29th March—strengthened the hope of an
early American entry into the war. The Staff talks ended with the
framing of 'a combined world strategy' in Mr. Churchill's words,
part of which was 'the broad design for the joint defence of the
Atlantic Ocean'.[2] Mr. Stimson saw the United States entering the
'valley of doubt' already in April. Mr. Churchill, in *The Grand
Alliance* pictured the President 'moving step by step ever more closely
with us' towards 'powerful intervention'. The 'powerful intervention'
began with six important decisions in April. One decision was the
repair of British warships in American yards. It came at a moment of
increased need as submarine attacks were shifting to the Western
Atlantic. It represented a large-scale reinforcement of British supply,
by way of docking space, labour and materials, equivalent to many
shiploads across the Atlantic. (This help was balanced by similar
British assistance to the American Navy after Pearl Harbour.) A
second decision was the allocation of lend-lease funds (on 14th April)
for the building of over 200 additional merchant ships. This more
than doubled the Emergency Shipbuilding Programme launched by
the Maritime Commission in March. A third decision was to set up
an American air-base in Greenland, from which American aircraft
could patrol in co-operation with British aircraft from the newly-
established British bases in Iceland.[3] Another decision was the
extension of the American security zone and patrol area beyond
Iceland. The possibility of the United States themselves convoying
American ships to Iceland, where the cargoes might be transhipped
for the United Kingdom, had been hinted by the President to Lord
Halifax as early as February. Fortunately, the President then pointed
out, the lines of the combat area under the Neutrality Act had been
drawn so that they fell east of Iceland (and of the Azores). Early in
April the Administration secured legal advice that it would be

---

[1] *Memoirs of Cordell Hull*, Vol. II, op. cit., p. 925.

[2] Churchill, *The Grand Alliance*, op. cit., pp. 119–21.

[3] This followed months of discussion on Greenland and the signing on 9th April, with
the Minister for Denmark in the United States, of the agreement for the protection of
Greenland by the United States. *Memoirs of Cordell Hull*, Vol. II, op. cit., pp. 935–37.

lawful both to carry goods to Iceland in American ships, and for the United States to convoy British ships to the limit of the Western Hemisphere. On 11th April, after a talk with the Ambassador, the President told the Prime Minister that he had decided to extend the United States security zone and patrol areas to cover 'all North Atlantic waters west of about West Longitude 26°'. He asked to be notified of the movements of British convoys 'so that our patrol units can seek out any ships or planes of aggressor nations operating west of the new line of the security zones'. If found, they would be notified to the British. The existence of this 'virtual sea frontier of the United States' was announced a week later.[1] Protection of British convoys to this 'frontier' did not come until August.

In the same message on 11th April the President announced still another decision—which had been made possible by the British capture of Massawa on 8th April. This was the ruling that the Red Sea and Persian Gulf were no longer combat zones. This opened these areas to all types of American goods carried by American ships.[2] Hitherto, virtually all supplies to the Middle East had been coming from the United Kingdom.[3] Direct shipment from the United States could only come slowly because of lack of both American ships and of American munitions. The President was not prepared to wait for the building of the new ships. On 30th April he wrote a letter to the Chairman of the Maritime Commission, calling on him at the earliest possible moment to secure, for 'our objective of all-out aid to the Democracies', 'at least two million tons of merchant shipping which now exists'. Interpreted as it was later as two million gross tons, say three million tons deadweight, this was a fair percentage of the existing American tonnage. The objective was difficult to secure and British estimates showed that before Pearl Harbour the United Kingdom had in continuous employment not more than 1·25 million deadweight tons of dry-cargo shipping. Part of the amount was obtained by requisitioning Axis shipping in American harbours, and part by purchase on the open market. To provide the three-quarters of a million tons of tankers included in the President's figure it was necessary to switch the oil traffic of the Eastern States from tankers to rail-cars and pipe-lines.[4]

One further important action by the President in April was to allot lend-lease funds for the building of bases in the United Kingdom

---

[1] Churchill, *The Grand Alliance*, op. cit., p. 122; Sherwood, op. cit., p. 292.

[2] *Memoirs of Cordell Hull*, Vol. II, op. cit., p. 944.

[3] A letter of Harriman to the Prime Minister, 30th April 1941, noted that from January to April only 4,000 tons of supplies had gone direct from the United States compared with 200,000 tons from the United Kingdom.

[4] Harold L. Ickes, *Fightin' Oil* (New York: Alfred A. Knopf, 1943), p. 22 ff. The transferred tankers were used on the 'shuttle service' across the Atlantic from New York to British ports.

to guard the North-Western approaches. On 25th April Purvis reported directly to the First Lord of the Admiralty that the President had approved lend-lease requisitions for the building of two destroyer bases and two air bases in Northern Ireland and Scotland. The President had allocated on 18th April $50 million 'for the procurement of materials for and the creation' of the bases.[1] The Navy Department, Purvis reported, was already assembling all the necessary construction equipment in Rhode Island for direct shipment to Londonderry and the Clyde. The minimum tonnage involved in the shipments was 200,000 tons. American engineers supervised the construction of the bases with the assistance of some 1,200 key technicians from the United States. The British Government paid the labour costs of all the Americans employed on the work, since such payments were not permissible under the Lend-Lease Act. Except for what could be supplied locally, all the materials, machinery and equipment necessary (even food and bedding needed by the personnel) were dispatched from the United States between June and August 1941.

As Purvis foresaw, this decision served as a basis for action in much wider fields. It enabled the Embassy to reopen with the State Department a question on which it had been working without success since early in the year, namely, the dispatch to the United Kingdom of American aircraft engineers and technicians. From this point the employment of American workmen and technicians by the British Government in the United Kingdom became a normal incident. The implication, as the Administration let it be known, was that any American who wanted to aid the British cause in this kind of way was free to go to the United Kingdom. At the same time, the way was being opened up for the training of British pilots on a large scale in the United States. Thus, early in May, the Prime Minister thanked the President for the offer, made through General Arnold, of a third of the United States Army's expanding capacity for pilot training; the first two batches of students, he said, would total 1,100.[2] At the same time, an offer of flying training facilities made by Admiral Towers on behalf of the United States Navy was gratefully accepted.

In April and May 1941 the war was going badly in Greece, the Levant and North Africa. Heavy shipping losses continued. For April they were over 500,000 tons sunk, and about half that amount damaged. The importing capacity of the United Kingdom, the Prime Minister told Hopkins in revealing these figures, was now less than half of the peace-time level. Because of public opinion and division in the Cabinet, the President still hesitated about convoying;

---

[1] Letter of the President to Secretary Knox, 12th June 1941, the date on which the contracts were let.

[2] See above, pp. 193–95. Churchill, *The Grand Alliance*, op. cit., p. 680.

and he resisted stubbornly pressures from various quarters.[1] A 'secret memorandum', left by Purvis amongst his papers, and dating from the second half of May, sums up well the atmosphere which then existed in Washington, though its authorship is uncertain. 'The President', it began, 'no longer doubts that he will have to enter the war in due course. But in spite of pressing advice from several of those closest to him, he puts it off. He is not at the moment in the mood to take advice from anyone. His reasons for delay are: (1) the obvious political difficulties, (2) a preference for producing an inevitable final outcome by gradually increasing the tempo of assistance; (3) the hope that if he waits the perfect pretext will present itself, and (4) above all, inadequate appreciation of the consequences of our losing Africa, and of the help he can give us in holding it.'

For a moment, however, with the proclamation by the President on 27th May of an 'unlimited national emergency', and the speech that accompanied it, the United States seemed to climb out of the valley of doubt.[2] The Embassy sent a report noting that there was no mention of neutrality; that the President said that he would take 'all additional measures necessary to deliver the goods . . .'; that he did not say such measures would be 'short of war'. 'There seems to be much confidence', it added, 'that the President's guarantee of delivery of supplies under the Lend-Lease Bill will be honoured . . . .' But no one knew quite how; and on the morrow the President denied that convoying was meant—a remark which left Stimson 'deeply discouraged' and Hopkins mystified.[3]

Next day, however, the President told the Prime Minister that the United States War and Navy Departments were ready to ferry and service aircraft to the point of take-off for the Atlantic crossing and that he hoped later to deliver to Iceland.[4] The Prime Minister gladly accepted. He referred the President to the Epistle to the Corinthians:

---

[1] The Foreign Secretary made it plain to the American Ambassador in London on 11th May that convoying supplies right across the Atlantic to British ports and turning the Atlantic Patrol into an offensive weapon against submarines would be the best help the United States could give. Stimson (6th May) and Knox both called for convoying; this was in public speeches, seen in advance by the President. Stimson asked for naval assistance to Britain and hinted war was close. Sherwood, op. cit., pp. 292–93; Stimson and Bundy, op. cit., pp. 370–71; and *Memoirs of Cordell Hull*, Vol. II, op. cit., p. 943.

[2] *Documents on American Foreign Relations*, op. cit., Vol. IV, 1941–42, Proclamation No. 2487. The Proclamation was issued by the President by virtue of the authority vested in him by the Constitution as well as by express statutes. It is an accepted principle of interpretation that the undefined powers derived directly by the President from the Constitution must be deemed to be adequate for the performance of his duties as President.

[3] Stimson and Bundy, op. cit., p. 371; Sherwood, op. cit., p. 299.

[4] This was the birth of the United States Army's Air Ferry Command—later Air Transport Command. Financed at first out of lend-lease funds to the amount of over $60 million—with an initial British requisition of $31·6 million in June—it reinforced the R.A.F.'s air ferry in the North Atlantic and expanded later into all theatres of the war. Stettinius, op. cit., Chapter XIII.

'For he saith, I have heard thee in a time accepted, and in the day of salvation have I succoured thee; behold now is the day of salvation.'

The next six months seemed an endless succession of days of packing for a journey that could never begin. Yet how restlessly the President was turning over in his mind things that could still be done, without risking the final irrevocable political act, was shown in a talk on 16th June 1941 with the Ambassador. The President spoke of the next important move which he was taking—the relieving of the British in Iceland, and the convoying by the Navy of supplies up to that point; the move would be easier if the Germans were unable —as he anticipated—to 'take it on the chin' and were to begin shooting. He spoke of American pilots flying bombers across to British bases in West Africa—not American bases, though the Prime Minister offered them—and of the possibility of flying fighters off American aircraft carriers to the British base at Takoradi.[1] He referred to the action just taken to freeze German and Italian assets in the United States and to close the German Consulates.

The defence of Iceland was declared vital to the United States on 1st July and the landing of American troops in the island was announced on 7th. The texts exchanged on the occasion with the Icelandic Government indicated that one of the purposes of the landing was to 'eliminate the threat against the steady flow of munitions to Britain'. British and Allied ships were admitted henceforward to American convoys going to Iceland; direct protection to British convoys was not given until August.[2] Jointly financed British-American air bases were established on the island. Solidarity against the Axis was shown also in July by the simultaneous freezing by the United States and the British Commonwealth (on 25th) of Japanese funds. This followed Japan's move into Indo China.[3]

Meanwhile, Hitler's attack on Russia on 22nd June 1941 had relieved the American public from some of their concern over the fate of Britain. But it brought also still closer collaboration between the British and American Governments. This was shown in the combined handling of supplies to Russia. Purvis served with Hopkins and the Russian Ambassador in a Washington Committee on aid to Russia. Hopkins acted now as the direct link between the President, the Prime Minister, and Stalin. In the interval since his visit to London in January, Hopkins had kept in the closest touch with the Prime Minister by correspondence and telephone and through

---

[1] This began in the autumn of 1941.

[2] Churchill, *The Grand Alliance*, op. cit., p. 129.

[3] The American black list of firms in South America trading with the Axis was published on 17th July; and on 30th the Economic Defence Board was set up to deal with economic warfare questions. *The United States at War*, op. cit., p. 67 ff. Medlicott, op. cit., Chapter XIV, iv.

Harriman, who was his representative in London. The latter sat in on British committees and had attended, since the beginning, the Battle of the Atlantic Committee. The second mission of Hopkins to London in the latter part of July, which was continued to Moscow, was even more significant than the first.[1] His activities covered a wide range of questions relating to supply and he spoke for the United States in an important strategic discussion on the relative importance of the Middle East campaign and the Battle of the Atlantic. This was in a meeting with the Prime Minister, the British Chiefs of Staff and the American Military Mission. He brought back what he had learned in London and from Stalin in Moscow to the Atlantic Conference, which began on 9th August.[2] New evidence of the closeness of the Anglo-American combination emerged from the Atlantic Charter and the joint message to Stalin, issued by the Prime Minister and the President on 12th August. Hopkins's suggestion of a combined Anglo-American supply mission to Moscow was adopted by the Conference.

There were some Staff talks at the Atlantic Conference, but as they had not been prepared in advance they were desultory and inconclusive. Details of the taking over by the United States Navy and the Royal Canadian Navy of convoying to the President's line beyond Iceland were settled. This the Prime Minister described in his report to his colleagues on his return as an 'unparalleled gesture of friendship by a neutral power'.[3] On the side of air supply, combined action was shown immediately after the Conference in the setting up of the South Atlantic air ferry to Africa, via Brazil, and the organisation of the air transport route across Africa to Egypt, the Middle East and Iran. Arrangements for the ferry (which was announced on 19th August) had been under negotiation since mid-July. On British requisitions a lend-lease allocation of $20·6 million was made for the service, which included air transport as well as the ferrying of bombers. The ferry was run by Pan American Airways until the United States Army took over in the autumn of 1942. The primitive British Trans-African air route to Egypt, already in use for the flying of aircraft from the United Kingdom, was developed with American aid and materials. Joint British-American aircraft repair

---

[1] Sherwood, op. cit., Chapter XV, and pp. 313–17; Churchill, *The Grand Alliance*, op. cit., pp. 377–78.

[2] Ibid., pp. 394–96. The mission to Moscow was led by Lord Beaverbrook and Mr. Harriman, who negotiated, and signed in Moscow on 1st October, the First Russian Protocol to regulate British and American supply to that country. On joint aid to the U.S.S.R.—which lies outside the scope of this volume, see Hancock and Gowing, op. cit., Chapter XIII, etc.; *Memoirs of Cordell Hull*, Vol. II, op. cit.; Sherwood, op. cit., Part II, Chapters XVIII–XX; Stettinius, op. cit., Chapter XI; J. R. Deane, *The Strange Alliance* (New York: The Viking Press, 1947).

[3] For the President's map and the discussions of Hopkins with Churchill, see Sherwood, op. cit., pp. 272–73, 300, 311, 371–72.

and maintenance depots were set up in the Middle East, and later
in Iran as the air routes lengthened into that country. This was only
part of a far larger combined effort extending from Africa across the
Middle East to Iran, which was launched in the autumn of 1941. It
was jointly financed, and jointly supplied and manned. It included
naval bases, assembly and repair depots for munitions and tanks,
roads, railways, hospitals, radio stations.[1] What all this involved in
terms of the supply from the United States of materials, equipment
and stores of all kinds, and the effect of this assistance on the North
African campaign, aid to Russia through Iran, the holding of the
Middle East, and recovery in South-East Asia after the Japanese
onslaught on Malaya and Burma, would require a separate chapter.
One item that may be mentioned by way of illustration was the
Prime Minister's request to the President at the beginning of
September for American transports to assist in the movement of two
British divisions to the Middle East. This request was met by the
release by the President of 'our best transport ships'.[2] The ships left
Halifax on 10th November 1941; the convoy was actually diverted
whilst at sea from the Middle East to the Far East.

Nevertheless, the President on his return to Washington from the
Atlantic Conference felt a certain chill in the air. He had not forgotten the warning on the last day of the Atlantic Conference,
12th August, when the Administration Bill for the extension of the
Selective Service Act escaped defeat by a single vote. He sensed what
the Embassy described in a report to London on 3rd September, as
the 'apathy and refusal to believe in the existence of a real crisis
threatening to change the day-to-day life of the American people'.[3]
He remarked that the country was no nearer to war as a result of
the Atlantic meeting and he told Congressional leaders on the 17th
August that he had made no new commitments for the United
States. The Embassy waited after the Atlantic Conference for the
big speech in which the President would galvanise the country into
complete acceptance of the Administration's policy of the defeat of
Hitlerism. The Ambassador thought that the President's broadcast
on Labour Day (1st September) left things much as they were. Not
even a dramatic incident would persuade the public of the imminence of war unless it were played up strongly by the President; but
the Ambassador thought the President's mind was not yet 'made up
to this'. None of the incidents that did occur involving American
destroyers—the mining of the *Greer*, the damage done to the *Kearney*,
the sinking of the *Reuben James* on 30th October—touched off the
powder. The policy of shooting at sight the Nazi 'rattlesnakes of the

---

[1] Stettinius, op. cit., Chapter XIII.
[2] Churchill, *The Grand Alliance*, op. cit., pp. 436–38; Sherwood, op. cit., pp. 376–77.
[3] See also *The New York Times*, 24th August 1941.

Atlantic' was announced on 11th September, and on 15th the convoying of British ships to Iceland. The revision of the Neutrality Act, which began in October and was concluded on 17th November, at last permitted American ships to deliver to British ports 'American goods under the American flag'.[1] But, as public-opinion polls and other signs indicated, public support was still lukewarm. On 11th November the Embassy reported that 'the mildness of the reaction to the sinking of the *Reuben James* (with the loss of ninety-nine lives) provides evidence of a danger already long foreseen that the present process of going gradually into war will make an outburst of popular anger unlikely, and without such an outburst there can scarcely be a declaration of war in this country, and without a declaration it will be difficult for the Administration to galvanise opinion to the point necessary for a united, concentrated and accelerated effort'—and for the acceptance of the necessary sacrifices.

Not many days later the final negotiations with the Japanese envoys began in Washington; and Tokyo began to count off the days to its fatal deadline. A series of disasters had befallen British sea power in the Mediterranean, and the reverses to British and American arms were to continue far into 1942. But Hitler had become mired in Russia; Britain's margin of survival had been increased by American lend-lease and mutual aid from Canada. British production—still the main arsenal of democracy—could be planned more freely because of assured supplies of raw materials and food from the nearest source outside Europe. Even the thin trickle of lend-lease supplies of aircraft was enough with British aircraft production to assure air superiority and forecast air supremacy. The Battle of the Atlantic was not over; but it had gone well enough for imports and home production to have exceeded consumption. Stocks (dry cargo) in the United Kingdom had risen by 3·26 million tons and oil stocks stood at 7 million tons compared with 4·5 million in June. On the side of production, much progress had been made towards acquiring the habit of combination with the United States. American war production could now burst through its peace-time chains. When Japan struck there was ready to hand a well-founded combined Victory Programme. This was the culminating achievement on the supply side in 1941. The production goals needed to surpass the enemy were ready waiting for the command to be given to industry. The evolution of the Victory Programme is dealt with in the next section.

---

[1] *Documents on American Foreign Relations*, op. cit., Vol. IV, 1941–42.

(v)

The Consolidated Statement of Production: British, Canadian, American

A combined programme to overtop Germany in armed force meant that America, whilst still formally at peace and still hoping to avoid war, would have to set out deliberately to take a series of practical steps *on the assumption of war*. These steps involved estimating American requirements, scheduling the production necessary to meet them, and placing at once all orders that required a long time for production. The obstacles in the way of a democracy taking such drastic action in peace-time were very great. It was not until July that pressures became great enough for the first steps to be taken. These pressures included the supply needs arising from the attack on Russia and the rapidly expanding American defence programmes.

A realistic programme for victory was different from any programmes of the past. It went beyond not only existing British production schedules, but also the sum total of British production, lend-lease aid, and the production planned for the armed forces of the United States. Even the 'Purvis Balance Sheet', bold though it had seemed, was only one wall of the four-square Victory Programme which he foresaw. It was not yet possible, from a political point of view, for his 'Balance Sheet' to go beyond British requirements up to the end of 1942. Its significance lay in its assumptions: it assumed that a British programme of this scale to the end of 1942 would have to be kept up on the same scale in the years beyond; that it must be paralleled up to 1942 by an American programme at least as large which in turn must continue into the years beyond on at least the same scale. Even this first instalment, which was to set the scale for this whole development, was not much more than a guess. For there was as yet no realistic measure of the resources of the enemy or of the speed at which American production capacity could turn out the weapons for a full victory programme.

Up to March 1941 there was not much profit to be had from dwelling on this distant goal. Arms from current production for immediate campaigns was the first concern and Purvis was the leader in the continuous battle of allocations in Washington. But after the Staff talks and the adoption of lend-lease the way lay open for a grand strategy of supply. From the beginning of 1940, Purvis had pressed at all times for maximum American production of every kind of war supply that Great Britain needed. He had done this for the simple reason that so long as the United States went on producing 'too little and too late' nearly all of the 'too little' was likely to be absorbed by the American Army and Navy. The purpose now widened. From March 1941 the goal which he and Monnet pursued steadily in their communications with London and in all the places open to them in Washington—in the British Supply Council, with the President and the heads of the American Administration and with the armed services—was to get production going at once on a scale large enough to produce by the end of, say, 1942 sufficient arms to ensure the defeat of the enemy.

The problem had to be attacked from three different angles: the angle of the military planners, the angle of the statisticians, and the angle of the production experts. The Staff talks had defined in the broadest terms the general strategical objective. (This was only a beginning; there would have to be continuous contact at the Staff level and further Staff talks.) Then came the turn of the statisticians on both sides of the Atlantic. They had to bring order and realism into several confused fields: (1) existing requirements figures had to be sifted and brought together into a single programme; (2) calculations had to be made as far ahead as possible of combined stocks and production; (3) enemy stocks and production had to be estimated as accurately as possible. (For the statisticians also this would have to be a continuous process, which must go on without interruption to the end of the war.) Meanwhile, the third element, the planners of production, would have to be continuously at work. Their field would have to be largely the United States, since British production was nearing its peak. They would have to translate requirements into orders to industry and strengthen all the weak points in production revealed by the statistical analysis. But they could not begin serious work in the United States until the President gave the sign and Congress voted the money.

In the American administration Purvis and Monnet found a number of individuals who not only thought as they did but were in a position to prepare the foundations; they included in the Office of Production Management Knudsen and Stacy May; and at the ministerial level Hopkins and Stimson. It was the latter who, when the time for action was ripe, took the decisive steps to set the American machinery at work to secure first a combined balance sheet of production and then a Victory Programme. In February 1941 Knudsen secured agreement in the O.P.M. Council on a 'single unified American defence program', to include British and foreign requirements for the fiscal year of 1942.[1] In March a first

---

[1] 18th February. *Industrial Mobilization for War*, op. cit., p. 134. Stacy May was director of the Bureau of Research and Statistics of the National Defence Advisory Council and the Office of Production Management of which Knudsen, with Hillman, was head.

attempt was made to arrive at a rough total of requirements by putting together all known elements—Army, Navy, Maritime Commission, British Commonwealth. The total was shown by Stacy May to be far in excess of the total value of all existing and projected American defence production (including lend-lease) which he put at roughly $50 billion.[1] By May statisticians on both sides of the Atlantic were working on the statistical approaches towards a consolidated statement of production.

The need of an 'over-all program for an all-out effort' was discussed by the Production Planning Board of the Office of Production Management on the 22nd May and again on 18th June. A 'general strategic plan' would make it possible first to calculate the 'munitions objective'; and second, to work out how 'the existing and potential munitions capacity of this country and its friends' could be utilised to achieve the objective. No such plan yet existed and O.P.M. was reluctant to take the responsibility for launching one; since no plan could be realised without drastic cuts in production for civilian use and this was dangerous ground from a political point of view.[2] The President's proclamation of an unlimited national emergency on 27th May gave Secretary Stimson a chance to act. In a note next day to Knudsen he asked for a survey of war production and suggested as a guide for making it 'trebling the overall production of this country both for the United States and the United Kingdom for delivery by the end of 1942'.[3] Hitherto, the Secretary noted, the United States had based their defence production on building entirely new factories or extending existing factories and facilities. This meant postponing production until new plants could be built. The national emergency, he warned, 'may not wait so long'. Therefore the O.P.M. should make an immediate survey of *existing* productive facilities which could be turned over rapidly from civilian goods to tanks, artillery and ammunition.

The next move was indicated a fortnight later by a note (9th June) circulated by Purvis to the members of the British Supply Council. It noted that the United States authorities wanted to build up a 'consolidated production picture' by securing a comprehensive monthly review of all North American war production on British (including British Commonwealth) or American account. Accurate long-term schedules of expected deliveries were wanted, and not merely contract schedules or programme figures. Monnet and the statisticians of the British Supply Council already had on hand most of the figures on the British Commonwealth. These figures covered: (1) all Canadian

---

[1] Ibid., pp. 134–35.
[2] Ibid., pp. 136–37.
[3] Secretary Knox joined in on the same lines on 3rd June. Ibid., p. 138.

production up to 1943 (on both British and Canadian account); (2) deliveries from British or British Commonwealth cash contracts in the United States. But the British Supply Council had no figures of the actual production expected month by month up to 1942 and 1943 from the American contracts let, or about to be let, to provide Britain with supplies under lend-lease. These figures, as well as those showing the yield expected from American War and Navy Departments' contracts, had to be assembled on the American side. The request, of which Purvis had thus given advance warning, was duly received from Secretary Stimson on 30th June. It took the form of a letter to Purvis and memoranda to the Office of Production Management, the Navy Department and the Maritime Commission. It asked for a consolidated balance sheet of American, British and Canadian war production. 'Efficient planning', Secretary Stimson wrote, 'requires a constant and overall knowledge of all equipment, material, shipping, etc., which are now being produced or planned in this country, the U.K. and Canada. . . . When the U.S. and foreign production programs are consolidated, it would be well to compare them with obtainable information of the production available to Germany.' The information as it came in would be assembled and consolidated into the Balance Sheet by the statistical officers of O.P.M. under Stacy May. In the letter to Purvis, Stimson ended with a significant remark, which Purvis underlined in sending the texts to London: 'It is impossible', Secretary Stimson wrote, 'to resolve the important question of allocation of United States production between our two countries until this Balance Sheet has been prepared.' The link between this 'Balance Sheet' and the 'Victory Programme' of September is clear from Secretary Stimson's remark.

Monnet left an account of a talk with General Burns, Lend-Lease Executive Officer, on 3rd July, in which the same link was shown. 'When the overall Balance Sheet was completed there would emerge the North American Production . . . as well as the United Kingdom Production. It would then be possible to set the totals of such production against the U.S.-U.K. estimate of the material required to overtake the enemy in material by the end of 1942. It was agreed that, over and above all production at present contemplated in the U.S., the U.K. or Canada, there would be a large deficiency for which provision would have to be made.' It was agreed in the talk that this deficiency would have to be made up from the War and Navy Departments' appropriations as distinct from lend-lease. Anxiety about the magnitude of this deficiency increased in July as a result of the demands from Russia and the increased needs of the American Army and Navy. The first lists of Russian requirements were received in July. The President, on the 15th, called for a large increase in tank output 'with the only limiting factor . . . the ability of American industry to produce the tanks'.[1] On the 21st he asked the War and Navy Departments and the Office of Production Management for a list of arms which they could recommend for immediate shipment to Russia. This led Secretary Stimson, at a meeting of the Council of O.P.M. next day, to point out the danger of conflict between the requirements for the Army, the Navy and lend-lease. He thought there was a 'need for an authoritative General Requirements or Strategy Board to look at the entire program and to determine its order of precedence . . . so as to attain strategic objectives. . . .'[2]

The danger of such conflict was increased by rapid expansion of American defence requirements as shown by the series of appropriation Acts from June to December. The main Defence Appropriation Act of 30th June 1941 was followed by three supplemental National Defence Appropriation Acts, passed on 25th August, 28th October, and 17th December. Together they provided for an army of three million (at least as regards orders for essential equipment such as tanks and artillery) as well as for large expansions in the Air Force and the Navy.[3] An account of the difficulties incurred as these programmes got under way—shortages of materials, the need of conservation orders, difficulties of organisation and jurisdiction—will be found in the official American accounts.[4]

Meanwhile, both sides had treated the preparation of the Consolidated Statement as a matter of extreme urgency. It was not difficult for London to produce quickly the British production figures. The Central Statistical Office, set up at the beginning of 1941 by direction of the Prime Minister, had been collecting from the statistical divisions of the Service and Supply Ministries the main figures of British production. It attempted to collate them with what American figures it could obtain. Figures were required for stocks and estimated new production over six quarters to the end of 1942. The British Supply Council cabled a classification of the items to be included. It comprised twenty-seven main chapters and over 100 subheadings covering all the different kinds of munitions, aircraft, naval

---

[1] *Industrial Mobilization for War*, op. cit., pp. 138–39.

[2] This need was met in some degree by the setting up of the Supply Priorities and Allocation Board (S.P.A.B.). Ibid., pp. 89, 110–13. *Minutes of the Council of the Office of Production Management* (War Production Board, Washington: 1946), p. 46. *The United States at War*, op. cit., p. 77.

[3] *Industrial Mobilization for War*, op. cit., pp. 127, 129. *The United States at War*, p. 80 ff.

[4] *Industrial Mobilization for War*, Part II. On the 'hopelessly confused' situation between O.P.M. and S.P.A.B., see p. 113. In October, the size of the tank programme (37,500 tanks) caused a shortage of armour-plate. In the same month alarm was caused by the growing shortage of machine tools, due to Russian and British and American demands; shortages of metals such as copper, aluminium, and steel forgings, began to appear about the same time. Conservation orders were introduced to safeguard supply. The first restrictions were introduced on the output of civilian goods. *Minutes of the Council of the Office of Production Management* (War Production Board, Washington: 1946), pp. 67, 68, 74.

vessels and raw materials.[1] Despite the magnitude of the task suddenly imposed on it, the British Government was able to supply most of the figures by 20th July. On the 25th Purvis forwarded to Secretary Stimson the British and Canadian figures, complete except for petroleum products. The two sides of the Balance Sheet were now ready in two roughly forged blocks. An attempt to weld them into the Consolidated Statement was begun early in August by a War Department Committee attended by the statistical expert of the British Supply Council. It became clear at once that differences in classification required consultations with London. Purvis had gone there on 1st August, Stacy May followed on the 7th, taking with him American production data and estimates of the arms output of Germany. The work of consolidation occupied most of August, but already the figures had begun to work.

On 5th August, the first sign of it came in a telegram sent in the Foreign Office series by Hopkins to the President, as Hopkins was boarding the *Prince of Wales* for the Atlantic Conference. He asked the President to 'bring production estimates of tanks, aircraft by month through 1942'.

From this point onwards the strategists were to take over the running. The wider implications of the Statement and its use as the starting point for the strategical discussions which led to the Victory Programme are discussed in the next section. But before leaving the statisticians it is necessary to say a word about the later history of the Anglo-American Consolidated Statement of Production, which was its final title. It was a plain, severely practical document of some sixty pages of tables, giving stocks and realistic forecast of the production of the United Kingdom, the United States and Canada by quarters up to the end of 1942. Besides munitions the first issue included shipbuilding, strategic raw materials and petroleum products. It gave no data on requirements. Only the first issue included the speculative element of British and American estimates, often divergent, of German strength.[2]

The importance of the Consolidated Statement was greatly increased by the steps, taken on the initiative of Secretary Stimson, to turn it into a regular statistical series. A form for this purpose was given to Monnet by the statistician of the British Supply Council in mid-September. Early in October Secretary Stimson, who had sent the Statement to the President and the General Staff, asked the

---

[1] This classification had been hastily concerted by British and American statisticians in Washington. The task of refining it so that different types became comparable was to continue long after the United States entered the war.

[2] Stacy May took the American estimates of German strength to London and brought back the best combined estimates which could then be made. In the British view it was misleading to include German munitions, much of which were being used against Russia, without adding also Russian figures.

United States Departments and the British Supply Council for a revision of the figures up to 1st October; it was to be prepared thereafter on a monthly or quarterly basis in the case of production, and quarterly or half-yearly in the case of stocks. The American production programme for 1942, sent to the President on 26th December, took as its starting point the figures of the third revision[1] of the Statement and indicated the necessary increases based on the Victory Programme of September. 'The Victory Programme', Secretary Stimson wrote in his covering memorandum to the President, 'is now on its way to becoming a reality.' The figures were to be greatly increased by the President's announcement, eleven days later, of the new targets for American war production. The task of keeping up to date and broadening and deepening the Consolidated Statement devolved upon the Combined Boards.

(vi)
The Victory Programme

Whilst the supply departments, American and British, and their statisticians were working through July and August at the Consolidated Statement of Production, the military planners on the British side were also at work; their task was to estimate requirements in the light of strategical objectives, in other words a victory programme. The two enquiries were independent but converged towards the same goal. Purvis left behind him—perhaps his last act—a remarkable paper which showed his clear vision of that goal. Some days before his death at Prestwick he wrote some notes which were found in his wrecked plane. They recorded the road he had travelled and the final step which he was hastening back to take in Washington. A British official with whom he talked in London on 13th August, the day before his death, has described him as full of excitement. He was impatient to get back to hammer at the iron, as he said, whilst it was still hot from the Atlantic meeting of the President and the Prime Minister. He was sure that at last the time had come when it was possible to secure from the President the 'greatest directive' yet made; it was one that would place all war production at last on a genuine war basis. This directive towards which the steps of the past had led —twenty-two of them as he set them out in order in his notes—he referred to as follows:

---

[1] The production figures for the third revision of the statement were received from the three countries by the end of November 1941, and the revised Statement was forwarded by Secretary Stimson to the Chairman of the British Supply Council on 18th December. See below, Chapter IX, Section (ii).

(23) Meantime following steps are vital as a follow-up to the Prime Minister's cable to the President:

    (*a*) Presidential directive immediately to U.S. General Staff calling for an appraisal of combined 'victory' requirements necessary to overtop enemy's material resources. (To be based on consolidated production data now being prepared.)

    (*b*) Presidential directive to U.S. War Department and O.P.M. and P.M. Directive to Chairman of North American Supply Committee to co-operate in taking production and appropriation steps to achieve such a 'victory' programme, whatever this involves in civil use interference.

This review of the past made by Purvis showed the central thread of his thought and action, namely, all-out production, limited only by the capacity to produce. This, as he saw it, involved two things: drastic restrictions on civilian production, and a complete breach with the mentality and policy which had limited production to an army of peace-time proportions. This he saw as a chain that fettered the minds of both the United States War Department and the British War Office.[1] The first 'break through', he recorded, came 'by obtaining letter from Stimson to Knudsen of May 28th' which is referred to above. Then followed the attempt of the War Department to get appropriations 'on other than a troop basis'. The document affords the only clues contained in the British records to several of his personal interventions at critical points.

His point '21' read: 'Stage now set by Prime Minister's cable to President of July 25th, 1941, for final action which will break impasse in production. . . .' In this message the Prime Minister wrote: 'We have been considering here our war plans, not only for the fighting of 1942, but also for 1943. After providing for the security of essential bases, it is necessary to plan on the largest scale the forces needed for victory. . . .' Amongst the supplies needed for victory Mr. Churchill placed the accent on heavy bombers, tanks, and special ships to bring the tanks to the beaches. He saw two steps which must be taken and without loss of a moment: first, the framing of 'an agreed estimate as to our joint requirements of the primary weapons of war . . .'—for which he proposed a meeting of the Combined Staffs in London; and second, consideration of 'how these requirements are to be met by our joint production'[2]—a matter for the technical experts on production.

The British Chiefs of Staff had advised the sending of such a message. And the advice arose from an attempt made to satisfy a wish expressed by the British Joint Staff Mission in Washington for an

---

[1] cf. *Industrial Mobilization for War*, op. cit., p. 119: 'In forecasting over-all requirements, the Services reflected their long peacetime experience with limited appropriations by gearing their requirements to minimum levels.' cf. *The United States at War*, op. cit., p. 81.

[2] Churchill, *The Grand Alliance*, op. cit., p. 722.

authoritative statement of British strategic policy for winning the war and the forces required for this purpose; such a paper they thought would be welcomed by the United States Chiefs of Staff. A paper prepared by the Joint Planning Staff in London, dated 17th July, gave preliminary estimates of military requirements, but concluded that the true joint British and American requirements could be ascertained only after joint study by both Staffs.

A direct reply to the Prime Minister's message was not received from the President until the end of August. Meanwhile, there were Staff talks at the Atlantic Conference. The British Chiefs of Staff, in the course of a review of strategy, assigned a high priority to the production of heavy bombers. Their report on the discussions indicated that the 'most distressing revelation' was the delay in American air-craft production. This meant the breakdown of the 'Slessor Agreement' whereby the greater part of the American heavy-bomber production was to be allocated to the United Kingdom.[1] Up to June 1943 the output from production, as then planned in the United States, would be about 4,600 heavy bombers; of these the United Kingdom could not count on much more than 1,000; its requirement (from the United States alone) was more than 6,000 machines. The American Chiefs of Staff were described in the report as 'very naturally obsessed with the shortage of equipment for their own forces', since it was hardly enough in many cases to provide for the training of the expanding American Army.[2]

A fortnight after this discussion the Consolidated Statement was finished in London. There was something like consternation in military planning circles when they first saw the American figures. Thus a letter on 29th August to the Secretary of the Joint Staff Mission in Washington referred to the 'incredible situation' shown by the Statement. '. . . It reveals the most astonishing state of affairs. The main point of interest is that it shows that by the end of 1942 the much-vaunted American production will not be much greater than that of our own and Canada combined.' The impact of the figures was increased in Washington by an analysis prepared by Monnet (for Lord Beaverbrook) on 19th August, and by a second analysis prepared in London by Sir Walter Layton at the end of the month. Stacy May took back the latter with him and used it effectively in conjunction with another document which had been given to him unofficially (it had not yet been circulated or approved in London). This second document contained the provisional estimates worked out by the

---

[1] See above, Section (iii), p. 309.

[2] The British Joint Staff Mission in Washington had reported (8th August) on the 'alarmingly small' allocations which were being made by the United States War Department. The Mission suggested discussions with the American Chiefs of Staff for the purpose of drawing up a 'joint Anglo-American estimate of the war material required to defeat the enemy'.

British Planning Staff in London in July; it showed how greatly British requirements alone would exceed American production of the prime weapons.

The analysis made in London by Layton compared expected American output to the end of 1942 with that of Canada and the United Kingdom combined. The comparison was all the more significant since it was based not on contracts placed but on the maximum production that could be got from existing capacity. It showed that the output of the United States would exceed that of Britain and Canada in some items, such as medium and light bombers, merchant ships, light tanks and army artillery. In a second group, including fighter aircraft, the output would be approximately equal. But in a vital third group, comprising heavy bombers, heavy and medium tanks, tank and anti-tank guns, British and Canadian production would exceed American. It was only towards the end of 1942 that for overall production the United States would begin to draw ahead of Britain and Canada; and even then the American stocks would still be much lower than theirs. The comparison brought out important divergencies between the programmes of the United States and the United Kingdom. Thus, British production was switching over to heavy and medium tanks and heavy bombers, whereas American production favoured light tanks and light and medium bombers. This obviously called for joint expert examination. Such an examination was all the more important since the nature of the strategical objective must affect the balance of the different types of equipment. If Germany could be subdued by bombing alone, then the all-important factor would be the heavy bomber. If the Continent had to be stormed by an army landing on a strongly held hostile coast then there would have to be a strong emphasis on tank landing craft and tanks. Both sides agreed that such a landing would probably be necessary but that it would require 'mainly armoured divisions with the most modern equipment'. As the report of the British-American Planning Committee noted later in the month, neither side visualised 'the employment of vast armies or infantry as in 1918'. Thus the statisticians had brought to light and defined quantitatively many questions which could be answered only by the military planners.[1]

Preparations for the Victory Programme Conference began in the last days of August 1941. On the 23rd Monnet telephoned from Washington to say the President accepted the idea and had given the necessary instructions. Messages followed at intervals from the American Military Mission in London, the American Ambassador, and Harry Hopkins, confirming the agreement of the President to a joint

---

[1] They had also presented a challenge to the production experts in the United States. In November the Chairman of the British Supply Council testified that the Consolidated Statement had been of the 'utmost value in promoting plans for an all-out programme of production in this country'.

discussion on long-term requirements and indicating his desire that the Conference should meet in London on 15th September as a preliminary to the British-American (Beaverbrook/Harriman) mission to Moscow on the 25th. The Conference was led on the British side by Lord Beaverbrook with representatives of the Service and Supply Ministries and the Chiefs of Staff, and on the American side by Averell Harriman, supported by a similarly composed delegation.

What had originally been conceived as two separate British-American conferences in London—on joint aid to Russia and the Victory Programme—became fused into one. Supplies to Russia had to be met out of what was now becoming a joint British-American pool. Close co-ordination was essential since each must know what requests had been made to the other and what the other was sending. The strategic effect of sending particular supplies had also to be considered; thus it was foreseen that the supply of fighters to Russia by the United Kingdom meant reducing air strength in the Middle East and inability to supply fighters for Malaya where they were to be desperately needed some months later. The need of co-ordination was demonstrated at the outset. The United Kingdom had agreed before the Conference was convened to meet half the Russian request for monthly supplies of 400 aircraft and 500 light and medium tanks. This was regarded as a commitment which had to be kept; but the United States at this stage lacked the tanks and aircraft needed to meet the other half of the commitment and a good deal of it fell to the United Kingdom.[1] This gave a keener point to Lord Beaverbrook's comment that the reduced forecast of American tank production, given at the Conference, meant 'a heavy reduction in our expectations'. (The President, however, soon gave assurances on tanks to be available by mid-1942, which the Prime Minister said 'more than restore the expectations we had prior to recent conference'.)

The question of war supplies required by the spring of 1943 in the British area of responsibility for the defeat of Germany and Italy was assigned to a Planning Committee of three British and four American Staff Officers. Their report on 'Victory Requirements' was signed on 19th September. The Committee discussed an American plan for the allocation of American aircraft on a percentage basis between the United States, United Kingdom, Russia, and other claimants. This came as a shock to the British representatives, since it disclosed that they would receive up to June 1942 1,800 fewer aircraft (600 heavy and medium bombers, 600 light bombers, 600 fighters) than had previously been expected. In particular, the loss of the heavy and

---

[1] A large part of the British reserve stock of aluminium was released to meet urgent Russian requirements. This was done in the hope—but without any promise—that the stock would be made up by the United States on whom the United Kingdom was already dependent for supply. American supply, however, meant restrictions on civilian consumption in the United States.

medium bombers was regarded as likely to have a grave effect on the British air offensive against Germany.

The general conclusion of the British delegates on the state of American production was given by Lord Beaverbrook as follows: 'There is a general retardation in the American production programme. The figures now supplied to us, particularly for the output of Army equipment, are much lower than anything we have had before and many of our minimum requirements cannot be met. It is imperative that the Americans should organise immediately a rapid increase of their production.' On the other hand, there was general agreement between the two countries on the basic strategy to be followed for the defeat of the Axis.

In the matter of victory requirements the Conference was not able to present any complete statement. British Army, Navy and Air Force requirements were put forward, but no corresponding estimates were given or yet available on the American side. The complete overall requirements given by the Royal Navy showed that the greater part of its needs was being met out of British production. The main assistance for which the Royal Navy looked to the United States was smaller vessels for the protection of convoys. As regards merchant shipping, requirements from the United States were given as five million gross tons in addition to tonnage already being built to British orders in that country. Some of these British figures were still provisional, and some revisions were made in October.

The report of the Planning Committee ended with clear recommendations as to the procedure to be followed 'in order to present a full picture of the overall victory requirements':

(a) Full United States requirements should be added. . . .

(b) The estimate of what is required to maintain Russian resistance should be added after the return of the delegations from Moscow.[1]

(c) The resultant totals, after deduction of British estimated production, should be referred to the Production Authorities in the United States, who should be asked to say how far these requirements can be met, within the time limits, and to what extent the demands for various items seriously conflict one with another.

(d) The modifications necessary to relate the total programme to the realities of United States and British Empire industrial production, to adjust any serious conflicts, and to fix relative priorities in greater detail, should be discussed between the United States and British Staffs in Washington and determined on a strategical basis.

Except for (b)—the Russian figures—action on these points moved slowly. The decisions taken to supply Russia called for rapid action under (c)—intensified production in the United States. The Prime

---

[1] It was not feasible to calculate Russian requirements for a longer period ahead than the First Protocol, i.e. to June 1942.

Minister referred to this in a message to Hopkins on 25th September. 'The offers which we both are making to Russia are necessary and worth while. There is no disguising the fact however that they make grievous inroads into what is required by you for expanding your forces and by us for intensifying our war effort.'[1] Britain would be unlikely, he pointed out, to be able to expand her programmes much further to meet the gap, but perhaps the United States could reach in the second half of 1942 the output then planned for the first half of 1943?[2]

The trouble was, as Monnet noted on 3rd October, that when the three totals, British, American and Russian, were finally added together the requirements would exceed the total production capacity of the United States and Great Britain. 'At that stage it will be necessary to decide on the highest grounds of strategy which requirements must be cut.' At the end of October it looked already as if raw materials would be the limiting factor which would force cuts. The British Joint Staff Mission in Washington, though still lacking the figures of American requirements, learned unofficially that 'U.S. requirements are great and, added to those of ourselves, Russia, etc., the totals would exceed the raw material resources. Consequently cuts will be inevitable, and this will necessitate high-level decisions, particularly with regard to the large Army and two-ocean Navy which we understand U.S. staffs envisage'.

The Joint Staff Mission had just received a letter in which the United States Chiefs of Staff confirmed their agreement on the procedure outlined in the report signed by their representatives in London on 19th September. The United States authorities, the letter said, after studying the figures would be ready to discuss adjustments with representatives of the British Chiefs of Staff. It added a warning that the signature of the London report by the United States Planning Officers was not to be taken as indicating that the United States Chiefs of Staff agreed either with the strategic concepts on which the report was based or had approved the supply to the British of the requirements they had then tabled. This communication indeed revealed at several points the distance that still remained between the two General Staffs. It was because the American Chiefs of Staff made little use of intermediaries such as the British Joint Staff Mission in Washington, or of its own Staff representatives in London, that Staff Conferences were of such importance.[3] The British Joint Staff Mission was led to expect further Staff talks on the Victory Programme

---

[1] Churchill, *The Grand Alliance*, op. cit., p. 416.

[2] The suggestion about anticipating output was made in the paper by Monnet of 19th August and was repeated by W. L. Batt at the Victory Programme Conference in London.

[3] British, American and Dutch Staff talks took place at Singapore in August 1941.

in mid-November, but they were never held. On 2nd December it reviewed the situation as regards the Victory Programme. It was now two months since the Chiefs of Staff in London had instructed it 'to ensure that the Victory Programme was not allowed to die of inertia'. It decided, however, that nothing could be done to speed American decisions since officials sounded out in the War Department thought it would not be politic for the Joint Staff Mission to approach the United States Chiefs of Staff at that stage. The United States had still four days longer to spend in the 'Valley of Doubt'.

Some light on what had been happening in these weeks to the Victory Programme on the American side is thrown by American official accounts. In September the Supply Priorities and Allocation Board had asked the United States departments for 'clear statements of their estimated requirements, based on military objectives, over the next two years'. The estimates of the War Department were given to the Office of Production Management towards the end of October. But 'the Navy Department and the Maritime Commission refused to submit programs at all until after the country was actually at war on the ground that they would never know what would be needed to defeat the enemy'. Finally the O.P.M. stepped into the breach by preparing a victory programme of total requirements in which it made its own assumptions as to the needs of these two departments.[1] The Supply Priorities and Allocation Board then proceeded in November to collect from industries estimates of their total requirements of critical material in 1942, including civilian as well as military.

Three days before Pearl Harbour, Donald Nelson—Executive Director of the Supply Priorities and Allocation Board, and soon to become Director of the War Production Board set up in January—received a 'final report on the feasibility of the Victory Programme in terms of the national industrial potential' and of its cost. The total expenditures foreseen by all the programmes involving United States supply, for their own Forces and for foreign countries, up to 30th September 1943 were estimated at some $150 billion. This meant doubling the entire programme of the United States up to that date —4th December 1941.[2] This was judged to be feasible but only under a full war-time economy. The political problem of how to overcome the national inertia in order to establish such an economy then seemed insoluble. It was to be solved unexpectedly three days later at Pearl Harbour.[3]

---

[1] *Industrial Mobilization for War*, op. cit., pp. 139–40. *The United States at War*, op. cit., p. 81, recorded that 'Figures presented initially by the services were practically worthless'. This referred to figures presented by all the services up to August 1941.

[2] Actual American (Federal Government) expenditures for war in 1941 totalled only $6·7 billion. *The United States at War*, op. cit., p. 93.

[3] *Industrial Mobilization for War*, op. cit., pp. 139–40, and Donald M. Nelson, *Arsenal of Democracy* (New York: Harcourt, Brace & Co. Inc., 1946).

CHAPTER IX

COMBINATION IN MID WAR, 1942

(i)

'The Giant Set Free'

WITH the entry of the United States into the war the story of British war supply from North America can be told on broader lines and in less detail. The financial troubles which complicated supply up to 1941 were now largely solved. The political difficulties which had beset supply from a neutral to a belligerent were completely removed. Common political policies and combined strategy made possible something like a pooling of supplies. Lend-lease procurement became more a matter of administration than of policy. War production would soon become so great that merely a fraction of it would suffice to meet all lend-lease requirements. The centre of interest shifted from procurement to combined allocation and assignment; it moved from supply to Britain to the broader aspects of the combined handling of war supplies—raw materials, munitions and foodstuffs, and their transport, and to the combined planning of war production. In the account that follows these broader aspects must receive some attention, but supply to the United Kingdom will still remain the major theme. For accounts of other aspects of the common war experience the reader must turn to the national histories of production, foreign policy, and combined military operations.

The unleashing of American war production was the cardinal factor in the year 1942. The factor next in importance was the combined machinery for strategy and supply. On the supply side this combined machinery steered war production and the allocation of resources. The rudder was a complex affair made up of the combined will and authority of the President and the Prime Minister, working through their national staffs and departments and in particular through the Combined Chiefs of Staff on the military side, and on the civilian side the Combined Boards. The Combined Boards were concerned with what can be described in a broad sense as the *strategy* of production, transport and supply. They expressed the principle of civilian, rather than military, control over supply. Even the Combined Munitions Assignments Board, which the President's and

336

Prime Minister's joint directive put 'under the Combined Chiefs of Staff', had civilian chairmen—Mr. Harry Hopkins in Washington and Mr. Oliver Lyttelton in London. On the production side there was no single commander-in-chief as there was for the Allied campaigns in North Africa, Europe and the Western Pacific. But just as no national military history of these campaigns can ignore the other half of the combination or the commanding role of the Combined Chiefs of Staff, so no national history of supply can ignore the part played by the Combined Boards. Yet during the course of the war the role of the Boards was difficult to assess by those immersed in the details of production and procurement. Their role consisted mostly —like that of a steersman—of innumerable adjustments rather than of spectacular turns. There had been much of this kind of adjustment before January 1942 and much of it might still have been secured by the continuance of the same kind of informal machinery as existed before Pearl Harbour. But it is probable that unorganised informality of this kind would have been quite inadequate to cope with the stresses and strains set up by full industrial mobilisation in the United States, as well as by the greatly increased scale and area of military operations.

Harmony between elements so numerous, diverse and complex as those involved in the war effort of the United States and the British Commonwealth was not achieved by accident. Combined strength could only have been brought to the high peak it attained by team work of a kind unique in the history of modern warfare. On the side of the Axis there was nothing which even remotely resembled it.

This account can deal with only that part of this combined machinery which was concerned with war production and supply. It was on the military side that combination reached its highest peak —both in unified commands and in combined operations such as the landings and campaigns in North Africa and Western Europe. This vast and intricate network of combined planning and action belongs to the specialised military histories. There will be some reference here to the Combined Munitions Assignments Board which, subject to the general strategy laid down by the Combined Chiefs of Staff, allocated military supplies for the different fronts. In the main, however, the study must confine itself to an outline of those parts of the combined machinery on the civilian side which affected most closely British war production, namely the Combined Raw Materials Board and the Combined Production and Resources Board. The account is written from British official sources, with some reference to American publications bearing on the same matters. The full account of the great partnership must wait on fuller publication of its American side. The account will be more intelligible if it can be read with some reference to the American background. For it was the vast turmoil of American

Y

war mobilisation that was the main factor in the life and work of the Combined Boards in the first part of their existence.[1]

Both from the point of view of military strategy and war supply, 1942 was the pivotal year of the war. It was the year in which the United States carried through their military and industrial mobilisation. Mr. Stimson ends his reflections on the meaning of Pearl Harbour with the words, 'the self-imprisoned giant was set free'.[2]

On the military side most of 1942 was a year of defensive warfare, during which the Allies suffered reverses whilst slowly gathering the power necessary to push back the enemy. The year's end saw the armies of the Axis checked at the points of their utmost expansion. The volcanic outburst of Axis power cooled at the edges as it flowed. The furthest points of its flow were reached by the autumn of 1942, with the German army at Stalingrad, Japan in occupation of much of New Guinea and part of the Aleutians, and Rommel in Egypt. In August the Americans landed in Guadalcanal; by September, as the Prime Minister told the President on the 17th, the British night-bomber offensive was having a disastrous effect on Germany. On 23rd October began the advance from El Alamein that was to push the Germans back on the long road to Tunis. On 8th November British and American armies landed in North Africa. On 17th November the President spoke guardedly of a 'turning point' in the war. By the end of the year there could no longer be much doubt that the tide was indeed turning in North Africa, on the Volga, and in the South-West Pacific.

The end of 1942 marked a favourable turn, no less definite, in the battle of production. British war production—two years older than American—reached its peak on many items in the autumn. By September 1942 all capital ships, aircraft carriers, cruisers and destroyers lost since Dunkirk had been replaced. In aircraft, British production long before this had reached parity with Germany.[3] The production of tanks, and of war-stores as a whole, was three times as high by the end of 1942 as at the beginning of 1941.[4] El Alamein was won by British Commonwealth forces using mostly British equipment, although American tanks, motorised equipment and aircraft played their part.[5]

---

[1] e.g. *The United States at War*, op. cit., pp. 103–33. The 1,000-page volume *Industrial Mobilization for War*, op. cit., devotes a dozen scattered pages to the Combined Boards. Gulick, op. cit., pp. 30–31. *Federal Records* of World War II (National Archives, Washington: 1950–51), two volumes. S. McKee Rosen, *The Combined Boards of the Second World War* (Columbia University Press: 1951).

[2] Stimson and Bundy, op. cit., p. 394.

[3] After the war it became clear from German documents that British production in operational types of aircraft reached parity with Germany in June 1940. Overall production of all types had caught up with German production in September 1939.

[4] See *Statistical Digest of the War*, op. cit., Table 117, and M. M. Postan, *British War Production*, op. cit., Tables 21 and 47.

[5] President's Press Conference, *The New York Times*, 7th November 1942.

On the American side, the War Administration had almost reached its final shape by the end of the year. By that time the conversion of civilian industry—the source of the greater part of the war production—was finished. The restriction of civilian supplies was shown in rising prices and the beginning of rationing. War production was now rising very fast towards the peak of $6 billion a month, which it was to reach in the last two months of 1943—a year earlier than if it had followed the British rate of expansion which had been restricted initially by the limitations of peace-time conditions. In December 1941 only about fifteen per cent. of the national industry of the United States was devoted to war production. By December 1942 the percentage was up to thirty-three. By June 1942 the United States output of finished weapons was greater in bulk than that of the United Kingdom, although in proportion to population it was still only about a third of that of Britain. In the last months of 1942 and the first months of 1943 the rising tide of production on both sides of the Atlantic was illustrated by the volume of exports of war supplies to Russia. But even in the year ending in October 1942 British and American supplies to Russia by the northern route alone reached very high figures—3,052 aircraft, 4,084 tanks, 30,031 motor vehicles, 831,000 deadweight tons of miscellaneous cargo, and over 100,000 tons of aviation spirit and fuel oil.

This was the key year also from the point of view of the building of the machinery of the British-American Combination. That machinery was set up in two stages in January and June 1942. By the end of the year each of the combined bodies had taken its final shape, had learned its business, and was playing its full part in the smooth working of the Combination.

The United States had greater inherent difficulties than the United Kingdom in gearing their economy to war. The difficulties arose in part from their continental size, their diversity, and the structure of government, based as it is on federalism and the division of powers. All this does not prevent intense national unity in time of grave crisis, but it does make it more important, if confusion is to be avoided, that the national forces should be directed from the outset towards clearly defined objectives. Some confusion there was bound to be because of the speed and magnitude of the conversion to a war economy. As the official accounts show very clearly, the confusion of 1942 was due to two main factors: the absence of clear-cut military and industrial programmes, and competition between agencies. If the intensity of the competition of men and institutions impressed British officials, schooled in the more orderly system of Whitehall, they were even more impressed by the speed with which munitions flowed from American production despite, or perhaps because of, the turmoil.

(ii)

The Setting Up of the Combined Machinery

The Arcadia Conference set the pattern for the series of great war conferences in which the Prime Minister and the President (and at Teheran and Yalta Generalissimo Stalin) conferred and shaped the strategy of the war.

The Prime Minister arrived in Washington on 22nd December 1941, accompanied by the British Chiefs of Staff, the Minister of Supply and supply officers. His discussions with the President in the White House occupied fourteen days, leaving just over a week for journeys to Ottawa (29th December to 1st January) and Florida (5th to 11th January). He left the White House on the night of 14th January. In this period there were eight main meetings of the Prime Minister, the President and their Chiefs of Staff; and the Combined Staffs met separately in twelve meetings. Parallel meetings took place between Cabinet Officers and high officials concerned with war production and supply. The main results were: (1) the setting up of the combined machinery composed of the Combined Chiefs of Staff and the Combined Boards; (2) decisions on the grand strategy of the war and the immediate problem of a commander-in-chief of the Allied forces resisting the Japanese advance in South-East Asia; (3) decisions on the production targets which the United States were to set for themselves in 1942 and 1943; (4) decisions on the immediate problem of the volume of American supplies for Great Britain which the Prime Minister had warned the House of Commons on the eve of his departure was likely to be reduced. Some reference to each of these four topics will be made but in the reverse order.

On (4) Mr. Churchill wrote in *The Grand Alliance*, 'Evidently the partition of supplies would require profound attention. . . .'[1] The immediate result of Pearl Harbour had been the freezing at the ports of all lend-lease supplies. The White House on 8th December issued a statement that lend-lease would continue in full operation. But the British Supply Council and the heads of the Joint Staff Mission, at a meeting that day in Washington, showed their preoccupation with the possibility of a wholesale diversion of supplies from the Atlantic to the Pacific sectors of the war. The Prime Minister reflected on this danger in his journey across the Atlantic—'all our future plans depended upon a vast flow of American supplies of all kinds such as were now streaming across the Atlantic. Especially we counted on planes and tanks, as well as on the stupendous American merchant-

---

[1] Churchill, *The Grand Alliance*, op. cit., p. 569.

ship construction'.[1] These fears vanished with the complete 'accord on all points affecting general strategy' reached at the first conference with the President on 23rd December.

The British Supply Council had foreseen that the entry of the United States into the war necessitated an immediate revision of British and Allied requirements in the United States. The third Lend-Lease Appropriation was expected in January, and requests for British figures had been received from several United States departments. The document covering commitments for 1942 was ready when the Prime Minister arrived on 22nd December. The total British and Allied requirements from the United States were put at $24·6 billion, a figure more than double the $9 billion contemplated by the United States Administration. The largest elements were $10·6 billion for aircraft, $7·6 billion for munitions, and. $4·2 billion for naval supplies. Air and naval supplies required to carry out British responsibilities under the Victory Programme were included, e.g. for the Navy, *inter alia*, fifty destroyers, twenty-two submarines and 470 convoy escort vessels. For the Royal Air Force, requirements to mid-July 1943 were set at 5,186 heavy bombers. Not included in this figure were commitments already made on British and lend-lease account for aircraft from the United States totalling 3,270 machines.

THE PRESIDENT'S PRODUCTION TARGETS

This lend-lease programme had only a minor influence on the immense targets set for American war production by the President in the message to Congress on 6th January. A more important influence was the comparative statement of British and American war production prepared by Monnet for the Supply Council, and used by him and Lord Beaverbrook in discussions during the Conference with the President, Harry Hopkins and the Service and supply staffs. The figures which the President's departmental advisers set before him on 26th December aimed at lower targets. They were contained in a paper submitted by Secretary Stimson on Anglo-American-Canadian war production 'based on the third revision of the Anglo-American Consolidated Statement'. American war production capacity in 1942 was estimated at $40 billion—$27 billion already earmarked for war contracts and $13 billion for new contracts to be placed immediately. A third of the total was to be for aircraft.

The general character of the estimates (which covered Army, Air Force and Navy supplies) is shown by the following typical figures. It was estimated that from stocks and new production the United States, Great Britain and Canada would have at the end of 1942

---

[1] Ibid., p. 569.

'striking forces' (front line backed by reserves) as follows: *Combat aircraft:* heavy and medium bombers, 3,700; light and dive bombers, 3,500; fighters, 5,300. *Tanks:* with some 5,000 medium tanks on hand in January, and 21,000 added during the year, the striking force by December 1942 was estimated at 400 heavy, 5,500 medium and 1,450 light. *Anti-tank guns:* with new production and stocks the striking force would be increased in 1942 from 1,600 to 6,100. *Anti-aircraft guns:* (over 20-mm) initial stocks (some 4,000 heavy and 4,500 light guns) would be increased to 7,200 heavy and 14,100 light guns by the end of the year.

In a letter to the President on 27th December, and in a series of later meetings on supply, presided over by the President or the Vice-President, Lord Beaverbrook pressed the case for bringing American production up to the levels of Great Britain and Canada. He took as basis Monnet's document of 10th December. Its conclusion was that 'United States production schedules at present indicated in 1942 should be capable of at least a fifty per cent. increase'. Lord Beaverbrook suggested that the United States should produce 45,000 tanks, 17,700 anti-tank guns, 24,000 fighter planes, as well as double their output of anti-aircraft guns. At a meeting on the 29th with United States production chiefs, Mr. Donald Nelson, who was present, records that the Minister of Supply emphasised 'over and over again the fact that we should set our sights higher in planning for production of the necessary war *matériel*'.[1] Lord Beaverbrook had discussed the air programme with General Arnold and Mr. Lovett on the 27th. He presented the case made out on the British side (in a note by the head of the British Air Commission) for an 'immense step up' in the scope of the joint air programme. If America built aircraft on the British scale, the note argued, this would mean an output of combat aircraft of 6,300 a month. The heavy-bomber target should be raised from 1,000 a month at the end of 1944 to 2,300 a month at the end of 1943. Both these targets were accepted by Hopkins in a talk with the head of the British Air Commission on New Year's Day. The President was convinced and issued the necessary directions to the Departments.[2] The Prime Minister cabled the figures to London on 4th January with the comment 'Max has been magnificent and Hopkins a godsend'.[3] In *The Grand Alliance*, writing of the President's production goals seven years later, he could record the verdict of history: 'These remarkable figures were achieved or surpassed by the end of 1943.' They were reached or passed for air-

---

[1] Letter of Lord Beaverbrook to the President, 27th December. *Industrial Mobilization for War*, op. cit., pp. 277–78. Churchill, *The Grand Alliance*, op. cit., pp. 610–12.

[2] *Minutes of the Council of the Office of Production Management* (War Production Board, Washington: 1946), p. 87.

[3] Churchill, *The Grand Alliance*, pp. 610–12.

craft, doubled for ships, doubled or trebled for some calibres of guns; if for tanks they were not reached, they could have been if it had been necessary.

The Combined Machinery. No less important than these far-reaching discussions on supply were the decisions of the Arcadia Conference on combined machinery. From these three weeks of intensive discussion there emerged the war-winning Anglo-American combination in its full maturity. Its character and objectives, its forms and mechanisms were alike decided here. Modifications and additions there might be later, but the central design remained unchanged throughout the war.

The Arcadia Conference gave for the first time precision to the word 'combined' by reserving it for the machinery and action of the British-American partnership.[1] The word 'joint' was left to describe purely national machinery, such as the United States Joint Chiefs of Staff. It was on the military side, both at and before the Conference, that the concept and the use of the word 'combined' emerged most clearly; though its free use on the civilian side is referred to above.

It was its use on the military side in the titles of the organ of the British and American Chiefs of Staff and of their Board for the assignment of munitions that determined its use for all the Combined Boards. The word was adopted on both sides of the Atlantic because it had been in free use for some time in military as well as civilian circles. Examples of its use on the American side on the eve of the Victory Conference discussion in London occur in a document of 11th September 1941, signed by General Marshall and Admiral Stark, which Mr. Sherwood refers to as 'one of the most remarkable documents in American history'. It was not of course an isolated document, and its antecedents go back at least to the Staff talks in February 1941. It was remarkable for several reasons. The most noteworthy was its forecast of the United States strategy to be pursued in the years that followed, with its emphasis on the concentration of the 'combined' forces on Germany as the prime enemy. Others were its references to the 'British Commonwealth' and its acceptance as amongst the 'major national objectives' of the United States of the 'prevention of the disruption of the British Empire'.[2]

Point one of the agenda for the Arcadia Conference was the 'fundamental basis of joint strategy'. A British outline statement was prepared on the outward voyage setting forth the strategic objectives and

---

[1] In current usage 'British' frequently included British Commonwealth countries, especially Canada which had a special relation to the Boards and was a member of two of them. The word 'combined' was not used in a wider 'Allied' context. Thus it does not appear in the declaration of the United Nations, issued on 1st January 1942. See above, p. 299.

[2] Sherwood, op. cit., p. 410 ff. The word 'combined' was in frequent use on the British side at this time: e.g. the phrase 'combined war strategy' used a month before Pearl Harbour in a note by Mr. Harold Balfour. Ibid., p. 420.

in broad terms the steps to be taken towards their achievement. Japan, according to this document, was to be held with the necessary minimum forces whilst Germany was defeated by all possible lines of attack—by the maximum production of munitions, by bombing with an unprecedented weight of explosives, by blockade, and by a continental invasion when the time was ripe. The British fear that recent events might have upset the agreement to regard Germany as the 'prime enemy' was not wholly without foundation. Views on the American side were still fluid. Thus Mr. Stimson, in a memorandum of 20th December discussing the possible theatres of American action in the near future, gave priority first to the South-West Pacific; second to West Africa, not as the base for a Mediterranean offensive but as protection for the sea routes to the East; third to Persia as the safest route for supplies to Russia; the Egypt-Libya theatre he regarded as of minor importance, except to British morale. However, the principle of 'Germany first' was supported by President Roosevelt and General Marshall and accepted without opposition. Not only was agreement reached on the broad lines of the British grand strategy document, but a number of practical decisions were soon taken to implement it. American bomber squadrons were to be established in England at the first possible moment. American ground forces were to relieve British forces in Iceland and Northern Ireland. There was to be a joint expedition to occupy French West and North Africa—Operation Super-Gymnast, which was eventually launched at the end of 1942 as Operation Torch.

The outlines of grand strategy having been thus determined, the next step was the devising of inter-Allied machinery to give it effect. Here the central issue, affecting both strategy and supply, was that of a combined higher direction of the war, narrowed down for the sake of speed and efficiency to Britain and America, as against a system of wider and more representative bodies, including the Soviet Union, China, the Dominions and the other Allies. The State Department, as Mr. Cordell Hull has indicated, favoured the latter policy; there was talk of a Supreme War Council to be responsible for both the political and military direction of the war. This was on the model of the last war. Britain and France had set up such an instrument in 1939, and the idea had been approved in principle by the British and American Staffs at their talks in February 1941.[1] The scheme, however, was not now looked on with favour in London. While the Prime Minister was at sea, the War Cabinet was warned from Washington of what was afoot, and at once cabled to him advising against the setting up of any formal co-ordinating body. The smaller belligerents could not well be excluded from such a body,

---

[1] Cordell Hull, Vol. II, op. cit., p. 1,124. See above, Chapter VIII.

but if they were included the necessary swiftness of decision would be lost. The War Cabinet therefore preferred a development along the lines of the existing methods of informal collaboration between the two main powers that had been followed so far in planning joint strategy, preparing the Victory Programme, apportioning munitions and arranging for their shipment. The Prime Minister expressed similar views in telegrams before and after his arrival. The substance of British-American leadership, he said, should not be sacrificed for some theoretical means of securing Allied unity. He saw several possible means of securing such unity at a later stage in the joint discussions. One was to bring Russia and China into conference. Another possibility was to confer with the five powers especially interested in the Pacific, and a third was to bring the smaller Allies into a discussion of 'uncontroversial topics', on the lines of the meetings held at St. James's Palace earlier in the year with the European Governments in exile.

Here again the British found a greater measure of agreement with their views in Washington than they had expected. The thinking of the American Joint Chiefs of Staff had arrived no less definitely than that of their British counterparts at the concept of Anglo-American combination as the means of directing the war both on the side of strategy and supply. Both disliked the apparent trend towards a multi-national superior authority. And the President himself took the same view. One reason was that Russia was not at war with Japan—nor China at war with Germany. But the real reason was the conviction that 'only Britain and the United States could really co-operate in . . . global strategy, and, most importantly, in determining the allocation of combined resources'.[1] Hence the President and the Prime Minister were able to agree at their first meeting that it was 'important to bring all (the Allies) in, but not to establish any permanent body that would limit the action or the capacity to take prompt decisions of the United States and Great Britain and Russia'.[2] The Prime Minister met at once on 23rd December with the representatives of the Dominions to indicate the nature of his discussions with the President on this and other matters. The President, he told them, was in favour of a meeting of the Pacific Powers, but they had both agreed that in the general interest the permanent body directly concerned with strategy and supply should be kept as small as possible. The British Chiefs of Staff would consult with Service representatives of the Dominions in Washington.

Here were the germs of two important developments which facili-

---

[1] Sherwood, op. cit., p. 467.

[2] The partnership here appears as a triumvirate. But Moscow was remote, geographically and otherwise; in practice the Russian front remained a separate war, and it was only in the Atlantic and Pacific theatres that real unity of direction was achieved.

tated the setting up of the combined war machinery: one was the ranging of the free nations of the world behind the Great Powers in a Grand Alliance. Hence the Declaration of the United Nations signed by twenty-six Powers on 1st January 1942. The other was the setting up of the two Pacific War Councils early in 1942, the first in London and the second in Washington. The two Councils flowered briefly in 1942 and then faded away. The United Nations, first launched as a symbol but soon to acquire a corporate entity, made the combined British-American machinery more palatable to American public opinion. It parried the traditional American distrust of exclusive alliances, particularly an alliance with the United Kingdom.

The main business of the latter part of the Arcadia Conference was to equip the British-American combination with permanent instructions. On the day after sailing in the *Duke of York* the British Chiefs of Staff had discussed the need for combined machinery; first to determine and direct strategy, but also to deal with vital problems involving manpower and war production. But their ideas, like those of their American colleagues, were somewhat nebulous at this stage. Both sides disliked any talk of 'special machinery' which might imply the setting up of formal inter-Allied bodies, and the general thesis was that use should be made of 'existing machinery', i.e. of the machinery of informal consultation which had been built up since the Staff talks of the previous February. It soon became apparent, however, that something more definite was needed. As might be expected in a so purely Anglo-Saxon affair, the development of the combined institutions came about as the result of practical experience rather than of preconceived schemes. The development of combination on the supply side has been dealt with above. On the military side the same kind of thing had been happening. One of the first actions of the British and American Chiefs of Staff when they met in Washington was to set up a joint planning committee, primarily to assist them in the immediate task of assigning priorities to the various operations projected in the Atlantic theatre in 1942. This body functioned so well that its continuance in some form after the Conference became obviously desirable. A more important factor, however, was the decision to establish unity of command in the South-West Pacific. For this led on to the combining of the British and American Chiefs of Staff and that in turn led to the Combined Boards on the supply side.

The command arrangements made for the control of the Far Eastern theatre led by a natural transition to the idea of a permanent joint body to direct the general strategy of the war as a whole. The earlier proposals for this theatre were criticised in London by the Acting Chiefs of Staff on the ground that no corresponding body was being set up for the German war and, further, that there was still no sign of 'an overriding authority for world strategy and for the allocation of men and material'. In fact, events were moving rapidly towards the creation of just such an authority, a 'joint strategy board', in the phrase used in many of the Washington documents in the last half of December. By 31st December the ideas of the British military leaders had crystallised further. They now envisaged the combined machinery as consisting of parallel joint bodies in both capitals on the following lines:

(1) A permanent joint planning organisation (comprising all the Services) to deal with strategy.
(2) A Joint Supply Board, to deal with production, the allocation of raw materials and similar questions.
(3) Joint Committees to allocate naval, military and air weapons.
(4) A Joint Shipping Committee.
(5) Other possible joint bodies, to deal with, e.g., economic warfare.

This was a close forecast of the four bodies agreed upon on 14th January:

(1) The Combined Chiefs of Staff.
(2) The Combined Raw Materials Board.
(3) The Combined Munitions Assignments Board.
(4) The Combined Shipping Adjustment Board.

The one respect in which this British plan was not followed (the idea of British and American Ministers of State to co-ordinate their respective teams) is referred to in a later study.[1]

American thinking at least on the mechanics of military collaboration was moving in the same direction. On 29th December the President drafted a text providing for a 'special body' of 'three American, three British to which there would be attached three persons for "consultation and advisory purposes", an Australian, a Dutchman and a New Zealander'. Hopkins noted next day that the talks on 'an appropriate joint body' were pointing towards a decision to have 'the Joint British and American Staffs assist the President'.[2]

Thus by the beginning of January the 'joint strategy board' had begun to take shape as the Combined Chiefs of Staff, though the final shape and the name were not given until the last meetings of the President and the Prime Minister between 12th and 14th January. The change of name was more than formal, since, partly through the insistence of General Marshall, the new body was not a joint secretariat limited to liaison and the pooling of information. It became the

---

[1] See *Studies of Overseas Supply*, Chapter VI.
[2] Sherwood, op. cit., p. 467.

organ charged with the taking of decisions on strategy, subject only to the final say of the President and the Prime Minister.

Both during and for some time after the Conference there remained some uncertainty as to the exact composition of the Combined Chiefs of Staff. The American view was that it consisted of the United States Joint Chiefs together with the representatives of the British Chiefs in Washington—i.e. the heads of the Joint Staff Mission (at that time Admiral Sir Charles Little, Lt.-Gen. Sir Colville Wemyss and Air Marshal Harris). The British on the contrary held that, while these might constitute the day-to-day working authority, the Combined Chiefs of Staff properly speaking were the American Chiefs in Washington plus the British Chiefs in London, and this indeed was what happened when the Combined Staffs met in the Great War Conferences. Some in London felt misgivings about the trend of war controls westwards—away from the Commonwealth, with its world-wide responsibilities, its seniority in belligerence, and its long experience of co-operation between independent states. The British War Cabinet believed that for practical reasons the controls over shipping, food, oil and raw materials should be centred in London. The planning of production would in due course have to be centred in Washington, but nothing should be done to disturb British production just as it was getting into full swing: 'the movement of the centre of gravity across the Atlantic is no doubt inevitable, but it should be gradual'. Nor did the War Cabinet wish to be committed at this stage to the assignment of finished munitions in Washington. The ideal of the British Chiefs of Staff was rather the creation of parallel controlling organisations in both capitals, with full-scale American representation in London to match the British missions in Washington.

In fact, however, the centre of gravity was moving rapidly westward. A step in this direction was taken at the beginning of January, when the Prime Minister decided that Field-Marshal Sir John Dill should remain in Washington as his personal representative: first, for liaison with the President; second, to provide a direct link with the United States Joint Chiefs of Staff; third, for liaison with the heads of the British civil missions. The Combined Chiefs of Staff was thus to be built round the private friendship of Sir John Dill and General Marshall; and this gave it an inner strength which no mere committee could possess. Such personal bonds were of the essence of the combination. They came into existence at the highest level when the Prime Minister and the President, after long correspondence, met at the Atlantic Conference, kindled to each other and formed a friendship which cemented an unbreakable partnership. Correspondence there was, and several meetings, with the heads of other Governments —Stalin and Chiang Kai-Shek. But nowhere else was there this personal intimacy, this deep mutual trust and confidence, this degree of sharing of secrets, this daily routine of working together in collaboration. The carrying right down the line of some part of this pattern, and its reproduction in full at a number of points, gave a unique strength and resilience to the British-American combination. In reporting to the War Cabinet on the setting up of the combined machinery, the Prime Minister (quoting Napoleon's maxim, 'A constitution should always be short and obscure') emphasised that it should be judged less by its formal structure than by the personalities behind it. In the same spirit the President had said that he did not much mind what went down on paper, since he, Churchill, Hopkins and Beaverbrook would be able to compose any difficulties that might arise.

The outline of the Combined Chiefs of Staff structure was soon filled in with a number of subsidiary institutions—the combined Secretariat,[1] the Combined Staff Planners, the Combined Military Transportation Committee and several others. The most important for our purposes, however, was the authority set up to deal with the assignment of munitions. Up to this point American munitions had not been regarded as pooled. Lend-lease was not a system of allocation.[2] Only for aircraft was there any sort of joint allocation, through the Joint Aircraft Committee. In the new situation the British urged strongly that finished weapons should be assigned according to strategic needs, that they should be allotted to whichever forces could make the best use of them at the time irrespective of their country of origin, method of procurement or any other consideration. The Americans were in entire agreement with this thesis, and the two Staffs drafted a minute to the Prime Minister and the President on 13th January in the following terms: 'We, the Combined Chiefs of Staff, agree in principle that finished war equipment shall be allocated according to strategic needs.' The result was a formal agreement on the highest level to the effect that 'the entire munitions resources of Great Britain and the United States shall be deemed to be a common pool'. Hopkins had proposed a two-man body to allocate munitions. This was the model used for the other Combined Boards, but in this case the British Chiefs of Staff, while prepared to have Hopkins and Dill as a court of appeal, insisted that the principle of strategic assignment could be implemented only by a body in which the two

---

[1] The secretariat system of the British Chiefs of Staff was adopted for the Combined Chiefs. The United States Joint Chiefs set up a similar system for their own secretariat needs.

[2] If munitions were pooled and there was an Assignments Board, what need was there of any separate lend-lease appropriations and a Lend-Lease Administration? It was argued on the British side that only United States departmental appropriations were needed and that the American Service Departments would defend British requirements —as they already did in part—before Congress. This view—which Monnet supported— did not prevail, and it was not put forward officially to the United States.

Staffs sat together. Hence the Combined Munitions Assignments Board was a multi-member agency composed of the three Service representatives of each Government with a civilian chairman to mediate between conflicting Service and national interests. The problem of a chairman was difficult: 'the only individual upon whom all elements could agree as bearer of the final responsible authority was Harry Hopkins'.[1]

Still more difficult was the problem of assignment to third countries. The British proposal was that the Munitions Assignments Board in Washington should make bulk assignments of American-produced munitions to the United States and Great Britain, while a corresponding body in London should make a similar division of British production. From the bulk allotments then received Britain and the United States would each make sub-allotments to the countries in its own sphere of influence: Britain to the Dominions and Colonies, the European Allies, Egypt and Turkey; the United States to China and Latin America. Supplies to Russia were in a special category, being governed by the joint Protocol.

Support for this scheme appeared to be forthcoming from the President, who at the end of the Conference proposed two separate Combined Munitions Assignments Boards, both independent of the Combined Chiefs of Staff, one in Washington with Hopkins as chairman and one in London under Lord Beaverbrook. General Marshall insisted successfully that this meant duplicating in London the Combined Chiefs of Staff, and that of this there could be no question. With the strong support of Hopkins, who consistently opposed the group system of assignment, he carried his point that the Combined Munitions Board must be under the Combined Chiefs of Staff in Washington. At the last meeting the President, in announcing the setting up of the Combined Boards, referred to the Munitions Board as a sub-committee of the Combined Chiefs of Staff whose representatives were its members and which could reject or revise its recommendations. The London Assignments Board was less important than the main Board in Washington. It was the latter which had to handle the biggest surplus of munitions, which all the United Nations, including Britain, needed. The sub-allocations made in London were subject, in theory, to revision by the main Board. Neither the Prime Minister nor Lord Beaverbrook looked with favour on the scheme for this Board, and agreed to it only as a provisional arrangement to be tried out for a month. 'C'est le provisoire qui dure', and the Combined Munitions Assignments Boards—the Board in Washington headed by Mr. Harry Hopkins and the Board in London headed by Mr. Oliver Lyttelton—lasted till the end of the war.

---

[1] Sherwood, op. cit., p. 470.

The remainder of the combined machinery was constructed very rapidly in the last few days of the Conference. The joint control of shipping resources, which had already emerged as the chief limiting factor on operations in 1942, was discussed by the Prime Minister and Hopkins on 12th January and by the Combined Chiefs of Staff on the following day. The arrangements made here were little more than a formalisation of the close contact already existing between Sir Arthur Salter and Admiral Land of the Maritime Commission. The chief difficulty was that the United States Government did not yet have the same strict control over shipping as was wielded by the British Ministry of War Transport. Executive power was left with the Ministry and the Maritime Commission. The function of the Combined Shipping Adjustment Board now set up in Washington was 'to adjust and concert in one harmonious policy' the work of the two controlling agencies. On the production side the structure was not yet complete. On 27th December Lord Beaverbrook had suggested that Hopkins should take charge of a 'committee of pro- duction'.[1] This was a formidable body designed to 'co-ordinate production between the United States, Great Britain and Canada, to mobilise and distribute raw materials and to dispose of the pro- duction requirements'. A similar body, as we have seen, formed part of the thinking of the British Chiefs of Staff. As yet, however, there did not exist the national machinery which would provide its basis. The 'Combined Production and Resources Board' had to wait until June 1942, when the War Production Board and the Ministry of Production had come into being. In one sector of the production field, however, co-ordination was already possible. A Combined Raw Materials Board, consisting of Mr. W. L. Batt, of the Office of Production Management, and Sir Clive Baillieu, who had just been appointed head of the newly-formed British Raw Materials Mission, was established to secure the 'speedy and efficient utilisation of raw material resources'. On the evening of 14th January the Prime Minister and the President reached formal agreement[2] on the setting up of the combined machinery for munitions assignments, raw materials and shipping. This concluded the Conference. Mr. Churchill flew home to report his high satisfaction with the evidence he had seen of the vigour with which the Americans were setting about the war, with the harmony established in general and with the Combined Boards in particular.

---

[1] Ibid., p. 470.

[2] *Co-ordination of the Allied War Effort, Agreements between The Prime Minister and The President of the United States of America*, Cmd. 6332, January 1942. See text in Appendix IV.

(iii)

The Combined Boards and the Combined Staffs

The Combined Chiefs of Staff and the development of war strategy belong to the military histories. Strategy, however, in the long run determined the general course of supply; and a brief reference must be made here to the Combined Chiefs of Staff and the strategic background of the Combined Boards. For the only serious impediment to the work of the Combined Boards in 1942 was the lack of guidance on basic strategy, and in the case of the civilian Boards the absence of full liaison with the Combined Chiefs.

In the midst of the Arcadia Conference, on 3rd January 1942, the secretary of the British Chiefs of Staff Committee reported that co-operation with the Americans was developing unexpectedly well and was very promising for the future. On the same day the Prime Minister cabled his colleagues in London: 'We live here as a big family in the greatest intimacy and informality. . . .' He referred to his very high regard and admiration for the President. 'His breadth of view, resolution and his loyalty to the common cause are beyond all praise. . . .' These messages recorded high hopes and gave clues to their realisation. One was the character and ability of the two leaders to work together and the family atmosphere in which British-American relations could be conducted. Mr. Stimson in his memoirs added a further explanation of the successful working of the machinery of combination at the highest levels. This was 'the organising genius and diplomatic skill of George Marshall', and the work of Sir John Dill, 'an equally disinterested and farsighted soldier-statesman'.[1] Mr. Stimson and Mr. Sherwood both emphasised the importance in the working of the Combined Chiefs of Staff of what Mr. Churchill referred to as the 'true comradeship and private friendship' between the two soldier-statesmen.[2] In Mr. Stimson's judgement it was their harmonious combination which made it possible for the Combined Chiefs of Staff to act 'not as a mere collecting point for the inevitable rivalries between services and

---

[1] Stimson and Bundy, op. cit., pp. 413–14. On the working of the combined machinery see *General Marshall's Report*, The Winning of the War in Europe and the Pacific (Biennial Report of the Chief of Staff of the United States Army, July 1 1943 to June 30 1945, to the Secretary of War) (New York: Simon & Schuster).

[2] Sherwood, op. cit., p. 358. Mr. Sherwood saw the beginning of this friendship at the Atlantic Conference in August 1941 as the only development of lasting importance to come from that conference.

nations but as an executive committee for the prosecution of a global war'. Mr. Churchill refers to the 200 formal meetings held by the Combined Chiefs of Staff during the war (eighty-nine of them at the conferences at Casablanca, Washington, Quebec, Teheran, Cairo, Malta and the Crimea). 'There was never a failure to reach effective agreement for action, or to send clear instructions to the commanders in every theatre . . . there never was a more serviceable war machinery established among allies. . . .'[1] In the words of General Marshall, the combined machinery produced

> the most complete unification of military effort ever achieved by two Allied nations.[2]

The Combined Chiefs of Staff was composed of the United States Joint Chiefs of Staff and the representatives in Washington of the British Chiefs of Staff. Each of the three Services on both sides were represented by a member, the British members being drawn from the Joint Staff Mission. The two national Staff organisations retained their separate identity and were not fused. They were only fully combined when they met in the Great War Conferences. The organisation at Washington shared a common office and worked through a combined Secretariat—each side of which kept its own records—and combined committees. Meetings of the Combined Chiefs of Staff were held weekly. It had its own small combined planning staff, but the main planning organisations on both sides remained national. Papers prepared in London or Washington were subjected to combined examination and decision. Thus complete continuity of thought and action was maintained.[3]

The wide authority of the Combined Chiefs of Staff and the

---

[1] Churchill, *The Grand Alliance*, op. cit., pp. 608–09. See p. 610 for the Prime Minister's tribute to the unique position held by Sir John Dill. That position had already been established by the end of February and the Ambassador reported to the Prime Minister on 1st March that Dill wielded an influence which 'no one else could'.

[2] *General Marshall's Report*, op. cit., p. 8.

[3] Responsible to the Combined Chiefs of Staff and forming part of its organisation in Washington were a number of combined committees, in addition to the Combined Munitions Assignments Board which ranked as a sub-committee of the Combined Chiefs. These were: the Combined Staff Planners, Washington; the Combined Military Transportation Committee, Washington; the Combined Communications Board, Washington; the Combined Intelligence Committee, Washington; the Combined Meteorological Committee, Washington (which also had representatives from Australia, New Zealand, South Africa and Canada); the Combined Administrative Committee, Washington; the Combined Civil Affairs Committee, Washington. There were also: the London Political Warfare Co-ordinating Committee; the Oil Rehabilitation Sub-Committee, London; and the Technical Sub-Committee for the Rehabilitation of Petroleum Resources, Washington. A British and an American representative of the Combined Shipping Adjustment Board were associate members of the Combined Military Transportation Committee. On the Combined Communications Board there were—in addition to American and British representatives—one representative from each of the Dominions of Canada and New Zealand and the Commonwealth of Australia.

central position of this body in relation to the Combined Boards are indicated by its terms of reference:

> Under the direction of the heads of the United Nations, the Combined Chiefs of Staff will collaborate in the formulation of policy and execution of policies and plans concerning:
>
> (a) The strategic conduct of the war.
> (b) The broad programme of war requirements based on approved strategic policy.
> (c) The allocation of munition resources based on strategic needs and the availability of means of transportation.
> (d) The requirements for overseas transportation for fighting services of United Nations based on approved strategic priority.
>
> In discharging the above responsibilities, the Combined Chiefs of Staff will constitute the agency for developing and submitting recommendations for decision by the President of the United States and by the British Prime Minister and Minister of Defence, on behalf of their Governments. In effecting the collaboration incident to their responsibilities, the Combined Chiefs of Staff will make use of appropriate combined or other bodies in Washington, London, and elsewhere, in order to avoid so far as practicable duplication of agencies.

As these terms of reference show the Combined Chiefs of Staff were to make use of 'combined or other bodies' and to prevent overlapping. The United States War Department's statement announcing the setting up of the Combined Chiefs of Staff (6th February 1942) spoke of it as 'a combined command post for the conduct of all joint operations of the two Governments in the war' and 'the control agency for planning and co-ordinating'. It was to ensure complete co-ordination of the war effort of the two countries '. . . including the production and distribution of war supplies'. In a general sense the Combined Boards were subordinate to the Combined Chiefs of Staff.[1] Thus in the case of the Combined Raw Materials Board the Ambassador agreed with the view expressed at the first meeting of the Pacific War Council that the allocation of raw materials should be made on the strategical advice of the Combined Chiefs.

The Combined Munitions Assignments Board was in theory a 'sub-committee of the Combined Chiefs of Staff'. The agreement between the President and the Prime Minister, published on 26th January 1942, referred to both the London and Washington Assignments Boards as being formed 'under the Combined Chiefs of Staff'. The principle governing assignment was: current strategical need within the broad strategical plans laid down by the Combined Chiefs of Staff. The Board therefore looked constantly to the Combined Planners for strategical guidance.

---

[1] The Combined Shipping Adjustment Board, however, had specific authority to refer direct to the Prime Minister and the President.

But apart from the Combined Munitions Assignments Board the Boards in practice had little direct contact with the Combined Chiefs of Staff. The 'co-ordination of production of war supplies' which the latter was supposed to exercise was only a remote control. The strategy of production is a much longer-term affair than assignment. Yet the Combined Production and Resources Board, as is indicated below, found itself unable to carry out its terms of reference, since the Combined Chiefs of Staff were not in fact prepared to enter into discussions on strategy with a civilian body. The Combined Production and Resources Board was unable therefore to secure the necessary strategical guidance to enable it to lay down the general priorities for production of war supplies.

Throughout the account that follows it has to be remembered that Combination was no mere matter of machinery. It was an all-pervading purpose which swept aside minor obstacles and minimised difficulties of organisation. Its vast extension was summed up by General Marshall in his Biennial Report at the end of the war:

> Strategic direction of all the forces of both nations, the allocation of manpower and munitions, the co-ordination of communications, the control of military intelligence, and the administration of captured areas all were accepted as joint responsibilities.[1]

PRODUCTION, ASSIGNMENT AND STRATEGY

Nevertheless neither on the side of production planning nor of assignment of current production was there adequate strategic guidance. The Combined Munitions Assignments Boards in Washington and London were formed, as the text of 26th January showed, to 'advise on all assignments both in quantity and priority . . . in accordance with strategic needs'. For the long view on strategic needs the assignors of war-stores required two sorts of guidance. The first was reasonably accurate estimates of production of the principal supplies month by month for a year or two ahead. These estimates were available in the Consolidated Statement of British, American and Canadian Production which became increasingly accurate as time went on. The second kind of guidance was strategic, long-term forecasts of when, where and how the armed forces were to be used. For this, however, the Assignments Boards, for at least the first third of their existence, waited in vain. Moreover without this strategic guidance there could be no proper combination in production. The figures in the Consolidated Statement might show what each side planned to produce but only a combined strategy could show what ought to be produced. Thus as later events were to show the Statement indicated many more tanks than would be needed and far too few landing craft.

---

[1] *General Marshall's Report*, op. cit., p. 8.

The Arcadia Conference merely agreed on combined strategy on the most general lines. It gave priority of defeat to the greater over the lesser enemy; but it did not attempt to answer the questions: When, Where and How? It gave merely a general compass direction leaving the routes to the goal still unmapped and the times uncalculated. Whilst the Allies were building up their power in the still mainly defensive war of 1942, long-term strategy was continuously under review in London and Washington. There was no serious disagreement on some of the main objectives set for the year; such as the steadily mounting bomber offensive against Germany in which American bombers would participate from bases in the United Kingdom, the maximum aid by way of supplies to Russia and China, and the holding at all cost of Australia, New Zealand and India. But there was considerable difficulty in coming to an agreement as to other offensive action in 1942, and on plans for the campaigns of 1943 and 1944.

There were some types of supply such as ships where it was clear, even without strategic guidance, that the amounts needed were virtually unlimited—although even here there were questions of relative urgency as between different types. Shipping remained for most of the period the greatest single limiting factor. A memorandum of 14th February, by the British head of the Combined Shipping Adjustment Board, drew the attention of the Combined Chiefs of Staff to the gravity of the shipping crisis. There was grave doubt until late in 1942 whether there would be enough ships for the full-scale landing in North Africa which was decided on in July but did not take place until November. Only the policy of cutting shipping to the bone made the landing possible in November. But it was even more important to save ships from being sunk than to build more; so that linked inseparably with shipping was the question of escort vessels. Still another limiting factor was the shortage of landing craft required in most theatres of the war for the battle of the beach-heads. Here a diversion may be permitted; since landing craft formed a good illustration of the relation between strategy, production and assignment.

In November 1941 the Prime Minister had drawn attention to the inadequacy of the Admiralty's landing-craft programme.[1] In the same month the United States had been asked to design (which they did with the help of a British group of consultants) and to produce a large landing ship capable of landing heavy equipment, including a number of heavy tanks, on enemy beaches. But the United States still had no large programme of construction of the several types of landing craft. Progress was retarded by many factors—such as the

---

[1] Churchill, *The Grand Alliance*, op. cit., p. 746.

absence of large orders, lack of experience in this type of construction, shortages of materials and low priorities. Merchant ships and escort vessels were regarded in the earlier months of 1942 as far more urgent than landing craft. The latter were not mentioned in the list of priorities drawn up by the President and Hopkins on 16th February, the day after the fall of Singapore.[1] In January 1942 landing craft were only eighth on the United States Navy's list of priorities; they slipped to the tenth place in March. The official history of the War Production Board stated that 'the Navy still did not consider the landing craft program as a very urgent one'. It was not until April that the first large construction programme was adopted in anticipation of North African and Pacific landings. In May the Prime Minister discussed landing craft at great length with Hopkins and General Marshall during their visit to London. By that time landing craft were becoming the most serious 'bottleneck' in all preparations for amphibious warfare.

Responsibility for the lag in production in the United States was due, according to the account of the War Production Board, not to any failure of industry or of the Board itself, but mainly to 'the failure of top officials responsible for strategic planning to anticipate the need for landing craft in the North African campaign sufficiently far in advance'.[2] Whatever the cause there was no doubt that the combined discussions in London in May 1942 brought to light, as General Marshall put it in his Biennial Report in 1945, a 'shortage which was to plague us to the final day of the war in Europe—the shortage of assault craft, L.S.T.s, L.C.I.s and smaller vessels'. This he described as 'the greatest by far' of all the problems.

By July 1942 landing craft were No. 1 on the United States Navy's list, with the highest priority for materials. The programme for 1942 called for 12,000 craft. Contracts of over a billion dollars were let to seventy-nine firms, many of them one or two thousand miles inland, and most without any previous experience of such construction. Neither the Navy nor the firms were experienced in the 'correct scheduling of procedures for the mass production of ships'.[3] As a result of these efforts and of British production there were enough landing craft for the North African landings. But the operation had to be delayed until the last-minute deliveries were made and landings were cancelled at several points where the Staffs had judged them to

---

[1] Sherwood, op. cit., p. 502.

[2] *Industrial Mobilization for War*, op. cit., pp. 46 and 535.

[3] *Landing Craft and the War Production Board*, April 1942 to May 1944, Historical Reports on War Administration: War Production Board, Special Study No. 11, Washington, 1944. The second programme, in preparation for the landings in Europe and the Pacific, began in August and September 1943; and peak deliveries were reached in May 1944. Many difficulties were created in 1942 by shortages of components, particularly diesel engines. In August the President gave instructions permitting landing craft to interfere, when necessary, with any other programme. See below, Chapter X, pp. 401–03.

be necessary.[1] Nevertheless the spurt of American production in the second half of 1942 had achieved remarkable results. Deliveries reached over 219,000 tons of landing craft, over twenty times more than in the first half of the year and twenty-seven times more than from July 1940 to the end of 1941.[2] By the time of the North African landing, production was high enough to permit a sharp drop to be made in the priority accorded to landing craft in the Navy's list. It was even possible to make a severe cut-back in the programme. By January 1943 landing craft, for the time being, had dropped out of the President's 'must' programme, which now listed only rubber, high octane fuel, aircraft, escort vessels and merchant shipping.

As this case illustrates, the lack of a clear-cut decision on future operations impeded but did not hold up production plans. It meant that assignments could only be made on a hand-to-mouth basis. Despite the absence of strategic decisions production went ahead because it was certain in any case that landing craft would be needed somewhere for objectives which the Staffs already had in mind, and in larger numbers than the combined industries could turn out in many months.

Up to July the decision of the Combined Staff Planners hung between a limited operation in France (Sledgehammer) and the invasion of North Africa (Gymnast). In March the latter was set aside for some months. The combined discussions in London and Washington, in which M. Molotov took part in May, pointed to the shortage of special landing craft as the barrier to any large-scale descent on the French coast in 1942.[3] Planning in May and June concentrated on the building up of American forces in the United Kingdom (Bolero) as a base for the main invasion of the continent in 1943 (Roundup). The fall of Tobruk in June led to some diversion of forces to Egypt. In the last week of July the President and the Prime Minister finally agreed to abandon 'Sledgehammer' and to concentrate on the invasion of North Africa (renamed Torch). This

---

[1] Ibid. Cited from *General Marshall's Report*, op. cit., p. 8.

[2] *Landing Craft and the War Production Board*, op. cit. *Wartime Production Achievements and the Reconversion Outlook* (Report by the Chairman of the War Production Board, Washington, 9th October 1945), p. 107, gives the following figures of United States production (for British figures see below, Chapter X, Section (i)):

	Thousands of tons displacement
1942	211*
1943	706*
1944	1,513
1945 (to 31st July) .	467

* Excluding L.S.T.s constructed by the Maritime Commission: 15 in 1942 and 60 in 1943.

[3] 'The main limiting factor', as a British *aide-mémoire* to M. Molotov indicated, 'is the availability of special landing craft.' For further reference to landing craft, see below, pp. 400–03.

was not to mean any slackening in the building up of American forces in Britain or the intensification of the air bombardment of Germany.

Thus it was not until the end of July 1942 that the Combined Munitions Assignments Board received some guidance on strategy, for which it had been asking since mid-February. But it was only a little guidance. It was not until the Casablanca Conference that there was enough agreement on the relative importance of the various theatres of war to serve as a basis for any longer-term assignments. In 1942 the basis was monthly assignment by countries. The British view, as put forward in March 1942, was that assignments should be on the basis of 'the provision of full equipment for existing units in available and active theatres of war'. Assignment on a country basis underlined the serious plight of the United States Army. General Marshall, in his role as Commander-in-Chief of the Army and Air Forces in the United States, was under severe pressure from all sides —from the Forces under his command, from Congress and from the general public. He indicated on 3rd March to the Combined Chiefs that out of thirty American divisions, formed for over a year, the majority still had only fifty per cent. of their equipment. Divisions in training had been deprived of arms to equip divisions going overseas. With the equipment in sight, he pointed out, the United States could only carry and maintain overseas in 1942 some fourteen divisions.

Already, in fact, the Ground Forces Sub-committee of the Assignments Board had been confronted with a statement that the United States War Department's policy now must be to suspend assignments to other countries until the immediate requirements of the American Army had been met. It was foreseen that a similar policy might be adopted for all war supplies, including aircraft. The British Heads of Missions therefore proposed that an 'Order of Battle' should be drawn up for all theatres, including the United States, to serve as a basis for assignment. The aim was to have a document which would forecast the situation in all the theatres in the immediate future and for the next six months. It would in effect show on strategic grounds the priorities between the different theatres. A separate paper on aircraft was asked for by the Heads of Missions; and from this point onwards the allocation of aircraft tended to be regarded as a separate question (see below p. 360 ff). On 19th March 1942 the question of strategic guidance for assignment formed the subject of an important meeting between the Munitions Assignments Board and the Combined Staff Planners. Hopkins as Chairman of the Board pressed for assignment on a military basis without consideration of political repercussions. But no solution was reached. There were serious differences of viewpoint between the American Services. 'The moment we start discussion of strategic aims', the British Staff Planners reported to the Joint Planners in London, 'we come up against fundamental differences of view between the United States Army, the Army Air Corps and the Navy.' There was a danger that the war might be conducted in watertight compartments unless an agreement on a strategic policy for 1942 could be reached. The United States Navy tended to regard the Pacific as its main theatre. This being purely an American theatre, it could operate without any of the entanglements of combination. The United States Army on the other hand tended to favour the European theatre. It could only employ its large army against Germany, which General Marshall steadily regarded as the prime enemy. The United States Air Force also favoured the concentration of its still limited fighting power in the United Kingdom for the offensive against Germany which was beginning to show results. The widespread dispersal of the air fleets in various theatres and the lag in the production of heavy bombers were viewed with some concern.

If the munitions assigners lacked guidance, the production planners were no better off. Their difficulty was shown by the fact that the Minister of Production on his Mission to Washington in November was not provided from London with a paper on strategy. This he needed for his talks on production plans for 1943. Sir John Dill stepped into the breach with a short informal paper summing up his understanding of the line of thinking in London. It was not until the last day of 1942 that the long-awaited London paper on American-British joint strategy was received in Washington. And there was still no American paper. The necessary guidance was given finally, however, by the Casablanca Conference in January. By this time the success of the combined armies in North Africa, the rise of British production to its peak and the rapid surge of American production had relieved the worst pressures.

The Minister of Production gave on his return from Washington at the end of 1942 a somewhat gloomy view of the lack of success in relating assignment to strategic needs. To the men on the spot the record on the side of military supplies was not regarded as bad. Testimony given in January 1943 in the London Munitions Assignment Board by the head of the British Army Staff was that the experience of 1942 proved that in general a reasonable British claim was usually satisfied by the Washington Board if a convincing case could be presented as to operational need. The Minister's report had emphasised especially the failure of the agreements for the allocation of aircraft; and this topic deserves a more detailed treatment.

The Crisis in Aircraft Assignments. Greater difficulties occurred in the assignment of aircraft than of other arms. The main causes of the trouble were visible already at the Atlantic Conference in August 1941 and the Victory Conference which followed in London in

September. Previous arrangements for the allocation of United States aircraft to Great Britain (the Slessor agreement) had broken down for three reasons: first, the diversion of supplies to Russia; second, the growing demands of American rearmament; third, the lag in output from American aircraft factories, particularly of heavy bombers.

In December 1941 the Prime Minister, in papers prepared on board the *Prince of Wales*, set out his conception of 1942 as the year of a great bomber offensive against Germany. 'We greatly desire', he wrote, 'American bomber squadrons to come into action from the British Isles against Germany. Our own bomber programme has fallen short of our hopes. It is formidable and is increasing, but its full development has been delayed.'[1] The allocation of aircraft was one of the most urgent questions awaiting the Combined Chiefs of Staff when they assembled in Washington, and it was discussed at the first meeting. It was one of the main reasons for the setting up of a Combined Munitions Assignments Board. The Prime Minister in a minute on 10th January noted that the United States Air Force would be brought into 'heavy action during 1942. Already it is proposed that strong bomber forces, based on the British Isles, should attack Germany and the invasion ports.' There were also to be American fighter squadrons in the United Kingdom. Two days later the Chief of the Air Staff and General Arnold signed what was to be known as the 'Arnold-Portal Agreement'. This was based on the recognition that it was not possible for the United Kingdom to plan strategy and production merely on the basis of monthly aircraft assignments. The agreement covered allocation to members of the United Nations for six months and included a tentative programme of allocations for a further six months. It served for a little time as the basis for allocations by the Joint Aircraft Committee. But assignments under it soon fell into arrears and the agreement was revised in June. The attempts to put allocations of aircraft on a longer-term basis continued however in a series of similar agreements which were used by the Combined Munitions Assignments Board as a basis for assignment.[2]

The failure of deliveries under the Arnold-Portal Agreement to come up to schedule became evident not long after the Arcadia Conference. Both sides eyed the agreement from a different angle.

---

[1] Churchill, *The Grand Alliance*, op. cit., pp. 576 and 620.

[2] With the setting up of the Munitions Assignments Committee (Air) the function of the Joint Aircraft Committee in relation to allocation of the output of complete aircraft to governments lapsed. It continued, however, to allocate aircraft components (engines, propellers, instruments, etc.) until these too were taken over by C.M.A.B. The Joint Aircraft Committee continued, however, to advise C.M.A.B. and the Combined Chiefs of Staff on matters relating to production. The British Service representatives on J.A.C. were also members of M.A.C. (Air) so that close liaison could be maintained between the two committees on the British side. Requisitions were given a tentative clearance by M.A.C. (Air) before they were formally lodged by J.A.C. This minimised the danger that M.A.P. might not receive assignments against its orders.

From the point of view of the R.A.F. the long-term deliveries provided for under the agreement were essential to the planning of expansion, training and operations. From the American side they began to look more like diversions from American requirements of a similar character needed urgently by the growing Air Force so that they too might take part in the fight.

One of the first tasks of the Combined Munitions Assignments Board acting on instructions from the Combined Chiefs of Staff was to review the aircraft production of the United Nations in the light of the requirements in the various theatres of war. On 29th March 1942 the Prime Minister asked the President to expedite the first instalment of American bombers which General Arnold had arranged to arrive in July: 'Never was there so much good work to be done and so few to do it.' The Prime Minister went on to refer to the growing bomber offensive against Germany and the 'most remarkable results' which were being achieved by radar. Meanwhile the diversion of aircraft from British assignments was becoming so serious that the Head of the British Air Commission in Washington wrote to General Arnold, Chief of the United States Army Air Force, specifying the main diversions since January 1942. 'The loss of allocated spares' was perhaps 'even more dangerous', since it was already immobilising some aircraft in the theatres, particularly in the Middle East. There must clearly be elasticity in any assignments system, the letter added, but sudden diversions, sometimes with little notice, should be avoidable.

The lag in production was the main cause of the trouble. A British memorandum of 8th May 1942, prepared as basis for a possible approach to Hopkins, noted that the President's objectives were 'badly down on combat types'—as much as thirty-four per cent. less than his targets for 1942. The memorandum foresaw the danger that the attempt to achieve the President's objectives on the basis of mere numbers might encourage the production of old types, at the expense of new types, and that it would intensify the problem of spares.

Meanwhile on 7th April the Combined Chiefs of Staff had called for an immediate survey of all United States and British air resources, including reserves, production, proposed expansion and present distribution of aircraft. Dill warned London at once that this move was based on the view that Britain was getting too many aircraft under the Arnold-Portal Agreement in view of the shortfall of American production. To make the survey a committee was set up which became known as the Arnold-Evill-Towers Joint (Aircraft) Committee; from this time on it usually dealt with combined aircraft requirements. Until a new basis was adopted the Combined Chiefs directed that the Arnold-Portal Agreement should continue as a basis for aircraft assignments.

In mid-April 1942 the really serious issue which underlay all these discussions emerged in conversations which the Canadian Prime Minister had during a visit to Washington. He informed a member of the Embassy staff that he had found a definite feeling on the American side that American forces should not serve except as complete American formations under American command. In other words aircraft should be retained in the United States until they could be fought by American crews in American squadrons. Hopkins took up the same point with Captain Balfour at the White House on 14th May. Public opinion, he said, was rising against the sending of aircraft to the United Kingdom whilst American pilots were left without aircraft to fly. In the President's view the Arnold-Portal Agreement, like the Slessor Agreement, no longer held good. Hopkins then referred to a recent request by the Prime Minister to the President for 200 American transports in June. In making the request the Prime Minister had referred to the promise of transports rather later in the year under the Arnold-Portal Agreement. General Arnold preferred, Hopkins said, that the transports should be sent complete with American crews and airborne troops. The President on 18th May informed the Prime Minister that plans were being made to train, equip and move air transport units to the United Kingdom as quickly as possible—204 by July, 416 by November.

Two days later the President raised the whole issue direct with the Prime Minister. The United States were anxious that every appropriate American-made aircraft should be manned and fought by its own crew; but the existing schedules of aircraft allocations did not permit this. American pilots and crews should be assigned to man American-made planes far more greatly than at present on the combat fronts. The Combined Chiefs of Staff, he suggested, should determine the strength of aircraft to be maintained in the respective theatres of the war; the maximum number of planes possible should be maintained in combat and a minimum number in reserve. Next day Dill and Evill talked with Hopkins on the President's message and Hopkins explained that the President was quite definite about not allowing his decision to weaken British strength in any area. While he wanted to have the maximum possible American forces fighting in the year 1942, this was not to be at the expense of reducing sensibly the air effort in any theatre of the war. In accepting the principle thus put forward by the President, the Prime Minister replied, 'God knows we have no right to claim undue priority in the ranks of honour'. The loss to the R.A.F. under the revised allocations would mean, however, that the United Kingdom would have in action by the spring of 1943 a hundred squadrons less than it had planned. About thirty squadrons in active theatres were awaiting aircraft at that moment. Unless these hundred squadrons could be replaced by American units on the various battlefronts by the dates expected, the Prime Minister added, 'the whole structure of our plans would collapse and an entirely new view of the war would have to be taken'.[1]

The talks that followed at the end of May and early June between the heads of the two Air Forces in London and Washington, resulted in a new Arnold-Slessor agreement which the President accepted in a cable to the Prime Minister on 13th June. The basic principle that American aircraft should be manned by American crews was accepted for heavy bombers. The original allocation to the United Kingdom of other types—light bombers and pursuits—was to stand. American units totalling some nineteen heavy and six light bombardment groups and eighteen pursuit groups would be distributed between the various theatres—United Kingdom, Middle East and India.

The episode indicated the difficulties of planning British production, training and operations, when plans depended on a somewhat variable margin of supply from the United States. There were bound of course to be crises in which one ally must be prepared to put all claims aside and rush supplies to a point of danger. One example was the rushing of 300 Sherman tanks and 100 105-mm. self-propelled guns to Egypt after the fall of Tobruk.[2] Another crisis the President foresaw and forestalled at Guadalcanal in mid-August, when in a minute to the Chiefs of Staff he noted that the United States would soon be engaged on two active fronts and had to have adequate support in both places 'even though it means delay in our other commitments, particularly to England'.[3] The combined supply machinery never worked better than when it faced such crises.

The new air arrangement was left undisturbed until the autumn. In mid-September the Prime Minister gave the President news of the devastating effect on Germany of the night-bombing offensive of the R.A.F. But he went on to express some concern on two points: the extent to which the programme for the building up of the American Air Force in the United Kingdom had been falling behind expectations; and second, the fact that American production seemed to be running behind schedule. He suggested once more that special emphasis should be given to the production of heavy bombers and pursuits. On 29th September the Minister of Production was informed that the President was considering an increase by twenty per cent. or more in aircraft production schedules for 1943. The sequel is told in the last section of this chapter.

---

[1] The Prime Minister put the 'loss' at 5,000 aircraft. Hopkins on the 19th had assured the Ambassador that the loss would be only 2,000.

[2] The American offer of an armoured division fell through because of the great inroads it would have made on the Bolero programme.

[3] Cited in Sherwood, op. cit., p. 623.

(iv)

Combination in Production—Raw Materials

At the Arcadia Conference the need for the maximum British-American combination in the fabricating of weapons was recognised. But it was decided that the only point in the field of production on which immediate action was necessary was to assure the supply of raw materials. Supplies of these were threatened by two immediate dangers. The first was the cutting off by Japan of such vital war supplies as rubber, tin, and fibres; the second was that the raw material requirements of the now mature British war industry would be threatened by the immense needs of the expanding American war factories.

References which were made in several of the documents of the Conference to a joint production body showed that the Conference was not unaware of the theoretical case which could be made out for the setting up also of a Combined Production Board. At the beginning of January the Combined Chiefs instructed their Combined Military Planners to examine the British and American Victory Programmes. There was no time for more than a very hasty examination of the figures; and in the midst of the scrutiny the whole basis of the calculations was changed by the President's new targets for production. In the circumstances all that the planners could do was to agree that first priority must go to heavy bombers, merchant ships, landing craft, aircraft carriers and convoy escort vessels. The report recognised that there were likely to be 'clashes of priorities'. It was assumed that 'some parallel body will be set up on the production side' to deal with such clashes and to co-ordinate production. The Conference disbanded, however, without setting up any parallel board for this purpose. The inference was that the Prime Minister and the President were not convinced that such a body was really necessary, or at any rate, that the time was yet ripe for it. If serious production problems arose they could always be discussed by some *ad hoc* arrangement between the Governments. Meanwhile, experience would be gained from the working of the one Combined Board directly concerned with production—the Combined Raw Materials Board.

Reference has been made in previous chapters to a number of adjustments in production made by the Governments by such *ad hoc* methods. As far back as 1940 important adjustments had begun in the production of aircraft and tanks as a result of combined discussion of production programmes, exchange of technical data and efforts to secure some standardisation of types. Other examples were the arrangement whereby the United States undertook to build transport planes whilst Britain concentrated on fighters and heavy bombers; and a somewhat similar arrangement whereby the United States took over the main burden of building merchant vessels whilst the United Kingdom concentrated its shipyards more on naval craft.[1] Similar arrangements could have been made without the benefit of any Combined Board in such matters as landing craft, escort vessels, tank transporters and the like.

STEEL

Even in the field of raw materials, where there was a highly efficient Combined Board, matters of the highest importance were dealt with by special arrangements outside the Board. Thus the two most important materials—steel the basis of munitions and aluminium the basis of the aircraft industry—were dealt with apart from the Board. This was a matter of history, policy and convenience. Steel was not really in short supply in the United States. British requirements were only a small fraction of the output. The shortages in the United Kingdom were due not so much to supply as to shipping. In these circumstances and for a commodity so vital to the whole American economy combined allocation was out of the question. The moment the War Production Board was able to institute an adequate control system in the United States—the Controlled Materials Plan—supply eased. It was for the War Production Board, and not for the Combined Raw Materials Board, to furnish the remedy; and the Combined Board wisely decided at the outset to leave steel alone. Any important questions on steel were discussed between W.P.B. and the steel division of the British Raw Materials Mission.[2]

ALUMINIUM

Aluminium was under a measure of combined control long before 1942. The working arrangements between Great Britain, Canada and the United States were not disturbed when C.R.M.B. was established. They afford a good example of combination as practised by the three Governments even in an early phase of the war. The basis of distribution of the main surplus, derived from the Canadian production of aluminium, was the contractual rights of the United Kingdom, the United States, and Australia. The British import requirements in the first stage of the war were secured mainly from

---

[1] In pursuance of these arrangements the United States built during the war 25,000 transport planes for the United Nations and 60 million tons of merchant shipping. The United Kingdom still built over a million tons of merchant shipping each year from 1941 to 1944 as compared with its output of 840,000 tons in 1940. See Section (v) below and Chapter X.

[2] There was later a Combined Steel Committee of C.R.M.B.–C.P.R.B., but it played a subsidiary part.

Canada.[1] British import requirements were estimated in 1939 at 60,000 tons, whilst domestic production was put at 30,000 tons a year. Canada had the double advantage over the United States, the other main potential source, of being already a war partner and also able to supply at a lower net dollar cost, because of her use of bauxite from the sterling area (the Caribbean). To expand Canadian production, however, additional capital was required and this was supplied by the British Government. Loans of about $40 million were made to the Aluminium Company of Canada in the first half of 1940; and a further sum of $16 million was advanced early in 1941. But before long still further expansion had to be provided in Canada to meet not only the requirements of the United Kingdom but also those of the United States. Canadian production was thus increased from 74,000 long tons in 1939 to over 400,000 long tons in 1943 and 1944.

There was a corresponding expansion in the United States. In mid-1941 the Truman Committee of the United States Senate brought to light a serious shortage of aluminium in the United States. In consequence several new American expansion schemes were adopted: the first, adopted in July 1941, was to add nearly 300,000 tons per year, and the second, adopted in February 1942, another 320,000 tons a year. As a result American production rose from 146,000 long tons in 1939 to nearly 700,000 long tons in 1944.[2] Whilst these new expansion schemes were getting under way Canada was able to augment American supplies by making large shipments of virgin aluminium to the United States—over 100,000 tons in 1942, 232,000 tons in 1943 and 214,000 tons in 1944.

There was a similar interlocking of supply arrangements between the three countries in the matter of fabricated aluminium. To secure additional light-alloy fabricating capacity overseas, the United Kingdom invested at the beginning of the war some $7 million on a large new tube and sheet mill at Kingston, Ontario. The United Kingdom began to draw on North America for fabricated aluminium in 1940.

---

[1] Orders from unsafe foreign sources—Switzerland and Norway—were diverted to Canada in 1940.

[2] The production of virgin aluminium in the three countries was as follows:

Thousand long tons

Country	1939	1940	1941	1942	1943	1944
United Kingdom .	25	19	23	47	56	35
Canada . .	74	97	191	304	443	412
United States .	146	184	276	465	821	693

Source: *The Mineral Industry of the British Empire and Foreign Countries, Statistical Summary 1938–44* (London, Imperial Institute, 1948)

The United Kingdom imports of fabricated aluminium (sheet, strip, bars, rods, etc.) during the years 1940 to 1944 totalled 13,000 long tons from Canada and more than 67,000 long tons from the United States.[1] For the latter the United Kingdom from the end of 1943 gave compensation in the form of deliveries to the United States of aluminium ingots from British and Canadian contracts in Canada.

To enable the three Governments to co-ordinate their relations in respect of aluminium and magnesium close informal contacts were maintained between the British Air Commission, the Department of Munitions and Supply and the War Production Board. These were reinforced by the setting up of the Combined Aluminium Committee in February 1943.

THE COMBINED RAW MATERIALS BOARD

The raw material crisis of December 1941 and the early months of 1942 was far too serious and involved much too wide a range of strategic materials to be handled by *ad hoc* methods of the kind that had worked well for steel, aluminium and magnesium. Nothing less than a Combined Board, with a combined staff at its disposal, able to command the fullest support and aid from the national raw material authorities, could have surmounted the raw material crisis of 1942. The speed and efficiency with which the crisis was handled was indeed remarkable. Within six months the Combined Raw Materials Board had become a highly effective instrument and was well on the way towards its goal.

By the end of its first year of operations it had solved or eased some of the most serious raw material problems of the Allies. Effective working arrangements were in operation which gave a reasonable assurance that all the important raw material problems likely to arise during the remainder of the war could be handled effectively. The habits of combined thinking and combined action had been firmly established. In presenting the first annual report of the Board W. L.

---

[1] United Kingdom imports of aluminium from Canada and the United States were as follows:

Thousand long tons

	1939	1940	1941	1942	1943	1944
Virgin aluminium						
from: Canada .	36	52	137	135	205	148
United States .	6·0	6·2	0·1	1·2	8·1	4·0
Fabricated aluminium						
from: Canada .	0·3	0·7	1·4	2·2	4·4	4·3
United States .	3·3	8·6	3·2	2·2	20·2	33·1

Source: Annual Statements of the Trade of the United Kingdom
(H.M. Stationery Office)

Batt, its American member, was able to say that 'the first twelve months of operations resulted in stabilisation of the raw materials situation'. As a result of the Board's activities 'world traffic in raw materials amongst the United Nations now flows in orderly fashion'.[1] The United Nations had not suffered any really serious shortage of the raw materials essential for war purposes. The supreme test of a Combined Board—its ability to produce agreements between the two Governments which both were able and willing to carry out—had been met. In July 1943 Sir Clive Baillieu, the British member, said in a broadcast: 'Every one of the Board's recommendations has been accepted and carried out by the Governments concerned.'

The year 1942 marked the beginning of a great expansion both of the requirements of raw materials and of their production. By the end of the year more than half of the necessary additions of machine tools and of plant had been made in the United States; and another quarter was added in 1943. The appetite for raw materials of the new factories thus brought into operation was immense; but it was met.

The scope of the Board, as set out in the directive of the Prime Minister and the President, was far wider than the allocation of British and American raw materials. It was directed by them:

(i) To plan the best and speediest development, expansion and use of the raw material resources under the jurisdiction or control of the two Governments, and make the recommendations necessary to execute such plans. Such recommendations shall be carried out by all parts of the respective Governments.

(ii) In collaboration with others of the United Nations, to work toward the best utilisation of their raw material resources, and, in collaboration with the interested nation or nations, to formulate plans and recommendations for the development, expansion, purchase or other effective use of their raw materials.

Its main business was thus to mobilise supplies of raw materials from the non-Axis world, to allocate them according to need, to secure price stability, to economise their use and to develop new supply where it was needed.

Although the first formal meeting of the Board was not held until 11th February 1942 and its Advisory Operating Committee did not meet formally until 2nd March, the Board and its staff were effectively at work long before these dates.[2] In mid-January 1942, or even earlier, the Combined Staff were already working on reports and

---

[1] War Production Board Release, 28th February 1943.

[2] As is shown in *Studies of Overseas Supply*, C.R.M.B. took over a going concern. Combination of a far-reaching kind in the handling of raw materials had been developing since 1940. C.R.M.B. took over as its staff the combined British and American teams which had been handling these matters. Combined arrangements for dealing with raw materials also existed between Ottawa and Washington.

framing interim decisions, and the Operating Committee was meeting informally. Work had begun even before mid-January on urgent cases of two kinds which were listed in a note by the British Secretary on 18th January. One kind was strategic materials threatened by the Japanese advance, notably rubber, tin, manila hemp and sisal. The other kind was materials, such as tungsten and nickel, in which shortages were developing as a result of the rapid expansion of war industry on both sides of the Atlantic. (Not only tungsten and nickel but all the other ferro-alloys were beginning to show shortages for the same reason.) It was around these two groups of commodities that the first reports and recommendations of the Board began to centre. Decision No. 1 of the Board was on tin. It included four recommendations to the Governments:

(1) An increase of tin smelting capacity in the United States.

(2) The re-examination of the world position as regards tin in the event of the loss of Malaya and the Netherlands Indies.

(3) Investigation of a Russian request for 18,000 tons of tin metal a year.

(4) Provision for the exchange of information between the two countries on conservation and restrictions on the use of tin.

In this historic first decision the Board, as was its invariable practice, assigned responsibility for the carrying out of its decisions.[1] The minutes record it thus: '*Responsibility:* United States, No. 1; Combined, Nos. 2, 3 and 4.' The first reports of the Board, both of which were already in existence by 18th January, were: Nickel No. 1 (recommendations confirmed by the Board in its Decision No. 3) and Manila–Sisal No. 1. The latter contained twelve recommendations on which there were interim decisions already on 16th January. The responsibility for seven of them was assigned to the United States, one fell to the United Kingdom, and five were combined.

Thus the Board spent no time on theoretical discussions as to its powers, programme and methods. It settled down to work at once on actual problems. The organisation, forms, procedures which it developed in the first two or three months remained with little change until the end of the war. After 1942 new scarcities could arise (sometimes quite suddenly as in the case of hides in 1943), but there were few really new problems. By 1943 some of the raw materials which had been critical in 1942 were no longer in short supply; others never ceased to be difficult and remained under close supervision until the end of the war. Cobalt is an example of a material for which a new

---

[1] Decision No. 2 of the Board included four recommendations to ensure that essential strategic materials awaiting shipment in the danger zones in the Far East were moved out as rapidly as possible.

technical advance, in this case jet propulsion, greatly increased the demand at a late stage in the war.

The imperative was used in its directive ('such recommendations *shall* be carried out . . .'). But it was no more possible for this Combined Board than for any of the others to become itself an executive body. It described itself in its first annual report as 'a clearing house for information and control point for action'. But so careful was the clearance of recommendations with all interested parties, before they finally reached the Board, that they amounted to decisions. In fact in the formal documents of the Board they were described as 'Decisions' which were set out in the form of 'Recommendations'.

The relations of the Board and its secretariat with the raw materials departments and agencies of the two Governments were extremely close. All the agencies whose consent was necessary to translate recommendations into action were represented on the Board's Advisory Operating Committee.[1]

The Operating Committee, which met weekly, was the chief working instrument of the Board. It played an important part in shaping the Board's recommendations, followed closely their carrying out, watched over shipments of materials, supervised the development of new supplies, arranged for the preparation of joint reports and kept them up to date.

The American member of the Board (Mr. W. L. Batt) was the Chairman of the powerful American Requirements Committee of the War Production Board. From its first meeting on 13th February 1942 to the end of the war this latter committee planned the distribution of American raw materials for war purposes, for civilian use and for export. The American staff of the Combined Raw Materials Board served also as the secretariat of the Requirements Committee. Both sides of the Board shared offices in the same building.

The Combined Reports on the critical raw materials were made as far as possible on a quarterly basis in accordance with a Reports Programme. By the end of June reports had been completed on no less than eighteen critical materials with three more nearly ready. The first revisions of these reports were under way in June. Serial numbers showed the number of revised editions through which a report had passed (e.g. Nickel No. 2). Although a large number of commodities were important enough to be included within the range of the Board—as many as 130—it gave little attention to commodities which were in easy supply. Its work was concentrated on raw

---

[1] On the British side the following Ministries were represented through officials in Washington: the Foreign Office, Ministry of Production, Ministry of Supply, Ministry of Economic Warfare. On the American side the agencies represented were: the State Department, War Production Board, Department of Commerce, Board of Economic Warfare, and Office of Lend-Lease Administration.

materials which were uncertain or were definite points of danger in the battle of production. Only those materials which were in such shortage as to endanger the war effort were brought under its full and authoritative review. During its first year it gave close attention to nearly thirty raw materials falling into this category. During the year recommendations based on comprehensive formal reports were made on the following: nickel, copper, tin, lead, zinc, antimony, mercury, phosphorus, manganese, chromite, tungsten, cobalt, vanadium, molybdenum, crude rubber, reclaimed rubber, manila hemp, sisal, nylon, shellac, mica, sheep shearlings, wool, graphite, asbestos, balsa wood, pyrethrum and kapok. Less detailed surveys were made of aluminium, bauxite, magnesium, cadmium, steel scrap, iron ore, and a number of other materials.

The speed and range of the Board's work was shown by its record at the end of the first quarter of 1942—two months after its formal constitution. By that time it had dealt with most of the materials threatened by the Far East crisis, had made arrangements in some cases for priorities as regards transport. It had dealt with carefully considered reports on tungsten, rubber, manila, sisal and tin. These reports pooled and co-ordinated all the data available from both sides. They gave the first authoritative and agreed view of the total position as regards each commodity. The Board had also made definite allocations in the case of rubber, nickel, tin, manila, sisal, nylon, tungsten and tin-plate. These allocations fell into several different categories. Some were regular quantitative allocations; others were temporary adjustments to tide over an emergency; still others were allocations of sources of supply. Already it was clear that quantitative allocations of supplies were not likely to be necessary in all or even in the majority of cases.

Its characteristic work on the development of existing or fresh sources of production was also clear in this opening phase. It confined its recommendations to selected areas where development was most likely to yield appreciable supply during the war. Thus in the case of nickel and aluminium it was essential, from the point of view of maximum output in the shortest time, to foster development in the main existing sources of supply—Canada for both metals and the United States for aluminium. Recommendations on conservation and substitution had also been made for a number of commodities. Another sphere of activity which had already assumed its characteristic pattern was combined purchasing. Arrangements of this sort had been recommended in certain cases, particularly for sisal and rubber. It had already worked out its characteristic hemisphere pattern, not only for co-ordinated purchasing, but also for the apportionment of world supplies, or of responsibilities for development. A hemisphere basis had been adopted in relation to fibres, rubber and tungsten.

CO-ORDINATED PURCHASING

Thus by co-ordinating the policies of the two Governments the Board had already begun to play an important part in securing price stabilisation and control of supplies in out-markets. The characteristic methods which were to be used by the Governments in carrying out the combined recommendations had also emerged. One means of control was long-term contracts made by the Government agencies with private producers. Another was control—through navicerts and otherwise—over shipping space. Import and export licensing and exchange control also played their parts. In some cases a third government (e.g. India in the case of jute) acted as the agent of the Board in the carrying out of recommendations.

The methods used had to be varied in accordance with the nature of the commodity and the circumstances. Mica afforded an example of co-ordinated buying combined with development, in which a third country, India, actively co-operated. In this case the Board was served by a special agency on the spot—the Joint United Kingdom-United States Mica Mission sent to India in July 1942. With a combined deficit of block mica (muscovite), amounting to five million pounds, foreseen for 1943 it was necessary to make careful arrangement for both purchasing and development in all the different mica-producing areas of the non-Axis world. The Joint Mission was sent to unify purchasing policy and to act as the regular agent of the Board for the purchase jointly of all new supplies of block mica in India.

Of all the methods used co-ordinated purchasing was perhaps the most useful expedient. It covered the widest range of commodities. It took various forms; thus both Governments might buy together under agreed ceilings and quotas; or one of them might act as sole purchaser on behalf of both. Such a co-ordinated system of purchasing of import needs was essential not only to save money but also to save shipping space. Almost every combined purchasing arrangement had its background of wasteful competition which had impeded the war effort. Wherever possible existing trade relations were taken into account in distributing the sources of supply. Where one government acted as sole purchaser it made arrangements to supply the other. Thus the United Kingdom bought on joint account, with an agreement to resell an agreed proportion of its purchases to the United States, the following commodities: hides (British East Africa), mica (India), rubber (Ceylon), long staple cotton (India). The United States, on the other hand, bought on joint account, with agreed allocations to their partner, certain commodities in South American countries such as balsa wood, glycerine, mica, quartz crystals and cotton linters. Examples of agreements to purchase within a fixed price ceiling and up to an agreed amount were flax in Canada and hemp, hides, horsehair and mercury in various countries. The first Annual Report of the Board indicated that co-ordinated purchasing arrangements then existed for thirty-one commodities. In most cases the agreements were made at the staff level without it being necessary to call in the Board.

No brief summary of this sort can do justice to the far-flung activities of the Board which covered raw materials throughout the entire free world. The United States and the United Kingdom were able to dispose of world supplies nearly as easily as they disposed of production facilities in their own countries. This was due to a variety of factors: the desire of the free peoples to aid the political cause for which the combination was fighting, its control of world shipping and shipping routes, its unrivalled purchasing power, and its efficient machinery for the clear-cut allocation to one government or the other (or more rarely to them both jointly) of responsibility for procurement in each area.

CONSERVATION

Conservation and economy in use and the substitution of materials was another highly important activity of the Board, the effects of which spread in wide circles throughout war-time supply. The United Kingdom had a longer experience in such measures than the United States and had developed more effective controls. Recommendations made by the Board on conservation and substitution ran into high figures. To handle the increasing exchange of information, much of it very technical, the Board set up in March 1942 a combined conservation liaison machinery. This became the channel for the exchange between Washington and London and other governments of a large volume of information on substitution, specifications, standardisation and simplification of products and manufacturing processes. Amongst the important examples of substitution recommended by the Board were the substitution of inferior grades of mica for certain purposes, the use of substitute fibres for manila and sisal, of steel for brass in cartridge cases. Substitution in the latter case enabled the American Army to save 77 million lb. of copper in 1942. Similar action was initiated in the United Kingdom, but as the supply situation improved it was discontinued. The Board's recommendations on substitution covered whole groups of inter-related materials such as the ferro-alloys and the various fibres. In the case of the ferro-alloys new metallurgical practices and specifications varied the alloy contents of different types of steel. This made possible very important savings in the most critical of the ferro-alloys such as nickel, tungsten and chromite, so that supply became adequate for requirements.[1] In the

---

[1] *Production, Wartime Achievements and the Reconversion Outlook* (War Production Board, Washington: 1945), p. 48.

case of the ferro-alloys, as also for rubber, mica, graphite, silk, nylon, hemp, sisal, cork and other commodities, the Board promoted the exchange of technical missions and visits by experts.

RUBBER

Perhaps the most important substitutions of all were those made for rubber. Thus in one case, mentioned in the War Production Board report on war production in 1942, by substituting cattle tail hair in linings of tanks and jeeps it was possible to save in a year 3 million lb. of rubber. Rubber was the most important, most difficult and most discussed of the problems confronting the Board during its existence. More of its 'decisions' were devoted to rubber than to any commodity—fourteen in 1942, nine in 1943, fourteen in 1944 and thirty-seven in 1945. The Japanese advance had cut off ninety per cent. of the crude rubber supplies—or a million tons a year. Ceylon, itself on the edge of the Japanese advance, supplied two-thirds of the rest (or 100,000 tons). If Ceylon also fell (and it was prudent to assume that it might) all the rest of the small producing areas together could not muster more than 50,000 tons a year.

There was only one place from which the gap in supplies could be filled and that was by the creation of a vast new synthetic rubber industry in the United States.

By strenuous and relentless efforts the two heads of the Board, Sir Clive Baillieu and Mr. William Batt, succeeded in getting production facilities for synthetic rubber laid down on the scale which was foreseen to be necessary. The capacity had to be capable of producing by 1944 800,000 tons or more of synthetic rubber a year. The arrangement whereby this responsibility was undertaken by the United States was one of the important production decisions of the war. Less than 30,000 tons of synthetic rubber were expected in 1942 and only 300,000 tons in 1943. Meanwhile the Allies had to live on stocks and reclaimed rubber and the trickle of new supplies of natural rubber. Using the limited quantities of synthetic rubber the United States could spare, the Allies had to learn the techniques for processing it. Under an arrangement with the United States rubber companies the Allied Governments undertook to furnish technical reports on their experience in processing the material.

For no commodity were the supply and requirements figures calculated more carefully over the critical years to 1944 than for rubber. Despite every effort in the matter of substitution and the development of new sources of supply of natural rubber a careful review by the Board in the spring of 1942 indicated that a drastic cut must be made in allocations. In reporting this decision to the Minister of Production on 22nd May Sir Clive Baillieu drew his attention to the Board's view that 'the firm decision to cut requirement figures given in the allocations would carry with it strategic and production consequences of the first order, and they cannot be certain that tentative allocations take proper account of all the factors involved, including strategic necessities, synthetic production likely to be available, economies and substitutions, best use of shipping and utilisation of manufacturing capacity'. The Board therefore recommended that the head of the War Production Board and the Minister of Production should review the whole situation immediately with the Combined Chiefs of Staff. Mr. Lyttelton replied on 27th May agreeing with this proposal and pointing out that it led to the general question of production. Before the Chiefs of Staff could judge the full implications for their strategic plans, 'they will need to know the effect of the scarcity of rubber on war production programmes. . . .'

In the case of copper, also, the careful study made by the Combined Raw Materials Board of supply and requirements pointed to the need of a wider combined planning of production than the Board itself could undertake. Its studies brought to light probable deficits in supply which might have forced drastic cuts in the munitions programmes of the United States, the United Kingdom and Canada. It was clear that the figures on the American side were still so speculative, and their controls as yet so inadequate, that there could be no certainty about the Board's conclusions. The head of the War Production Board was already wrestling with the problem and he had begun to envisage, as a possible solution of this and other problems, the setting up of a Combined Production and Resources Board. By agreement between the two Ministers the two problems of rubber and copper were referred therefore to the Combined Production Board as soon as it was established in June. The events leading up to it must now be reviewed.

(v)

The Combined Production and Resources Board

The time was ripe to fill the gap in the combined machinery which had been noted in January 1942 by the British and American Joint Staffs—the need of 'some parallel body . . . on the production side', parallel, that is, to the Combined Chiefs of Staff. Two important developments since January had made the step possible and necessary. One was the setting up in both countries of departments to co-ordinate national production. The other was the emergence of practical problems which called for a new combined board.

When the Arcadia Conference disbanded, the American War Production Board was still not in existence. It was set up under Mr. Donald Nelson in mid-January; its Planning Committee was appointed in February. In the United Kingdom the Production Executive gave way in February to a new Ministry of Production under Mr. Oliver Lyttelton;[1] and its Joint War Production Staff was created in March. Like the War Production Board the new Ministry did not have direct charge of any branch of production. The primary functions of the Minister were twofold: (1) co-ordination of action in relation to the Combined Boards in Washington and representation of the British Government in negotiations with the War Production Board and the Office of Lend-Lease Administration; (2) the broad planning of future munitions production. Within the general production programme the existing Supply Ministries retained their responsibility for actual production. The strength of the Minister of Production came from his seat in the War Cabinet, from his powers over import programming, manpower and the allocation of raw materials and machine tools, and from his role in relation to the Combined Boards and the American production authorities.[2]

CIVIL AND MILITARY PLANNERS — THE GULF IN THE UNITED STATES

The Joint War Production Staff, which met first on 30th March 1942, brought together into a permanent body the main military and civil planners from both the Services and the three Supply Ministries. It took over much of the existing work of the Defence Committee (Supply) which henceforward met only on special occasions. Its function was to ensure enough weapons at the right time, i.e. to serve as a link between production and strategy. More specifically, it was to advise the Minister of Production on adjustments or extensions of programmes in the light of strategic needs and of production in other countries, to keep the Chiefs of Staff informed as to production possibilities, and to supply information to the Combined Boards. One of its tasks was to negotiate a long-term understanding on production with the United States. The most important part of the organisation was the permanent staff, the Joint War Planning Group, headed for the first twelve months by Sir Walter Layton. American representatives in London were invited from time to time to its meetings.

---

[1] Lord Beaverbrook was Minister of Production for a brief period before Mr. Lyttelton.

[2] *Office of the Minister of Production*, Cmd. 6337, February 1942; statement of the Prime Minister in House of Commons, 12th March 1942, H. of C. Deb., Vol. 378, Cols. 1205–07. See also Postan, op. cit., Chapter V, Section 5. The Admiralty, which had a large peace-time production establishment, continued to handle naval production during the war. The Ministry of Supply had been set up on the eve of the war to deal with army supplies and most raw materials. The Ministry of Aircraft Production had been set up in 1940 to handle aircraft production.

The initiative towards an understanding with the United States on production came from the British side and this was not accidental. In the spring of 1942 the American war output caught up with and passed that of the United Kingdom. Though the British still had 'something on hand', as the Minister of Production told the President in June, they were 'not far short of the peak of [their] war effort'.[1] The war against Japan brought about important changes in the planned strength of the British Army and the Armies of other members of the British Commonwealth; and this in turn brought changes in the production programmes of the supply ministries. As British production reached towards its ultimate limits, its dependence on American production must inevitably increase; it was already so important for such major items as aircraft, merchant ships and tanks that it was becoming a substantial element in British production planning. It was important that the dependence on the United States should be such as to give a firm and calculable basis for British planning. There was the standing example of Canada to show how far certainty could go in an ideal situation. Canada had been a full war partner from the outset; her divisions, armed largely with British-type munitions, were combined with British divisions in a single army; her war production was so closely geared with that of the United Kingdom that it could be counted on with complete certainty in British supply calculations.

The first move towards the new Combined Board came in mid-February 1942 from the British Supply Council in Washington, with Monnet as the prime mover. All the heads of the British missions in Washington, including the Service members, agreed that a new Combined Board was needed to co-ordinate production in the British Commonwealth and the United States. Combined war production as defined by the British Supply Council involved five functions:

> determination of strategic concept and its expression in military requirements; translation into terms of raw materials necessary to their production; production itself; assignment of finished weapons; shipping.

Only for 'production itself' was there no specific combined body. Production in the British Commonwealth and the United States, all their munitions workers and their machines, drew upon certain common elements, such as shipping, steel and other strategic materials, machine tools and components. Thus changes in one programme affected the others. To avoid confusion, and to ensure maximum efficiency, strategy must be adjusted to available production and production to strategy. These conclusions, the united view of the heads of every British body in Washington, were discussed in many messages

---

[1] In the twelve months to June 1943, he told the President, the United Kingdom planned the following increases in output: naval vessels, 20 per cent.; army supplies, 60 per cent.; aircraft, 100 per cent.

and memoranda exchanged with London during March, April and May.

There was general agreement with this view in London. Hopkins was there on a visit in April and the matter was discussed with him. The Prime Minister, on 21st April, suggested to the President that additional combined bodies seemed necessary. One was required for food. Another was needed to handle 'our long-range programmes of war production'; it might also meet the need for a 'single controlling body over the Combined Boards'. The idea was that a Production Board would co-ordinate the civilian combined bodies, as the Combined Chiefs of Staff did the military. The sequel was the visit of the Minister of Production to Washington, and the setting up on 9th June of the Combined Production and Resources Board headed by himself and Mr. Donald Nelson.[1] The Combined Food Board, headed by Mr. Wickard, Secretary of Agriculture, and Mr. R. H. Brand, head of the British Food Mission, was set up at the same time.

The new Board for Production was the outcome not only of a general need but also of certain immediate and specific problems. One was purely American—the 'gulf between U.S. military and civilian staffs', as it was put in a meeting of the British missions in May. The War Production Board, as its history indicates, never succeeded in creating a close organic relationship between itself and the United States Joint Chiefs of Staff.[2] Mr. Lyttelton mentioned this difficulty in a report which he made to the War Cabinet in September 1942:

> The Americans have never been accustomed, in consideration of military or quasi-military matters, to link harmoniously the civil and military interests. They have no War Cabinet and they have no Defence Committee at which requirements, both civil and military, can be scrutinised, and programmes framed with due regard for the merits of the case. Nor have they any means by which the conflicting views of the several agencies can be harmonised and a common policy reached. The whole burden of grouping the extravagant demands of the War Department and of co-ordinating the action of the many agencies which have been created falls on one man—the President.[3]

A Combined Production and Resources Board was seen on the American side as 'the capstone of the combined board structure' and as a possible means of bridging the gap between the civil and military authorities. Created by a clear-cut directive issued by the President and the Prime Minister, it seemed, as the War Production Board

---

[1] With Sir Robert Sinclair and Mr. J. S. Knowlson as their deputies.

[2] *Industrial Mobilization for War*, op. cit., pp. 253–55. Considerations of security entered into the reluctance of the Services to work through civilian channels. Sherwood, op. cit., p. 756.

[3] There were some minor jurisdictional problems on the British side which are referred to in *Studies of Overseas Supply*.

history has noted, to raise Mr. Nelson above his status as W.P.B. Chairman and to place him on a par with the Combined Chiefs of Staff.[1] But no Combined Board could bridge this American gulf, if the War Production Board and the Joint Chiefs could not do it for themselves.

By April both countries were conscious that it was now a practical necessity to adjust their production programmes in the light of an agreed strategic plan. Staff discussions in London in that month with General Marshall led to the decision to work out a combined Order of Battle. The American Joint Chiefs were unable to produce theirs for many months. The British Chiefs had ready within a matter of weeks the British Order of Battle showing the scale and character of the British forces to be equipped and deployed in all theatres of the war by 1st April 1943. The plan called for about fifty-three infantry divisions, twenty-one armoured divisions and some 6,700 first-line aircraft. The latter figure meant a total of 30,000 aircraft of which about a third would be needed from the United States. The United Kingdom would also depend on the United States for a third of its medium and heavy tanks and nearly all of its light tanks and self-propelled guns. The supply by the United States of tanks, armoured cars and self-propelled artillery seemed to be fairly well assured by the recent British Tank Mission. But there were other deficiencies which were not covered. They included: destroyers, of which the Royal Navy had only about half its needs; escort vessels, of which the United Kingdom was producing sixty per cent. of its needs; and merchant ships, for which it was depending almost entirely on the United States.

As regards aircraft the Arnold-Portal Agreement appeared to have assured the third of the British requirements looked for from the United States. In this case combination in production was already being looked after by an existing body, the Joint Aircraft Committee. This was itself 'a combined production board for aircraft'. The Director of the British Air Commission in Washington pointed out that on this committee the British had a 'fortunate' and 'unique position', which must not be jeopardised by the creation of the new production board.[2] British dependence on the United States involved not merely complete aircraft but also components. Thus, as a British document pointed out:

> The problem of balance in the aircraft programme is inevitably a combined one, since the United States make engines, propellers, guns and radios, etc., for airplanes produced in England, Canada and Australia.

---

[1] *Industrial Mobilization for War*, op. cit., p. 225.

[2] The charter of the Combined Production and Resources Board permitted it to 'utilise', not to displace, the Joint Aircraft Committee.

Thus the British Order of Battle showed clearly, as the Joint War Production Staff noted, that the British production programme must be integrated with that of the United States; it must be 'balanced both internally and internationally and properly timed'. Examples of unbalance were noted in a British Supply Council memorandum sent to Hopkins and Nelson at the end of April. One was Sten guns. British requirements were two million. British capacity, however, was enough to produce five million by the end of 1943, and the United Nations needed such a weapon in such numbers. But the ammunition (9-mm. parabellum), which was non-common, would have to come in large measure from the United States.[1] This seemed possible since the United States at this time were planning to produce ·30-inch ammunition at rates which London regarded as fantastically high. But there had been no consultation between London and Washington before manufacture of the Sten gun was undertaken.

Apart from the general need to combine the British and American war production programmes, the Lyttelton Mission had another very practical objective. The Minister of Production came to the rescue of the British percentages, which seemed likely to be swamped by American Army programmes, which in turn were based on impossible production targets. Experience had taught the British missions that it was dangerous to present British requirements as if they were merely marginal figures. If looked at out of the context of British production they appeared as a small and seemingly unimportant fraction of American production. The wiser policy was for both sides to table an agreed statement of their total requirements and to link it with a strategic plan. If this were not done it was foreseen that the bulk of American production would be assigned to the American forces which had presented inflated requirements. The fixed charge of the Russian protocol would absorb most of the rest, and the British would get what was left over, if any.

In May Hopkins gave the warning (referred to above) about the President's desire to equip the maximum American forces in the shortest time, which seemed to mean that aircraft and equipment supplies would be reserved for American pilots rather than given to other nations. The only way to protect British supplies from the United States, he suggested, was to make them part of a combined production programme agreed between the two countries. British munitions production, as well as aircraft, was already being held up by lack of key components from the United States. Thus the Minister of Supply cabled on 10th June about the 'impossible situation created here by non-fulfilment of American promise on which our production projects have been based'. A fall in deliveries of transmissions and

---

[1] Later in the war there was a considerable production of 9-mm. ammunition in the United Kingdom.

suspensions for the Valentine tank had cut production by fifteen per cent. Deliveries of tank tracks were falling behind and shortage in gun mountings from the United States threatened to stop the production of Humber Mark IV armoured cars.

It was from the American side, however, that the first important move came towards a combined programme. It was taken by Mr. Nelson in a letter to the Chairman of the British Supply Council on 23rd April. It was then clear that the President's January production targets had been set far too high. Production was running far behind schedules. By the end of May only a quarter of the total production fixed for the year had been completed. The degree of inflation in the programme was well shown in the case of tanks. The programme as it then stood called for 77,000 tanks in 1943; but the number actually produced in that year was 29,497.[1] The President's production targets had been based on the assumption of a total output in 1942 of $40 billion; and in 1943 of $75 billion. But by the time the Service Departments and the Maritime Commission had built their full programmes round the President's key figures the totals stood at $62 billion for 1942 and $110 billion for 1943. These totals were so clearly impossible that Nelson, with the support of the President, embarked on the task of reducing them to a realistic level. Apart from plant and machine tools the schedules had to be adjusted to the available supplies of critical raw materials and of semi-manufactured products, such as steel plate. In his letter the Chairman of the War Production Board urged that since the American programme must now be revised the opportunity should be taken for a joint review of the programmes of both countries. This would ensure that the revised American production plan made adequate allowance for British needs. The matter was discussed by the British missions. Monnet thought that out of such a joint review would emerge a Combined Production Board headed by Nelson and Lyttelton. It was recognised that the review could not be made without the help of the Combined Chiefs of Staff; but Sir John Dill doubted whether the American Joint Chiefs would have become sufficiently accustomed to work with a civilian agency to make such a joint review possible.

A COMBINED BOARD WITHOUT A COMBINED PROGRAMME

He proved to be right. Mr. Lyttelton was able to secure a Combined Board[2] but not a combined programme. He found on his arrival that the President, Hopkins, Nelson and the War Department were ready to set up a Combined Production Board. An exchange of

---

[1] Without counting tank chassis for self-propelled guns the output of tanks in the United States was: 1942, 23,884; 1943, 29,497; 1944, 17,565; 1945 (7 months), 13,137.

[2] The Board originally consisted of representatives of the United Kingdom and United States. A representative of Canada was added in November 1942.

telegrams between the President and the Prime Minister cleared the way for the public announcement on 9th June 1942 giving the directive which set up the Combined Production and Resources Board. The directive put as the first of the Board's tasks a combined production programme based on strategic requirements which the Combined Chiefs of Staff were to indicate. The Board was given a second task, that of making adjustments. But in its third paragraph the directive turned again to its main theme, production in relation to strategy. There was little trace in the last paragraph of the earlier idea of the Board as a 'single controlling authority over the Combined Boards'; for this could hardly be deduced from the vague phrase about utilising 'existing combined or national agencies of war production'. The text ran as follows:

The Board shall:

(*a*) Combine the production programmes of the United States, the United Kingdom and Canada into a single integrated programme, adjusted to the strategic requirements of the war, as indicated to the Board by the Combined Chiefs of Staff, and to all relevant production factors. In this connection the Board shall take account of the need for maximum utilisation of the productive resources available to the United States, the British Commonwealth of Nations, and the United Nations, the need to reduce demands on shipping to a minimum, and the essential needs of the civilian population.

(*b*) In collaboration with the Combined Chiefs of Staff, assure the continuous adjustment of the combined production programme to meet changing military requirements.

To this end the Combined Chiefs of Staff and the Combined Munitions Assignments Board shall keep the Combined Production and Resources Board currently informed concerning military requirements, and the Combined Production and Resources Board shall keep the Combined Munitions Assignments Board currently informed concerning the facts and possibilities of production.

To facilitate continuous operation, the members of the Board shall each appoint a deputy, and the Board shall form a combined staff. The Board shall arrange for such conferences among United States and United Kingdom and Canadian personnel as it may from time to time deem necessary or appropriate to study particular production needs, and utilise the Joint War Production Staff in London, the Combined Raw Materials Board, the Joint Aircraft Committee and other existing combined or national agencies for war production in such manner and to such extent as it shall deem necessary.

On paper the first and third paragraphs seemed to assure a combined production programme by bridging the gap in the United States between the civilian and military sides. It used words of command: 'shall keep the new Board informed concerning military requirements. . . .' The first step, then, for the Board was to secure the combined military requirements. This point was made in a memorandum of 13th June given by Nelson and Lyttelton at the White House to Hopkins, General Marshall and Admiral King. But, as the memorandum pointed out, the Combined Chiefs of Staff would have to complete first the Combined Order of Battle for the spring of 1943: 'The Order of Battle, translated into terms of munitions, will furnish a schedule of requirements which can then be compared with a statement of the supplies that will be available by the end of 1942.' The comparison would show up deficiencies and excesses which could then be adjusted. The result would be 'a combined programme related not to overall establishments or gross figures of ultimate strengths, but to actual operational needs at a given date'. The British Chiefs of Staff in April had produced their Order of Battle, translated into munitions, at a few days' notice. The Lyttelton Mission seems to have assumed that the Americans would produce theirs in June before the Mission left Washington.[1] At its first meeting on the 17th the Combined Production and Resources Board formally invited the Combined Chiefs of Staff to direct the Service authorities to furnish the Board with two statements: one to show the munitions which the Combined Staffs required to be produced by the end of 1942; the second to show requirements by the end of 1943 for the Combined Order of Battle in April 1944. Next day Mr. Lyttelton attended a meeting of the Combined Chiefs to explain the proposals; they accepted the Board's invitation and instructed their planning staffs to get to work. The Minister returned believing that all was well.

A month later the Combined Production and Resources Board reported that the work on the April 1943 Order of Battle was advancing. But the assembling of the American figures had been so slow that they were now too late to affect actual production in 1942. The Board's effort was then concentrated on the data for 1943 (for the campaigns of 1944) which it wished to receive by 1st September. The information would be of little use for planning purposes if it was not available by October at the latest. The President, on 19th August, in accepting the Board's first report, undertook to see that the American requirements were produced; and on the 28th the Combined Chiefs agreed to make every effort to give the Board the data it needed. The British Order of Battle for 1944, translated into munitions, was again produced quickly. But the American side still could not produce its figures. Nor was there any immediate prospect of agreement on a combined strategic plan. Finally, on 8th September, the Board learned that the United States Joint Chiefs had declined to produce their part of the Order of Battle, on the ground that it was not feasible to do so at such an early stage in the organisation of the American

---

[1] At a British Joint Staff Mission meeting on 13th June the American Order of Battle was expected to be ready on the 16th.

forces. Instead the Joint Chiefs proposed to calculate their requirements on the following basis: (*a*) total forces that could be transported and maintained overseas (this was based in principle on a forecast of available cargo vessels and convoy escort vessels); (*b*) total American forces needed for defence of the Western Hemisphere in training or for use as strategic reserves. The trouble was in the blank cheque which (*b*) seemed to give to the United States War Department. It meant that requirements would be given on a numerical basis for the whole of the American forces wherever situated; they would not be related to strategic plans for operations in the active theatres of the war. There could then be no check on the element of inflation in the American Army supply programme.

The upshot was that the Combined Production and Resources Board was never able to obtain 'realistic requirements based on a Combined Order of Battle'. The attempt to secure a combined Order of Battle was not abandoned, however, by the Combined Chiefs and the Combined Staff Planners. On 7th December the latter reported that American requirements, together with British needs from the United States, had been submitted to the Combined Production and Resources Board, but that they could make no further progress towards a combined Order of Battle in the absence of agreement on the basic strategic concept. The sequel is referred to in the next chapter. Unable to work effectively through a Combined Board the Prime Minister and the President had to resort to direct discussion on the ministerial level.

Although the main advance of the Combined Production and Resources Board was blocked, its endeavours helped to produce some useful indirect results before the year ended. One was the closer scrutiny of American Service requirements ordered by the President in October. Separate statements of British and American Service requirements were obtained, but these were never combined by scrutiny and approval by the Combined Chiefs of Staff. Adjustments between the national war production programmes were made, but they had to be made on a unilateral basis, though not without consultations. Further the British side of the Combined Production and Resources Board, by dwelling on the value of the British Joint War Production Staff, played an indirect part in the decision by the War Production Board to set up the Production Executive under Charles E. Wilson. This body linked the American production and Service departments. Another valuable development was the growth of combined statistics. Under the Board the first Consolidated Statement grew into a regular flow of statistical information about production from both sides of the Atlantic.

Thus long before 1942 was ended it was clear that in practice the scope of the Combined Production and Resources Board must be narrower than its design had promised. If indeed the original concept had worked, the Board's field would have covered the great bulk of production in both countries. This involved a diversity enormously greater than for any of the other Boards which dealt with a comparatively small number of relatively simple and identifiable things like copper or wheat or shipping tonnage. It was therefore inevitable that the joint planning of production in any wide sense should collapse before it could even get under way.

'CONTINUOUS ADJUSTMENT'

The Combined Production and Resources Board now turned to the second task under its directive, that of 'continuous adjustment' between the production programmes. Towards the end of 1942 a further important task emerged which was covered by the phrase in the Board's directive referring to 'the essential needs of the civilian population'. The important task of securing combined programmes for the production of civilian supplies was handled by the Board through a combined Non-Military Supplies Committee. Combined programming began with textiles and medical supplies and was soon extended to many other commodities such as transportation equipment, internal combustion engines, agricultural and mining machinery, electric motors, pumps, compressors and footwear.

Some reference will be made in Chapter XI to the problem of adjustments between the national systems of war production. Here some of the matters taken up by the Board in its early months may be mentioned. It soon became clear that far-reaching adjustments would not be much less difficult than the achieving of a fully combined production programme. The systems of national production and the organisation and supply of the armed forces were already set in their ways. Only adjustments of a limited kind could be made. It was not possible for the combined bodies to secure basic changes such as a real standardisation of weapons and types. It was hardly within the competence of the Board to suggest changes of an administrative kind, such as a tightening of the loose American system of programming for army supply. Yet a margin of inflation of a few per cent. in the American Army supply programme could involve quantities greater than those furnished under lend-lease, and swallow up assignments to the United Kingdom.[1]

Much of the early discussion on adjustment turned on questions of shipping. One trouble was that whilst global shipping was the

---

[1] Important administrative adjustments did not have to wait on any Combined Board. Thus a proper system of allocation of key raw materials (the Controlled Materials Plan) was introduced by the War Production Board late in 1942. It was based on the British system which was studied on the spot by an American mission to the United Kingdom and explained in Washington by a mission of British experts led by Professor Arnold Plant.

limiting factor for global production, it was a bad guide in particular cases. There was necessarily an element of doubt in shipping forecasts. Small changes, such as cuts in the shipment of food or raw materials, or a change due to a strategic factor in the delivery point of munitions —Red Sea, or Pacific, or North Atlantic—could make a big difference in the numbers of ships available at a given time. An early (1941) example of an adjustment on the ground of shipping was the supply of vehicles to the Middle East from the United States instead of from the United Kingdom. The major example was the large quantities of supplies of many kinds furnished to American and Canadian troops in the United Kingdom. Later in the war jerricans afforded a clear-cut example of a switch in production from the United States to the United Kingdom on shipping grounds. On the same ground the United Kingdom undertook to provide locomotives for the United States forces in Britain and France at the cost of 900 fewer tanks from British tank factories. These were comparatively minor adjustments; they saved less Atlantic shipping space than might have been saved if the United States Army could have adopted certain British types of weapons, such as the 25-pounder field gun. Other possible adjustments were discussed and dropped. One was the idea, suggested by Mr. Harriman in the London Combined Production and Resources Board in July 1942 and taken up again by Mr. Lyttelton in Washington in November, of building American Mustangs in the United Kingdom. Mustang aircraft used the Packard-built Rolls-Royce engine; if the frames could be built in the United Kingdom, shipping space could be saved. Alternatively Mustang frames from the United States could be assembled in the United Kingdom. The United Kingdom might receive an equivalent number of American aircraft in some other theatre. But in such a case both countries would have to make long-term assignments— since neither could forgo production of its own aircraft without a guaranteed replacement.

Most of the adjustments affected American production. At its first meeting in June the Combined Production and Resources Board gave a useful decision which settled in part a long-standing problem affecting the supply to the United Kingdom of non-common weapons, spares and components (such as ·303-inch rifles, 3·7-inch predictors, landing-craft engines, tank transporters, tank components, etc.). Most of the items were vital to the British Army programme. The Board ruled that British requirements should be assigned a priority rating equal to that given to American weapons of equivalent strategic importance. The Board remained guardian of such decisions and was available as a court of appeal. Another decision affected the raw material content of finished weapons assigned to the United Kingdom by the Combined Munitions Assignments Board.

A decision of the Combined Munitions Assignments Board (which its sub-committee for ground supply had questioned), that the copper content of certain shells was not to be debited against the British copper allocation, was upheld on appeal by the C.P.R.B. It laid down the principle that 'transfers . . . of semi-finished or finished munitions should be made independently of their raw material content'.

One of the best examples of adjustments in the war production programmes was afforded by steel plate. The Combined Chiefs of Staff and all the Combined Boards, save Food, had an interest in steel plate. It affected a number of the most critical programmes— merchant ships, landing craft, escorts and other naval vessels, armoured cars and tanks. Steel itself was tight, but the main trouble was fabricating capacity.[1] The C.P.R.B. reported to the Combined Chiefs of Staff in July a deficit of about half a million tons of steel plate. The decision as to where cuts should be made was a matter of strategic importance. A Combined Committee, composed of representatives of the Combined Staff Planners and three Boards (Munitions, Production and Resources, and Shipping) proposed to cut merchant shipping. But the supply of steel plate was improving and further studies by the Production and Shipping Boards showed that a cut could probably be avoided. Towards the end of the year the President decided to increase the production targets for 1943 for both cargo ships and escort vessels. Again in April 1943 the Chairman of the C.P.R.B. warned the Combined Chiefs of Staff of a shortage of steel plate in the third quarter. This time the cuts were made by a reduction of fifteen per cent. in the steel allocation to the Services and of ten per cent. in the allocation to the United Kingdom and Canada.

After this diversion we must now return to the main theme. The Minister of Production reported to the War Cabinet at the end of September 1942 that the Combined Production and Resources Board was unable to fulfil its main purpose. Since there was no real link between the civilian and military sides in the United States, he suggested that the Prime Minister should now appeal directly to the President. The Prime Minister's message, sent on 4th October, noted the formidable difficulties in the way of producing any combined statement of requirements as far ahead as April 1944. He suggested that it was necessary, nevertheless, to scrutinise production targets more closely and to relate them to strategic needs. Otherwise a

---

[1] In the last quarter of 1942 the United Kingdom agreed to a reduction of its steel quota from the United States from 420,000 to 335,000 tons per month. This cut, made largely on shipping grounds, helped to relieve the pressure on steel supplies in the United States. At the end of July 1942 unshipped military stores at seaboard in the United States totalled 615,000 tons, whilst monthly shipments to the United Kingdom had been running at only 175,000 tons.

serious waste of resources and materials could occur. Thus the combined tank programme for 1943 provided for 87,000 tanks. This was enough for 200 armoured divisions, with 225 tanks each and 100 per cent. reserves, and was 'out of all proportion to anything that can be brought to bear on the enemy in 1943'. He gave ball ammunition as another example. The programmes called for 22,000 million rounds for use in 1943; but so far in the campaigns in the Middle East only 200 million rounds had been used. Inflated demands for arms that were not really needed would inevitably endanger combined production of 'such vital requirements as escort vessels, ships and aircraft of which it is almost impossible to have too many'. The President replied on 13th October in a telegram approved by the United States Joint Chiefs of Staff. He agreed that programmes should be re-examined from time to time with reference to raw material content and other factors. Such reviews should be made by the Combined Munitions Assignments Board and the Combined Chiefs of Staff, which should look at once into the matter of tanks and ball ammunition.[1] The role of the Combined Production and Resources Board, the President thought, should be, not to question specific requirements, but to analyse total American and British requirements. The Board should advise the Combined Chiefs of Staff if it found that the 'realities of production' made any adjustments necessary.

The Prime Minister sent a message to Hopkins three days later in which he said that the Government was 'frightfully anxious about the future of the American air programme and what our assignments in it are to be'. Aircraft were the centre of animated discussions which were then going on at high levels in Washington on the American production programme for 1943 and 1944. They had begun at the end of August 1942 when the President ordered a full review of war production. At that date the War Production Board estimated that production in 1943 could not exceed $75 billion. Yet the arms programmes added up to about $93 billion. The largest figure was $37 billion for the 100,000 aircraft which the President wanted to set as the target. Obviously when the cuts came to be made lend-lease was most likely to suffer heavily, and cuts seemed to be threatened even in the most critical items such as aircraft, cargo shipping and escort vessels. Early in October the President asked the United States Joint Chiefs of Staff for a statement showing the number of each type of aircraft—combat, transport and communication—which they wanted within the total of 100,000 to be produced in 1943. On the 24th he told the Prime Minister that after numerous conferences he had agreed to reduce his figure to 82,000 aircraft in 1943, but he expected this number to be delivered. He gave news

---

[1] The American production objectives for tanks had already been reduced, the President pointed out, to about 54,000 in 1943.

also of his plans to build in 1943 seventy additional escort vessels, and two million additional tons of merchant shipping. Since British requirements for 1943 and 1944 were involved in all these plans, Sir Robert Sinclair—who represented the Minister of Production on the Combined Production and Resources Board—urged early in October an immediate visit by the Minister to ensure that the British and American programmes were examined together. A Washington message to the Chiefs of Staff, sent at the same time, reported that all programmes had now become 'malleable if not actually in the melting pot'.[1] The size of the American Army was at last fixed at $7\frac{1}{2}$ million for 1943, a reduction of nearly $1\frac{1}{2}$ million on previous estimates.

The Lyttelton Mission arrived on 4th November 1942 and returned on the 30th. It came at an important moment in the supply history of both countries. It had as its military background the British victory at El Alamein and the combined invasion of North Africa. The one improved the British claim for supplies from the United States; but the other could be used to resist demands for arms which might be useful to American forces. This danger was less than was feared in London, because, as the Minister reported, the United States had now turned the corner in their production. The autumn months were demonstrating their enormous industrial capacity. The output of the principal weapons reached levels from two to six times those of November 1941. But combined discussions were still of great importance, since the Administration was now fixing the main lines of its production programmes for the next eighteen months. It was doing this on a realistic basis, thus deflating some of the expectations of the armed forces, and increasing the danger of disproportionate cuts in British requirements. A meeting of British Missions in Washington late in October welcomed a realistic United States programme, but warned that the United States Services were working on the basis of a twenty-five per cent. cut in the Army supply programme for 1943, involving possibly a cut of twenty-five per cent. in the lend-lease programme.

On the British side the supply crisis was of a different kind. The final decisions had now to be taken to divide up the reserves of manpower between 'fighting and fabrication'. The position was summarised in a communication dated 14th October 1942 from the Minister of Production to the Prime Minister:[2]

> . . . as we must allocate almost all the remaining reserves of our manpower within the next few months we must reach some understanding with the Americans. Without such an understanding, we

---

[1] The Prime Minister wanted Hopkins to come over to discuss the matter before the Lyttelton Mission left, but Hopkins saw 'no awfully good reason' for a visit at that moment.

[2] Quoted in M. M. Postan, *British War Production*, p. 242.

cannot risk increasing the manpower in the Services on a scale involving substantial dependence on the United States for equipment.
If we cannot reach it we must adjust the balance between our industrial effort and the intake into the Services.

Because these were the last manpower reserves the need for long-
range assignments from American production were more urgent than
ever. British requirements could be pruned a little, but the important
thing was to be sure of the residue. As the Minister of Production put
it before leaving London, 'I do not propose to ask for a Protocol, but
I aim to secure its equivalent'. The real point was that the British
Government could not take the risk of continuing the mobilisation
of such a high proportion of its adult population for war purposes
unless it could count on getting the munitions from the United States
on which this arrangement was based. A memorandum used by the
Mission in Washington put the figure of mobilisation at thirty per
cent. of the adult population. The 'last reserves' still left to mobilise
were $1\frac{1}{2}$ million persons. Out of 32 million adults of working age
9·6 million were already in the armed forces, civil defence and
munitions industry. Munitions were being provided not merely for
the 4·1 million in the armed services of the United Kingdom, but
also for 2·7 million in the armed forces of the Dominions, India and
Allies. This mobilisation involved a growing dependence on the
United States. The memorandum gave some examples of the degree
of British dependence on the United States for important types of
supply:

	Per cent.
Synthetic rubber	100
40-ton tank transporters and 10-ton lorries	100
Self-propelled artillery	nearly 100
Transport aircraft	nearly 100
Auxiliary aircraft carriers	85
Escort vessels	68*
Light bombers and G.R. landplanes	68
Tanks	50–57
Tank engines and track (for United Kingdom tank production)	40–50
Fleet Air Arm aircraft	40
Alloy steel	34
Carbon steel	28

* Represents United States percentage contribution to pool of new
construction in 1943.

The Minister of Production took back with him on 30th November
1942 a letter written that day by the President to the Prime Minister
in which the agreements reached with the Mission were summarised.
(As the next chapter shows the President's letter failed to 'carry
down the line' on a number of points, but its importance at the time
seemed considerable.) The President put shipping first and devoted
half of his letter to it. There were two main aspects, the building of
new ships and the maintenance of the British import programme.

On the latter the President's assurance that 'from our expanding fleet you may depend on the tonnage necessary to meet your import program' seemed at the time to the Ministry of Shipping to be hedged round with qualifications which 'might go far to destroy its value' and did in fact do so. The President put the minimum shipbuilding target for 1943 at 18·8 million deadweight tons with the intention of increasing it if possible to 20 million tons.[1] This settled a controversy (in the President's words) about 'the relative need of merchant ships versus escort vessels. In this case I believe we should try to have our cake and eat it too.' A total of 336 escorts were to be built in 1943— an increase of seventy. The principle of a *pro rata* allocation of American-built escorts was agreed; and the ratio was fixed later at 1 British to 1·37 American.

Then came aircraft, on which the President had two main points. The first was his target of 82,000 combat planes to be produced in 1943. He had no misgivings about reaching the target and that without any sacrifice of quality to numbers. The other point was about assignment. He put aside as of secondary importance the mid-summer policy that American planes must be flown by American crews. If, he wrote, 'you can get at the enemy quicker and just as effectively as we can, then I have no hesitancy in saying that you and the Russians should have the planes you need'. Assuming eighty per cent. fulfilment of the American production programme, a new and detailed 'Agreement on Air Supplies to the British in 1943' was reached some days later. On the assumption that eighty per cent. of the President's target would be produced it assured the British of 9,212 aircraft in 1943 (for the Royal Air Force 4,611; for the Fleet Air Arm 2,201; 600 transports; and for the R.A.F. for U.S.S.R. 1,800 fighters). As an offset the United Kingdom was to provide 600 Spitfires for the United States Army Air Force.

Finally, the President's letter referred to ground army equipment. Negotiations were not then concluded; but the President gave an assurance that every effort would be made to include 'your essential requirements in our Army Supply Programme'. An agreement— known as the Somervell-Weeks-Riddes Agreement was reached some days later and the Minister gave the text of it in his Report to the War Cabinet on 9th December. This matter is referred to in the next chapter. A cut of twenty-five per cent. was to be made in British requirements—corresponding to a similar cut in the American pro-grammes. But the aim was to provide the minimum needed to cover the deficit on British production; thus for tanks the United Kingdom was to get ten out of nineteen up to April 1943.

The various 'agreements' secured by the Lyttelton Mission looked

---

[1] Production by the Maritime Commission in 1943 reached 19,296,000 deadweight tons.

like long-term assignments. But all such agreements were in fact subject to review; and no attempt to make them completely binding ever succeeded. The aircraft agreement itself provided that allocations were to be reviewed in May 1943. In the hope of making the agreements firm, the Minister (in accordance with the President's own wish) had adopted the policy of carrying the negotiations 'down the line' with the Services before coming to the President himself. In any case the principle that the programming of production must be a combined affair had been vindicated; and the planners in London could go forward with greater assurance. The President in his letter to the Prime Minister ended with a promise that the 'flow of materials, machine tools, components and complementary items from America . . . will be maintained'. He added that he wanted the Prime Minister to feel that the letter and the agreements gave him 'the assurances you need in planning your own production', and the 'firm base upon which to make the allocations of your remaining reserves of manpower'.

CHAPTER X

THE HARVEST OF MUNITIONS AND COMBINED SUPPLY

(i)

Supply and Strategy

'WHATSOEVER a man soweth, that shall he also reap.' In 1943 and 1944, the years of peak production, the Allies reaped the harvests planned and sown in the earlier war-years. On the supply side these were years of harvesting, rather than of planning and of policy-making for the future. The machine industries of the United States and the United Kingdom and Canada, without counting other members of the British Commonwealth, together produced arms on a scale never before attained in the history of warfare. The main emphasis of planning could now pass over to the side of strategy. The harvest of munitions gave at last the strategic initiative to the United Nations. They could abandon their defensive roles and begin to pass over finally to the attack. The history of the war, like a river at the peak of its flood, had now reached its fullest expanse. The main tributaries of supply which this volume has been tracing become more difficult to follow in the vast widening flood. The chapter on procurement in *Studies of Overseas Supply* shows the flow of supplies to the United Kingdom in this period. The flow ran at its highest levels, but so smoothly that there were relatively few policy issues or serious difficulties.

Two-thirds of the total lend-lease aid to the British Commonwealth during the war and the bulk of Canadian mutual aid were given in the years 1943 and 1944; so was the bulk of British reciprocal aid. Munitions made up about seventy per cent. of the total lend-lease supplies in these two years. No account of this flow of supplies from North America can be intelligible unless the figures are shown within their context of combined supply and total production. The various items of overseas supply, the periods in which they were received, the percentages which they formed of British, American and Canadian production and of total combined supply, are like bits of stone in a mosaic—their significance lies in the patterns of which they form part. Only a suggestion of these patterns can be given here.

One or two illustrations can be given of the way in which strategic plans affected production and supply, and how these in turn determined the scope and timing of particular operations. Something can be said also to illustrate the relation of production in Britain to production in the United States, to show their contributions, with that of Canada, to combined production, and to throw some light thereby on the significance of the mutual-aid sector of combined supply. Illustrations can also be given to show how complex the problem of lend-lease could be in particular cases, and how embarrassing could be the dependence of Britain on the United States for a percentage of her needs if the supply were uncertain. Only a passing reference need be given here to the combined machinery during these years, since some space will be devoted to this topic in *Studies of Overseas Supply*. All this can only be in the nature of a slight sketch of the full picture, which it will not be possible to reconstruct until the national histories of production and supply become available. Even these histories cannot tell the full story. For the war efforts of the British Commonwealth and the United States were so interlocked that the full significance of their combination in one particular aspect of supply can only emerge from the final record of their action together in the field. Thus on the air side only the history of combined air operations—particularly the combined bomber offensive against Germany, the most sustained and continuous military operation of the war—could give final meaning to the data in this study, to the numbers and types of aircraft, to percentages of total requirements, to financial and other factors.

Only in such a history of operations could there be a final accounting for a vast variety of separate elements. These include such diverse things as the training of British aircrews in the United States and the advanced training of American crews in Britain; the provision of 133 airfields for American use in the United Kingdom; the exchange of all technical air data and of inventions; the magnetron valve and the Rolls-Royce Merlin engine and the jet engine. They include also the American contribution to the Royal Air Force of complete aircraft, components and armaments; and the innumerable smaller yet significant items such as the British spark-plugs—well over a million by D-Day—with which American bombers in all theatres were equipped, and the quarter of the 1,000-lb. bombs dropped by Bomber Command in 1944 which the United States supplied.

The strategic planning for 1943 and 1944 was closely linked with supply programmes and especially with the combined output of ships and the main offensive weapons. The passing to the United Nations of the strategic initiative meant that Britain no longer needed to place the main emphasis on the mass production of defensive weapons in the shortest possible time. Henceforward the United

Kingdom as well as the United States could concentrate on weapons of offence, such as the heavy bomber and tanks, and on the development of new weapons and secret devices in radar, artillery, explosives and other fields. The results from such devices were reflected in increased mastery over the submarine, the achievement of naval superiority in the Pacific, and the growing success of the air offensive against Germany. The production plans for a greatly increased output of heavy bombers on both sides of the Atlantic were geared to the new kind of systematic air offensive which mounted in fury all through 1943 and 1944. This was a combined offensive of a type that no other country, Allied or enemy, was able to mount and sustain during the war. By the end of 1943 the offensive could be stepped up from Italian bases to reach into the farthest corners of German-held Europe to destroy basic industries, transport and fuel supplies.

From the outset the United States, immune from serious attack, had been free to concentrate their main production on offensive weapons. They were able therefore to contribute to the common pool a larger proportion than the United Kingdom of such weapons for the assault on the Continent. The time for that vast operation had not yet come since supplies were not yet adequate. The year 1943 had thus to be a year of intermediate objectives. It was to be the main war production year of the United States in which they would finish the initial equipment of their own forces and furnish a large surplus for their allies. But amidst the many operations of 1943 against each of the three enemies—for this was the year of the heightened bomber offensive against Germany, the sustaining of Russia, the defeat of Italy and the beginning of the rolling back of the Japanese in the Pacific—preparations went forward increasingly for the main purpose for which the production of both 1943 and 1944 was to serve—the invasion of Europe. All the main conferences of 1943—Casablanca in January, Washington in May, Quebec in August, Cairo and Teheran in November and December—served this purpose. Before that enormous amphibious operation could be mounted there were still all sorts of special production programmes to be executed, including landing craft, Mulberry harbours, cross Channel oil pipelines (Pluto) and a number of others. The core of the problem was shipping in its manifold forms—cargo boats, tankers, convoy protection ships, landing craft and the many types of naval combat vessels. This chapter is directly concerned with only one of the many aspects of the problem of ocean transport—that of the supply of new ships from North America, and even for that there is space for only a brief reference.[1]

---

[1] See Hancock and Gowing, op. cit., Chapter XIV, and the forthcoming volume in the Civil Histories Series on Shipping, by Miss C. B. A. Behrens.

SHIPPING AND ESCORT VESSELS

The limiting factors of supply, above all shipping, were the main notes struck by the President and the Prime Minister in their joint message to Stalin on 26th January 1943, giving the results of their meeting in Casablanca. In Europe, the message explained, the main desire was to divert German forces from the Russian front whilst maintaining maximum supplies to Russia by all available routes. The clearing of the Axis out of Africa would free supply lines in the Mediterranean route and open Axis centres in southern Europe to air bombardment. The opening soon of large-scale amphibious operations in the Mediterranean would involve a considerable concentration of Forces, shipping and landing craft. Shortage of shipping in general, and above all special types of ships, naval and military, continued to dominate strategic planning from Casablanca in January 1943 to the eve of D-Day in the spring of 1944. The main naval and military deficiencies were escorts to destroy submarines and so win the battle of the Atlantic passage and approaches, and landing craft for amphibious operations in all theatres of the war.

Under the January 1942 agreements the shipping resources of the two countries were 'deemed to be pooled' and were to be administered by the Combined Shipping Adjustment Boards in London and Washington in 'one harmonious policy'. Shipping was much more directly and closely connected with strategic operations than the work of the other Combined Boards—perhaps more closely even than the Combined Munitions Assignments Board. At most conferences of the heads of Governments the shipping experts of both countries met to consider the shipping aspects of any plan under consideration. Account was taken in such discussions both of ships already existing and the timetables for the completion of new ships. Such conferences dealt with a series of facts or probabilities, some of which it was not too difficult to estimate—such as existing tonnage, rates of production, rate of sinkings. Thus at Casablanca in January 1943 shipping —including landing craft and escort vessels—played a major part in the choice between a series of operations—in France, Sicily, Burma, the Pacific.

The limitations of ocean transport and the rate of new building led to decisions of the highest importance as to the use of manpower, the size of armies, and the nature and extent of lend-lease supplies to the United Kingdom. They brought about a drastic reduction of the planned size of the American Army and the use of a relatively larger proportion of manpower in the armed forces of the United Kingdom. The original American plans in 1942 for an armed force of 16 to 17 million were discarded on the advice of the Combined Chiefs of Staff. The reasons were that such a large force could not have been equipped quickly enough, nor shipped and supplied by sea, nor even deployed against the enemy. The more economical plan from a shipping point of view was to make the maximum use of manpower in the United Kingdom, e.g. by the use of lend-lease supplies to diminish the need of dollar-earning exports. But this in turn depended on enough new ships being made available to the United Kingdom to maintain the import programme.[1]

From a longer range point of view the crux of the problem of shipping was that sinkings of merchant ships still exceeded replacements and that there was a serious lag in the combined production of escort vessels—the means to prevent sinkings. In 1942 the United States, the United Kingdom and Canada produced 10·6 million deadweight tons of merchant shipping. But even this large total was exceeded by sinkings; and the merchant fleet of the United Nations was smaller at the end of the year than at the beginning. In the United Kingdom, since the shipping crisis of 1941, escort vessels, destroyers, frigates, corvettes, etc., had been given the highest priority. Orders for corvettes had been placed by the United Kingdom in Canada, but it was to the United States that Britain looked for the main supply of ships of this type. This hope had been disappointed. After Pearl Harbour most of the American production was required for the protection of American ships in the western Atlantic and in the Pacific. So great was the American need that the United Kingdom had agreed to loan anti-submarine trawlers to the United States and to divert to the United States Navy 25 corvettes under construction on British account in Canada. Despite the highest priority, the production of escorts in the United Kingdom in 1942 was far below need; but 72 destroyers were completed out of 135 under construction. In the late summer the Royal Navy had only 445 escorts as against requirements put by the Admiralty at 1,050. Corvettes and frigates could be built faster, but even in 1943 only 50 of them were completed in the United Kingdom.[2] Altogether the United Kingdom built during the war 479 ocean convoy vessels,[3] whilst Canada built 122 corvettes, 70 frigates and 103 minesweepers.

In the United States the building of escorts had fluctuated with the rate of sinkings and the demand for landing craft. In the summer of 1942 landing craft, urgently needed for the invasion of North Africa, pushed escorts from their position of top priority. Only four destroyer escorts were in fact scheduled for completion during the year and none was finished. The number programmed for 1943 was

---

[1] Hancock and Gowing, op. cit., Chapter XV, on Manpower. British reciprocal aid was also a device to save shipping. At the end of 1944 it was estimated that the equipment furnished in Britain to the United States Army Air Force alone saved well over 600,000 tons of shipping space.

[2] Postan, *British War Production*, pp. 290–92.

[3] Corvettes 184; frigates 86; hunts 86; sloops 32; minesweepers 91.

reduced in October 1942 from 241 to 200.[1] At the end of that month, however, the President restored escorts to first priority and they held this place until late in 1943.

The combined merchant shipbuilding programme for 1943 was set at some 23 million tons. To protect these ships, construction of about 1·1 million displacement tons of escort vessels was planned in the United States, the United Kingdom and Canada. There was pressure from the British side to speed up the output of escort vessels in the United States. The Combined Chiefs of Staff on 2nd January 1943 took the unusual step of making a direct approach to the Combined Production and Resources Board asking for any action possible to increase production. Rapid production was facilitated by a considerable degree of standardisation of design secured through the Combined Shipbuilding Committee (Standardisation of Design) established early in 1943 largely through the efforts of C.P.R.B.[2]

By the summer of 1943 combined merchant ship construction was nearing its peak. The rate of sinkings had been dropping for several months. At the end of June the Combined Production and Resources Board circulated a graph to show that by September the curves of ship construction and sinkings would meet. Construction by the United Nations in the first half of the year reached 10 million tons; eighty-five per cent. of the total came from American shipyards and the rest from the United Kingdom and Canada. The curve of total new construction showed a steady upward movement. It rose above the 10-million tons mark in the late summer of 1942 and then swept upward to pass the 20-million mark in the following spring. At the Quebec Conference in August 1943 the Chiefs of Naval Staffs assumed that the worst was over in the Battle of the Atlantic. At the end of the year the Combined Production and Resources Board reported that almost a million tons of ocean convoy vessels had been delivered in 1943 as compared with just over 100,000 tons in 1942. Combined construction of merchant shipping had reached 21·5 million deadweight tons during the year.

Since total construction had come close to programmes, whilst losses had been far less than anticipated, there was a large net addition to the total shipping resources of the United Nations. At the end of 1943 they amounted to 63 million tons, 15 million more than in December 1941, and with a high proportion of new ships.

Meanwhile there had been much anxiety in the United Kingdom for many months about the rapid shrinking of the British cargo fleet

---

[1] *Industrial Mobilization for War*, op. cit., pp. 537–38.

[2] The Committee was set up on 5th March 1943 by the Combined Chiefs of Staff on the recommendation of C.P.R.B. to advise agencies on standardisation. Its membership included the naval and shipping departments of the United States, United Kingdom and Canada.

and of vital imports of food and raw materials.[1] The seeming commitment of the President in his letter of 30th November 1942 referred to above, although taken by the British Government as firm, was to disintegrate at the departmental level. This had happened several times before and was to happen in other cases several times again, as later pages show. It increased the difficulty of planning, both on the side of production and on that of supply. *British War Economy* quotes the note of concern that emerged in a War Cabinet paper: '. . . We must know where we stand. We cannot live from hand to mouth on promises limited by provisos. This not only prevents planning and makes the use of ships less economical; it may in the long run even imperil good relations.'[2]

The matter continued to be discussed at the highest level between the two Governments through the first half of 1943. On 7th June the President informed the Prime Minister by letter that he had arranged for the transfer to the British flag 'for temporary war-time duty' of fifteen to twenty ships a month.[3] Thus by mid-1943 the shipping crisis can be said to have been surmounted.

The President referred in his letter to the general principle of combination in production, as agreed between himself and the Prime Minister in their conference after Pearl Harbour. This was for 'each to concentrate on doing those things which each of us was best qualified to do'. As applied to shipping, the President went on, the agreement was that the United States was to be 'the predominant cargo shipbuilding area for us both, whilst your country was to devote its facilities and resources principally to the construction of combat vessels'. As the President's letter showed, combination, with lend-lease as its instrument, was not merely a method of adjusting resources in shipping, but also in manpower. The United States had built a vast tonnage of cargo vessels and could man only a limited portion. The transfer of ships made it possible to make use of the growing pool of trained seamen in the United Kingdom, due to destruction of British ships.

LANDING CRAFT

In the process of stepping up the building of escort vessels the production of landing craft had slackened towards the end of 1942 on both sides of the Atlantic.[4] The United Kingdom had led the way in

---

[1] The course of events is set out in the volume in this series on *British War Economy*, op. cit., Chapter XIV. See also the forthcoming volume on Shipping, op. cit.

[2] Hancock and Gowing, op. cit., p. 430.

[3] In giving the text of this letter to the House of Commons on 3rd August 1943 the Prime Minister noted that the discussions had been 'furthered in great detail by the Minister of War Transport'. He informed the House that the transfer over the next ten months of 150 to 200 new ships built in the United States (and of a proportionate number from Canada) had already begun. H. of C. Deb., Vol. 391, Cols. 2088–90.

[4] On the earlier phase of landing craft see above, pp. 356–58.

landing-craft construction with a programme of 128 set in the spring of 1940; and on the eve of Pearl Harbour 348 were under construction. By mutual agreement British programmes concentrated mainly on smaller types, leaving the larger landing ship tanks to the United States and Canada. In the end the United Kingdom produced a higher proportion of landing craft than originally planned and received less from the United States than had been expected. Total production in the United Kingdom during the war of landing craft of all types was 4,133,[1] or twenty-six per cent. of the total tonnage of new naval construction during the war. The rise in production in the United Kingdom is shown in Table 12.

Deliveries of United Kingdom landing craft[2]

TABLE 12   Number

	September 1939 to December 1941	1942	1943	1944	First half 1945	Total
Major landing craft[3] .	89	192	442	418	123	1,264
Minor landing craft .	319	329	1,017	887	317	2,869
TOTAL . .	408	521	1,459	1,305	440	4,133

The table shows that 1943 was the peak year for these craft. In the autumn of 1943 the Admiralty gave first priority to landing craft over everything else. Some orders were placed for the larger L.C.T.s and L.S.T.s; in December forty-four of these 4,800-ton vessels were ordered in the United Kingdom and thirty-five in Canada. These were mostly for completion in 1945. The method of prefabrication for both landing craft and corvettes, by using inland firms for the construction of sections, was in full swing in the United Kingdom by the second half of 1942.[4]

In the United States the landing-craft programme had been cut back sharply early in 1943 to make way for escorts. Landing-craft deliveries, which were 88,000 displacement tons in January 1943 and 106,000 tons in February, had fallen by July to 51,000 tons. The lack of landing craft was singled out as the main barrier to the amphibious operations planned at Casablanca in January. Twelve months later, at the Cairo and Teheran conferences in November and December 1943, this was still the greatest obstacle. Production in the United

---

[1] See *Statistical Digest of the War*, op. cit., Table 112.

[2] In addition three L.S.T.s were built in 1943, one in 1944 and eighteen in the first six months of 1945.

[3] Landing craft tank, landing craft infantry, landing craft flak (large), landing craft gun (large and medium).

[4] Postan, op. cit., p. 296.

States had continued at such a low level through most of the year that the combined planners (C.O.S.S.A.C.), who had been at work in London since the early summer on plans for the invasion of Normandy (Overlord), doubted whether there would be anything like enough landing craft to ensure the success of the operation. This was 'the nightmare that was to haunt C.O.S.S.A.C. to its dying day', and then to haunt S.H.A.E.F., even into the days after the first landings in Normandy.[1] In the autumn of 1943 the supply situation seemed to move from bad to worse.

All the discussions on operations at Teheran and Cairo in the late autumn of 1943 turned on the numbers and types of landing craft that could be made available at different times and in different theatres by a complicated process of juggling timetables. The dates at which particular operations could be launched in Europe—the landing of extra divisions in Italy to pin down German troops in that country, the secondary landing of several divisions in the South of France (Anvil) to coincide more or less with Overlord, whether or not operations would be practicable in the Bay of Bengal early in 1944, were all discussed at Cairo and Teheran on the basis of the production figures for landing craft and timetables of movements.

The feasibility of such operations at particular dates depended on margins as narrow as several weeks, or at most, months of new production of particular types of landing craft.[2] The competition for landing craft between various operations continued until the eve of the invasion of Normandy. It was in April 1944 that the Prime Minister wrote to General Marshall: 'The whole of this difficult question only arises out of the absurd shortage of the L.S.T.s. How it is that the plans of two great empires like Britain and the United States should be so much hamstrung and limited by a hundred or two of these particular vessels will never be understood by history.'[3]

Meanwhile the large-scale emergency programme for landing craft for which the situation called had been put into effect by all three countries—the United States, the United Kingdom and Canada—before the end of 1943. The President himself, whilst still at the conference in Cairo, gave the order to restore landing craft in the United States to the highest priority.[4] This programme for landing craft meant sacrificing other types of shipbuilding. Landing craft,

---

[1] Lieutenant-General Sir Frederick Morgan, *Overture to Overlord* (London: Hodder & Stoughton, 1950), pp. 100–01, 148–49, 154, 176–77. Also published in the United States under the same title (Garden City, New York: Doubleday & Co. Inc., 1950), pp. 92–93, 143, 145, 170.

[2] Thus sixty-eight L.S.T.s—three months' production—had to be shifted from the Mediterranean to the Channel by 15th January 1944 if the date set for Overlord was to be kept. *General Marshall's Report*, op. cit., pp. 27, 30.

[3] Churchill, *Closing the Ring*, op. cit., p. 454.

[4] *Industrial Mobilization for War*, op. cit., p. 608; *Landing Craft and the War Production Board* (War Production Board, Washington: 1944).

escorts, major naval vessels and merchant ships were all competing programmes. All drew together upon shipyards and their man-power, and upon steel plate, engines and innumerable components. The necessary cuts were made in merchants ships and escorts rather than in major combat ships. Combined deliveries of merchant ships fell in consequence to 17·3 million deadweight tons in 1944 (14·8 million in the United States, 1·3 million in the United Kingdom, 1·1 million in Canada and a small number in Australia). High landing-craft production targets, starting at 102,000 tons a month and rising month by month, were set in the United States; and to ensure that the targets were met overriding priorities were given in materials, components and manpower. At D-Day 233 of the large L.S.T.s and 835 L.C.T.s were ready for the assault on the beaches.[1] Combined construction of landing craft reached its peak in May 1944 with the delivery of 198,000 tons in the United States and in the United Kingdom. United States output for the year 1944 was 27,388 craft totalling 1·5 million displacement tons, as against 16,000 in 1943 (0·7 million tons), 6,900 in 1942 (0·2 million tons) and a mere 995 of smaller craft in 1940–41.[2] The production of landing craft in the United States from July 1940 to June 1945 was 63,218 craft totalling 2,978,000 displacement tons or thirty-six per cent. of total new naval construction. Landing craft thus illustrate the close interlocking between the United States, the United Kingdom and Canada in strategy and production and in the use of war equipment. The spectacle of craft from the several countries shuttling back and forth across the Channel, carrying impartially in combined operations American, British, Canadian and other troops and their supplies, showed how little meaning there was from a practical point of view in fine distinctions between lend-lease, mutual aid and reciprocal aid.

(ii)

The Combined Machinery and Adjustments in Production and Supply

Thus strategy determined production and supply determined strategy in an endless process of interaction. Despite the chaos of particulars there was an essential unity about the process which was

---

[1] Dwight D. Eisenhower, *Crusade in Europe* (Garden City, N.Y.: Doubleday & Co. Inc., 1948), p. 53. Also published in the United Kingdom under the same title (William Heinemann Limited, 1948).

[2] *Production, Wartime Achievements and the Reconversion Outlook* (War Production Board, Washington: 1945), p. 30.

perpetually demonstrated by the final unity of action in the field. Waging the most mechanical, scientific, high-speed and complex war in history, the British-American combination nevertheless retained a high degree of fluidity in its arrangements. Its ability to make rapid adjustments in the processes of production and supply in the light of changing need and experience was an important factor in victory.

These adjustments were innumerable and only a few will receive any special mention in this history. Successful combination was an endless process of particular agreements, not all of them even recorded in the millions of files and many millions of pages of paper that make up the archives of the war. Supplies were bought, shared, allocated, manufactured and again allocated, assigned, distributed and used in particular theatres by a continuous process of agreement. If there was disagreement, it was almost always resolved in agreement at some point along the line.

Combination was no formal process which could be demonstrated on charts of organisation. The processes of production and supply, hardly less than on the military side, were combined at a multitude of points on both sides of the Atlantic. There was more combination outside than inside the Combined Boards. The control of production and supply remained in the hands of the national production authorities. There was a great deal of direct traffic between the national systems by many roads. The Combined Boards in a sense were merely traffic junctions of special importance. Their most important tasks were those of exercising a general oversight over part of the process and of making adjustments where needed. It was easy, especially in the early stages, as Chapter IX showed, for national production authorities, intent on speedy results, to throw the production of particular kinds of equipment out of balance. It was the function of the various boards, each from its special angle, to watch the processes of production and supply in order to prevent or correct unbalance of this sort.

The Casablanca conference in January 1943 finally supplied the strategic guidance which all the Combined Boards had lacked in 1942. The conference of heads of Governments that followed in May, August, November and December gave the whole combined organisation a surer sense of direction and kept it running smoothly. The whole combined organisation was fully developed by the end of 1942 and was working efficiently. The Casablanca conference was the longest and most complete of the series of meetings of the civil and military heads held since 1941. Indeed, at the end of it the Prime Minister declared that 'there never has been, in all of the inter-allied conferences I have known, anything like the prolonged professional examination of the whole scene of the world war in its military, its armament production and its economic aspects'.[1] Continuity between conferences and liaison between the Combined Chiefs and the Combined Boards was easier when, as in the case of Trident in May 1943, the Heads of Government conference was held in Washington, the headquarters of the combined organisation; or at least on the same side of the Atlantic, as in the case of Quadrant, held in Quebec in August.

The basic pattern of the machinery of Combination was already firmly fixed in 1942 and was to remain unchanged to the end of the war. The possibility of change was never discussed except in one context, the idea that closer co-ordination with the other Allies might be secured by some modification in the exclusively American-British (or British Commonwealth) character of the combined organisation. When the point arose, as it did on more than one occasion in connection with the work of one or more of the combined boards, the conclusion was always the same: that from the point of view of swift action and efficient working it was better to preserve the principle of British-American combination and to confer when necessary with other countries on an informal basis. The Combined Chiefs, when they raised the same question at Cairo at the end of 1943, in connection with the possibility of closer liaison at the staff level with the U.S.S.R. and China, arrived at the same conclusion.

For the British missions in Washington, mid-1943 was the central point of calm in the war. It lay midway between the anxieties of 1941, the shortages of 1942 and the uneasiness that began in the second half of 1944 about the possible loss of supply through the ending of lend-lease. By May 1943 the U-boats had been thwarted; shipping was easing; production was running full throttle. There were enough supplies to meet most needs. The Chiefs of Staff could report at Trident in May that there were now available enough men, weapons and material for all proposed operations—with the big exception of landing craft. British requirements programmes were being accepted by the American agencies without difficulty. Assignments were secured easily from the Combined Munitions Assignments Board.

Combined activities in 1943 and 1944 in the matter of raw materials and war production (both inside and outside the two Combined Boards which shared this field) were determined largely by the degree of maturity reached by particular production programmes at particular points of time. In retrospect, the United States official accounts showed the United States as passing through a sequence of shortages.[2] First, productive capacity (buildings and machine tools); second, raw materials (basic metals and minerals); third, inter-

---

[1] Cited in Sherwood, op. cit., p. 684.

[2] *United States at War*, op. cit., and *Industrial Mobilization for War*, op. cit.

mediate manufactured products (metal fabrications and manufactured components), with another batch of raw material shortages, largely forest, agricultural and animal products; fourth, manpower. By 1943 the United States were in the third stage. The United Kingdom, at least a year ahead in maturity of war production, was already deep in the fourth.

In both countries requirements of capital equipment, particularly machine tools, had been largely met by the end of 1942. Production planning in the United Kingdom at the beginning of the war had foreseen the early months of 1942 as the point at which the phase of capital equipment should come to an end. But changes and expansion in certain parts of the production programme had led to increased orders for plant and machine tools in 1942, mainly in connection with shipbuilding and the heavy-bomber programme.[1] In 1941 and 1942 some twenty per cent. of British machine-tool requirements were still being met by the United States. The demand slackened in 1943 and the removal of machine tools from lend-lease in November marked the end of the machine-tool phase. The final settlement in connection with machine tools, which is referred to below,[2] came fourteen months later, much in advance of the general lend-lease settlement. The Combined Production and Resources Board in mid-1943 noted that broadly speaking 'the problem of machine tools supplies has disappeared'. Even in the United States, it noted, the provision of machine tools was 'rapidly declining'. By this time the productive capacity of the industry in the United States and Canada, which in 1942 was more than five times as great as in 1939, had more or less cleared up the heavy backlog of orders that had accumulated in 1941 and 1942.

As regards raw materials two of the three main problems of 1942 had been largely solved by the spring of 1943. One, referred to below, was the chronic problem of imports into the United Kingdom. The other two were the grave shortages in the supply of some twenty-five basic materials, due to the sudden Japanese conquest of South-East Asia and the placing of vast American war contracts; and faulty control of distribution in the United States. Solutions of both these problems had been worked out by the beginning of 1943. The supply of most of the basic materials, especially base metals and minerals, had been assured by the processes of international allocation, the confining of use to essential war needs, the development of old and new sources, conservation, and co-ordinated purchasing of supplies throughout the non-Axis world. The problem of distribution in the United States was solved by the putting in force in the spring of 1943 of the Controlled Materials Plan for allocating supplies of steel,

---

[1] Postan, *British War Production*, op. cit., pp. 203–04.
[2] Chapter XI, pp. 448–49.

aluminium and copper. Here too increased production played a vital part; since 1939 the output of steel in the United States had been doubled, that of aluminium multiplied five times and of magnesium fifty-five times.[1]

The introduction of an effective system of allocation in the spring of 1943 helped war production in the United States to settle into a more orderly routine. In the words of the official account, the Controlled Materials Plan became 'the central instrument for adjustment of production programs in accordance with strategic requirements and prospective supply of critical resources'.[2] Henceforth programmes of requirements put forward by the Services and other claimants had to justify themselves in terms of raw materials before they could obtain allocations under the Controlled Materials Plan. Moreover, final acceptance in the spring of 1943 of the principle of civilian direction of war production by the War Production Board led to a more harmonious relationship between the civil and military sides. The Services were now able to give more precise data as to their requirements both of materials and of manufactured components.

Fresh raw material shortages developed, however, in other materials, both in the United States and elsewhere. These materials included in particular forest products (lumber, pulp and paper) and animal products such as hides and leather. Such shortages were due mainly to lack of manpower, seasonal factors and difficulties of expanding output. There was also the perennial problem of rubber. The end of the year marked the long-foreseen critical point at which it would be clear whether the United Nations were succeeding or failing in their efforts to fill the gap in the supply of natural rubber by the production of synthetic. It became clear then that a disastrous failure of rubber supplies would be averted. It was even possible to make some cuts in the production of certain types of synthetic rubber. This was done in favour of a still more critical product—high octane gasoline,[3] which competed for the same materials as synthetic rubber.

The problem of keeping raw material stocks in the United Kingdom at the levels necessary to maintain British war production was more intractable. This was primarily a matter of shipping rather than of shortage of supplies. The 'target' figure for raw material imports in 1942, as fixed in the previous November, was 14 million tons—about half the total imports by volume. Continued shipping losses threatened to cut the figure by a million tons; mainly at the expense of non-

---

[1] There was also a threefold increase in the United States in the principal chemicals and in plant products, textiles and fibres. *Industrial Mobilization for War*, op. cit., Part IV.

[2] Ibid., p. 632.

[3] Ibid., pp. 663, 648–49. A study made at the end of 1942 which showed a deficit of about 100,000 barrels of high octane gasoline per day led to a decision to expand production to cover the deficit. The United Kingdom had received about a third of the amount covered by its requisitions over the previous four months. In November the head of the British Petroleum Mission reported: '*We are now in a very bad situation.*'

ferrous metals and of steel from the United States. Actual imports for
the year were 11·5 million tons. At the end of 1942 the 'target' for
1943 was fixed again at 14 million tons. The drain on shipping in
1942 had already lowered stock levels and an increase of consumption
by war industry was expected in 1943. It was calculated at the time,
although historical research may throw some doubt on the validity
of the estimate, that an import of 14 million tons of raw materials
would mean a stock level of only three or four weeks' consumption.
To increase stocks to a safer level a cut in consumption was ordered
by the Prime Minister. The import figures were so bad in the early
months of the year that the Minister of Production thought that raw
material imports for the year might be as low as 11 million tons. The
possibility of a serious cut in war production was averted by the
passing of the shipping crisis. Raw material imports for the year ending June 1943 were 11·4 million tons. From this point stocks began
to rise again slowly. In the first half of 1944 the import rate was still
only 11·8 million tons a year; but there was some decrease in consumption due to manpower shortages. At no time between Pearl
Harbour and the end of the war, Professor Postan notes, 'was munitions production in the country interrupted or even slowed down by
a failure in the supply of raw materials'.[1]

By 1943 the United Kingdom had achieved an increase as compared with 1938 of about forty per cent. in total industrial production
and this had been secured with only forty per cent. of the pre-war
volume of imports of raw materials.

With the eighty per cent. increase in American production goals
in 1943, as set at the beginning of that year, there was little margin
for wasteful use of raw materials, components and manpower. Shortages had begun to shift at the end of 1942 from the supply of the more
basic raw materials to the supply of particular shapes and forms of
steel, copper and aluminium (i.e. semi-fabricated materials). Serious
shortages appeared also in a group of manufactured products, such
as valves, compressors, diesel engines and electric motors, which
served as components in many different types of products. A scheduling order, M.293, published by the War Production Board on 26th
February 1943, regulated the manufacture of thirty-six classes of
critical components. In essence it was a means of regulating the flow
of steel, copper, aluminium and other materials into the manufacture
of components, and thereby controlling their distribution to the
different end-products such as ships, tanks and aircraft.[2] Every control of this kind had its repercussions on British supply. This order

[1] Postan, *British War Production*, op. cit., Chapter V, p. 214; and Hurstfield, *The Control of Raw Materials*, op. cit., Chapter XIV.
[2] *Industrial Mobilization for War*, op. cit., pp. 632–34 and 685 ff. *United States at War*, op. cit., p. 312 ff.

made it necessary for the British Government to anticipate its needs still further in advance if it was to be certain of supply. Another general directive affecting components, issued on 30th April, caught British supply in its backwash. It lowered the priority given to what appeared to be miscellaneous British requirements for equipment and components included in Part III of the United States Army supply programme. The effect on the British war production programme was shown in an appeal which the British Chiefs of Staff lodged immediately with the Combined Chiefs. In some cases the British requirement, small though it might seem in the mass of American production, was in fact the whole British programme for that particular item. To assign it anything lower than top priority might imperil a whole production line of tanks or guns, or some vital kind of engineering equipment. The adjustment made in this case was a compromise. Out of the total value of $730 million affected by the directive, top priority was assigned to $200 million, for items to be selected by the British missions in consultation with the United States War Department. The meeting of 16th June 1943, in which British officials worked out this solution with Generals Somervell and Clay, was typical of the continuous process of adjustment needed in what the record of this meeting called 'the interlocking problems arising out of the United Kingdom and United States programming arrangements'.

Although each country controlled its own war production programmes, these interlocked at many points. Both countries drew more or less on the same pools of raw materials, machine tools, ships and components; they made use at some points of each other's designs, techniques, and even manpower. The principle of combination made possible a certain degree of specialisation by each country which increased their interdependence. Constant adjustment between them was thus essential. Such adjustments were the general province of the Combined Production and Resources Board; and, in their special fields, of the Combined Raw Materials Board and the Combined Shipping Adjustment Board. The adjustments which were necessary were legion, and the Boards handled only a limited number of the more important cases. A few of the cases have been mentioned in this volume. One was the basic adjustment, forced by lack of enough ships, whereby the United Kingdom put a higher percentage of its manpower into its armed forces, whilst the United States made up for a smaller army than originally planned by producing more munitions. Another was the American undertaking to construct the greater part of the merchant ships and nearly all the transport aircraft needed to meet the combined requirements. Still others are referred to below and some are mentioned in *Studies of Overseas Supply*.

Adjustments were needed for many different reasons. Some arose from the marked difference in the stage of development reached by the two war administrations. One had bought maturity at the cost of mistakes. The other was new and needed time to settle down. It still had its mistakes to make, and in accordance with the rule that a country learns more from its own experience than from the experience of another, it often preferred to repeat the mistakes of the other before reaching similar solutions. One of the best examples was the wrong turnings taken before the United States introduced the Controlled Materials Plan. Other adjustments arose from the radical differences between the industries of the two countries. One has just been mentioned—the almost complete dependence of the United Kingdom on imported raw materials. Another was the concentration of British industry in the past on a wide variety of goods for the export trade, whilst the United States, with their large internal market, had developed mass-production methods on a unique scale and had invested their savings in a constant modernisation of their machinery and plant. The large-scale application of mass-production methods to the making of munitions was facilitated by the billions of dollars of British cash orders and capital investment poured into the United States in the opening years of the war. This money helped to put to work idle factories, to build machine tools and to begin the process of channelling into war production some of the $8\frac{3}{4}$ million unemployed workers.

War production in the United States was thus largely superimposed on civilian production. War requirements were met mainly by a very large increase in the total output of the economy, which rose from $120 billion in 1941 to almost $200 billion in 1944; forty-three per cent. of the latter figure was for war purposes.[1] Free from any direct interference by the enemy, immune from bombing, blackouts and dispersion, possessing abundant plant and machine tools, raw materials and managerial skill, and an immense reservoir of trained workers, American mass production was able to achieve a remarkable output in a short period of time. The high acceleration in the rate of output is illustrated in the tables later in this chapter. Early in 1942 the volume of munitions production in the United Kingdom was still greater than that of the United States; but it was soon overtaken. In 1944 the United States produced nearly six times as much munitions as the United Kingdom. Yet the historian of British war production rightly pays tribute to the elasticity of American war industry and its ability, despite its mass-production techniques, to make the changes in the design of weapons made necessary

---

[1] *Industrial Mobilization for War*, op. cit., p. 766. So great was the productivity that 'consumer purchases of goods and services were somewhat larger in each of the war years than in 1939'. Ibid., p. 964. In the United Kingdom the purchase of consumer goods and services fell by twenty-one per cent. between 1938 and 1944. *Statistics Relating to the War Effort of the United Kingdom*, Cmd. 6564, November 1944, p. 26.

by war experience.[1] The major shifts in military requirements caused by inadequate tank performances in North Africa, landing craft at Tarawa and artillery in Italy were taken by American industry in its stride.[2] If need be it always had enough margin to provide a separate factory for the making of a redesigned weapon. Thus in practice American war production largely avoided the dangerous rigidity which it had been feared might set in once the production lines were fixed.

British industry, adjusted to the varying needs of export markets, and less developed on mass-production lines, showed an even greater ability to adapt itself to new requirements. This quality was never better shown than in the year before the invasion of Europe. Manpower had become so short that a new production requirement could be met only by taking labour away from other programmes. The island was an armed camp crowded with the armies of three nations, all of which had to be provided with transport, housing, airfields, training grounds and a multitude of goods and services. Yet in this period the United Kingdom not only maintained—in its dispersed factories within an hour's flight of enemy aircraft—large programmes for the production of still heavier bombers, heavier tanks, and more powerful artillery; it also added extensive new programmes. These included masses of special invasion equipment, special radar, special equipment for airborne divisions, special craft and apparatus to get troops and their tanks and trucks across the Channel, to land them dry on the beaches and in prefabricated harbours, to bridge the roads ahead of them into Germany—and to carry their petrol, which alone meant providing the American Army with seven million jerricans. All this was part of the peculiar contribution which could be made only by a country which formed an advanced base on the very frontier of the enemy. There were other enterprises which only the United States could undertake. The greatest of them was the production of atomic power. The British scientific and technical contributions in the initial stages were of the highest importance, but only the United States had the margins necessary to undertake the vast industrial projects required to carry through the enterprise.[3] Some need of adjustment arose from the fact that the timing of war production on both sides of the Atlantic was different. If the stages of development had coincided the planning of supply would have been much easier. War production began earlier in the United Kingdom than in the United States. It rose steadily and relatively fast to a high level which it retained longer than in the case of any of the other powers. The timing in Canada was a little slower with peak production to-

---

[1] Postan, op. cit., p. 244.

[2] *Industrial Mobilization for War*, op. cit., p. 635.

[3] See *Studies of Overseas Supply*, Chapter VIII by J. D. Scott.

wards the end of 1943. The United States began later than either, but they moved much faster when once they had gained momentum. The British peaks for ground army supplies were reached in 1942 or early in 1943, roughly about a year before those of the United States. In the United States peak production was reached for most items in November 1943. This was the period planned for maximum output of aircraft, armoured fighting vehicles and major naval vessels. This level once reached was maintained more or less to D-Day. As in the United Kingdom, special production efforts were needed in the first half of 1944 for various supplies such as landing craft, troop transports, aircraft radar, heavy bombers, heavy trucks and tractors. For munitions generally, including aircraft, the combined peak was reached in March 1944.

Aircraft reached peak production in both the United States and the United Kingdom in the first half of 1944. The output for the year in the United States was 96,000 aircraft, 10,000 more than in 1943, and 962 million lb. of weight as against 655 million lb. in 1943.[1] In the United Kingdom aircraft still retained in 1944 the high priority they had held throughout the war. Numbers, which hovered just above 2,000 a month from 1942 to 1944, were no clear index to output. As in the United States, there was a steady upward increase in structure weight from the 10 million lb. a month reached in the spring of 1942.[2] The output of heavy bombers, which had lagged behind the programme, caught up with it in the first half of 1943 and held fairly steadily to it thereafter up to the peak just before D-Day. Total combined annual deliveries of heavy bombers rose from over 4,000 in 1942 to over 20,000 in 1944.

The peaks for ground army supplies in the United Kingdom were reached more or less in accordance with plan. Maximum output of Ministry of Supply war-stores in general was reached in the first quarter of 1943; but the peak for some kinds of motor vehicles was about the middle of 1942, and for gun ammunition September 1942. For signal stores and small arms ammunition, however, the peak was late in 1943, and for engineer stores, armoured and scout cars just before D-Day.[3] The War Office and the Ministry of Supply had adopted early in the war the expedient, later used by the United States War Department, of an army supply programme covering two years' requirements ahead and revised every six months. From 1940, as the history of *British War Production* shows, the British programme set a clearly defined timetable with strict quantitative limits for different parts and stages in the equipping of the Army. In these plans

---

[1] *Industrial Mobilization for War*, op. cit., pp. 753–54.

[2] In March 1944, which was an exceptional month, the figure reached 20 million lb.

[3] *Statistical Digest of the War*, op. cit., Tables 126 and 127; Postan, *British War Production*, op. cit., Tables 47 and 48.

1942 was foreseen as the year of maximum output.[1] By the end of that year the initial equipment of the army of fifty-five divisions was expected to be completed, provided maintenance and war wastage requirements were not excessive. Several factors, however, disturbed these plans. In each revision of the programme allowance had to be made for more and heavier tanks and armoured fighting vehicles. A still more important factor was the effect of the entry of Japan into the war. This brought a sharp upward revision of the planned strength of the British Army. The Order of Battle, fixed in May 1942 for April 1943, was now based on some ninety-seven divisions—twenty-three armoured. The resulting increase in munitions requirements, for both the British Army and the overseas armies of the Commonwealth, was formidable. A good deal of the increase was to come from the United States and some from Eastern Group countries; but by far the heaviest part fell to British war production. Full use could be made, however, of the very large productive capacity created in the United Kingdom to meet the initial equipment of the Army, and British industry proved equal to the task. The production goals were met despite a sharp decrease in the labour force available to the Ministry of Supply in 1943. Manpower was being drained off into the armed forces and into other channels, such as aircraft production and special ship-building programmes.[2] This was also the peak year of naval construction, including landing craft and escort vessels; nearly 500,000 tons of naval shipping was completed.[3]

Even at this late stage it was still possible for a great expansion to take place in a section of British war industry on the basis of a technical invention, and to have important consequences for North American supply. What was virtually a new industry was developed in 1942 on the basis of the cavity magnetron valve, brought to the United States by the Tizard Mission in the autumn of 1940. The intense manufacturing activities in the production of new secret radar devices are described in *British War Production.*[4] Out of the magnetron valve came a whole series of secret devices including centrimetric radar, A.S.V., OBOE and H_2S, which transformed anti-U-boat warfare and night bombing at the end of 1942; gun-laying devices and the proximity fuse. The latter, manufactured in the United States under a special 'crash' programme, helped to defeat the flying bomb.

One measure of the new industry was the astronomical rise in the demand for radio valves. The forecast of British valve requirements rose from 24·4 million for 1942 to over 50 million for 1943 and even

---

[1] Postan, op. cit., p. 346.

[2] Ibid., p. 225. On Eastern Group countries see *Studies of Overseas Supply*, Chapter IX.

[3] See Cmd. 6564, *Statistics relating to the war effort of the United Kingdom*, Table 8. This figure is in terms of standard displacement. Tables 111 and 112 in the *Statistical Digest of the War*, op. cit., show the types and tonnage of the various vessels completed.

[4] Postan, op. cit., pp. 361–63. On radar see *Studies of Overseas Supply*, Chapter VIII.

higher for 1944. It was planned to secure 15 to 20 million valves from the United States. The supply of radio valves from the United States to the United Kingdom rose from 1·4 million in 1942 to 2·3 million in 1943, and then jumped to 17·4 million in 1944, a figure which was still only a small part of American production.[1] The value put on assignments of all United States-produced radio and radar equipment rose from $10 million in 1942 to $92 million in 1943 and $254 million in 1944. This was in addition to the value of radio and radar equipment installed in complete aircraft supplied under lend-lease. For the years 1941 to 1945 this latter figure was estimated at $256 million.

Radar illustrates very clearly the growth from 1940 onwards of full British-American-Canadian combination in war production and supply. Its pattern was woven from many threads; the contribution of basic British inventions, their rapid translation into finished devices for industrial production, the perfection of both British and American devices in the United States and the application there and in Canada of mass-production methods, the formidable combined production which resulted, and the provision of part of Britain's needs from the output of American and Canadian factories.

Nevertheless, although some expansion occurred in British production at special points from 1943 to 1945, the Services and the supply departments looked to the United States for most new or belated British requirements, or increased demands for existing types of munitions supplies which could not be met easily by British industry.[2] The general nature of British requirements in the United States in the next phases of the war was outlined in the joint war plans drawn up in the autumn of 1942. Two of the main items of supply have been mentioned above; the United Kingdom was to look mainly to the United States for merchant shipping and transport aircraft. In addition it was assumed that the United States would supply nearly all the self-propelled guns, the 40- and 20-ton tank-transporters and 10-ton trucks, as well as a high proportion of British requirements in tanks and landing craft, light bombers and auxiliary aircraft carriers.

This was part of what was known as the Somervell-Weeks Rootes Agreement. It sought to do two things: (a) to provide a firmer basis for the combined planning of war production by setting down the principles which were to govern supply from the United States to the United Kingdom; (b) to draw up an agreed list of thirty-one stores, covering the main items of munitions supply, and indicating the amounts which the United Kingdom was to receive from the United States. It was an outcome of the Lyttelton Mission in the

---

[1] Postan, op. cit., Chapter VI, section 6. Some contracts for radio valves were also placed in Canada.
[2] Postan, op. cit., p. 246.

late autumn. Months of discussion and uncertainty as to the amounts of different types of munitions the United Kingdom could count upon from the United States for the next two years had preceded this step. The unsatisfied and insatiable needs of the expanding American Army threatened to crowd out British requirements. But adjustments of this sort, which made the United Kingdom dependent on the United States for a definite proportion of its requirements, had their disadvantages. Any failure to secure the fixed proportion or to secure it in time, or any serious falling-off in assignments, was likely to throw the supply of the armed forces out of balance.

The agreement tried to set out for both countries the principles on which they were to act. The United Kingdom was not to over-state its requirements; they should be put at the minimum necessary to cover the deficit in British production. (Even the British missions in Washington had expressed the feeling at times that London tended to overstate its requirements.) From this a second point followed: the United Kingdom was not to ask for supplies in excess of British capacity to man and use them in all the areas of British strategic responsibility. Then followed a statement of American responsibilities which proved to be more difficult to carry out. They were designed to remove the element of uncertainty in the planning of British production and the disposition of British forces which is referred to at several points in this study. The agreement stated that the inclu-sion of British requirements in American programmes 'shall carry an equal obligation to produce and make available to both forces' the quantities involved. If it were not possible to meet the monthly schedules of production, then the quantities assigned would be scaled down 'in the proportion to the requirements accepted'. In other words the United Kingdom was not to be the residual legatee who would receive what was left over when the American forces had taken what they wanted. Both parties would have to consent to any changes in the agreement, and a change could only be made in the event of 'a major unforeseen change in the strategical situation'. Provision was made for adding unforeseen British requirements by a 'spot' procedure. The flow of components needed by the British production programme was also assured. The agreement was obscure as to its application to British contracts in Canada. The United Kingdom assumed these remained at the disposal of the British Government save for American contracts placed with War Supplies, Limited. But the United States War Department interpreted it as extending beyond those contracts.

It was rather a moot point whether it was good policy to try to assure supply by such general agreements. They were rather an exception to the usual procedure for securing supplies. They in-cluded, in addition to the Somervell-Weeks-Rootes agreement, the

aircraft agreements referred to in earlier chapters, an agreement on
tanks negotiated by a British tank mission early in 1942 and the
Stage II agreement at the end of 1944 which is referred to in the
next chapter. None of them worked very well. If there was plenty,
the United Kingdom usually secured its requirements. If there was
a shortage there had to be discussion and allocation in accordance
with the circumstances at the time, which no general rule could
foresee.

In some cases listed in the agreement, such as tanks and certain
types of trucks and tyres, combined production never caught up
with requirements. In the case of tanks combined planning narrowly
avoided a decision that might have had serious consequences. An
American suggestion was made at the end of 1943 that British tank
production should be reduced. Combined tank production was to be
concentrated largely in the United States and the British Army was
to turn over increasingly to American Sherman, M-4, tanks. The
argument for concentrating tank manufacture mainly in the United
States was that it was uneconomical to use machine tools and material
to produce British models which in any case were regarded as
inferior to the Sherman. Fortunately, as events showed, British tank
manufacturing was maintained. The Sherman—which was a joint
United States-British design, was only a stage in the evolution of
tank design and in 1944 the United States changed over to heavier
models with better armour and larger guns. In the meantime a
number of Shermans supplied to the United Kingdom had been
fitted there with the seventeen-pounder gun with great advantage
as regards hitting power. It became clear later that the assumption
that enough American tanks would be available for the British Army
was ill-founded. The United States Army supply programme for
1944 provided for nearly 9,000 Shermans for the United Kingdom.
This represented two-thirds of the total prospective United Kingdom
supply of medium gun tanks in that year; the remaining 4,000 were
to come from United Kingdom production. Only sixty per cent. of
the Shermans were in fact received during the year and those mostly
of the older types. During the year United States tank reserves in
Europe had fallen dangerously low. Since October therefore the
United Kingdom had given up all the Shermans which would
normally have come to it, and in addition had transferred some tanks
in the field; in all it had forgone in this way nearly 5,000 tanks.
Some British armoured formations which had been converted to
United States tanks had to be reconverted to British tanks. A
memorandum by the British Staff of the Combined Production and
Resources Board in January 1945 concluded that there would have
to be an immediate increase in the combined tank programme. It
was clear that 'combined planning has taken a nasty blow'.

Despite the Somervell-Weeks-Rootes Agreement, difficulty arose almost immediately over the supply of trucks to the United Kingdom, especially 'heavy heavies' (i.e. six to ten tons). The proportion of this type desired by the United Kingdom was regarded as too high. The matter was referred through the Combined Production and Resources Board to a Combined Truck Committee which reported in April 1943 on the results of an investigation of the production of wheeled vehicles in the United States and the British Commonwealth, and a study of requirements in relation to shipping and other factors. The report indicated a gap between British production and British requirements of nearly 700,000 trucks of various types. Canada could provide only about a fifth of the deficit. The United States could supply all their own requirements; but the United States Army supply programme had provided for only 112,921 vehicles to meet the needs of the United Kingdom and Canada. The deficit was most serious in respect of heavy trucks, especially tank-transporters, of which there was little or no production in the United Kingdom. Here a difference of military doctrine impeded supply. British military experience showed that tank-transporters were very important. The United States Army still had to learn this in North Africa. The Committee advised waiting until this experience could filter through from the field into the programming of supply. Before more 'heavy heavies' could be produced in the United States allocations of the necessary steel, copper, aluminium and rubber had to be made. But the main 'bottleneck' was the lack of enough forgings and castings, which meant serious shortages of axles, transmissions and engines. 'Heavy heavies' remained short to the end. In 1944 out of total British requirements of 35,737 heavy trucks and tractors (four tons and over) only sixty-five per cent. could be met—less than a third from the United Kingdom production and over two-thirds from the United States. For other kinds of trucks assignments had more or less caught up with British requirements by the end of 1943. A British report from Washington in May 1944 noted the rapidity with which trucks were moving: 'Vehicles are made available within one month of assignment and exported one month later.'

The supply of tyres from the United States was one of the most difficult problems of the later war-years. Apart from the shortage of the basic raw material, rubber, there was a shortage of fabricating capacity. Tyres were an important civilian requirement as well as a vital necessity for the armed forces. They were one of the few manufactured products to come under full combined allocation. There was the added complication in the United States that a vital British military requirement remained until the end of 1944 under a civilian agency, the Procurement Division of the Treasury. This was a difficulty for the United Kingdom because the United States Army could command higher priorities.

Already in 1941 the British Commonwealth had presented large requirements in the United States, including two million giant tyres. Because of lack of shipping space in 1942 unshipped tyres piled up at seaboard and British requirements had to be reduced. By the autumn of 1943, at the point of switching over from natural to synthetic rubber, a world shortage of six million truck tyres was revealed. The Rubber Director in September 1943 suspended production on lend-lease contracts for supply to the United Kingdom. In November the long-felt need of closer combination in the tyre production programmes of the United States, the United Kingdom and Canada was met when the Combined Production and Resources Board set up the Combined Tyres and Tubes Committee in Washington, whilst in London a Tyre Working Party was established. The task of these bodies was to review requirements and to estimate what new production was needed. The Combined Committee, however, did not possess the power to allocate—a point which authorities in London were slow to realise. It could merely recommend; allocation of American production for foreign requirements remained a function of the War Production Board and the Foreign Economic Administration. Allocations for the 'British Empire' were made to the British Supply Council which apportioned them amongst all countries of the Commonwealth. Finally, in 1944, the limitations of civilian procurement of a military requirement, the difficulties of estimating requirements and planning production of a great many different types of tyres, both for military and civilian use, the disparity between needs in a small island and in a continental area, caused a breakdown in procurement. Critical British tyre requirements remained unsatisfied until the War Department took over on 1st January 1945 and tyres began to be assigned by the Combined Munitions Assignments Board. From this date British civilian requirements from the United States (except for tyres not normally manufactured in the United Kingdom, such as tractor types) were taken off lend-lease and purchased for cash.

(iii)

Combined Munitions Production and the Mutual Aid Sector

The secret of combination is not to be found in any study of comparative war effort. Combination was no mere sum of parts. It was a multiplier of forces.

The most spectacular sign of the success of combination was the fact that by 1944 the super-priority lists both in the United Kingdom and the United States had become practically identical. Both countries had a list of the things which were of supreme importance and the lists were the same. By 1944 it was hardly possible for any weapon to be plentiful in one country and scarce in the other; and it could be said with confidence that for practical purposes waste due to failure to co-ordinate effectively had been eliminated.

COMPARISON AND TRENDS

In this section an attempt is made to sum up in the matter of munitions production the total forces generated by the combination. Only against such a background is it possible to judge the proportions and functions of mutual aid. The figures are mostly allowed to speak for themselves. The highly complex question of comparative war effort can hardly be touched upon in this book; it is referred to in a few words at the end of this section.[1] The war was not fought on the basis of any such comparisons. Each side was making the best use it could of its resources, manpower and skills. Each complemented the other and was able to use special facilities and assets not possessed by the other. This and many other factors made comparisons difficult. Yet it is true that comparisons were made by departments on both sides from time to time in the form of rough-and-ready tabulations of figures. One such was made by the Ministry of Production in January 1945 (Table 13).

United States munitions output in terms of United Kingdom population, December 1941 to June 1944

TABLE 13   Number

	September 1939 to June 1944	December 1941 to June 1944		
	Production in U.K.	Production in U.K.	U.S.	U.S. output in terms of U.K. population
Aircraft	103,000	66,300	171,700	62,400
Armoured fighting vehicles .	100,000	77,500	154,700	56,300
Wheeled vehicles . . .	919,100	511,000	2,036,800	740,700
Artillery equipments over 20-mm.	64,000	49,300	70,000	27,600
Gun ammunition (million rounds)	161	120	280	100
Small arms (thousand) . .	6,012	5,700	12,800	4,700
Small arms ammunition (million rounds)	8,285	6,620	33,800	12,300

[1] See also Chapter XI, Section vi.

Since the population of the United Kingdom was only a third of that of the United States the comparison was to the advantage of British war production. The table was not intended to be in any sense a complete comparison. It covered for example only ground army equipment and aircraft, and manufacture in the United Kingdom was spread over a longer period than in the United States. If other large areas of war production, such as merchant ships and naval vessels, were included the comparison would be less favourable to the United Kingdom. Moreover the rate of American production was rising much faster than that of the United Kingdom, so that if the comparison had been based on 1944 alone the proportions shown for the United States would have been higher.

A broad comparative study of 'Munitions Output in World War II' was made after the war by an American authority, Dr. Raymond W. Goldsmith.[1] The study centres round two highly condensed statistical tables. One shows, so far as data permit, the volume of munitions production of the major belligerents in terms of annual expenditure. The other shows the trend of production in each case. The first table shows an expenditure on combat munitions by the United States of $107½ billion over the period 1935 to 1944 and by the United Kingdom of $43½ billion. Multiplied by three for a population equal to that of the United States, this would make a total of $130 billion for the United Kingdom. The table is not complete since it covers only combat munitions production; it thus excludes from the comparison other factors (merchant ships, mechanical transport and miscellaneous military stores) in which combined production, particularly that of the United States and Canada, was of great importance in contributing towards victory.[2]

Volume of combat munitions production of the major belligerents in terms of annual expenditure

TABLE 14　　　　　　　　　$000 million (1944 U.S. munitions prices)

Country	1935–39	1940	1941	1942	1943	1944
United States .	1½	1½	4½	20	38	42
Canada . .	0	0	½	1	1½	1½
United Kingdom	2½	3½	6½	9	11	11
U.S.S.R. . .	8	5	8½	11½	14	16
Germany . .	12	6	6	8½	13½	17
Japan . .	2	1	2	3	4½	6

[1] Dr. Raymond W. Goldsmith, Director of the General Economic and Planning Division of the Civilian Production Administration (formerly War Production Board), 'The Power of Victory, Munitions Output in World War II', in *Military Affairs, Journal of the American Military Institute*, Vol. X, Spring, 1946.

[2] Thus these additional items would double the total shown for Canada in Table 14, bringing it to $9 billion. See Table 17 below.

Trend of combat munitions production of the major belligerents
1944 = 100
TABLE 15

Country	1938	1939	1940	1941	1942	1943	1944
United States	2	2	5	11	47	91	100
Canada	0	2	6	27	73	102	100
United Kingdom	4	10	34	59	83	100	100
U.S.S.R.	12	20	30	53	71	87	100
Germany	16	20	35	35	51	80	100
Japan	8	10	16	32	49	72	100

The tables show that when the United States really began to arm in 1942 the process went forward with enormous acceleration. For combat munitions the production of the United States in 1944 is shown to be about four times that of the United Kingdom. It was about fifty per cent. more than the whole production of America's allies; and also about fifty per cent. more than all its enemies produced together in that year. The United Kingdom, on the other hand, began to reach a high rate of production as early as 1940, neared peak production in 1942 and reached it in 1943. The most remarkable feature illustrated in the table is the early start of Germany and her belated finish—the levelling off in 1940-41 of both Germany and Japan, the slight rise of Germany in 1942 and its rapid acceleration in 1943-44. At the end German production, split between a two-front war, was hardly enough to equal that of the U.S.S.R. alone, without counting the vastly greater combined production of the United States, Great Britain and Canada. The combined production of these three countries in 1944 totalled about $55 billion compared with about $16 billion for the U.S.S.R. and $23 billion for the Axis countries.

On the last day of the war the statistician of the British Supply Council in Washington (Professor R. G. D. Allen), reduced to a few simple tables the combined munitions production and supply data of the war. The figures given below, which are taken mainly from these tables, illustrate: (a) combined munitions production, showing the broad relation of national munitions production in the United Kingdom to national munitions production in the United States and Canada; (b) the sources of the munitions supply of the British Commonwealth; (c) the magnitude of the contribution made by British production to the total munitions needs of the Commonwealth; (d) the extent of the American lend-lease and Canadian mutual-aid sectors in the munitions supply of the Commonwealth; and also the extent of the reciprocal aid contributed by the United Kingdom.[1] The national war production in the United Kingdom,

[1] The extent of Canadian mutual aid is shown above in Chapter VII. See also Chapter XI.

Canada and the United States is summarised in the following three tables.

The trend of munitions production in the United Kingdom is indicated by various indexes used by the British Ministries concerned with production.[1]

Indexes of United Kingdom munitions production,
September 1939 to June 1945

TABLE 16

Year	Aircraft (based on structure weight and man-hours per airframe)	Total warlike stores (Ministry of Supply)
	Production in January 1942 =1,000	Average production, September to December 1939 =100
1939 (September to December) .	319	100
1940	552	226
1941	803	406
1942	1,192	714
1943	1,587	738
1944	1,692	634
1945 (January to June) . .	1,279	498

The munitions production of Canada, as shown in Table 17, totalled $8,978 million (valued at 1944 costs). About half of Canada's production was in ordnance and vehicles. The percentage of the whole made up by aircraft and ships, namely thirty per cent., was much lower than in the case of the United States or the United Kingdom.

Canadian munitions production, January 1940 to June 1945
(valued at 1944 costs)

TABLE 17   Canadian $ million

	1940	1941	1942	1943	1944	(first half) 1945	5½-year total Value	Per cent.
Aircraft	43	106	222	337	385	162	1,255	14·0
Ships	61	127	265	405	379	185	1,422	15·8
Guns and small arms .	1	17	150	177	144	32	521	5·8
Ammunition . . .	18	160	407	423	432	140	1,580	17·6
Combat and motor vehicles	148	273	510	552	528	211	2,222	24·7
Signals and instruments .	3	14	78	153	196	73	517	5·8
Other munitions . .	87	163	282	392	348	189	1,461	16·3
TOTAL . .	361	860	1,914	2,439	2,412	992	8,978	100·0

[1] See *Statistical Digest of the War*, op. cit., Table 132, and Postan, op. cit., Tables 21 and 47.

The munitions produced in Canada for these expenditures included such items as the following[1] (in round numbers): major merchant and naval units 1,000; smaller craft 7,000; automotive and armoured fighting vehicles 800,000; tanks and tank chassis 5,613; aircraft 16,000; heavy field and naval guns 28,000; machine guns, rifles and small arms 1,700,000; heavy shells (filled rounds) 100 million; small arms ammunition (rounds) 4,600 million; chemicals and explosives, over two million tons.

For the United States the table that follows shows a grand total expenditure on munitions of $182,135 million in five years. Nearly two-thirds of the total fell in the two peak years of 1943 and 1944. In December 1943 peak production in the United States reached the annual rate of $63,000 million.[2] Aircraft and ships (naval vessels, landing craft and merchant ships) made up nearly half of the total expenditure of the five years.

United States munitions production, July 1940 to June 1945[3]

TABLE 18   U.S. $ million

| | 2nd half 1940 | 1941 | 1942 | 1943 | 1944 | 1st half 1945 | Five-year total | |
							Value	Per cent.
Aircraft . .	342	1,737	6,095	12,519	16,046	6,855	43,594	23·9
Ships . . .	391	1,852	6,957	12,498	13,431	4,884	40,013	22·0
Guns and fire-control equipment . .	82	396	2,007	3,647	3,120	1,394	10,646	5·9
Ammunition . .	89	454	2,931	5,549	6,385	3,851	19,259	10·6
Combat and motor vehicles . .	260	1,340	4,943	6,524	5,372	2,695	21,134	11·6
Communication and electronic equipment . . .	27	226	1,512	3,043	3,739	1,906	10,453	5·7
Other munitions .	806	2,320	6,263	10,430	11,033	6,184	37,036	20·3
TOTAL .	1,997	8,325	30,708	54,210	59,126	27,769	182,135	100·0

The scale of the mutual-aid sector of combined supply has to be visualised in terms of quantities as well as money values. To provide a rough scale figures are given showing combined production for four groups of munitions; aircraft, ships, vehicles, guns and ammunition. The percentages of United States munitions production formed by lend-lease supplies to the British Commonwealth for these four

---

[1] Statement by Minister of Munitions and Supply, H. of C. Deb., Canada, Vol. XXXXIV, No. 52, p. 2,270; and Ministry's Press release, 30th December 1945.

[2] See also tables in *Industrial Mobilization for War*, op. cit., p. 962, and *Production, Wartime Achievements and the Reconversion Outlook* (War Production Board, Washington: 1945) which cover slightly different periods.

[3] Valued at W.P.B. standard costs.

groups in the two peak years 1943 and 1944 were as follows: aircraft 12·7 per cent.; ships (including equipment and repairs) 9·2 per cent.; vehicles and equipment (tanks, trucks, etc.) 28 per cent.; guns and ammunition 9·4 per cent.

THE PRINCIPAL MUNITIONS GROUPS

Aircraft. The total combined production by the United States, the United Kingdom and Canada of military aircraft from September 1939 to June 1945 was 427,447. The United States produced from July 1940 to June 1945 284,318 military aircraft, or sixty-six per cent. of the combined total. The total structure weight was about 2,402 million pounds. The United Kingdom produced 123,819 aircraft, or twenty-nine per cent. of the total, with a total structure weight of approximately 759 million pounds; Canada with 16,431 aircraft and Australia with 3,393 together produced five per cent. The peak of combined production was reached in March 1944 with 12,118 aircraft. There was a sharp rise in structure weight in both the United States and the United Kingdom from 1942 onwards, as both countries turned increasingly to the production of heavy bombers. By 1944 the structure weight of the combined output of aircraft was nearly eight times the monthly output in 1941; but in numbers of machines it was only 3½ times. In the United Kingdom deliveries of heavy bombers rose from forty-one in 1940 to 5,507 in 1944; in the United States from forty-five in the second half of 1940 to 14,871 in 1944.

Production of military aircraft in the United Kingdom and the United States

TABLE 19

Year	United Kingdom (Sept. 1939 to June 1945)		United States (July 1940 to June 1945)	
	Number	Structure weight (million lb.)	Number	Airframe weight (million lb.)
1939　Sept. to Dec.	2,924	11.25		
1940	15,049	50.04	3,777	13.4
1941	20,094	87.25	19,410	81.5
1942	23,671	133.38	47,031	274.9
1943	26,263	185.25	83,007	650.6
1944	26,462	208.52	93,623	951.6
1945　Jan. to June	9,356	74.82	37,470	429.9
	123,819	759.31	284,318	2,401.9

Ships, Naval. During the war the combined construction of naval vessels totalled about 11 million displacement tons of new building; the United States 8·2 million tons; the United Kingdom 2·4 million tons;[1] Canada ·373 million tons. In the United States combat vessels (battleships, cruisers, carriers, carrier escorts, destroyers, destroyer escorts and submarines) formed forty-six per cent. and landing craft thirty-six per cent. of total naval construction. In the United Kingdom major combat vessels (battleships, cruisers, carriers, destroyers, submarines and landing-force ships) were thirty-nine per cent. of the naval construction, landing craft twenty-six per cent., and ocean convoy vessels nineteen per cent.

Merchant Ships. Combined construction of merchant ships in the three countries was 61·1 million deadweight tons; the United States 50 million;[2] the United Kingdom 8·3 million; Canada 3·6 million. Four-fifths of the total was thus produced in the United States. The year of peak production was 1943 when combined construction almost reached two million tons a month.

Combined merchant vessel construction

TABLE 20   Thousand deadweight tons

	1939 4th qtr.	1940	1941	1942	1943	1944	1945 1st half	Total
Tankers	—	200	810	1,498	3,825	4,277	1,947	12,557
Dry cargo	336	1,048	1,459	9,059	17,548	12,520	5,166	47,136
Minor types	—	27	25	126	659	429	157	1,423
TOTAL	336	1,275	2,294	10,683	22,032	17,226	7,270	61,116

Tanks, Carriers, Armoured and Scout Cars. The United States produced about seventy-five per cent. of the combined number of tanks and tank chassis produced in the three countries from September 1939 to June 1945, the United Kingdom twenty-one per cent. and Canada four per cent.[3] The exact proportion of the total tank output that was produced in each country, however, depends largely on the definition and classification of tank vehicles. If light tanks are defined as tanks of less than twelve tons the proportion would be considerably influenced by the fact that in the United States sixty-five per cent. of the total number of tanks produced were medium tanks, nearly thirty-four per cent. light tanks and less than two per cent. heavy tanks, whilst in the United Kingdom only a small number of light

---

[1] Built in United Kingdom for Royal Navy, 3rd September 1939–31st August 1945, 7,562 naval vessels, 2,351,492 tons; built in United Kingdom for Dominions, 35 naval vessels, 36,305 tons.

[2] In addition, 1½ million tons of army transports were constructed by the Maritime Commission for the United States Navy.

[3] Canada produced 5,678 tanks and tank chassis, about two-thirds of them gun tanks.

tanks were produced in the war-years. More than fifty per cent. of the total United Kingdom tank production were infantry tanks and about forty per cent. were cruiser tanks of more than twelve tons.

On the other hand, if the definition of light tanks is extended to include tracked and armoured vehicles of the Bren carrier size (as in Russian and some German statistics of tank output) then the British figure of tank output will be greatly swollen by the large number of tracked and armoured carriers made in the United Kingdom. Out of the total number of armoured carriers and scout cars produced in the three countries just over forty per cent. were produced in the United States, just under forty per cent. in the United Kingdom and nearly twenty per cent. in Canada. Probably a better way of comparing the achievements of the three countries would be by figures of structure weight corrected by man-hours similar to those used for measuring aircraft production. Such figures, however, were never computed and are, therefore, not available.

Of the total combined output of armoured cars nearly fifty per cent. were produced in the United States and twenty-five per cent. each in the United Kingdom and Canada.

Number of armoured fighting vehicles produced in the United Kingdom and the United States

TABLE 21   Number

	United Kingdom (from September 1939 to 30th June 1944)		United States (from July 1940 to June 1945)	
Gun-tanks . . . . {	Infantry	13,604	Heavy	1,491
	Cruiser	11,013	Medium	55,752
	Light	498	Light	29,242
Bren carriers	27,043		13,497	
Other tracked and armoured carriers	33,082		Nil	
Scout cars	8,331		73,646	
Armoured cars	6,099		16,335	

Motor Vehicles. The combined production of military trucks of all kinds was about four million. The United States produced sixty-seven per cent.; Canada twenty per cent.; the United Kingdom seventeen per cent. The peak for trucks generally was reached in 1942 with a combined output of 80,000 a month. It was down to 69,000 per month in the first half of 1945. For 'heavy heavies', however, production kept rising up to V.E.-day, but never fast enough. The contributions of each of the three countries for each main class of trucks is shown in the following percentages. (Table 22.)

Ordnance and Ammunition. Supplies under lend-lease to the British Commonwealth in 1943 and 1944 formed 9·4 per cent. of American production under this head.

Percentage distribution of combined truck production
September 1939–June 1945

TABLE 22   Per cent.

	U.S.*	Canada	U.K.	Combined
Heavy-heavy (over 2½ tons) . .	7	—	4	5
Light-heavy (2½-ton type) . .	34	53	} 52	} 55
Medium (1½-ton type) . .	18	10		
Light (under 1½ tons) . . .	41	37	44	40
	100%	100%	100%	100%

* Excluding production prior to July 1940.

Artillery, Anti-tank and Ground Anti-aircraft Guns. The combined production from September 1939 to June 1945 totalled 177,674 units. Of these weapons about two-thirds of the total were produced in 1942 and 1943. Of the combined total the United States produced fifty-six per cent., the United Kingdom thirty-eight per cent. and Canada six per cent.

Small Arms and Infantry Weapons. No less than 27 million small arms and infantry weapons—rifles, carbines, machine and sub-machine guns, anti-tank projectors, 20-mm. guns of all types, and mortars— were produced by the three countries. The overall percentages were: the United States 61⅔ per cent., the United Kingdom 33⅓ per cent. and Canada 5 per cent. But the overall percentages masked wide differences for particular weapons; thus the United States produced seventy-nine per cent. of the rifles and carbines, the United Kingdom sixty-four per cent. of the sub-machine guns and forty-seven per cent. of the 20-mm. guns.

Ammunition. The combined production of ammunition corresponding to this vast output of weapons is shown in Table 23.

Ammunition: total production and percentage distribution
of combined output

TABLE 23

	Total production to June 1945	Percentage distribution of combined output between:		
		U.S.	U.K.	Canada
		%	%	%
Heavy and medium artillery (thousand rounds)	48,881	65	23	12
Light field, tank and anti-tank (thousand rounds)	429,003	68	25	7
Anti-aircraft, ground (thousand rounds)	151,820	49	36	15
Mortar bombs (thousands) . .	199,695	49	45	6
Anti-tank mines (thousands) . .	40,393	45	43	12
Grenades (thousands) . .	217,107	49	44	7
20-mm. (all types) (million rounds) .	2,162	71	26	3
S.A.A. under 20-mm. (million rounds)	56,190	75	17	8
Aircraft bombs (thousand short tons) .	7,150	80	20	*

* Negligible.

THE MUTUAL-AID SECTOR

Against this background of combined production the broad outlines of the mutual-aid sector become clear. A table prepared by
Professor Allen shows the various sources of munitions supply to the
British Commonwealth during the war with the percentages coming
from each source: British war production, production in Canada, in
other parts of the British Commonwealth and in the United States.[1]

*Total British Commonwealth supplies of munitions and percentage
from each source*

TABLE 24

	1939 (Sept.–Dec.) and 1940	1941	1942	1943	1944	1945 (1st half)	Total
Total supplies ($ million) .	9,200	13,000	19,900	24,800	24,700	9,300	100,900
Per cent. from:	%	%	%	%	%	%	%
United Kingdom . .	90·7	81·8	72·6	62·4	61·2	66·1	69·5
Canada . . .	2·6	5·2	8·6	8·8	8·9	10·0	7·9
Eastern Group . .	1·1	1·5	1·9	1·9	1·2	1·7	1·6
Purchase in United States	5·6	9·1	4·7	2·4	1·5	1·2	3·7
United States lend-lease .	—	2·4	12·2	24·5	27·2	21·0	17·3

The table indicates that by far the greatest part of the munitions
used by the British Commonwealth during the war was provided by
the United Kingdom. Up to the end of 1940 the United Kingdom
provided nearly ninety-one per cent. of the total. From then on
supplies from North America began to tell. Over the whole period,
however, the United Kingdom provided about seventy per cent. of
the total munitions supplies used by the British Commonwealth. In
1940 North America provided eight per cent.; and in 1941 seventeen
per cent. The amounts steadily increased in the next two years until
in 1944 they reached 37·6 per cent. Over the whole period North
America provided nearly 29 per cent. (from the United States 17·3
per cent. under lend-lease and 3·7 per cent. for cash, and from
Canada nearly 8 per cent.). The Eastern Group countries (mainly
Australia, New Zealand, India and South Africa) provided only
1·6 per cent.; and in no year did their contribution rise above 1·9 per
cent. Their main contribution on the economic side took the form
of raw materials and foodstuffs which do not appear in the table. For
this reason the table understates their contribution, as it does that
of Canada.

---

[1] This and the following tables are taken from the article by Professor R. G. D. Allen,
'Mutual Aid between the U.S. and the British Empire, 1941–5,' *Journal of the Royal
Statistical Society*, Vol. CIX, Part III, 1946, pp. 243–71, to which the reader should turn
for full and authoritative analysis of this complex subject. Professor Allen was also
responsible for the Ministry of Production statistical study referred to above (p. 419).
The average conversion rate used in the tables for munitions, allowing for differences in
costs, was £1 = $7.00; and for non-munitions £1 = $4.00.

To bring out the role of British cash purchases in the United States in the earlier period before Pearl Harbour, Professor Allen has provided the table given below. The British Commonwealth and Empire obtained during the war about twelve per cent. of the total United States munitions output—two per cent. for cash and ten per cent. under lend-lease. The cash expenditure (almost wholly by the United Kingdom), provided only a small proportion of total British Commonwealth supplies, but it paid for a considerable percentage of United States production during that period and in so doing laid the basis for a large munitions industry outside the American Government arsenals. It was of special importance, as earlier chapters have shown, for aircraft, aircraft engines and tanks.[1] The output from the British (including the French) contracts amounted to about forty per cent. of aircraft production in the United States up to Pearl Harbour. 'It was British ordering', Professor Allen points out, 'which established United States production of such important types as the Mustang fighter (developed from the Spitfire design), the Hudson and Ventura bombers and the Harvard trainer.' The Mustang was adapted to the Rolls-Royce Merlin engine built by the Packard Company in the United States.

British Commonwealth supplies of munitions from the United States[2]

TABLE 25

	Commonwealth supplies from the United States			United States production	
	Purchases	Lend-lease supplies	Total	Total	Percentage to Commonwealth
	$ million	$ million	$ million	$ million	%
All munitions:					
1940 (second half) .	400	—	400	2,000	19·1
1941 . . .	1,200	300	1,500	8,600	17·3
1942 . . .	900	2,400	3,300	32,000	10·5
1943 . . .	600	6,100	6,700	54,400	12·3
1944 . . .	400	6,700	7,100	57,700	12·3
1945 (first half) .	100	2,000	2,100	25,500	8·1
TOTAL (five years) .	3,600	17,500	21,100	180,200	11·7
of which:					
Aircraft and equipment .	2,100	5,600	7,700	47,300	16·3
Ships, equipment and repairs . . .	200	3,300	3,500	41,100	8·5
Ordnance and ammunition	700	3,000	3,700	34,200	10·8
Vehicles and equipment .	400	3,700	4,100	19,300	21·2
Other munitions . .	200	1,900	2,100	38,300	5·5

[1] See above, Chapter VII.
[2] *Journal of the Royal Statistical Society*, Vol. CIX, Part III, 1946, op. cit., p. 267.

The composition of lend-lease aid to the British Commonwealth is shown in the following tables prepared by Professor Allen:[1]

United States Lend-Lease Aid to the British Commonwealth

TABLE 26 $ million

	1941 (Mar. to Dec.)	1942	1943	1944	1945 (Jan. to Aug.)	Total
Ship (sail away) . .	65	195	1,078	540	229	2,107
Munitions destined for:						
United Kingdom . .	86	987	2,797	3,807	971	8,648
Rest of Commonwealth and other war theatres.	100	1,158	2,131	2,294	1,203	6,886
Other goods destined for:						
United Kingdom . .	576	1,404	1,782	2,405	1,275	7,442
Rest of Commonwealth .	10	227	436	583	390	1,646
Services	245	786	807	1,137	369	3,344
Total aid to British Commonwealth . . .	1,082	4,757	9,031	10,766	4,437	30,073
Aid to Russia . . .	20	1,376	2,436	4,074	2,764	10,670
Aid to other countries .						2,872
Total lend-lease aid . .						43,615

Composition of United States Lend-Lease Aid to the British Commonwealth

TABLE 27

	1941 (Mar. to Dec.)	1942	1943	1944	1945 (Jan. to Aug.)	Total
$ million:						
Total lend-lease aid . .	1,082	4,757	9,031	10,766	4,437	30,073
Less petroleum . . .	83	232	372	799	656	2,142
Total, excluding petroleum	999	4,525	8,659	9,967	3,781	27,931
Per cent:						
Aircraft and equipment .	2·0	17·8	18·8	23·6	27·7	21·0
Ships, equipment and repairs	14·1	8·5	17·9	9·3	9·2	12·0
Ordnance and ammunition.	7·0	15·4	12·1	9·0	7·8	10·0
Vehicles and equipment .	6·7	9·5	17·0	14·6	9·4	13·5
Other munitions . .	1·1	2·3	4·5	11·0	10·2	7·1
Total munitions . .	31·7	53·6	70·3	67·5	64·3	64·4
Foodstuffs . . .	29·1	14·3	9·5	11·7	12·7	12·2
Other agricultural produce.	8·0	3·2	2·4	2·4	3·7	2·9
Metals	9·3	6·4	4·9	3·5	5·4	4·8
Machinery . . .	2·4	4·2	3·4	2·7	2·6	3·1
Other manufactures . .	1·5	2·7	1·1	1·8	2·4	1·8
Services, excluding ship repairs . . .	17·9	15·5	8·4	10·6	9·0	10·8

[1] Ibid., pp. 250 and 263.

As the tables indicate munitions constituted the largest element in United States lend-lease aid, about sixty-five per cent. Services (mostly shipping) made up ten per cent. Other supplies (non-munitions) made up twenty-five per cent., of which half was food. The importance of the non-munitions element to British war production was greater than the low and fairly steady percentages of United States production, shown in the next table, might seem to indicate. The machine tools could not be obtained from any other source. The food and raw materials cost far less in terms of shipping than any other source of supply save Canada; and they made possible the very high degree of mobilisation of British manpower for war production and for fighting. The percentages of American munitions production provided as lend-lease were higher and more fluctuating. For the main groups they reached their peaks in 1943 and 1944. Some idea of the total production of supplies which these percentages represent is given earlier in this section.

United States Lend-Lease Aid to the British Commonwealth in relation to total United States production[1]

TABLE 28   Per cent.

	1942	1943	1944	1945 (first half)
Lend-lease as per cent. of total production:				
Aircraft and equipment	12·4	11·9	13·5	11·8
Ships, equipment and repairs	5·5	11·8	6·7	5·4
Ordnance and ammunition	10·4	10·0	8·8	4·6
Vehicles and equipment	9·8	26·7	29·4	12·1
Other munitions	1·4	3·4	9·9	5·5
Total munitions	7·6	11·2	11·7	7·6
Foodstuffs	4·3	4·4	5·4	3·9
Other agricultural produce	4·3	5·6	4·4	5·0
Metals	3·9	4·2	3·4	3·5
Machinery	2·6	5·7	7·1	4·2
Other manufactures	0·7	0·6	1·1	0·7

The reverse side, lend-lease as compared with the reciprocal aid accorded to the United States by the United Kingdom and other members of the British Commonwealth, so far as it was recorded, is shown in the following table by Professor Allen:[2]

---

[1] Ibid., p. 264.

[2] Ibid., p. 258, and Hancock and Gowing, op. cit., p. 353. Sterling converted at £1 = $7.00 for military stores and ships; for other goods and services, £1 = $4.00. For Canadian mutual-aid figures see above, Chapter VII.

Comparison of Lend-Lease Aid to the British Commonwealth and
Reciprocal Aid to the United States to VJ-Day

TABLE 29

	In $ million		In £ million sterling	
Government account	Lend-lease aid from United States	Reciprocal aid to United States	Lend-lease aid from United States	Reciprocal aid to United States
United Kingdom:				
Ships and construction .	2,107	910	301	227
Military stores . .	13,823	2,014	1,975	288
Petroleum . . .	1,850*	1,187	462*	297
Other goods . . .	6,263*	361	1,566*	90
Services . . .	2,980	1,195	745	299
TOTAL . . .	27,023	5,667	5,049	1,201[1]
Australia . . .	1,570	1,041	296	216
New Zealand . . .	271	248	52	54
South Africa . . .	296	1	53	†
India . . .	913	610	178	134
TOTAL . . .	30,073	7,567	5,628	1,605

* Approximate division between petroleum and other goods.
† Less than £0·5 million.

What British production and its reciprocal-aid sector meant in
terms of comparative war effort is discussed in other volumes in this
series[2] and in Professor R. G. D. Allen's paper cited above. They
analyse in detail the means by which—by mobilising in war industry
and the armed forces a higher percentage of manpower than any
other belligerent, by working longer hours, by lowering standards of
living, by sacrificing financial reserves, by incurring war debts abroad,
and by the help of lend-lease—the United Kingdom was able to play
such a large role in proportion to its limited resources and production. It was able in the first place to produce about seventy per cent.
of the munitions used by the 8¾ million men in the armed forces of
the British Commonwealth of Nations. In the second place, it was
able, together with the other Commonwealth countries, to furnish
reciprocal aid to the United States which was almost equivalent in
proportion, if not in amount, to the lend-lease aid given by the
United States. Professor Allen's analysis came to two main conclusions: first, that both the United States and the United Kingdom

---

[1] This figure is given in Cmd. 6931, October 1946, as £1,241,400,000. See also a
statement by the Chancellor of the Exchequer in answer to a question in the House of
Commons, 5th December 1950, which gave a grand total for United Kingdom reciprocal
aid of £2,078·4 million, made up of £1,241·4 million to the United States and £837
million to foreign countries. The total did not include £153 million to U.N.R.R.A. and
£22 million to the International Refugee Organisation. H. of C. Deb., Vol. 482, Written
answers to questions, Cols. 38–40.

[2] Hancock and Gowing, op. cit., p. 365 ff.

contributed about 4¾ per cent. of their national income to mutual aid; second, that the United States contributed about eleven per cent. of their war expenditure as lend-lease to the British Commonwealth, as compared with nearly nine per cent. of war expenditure contributed by the United Kingdom as reciprocal aid to the United States. This latter point is referred to at the end of this volume in the section on the financial settlements. Each was able to give so much because each received so much from the other. The strength was in the bundle of faggots tied together—British Commonwealth and American leadership, their combined manpower, their territories, their bases, the raw materials they controlled, their production facilities, their inventions and technical skills.

CHAPTER XI

THE ENDING OF WAR SUPPLY
FROM NORTH AMERICA

WHEN the harvest of munitions was gathered the assault was launched on the sea walls of Europe. The invasion of Normandy marked the high point of the British Commonwealth-American combination. From this point onwards the history of war supply from North America slackens in interest. The centre of interest lies in the military history of the combination. Whilst American, British and Canadian armour was thrusting into Germany, the Japanese were being pushed back steadily in the Pacific—westwards, 3,000 miles across the central Pacific; and northwards, 1,500 miles from New Guinea to the Philippines. This chapter is not concerned with the military campaigns; its theme is the transition to peace on the supply side. Its centre of interest lies in what was still an undertone in 1944, but was to become dominant as the war neared its end.

Since 1942 the future had been conceived of as in three stages. Stage I was the period set for the defeat of the prime enemy, Germany. Stage II began with the defeat of Germany and ended with the defeat of Japan. Stage III was what came after—the period of military and economic demobilisation and the restoration of an economy of peace. These were planning concepts. The duration of each stage was guesswork. The chief uncertainty was the duration of Stage II, for which estimates ran from six months to two or three years. It actually lasted only fourteen weeks. It is upon Stage II that this chapter is centred. But it stretches back well into Stage I, in which Stage II was rooted; and it reaches forward into Stage III. Its central thread is still war supply from North America; but woven with it is a thread of a different colour, that of general economic aid from North America in the transitional period.

The chapter shows how four questions were asked and answered both in respect of Stage II and Stage III. Would Canada and the United States continue to finance essential supply from the dollar area? At what levels? Under what conditions? For how long? It was with these questions that planning in the United Kingdom was preoccupied in the first nine months of 1944. They seemed to receive an answer in the Stage II agreements towards the end of the year. The agreements broke down in mid-1945 and the answers had to be worked out afresh. For planning purposes, the first set of answers, the Stage II agreements, related to a period of eighteen to twenty-four months from 1st January 1945. But the period had hardly begun to run when the agreements collapsed. The Governments had to face again what was still essentially the same problem, and—still using the same data—to find a second set of answers. These were given in the post-war financial agreements between the United Kingdom, the United States and Canada.

(i)
Lend-Lease Passes its Peak

The note of transition to peace began faintly at the moment when munitions production reached its peak in the United States at the end of 1943—as if that great industrial country felt that the end was already looming in sight when its factories had performed their task of arming its forces. The history of the War Production Board notes that 'as the peak of war production passed in November, Nelson began to think and talk increasingly about orderly reconversion of industry'.[1] A Congressional committee at this time investigated post-war economic policy and planning; and the President in his message to Congress in January 1944 mentioned reconversion—linking it with maintenance of a high standard of national income and living. Thereafter problems of reconversion in Stage II were kept under review both by the War Production Board and the Office of War Mobilization, which added the word Reconversion to its title later in the year. A statement of W.P.B. policy on reconversion was issued in September, but opposition from the Services and a turn for the worse in the war in Europe put an end to further important moves in this direction for many months.[2] The British Government meanwhile was much concerned about the economic problems that had to be faced at the end of the war with Germany. It foresaw that in Stage II there must be some release of manpower and a little easing of austerity, and it foresaw the shape of the immensely difficult problems of Stage III. Some reflections were given already in May 1944 in a White Paper on Employment Policy after the war.[3]

There were also other signs of concern about the transition to peace. One was revealed in mid-1944 in a rather sudden burst of public criticism of the Combined Boards. Others were visible in lend-lease policies and practices and in military assignments. The Com-

---

[1] *Industrial Mobilization for War*, op. cit., pp. 553 and 575.

[2] Ibid., p. 817.

[3] *Employment Policy*, Cmd. 6527, May 1944. The studies in full employment after the war began as far back as 1941. Hancock and Gowing, op. cit., p. 539.

bined Boards were discussed and criticised in July 1944 in Congress and in articles in American business papers and in meetings of trade associations. One of the grounds of criticism of the Boards was their alleged lack of responsibility; since they were set up under Executive Orders of the President, they were not directly accountable to Congress. It was also charged that they eliminated normal commercial competition and divided up foreign markets, sometimes to the disadvantage of American exporting interests. Thus secret marketing agreements were reported to exist between the United States and the United Kingdom for the control of the exports of industrial leather belting and textiles. Attacks were also made on bulk purchasing and on the arrangements whereby the United States undertook supply responsibilities related to the Western Hemisphere whilst the United Kingdom did the same for the Eastern Hemisphere. Most of the criticism was evidently based on the assumption that peace was not far ahead; and that it was undesirable to permit these war-time agencies to continue their operations into the peace, since they might impede a return to normal trading conditions.[1]

The usefulness of the Combined Boards was far too great, however, for them to be disturbed seriously by such attacks. Hopes of an early end of the war faded in the autumn of 1944. In any case the Boards were needed for the transition to peace as well as during the war. Already at the end of 1943 the shift of interest to non-military supplies had considerably strengthened the position of the Combined Production and Resources Board. Thus in 1944 it was dealing with general shortages in certain commodities, of as much interest to civilians as to the Services, such as textiles and coal. The Combined Boards had begun to undertake new activities in connection with relief and rehabilitation. They were designated in the Charter of the United Nations Relief and Rehabilitation Association as the intergovernmental agencies responsible for determining the sources of supply for commodities required by the liberated areas—a function which continued to be important until the end of the war. Generally speaking the action of the Boards was limited to goods in short supply. These were listed in the reserved commodity lists issued in November 1944. The Combined Production and Resources Board's reserved list included public utility and transportation equipment, coal-mining and agricultural machinery, footwear and leather products, coal and coke, textiles and a few medical supplies. The Combined Raw Materials Board's reserved list included some thirty raw materials of varying degrees of shortage.

The Combined Chiefs of Staff Organisation was also affected by the changing character of the war. Its central activities declined. Its

---

[1] e.g. *The Wall Street Journal*, 5th–8th and 10th July 1944; *The Journal of Commerce*, 2th, 18th, 19th July 1944.

combined committees, however, continued to be active; and one new committee was set up. In accordance with a request made by the Supreme Allied Commander in July 1944 the Combined Chiefs agreed, early in November, to the setting up in Washington of the Combined Liberated Areas Committee.[1] The Committee was designed to secure continuity of policy in the matter of civilian supplies in liberated Europe in the period immediately following the end of military responsibility.

The slackening of activity in the Combined Chiefs of Staff was evident soon after D-day. The Dill-Marshall team was broken by the former's death on 4th November 1944. With the launching of the invasion of Europe, the stage of planning was drawing to a close. The emphasis was passing in all the theatres of the war from plans to execution. The initiative fell largely into the hands of the commanders in the field and there was much less business for the central organisation in Washington. In the Pacific theatre the control of the Combined Chiefs of Staff had never been more than nominal. Since May 1944 combined meetings in Washington had become less frequent and more mechanical. On the British side it was admitted that there were few questions on which general discussions would be profitable, but it was hoped that the machinery would still continue to function. The American side agreed that the organisation should be kept intact. But the American Joint Chiefs wanted to leave responsibility mainly to the theatre commanders on the ground that a committee could not conduct a campaign; the agencies of the Combined Chiefs of Staff, it was felt, could never act fast enough to keep up with situations as they developed in the field.

The work of the Combined Munitions Assignments Board—the Board which was closest to the Combined Chiefs of Staff—also diminished during this period. The falling off of assignments to the United Kingdom in the second half of 1944 is dealt with below. One reason was the feeling that there were supplies enough in Europe to finish the job. There was also the American Government's fear (mentioned above) of having a very large arms surplus left on its hands in the event of a sudden collapse. To diminish this risk a scheme known as the Supply Control Plan was adopted by the United States War Department. The plan called for a monthly progress report on supply and production. Thus from December onwards British programmes were required to show the rates of delivery desired each month; each month they were subjected to a close scrutiny.

All this was linked up in turn with the evolution of lend-lease policy. Up to D-Day questions of eligibility had been raised mainly

---

[1] The Committee was represented in London by the fully combined London Co-ordinating Committee which in fact had already been at work since October.

in relation to particular lend-lease requisitions. A first sign of a new phase, in which whole categories of goods might cease to be eligible, had occurred in November 1943. In that month a list of capital goods—mostly machine tools and equipment for projects of a permanent nature—were removed completely from lend-lease.[1] A few more items were added to the list in January. Altogether these removals cost the British Commonwealth roughly $200 million a year. Although there were no further large cuts up to June 1944, the very magnitude of the flow of lend-lease supplies in the five months before D-Day was itself a danger signal. The flow of munitions had almost doubled in this period. In the thirty-one days of May, the peak period, munitions supplies to the United Kingdom reached the total of $594 million.[2] Aircraft supplies in the five months totalled $1,474 million, as compared with $1,611 million for the whole of 1943, and $706 million for 1942.[3] The magnitude of the flow did not mean any slackening in the scrutiny of particular requisitions. In fact requisitions of all kinds were challenged on the ground of eligibility more frequently in this period than in 1942. Each requirement had to be justified more minutely, and more detailed information had to be given as to needs and to production within the Commonwealth. It became increasingly difficult to secure military assignments for non-active theatres of the war; and the right of the United Kingdom to re-transfer goods of lend-lease origin was more often questioned.

The phenomenal expansion both of American war production and of lend-lease aid presented political problems for the Administration. That the political aspects were well understood on the British side was shown by a letter by Sir John Dill of 17th June 1944 in which he commented on the cost of a proposal to keep the production of the Merlin engine at a high level. Fifteen thousand more Merlins would cost some $230 million, he wrote:

> Following the success of the American production as a whole, the matter of the huge expenditure is looming up ominously. The Americans who approve these schedules and their corresponding expenditure have behind them the shadow of the Truman Committee, the Bureau of the Budget, the Congressional investigation and the whole political situation generally.

The British Air Commission also noted in June that it was becoming more difficult to obtain aircraft supplies under lend-lease. It was not because supplies were scarce, it pointed out, but because of the

---

[1] See p. 280.

[2] *Twenty-first Report to Congress on Lend-Lease Operations*, for the period ended 30th September 1945, p. 22.

[3] There were also cash purchases of $306 million which brought the total for 1942 up to $1,112 million.

political and financial pressures which were being put upon the War and Navy Departments to check expenditure on unnecessary production. The British Admiralty Delegation added a report that the United States Navy Department had begun to reject requisitions for naval supplies under lend-lease which involved deliveries more than eighteen months ahead.

In June 1944 the trends and future of lend-lease were discussed in a meeting in London on the basis of a study made by the British Supply Council. Current pressure by the Foreign Economic Administration on the use of lend-lease for the supply of civilian goods, and on raw materials for manufacture into civilian goods, was thought to be due to fear of a political inquest into rising British gold and dollar holdings. Nevertheless Congress had just passed the Fifth Lend-Lease Appropriation Bill at a level much the same as that of the previous year. The sums voted seemed likely, on the basis of past experience, to exceed requirements by as much as $1,500 million. For non-munitions the figures were: 1943–44, $4,670 million; 1944–45, $4,340 million. There had never been much fear that lend-lease would cease for military supplies; and such supplies seemed likely to continue in Stage II although on a reduced scale. But a continuation of lend-lease for non-military supplies in Stage II seemed uncertain; they had been rather an afterthought in 1941, and had always been more vulnerable than munitions. The Supply Council's study recognised that lend-lease would terminate at the end of the war, and cited pledges to that effect given by the Administration to Congress during the hearings on the Bill. To avoid disputes as to eligibility, and to give a firm basis for British supply planning for the remainder of the war, the study favoured a protocol arrangement (like that with Russia), setting out exactly what quantities and types of supply the United Kingdom should receive. This idea was adopted and was put forward by the British team during the Stage II negotiations. In the end it proved unacceptable to the American side. If adopted it would have restricted considerably the activities of the Combined Munitions Assignments Board.

During the summer there were some very cautious soundings at a high level on the large issues of policy which were involved, whilst at a lower level there was some exchange of data. The United States War Department began to draw up a munitions programme for Stage II in May and a request was made for figures of British Stage II requirements. London was reluctant to commit itself to figures before a joint discussion had taken place on policy issues. Calculations were made in March on the assumption that the war effort against Japan would require about sixty-five to seventy-five per cent. of the manpower mobilisation needed for the war against Germany. By the end of the first year of Stage II it was calculated that the munitions labour force available in the United Kingdom would in any case have dropped to about sixty to sixty-five per cent. of the numbers available at the end of 1944. The assumption was made that lend-lease aid would continue on a proportionate basis for munitions. But since non-munitions supplies would be needed at the same level the overall reduction in lend-lease aid should not be more than about twenty per cent. Figures of munitions requirements were regarded as highly uncertain until the Combined Chiefs of Staff had worked out a strategic plan for the combined offensive against Japan. When London finally gave in mid-July its preliminary estimates for munitions, it did so with reservations. The United States War Department replied at once that the figures were greatly in excess of what it had expected. It proceeded to make its own estimates of British requirements apparently on the basis of two assumptions: (a) lend-lease munitions were to be given solely for use against Japan; (b) the United Kingdom would supply itself with as much as it was capable of producing.

If no cut was to be made in British war production, and it was to get nothing on lend-lease which it could produce itself, then theoretically it could produce most of its own requirements. But this would mean that British war production would be maintained whilst American war production was cut back by perhaps one-third to the amount required to deal with Japan. Thus the production of, say, Rolls-Royce Merlin engines in the United States would cease whilst the output of Merlins in the United Kingdom was maintained at the old level. On this basis the United Kingdom might get much less than half of what it had been receiving under lend-lease. Any such formula would mean, as the British Missions noted, that lend-lease aid would be frittered away in 'case-law difficulties' at lower levels. Indeed this was likely to be the fate of any general formula which merely said that Britain was to receive lend-lease on a proportionate basis. The only way to prevent this, the British side in Washington advised in August, was to secure an explicit recognition of the need for

a reasonable measure of recovery of the United Kingdom civilian economy and a progressive increase of the United Kingdom export trade as being essential to the effective fulfilment of British responsibilities during the Japanese war and thereafter.

By now Hopkins, after his illness, was back once more in harness and his aid was repeatedly sought in the weeks leading up to the Quebec Conference in mid-September. Finally the President issued instructions that pending the discussion he was to have with the Prime Minister, the American agencies should continue to plan for lend-lease supply in Stage II on the old basis.

Up to this point the American departments were still very much in the dark as to the real nature of the problems confronting the British Government. Despite strong pleas from the Washington Missions, London had been unwilling to release to the American Government the all-important British figures on exports, the shrinkage of manpower and on finance. The figures were withheld to enable the Prime Minister to present them to the President in person at Quebec, which was done on 14th September.[1]

(ii)

The Stage II Negotiations

One of the reasons for this caution was the extreme delicacy of the issues, which seemed to involve the economic fate of Britain and her future relations with the United States. Their delicacy had been shown by cautious soundings at a high level in Washington between April and July. Informal talks were had by the Ambassador and several other British representatives with one or two members of the President's Cabinet. They were hampered by the absence of Hopkins; when he was away ill, as on this occasion, there was no central channel through which such informal talks could be conducted without risk of interdepartmental friction and possible leakage. The soundings led to a hint on the American side that lend-lease might be restricted in Stage II, but assurances were received that the Administration was anxious to assist in restoring the economic strength of the United Kingdom. The possibility of doing this by a loan bearing interest at 2 or $2\frac{1}{2}$ per cent. was mentioned. This suggestion drew a cold reply from the Chancellor of the Exchequer. He warned the British side in Washington that there must be no encouragement whatsoever to the idea of a debt during the war.

> It must be the first object of our financial policy not to repeat previous experience and incur indebtedness to the United States Government which we are not able to meet.

The United Kingdom would need some financial aid after the war but it could not take the form of a loan on such terms. The line taken on the British side, in talks with the Lend-Lease Administrator, was that Britain's grave transitional problems after the war had arisen wholly from the sacrifice 'of every precaution for the future in the interests of immediate strength'; it was essential in Stage II, as in Stage I, 'to adhere to the pooling principle and to avoid creating a war debt'. If the United Kingdom was to play its full part in Stage II,

---

[1] On grounds of security it was not yet judged wise to release such data to the public. See pages 298 and 491.

and to make the first steps towards economic recovery, then full lend-lease aid, for munitions and non-munitions alike, should continue.

There was a Stage II also in relation to supply from Canada. Estimates made in London in the summer suggested that the United Kingdom would need from Canada munitions to the amount of about $1,200 million and non-munitions supplies of about $1,000 million. Only a part—and not the greater part—of this would be required under mutual aid. A British Mission led by Lord Keynes worked out the programmes with the Canadian authorities in Ottawa during the autumn. It was arranged that British requirements in the first five months of the financial year beginning April 1945 would be covered by an Appropriation Act and that the new budget which would follow would make any further provision that might be needed.[1]

Before the British Prime Minister and the President could broach the economic issue at Quebec, there was a matter of grand strategy to be clarified: namely the part which the United Kingdom was to play in the war against Japan. It was the United States that had been struck first and hardest by Japan. The American public and the Navy Department, if not the Army leaders and the President, had always tended to regard the Japanese war as peculiarly an American war. It was assumed that in Stage II Britain would give less attention to Japan than the United States and would devote part of her energies to reconstruction and exports. There were warnings from the American side that in this case there would be a loss of sympathy for Britain, and a more critical attitude towards lend-lease aid. The British Commonwealth, however, had suffered just as much from the Japanese as the United States and was as deeply committed to Japan's defeat. Full-scale military participation was dictated by British obligations: to her own peoples who had suffered invasion, to other Commonwealth countries and to the United States. The State Department also attached importance to full British participation. The Prime Minister left no doubt on this score at the Quebec conference. The only question was one of physical limitations; how far Britain could play her full role as senior partner in the Commonwealth, given the factors of distance, shipping, type of equipment and degree of economic exhaustion. For a full discussion of the economic factors which were involved, the reader must be referred to *British War Economy*.[2] (Some of the financial factors are referred to in Chapter VII of the present study.) The relation of Stage II planning to British war mobilisation, the distribution of the nation's manpower and resources in the mid-war years, and the changes expected when the

---

[1] See p. 484.
[2] Hancock and Gowing, op. cit., Part V.

greater war with Germany ended and energies could be concentrated on the lesser war against Japan, are all dealt with in *British War Economy*. Since that volume deals with the Stage II negotiations in Washington, only a brief summary of them need be given in this chapter.

The basis for the negotiations was laid by an agreement between the President and the Prime Minister which both initialled at Quebec on 14th September 1944. The agreement, and the record of the conversation that led to it, noted that they had discussed:

> the question of the scope and scale of mutual lend-lease aid between the United States and the British Empire after the defeat of Germany and during the war with Japan.

They agreed to set up a Combined Committee over which Secretary Morgenthau presided, assisted by Mr. Stettinius and Mr. Crowley. The British members—Lord Keynes, Mr. Ben Smith and Sir Ronald Campbell—were appointed later. In the light of the agreement, and the record of conversation, the Combined Committee was to

> agree and recommend to the Heads of their respective Governments the amount of mutual aid in munitions, non-munitions and services which will be provided for the most effective prosecution of the war.

The record of conversation noted that the President had accepted the Prime Minister's point that 'during the war with Japan' the United Kingdom would continue to get not only munitions, but also food, shipping, etc., from the United States 'to cover our reasonable needs'. The figures discussed by the two leaders, with Mr. Morgenthau who was present, were as follows: for munitions assistance in the first year, $3,500 million; for non-munitions requirements, all of which should be 'on lend-lease', the amount mentioned was $3,000 million gross, 'against which a considerable amount would be set off for reverse lend-lease'. There was also an important passage in which the President recognised that no impediment should be set to the re-establishment of the British export trade. The negotiations in Washington lasted through most of October and November. The issues were complex; but no British case presented in Washington during the war had been better prepared. To provide a fully documented basis for the negotiations in Washington the British Government prepared a memorandum on British requirements for the first year of Stage II. This was presented by the British members of the Combined Committee to their American colleagues with the expressed hope that:

> (i) Munitions should be made available on lend-lease during the first year of Stage II on a scale sufficient not only to provide those categories of requirements which only the United States can

produce in the time, but also to make possible the release of manpower from munitions production in the United Kingdom to the extent explained herein.

(ii) In the sixth year of war the British civilian is entitled to such moderate easements as are practicable without interfering with the prosecution of the war, both by some release of manpower in the United Kingdom to increase production for civilian use, and also by a lend-lease programme, especially for food, which will allow some raising of standards.

(iii) There should no longer be any restrictions or avoidable handicaps on the recovery of the British export trade so that the United Kingdom may begin to be more self-supporting in respect of overseas payments at the earliest possible date.

From these three points, based on the Quebec decisions, a fourth emerged which the British members defined as follows:

(iv) It is in the mutual interest that the British reserve of gold and dollars, which is already dangerously inadequate, should not suffer by the end of 1945 any significant deterioration below its present level.

Of these points the third, the freeing of exports, was the most important. The restrictions on British exports accepted in the British Lend-Lease White Paper of September 1941 were an insuperable barrier to any expansion of the export trade. Desultory conversations on the revision of the White Paper which had begun in May 1943 had been shelved in August 1944 on the ground that this was part of the area that would have to be covered in the Stage II talks. The problem was difficult from the point of view of American politics. The President's agreement at Quebec that lend-lease aid should continue, whilst British exports were to be liberated, was taken by Mr. Cordell Hull as meaning unfettered credits for Great Britain and a breakdown of the endeavours to use Article 7 of the Master Lend-Lease Agreement to put an end to Imperial Preference. He quotes in his Memoirs a sentence from the President's message to him from Quebec which the President emphasised with a double inked line: 'The real nub of the situation is to keep Britain from going into complete bankruptcy at the end of the war.'[1] From this it appeared that the President placed less emphasis on the continuation in Stage II of lend-lease on much the same scale than upon American aid in securing British economic recovery. This was quite a new issue on which neither Congress nor public opinion had as yet been prepared, whilst lend-lease was merely the continuation of an existing war measure.

The economic strength of the United Kingdom had been brought

---

[1] *Memoirs of Cordell Hull*, Vol. II, op. cit., pp. 1619–20; Stimson and Bundy, op. cit., pp. 592–93.

to this low ebb, as Lord Keynes wrote at the time, by 'financial imprudence which has no parallel in history'. 'We threw good house-keeping to the winds. But we saved ourselves and helped to save the world.' The greatest act of 'imprudence' had been what he referred to as 'abandonment' of Britain's export business in order to devote most of her manpower to war. The manpower percentages for 1939 and 1944, as given in the British statement, told their tale. In 1939 only 22·2 per cent. of manpower was devoted to 'Government work', (including armed services and war industry); whilst 9·5 per cent. was used for 'export' and 68·3 per cent. for 'home market'. In 1944 the percentages had become: 'Government work', 67·5; 'export', 1·9; 'home market', 30·6. The abandonment of most of the exports was possible because lend-lease and mutual aid provided a substitute. In 1944 exports were less than thirty per cent. of the pre-war level. They were not enough to finance a tenth of total British overseas require-ments, or one-seventh, if allowance were made for lend-lease and mutual aid. The need both for large exports and large liquid reserves was shown by the overseas indebtedness. Overseas war debts already totalled some $10,000 million and would rise further in 1945. In addition British assets worth $4,000 million had also been sacrified which before the war had financed a substantial part of the imports of raw materials and food. To meet overseas liabilities, and to import at the level of 1938, exports would have to be raised to five times the 1944 level, i.e. 150 per cent. of the pre-war level. Even if a start were made at once, it would be years before such a figure could be reached. Meanwhile imports would have to continue, perhaps without North American financial aid to pay for them, interest would have to be paid, and a part at least of the war credits would have to be refunded. The British proposal for freeing exports was that the White Paper should be withdrawn on 1st December 1944, leaving exporters free to export anything anywhere. But this ran into political difficulties in the United States. The best that could be done was to postpone the date formally until the end of the German war; whilst the Adminis-tration gave the substance at once by refraining from administrative interference with British exports. The move was facilitated by the agreement that from 1st January 1945 the United Kingdom would no longer receive under lend-lease (as the Prime Minister explained to the House of Commons on 30th November), shipments of

any manufactured articles for civilian use which enter into export trade, nor of many raw and semi-fabricated materials, such as iron and steel and some non-ferrous metals.[1]

Thus even under the White Paper exports would be free over a wide

---

[1] At the same time the United Kingdom reaffirmed its intention not to undertake any 'general reconversion of industry or expansion of exports before VE-Day'. H. of C. Deb., Vol. 406, Cols. 69–73.

range of goods. This provision was not affected by the subsequent breakdown of other parts of the Stage II agreement.

There was less success in meeting the point about British gold and dollar reserves. Reserves stood at the end of August 1944 at their peak, $1,748 million. The rise from the lowest point reached during the war—$12 million in April 1941—had been due largely to payments by American troops stationed in the United Kingdom and Australia. But these payments were diminishing rapidly. In a year's time reserves were likely to be at a dangerously low level. Meanwhile overseas debts would have increased and the running adverse balance on current account would continue to mount for several years after the war. Reciprocal aid, including that given in the shape of raw materials and foodstuffs from colonial areas for which the British Government paid, was eating into revenues from dollar-earning exports. But the United Kingdom insisted on the continuance of such aid because of the importance it attached to the principle of pooling.[1] Moreover, the removal from lend-lease of items like machine tools meant increased dollar expenditure in the United States. This, and the American suggestion to include raw materials under reciprocal aid, were both due, as the British Stage II statement pointed out, to 'a livelier awareness by the United States Administration of this recovery in our reserves than of the much greater increase of our liabilities'. A reduction had been made on the same ground in the Fifth Lend-Lease Appropriation. The same factor was at work in the reductions made in the Stage II programmes by the exclusion of raw materials and many manufactured goods; this meant increased dollar expenditure by the United Kingdom in the United States. The case was so well demonstrated that the American delegation sought to relieve the pressure on reserves to the extent of $400 to $500 million. For this purpose various expedients were examined, including the restoration to lend-lease of Cuban sugar, civilian tobacco and machine tools; the payment of suspended British claims on old contracts taken over by the United States, and making provision under lend-lease for emergency houses. The latter proved possible, the others not. Nevertheless, when various items were added together the relief provided was still substantial.

The same spirit of good will was shown in the treatment of British lend-lease programmes for munitions and non-munitions in Stage II. They were passed without any very serious reduction after close scrutiny by the Departments concerned—War, Navy and Foreign Economic Administration. Munitions requirements were to be provided in the first year of Stage II—which was assumed to be the calendar year 1945—up to about fifty-four per cent. of the total of the programme for 1944. The original British submission for muni-

---

[1] A formal undertaking was given to continue reciprocal aid during Stage II.

tions was amended and of the amount as it stood after amendment ninety-eight per cent. was granted. The total value accepted by the Admiralty was $2,585 million; well over half the total was for aircraft and aircraft supplies. On the side of non-munitions, requirements were to be met to a total of $2,596 million. This was made up as follows: shipping, $852 million; petroleum, $371 million; food and tobacco, $1,022 million; raw materials, $260 million; miscellaneous and manufactured goods, $91 million. The programme provided, as was noted on the American side, 'a moderate degree of easement in the standard and conditions of life in the United Kingdom in Stage II'.

The negotiations were conducted with a high degree of skill on both sides and with the utmost good will. When they were completed towards the end of November, all seemed set fair. The Service departments accepted the figures for munitions, as set out in the schedules, as production requirements on the United States. But there were some reasonable qualifications as to procedure. The departments agreed to make all practicable efforts to produce the amounts or to supply from stocks; but they did not undertake to set up any new production facilities. Deliveries were subject to the 'established procedures' of the Combined Boards.

The agreements took the form of letters to Mr. Morgenthau, which were signed by heads of the American Departments concerned, and by the British negotiators. The munitions agreement was referred to on the American side in the negotiations as a 'firm commitment' subject to the conditions mentioned above. But none of the texts was incorporated in any binding document signed and sealed by both sides—such as the protocol desired by the United Kingdom. Indeed, at the last meeting, after the letters had been presented, it was agreed that the next step was for Mr. Morgenthau to make an 'informal report' to the President. There the matter ended. The Combined Committee was allowed to lapse, although the United Kingdom would have liked to keep it intact. The 'agreements' lay crumbling on the shelf as the German war dragged on month after month.

(iii)

Lend-Lease in Decline

The high tide of the German effort was reached two days after Christmas at the turn of the year.[1] The worsening of the war in Europe up to that point had pushed the Stage II agreements into the background so that interest in them in the United States had died away.

---

[1] Annual message of the President to Congress, 6th January 1945.

But as yet there was no visible sign of change. Lend-lease and mutual aid, combined assignments and allocations by the Combined Boards, went on with little change until the end of the war with Germany. In the first months of 1945 the demand, both in Congress and outside it, was for all-out production to finish the war. All talk of reconversion was stilled. The Director of War Mobilisation and Reconversion warned Congress that maximum war production was incompatible with any move towards reconversion. War production had reached a figure of $61·3 billion in 1944; the programme for 1945 was set in January at $62 billion, over $5 billion more than had previously been thought necessary. The combined munitions programmes were four per cent. less than for 1944. Until April there was little sign of relaxation of the bans on civilian production. There was, indeed, a further curtailment of the supplies of civilian goods available in the United States, since increasing demands from liberated areas had to be met. Even the steps taken after April towards reconversion produced little visible result before the end of the war with Japan. Although scores of limitation orders were lifted, there were still serious shortages of raw materials and components.

In reviewing before Congress, on 6th January 1945, the progress of the war, the President warned the nation against tensions between allies—tensions due to the slowing down of Allied progress as well as to enemy propaganda. At the time British policies in Italy, Greece and Poland were drawing fire from the American press. The British people were now in the midst of their sixth winter of war; and there was some counter-fire, sharper than usual, from the British press.

Such eddies had no effect, however, on the solid structure of the British-American combination either on the side of strategy or supply. On the supply side an opportunity to remind the public of the valuable work of the Combined Boards was given by the announcement of 19th January, by the Prime Ministers of Great Britain and Canada and the President, that the Combined Raw Materials Board, the Combined Production and Resources Board and the Combined Food Board would continue to operate until the end of the Japanese war. The Combined Boards were now entering on the fourth year of their work, of which the public still had little knowledge.

How far combination in war production had travelled since 1940 was indicated by the announcement at the end of January 1945 of the purchase by the United Kingdom of 58,000 lend-lease machine tools. It was a reminder that the machine-tool phase of the war was long past. The tools had been supplied under lend-lease by the United States from March 1941 to November 1943 when they were taken off lend-lease. The purchase price paid by the British Government was $31½ million for tools valued originally in the lend-lease records at $166 million. By this time the tools had played their main part in expanding British war production. The price paid was a recognition of their value as durable capital equipment for the use of British industry after the end of the war. The sale was welcomed by the Administration as a reminder that Britain was neither receiving nor using lend-lease goods for post-war purposes. The press release issued by the Foreign Economic Administration seized the opportunity to illustrate the proportion of lend-lease in the British war effort: 73 per cent. of British machine tools were supplied during the war by British manufacturers, $14\frac{1}{2}$ per cent. purchased for cash from the United States, $12\frac{1}{2}$ per cent. supplied under lend-lease. The Administration was making a serious effort at this time to inform Congress and the public of the importance of British reciprocal aid to the United States and its armed forces in the various theatres of the war. Thus the War Department distributed to the armed forces in all theatres of war a million copies of a pamphlet entitled 'Invisible Weapon' dealing with the strategy of lend-lease and 'reverse lend-lease'.[1]

The tempo of supply history moved slowly through February and March. The renewal of the Lend-Lease Act became necessary in the latter month. The Bill was voted by the House of Representatives on 2nd March and by the Senate on 10th April. The sudden death of President Roosevelt occurred two days later and the Act was signed by his successor on 16th April. It contained a significant amendment forbidding the use of lend-lease for 'post-war relief, post-war rehabilitation or post-war reconstruction'.[2] A Bill to provide for the sixth lend-lease appropriation for 1945–46 then became necessary, and the preparation of estimates began even before the renewal Act was passed.

From April 1945 the tempo quickened. The British missions in Washington reported to London on 1st May that the United States War Department had adopted the assumption that Stage I was now at an end. Stage II began formally on 8th May when Germany capitulated. Stage II was to last for only three months. It came to an end for practical purposes with the capitulation of Japan on 14th August. VJ-Day was proclaimed on 15th August and the instruments of surrender were signed on 2nd September.

In the early spring, however, the duration of Stage II could not be foreseen. For planning purposes the War Department, late in March, adopted the formula: the German war to end by 30th June and

---

[1] Some conception of the magnitude of the British effort was given by two White Papers published late in 1944: *Statistics Relating to the War Effort of the United Kingdom*, Cmd. 6564, November 1944, and *Mutual Aid Second Report*, Cmd. 6570, November 1944. The United States Foreign Economic Administration conducted a useful publicity campaign to show the importance of mutual aid, by means of the 'President's Reports to Congress on Lend-Lease Operations', etc.

[2] *Nineteenth Report to Congress on Lend-Lease Operations.*

Stage II to continue to 31st December 1946. At this time it was making fresh calculations of British requirements for 1945 and using for this purpose the British Stage II figures as submitted by the Keynes Mission on 23rd October 1944. London was now asked to bring the figures up to date. It seemed clear that the combined understandings of the autumn of 1944, and the lend-lease programmes based on them, still held good.

Thus at first the transition from Stage I to Stage II hardly seemed to ruffle the surface of British supply from North America. Lend-lease, and mutual aid from Canada, went forward steadily. The first British estimates for the sixth lend-lease appropriation, presented before the end of the war with Germany, showed little change from the totals for the fifth appropriation. The estimate for non-munitions was $3,676 million for the sixth appropriation, which was later pruned to about $3,000 million, whilst the Stage II total was $2,596 million. The hearings for the appropriation went smoothly and the Act was voted by Congress on the last day of June. For once, however, the real trends were clearer at the lower working levels of assignment and delivery than at the higher levels of planning and programmes or even of requisitions. From April onwards British officials in Washington, watching events closely at these lower levels, could see the brakes coming on slowly at many different points.

The transitional character of the period has to be remembered. Major phases of the war were ending; new phases were beginning that reached forward into the post-war world. To the general public in the United States, lend-lease had almost completed its main historical purpose. In the interest of American defence it had helped Britain to survive in the European war. Liberated areas were now making heavy demands on the American—as on the British—economy. As the Anglo-American combination neared the end of its first great objective new international alternatives to the combined machinery seemed to be emerging. These included the United Nations Relief and Rehabilitation Administration set up in the autumn of 1943. A year later provision was made for a United Nations Food and Agriculture Organisation. The Bretton Woods Conference in the summer of 1944 provided for the setting up of the International Bank for Reconstruction and Development and the International Monetary Fund. As the war with Germany was ending, the United Nations Conference in San Francisco was working out the Charter of the United Nations.

For over a year lend-lease requisitions had been subjected to more stringent tests as to eligibility. Once Germany had surrendered, lend-lease aid to the United Kingdom obviously became more vulnerable and the scrutiny became more close than ever. It is true that the autumn agreements covered supply, not merely for the British war effort against Japan, but also for some easement for the civil population of the United Kingdom. But the agreements were known only to the higher officials; they had long been on the shelf, and there were no clear rules for their interpretation. Each fresh requisition now provoked new questions. Would it serve any war purpose? Or would it merely enable the United Kingdom to reconvert its industries faster than the United States and so capture export markets? It was the duty of the Combined Production and Resources Board, under the Stage II agreements, to watch and report on the progress of reconversion. At a meeting on 17th April 1945 the Board placed formally on record the fact that the rates of munitions cut-backs foreshadowed for the United Kingdom, the United States and Canada were in general correspondence as to scale. The judgement seemed to support the assumption that the Stage II agreements, including the amount of lend-lease aid which Britain was to continue to receive, remained in full effect. But such a general pronouncement could not prevent officials at the lower levels of supply from challenging more and more freely the eligibility of particular requisitions.

Moreover the part which Britain was to play in the final stages of the war against Japan was not very clear to the average American official. Indeed, at no time had the British Commonwealth's part in this theatre received much favourable publicity in the United States. For its main effort in the later stages of the war was made in South-East Asia; and this for many Americans was a 'colonial' area in which the motives of Britain were less than pure.

The ease with which long-term supply programmes, and even requisitions, were being accepted by the United States, was deceptive. Even in June lend-lease requisitions were still being filed at the rate of 7,000 a year. The real trend was shown, however, by an analysis of assignments made for the British Supply Council at the end of April. It concluded that 'securing assignments is becoming more difficult than getting programmes accepted'. In fact, as they watched developments in Washington on the working level of requisitions and assignments, the British missions had begun to feel that the system of assignments, if not the whole basis of lend-lease itself, was crumbling. The marked falling off of lend-lease supplies in the first half of 1945 as compared with the year 1944 can be seen in several of the tables given in Chapter X.

Assignments and Supply. On the munitions side the decline would be more apparent if the comparison were made with the first half of 1944 when the flow of supplies was greater than at any period of the war. In the past a shortage in the production of munitions was the main cause of any failure to secure from the Washington Combined Munitions Assignments Board the assignments to which British production plans were geared. There were still shortages even in

1945; this, indeed, was the main reason for the falling off of air assignments. But the shortages occurred largely because production programmes for aircraft had been cut heavily on both sides of the Atlantic in anticipation of the war with Germany ending by 1st January 1945. Shortages alone, however, could not explain the acute decline revealed in the analysis of assignments by the British Supply Council which is referred to above. It showed that in the first four months of 1945 the British Army had received only a sixth of the year's total provision of $1,000 million made to it by the United States Army supply programme.

There had been a sharp falling-off in assignments for the Ground Army in the second half of 1944 as compared with the peak year of 1943; but this was nothing like the spectacular fall in the first third of 1945. The rate in these four months was only fifty per cent. satisfaction of Ground Army requirements from the United States on a Stage I basis; or two-thirds on the lower Stage II basis. The percentage of satisfaction had averaged eighty-five per cent. in 1943 and seventy-five per cent. in 1944.[1]

The falling off of assignments posed a grave issue for British planning. Matters came to a head in April. Assignments expected from the April production of radio sets and assault wire, on which forward planning had been based in the United Kingdom, were not

---

[1] The following table shows for 1943 and 1944 the relation between the value of the provision for British requirements (Ground Army) as made in the United States Army supply programme, and the value of assignments to the United Kingdom.

$ million

	Provision		Assignment		Percentage of satisfaction	
	1943	1944	1943	1944	1943	1944
'A' vehicles[a] . . .	1,042	778	938	501	90	64
'B' vehicles[b] . . .	296	291	284	243	96	84
Weapons and instruments	246	74	246	73	100	99
Small arms . . .	106	21	86	20	81	95
Gun ammunition .	369	221	221	167	60	76
Small arms ammunition ,	182	58	146	50	80	100
Signal stores . .	227	247	195	237	86	96
Clothing and textiles .	126	49	115	48	91	98
Engineer stores . .	232	210	182	150	78	71
Transportation stores .	62	72	53	58	85	81
General Q.M. stores .	11	47	—	43	—	91
Chemical warfare . .	35	13	—	10	—	77
Explosives . . .	59	31	—	30	—	97
Medical stores . .	30	25	—	18	—	72
	3,023	2,137	2,466	1,656	85	77

The value of assignments in 1942 (according to a very tentative estimate made during the Lyttelton Mission) was $1,500 million.
   [a] i.e. tanks, armoured and scout cars, armoured carriers.
   [b] i.e. all other military motor vehicles.

forthcoming. The United States Joint Chiefs of Staff were asked to reopen the matter and to confirm the principle that where provision was made in the Army supply programme for British requirements, assignments could be expected unless urgent and unforeseen circumstances arose. Unless such provision meant a reasonably firm commitment, the planning of production in the United Kingdom was left hanging in the air. The Joint Chiefs were unwilling either to reopen the particular case or to accept the general principle.

The British Joint Staff Mission decided, therefore, to carry the matter to the Combined Chiefs of Staff. Now that President Roosevelt was dead and Harry Hopkins incapacitated, the Combined Chiefs seemed the last court of appeal. Hopkins, though formally chairman of the Combined Munitions Assignments Board to the end of the war, had played no part in the affairs of the Board for a number of months. His absence removed the keystone of the arch of munitions assignments—the institution of the 'neutral' chairman. The only solution, the Joint Staff Mission thought, was to find another 'neutral' chairman. More and more, it explained to the Chiefs of Staff in London, American production and resources were being reserved for American needs; the United Kingdom had to establish an extremely complete case in order to have any chance of receiving an assignment. All foreign requirements were subjected to a very detailed scrutiny and had to be backed by complete statistical data and justification on the operational side. It was not an adequate plea that British war production had been planned on the basis of a reasonable expectation of the delivery of certain kinds of munitions for which provision had been made in British programmes. The Mission expressed concern about what would happen in Stage II. It seemed likely that the Americans would insist on complete priority being given to the main operations against Japan. The London Munitions Assignment Board in reply took a broad view of the situation. It paid a tribute to the working of the assignments machinery. Up to this point it had 'worked extraordinarily well' on the whole. Despite all the difficulties the United Kingdom in the end had seldom 'failed to receive reasonable assignments'. Since the American forces were now fully deployed and were taking the major part of the burden of both the German and Japanese wars, it was only natural, the London Board thought, that charity should begin at home.

These words were timely; since they were to prove in effect a farewell tribute to the Combined Munitions Assignments Board. Eleven days later came VE-Day, and with it assignments to the United Kingdom slowed down to a standstill. The first and main breakdown occurred in the air programme. There had been discussions in Washington late in April, in which British air authorities had taken part, on a revision of the allocation of aircraft to the

United Kingdom for the second half of 1945. The American air authorities observed that substantial cut-backs had been made, or were to be made, in the British aircraft production programme, and they went on to note that some production of civilian types for export was contemplated in the United Kingdom.[1] They found this difficult to reconcile with British requests for military aircraft; and they added that the United States Army Air Force was itself under pressure to cut back its own production. The British negotiators founded their case on the Stage II agreements. It then became clear that the American side did not regard these agreements as binding on the Administration even though they had been approved by the Morgenthau Committee and the United States War and Navy Departments. The Administration could not be regarded as having undertaken any firm commitment to the United Kingdom since there was no record that the President had ever formally approved of the undertakings. This view, it seemed, was shared by Mr. Morgenthau himself. The 'agreements' were documents and programmes required by the Administration for its own budgetary and production purposes. As for aircraft, all the United States air authorities could do was to recommend the allocation of the aircraft necessary to maintain existing units in the South-East Asia Command. If the British needed more aircraft than this, they would have to produce for themselves by keeping their production at Stage I levels. The conclusion defeated the purpose of the autumn agreements since it meant an increase rather than a decrease of British aircraft production in Stage II. Following the agreements, British production had been reduced to the point where it was inadequate both as to numbers and types to enable the British air forces to carry out the tasks assigned to them in the war with Japan.

The trouble over aircraft, as the British Joint Staff Mission warned London at the beginning of May, was likely to expand to the whole field of lend-lease. Already similar arguments had been met on high levels in the United States War Department. After a discussion at the Pentagon, the Mission reported: '*De facto* and *de jure* we are where we were before the Keynes discussions.' The British Supply Council, however, drew some comfort from the fact that so far the validity of the Stage II agreements for non-munitions had not been challenged. It noted that the Administration was afraid of criticism by Congress if the United Kingdom were given war supplies which it could produce for itself by delaying reconversion of its war industries. Such criticism ought to be easy to counter, the Council

---

[1] There was by this time a serious shortage of transport types in British Commonwealth countries. By arrangement with the United States, British aircraft construction facilities were devoted during the war mainly to combat types whilst a large proportion of United States facilities was devoted to the construction of transport types.

thought, by referring to American steps towards reconversion and to the agreement at Quebec of President Roosevelt and the Prime Minister. But it feared that there was no one who would 'put the case forcefully to Congress'.

A serious view of these developments was taken by ministers in London. A private message was sent by the Chancellor of the Exchequer on 7th May to the head of the Foreign Economic Administration (Mr. Crowley) to remind him that both the Prime Minister and the Chancellor had announced the Stage II arrangements in Parliament in the autumn of 1944. This had been done after consultations with the United States Administration which had issued simultaneously a press release in Washington. British plans since then, the Chancellor added, had been based on these understandings. He recognised that conditions had since changed. This pointed, however, not to a unilateral withdrawal from the common understanding, but rather to fresh discussions by the Combined Committee that had made the original agreements.

(iv)

Stage II and the Collapse of Financial Aid from North America

For some days longer a feeling persisted in British circles in Washington that the basic principles of the Stage II agreements would still be honoured.[1] Good progress was being made on the lend-lease appropriation for non-munitions. But such optimism proved to be ill-founded. In the third week of May the Supply Council referred to a 'serious deterioration' in the attitude of the War Department to the Stage II 'munitions agreements'. A 'wave of economy' had swept over Washington. British air representatives were told that for several reasons the air agreement could not be carried out. It was again pointed out that the President had never ratified the agreement. Another reason was that the economy wave had produced a heavy cut in the budget and programmes of the United States Army Air Corps. This in turn imposed a drastic cut in allocations to the Royal Air Force, both for complete aircraft and for American components required for aircraft under construction in the United Kingdom and Canada. Finally came a clear statement of policy on an essential point. The United States Army Air Corps could only agree to aircraft

---

[1] Support for an optimistic view was found in a statement on the basis and future of lend-lease issued from the State Department on 14th May by the Acting Secretary of State, Joseph C. Grew.

supplies for Britain if they were clearly necessary for use in the Pacific theatre in the war against Japan. Moreover, all allocations would have to have the specific approval of the United States Joint Chiefs of Staff.

The conclusion drawn from all this by the British missions was that the time had come to play their last card—a direct message from the Prime Minister himself to the President. But first the Chancellor of the Exchequer and the Minister of Production tried their hand in a direct message to Secretary Morgenthau and Judge Vinson. The message cited the dates and character of the four agreements emanating from the combined Morgenthau-Keynes Committee between 23rd October and 10th November. These were referred to as 'agreements between representatives of the United States Navy and War Departments on the one hand and representatives of our Service and Supply Departments on the other hand'. The message noted that time had made necessary some reductions of the air and army programmes; but in any revision the same principles should apply. On the air side, London had, in fact, decided to reduce its claim by over $200 million. The Prime Minister's message to the President followed on 28th May. Its theme was 'the machine has come to a standstill'. The Prime Minister noted that when he met President Roosevelt in September 1944 at Quebec, they had initialled together 'an agreement about lend-lease after Germany was defeated'. It was in accordance with that agreement that a detailed plan had been worked out with the American Administration by the Keynes-Sinclair Mission. British production plans had been made on the basis of this plan. He went on to refer to the War Department's expectation of such a large cut in its budgetary appropriations for the United States Army Air Corps that supplies to the United Kingdom would be 'drastically curtailed below the statement of our requirements' as they had been agreed in the preceding autumn. This, he thought, called for discussions between the Chiefs of Staff on both sides. Seven weeks elapsed before the President gave his answer to this message. It was in the form of a memorandum handed to the Prime Minister at the Potsdam Conference on 17th July.

Meanwhile in Washington during this period of waiting the assignments machine continued to stand more or less idle. At the end of June 1945 only about twenty per cent. of the assignments required for the Far Eastern war had been obtained. Early in July the Joint Staff Mission urged that the matter should be put on the agenda of the Potsdam Conference. 'We have been in very deep water for some time', it added. Most current committee work was held up because American departments lacked guidance on policy. 'Direct use against Japan' was the only point on which American officials felt sure of their ground. It was not clear whether lend-lease could be applied to supplies for British occupational forces in Germany or to her forces in the Middle East. It was uncertain whether lend-lease was available for spare parts needed for equipment already delivered, but which was not then in direct use against Japan. Complete uncertainty as to delivery of the planned margins from the United States now threatened the whole basis of the supply plans of the British Ministries.

The uneasiness caused by the absence of any direct reply by the President to the Prime Minister's message was relieved somewhat by private assurances from Administration leaders that the Administration was still disposed to carry out the terms of the Stage II agreements. The President, it was said in mid-June, had given the 'green light' to all United States Departments on the Stage II agreements. Assurances about the 'green light' had become so definite by 20th June that the Missions reported to London that the impasse was about to be broken for aircraft; this in turn would ease the way for the Army's programme. The position as to the Navy had all along been satisfactory. To help this favourable trend, the British Chiefs of Staff in Washington laid before the Combined Chiefs of Staff a statement of the British Government's understanding of the principles and conditions underlying the Stage II agreements.[1] Another favourable sign was the acceptance by Congress on 30th June of the Sixth Lend-Lease Appropriation Bill which provided upwards of $3 billion lend-lease money for non-munitions supplies to the United Kingdom in the fiscal year 1945–46. In the final hearings on the Bill, the Administration spokesman gave Congress two assurances: first, that lend-lease would not be used directly or indirectly as an aid to post-war rehabilitation; and second, that lend-lease would be discontinued at the date of, or very shortly—'perhaps thirty days or something like that'— after the Japanese surrender. It was then assumed that the end of the war with Japan was at least six months ahead; perhaps a year; even eighteen months. Actually it was only six weeks away.

All July, and even into the first days of August, the winds of Washington blew hot and cold on lend-lease. On 5th July the President issued a directive to Departments to the effect that approval of the issue to Allied Governments of lend-lease munitions and war-stores was to be limited solely to use in the war against Japan. There was to be no issue for any other purpose. Some days later there were again private assurances about the 'green light' having been given. London was told on 6th July it must lodge lend-lease requisitions for non-munitions supplies. But four days later it was warned that the July assignments on the air side still hung fire; even assignments of components for aircraft, and other similar requirements, needed 'to

---

[1] A copy was also sent, by the Chairman of the British Supply Council, to the Director of War Mobilisation to whom the President had told American Departments they were to turn for guidance on the agreements.

keep production flywheels turning in the United Kingdom and Canada' remained in suspense. The position was better in respect of ground army requirements for direct use against Japan. To the end of July there was still some movement of military stores due for shipment from the United States to various British theatres, including even the United Kingdom. Clearance was refused only for a small percentage of the total tonnage on the ground that the items were not required for use against Japan. But there were no assignments from July production and the British Supply Council in mid-July expressed to the War Department its grave concern at the effect of 'the lack of approval of many of our bids'. In the hope of speeding air assignments it gave a list of the most critical items needed to maintain Royal Air Force operations against Japan, and to avoid a breakdown in planning and supply.

For non-munitions in July the wind still seemed favourable. Mr. Crowley, in a letter to the Chairman of the British Supply Council, expressed his belief that 'the British Commonwealth's requirements will be adequately taken care of during the coming fiscal year and that the general understandings concerning Lend-Lease Aid to the British Commonwealth during Stage II will be fulfilled'. At the same time there was a sharp increase in the items for which dollars were needed. The supply of maintenance items for American military equipment in the hands of British armed forces was put on a payment basis as from 1st August. If this were extended to food for the armed forces the financial consequence would be very serious. Food was then being shipped on lend-lease direct to British armed forces overseas at the rate of $320 million a year, with another $220 million worth going to the armed forces in the United Kingdom. Only a small fraction of this grand total of $540 million was being shipped direct to British forces in the Far Eastern theatre. The Supply Council discussed a clause which for some time had been included in lend-lease requisitions for timber and other commodities to cover a possible change in eligibility during the course of the requisition. The Treasury was thereby incurring a dollar liability of unknown extent if the commodity should be declared later to be ineligible for lend-lease.

Meanwhile at the Potsdam Conference, in the second half of July, there had been important discussions between the President and the Prime Minister on the future of lend-lease. In the President's reply to the Prime Minister on 17th July he wrote that the United States intended to furnish lend-lease to the British Commonwealth for the war against Japan, in accordance generally with the schedules of requirements worked out in October and November 1944. These estimates, he pointed out, were subject to various factors, such as changing strategic demands, conditions of supply, procurement and allocation, and the voting of the necessary funds by Congress. He then went on to make the point that the British gold and foreign exchange holdings were now considerably higher than was anticipated at the time of the Stage II discussions. He hoped, therefore, that the British Government would be able to relax its position in the matter of paying dollars for supplies, particularly for items likely to lead to political criticism in the United States. The reference to the British gold and foreign exchange holdings drew from the Chancellor of the Exchequer the comment that the United Kingdom was 'in worse financial straits to-day, especially with the eventual end of lend-lease in sight, than we have ever been before'. Reserves were at a level which the United States Treasury in the preceding autumn had agreed were a reasonable minimum, having regard to the size and inevitable growth of British overseas liabilities. There had been some gain because the delay in the ending of the German war had meant more expenditure by American troops in the United Kingdom. But the gain was greatly outweighed by the increase in overseas obligations due to the same cause. The net reserves of gold and dollars at that moment were \$1·8 billion whilst overseas liabilities against them were approximately \$13 billion.

In a conversation with the Prime Minister on the 24th the President explained frankly his difficulties. As Vice-President he had played an important part in the renewal of the Lend-Lease Act and regarded himself as personally responsible to Congress for seeing that lend-lease supplies were given only for use against Japan.[1] He was anxious to interpret the Act as broadly as possible to avoid undue embarrassment to the United Kingdom in the use of its forces against Japan. But he had to work within the Act, which forbade the use of lend-lease funds for reconstruction and rehabilitation in the United Kingdom. He foresaw the possibility that he might have to ask Congress for additional legislation.

After further intermittent discussion at Potsdam letters were exchanged at the end of July. The President on the 29th sent, with a covering letter to the Prime Minister, a copy of a directive he had issued that day to the United States Joint Chiefs of Staff. It followed, but defined more clearly, the line already set on 5th July. The requirements for occupational forces in Axis countries were eliminated definitely from lend-lease. Military and naval lend-lease was confined to material for the use of forces employed directly or indirectly in the war against Japan. In short, as a British official put it, the intention was 'to cover our scheduled (Stage II) requirements as now revised, less the requirements for occupational forces. . . .' Whilst not wholly satisfactory, it was 'the best we can get'. The President in his covering

---

[1] The President made the same point at a press conference on 24th August.

letter accepted a suggestion made by the Prime Minister in the earlier talks that post-war economic arrangements should be discussed later in the summer in Washington.

The Ending of North American Financial Aid. Faced with what London considered to be a 'unilateral decision' and a 'departure from the agreements of last autumn' the British Supply Council held a special meeting on 3rd August to consider the situation. It examined the complex administrative problems of disentangling' eligible from non-eligible supplies and sought to count the cost of the latter. A tentative estimate put the cost for military supplies for forces of occupation at $300 to $400 million. This sum was only part of the total cost, but it was enough, the Treasury representative pointed out, to reduce the gold and dollar reserves by a quarter.[1]

With victory looming, and the end of lend-lease in sight, August was a month of anxious discussion in Washington. All the Missions of the British Commonwealth were in daily touch with each other. The Supply Council held another special meeting on 8th August—in between the two atomic bombs. There was at first a hopeful report that the Foreign Economic Administration regarded lend-lease for non-munitions supplies as outside the President's directive. But during the meeting itself, word was received of a draft directive which would stop practically all military lend-lease deliveries pending a re-examination of British requirements.

The British Merchant Shipping Mission on 10th August advised the Ministry of War Transport that sailings of all United States ammunition ships had been suspended. It predicted the imminent collapse of lend-lease. Under the head of shipping alone the end of lend-lease would involve the United Kingdom in a monthly dollar expenditure of about $60 million.

The Japanese surrender was expected hourly. The uncertainty led to the postponement of a special combined meeting, fixed for 13th August at the Pentagon, to work out the practical application of the President's directive. On that day the British Supply Council met again. It learnt that the War Department had just stopped all shipments of munitions under lend-lease; and it warned London that unofficial indications pointed to the end of supplies of food, raw materials and civilian goods to the United Kingdom under lend-lease within thirty days or less of VJ-Day. Supplies and services for the Far East would continue, it thought, and so might shipping and oil programmes, since these were balanced by British Mutual Aid. A further message warned that lend-lease would automatically stop if Congress by resolution declared the emergency ended. 'The basic difficulty is legislative authority'; for the Act ruled out post-war aid.

---

[1] Spares alone for lend-lease equipment in Europe would cost $50 million.

Further bad news came from Ottawa in the form of an official announcement by the Canadian Government (which was not made public) that Canadian Mutual Aid would end at VJ-Day.

When the Pentagon meeting was held finally on the 17th August, the situation was still not clear. Continuation of lend-lease for forces still engaged in the Far Eastern theatre seemed to the British representatives to be within the law; fighting might flare up in the outlying areas still held by the Japanese. On this it was agreed that the Joint Chiefs of Staff would have to advise the President. The President provided later for this contingency by a directive of 5th September to the Joint Chiefs that lend-lease aid could still be given, if needed for any Allied forces still engaged in putting down Japanese resistance, or in cases where abrupt cessation would cause undue hardship, e.g., rescue of prisoners of war.

On 18th August a letter from Mr. Crowley asked the British Supply Council to begin discussions immediately on the 'discontinuance . . . of Lend-Lease Aid to the British Commonwealth in an expeditious manner which will best promote our mutual interests'. He suggested payment for any supplies in the 'pipeline' which the British Government might still want. Lend-lease procurement machinery could be used for sixty days for such cash transactions. The letter asked for an inventory of lend-lease supplies 'still under the control of the British Commonwealth' as at VJ-Day. The Administration's decision to end lend-lease followed swiftly before discussions could begin. The President announced it at a press conference on the 21st; and a meeting of the British Supply Council was interrupted by a messenger with the news. The President announced that he had directed the Foreign Economic Administration to wind up lend-lease immediately. A British Embassy message to London on that day reported that: 'The dollar sign is back in the Anglo-American equation'; there was 'a certain contraction of view' on some of the broad aspects of British-American relations.

From London Edward R. Murrow reported on the 24th, 'there is considerable resentment in the air over here'. The President's announcement of the end of lend-lease came the day after Ministers in London had informed the British people of further cuts in their clothing and food rations. But perspective was not lost. *The Times* declared that: 'The timely and generous help . . . when this country was fighting alone and had spent her last dollar in cash-and-carry, will never be forgotten.' Mr. Churchill in the House of Commons on the 24th, following a statement by the Prime Minister, summed up the general feeling: the manner might be 'rough and harsh' but he reminded the House that he had judged lend-lease to be 'the most unsordid act in the history of the world'.

The Prime Minister, Mr. Attlee, also paid his tribute to lend-lease whilst regretting its abandonment 'without consultation and prior discussion of the difficult problems involved in the disappearance of a system of so great a range and complication'.[1] He announced that the British Government accepted the invitation of the Foreign Economic Administrator to enter into negotiations regarding the discontinuance of lend-lease and reciprocal aid. Lord Halifax and Lord Keynes, with representatives of the departments concerned, were to widen their mission to Washington on post-war economic and financial questions by adding to it the settlement of lend-lease and reciprocal aid. The mission had been arranged at Potsdam and its scope was being defined at this time in talks in London with Mr. W. L. Clayton. It was at first suggested by the Foreign Economic Administrator, and announced by him at a press conference, that the terms of payment for lend-lease supplies in the pipeline should be fixed at once on the basis either of cash or of a thirty-year credit with interest at $2\frac{3}{8}$ per cent. This was regarded in London as a departure from the arrangements which had just been negotiated with Mr. Clayton. The Prime Minister, at the end of August, intervened with the President and it was agreed that payment for pipeline supplies should be one of the matters to be settled in the negotiations about to open in Washington.

The essential point was that the pipeline was not suddenly broken. It did not begin to 'suck air' as had been feared. The flow slackened greatly but supplies continued to move. Concessions were made on both sides. Thus it was agreed that ocean freight charges should be met under lend-lease by the United States for a period of sixty days after VJ-Day. This prevented the sudden disruption of the international shipping pool.[2] The United Kingdom on its side agreed to continue to furnish supplies under reciprocal aid to the United States, and especially to the United States Army abroad. The cost was to be offset in the final settlement against sums due for lend-lease pipeline supplies since VJ-Day.

Before this final settlement is considered something must be said on two points. One relates to the winding up of the combined machinery of the war. The other is a reflection on the breakdown of lend-lease arrangements as traced in this chapter.

---

[1] H. of C. Deb., Vol. 413, Cols. 955–57, 24th August 1945. In a magazine article two years later (*Colliers*, 18th October 1947), Mr. Morgenthau, who was no longer in office, used stronger language. 'On August 21, the United States Government, without warning, brutally terminated the operation of the Lend-Lease Act.'

[2] *Twenty-first Report to Congress on Lend-Lease Operations*, p. 8.

(v)

The Dismantling of Combined Machinery

To the American public, the end of lend-lease seemed a minor incident of American reconversion, the cutting out of a small and not very popular part of the vast American war expenditure, and the disposal of some surplus stores abroad. During the war the American Government had become the purchaser of almost half of the products of American industry. Lend-lease stores abroad were only a fraction of the vast surplus of war supplies in the United States itself. Public attention centred naturally on the main process of reconversion which involved the return of forty-five per cent. of the nation's labour force from its armed forces and war industries. New industrial plants on which the Government had spent some $16 billion had to be turned over to peace-time uses. Reconversion meant the demobilisation of everything that could be demobilised and the ending of all controls. The public, normally intolerant of controls, had accepted them on the assumption that they would end with the war. The demand for the sweeping away of controls on raw materials, transport, prices, wages, trade and manpower would not wait for VJ-Day. The process began some months earlier. From July onwards the Controlled Materials Plan for steel, aluminium and copper was 'open ended'; in other words, free bidding was permitted for any supplies of these materials left over after military and civilian needs had been met. By the beginning of August the War Production Board had removed over 250 restrictive controls of various kinds, mostly limitation and conservation orders. Limitation orders were continued only on certain important consumer goods and on the distribution of a few scarce raw materials. By the end of August the only metals still under full control were tin, lead and antimony. The President, on 18th August, instructed Federal agencies 'to move as rapidly as possible without endangering the stability of the economy toward the removal of price, wage, production, and other controls and toward the restoration of collective bargaining and the free market'.[1] Wholesale cancellation of Government contracts began in mid-August. By the end of the month a fair proportion of the more than 350,000 contracts let by the Government during the war had been cancelled. Employment in the principal war industries, such as aircraft, ammunition and shipbuilding, fell during that month to almost half the level of May.[2]

---

[1] Executive Order 9599, *The United States at War*, op. cit., p. 491.
[2] Ibid., p. 472.

The demobilisation of the armed forces proceeded likewise at phenomenal speed, limited only by the shipping available. It went much faster than the Army leaders had hoped and planned, but never fast enough to satisfy public opinion.[1]

Administrative demobilisation followed close on the heels of the demobilisation of industry and of the armed forces. Before the end of the year most of the special war-time agencies, as well as three of the Combined Boards, were abolished. Their functions, in some cases, were transferred to the regular departments of government.[2]

The first sign of the winding up of the combined organisations came in June. It was a step towards the narrowing down of collaboration in the matter of aircraft design and development; and it led on in September to the winding up of the Joint Aircraft Committee. The desirability of continuing full collaboration with the United States on defence research and development was discussed on the British side in June. The British Chiefs of Staff considered that the collaboration should continue, not merely for the war with Japan, but for a period of years to follow. Combination in research and development included at that stage not only close contacts between the Services of the two countries, but also between their supply departments, and between the British Commonwealth Scientific Office and the American Office of Scientific Research and Development. There was also an important exchange of data through the Combined Production and Resources Board. A serious difficulty in continuing the collaboration was that the authority under which the American officials disclosed scientific or technical information derived from the Lend-Lease Act (Sections 2 and 3). Likewise the Patent Interchange Agreement was limited to the war. The United States authorities in general favoured collaboration to the end of the war with Japan, irrespective of whether the results could be applied in the Japanese war.

The United States Army Air Force, however, preferred a more restrictive policy. Thus, on 27th June, the State Department in a memorandum for the Joint Aircraft Committee, moved to discontinue the standardisation and exchange of technical information on the air side, except for weapons for use in the war against Japan. Collabora tion in design and development on work still on hand and unfinished which might be of use in the war against Japan before 1st March 1946 could continue. In the circumstances it did not seem worth while to

---

[1] Ibid., p. 471.

[2] *The United States at War*, op. cit., p. 500, gives a list of eighteen agencies terminated between June and December 1945. In each case, except those of the Combined Boards, termination was by Executive Order of the President. The Washington Munitions Assignments Board was terminated on 8th November 1945 by the United States Joint Chiefs of Staff with the approval of the President and the Prime Minister of the United Kingdom. The other two Combined Boards were terminated on 31st December 1945 by an agreement between the Prime Ministers of the United Kingdom and Canada and the President, which was announced on 10th December.

continue the Joint Aircraft Committee and the Joint Radio Board, its sub-committee. With the agreement of the British Government, both were wound up on 12th September. This was the fifth anniversary of the Joint Aircraft Committee. The British Minister of Aircraft Production, in a message to the United States Secretary of War, noted that the Committee by its continuous planning since 1940 had made it possible at all stages of the war for the aircraft industries of the two countries to maintain their maximum impact upon the enemy. It still remained possible in theory to continue collaboration on research, design and development through the regular channels of the two Governments. Thus, on the air side, the United States Aeronautical Board undertook to carry out, on a joint United States Army and Navy basis, any of the functions of the Joint Aircraft Committee and the Joint Radio Board which the United States desired to continue.

The Combined Boards were part of the organisation of the Combined Chiefs of Staff; whether they were to continue depended in part on the decision as to the continuation of the Combined Chiefs. There was an inconclusive discussion at Potsdam in July on the future of the Combined Chiefs of Staff organisation. Whilst the British view was that the organisation should continue after the war, the American Chiefs regarded any discussion as premature, since American policy was still undefined. At the end of August the matter was discussed again by the British Joint Staff Mission in Washington; it concluded that, with the exception of the Combined Staff planners, all the combined committees of the Combined Chiefs of Staff had work to do which would carry them over the next months.

The work of the Combined Munitions Assignments Board, on the other hand, was clearly finished. The decision to wind up both the Washington and London Boards was taken by the Prime Minister and the President in October. A suggestion to wind up the Washington Board had been made by the President to the Prime Minister at Potsdam in July. The ground was that the resources of the two countries were now generally more than sufficient to ensure the success of combined strategy. American supplies had been allocated under lend-lease without a board before the United States entered the war. The British view, however, was that, so long as the Combined Chiefs directed strategy, it was useful to continue the Munitions Assignments Boards and their committees as instruments through which the Combined Chiefs could guide the allocation of munitions. The Prime Minister emphasised the importance of continuing the interchange of information as to the availability and disposal of munitions, including captured war material. He desired that a 'neutral' chairman should again head the Washington Board. In fact only ground assignments were involved in the dissolution of the main Washington Board; since for some time both naval and air supplies had been handled by direct negotiations between representatives of the Services. The final messages which were exchanged when the Washington and London Boards were abolished emphasised the harmony that had been maintained in their work despite the pressure of conflicting claims and the stress of war.

There remained the question of the other Combined Boards. On 29th August the President and the Prime Ministers of Great Britain and Canada announced their decision to maintain them for the time being. The purpose was to avoid 'serious dislocations of supplies'. The continued exchange of statistical data on production and supply, for which the Combined Production and Resources Board had been the channel, was felt to be desirable. There was also some advantage in continuing to allocate a few scarce raw materials—especially for the United States, since these were mostly from sources controlled by the United Kingdom. The Combined Raw Materials Board decided on 11th September that all its recommendations were terminated for eighteen raw materials.[1] The Board's reserved commodity list, comprising over fifty raw materials, had been completely revised in the previous weeks and reduced to thirteen commodities.[2] A few other revisions were made before December. The agreement of the two Governments to terminate the Combined Raw Materials Board and the Combined Production and Resources Board as at 31st December 1945 was announced by the President and the Prime Minister on 10th December. The removal of controls made combined allocation no longer a practicable procedure; and it was necessary to broaden the basis of international collaboration for the few remaining commodities that were still difficult. Plans were made therefore at the beginning of December to continue allocation arrangements into 1946 for a few important commodities that were still in short supply; namely, hides and leather, rubber and tin metal. The machinery devised for this transitional period was that of independent multilateral commodity committees.[3]

Reflection on Two Systems. The manner of the ending of lend-lease illustrated an important point in the experience of British officials in working with their American colleagues. The point was that within the fundamental identity of aims, purpose and outlook between the two peoples there lurked important differences. Working relations were based on the fact of this fundamental identity. It was the foundation of the extraordinarily intimate and successful British-

---

[1] These were: antimony, asbestos, bismuth, cadmium, carbon black, casein, chromite, copper, gluebones, gluestock, graphite, kapok, manganese ore, nickel, nylon, platinum, pyrethrum, pyrites.

[2] These commodities were: copal gum, cordage fibres, hides, skins and leather, hog bristles, jute (including Belgian Congo jute), lead, lumber, mica, newsprint, pine rosin, rotonone, rubber, tin.

[3] See *Studies of Overseas Supply*.

American combination, at thousands of points daily, over two and a half years of war waged together and the earlier two years in which the United States were a helpful but neutral friend. The differences, though obscure, were important, because they arose from divergencies in tradition, experience and constitutional systems.

An exploration of these differences would lead beyond the scope of an official history which can be based only on one side of the total experience. What is said here can only be in the nature of an 'aside'.

It was not for lack of foresight that the British Government failed to begin the Stage III negotiations before the surrender of Japan. There is evidence that the matter was discussed in London in March but put aside on the ground that to raise the issue then in Washington might prejudice the success of the Stage II agreements. Through the critical months from May to July London waited, hoping to clear up the mystery as to whether the Stage II agreements were alive or dead. The view of the British missions in Washington, as recorded in a discussion in May, was that even if no binding agreement had been entered into by the United States Government, the United States Service Departments were at least 'under an obligation to support the request for the necessary appropriations by Congress'.

But the continuity of administrative memory in Washington was overestimated. The agreements themselves, and still more the impressive demonstration of Britain's financial crisis given by Lord Keynes in the autumn of 1944, had almost dropped out of sight and of mind. In the competitive American system there is no 'once and for all'. A case has to be kept to the forefront by constant discussion. The relations of a foreign government with the United States must centre in the President, not in the Cabinet, and still less in Congress; and there can be no loss of continuity so great as that which may come with the death of a President. Apart from the death of President Roosevelt an explanation of the breakdown of the Stage II agreements and the sudden ending of lend-lease could be found in external events and the law. The external events were the sudden and unexpected ending of the war with Japan. This in turn, like a breaking dam, unleashed the flood of American reconversion and demobilisation. A hint of the breaking of the dam was given in a report to London in May. The War Production Board was convinced, it was reported, that reconversion was too complex to be planned in detail and that the only thing to do at the end of the war was to get rid of all controls as quickly as possible. But at that time the end of the war still seemed a remote contingency.

As for the law, it was clear enough that lend-lease was a war measure which must end with the war. Administration leaders, in defending the manner in which lend-lease was ended, pleaded that the end was fixed in the law and that the President had no discretion.

But the real reason for the haste of the Administration was Congress and public opinion rather than the law. For the law itself gave some discretion as to the fixing of the legal date of the end of the war. The impression in London seemed to be that the President could use this discretion and could find some way of getting the support of Congress for his action.

In announcing the Stage II agreements to Parliament the Prime Minister had said:

> Let me remind the House that it is no part of the purpose of the Lend-Lease Act to provide general relief, or to prepare for post-war reconstruction, or to aid our export trade.[1]

Neither Congress nor public opinion was in any mood in the summer of 1945 to provide Britain with lend-lease aid beyond the immediate necessities, and certainly not beyond the war. This was shown in the spring by the amendment of the Act barring the use of lend-lease funds for post-war needs. The amendment ran counter even to the small 'easement' for the civilian population envisaged under the Stage II agreements. However it might seem in London, it was clear enough in Washington that assistance from the United States to tide over the United Kingdom until it could break even in its balance of payments and begin to pay off the accumulated debts of the war was a new issue with the most far-reaching implications. Yet the difficulty of the issue, and the scale of the campaign needed to prepare Congress and public opinion, was not realised early enough by the Administration. Mr. Stimson has recorded his opposition in the Cabinet in October 1944 to the use of lend-lease for post-war rehabilitation. In his view the assumption that the lend-lease machinery could be used for this purpose prevented the preparation before the war ended of a bolder and more effective method of achieving the same goal.[2] A hint as to the magnitude of the task of preparing public opinion was shown by a public opinion poll in June 1945. The results implied that the majority of the public, though doubting Britain's capacity to pay, nevertheless wanted the United Kingdom to repay in full for lend-lease aid, even for material which British soldiers and airmen had used up in fighting the common enemy. The wording of the questions was open to challenge and the results were not published; but they seemed to be confirmed by another poll on the same subject published at the beginning of October.

These episodes, like many before them, showed how easy it was to project British constitutional ideas and practices into the American scene. It was never easy for British Ministers and officials to grasp the

---

[1] Mr. Churchill in the House of Commons, 30th November 1944. H. of C. Deb., Vol. 406, Col. 71.

[2] Stimson and Bundy, op. cit., pp. 592–93.

full implications of the roles of various forces and bodies in the American system—the President and his Cabinet, 'the complex politics of Congress' and the 'immeasurably remote public opinion of the United States'.[1] It was never easy for London to envisage clearly a system in which there was no smooth harmony and no ready access between Government and Congress. Although British officials in Washington had a unique opportunity to understand the differences between the two constitutional systems, it was difficult for them to convey their knowledge across the Atlantic. They learned from practical experience the important consequences that flowed from the doctrine of the division of powers between the President and Congress. In the system to which they were accustomed in London, Government, though separated from Parliament, is also in Parliament. The Queen's Ministers sit in Parliament and lead in the conduct of its business. They control the introduction of legislation and can be reasonably certain in advance of its acceptance. If discussions abroad show the need of a new law or a change in an existing law they can negotiate on the assumption that Parliament will be ready to legislate. Ministers are responsible to Parliament for their departments and the actions of their subordinates. It is the civilian heads of the Service Departments, not the generals and admirals, who appear and answer in Parliament.

The British missions in Washington had to understand how things were done, or left undone, in a system with none of these elements. The first impression of Washington as a scene of disorder, of endless committee discussions mixed with uncoordinated activities by individuals and agencies, gave way to a sense of movement on a vast scale. Mr. Churchill commented during the second Quebec Conference: 'there is so much free speech in the United States that one thing cancels out the other, and the great machine crashes on.' The Washington part of the machine seemed strangely different from that of Whitehall. Neither the President nor the members of his Cabinet sit in Congress. They are not there to introduce legislation nor to answer questions, nor to stand between their officials and Congress. Congress may order an inquiry into the administration of the law and summon before it high officials, generals and admirals—as well as officials and officers far down the line. The effect of this last point on the attitude of American officials—their preoccupation with the knowledge that they might at any time be summoned as individuals before a Congressional committee to justify their actions—was referred to on many occasions during the war in British dispatches and cables to London. British officials were no less impressed with the fact

---

[1] The phrases quoted were used by Lord Keynes in his explanation in Parliament of the difficulties of the negotiations for the loan agreement. H. of L. Deb., Vol. 138, Col. 780, 18th December 1945.

that in the American system neither the President nor the members of his Cabinet could count with assurance on legislation by Congress or could pledge in advance any action by Congress on any matter. As Lord Keynes put it in a letter written during the loan negotiations: 'There is no such thing as certainty in Washington.'

One consequence of these differences of system was the difference in the ability to make and to maintain agreements. In the more unified British system it was possible, as American officials learned early and not without astonishment, for a senior British official in close touch with his Department to undertake a commitment involving legislative action with a reasonable assurance that all the Ministries concerned and Parliament would uphold the agreement. The American official, or even a member of the President's Cabinet, laboured under far greater difficulties. It was often not easy to be sure that an agreement between the different agencies would hold good; and never in any circumstance could legislation by Congress be counted on in advance. Here, perhaps, it may be mentioned that, on learning of the project to write this history, one of the most eminent of the American members of the Combined Boards made the following remark to the author: 'Be sure that you mention one chief lesson of this experience. You British can make agreements that will stick. We cannot—or at least it is much more difficult for us. There has to be something provisional about agreements we make with you. What they mean is that we pledge ourselves to try to make them stick with all the other agencies of the Government. Least of all can we make binding agreements that involve action by Congress, since we can have no say at all in that.'

The two problems, how to ensure agreement between the American agencies, and how to make the agreement binding, were carefully discussed by the British missions in Washington when they were preparing the Stage II negotiations. The record of a meeting on 27th September 1944 noted:

> Past experience had taught us that an agreement in general terms made at a high level on behalf of the United States Government was not necessarily regarded as binding by all United States Departments. Our problem was not only to reach a firm agreement with the United States Government but also to make this agreement binding.

The difficulties confronting British officials on the spot had been noted earlier in a report by a British War Cabinet Office official who studied the situation in Washington at the end of 1942: 'There is no United States Cabinet in our sense of the word', he reported, 'and there is no machinery by which policy questions can be examined by all the Departments or "agencies" concerned and then be referred to higher authority with the pros and cons established—nor when a decision is reached is it followed up by any central body like the War

Cabinet secretariat in London. There is in fact no Government machine as we know it.' The difficulties of British officials were increased considerably by interdepartmental jealousies and jurisdictional quarrels on the American side.

The functions of the different agencies and their relations with each other made it necessary for British representatives to keep in personal touch, not only with the State Department, but also with the Treasury, with the Foreign Economic Administration and with the War and Navy Departments. A mitigating feature was the preponderant influence of the two latter Departments in time of war—though not in peace. Their powers went beyond those of the Service Departments in London and once agreement on a matter was reached with them during the war action was likely to follow. But there was no one central channel through which British officials could act. To go from one department to another might be like ploughing in water with the furrow closing behind. To try to work through one department might make the others feel, as Lord Keynes put it in a discussion on tactics in October 1944, that they were being faced with a 'dictate from above'. In reply to the complaint of the head of one department that it was a mistake to go 'shopping around' amongst the different agencies (with a hint that it was better to use him as a channel), a British representative replied tactfully that 'British officials were only too anxious to know where to go in Washington to obtain proper decisions'.

If the system did not provide an answer it might be found at particular times in a personality such as Harry Hopkins. When some step of special importance involving several of the main agencies had to be prepared, Hopkins was turned to for advice. Sometimes, on complex and difficult issues his advice was judged to be so important that action was held up whilst he was away ill. Thus the Stage II preparations were held up from March to May 1944. The telegrams referred frequently to him: 'By this time Hopkins should be back', 'We need his advice. . . .' His advice was followed, for he was the best guide to personal relations and channels within the Administration.

(vi)

Overseas Supply in the Transition: The Financial Settlements

The story of the financial background of British supply from North America, the earlier part of which was told in Chapter VIII, can now be completed.

Victory brought with it the end of the war-time system of financing British supply from North America. This, in Lord Keynes's phrase, could have been an 'economic Dunkirk'. Deprived of the means of financing supplies from North America, Britain would have been forced to cease importing from that continent, and a deep chasm would have begun to open between the sterling and dollar areas. These dangers were recognised and avoided. The Canadian and United States Governments both hastened to make temporary arrangements in order to keep essential supplies moving on a credit basis until long-term financial arrangements could be made. The dates of the financial agreements of the United States and Canada with the United Kingdom, 6th December 1945 and 6th March 1946, are historical landmarks of no mean importance. This is a theme which belongs to the history of the peace. Only one part of it concerns this volume—the balancing of the accounts in the international system of mutual aid; and even to that only a summary reference is appropriate since its full significance can only be made clear in the history of the peace.

By way of preface to the financial settlements a reminder must be given of the special character of the British war effort which brought lend-lease and mutual aid into existence. The matter was best stated in the announcement made by the Prime Minister in the House of Commons on 24th August 1945:[1]

> The system of lend-lease from the United States, mutual aid from Canada, and the accumulation of sterling by the sterling area countries have been an integral part of the war organisation of the Allies. In this way it has been made possible for us in this island to mobilise our domestic manpower for war with an intensity unsurpassed elsewhere, and at the same time to undertake expenditure abroad on the support of military operations over a widely extended area, without having to produce exports to pay for our imports of food and raw materials or to provide the cash we were spending abroad. The very fact that this was the right division of effort between ourselves and our Allies leaves us, however, far worse off, when the sources of assistance dry up, than it leaves those who have been affording us the assistance. If the role assigned to us had been to expand our exports so as to provide a large margin over our current needs which we could furnish free of charge to our Allies, we should, of course, be in an immeasurably stronger position than we are to-day.

Under this system the war was planned from 1941—even earlier—on a combined basis. The principle of the international 'division of labour' which the system embodied made possible an earlier and greater impact upon the enemy. When the combination became complete with the entry of the United States into the war, it became

---

[1] H. of C. Deb., Vol. 413, Cols. 955–56.

possible to time lend-lease aid with greater precision so that the maximum force could be brought against the enemy at a given point in time and space. The timing was shown in the movement of supplies, especially of munitions, so that they reached their maximum flow in the months just before D-Day. The timing was reflected also in the peak rate of $12 billion a year reached by lend-lease aid in the first half of 1944 and the decline by the end of that year to a yearly rate of $9 billion. Lend-lease, mutual aid and sterling credits made it possible to utilise in full the geographical position of the United Kingdom as an island-base close to the enemy, provided with a large reservoir of manpower and industrial capacity which did not have to be transported across the oceans. It thus became possible for the United Kingdom to maintain a much higher proportion of its manpower in the armed forces than the United States or Canada. In addition, a higher proportion of civilians were mobilised in war industry and other war work, such as the building up of a base for large armies from North America and the repair of bomb damage. By mid-1944 fifty-five per cent. of the total labour force of the United Kingdom was in the Services or on war work as against forty per cent. of the total labour force in the United States. Table 30 shows the result of a comparison made by the statistician of the British Supply Council on the eve of VJ-Day between the percentages of the total labour force in the armed forces in Great Britain and the United States.

The Armed Forces as a percentage of the total labour force in Great Britain and the United States[1]

TABLE 30   Millions of persons at mid-year

	1941	1942	1943	1944
Great Britain				
Total labour force	21·4	22·1	22·3	22·0
Armed forces	3·8	4·5	5·1	5·2
Percentage of total labour force	18%	20%	23%	24%
United States				
Total labour force	54·0	56·1	60·8	62·2
Armed forces	1·7	3·7	9·2	11·5
Percentage of total labour force	3%	7%	15%	18%

Munitions production in the United Kingdom itself was not sufficient to maintain such a high proportion of its manpower in the fighting forces. The difference was made up by supplies of munitions

---

[1] cf. *The Impact of the War on Civilian Consumption in the United Kingdom, the United States and Canada* (Report of a Special Combined Committee set up by the Combined Production and Resources Board, Washington: September 1945); and R. G. D. Allen in *Journal of the Royal Statistical Society*, Vol. CIX, 1946.

from the United States and Canada. In the same way the higher percentage of manpower both in the armed forces and in war industry was sustained by the import of food, raw materials, and other supplies from both hemispheres.

The sudden drying up of these special sources of assistance left the United Kingdom far worse off than the United States and Canada or indeed most of the other victorious countries. Alone amongst them it was saddled with unproductive war debts owed abroad, which were as high as the highest reparations that might have been—but were not—imposed on a defeated Axis country. The deficit in the external balance of payments was immense. Expenditure abroad, as the Prime Minister indicated in his statement, was then at the yearly rate of £2,000 million. To meet this expenditure the United Kingdom had an income from all sources of some £800 million. Its exports, the main means of external payments, were less than a third of their pre-war volume; and even with some recovery they would not be more than enough to cover half of the expenditures abroad in 1946 for minimum imports and other payments. The situation as regards exports was illustrated by the manpower figures in mid-1945:[1]

Manpower in direct export industries	0·4 million
Manpower in the armed forces, civil defence and war industries	9·2 million

Other normal means of foreign payments, such as shipping services and income from investments, were heavily cut. Shipping tonnage was about three-quarters of the pre-war figure. Income from foreign investments (which had met the cost of about a quarter of the pre-war imports of the United Kingdom) was halved. Total external disinvestment was put at £4,198 million.

External Disinvestment: United Kingdom, September 1939–June 1945

	£ million
Sale of investments abroad . . .	1,118
Increase in external debt . . .	2,879
Reduction of reserves of gold and dollars .	152
Unallocated	49
TOTAL	£4,198[2]

The immediate problem as regards the deficit in the balance of payments was to find the means of payment across the exchanges for supplies from North America. The only means whereby supplies could continue on an adequate scale from the dollar area was by loans large enough to cover the deficit during the several years of transition that must elapse before the export trade could be built up

---

[1] *Statistical material presented during the Washington negotiations*, Cmd. 6707, December 1945.

[2] Ibid. The White Paper noted that in addition to external disinvestment, recovery was affected by internal disinvestment and physical destruction involving over £2,000 million. Altogether national wealth in the United Kingdom had diminished during the war by about twenty-five per cent.

to the point at which the United Kingdom could begin to pay its way. The burden of debt was a problem with a longer span. It was closely linked with the settlement of lend-lease and mutual aid; since, if the settlements were such as to add fresh debt, it might be impossible to pay for both the annual interest and the barest minimum of imports.

The total external liabilities of the United Kingdom were put at £3,355 million at 30th June 1945 as against liquid assets of £453 million. Of this amount £2,723 million were owed to countries in the sterling area.[1] Since Britain still had large armed forces abroad, and had to import supplies without the means of payment, the debt was still mounting rapidly in the months after the war. By December 1945 liabilities stood at £3,600 million, an increase since June of over £200 million.

The matter of the sterling balances belongs to the financial history of the war, and little need be said about it in this volume. Its interest is by way of contrast. Unlike supply from North America, the problem of financing supply from the sterling area was solved with comparative ease; it caused no serious crises during the war although it left heavier burdens. The acute problems were those of production and transport, rather than of finance. The existing banking arrangements of the sterling area gave it the experience, the instruments, and the methods necessary to finance war-time supply within the area. At the end of the war, sterling remained a stable currency freely usable over a large part of the world. It was the only firm standard of reference that could give any sort of stability to European currencies. But this stability, in turn, depended on the United Kingdom having sufficient liquid reserves to maintain some sort of equilibrium, and at the end of 1945 the liabilities were eight times as great as the liquid reserves in gold and dollars. One of the arguments in favour of scaling down sterling balances was that in most countries —e.g., India, Egypt, Australia, New Zealand and the Colonies— they were mainly in the hands of central banks and Governments. Whether held by Governments and central banks or privately, the sterling balances were still in large measure war debts for which there were no corresponding productive assets. India, Egypt, Eire, Palestine, Australia, New Zealand and South Africa had improved considerably their overseas financial position as a result of their large sterling balances accumulated in London; two-thirds of the sterling debt was owed to the first four of these countries. Most of this two-thirds was spent on the defence of the Middle East, Egypt, India and Burma. The United Kingdom had to maintain large military forces in these areas and this involved very large expenditures for troop

---

[1] Ibid., Tables 6, 7, 8.

pay, munitions, military construction and communications. As Lord Keynes wrote during the Stage II negotiations:

> For five years we, and we alone, have been responsible for practically the whole cash outgoings for the war over the vast territories from North Africa to Burma.

Only a little more than a third of the total sterling liabilities was due to the excess of British war-time imports over exports, and most of these imports were used up in war production. British exports could pay for only a fraction of all this expenditure; the rest involved 'huge debts in the form of accumulated sterling balances'.[1] Because the debts incurred in these various ways were largely war debts, there was a strong case for attempting to scale them down to a reasonable level. But this was rendered difficult by the circumstances of their origin, the prevailing political and economic conditions, and the opposition in the majority of the creditor countries to any serious scaling down of debt. The holders of the debts were also the suppliers of scarce and much-needed foodstuffs and raw materials. There was no sign of any glut or fall in world prices which might have increased the bargaining power of the United Kingdom. Moreover, negotiations for a settlement of the sterling balances could not begin with any hope of success until liabilities to the dollar area had been determined by financial settlements with Canada and the United States.

The liabilities of the United Kingdom in respect of dollars were much less than its sterling debts. Total liabilities to North and South America were given in the White Paper as £303 million in mid-1945; but the full total could not be known until the lend-lease and mutual-aid settlements had been made. In the case of Canada the debt, which replaced a favourable pre-war balance of payments, totalled about $1,000 million; this included the $700 million loan and the liability under the Air Training Plan. To the debt had to be added the forced sale of about a billion dollars of British-owned Canadian securities. British income from this source had fallen from some $80 million before the war to about $55 million in June 1945.

Altogether, by the sacrifice of investments, which were the accumulated reserves of the past, by using up present liquid reserves and by throwing in all current dollar earnings, the United Kingdom had spent $6,000 million on the purchase of supplies and services from North America before the introduction of lend-lease and mutual aid. Roughly $2,000 million were obtained by the sale of securities and a further $2,500 million by the net depletion of reserves. As Lord Keynes pointed out in a British Commonwealth meeting in Washing-

---

[1] Cmd. 6707, op. cit. Post-war sterling gifts totalling $38 million were made to the United Kingdom by Australia and New Zealand, *United Kingdom Balance of Payments 1946 to 1949.* Cmd. 7793, October 1949.

ton during the loan negotiations, the United Kingdom had never been able to recover from the initial burden caused by those huge cash payments for munitions and food from North America. The trade of a large part of the world, he added, was clogged by the indebtedness of Great Britain.

It was on this last point that the settlement and loan negotiations largely turned in both Washington and Ottawa. The alternatives were presented starkly at Ottawa. Without loans and burdened with war debt, the United Kingdom would be isolated and forced back into 'the grimmest form of bilateralism'. There would be a grave shrinkage in international trade. The common goal of the United Kingdom, Canada and the United States, the freeing and expansion of world trade, would be defeated. The goal was stated clearly in the Master Lend-Lease Agreement with the United Kingdom, dated 23rd February 1942, and in the Canadian Mutual Aid Agreement with the United Kingdom, signed on 11th February 1944. Both agreements laid down, in almost identical words, the principle that the lend-lease settlement after the war should be such that it did not 'burden commerce between the two countries', but promoted 'mutually advantageous economic relations between them and the betterment of world-wide economic relations'. Funds that had to be paid out as interest and principal on unproductive war debts would not be available for the purchase of imports. Payments abroad had to come from a single source, present British production, and invisible exports of British services. That source was too small to pay both for large war debts not represented by any productive assets, as well as the interest and amortisation charges on the large dollar loans needed as working capital in the transition period until the United Kingdom could break even in its external balance of payments.

The Settlement with the United States. The general scope of the lend-lease settlement, as well as the subordinate part played by it in the Washington loan negotiations, is indicated by the title of the agreement, dated 6th December 1945: 'Financial Agreement between the Governments of the United States and the United Kingdom, together with a Joint Statement regarding Settlement for Lend-Lease, Reciprocal Aid, Surplus War Property and Claims.'[1] The agreement was

---

[1] The text of the 'Joint Statement' is annexed to this volume, see Appendix VII. See also Cmd. 6707, op. cit.; *Financial Agreement between the Governments of the United States and the United Kingdom*, Cmd. 6708, December 1945; *Proposals for Consideration by an International Conference on Trade and Employment*, Cmd. 6709, December 1945; *Specific Agreements Regarding Settlement for Lend-Lease, Reciprocal Aid, Surplus War Property and Claims*, Cmd. 6778, March 1946; *Twenty-First Report to Congress on Lend-Lease Operations*; *Agreement between the Governments of the United Kingdom and the United States of America for a Settlement of Claims under the Specific Agreements of 27th March 1946*, Cmd. 7471, July 1948. Letter from U.S. Secretary of State to Senator Mead, 7th March 1946, Senate Doc., 79th Congress, 2nd Session, Report No. 110, Part 5, Appendix XVIII. Also 'Mutual Aid between the United States and the British Empire, 1941-1945', by R. G. D. Allen, in *Journal of the Royal Statistical Society*, Vol. CIX, Part III, 1946.

accompanied by a joint statement by the President and the Prime
Minister which indicated that the discussions between the two
Governments, lasting from 11th September to 5th December, had
ranged over the major problems affecting the basic economic relations
of the two countries. They included 'the question of financial assistance from the United States to the United Kingdom, the demobilisation of war-time trade and monetary restrictions, the settlement of
lend-lease, the disposal of surplus war property in the United Kingdom owned by the United States, and finally long-range commercial
policies in the broad sense. . . .' The British view from the outset
was that the question of a loan was the main thread in this complex
of issues. This did not mean that the close link between the post-war
deficit and the huge cash payments of the 'cash and carry' period was
forgotten. There was a certain retrospective justice in the idea put
forward by the Chancellor of the Exchequer to Lord Keynes at an
early stage in the negotiations. The idea was that a basis might be
found in these 'cash and carry' payments for a substantial 'grant-in-
aid' to the United Kingdom. This would have been a kind of retroactive lend-lease—'pensioning the past' Lord Keynes called it. But
for reasons which he explained later the idea made no headway. A
basis could not be found in the past—littered as it was with the debris
of unpaid war debts and American neutrality; it could be found only
in present need and the hopes that would be wrecked if the need were
not met. Only a moderate loan was judged to be acceptable to Congress; and, despite all the efforts of the British negotiators, it had to be
an interest-bearing loan. Lord Keynes never ceased to regret, as he
confessed in Parliament, that he failed to bring back to London 'the
balm and sweet simplicity of no per cent'.[1] But even with interest the
loan was never safe until it was finally voted by Congress and signed
by the President on 15th July 1946. The line taken steadily by the
Administration was that the arrangement as a whole was necessary
to 'put an end to an economically divided world'.[2] The arrangement
linked together two elements: (*a*) the loan, or rather 'line of credit', to
the United Kingdom, which was fixed at $3,750 million; (*b*) the
payment by the United Kingdom of $650 million in 'complete' and
'final settlement of the financial claims of each Government against
the other arising out of the conduct of the war'. This sum of $650
million was a liability to be discharged by the United Kingdom on
the same terms as the loan. (It was not, however, subject to approval
by Congress.) The loan could be drawn on up to 31st December 1951,

---

[1] H. of L. Deb., Vol. 138, Cols. 784 and 787, 18th December 1945. Yet interest was not
really the main point in the discussions in London on the loan agreement. Its most
unpalatable features were the strings attached to it: namely, convertibility and non-
discrimination.

[2] Statement by Secretary of the Treasury before Senate Committee on Banking and
Currency, 5th March 1946.

at which time interest would become due on the total sum of $4,400 million at two per cent.[1]

What the lend-lease settlement did was to wipe out all claims between the two Governments arising out of the war. This marked the end of what Lord Keynes called the 'uncomfortable and uncertain obligation' of the 'consideration' which the President might ask for in return for lend-lease—the subject of much worried discussion on the British side during the whole life of the Act.[2] All American lend-lease and British reciprocal-aid stores and services supplied up to VJ-Day, and consumed, lost or destroyed during the war, were wiped off the slate. Munitions on hand on VJ-Day could be retained subject to recapture on both sides. For civilian stores and facilities supplied by either Government and still on hand at VJ-Day, or shipped since then, a balance was struck; it showed a debit to be paid by the United Kingdom under this head of $650 million. In return, the United Kingdom received title to such stores and facilities in the United Kingdom and the Colonies. Military supplies, including aircraft and shipping in the hands of British forces on VJ-Day could continue to be used by the United Kingdom, but the United States reserved the right of recapture. But, as the Joint Statement recorded, 'the United States has indicated that it does not intend to exercise generally this right of recapture'. Ships in existence on VJ-Day, naval vessels and all merchant ships of 100 gross tons and more, supplied by either Government, were to be returned to that Government. The amount to be paid by the United Kingdom for civilian stores and facilities (including some transport aircraft) was a compromise figure. It was less than the American negotiators wanted, but more than the British thought the stocks in the United Kingdom were worth. On the whole, as Lord Keynes assured a meeting of the Commonwealth countries on 5th December, it represented 'fair and reasonable value', since the stocks had been well picked over already by the United States and the United Nations Relief and Rehabilitation Administration. The Americans, he thought, had taken a 'very generous line'.

The sum was distributed amongst the following elements:

$ *million*

1. Amount due to United States under the offsetting arrangements for mutual aid between the two countries after VJ-Day. (Lend-lease pipeline supplies less British reciprocal aid) . . . . 118[3]

---

[1] For the total duration of the loan—fifty years—the interest worked out at about 1·6 per cent. In addition to the six years' moratorium on interest, there was provision for a complete waiver—cancellation—of interest in any year in which British exports fell below a certain level.

[2] H. of L. Deb., Vol. 138, Cols. 786–87, 18th December 1945.

[3] Later reduced to $90½ million. Cmd. 7471, July 1948.

$ *million*

2. Payment for United States property in the United Kingdom 60
3. Payment in final settlement for stocks of lend-lease goods of civilian types held by the United Kingdom on VJ-Day 472

TOTAL 650

The general lend-lease settlement was embodied in nine 'Specific Agreements' which were negotiated between December 1945 and March 1946 and signed on the 27th of that month. The nine agreements covered the following subjects:

1. Lend-Lease and Reciprocal Aid Pipelines and Offsetting Arrangement.
2. Settlement of Inter-Governmental Claims.
3. Civilian Holdings.
4. Military Holdings.
5. Lend-Lease Aircraft (Non-combat) and Spares.
6. Petroleum.
7. Lend-Lease and Reciprocal Aid Installations.
8. United States Army and Navy Surplus Property and Surplus Installations in the United Kingdom.
9. Tort Claims.

Aircraft proved the most difficult subject. No difficulty arose over military aircraft which were retained by the United Kingdom subject to recapture. A compromise was made for non-combat aircraft, such as transports, which were *prima facie* capable of civilian use. Full title was given to 672 Dakota aircraft and 43 aircraft of other types, which were regarded as covered by the total sum fixed on 6th December; an equal number of Dakotas was taken over by the United Kingdom under a temporary leasing arrangement.[1]

From 1942 onwards, finance as such had played little part in the combined planning of supply. Plans were made and programmes of requirements and supplies drawn up, not in terms of dollars and pounds sterling, but of units of equipment and quantities of raw materials and food. The reappearance of the dollar sign in the final balancing of accounts was a necessary formality, although in fact the contribution of each country to the other was beyond any financial accounting. The Joint Statement of 6th December recorded that in arriving at the settlement 'both Governments have taken full cognizance of the benefits already received by them in the defeat of

---

[1] Cmd. 6778, March 1946.

their common enemies'. 'Full cognizance of the benefits' covers all those things which, even though physical elements enter into them, are measureless and imponderable, like Dunkirk, the Battle of Britain, and the Fifty Over-Age Destroyers. The value of the exchange of scientific and technical data could not be expressed in figures. Nor was it possible to assess the value to the United States of the armament industry created by British cash contracts in the 'cash and carry' period.

Even the figures set down in the ledgers on both sides for actual goods and services exchanged were hardly comparable. To convert pounds into dollars and dollars into pounds at official rates of exchange had little meaning, because of the differences in the relative cost structures in the countries of the British Commonwealth, and the United States. American lend-lease aid to the United Kingdom was about $27,000 million. After making a rough equation of costs, Professor R. G. D. Allen arrived at a figure of British reciprocal aid to the United States of $6,000 million. Taking into account the disparity in size of population and relative industrial power, he concluded that reciprocal aid of $6,000 million from the United Kingdom was equivalent to some $20,000 million from a country the size of the United States, and this, he added, was a sum 'within hailing distance of the $27,000 million of lend-lease aid'.[1] Using figures from the combined study entitled 'The Impact of the War on Civilian Consumption', he checked this conclusion by a comparison between total war expenditure, national income and gross national production with the result shown in Table 31.

Mutual Aid in relation to war expenditure and national income

TABLE 31   Per cent.

	United States lend-lease aid to the British Commonwealth ($3\frac{1}{2}$ years, January 1942 to June 1945)	United Kingdom reciprocal aid to the United States (3 years, July 1942 to July 1945)
	%	%
Percentage of:		
War expenditure	10·9	8·6
National income	4·8 (4·1)	4·6
Gross national production	4·1 (3·4)	3·0

The figures in brackets were the result of a fresh calculation based on a point brought out in the discussion of his paper. The comparison

---

[1] Allen, op. cit., p. 259; see Table 27, p. 430, above. The differences in costs between the United States and the United Kingdom are referred to in the first British White Paper on Mutual Aid, Cmd. 6483, November 1943, para. 30.

2H

would be more favourable to the United Kingdom, it was pointed out, if allowance were made for the relative dearness of munitions in the United States and the fact that they bulked larger in lend-lease than in total production.

Such considerations were not absent from the minds of the American negotiators; and they were fully aware of all the 'benefits' for which there could be no dollar sign. If the case was not argued by them on these grounds before the bar of American public opinion, it was for the reason put by Lord Keynes to Parliament. 'The Americans—and are they wrong?—find a post-mortem on relative services and sacrifices amongst the leading allies extremely distasteful and dissatisfying.' However it was looked at, there was still the fact that $16,000 million, or over $20,000 million—for there was some discrepancy in the estimates—of lend-lease 'credit' was wiped off the slate. Lord Keynes, who was in a better position than most others to judge, referred to the settlement as 'an act of unprecedented liberality'. He saw in it an expression of the 'liberal purposes and intense good will towards this country of the American people', and the desire to see the United Kingdom as a 'strong and effective partner' in a troubled world.[1] Thus in the end the 'lending' was true to its old English root: *laenan*, to give.

The Settlement with Canada. Something must now be said about the last phase of Britain's financial relations with Canada, to complete the account given in Chapter VIII. A British Treasury minute of August 1946 summed up these relations during the war in a sentence. The requirements of the United Kingdom in Canada were covered throughout the war without 'any undue legacy of debt or any undue strain on our depleted resources'. Canada, it should be noted, gave mutual aid to the United Kingdom on a large scale without asking for or receiving either British reciprocal aid or American lend-lease.[2]

At the end of the war the Canadian Department of Finance prepared for publication in a combined report, a single table

---

[1] H. of L. Deb., Vol. 138, Cols 779, 782, 787, 18th December 1945.

[2] The United Kingdom paid Canada all it could pay across the exchange; Canada provided the rest free. In general the principle of mutual aid was the basis of war relations within the family system of the British Commonwealth. The Mutual Aid Agreement of 11th February 1944 recognised this in providing that the United Kingdom should 'continue to contribute to the defence of Canada and the strengthening thereof and will provide such articles, services, facilities or information as it may be in a position to supply and as may from time to time be determined by common agreement in the light of the development of the war'. Aid furnished by the United Kingdom to Canada and to Canadian forces abroad was not counted formally as reciprocal aid. The latter was given by the United Kingdom from 1939 to 1945 to fourteen countries, all outside the Commonwealth, namely: Belgium, China, Czechoslovakia, Denmark, France, Greece, Netherlands, Norway, Poland, Portugal, Turkey, United States, U.S.S.R., Yugoslavia. The total amount was £2,078.4 million, of which £1,241 million was in respect of the United States. *Mutual Aid, Third Report*, Cmd. 6931, October 1946. See also below, Appendix VIII.

summarising Britain's war-time requirements from Canada and showing how they were financed.[1]

War-time requirements of the United Kingdom in Canada and the sources from which they were financed

TABLE 32   Canadian $ million at current prices

	1940	1941	1942	1943	1944	Total
United Kingdom requirements:						
Munitions and military supplies .	50	353	643	916	978	2,940
Food	239	320	325	384	470	1,738
Raw materials (wood and metals) .	185	191	176	229	209	990
Other exports	68	50	90	65	55	328
Freight	60	110	114	128	124	536
Air training and other war services .	32	145	196	202	208	783
Miscellaneous current requirements .	27	24	23	23	29	126
TOTAL	661	1,193	1,567	1,947	2,073	7,441
Sources of finance:						
Mutual aid and 1942 contribution from Canada	—	—	1,000	501	775	2,276
Provision of supplies and services in exchange by the United Kingdom to Canadian forces abroad . .	20	40	85	430	1,005	1,580
Net accrual to the United Kingdom of normal commercial credits from exports and other current transactions	154	244	304	207	195	1,104
Loans, book credits, security purchases, gold payments and other capital transactions (net) . .	487	909	178	809	98	2,481
TOTAL	661	1,193	1,567	1,947	2,073	7,441

The complex financial arrangements indicated by the table can be summarised briefly as follows. At first, in accordance with the normal practice, sterling balances held in London by the Bank of Canada were kept from rising too high by the shipment of gold and the sale of United States dollars to Canada. As British purchases increased, the United Kingdom resorted in addition to the repatriation or sale of British-held Canadian securities. By the end of 1941 these sources of payment were practically exhausted and the Canadian Government had accumulated considerable balances in sterling. In April 1942 this past accumulation of sterling was consolidated in the form of a loan of $700 million which was made free

---

[1] *The Impact of the War on Civilian Consumption* (Washington: 1945, p. 148). Something of the pre-war scale of supply from Canada is indicated by its exports to the United Kingdom in 1939. (Millions of dollars)—Agricultural and vegetable products, 94.2; Animals and animal products 73.6; Fibres, textiles and textile products 3.5; Wood, wood products and paper 43.9; Iron and iron products 16.0; Non-ferrous metals and products 83.4; Non-metallic minerals and their products 3.4; Chemicals and allied products 5.7; Miscellaneous commodities 4.4; *Canada at War, Recapitulation Issue*, op. cit., pp. 107–13.

of interest until the end of the war.[1] The continuing dollar deficit of
Britain (and other sterling-area countries) was then taken care of by
the free gift of $1,000 million. This was only enough to cover British
requirements to January 1943. British supply needs were tided over,
until the Mutual Aid Bill could be introduced in April, by various
expedients. These included sales by the United Kingdom of United
States dollars and the repurchase by Canada, for some $200 million,
of munitions plants which the United Kingdom had financed in
Canada. The first Mutual Aid Appropriation of $1,000 million in
April 1943 was followed by a second appropriation of $800 million
in the spring of 1944.[2] Later in that year additional funds were made
available by Canada. This was done by an upward revision of the
basis on which payments were being made to the United Kingdom
for the cost of advanced training and maintenance of Canadian
armed forces overseas, including the cost of reserve stores and stores
in transit provided by the United Kingdom for these forces. In
April 1945 the Canadian Government secured an interim war
appropriation of $2,000 million to cover all Canadian war expendi-
tures, including mutual-aid requirements for the next five months.
This arrangement, whereby in effect mutual aid was eliminated for
munitions and charged direct on the Canadian defence appropriation, was one that Lord Keynes had advocated when he visited
Ottawa in August 1944. The appropriation actually covered British
requirements up to the surrender of Japan on 2nd September, the
date at which Canadian mutual aid terminated. From that date, until
the final settlement at the beginning of March 1946, the deficit of the
United Kingdom in Canadian dollars was met on an overdraft basis.

All these arrangements were made by a continuous process of
discussion and agreement between the two Governments, in which
the hard facts of finance were dealt with in a spirit appropriate to the
family relations of members of the Commonwealth. The Government
of Canada showed throughout a rare understanding of the harsh
realities facing the United Kingdom. One of the difficulties which it
brushed aside was the fact that the United Kingdom was incurring
war debts to sterling countries but not—apart from the $700 million
loan of 1942—to Canada. There was no precise analogy between a
sterling and a dollar debt, but the point was not easy to make clear
to the general public.

The first move towards defining the conditions of a post-war
settlement came from Ottawa in February 1945 in several messages
exchanged between the Canadian and British Prime Ministers. The
Canadian Government had three main preoccupations: (a) the

[1] By the agreement of 6th March 1946 the interest-free provision was extended to the
end of 1950.
[2] For the texts of the Canadian Mutual Aid Acts see Appendix VI.

financial difficulties of Britain at the end of the war—a matter which Lord Keynes had explained forcefully in Ottawa in the previous autumn; (b) the effect of these difficulties on Canadian exports; (c) the contribution of mutual aid towards the adoption of liberal principles of trade after the war. The Canadian Government was concerned lest the arrangements for facilitating the transfer of war supplies should 'burden post-war commerce or lead to the imposition of trade restrictions'. The specific problem it faced was that, despite some fifty years of preferential treatment of British exports in Canadian markets, Britain might be forced out of sheer necessity to discriminate against the purchase of Canadian products in favour of purchases within the sterling area. The Canadian Government recognised that in the transition period there must be some restriction of dollar imports by sterling-area countries; but it should not be such as to set a pattern for the future. It recognised also that in the transition some borrowing abroad by the United Kingdom would have to be agreed to by dollar countries as a necessary step toward the adoption by Britain of a liberal and expansionist trade policy. It was well understood in Ottawa that interest on such loans must be such as not to jeopardise the future balance of payments. Satisfaction was soon given to Canada by the British Government in the matter of non-discrimination as between imports from Canada and from the sterling-area countries. But the wider issues of post-war policy concerned the United States as much as Canada. The British Government was anxious that any discussions with Ottawa should run in step with talks with Washington. But to attempt to discuss Stage III with the United States whilst Stage II was still unsettled was judged to be unwise.

There were always some links between American and Canadian financial aid to the United Kingdom. As lend-lease began to end for particular commodities there was some risk that British requirements would be transferred to Canada. Canada on the other hand had the same interest as the United States in seeing that demands on Canada were cut down as the war neared its end. British Stage II programmes were examined in July 1945 from this point of view by the Mutual Aid Board in conjunction with the British Supply Council. Reductions made by the United Kingdom in its aircraft and truck requirements from Canada were welcomed.

The sudden ending of the Japanese war brought a no less sudden notification on 15th August of the termination of mutual aid under Clause 8 of the Mutual Aid Agreement. There was no public announcement, however, and discussions in the next few days between the two Governments soon made it clear that there was no intention on the part of Canada to stop the flow of supplies other than munitions. What the notification meant in effect was that when mutual aid ended on 2nd September the Mutual Aid Board would 'start a fresh ledger'. Further transactions would be entered in this new ledger and this would give the two Governments time to discuss a financial settlement—and one in which, as Ottawa hinted, the whole burden of payment would not necessarily fall on the United Kingdom.

From September to December Canada followed closely day by day the negotiations in Washington. The Canadian Government announced in Parliament on 7th September its intention of finding some mutually acceptable method of continuing supply to the United Kingdom on a credit basis. Lord Keynes, on his way to Washington for the financial discussions with the American Government, had had a preliminary talk with Canadian authorities in Ottawa. A statement in the Canadian House of Commons on 10th December, after the publication of the financial agreement with the United States, indicated that some preliminary talks had already taken place with the British Government on financial arrangements between the two countries.[1] The main negotiations opened in Ottawa on 11th February 1946. Financial and trade relations, past and future, were discussed against the background of the agreements already concluded with the United States but still uncertain until Congress made up its mind about them. The discussions were brief, for they began with a large measure of agreement on essentials. There was full agreement on the basic objective of freeing and expanding world trade, and, as a means to this end, making sterling once more a fully convertible currency. On 6th March two main agreements, somewhat on the lines of those made at Washington, were concluded between the two Governments. These were: (a) an 'Agreement between the Government of the United Kingdom and the Government of Canada on the Settlement of War Claims', providing for a 'final settlement of all outstanding accounts between them arising out of the war'; (b) 'A Financial Agreement between Canada and the United Kingdom', providing for a loan to cover Britain's dollar needs in the transitional period.[2]

Only a passing reference can be made to the loan agreement, which is outside the scope of this volume. The question of interest caused some discussion. The British view was that this was no ordinary self-amortising loan, that credit should carry no interest since interest would add debt to debt and hinder the clearing of sterling and the freeing of trade; but this argument ran into the difficulty that for political reasons the Canadian loan could hardly

---

[1] *Journal of the Parliaments of the Empire*, Vol. XXVII, No. 1, p. 120.

[2] Cmd. 6904, March 1946, and Canada Treaty Series Nos. 9 and 10, 1946. The agreements with Canada were to come into effect at the same time as the agreements with the United States. Part came into effect on 30th May and other clauses on 16th July.

be made on easier terms than the loan given by the United States. The figure of $1,250 million was fixed as the amount of the credit. The conditions as to interest (two per cent. as from 31st December 1950 with waiver clause) and duration (fifty years) paralleled those in the financial agreement with the United States.

The agreement on 'war claims' looked to the future rather than to the past. The Mutual Aid Agreement of 11th February 1944 (Articles VI, VII, VIII, IX) made some reference to a post-war settlement. It reserved the right of Canada to request the return of 'aircraft and automotive equipment' after the war on conditions to be arranged in a final settlement; but otherwise it ruled out any obligation on the part of the United Kingdom to re-deliver supplies at the end of the war. The only express exception was made for cargo ships to which Canada retained title. In general, supplies still in Canada at the end of the war, or in ocean transit, were to revert to Canadian ownership. In the final settlement negotiated in Ottawa both sides were guided by practical considerations. It was agreed that any legacy of war debt between the United Kingdom and Canada must be avoided. The outstanding liabilities of the United Kingdom to Canada then totalled about $1,200 million. These sums, as the British Treasury representative who led the British negotiators pointed out, 'were entirely in respect of war debts and represented non-productive expenditure'. They consisted of two main items, the $700 million loan of 1942 and $425 million in respect of the British contribution in Canada to the British Commonwealth Air Training Plan. There were also substantial liabilities in respect of supplies received by the United Kingdom from Canada since the termination of mutual aid. On the credit side certain payments were due to the United Kingdom from Canada in respect of Canadian forces overseas and war-stores. Under the Claims Agreement, on consideration of a payment by the United Kingdom of $150 million, all claims both ways for the entire period 1st September 1939 to 1st March 1946 were wiped out. Only one exception was made, the $700 million loan of 1942; but its interest-free provision was extended to the end of 1950. A parallel agreement cancelled the $425 million liability under the British Commonwealth Air Training Plan.

The wheel had now come full circle. The gap was closed between British dollar cash payments (which had continued on a large scale in the later war-years) and the total dollar cost of supplies from Canada. Canadian financial aid to the United Kingdom, provided freely without charges or conditions, reached a grand total of $3,468 million, made up as follows:

1942 Gift	$1,000 million
1943–45 Mutual Aid	$2,043 million
1946 Cancellation of Air Training Debt .	$425 million

This free contribution of money met only part of the total cost of British war-time requirements in Canada. The Canadian Government, in the table given at the beginning of this section, put the cost of those requirements at $7,441 million to the end of 1944. It gives payments by Canada in respect of its forces abroad as $1,580 million, and the amount found by the United Kingdom out of its current earnings as $1,104 million. The rest was met by the sale of securities, gold payments and other means.

Money was only a measure of goods. Most of Canada's production of war materials of all sorts during the war went to the United Kingdom.

Deliveries of Canadian war materials, September 1939 to March 1945[1]

TABLE 33	Per cent.

Percentage of Canadian war materials delivered to:	
Canada	34
United Kingdom and rest of the Commonwealth .	53
United States	12
Other United Nations	1
	100

The content by main groups of the exports to the United Kingdom is shown in Table 32. It illustrates two points: how Canada increased in importance as a main source of Britain's overseas supplies of raw materials and food; and how, by trebling her industrial capacity during the war, Canada became a second major source of munitions within the Commonwealth.

The economic side in turn was only part of a larger whole. On VE-Day the British Prime Minister sent the Prime Minister of Canada a message of congratulation to the Government and people of Canada on their contributions to victory. He referred to the part played by Canadian forces on land, air and sea, to the 'immense achievement of the British Commonwealth Air Training Plan under Canadian administration', to the 'aid so generously accorded in the sphere of finance . . . of munitions . . . of naval and merchant vessels . . . of foodstuffs'.

---

[1] *Canadian Mutual Aid Board* (Second Annual Report to March 31, 1945).

(vii)

Retrospect

The theme of this book is North American Supply. It deals with an important aspect of the great partnership—the combination of the British Commonwealth of Nations and the United States of America. It is this greater theme in the background which illuminates the dull facts of supply that inevitably crowd the front of the stage. The lighting of the foreground changes as the scene shifts slowly: from the limited partnership between a fighting Commonwealth of Nations and the great neutral United States to the building of the complete machinery of the Combination; and then to the marshalling by it against the enemy, with a speed and completeness without parallel in history, of the production and resources of the world. In every chapter the facts of supply are drawn against that great background and there is no need to return to it here.

It may be useful, however, to draw attention in these last words to another central theme, less important but still significant, which can be traced throughout the complex pattern of North American Supply. It began to emerge in the first year of the war, became dominant in the second year, and then was submerged for a time until in the fifth year, the year of victory with which this chapter closes, it returned again to the centre of the stage. This is the theme of the financial and economic consequences of British dependence during the war on overseas supply and particularly on supply from North America.

Before the war British requirements from the United States were both minimal and incalculable—minimal because of the difficulty of payment in dollars, incalculable because of American neutrality. 'Cash and carry' removed the second difficulty but made payment in dollars more difficult. In order to survive and fight back after Dunkirk the United Kingdom was forced to increase its armed forces far beyond the limits of the normal capacity of its economy. In living beyond its means, in order to live at all, it had to forgo exchange-earning exports and to concentrate most of its production on war material for the arming of British as well as Commonwealth and Allied forces. The munitions which it could not produce in time and the raw materials which it could not import out of current earnings and which had to be obtained by the shortest sea routes were purchased from North America by using up the nation's accumulated reserves of gold, dollars, securities and investments. No small part of them was used in financing American and Canadian munitions factories in order to speed up war production in North

America. The means of further British payments across the exchanges were exhausted by March 1941. The theme of this book would have come to an abrupt end in that year but for the Lend-Lease Act of March 1941 and Canadian support of sterling.

Lend-lease was far more than a financial measure to ensure the giving of the arms for which Britain could no longer pay. Although she could no longer pay in gold and dollars Britain continued to give value for value received. She was doing the job for which she was receiving the tools. She was paying in terms of a higher degree of mobilisation of her manpower than any other belligerent, and in fighting on all fronts a war on which hung the fate of the whole free world. Lend-lease was an American necessity. It was the only means whereby an America at peace could buy time to rearm fast enough so that it too might survive. It was 'An Act', as its title said, 'to Promote the Defense of the United States'.

Nevertheless the financial conception implied in the phrase 'lease and lend' was to exercise a fateful influence on the financing of overseas supply throughout the war and far into the peace. It was to have a profound effect on the economic situation of the United Kingdom after the war. Lend-lease and mutual aid themselves were cancelled by the wise and generous action of the United States and Canada. But the conception of lending and repayment had set the political and economic pattern for Britain's post-war financial arrangements with both the dollar and the sterling areas. The fact that in theory if not in practice the 'dollar sign' had remained was a barrier to the removal of the rupee sign and all the other signs in which supplies from overseas were recorded. Because these signs could not be removed British war debts were incurred in the shape of the sterling balances.

At the height of the war the lend-lease formula seemed to be filed away in the archives of history as the brilliant invention by which at the end of 1940 the President had solved the political dilemma posed to him by Mr. Churchill in his first message as Prime Minister: 'We shall go on paying dollars for as long as we can but I should like to feel reasonably sure that when we can pay no more you will give us the stuff all the same.'[1] But by an irony of history the formula had raised all over the world political and legal barriers against the logic of pooling. That logic demanded that all countries should bear both in the war and the peace the cost of their contributions of war supplies for the common enterprise.

The Lend-Lease Act represented in the minds of the American people two separate ideas and goals: Aid to Britain and Defence of America. The President designed it so that so long as America was

---

[1] Churchill, *Their Finest Hour*, op cit., p. 23.

at peace its weight would fall equally upon both ideas, but in war mainly upon the second. From Pearl Harbour, until the defences of Germany began to collapse, lend-lease was primarily an instrument of American defence. It continued as an essential piece of mechanism which enabled the British-American combination to function. The keynote of the combination was equality of sacrifice, each partner seeking to give the utmost possible 'mutual aid' to the other in the common cause.

The plans for the future, for the last phase of the war and the first phase of peace (Stages II and III) were laid in the war-years, when the idea of full partnership was at its height and there was a strong sense of a common cause and a common destiny. The agreements or understandings were based on the assumption that, for several years of gradual transition, aid to Britain must continue in order to wind up the common obligations of the war, to safeguard American interests in a stable peace and to achieve the goals set by the Administration of an expanding and free world economy.

But it is in the nature of the American political process that the American Administration cannot make with another country at one stroke binding agreements of this kind. What to that other country may seem to be by all its own standards and tests an *agreement*, has to be called an *understanding* when it is translated into the American political language. For in the semantics of American politics such an understanding cannot become an agreement until by a political and educational campaign the Administration has won for it the support of public opinion and of Congress.

In the case of the Stage II and Stage III agreements a fatal delay postponed the taking of this second step until it was made impossible by sudden and unforeseeable strokes of death and war—the death of President Roosevelt and the collapse of Germany. The distractions and hesitations, natural enough in Washington when an Administration stands on the brink of a difficult political campaign, were reinforced by a hesitation in London due to quite different reasons. To wage a swift and effective publicity campaign in the United States as soon as the Stage II and Stage III understandings were made the Administration needed the release by London of full statistical data on the British war effort. This information would have revealed to the American public how much greater than theirs had been the deprivations and the sacrifices of the British people. But considerations of security seemed to forbid the giving out in the face of the enemy of data which might have aided him by showing him how far America's ally was extended.

Thus all the promise of an orderly transition was swept away in the sudden ending of the war and the back-to-peace stampede in the United States. The abrupt ending of lend-lease supply was accompanied by the collapse of the machinery of British-American combination. The Administration in Washington was left with a dying statute in its hands; for it had given a pledge that the Lend-Lease Act would end with the war. In the public mind the symbols of partnership and equality of sacrifice had already faded from the Act. It was now shrunken to its smallest dimension—an Act for aid to Britain in a war which was already finished.

It lies beyond the scope of this book to tell the story of the frailness of the bridge which the Washington loan negotiations at the end of 1945 designed for the transition. That the United States were still able to build such a bridge out of the debris of broken machinery, crumpled plans and faded hopes was no mean feat. Given the changes in outlook, capacities and goals, which sudden peace always brings in a democracy, it was an achievement not unworthy of the great war partnership.

Appendices

APPENDIX I

Purchase of United States Army Surplus Equipment
June 1940

The documents printed below relate to the transaction, described in Chapter V, by which in June 1940 the British Government purchased, through the United States Steel Export Company as intermediary, surplus equipment of the United States Army. The material was purchased first by the Anglo-French Purchasing Board on 11th June. A week later it was taken over by the British Purchasing Commission (letter of 18th June).

ANGLO-FRENCH PURCHASING BOARD
725-15th Street, N.W.
Washington, D.C.
June 11, 1940.

United States Steel Export Company,
30 Church Street,
New York, N.Y.

Dear Sirs:

Pending the execution of a definitive contract between us and to avoid delay in the purchase and shipment of certain material, a list of which is attached hereto, made a part hereof and marked Exhibit A, we agree to purchase such material from you and we will pay you as demanded from time to time, the total sum of $37,619,556.60 against the purchase price of such material all of which you purchased from the United States Government by a contract executed June 11, 1940. We hereby agree to pay you in addition, your out-of-pocket expenses and disbursements in connection with this transaction, including the cost of packing, handling and freight charges.

We agree to accept and take title to the material listed in Exhibit A, f.o.b. cars "as is", "where is". It is understood that you will act as our agent in arranging for shipment to seaboard, where necessary, and that payment for any material covered hereby, including freight to seaboard, will be made by us against presentation of railroad bills of lading covering such material.

It is understood that with respect to the material covered hereby, you make no guarantee or warranty as to its present condition, usefulness for the purpose for which manufactured or contemplated by us. It is further understood that you may invoice the items in Exhibit A in the form in which they are enumerated and described by the United States Government to you, without inspection or verification by you.

We agree to save you harmless from any loss or damage to you or other parties occasioned by the use of handling of the material listed in Exhibit A after title has passed to you.

It is expressly understood that you have no obligation to do anything which will violate the terms of the Neutrality Act of 1939, or the Johnson Act.

Please confirm that the foregoing sets forth your understanding by signing and returning six copies of this letter.

Yours sincerely,

BRITISH PURCHASING COMMISSION

(Sgd.)   Arthur B. Purvis,
Director General.

FRENCH PURCHASING MISSION

(Sgd.)   J. F. Bloch-Lainé,
Director General.

ACCEPTED:
UNITED STATES STEEL EXPORT COMPANY
By (Sgd.) Geo. W. Wolf, President.

EXHIBIT "A"

LIST A

Item	Appraised value
13,000,000 Cal., 30 Ball	$3,900,000.00
17,000,000 lbs. TNT	2,550,000.00
6,693,000 lbs. smokeless powder 155G	3,651,060.00
1,000,000 lbs. smokeless powder 155H	420,000.00
97,680 Shell, 3§ Stokes (used)	125,030.40
1,000,000 rds. 75 m/m (C.H.) w/uk III fuzes	10,450,000.00
75,000 rounds 75 mm Shell, H.E., Normal charge, complete with uk III fuzes, at $10.45	783,750.00
Total Appraised value	$21,879,840.40

LIST B

Item	Appraised value
500,000 Rifle, cal. .30, M1917 (used)	3,750,000.00
1,157 Lewis M.G.	39,245.44
7,071 Vickers, M.O.	927,927.33
2,602 Marlin M.G. (tank)	193,458.70
15,638 Marlin, M.G. (aircraft)	362,176.08
5,124 Vickers M.G. (aircraft)	173,806.08
38,040 Lewis M.O. (aircraft)	1,290,316.80
308 Mortar 3§ Stokes	3,850.00
20,000 Revolvers, cal. .45	145,000.00
395 Guns, 75 mm M1917 w/Limber & Sights	603,402.00
500 Gun 75 mm. M1897	2,243,750.00
1,950 Caisson for 75 m/m	168,750.00
1,350 Limber for 75 m/m	101,250.00
10,000 Guns. B. M.G. M1917	2,154,900.00
10,000 Tripods M1918	260,000.00
100,000 Ammunition Belts	181,000.00
100,000 Ammunition Chests	360,000.00
10,000 Water Chests	129.000.00
10.000 Steam Condensing Device	19.600.00
3.333 Belt Filling Machines	163.283.77
25.000 Rifle. B.A. M1916	1.519.000.00
1.000.000 20-round magazines	950.000.00
Total	$15.739.716.20
Add List A	21.879.840.40
Total Contract Value	$37.619.556.60

June 18, 1940.

United States Steel Export Company,
30 Church Street,
New York, N.Y.

Dear Sirs:

We reaffirm the contents of the letter to you dated June 11, 1940 signed by the French Purchasing Mission and the British Purchasing Commission.

We agree to purchase from you such other or additional material to that listed in Exhibit A attached to our letter dated June 11, 1940 to you, as you may purchase from the United States Government.

We likewise agree that such changes or deletions in said Exhibit A as you determine are necessary may be made.

We agree that we will pay you, as demanded, such additional amounts in excess of $37,619,556.60, as may be occasioned by said changes or deletions, with the express understanding that the total sum, exclusive of your out-of-pocket expenses and disbursements in connection with this transaction, including the cost of packing, handling and freight charges, shall not exceed $50,000,000.00.

Very truly yours,

HIS MAJESTY'S GOVERNMENT IN THE
UNITED KINGDOM
By BRITISH PURCHASING COMMISSION
By *(Sgd.) Edgar S. Bloom,*
Director of Purchases.
By *(Sgd.) F. Johnson,*
Director of Administration for and on
behalf of the Director General.

ACCEPTED:
UNITED STATES STEEL EXPORT COMPANY
By *(Sgd.) Geo. W. Wolf,* President.

APPENDIX II

Assignment of the French Contracts in the United States

June 1940

The following documents illustrate the transaction as described in Chapter V. The first two documents are the Assignments and Agreements, dated 16th June, by which the Director General of the French Purchasing Commission, representing the French State, transferred to the British Government, as represented by the Director of the British Purchasing Commission, the French aircraft and other war supply contracts in the United States. The list of the aircraft contracts referred to in the first document as 'Exhibit A' is not reproduced here. There was no list of the contracts other than aircraft involved in the agreements. It was not until the end of September 1940 after an exhaustive enquiry by an American accounting firm engaged by the British Purchasing Commission, that a clear summary of the financial consequences of the transaction as a whole became available to the British Government. The parallel letters exchanged at Bordeaux on 17th June 1940 between General Weygand and the British Ambassador to France are also reproduced. See discussion of the 'Weygand Agreement' in Chapter V, Section (iv).

ASSIGNMENT AND AGREEMENT dated June 16, 1940, by and between THE FRENCH STATE, represented by *the Directeur Général des Achats* with offices in New York City (hereinafter called the ASSIGNOR) and His Majesty's Government in the United Kingdom represented by the BRITISH PURCHASING COMMISSION, acting through the DIRECTOR-GENERAL, WITNESSETH: The Assignor has heretofore entered into certain agreements for the purchase in the United States of America of aeroplanes and equipment, including engines and arms, a list thereof being attached hereto and made a part hereof marked Exhibit A.[1] The Assignor and the Assignee have collaborated with respect to purchases of material in the United States of America and now desire to transfer to and vest in the Assignee all of the right, title and interest of the Assignor in, to and under each and all of the above agreements and all things purchased and to be purchased thereunder.

In consideration of the foregoing and for the sum of One Dollar ($1) to the Assignor by the Assignee paid and for other good consideration the parties hereto hereby take the following action and make the following agreements: FIRST: The Assignor hereby transfers, assigns and sets over unto the Assignee, all the right, title and interest of the Assignor in, to and under each and every of said agreements heretofore entered into by the Assignor and listed in said Exhibit A and all right, title and interest in and to all material already delivered or to be delivered thereunder.

The Assignor agrees with the Assignee and with each of the contracting parties under each of said agreements that from the time and date hereof,

---

[1] Exhibit A: not printed.

the Assignee shall have the sole and exclusive benefit and ownership of, and control and power of disposition over, each and all said agreements and all matters arising thereunder, and all material delivered or to be delivered thereunder.

The delivery of a copy of this Assignment and Agreement to any of the said contracting parties will constitute irrevocable instructions and authority to said contracting parties to recognise the right and power of the Assignee, to the complete exclusion of the Assignor, as from this time and date, in all matters pertaining to said agreements and material.

The Assignor directs each of said contracting parties to credit all payments heretofore made by the Assignor under said agreements to the account of the Assignee and to accept the instructions of the Assignee with respect to any such credits as well as in respect to all other matters pertaining to said agreements and material.

SECOND: The Assignee hereby accepts the foregoing assignment from the time and date hereof and hereby agrees to assume and carry out all of the obligations of the Assignor heretofore assumed by the Assignor under and pursuant to said agreements. Each agreement covered hereby is assigned and transferred severally and the effect of the assignment or transfer of any one agreement shall not affect the assignment or transfer of any other agreement.

THIRD: The Assignee shall have complete authority in its own name and without any further act on the part of the Assignor to take all action under all said agreements deemed advisable by the Assignee either in carrying out or amending or terminating said agreements or any of them, as the Assignee may determine, such authority to vest in the Assignee with respect to all agreements originally entered into by the Assignor alone or the Assignor and the Assignee together.

In witness whereof the parties hereto have executed this instrument as of date herein above mentioned.

Witness   THE FRENCH STATE
GEO. S. MONTGOMERY, JR.   By J. F. BLOCH-LAINÉ,
                             Directeur Général des Achats.
Witness   HIS MAJESTY'S GOVERNMENT
                          IN THE UNITED KINGDOM
                          ·By British Purchasing Commission,
T. W. CHILDS.   By ARTHUR B. PURVIS,
                          Director General.

ASSIGNMENT AND AGREEMENT dated June 16, 1940, by and between THE FRENCH STATE, represented by *the Directeur Général des Achats* with offices in New York City (hereinafter called the ASSIGNOR) and His Majesty's Government in the United Kingdom, represented by the BRITISH PURCHASING COMMISSION, acting through the DIRECTOR GENERAL, WITNESSETH: The Assignor has heretofore entered into certain agreements for the purchase in the United States of America of airplanes and equipment and arms, munitions, explosives and other implements of war and materials and articles pertaining thereto or to their manufacture. The Assignor and the Assignee have collaborated with respect to purchase of material in the United States of America and now desire to transfer to and vest in the Assignee all of the right, title and interest of the Assignor in, to and under each and all of the above agreements, and all things purchased and to be purchased thereunder.

In consideration of the foregoing and for the sum of One Dollar to the Assignor by the Assignee paid and for other good consideration the parties hereto hereby take the following action and make the following agreements: FIRST: The Assignor hereby transfers, assigns and sets over unto the Assignee, all the right, title and interest of the Assignor in, to and under each and every agreement heretofore entered into by the Assignor in the United States of America for the purchase of airplanes and equipment and arms, munitions, explosives and other implements of war and materials and articles pertaining thereto or to their manufacture, and all right, title and interest of the Assignor in and to all material already delivered or to be delivered thereunder.

The delivery of a copy of this Assignment and Agreement to any of the said contracting parties will constitute irrevocable instructions and authority to said contracting parties to recognize the right and power of the Assignee, to the complete exclusion of the Assignor, as from this time and date, in all matters pertaining to said agreements and material.

The Assignor directs each of said contracting parties to credit all payments heretofore made by the Assignor under said agreements to the account of the Assignee and to accept the instructions of the Assignee with respect to any such credits as well as in respect to all other matters pertaining to said agreements and material. SECOND: The Assignee hereby accepts the foregoing assignment from the time and date thereof and hereby agrees to assume and carry out all of the obligations of the Assignor heretofore assumed by the Assignor under and pursuant to said agreement. Each agreement covered hereby is assigned and transferred severally, and the effect of the assignment or transfer of any one agreement shall not affect the assignment or transfer of any other agreement. THIRD: The Assignee shall have complete authority in its own name and without any further act on the part of the Assignor to take all action under all said agreements deemed advisable by the Assignee either in carrying out or amending, or terminating said agreements or any of them, as the Assignee may determine, such authority to vest in the Assignee with respect to all agreements whether originally entered into by the Assignor alone or the Assignor and the Assignee together.

In witness whereof the parties hereto have executed this instrument as of the date herein above first mentioned.

Witness   THE FRENCH STATE
(Sgd.)   GEO. S. MONTGOMERY, JR.   By (Sgd.) J. F. BLOCH-LAINÉ,
                                       Directeur Général des Achats.
                                     HIS MAJESTY'S GOVERNMENT IN
                                       THE UNITED KINGDOM
Witness   By British Purchasing Commission,
(Sgd.)   T. W. CHILDS.   By (Sgd.) ARTHUR B. PURVIS,
                                       Director General.

June 16, 1940.
THE FRENCH STATE

Dear Sirs:

You and we are entering into two agreements today, under which you assigned to us agreements made by you in the United States for the purchase of materials. In consideration of your allowing to us the benefit of all payments heretofore or hereafter made by you under said purchase agreements, we agree to pay to or credit you from time to time as follows:

(1) With respect to payments which you may make on or after June 17th, 1940, under any of said purchase agreements, we agree to pay you in New York in lawful money of the United States of America the amount of all such payments (other than payments made with respect to material of which you take and retain delivery) promptly after we shall have been substituted in your place under the purchase agreement under which you shall have made such payments.

(2) With respect to payments which you have heretofore made under any such purchase agreements, we shall pay the amount thereof to you by paying to you a proportionate amount of each such payment as and when the materials with respect to which such payment was made shall have been delivered to and received by us, such payment to be made to the Bank of Canada for your account in lawful money of the United States of America.

In the event that after we shall have been substituted in your place under any such purchase agreement under which you have heretofore made any payment, such purchase agreement shall be terminated for any reason prior to the completion of deliveries thereunder, all losses incurred by the purchaser thereunder on account of such termination shall be borne equally by you and by us, and the deposit to your credit in the Bank of Canada referred to in paragraph (2) above shall be increased or decreased by the difference between that part of the payment heretofore made by you under such contract not previously paid to you and one-half of the losses incurred on account of the termination thereof.

Please confirm that the foregoing sets forth your understanding by signing and returning the copy of this letter enclosed herewith.

Very truly yours,
HIS MAJESTY'S GOVERNMENT IN THE
UNITED KINGDOM
By British Purchasing Commission,
By (Sgd.) ARTHUR B. PURVIS,
Director General.

Accepted: June 16, 1940.
THE FRENCH STATE
By (Sgd.) J. F. BLOCH-LAINÉ,
    Directeur Général des Achats.

BRITISH PURCHASING COMMISSION
New York
June 16, 1940.

THE FRENCH STATE

Dear Sirs:

You and we are entering into two agreements today, under which you assigned to us agreements made by you in the United States for the purchase of materials. This letter is to express our mutual understanding of the existence, in the agreements so assigned, of a preferential right in favor of the "French Territories" as hereinafter defined, upon the following terms:

1. "French Territories" as used in this letter shall mean the government of any part of the present French Empire, including all possessions, colonies, mandates, protectorates and other lands now directly or indirectly subject to the control of the Republic of France.

2. If at any time during the effective period of any of the contracts which you have today assigned to us, any of the materials covered thereby shall be required by any of the French Territories in connection with the organization or maintenance of their national defense for the purpose of the prosecution of the present hostilities, we agree forthwith to give such French Territory a preferential right to receive any of such materials not theretofore delivered to us and shipped by us from the United States of America, and to use our best efforts to accomplish the delivery of such material to such French Territory.

3. In any such event it is understood and agreed that such French Territory or yourselves shall pay to us any amounts theretofore paid by us on account of the purchase price of the materials so required by such French Territory, and shall pay to the supplier any balance due with respect to the purchase price thereof. You hereby guarantee the performance by any such French Territory of any obligation imposed upon it pursuant to this letter.

Please confirm that the foregoing sets forth our mutual understanding by signing the copy of this letter enclosed herewith.

Very truly yours,
HIS MAJESTY'S GOVERNMENT IN THE
UNITED KINGDOM
By British Purchasing Commission,
By (Sgd.) ARTHUR B. PURVIS,
Director General.

Accepted: June 16, 1940.
THE FRENCH STATE
By (Sgd.) J. F. BLOCH-LAINÉ,
Directeur Général des Achats.

SUMMARY OF FRENCH CONTRACTS ASSIGNED TO
B.P.C. AT JUNE 16, 1940†

CONTRACT *Classification*	Outstanding Commitment at June 16, 1940		
	To Contractors	*To French* (*for advances*)	*Total*
	$	$	$
Airframes	138,746,853	44,181,136	182,927,989
Engines	97,207,661	65,450,395	162,658,056
Propellers	8,876,427	7,432,354	16,308,781
Miscellaneous	28,650,093	12,464,480	41,114,573
French advances on contracts exe- cuted by B.P.C. . . .	—	22,326,800	22,326,800
Total for Air Contracts . . .	$273,481,034	$151,855,165	$425,336,199
Machine Tools (see also * below) .	50,397,453	36,396,849	86,794,302
Armament	3,550,366	1,478,935	5,030,301
Automotive Equipment, etc. . .	18,591,634	7,758,677	26,350,311
Benzol and chemical . . .	1,787,288	100,000	1,887,288
Toluol	692,075	—	692,075
Brass and Zinc	8,709,590	597,540	9,307,130
Cotton Linters	264,018	—	264,018
Gasoline	18,026,469	—	18,026,469
Steel (Note 1)	—	325,231	325,231
U.S. Steel Export Corp. (Note 2) .	—	16,000,000	16,000,000
Atlas Powder Co. (Note 3) . .	—	951,333	951,333
Tennessee Powder Co. . . .	—	8,600,000	8,600,000
Contracts cancelled or in process of can- cellation as at Sept. 30, 1940			
*Machine tools	1,429,409	82,067	1,511,476
Miscellaneous	8,603,539	2,611,575	11,215,114
Total for all contracts . .	$385,532,875	$226,753,372	$612,291,247

Note 1. Except for relatively unimportant quantities of steel manufactured or in process of manufacture at June 16, 1940, all commitments for steel which had been entered into by the French Purchasing Commission were taken over by the British Iron & Steel Corporation Ltd.

Note 2. Prior to June 16, 1940 the Anglo-French Purchasing Board had entered into a contract with U.S. Steel Export Corporation for the purchase of surplus arms. No deliveries had been made prior to June 16, 1940 and the contract was taken over in its entirety by the B.P.C. as at that date. Advances of $16 million made by the French were refunded by the B.P.C.

Note 3. The amount of $951,333 advanced by the French to Atlas Powder Co. represented a two-third interest, by assignment from the B.P.C., in an agreement for capital assistance in the construction of a powder plant. Under the terms of the general assignment all interest in the contract reverted to the B.P.C.

† *Author's Note.*—This summary (based on the records of the French Purchasing Commission and enquiries made with all the suppliers) was presented to the British Purchasing Commission at the end of September 1940 by the accounting firm of Price, Waterhouse and Company.

TRÈS SECRET

Bordeaux, le 17 Juin 1940.
L'Ambassadeur de Sa Majesté Britannique
à
Monsieur le Général Commandant en Chef
Ministre de la Défense Nationale.

Monsieur le Ministre,

Vous avez bien voulu me faire parvenir une lettre datée le 17 Juin conçue dans les termes ci-après:

"Comme suite à la demande que vous m'avez adressée, j'ai l'honneur de vous confirmer par la présente lettre que le Gouvernement français transferera à dater de ce jour au Gouvernement britannique le bénéfice et les charges de tous les contrats de fournitures, de quelque nature qu'ils soient, actuellement en cours à son profit direct ou indirect aux Etats-Unis d'Amérique.

J'ai l'honneur de vous prier de m'indiquer votre accord en vous engageant, au nom du Gouvernement britannique, à faire face, aux lieu et place de L'Etat français, aux charges de toutes natures pouvant résulter de ces contrats."

J'ai l'honneur de vous donner l'accord du Gouvernement britannique sur l'opération de transfert ainsi définie.

Veuillez agréer, Monsieur le Ministre, les assurances de ma haute considération.

TRÈS SECRET

Bordeaux, le 17 Juin 1940.
L'Ambassadeur de sa Majesté Britannique
à
Monsieur le Général Commandant en Chef,
Ministre de la Défense Nationale.

Monsieur le Ministre,

Par échange de lettres en date de ce jour, le Gouvernement français a transféré au Gouvernement britannique le bénéfice et les charges de tous les contrats actuellement en cours à son profit aux Etats-Unis d'Amérique.

J'ai l'honneur de vous confirmer par la présente que le Gouvernement britannique se reconnait redevable vis-à-vis du Gouvernement français des sommes que celui-ci a engagées jusqu'à la date du 17 Juin 1940 pour l'exécution des contrats dont la suite sera reprise par le Gouvernement britannique.

Veuillez agréer, Monsieur le Ministre, les assurances de ma haute considération.

APPENDIX III

The Lend Lease Act

[PUBLIC LAW 11—77TH CONGRESS]
[CHAPTER 11—1ST SESSION]
[H.R. 1776]

AN ACT

Further to promote the defense of the United States, and for other purposes.

Be it enacted by the Senate and House of Representatives of the United States of America in Congress assembled, That this Act may be cited as "An Act to Promote the Defense of the United States".

SEC. 2. As used in this Act—

(a) The term "defense article" means—

(1) Any weapon, munition, aircraft, vessel, or boat;

(2) Any machinery, facility, tool, material, or supply necessary for the manufacture, production, processing, repair, servicing, or operation of any article described in this subsection;

(3) Any component material or part of or equipment for any article described in this subsection;

(4) Any agricultural, industrial or other commodity or article for defense.

Such term "defense article" includes any article described in this subsection: Manufactured or procured pursuant to section 3, or to which the United States or any foreign government has or hereafter acquires title, possession, or control.

(b) The term "defense information" means any plan, specification, design, prototype, or information pertaining to any defense article.

SEC. 3. (a) Notwithstanding the provisions of any other law, the President may, from time to time, when he deems it in the interest of national defense, authorize the Secretary of War, the Secretary of the Navy, or the head of any other department or agency of the Government—

(1) To manufacture in arsenals, factories, and shipyards under their jurisdiction, or otherwise procure, to the extent to which funds are made available therefor, or contracts are authorized from time to time by the Congress, or both, any defense article for the government of any country whose defense the President deems vital to the defense of the United States.

(2) To sell, transfer title to, exchange, lease, lend, or otherwise dispose of, to any such government any defense article, but no defense article not manufactured or procured under paragraph (1) shall in any way be disposed of under this paragraph, except after consultation with the Chief of Staff of the Army or the Chief of Naval Operations of the Navy, or both. The value of defense articles disposed of in any way under authority of this paragraph, and procured from funds heretofore appropriated, shall not exceed $1,300,000,000. The

value of such defense articles shall be determined by the head of the department or agency concerned or such other department, agency or officer as shall be designated in the manner provided in the rules and regulations issued hereunder. Defense articles procured from funds hereafter appropriated to any department or agency of the Government, other than from funds authorized to be appropriated under this Act, shall not be disposed of in any way under authority of this paragraph except to the extent hereafter authorized by the Congress in the Acts appropriating such funds or otherwise.

(3) To test, inspect, prove, repair, outfit, recondition, or otherwise to place in good working order, to the extent to which funds are made available therefor, or contracts are authorized from time to time by the Congress, or both, any defense article for any such government, or to procure any or all such services by private contract.

(4) To communicate to any such government any defense information, pertaining to any defense article furnished to such government under paragraph (2) of this subsection.

(5) To release for export any defense article disposed of in any way under this subsection to any such government.

(b) The terms and conditions upon which any such foreign government receives any aid authorized under subsection (a) shall be those which the President deems satisfactory, and the benefit to the United States may be payment or repayment in kind or property, or any other direct or indirect benefit which the President deems satisfactory.

(c) After June 30, 1943, or after the passage of a concurrent resolution by the two Houses before June 30, 1943, which declares that the powers conferred by or pursuant to subsection (a) are no longer necessary to promote the defense of the United States, neither the President nor the head of any department or agency shall exercise any of the powers conferred by or pursuant to subsection (a); except that until July 1, 1946, any of such powers may be exercised to the extent necessary to carry out a contract or agreement with such a foreign government made before July 1, 1943, or before the passage of such concurrent resolution, whichever is the earlier.

(d) Nothing in this Act shall be construed to authorize or to permit the authorization of convoying vessels by naval vessels of the United States.

(e) Nothing in this Act shall be construed to authorize or to permit the authorization of the entry of any American vessel into a combat area in violation of section 9 of the Neutrality Act of 1939.

SEC. 4. All contracts or agreements made for the disposition of any defense article or defense information pursuant to section 3 shall contain a clause by which the foreign government undertakes that it will not, without the consent of the President, transfer title to or possession of such defense article or defense information by gift, sale, or otherwise, or permit its use by anyone not an officer, employee, or agent of such foreign government.

SEC. 5. (a) The Secretary of War, the Secretary of the Navy, or the head of any other department or agency of the Government involved shall, when any such defense article or defense information is exported, immediately inform the department or agency designated by the President to administer section 6 of the Act of July 2, 1940 (54 Stat. 714), of the quantities, character, value, terms of disposition, and destination of the article and information so exported.

(b) The President from time to time, but not less frequently than once every ninety days, shall transmit to the Congress a report of operations under this Act except such information as he deems incompatible with the public interest to disclose. Reports provided for under this subsection shall be transmitted to the Secretary of the Senate or the Clerk of the House of Representatives, as the case may be, if the Senate or the House of Representatives, as the case may be, is not in session.

SEC. 6. (a) There is hereby authorized to be appropriated from time to time, out of any money in the Treasury not otherwise appropriated, such amounts as may be necessary to carry out the provisions and accomplish the purposes of this Act.

(b) All money and all property which is converted into money received under section 3 from any government shall, with the approval of the Director of the Budget, revert to the respective appropriation or appropriations out of which funds were expended with respect to the defense article or defense information for which such consideration is received, and shall be available for expenditure for the purpose for which such expended funds were appropriated by law, during the fiscal year in which such funds are received and the ensuing fiscal year; but in no event shall any funds so received be available for expenditure after June 30, 1946.

SEC. 7. The Secretary of War, the Secretary of the Navy, and the head of the department or agency shall in all contracts or agreements for the disposition of any defense article or defense information fully protect the rights of all citizens of the United States who have patent rights in and to any such article or information which is hereby authorized to be disposed of and the payments collected for royalties on such patents shall be paid to the owners and holders of such patents.

SEC. 8. The Secretaries of War and of the Navy are hereby authorized to purchase or otherwise acquire arms, ammunition, and implements of war produced within the jurisdiction of any country to which section 3 is applicable, whenever the President deems such purchase or acquisition to be necessary in the interests of the defense of the United States.

SEC. 9. The President may, from time to time, promulgate such rules and regulations as may be necessary and proper to carry out any of the provisions of this Act; and he may exercise any power or authority conferred on him by this Act through such department, agency, or officer as he shall direct.

SEC. 10. Nothing in this Act shall be construed to change existing law relating to the use of the land and naval forces of the United States, except insofar as such use relates to the manufacture, procurement, and repair of defense articles, the communication of information and other noncombatant purposes enumerated in this Act.

SEC. 11. If any provision of this Act or the application of such provision to any circumstance shall be held invalid, the validity of the remainder of the Act and the applicability of such provision to other circumstances shall not be affected thereby.

Approved, March 11, 1941.

APPENDIX IV

The Setting up of the Combined Boards:

Agreements between the Prime Minister and the President of the United States of America, January 1942

The agreements on the setting up of the first three Combined Boards were concluded during the Arcadia Conference between the Prime Minister and the President in January 1942. The texts were agreed at their final meeting on 14th January. A few changes, largely of a drafting character, were made by an exchange of cables after the return of the Prime Minister to London. The text as given below is that presented by the Prime Minister to Parliament and published in Cmd. 6332, January 1942. It was published on 26th January 1942 simultaneously in London and Washington. The Washington version appeared in a State Department press release and in the Bulletin of the State Department of 31st January 1942. Due no doubt to the difficulty of drafting amendments by cable there are certain discrepancies between the American and British texts. (Thus the American text mentions C.R.M.B. as the first of the Combined Boards whilst the British text puts it last. The latter also omits a sentence —which was in the draft of 14th January—regarding the power of C.R.M.B. to appoint its staff. There are also minor differences of wording in the preamble.)

CO-ORDINATION OF THE ALLIED WAR EFFORT

To further co-ordination of the Allied War Effort the President and the Prime Minister have set up bodies to deal with Munitions Assignments, Shipping Adjustment and Raw Materials. The functions of these bodies are outlined in the following documents. These bodies will confer with representatives of the U.S.S.R., China and such others of the United Nations as are necessary to attain common purposes and provide for the most effective utilization of the joint resources of the United Nations.

(i) *Munitions Assignments Board*

1. The entire munition resources of Great Britain and the United States will be deemed to be in a common pool, about which the fullest information will be interchanged.

2. Committees will be formed in Washington and London under the combined Chiefs of Staff in a manner similar to the South West Pacific agreement. These Committees will advise on all Assignments, both in quantity and priority, whether to Great Britain and the United States or other of the United Nations, in accordance with strategic needs.

3. In order that these Committees may be fully apprised of the policy

508

of their respective Governments, the President will nominate a civil Chairman, who will preside over the Committee in Washington, and the Prime Minister of Great Britain will make a similar nomination in respect of the Committee in London. In each case the Committee will be assisted by a Secretariat capable of surveying every Branch and keeping in touch with the work of every Sub-Committee as may be necessary.

4. The civilian Chairmen in Washington and London may invite representatives of the State Department, the Foreign Office or production ministries or agencies to attend meetings.

(ii) *Combined Shipping Adjustment Board*

1. In principle, the shipping resources of the two countries will be deemed to be pooled. The fullest information will be interchanged.

2. Owing to the military and physical facts of the situation around the British Isles, the entire movement of shipping now under the control of Great Britain will continue to be directed by the Ministry of War Transport.

3. Similarly, the appropriate authority in the United States will continue to direct the movements and allocations of United States shipping, or shipping of other Powers under United States control.

4. In order to adjust and concert in one harmonious policy the work of the British Ministry of War Transport and the Shipping authorities of the United States Government, there will be established forthwith in Washington a Combined Shipping Adjustment Board consisting of a representative of the United States and a representative of the British Government who will represent and act under the instructions of the British Minister of War Transport.

5. A similar Adjustment Board will be set up in London consisting of the Minister of War Transport and a representative of the United States Government.

6. In both cases the executive power will be exercised solely by the appropriate shipping agency in Washington and by the Minister of War Transport in London.

(iii) *Combined Raw Materials Board*

A planned and expeditious utilisation of the raw material resources of the United Nations is necessary in the prosecution of the war. To obtain such a utilisation of our raw material resources in the most efficient and speediest possible manner, we hereby create the "Combined Raw Materials Board".

This Board will:—

(*a*) Be composed of a representative of the British Government and a representative of the United States Government. The British member will represent and act under the instruction of the Minister of Supply.

(*b*) Plan the best and speediest development, expansion and use of the raw material resources under the jurisdiction or control of the two Governments, and make the recommendations necessary to execute such plans. Such recommendations shall be carried out by all parts of the respective Governments.

(*c*) In collaboration with others of the United Nations work toward the best utilisation of their raw material resources, and, in collaboration with the interested nation or nations, formulate plans and recommendations for the development, expansion, purchase, or other effective use of their raw materials.

January, 1942.

APPENDIX V

The Master Lend-Lease Agreement

The following text—Treaty Series No. 7 (1942), Cmd. 6391—reproduces the agreement between the United Kingdom and the United States on the 'Principles applying to Mutual Aid' of 23rd February 1942, commonly known in the United States as the Master Lend-Lease Agreement. Similar agreements were made by the United States with other countries in receipt of lend-lease aid. See above, Chapter VII, Part II, sections (vii) and (viii), and Chapter VIII, section (i).

AGREEMENT BETWEEN THE GOVERNMENTS OF THE UNITED KINGDOM AND THE UNITED STATES OF AMERICA ON THE PRINCIPLES APPLYING TO MUTUAL AID IN THE PROSECUTION OF THE WAR AGAINST AGGRESSION.

[*Washington, February 23, 1942.*]

WHEREAS the Governments of the United Kingdom of Great Britain and Northern Ireland and the United States of America declare that they are engaged in a co-operative undertaking, together with every other nation or people of like mind, to the end of laying the bases of a just and enduring world peace securing order under law to themselves and all nations;

And whereas the President of the United States of America has determined, pursuant to the Act of Congress of the 11th March, 1941, that the defence of the United Kingdom against aggression is vital to the defence of the United States of America;

And whereas the United States of America has extended and is continuing to extend to the United Kingdom aid in resisting aggression;

And whereas it is expedient that the final determination of the terms and conditions upon which the Government of the United Kingdom receives such aid and of the benefits to be received by the United States of America in return therefor should be deferred until the extent of the defence aid is known and until the progress of events makes clearer the final terms and conditions and benefits which will be in the mutual interests of the United Kingdom and the United States of America, and will promote the establishment and maintenance of world peace;

And whereas the Governments of the United Kingdom and the United States of America are mutually desirous of concluding now a preliminary agreement in regard to the provision of defence aid and in regard to certain considerations which shall be taken into account in determining such terms and conditions, and the making of such an agreement has been in all respects duly authorised, and all acts, conditions and formalities which it may have been necessary to perform, fulfil or execute prior to the making of such an agreement in conformity with the laws either of the United Kingdom or of the United States of America have been performed, fulfilled or executed as required;

The undersigned, being duly authorised by their respective Governments for that purpose, have agreed as follows:—

ARTICLE 1

The Government of the United States of America will continue to supply the Government of the United Kingdom with such defence articles, defence services, and defence information as the President shall authorise to be transferred or provided.

ARTICLE 2

The Government of the United Kingdom will continue to contribute to the defence of the United States of America and the strengthening thereof, and will provide such articles, services, facilities or information as it may be in a position to supply.

ARTICLE 3

The Government of the United Kingdom will not, without the consent of the President of the United States of America, transfer title to, or possession of, any defence article or defence information transferred to it under the Act, or permit the use thereof by anyone not an officer, employee or agent of the Government of the United Kingdom.

ARTICLE 4

If, as a result of the transfer to the Government of the United Kingdom of any defence article or defence information, it becomes necessary for that Government to take any action or make any payment in order fully to protect any of the rights of a citizen of the United States of America who has patent rights in and to any such defence article or information, the Government of the United Kingdom will take such action or make such payment when requested to do so by the President of the United States of America.

ARTICLE 5

The Government of the United Kingdom will return to the United States of America at the end of the present emergency, as determined by the President, such defence articles transferred under this Agreement as shall not have been destroyed, lost or consumed, and as shall be determined by the President to be useful in the defence of the United States of America or of the Western Hemisphere or to be otherwise of use to the United States of America.

ARTICLE 6

In the final determination of the benefits to be provided to the United States of America by the Government of the United Kingdom, full cognisance shall be taken of all property, services, information, facilities or other benefits or considerations provided by the Government of the United Kingdom subsequent to the 11th March, 1941, and accepted or acknowledged by the President on behalf of the United States of America.

ARTICLE 7

In the final determination of the benefits to be provided to the United States of America by the Government of the United Kingdom in return for aid furnished under the Act of Congress of the 11th March, 1941, the terms and conditions thereof shall be such as not to burden commerce between the two countries, but to promote mutually advantageous economic relations between them and the betterment of world-wide economic relations. To that end, they shall include provision for agreed action by the United States of America and the United Kingdom open to participation by all other countries of like mind, directed to the expansion, by appropriate international and domestic measures, of production, employment, and the exchange and consumption of goods which are the material foundations of the liberty and welfare of all peoples; to the elimination of all forms of discriminatory treatment in international commerce, and to the reduction of tariffs and other trade barriers; and, in general, to the attainment of all the economic objectives set forth in the Joint Declaration[1] made on the 14th August, 1941, by the President of the United States of America and the Prime Minister of the United Kingdom.

At an early convenient date conversations shall be begun between the two Governments with a view to determining, in the light of governing economic conditions, the best means of attaining the above-stated objectives by their own agreed action and of seeking the agreed action of other like-minded Governments.

ARTICLE 8

This Agreement shall take effect as from this day's date. It shall continue in force until a date to be agreed upon by the two Governments.

Signed and sealed at Washington in duplicate this 23rd day of February, 1942.

> For the Government of the United Kingdom of Great Britain and Northern Ireland:
>
> (L.S.) HALIFAX.
> *His Majesty's Ambassador Extraordinary and Plenipotentiary at Washington.*
>
> For the Government of the United States of America:
>
> (L.S.) SUMNER WELLES.
> *Acting Secretary of State of the United States of America.*

---

[1] Cmd. 6388.

2K

APPENDIX VI

The Canadian Mutual Aid Acts (1943–44)

and the Mutual Aid Agreement between the Governments of Canada and the United Kingdom, 1944

The following texts are reproduced from the Second Annual Report of the Canadian Mutual Aid Board, published in Ottawa in 1945. See discussion above in Chapter VII, Part I, Canada.

AN ACT FOR GRANTING TO HIS MAJESTY AID FOR THE PURPOSE OF MAKING AVAILABLE CANADIAN WAR SUPPLIES TO THE UNITED NATIONS.

(Assented to 20th May, 1943.)

Preamble

Whereas Canada, in association with other nations, is at war with Germany, Italy, Japan and their associates; and whereas it is essential to the defence and security of Canada and to the cause of world freedom that Canada should make the utmost contribution to the victory of the United Nations; and whereas it is necessary that the products of Canadian war industry be made available not only for use by Canadian forces, but also to other United Nations, in accordance with strategic needs, in such manner as to contribute most effectively to the winning of the war; and whereas it is expedient that the conditions upon which Canadian war supplies are made available to other United Nations should not be such as to burden post-war commerce or lead to the imposition of trade restrictions or otherwise prejudice a just and enduring peace: Therefore His Majesty, by and with the advice and consent of the Senate and House of Commons of Canada, enacts as follows:

Short Title

1. This Act may be cited as *The War Appropriation (United Nations Mutual Aid) Act, 1943.*

Definitions

2. In this Act and in any regulation made thereunder, unless the context otherwise requires:

"Board"

   (a) "Board" means the Canadian Mutual Aid Board constituted by section three of this Act;

"Regulation"

   (b) "regulation" means a regulation made under the authority of section six of this Act;

"United Nations"

   (c) "United Nations" means the signatories to the Declaration by United Nations, done at Washington on the first day of January, one thousand nine hundred and forty-two, and includes any other nation or authority which may be designated by the Governor in Council as being associated with Canada in the prosecution of the present war;

"*War Supplies*"

(d) "war supplies" means

   (i) any weapon, munition, aircraft or ship;

   (ii) any machinery, facility, tool, material or supply necessary for the manufacture, production and processing, repair, servicing or operation of any article described in this paragraph;

   (iii) any component material or part of or equipment for any article described in this paragraph;

   (iv) any agricultural product; and

   (v) such other commodities, articles or services as may from time to time be designated by the Governor in Council as essential to the conduct of the war or to the relief and maintenance of any United Nation.

Canadian Mutual Aid Board

3. (1) There shall be a Board to be called the Canadian Mutual Aid Board consisting of the Minister of Munitions and Supply, the Minister of National Defence, the Minister of Finance, the Minister of Agriculture and the Minister of Justice, acting as a committee of the King's Privy Council for Canada, which shall be charged with the administration of this Act.

Chairman

(2) The Minister of Munitions and Supply shall be the chairman of the Board.

Officers, Clerks and Employees

(3) The Board, with the approval of the Governor in Council, may appoint and fix the remuneration of such officers, clerks and other employees as are necessary for the proper conduct of its business and for that purpose may require the services of any department or agency, or of any officer or employee of any department or agency, of the Government of Canada.

Board May Make War Supplies Available to the United Nations

4. (1) The Board may, on behalf of His Majesty, in accordance with the strategic needs of the war, contribute, exchange, deliver, transfer title to or possession of or otherwise make available war supplies to any of the United Nations other than Canada and for that purpose or as incidental thereto may cause to be purchased or otherwise acquired or procured war supplies in Canada through the agency of the Minister of Munitions and Supply or any other agency of His Majesty and, subject to the provisions of section five of this Act, may provide or make available the funds required to pay expenditures incurred in carrying out the purposes described herein.

Consideration
Terms and Conditions to be Approved by the Governor in Council

(2) It shall be good and sufficient consideration for making war supplies

available to any of the United Nations hereunder that the said war supplies are to be used in the joint and effective prosecution of the war, but no war supplies shall be so made available to any of the United Nations except upon terms and conditions approved by the Governor in Council or by regulations, and the Governor in Council may require, in respect of specific classes of supplies or any specific transfer of supplies under subsection one of this section, such payment or repayment in kind or property or such reciprocal action or provision of supplies or such other direct or indirect benefit as the Governor in Council deems appropriate.

$1,000,000,000 May be Paid Out of the C.R.F.

5. There may be paid out of the Consolidated Revenue Fund, for the purposes of this Act, a sum or sums not exceeding one thousand million dollars ($1,000,000,000) exclusive of any sums paid for war supplies for which payment shall be made in cash by any of the United Nations to which such supplies shall be made available hereunder.

Regulations

6. The Governor in Council may, on the recommendation of the Board, make regulations for the purpose of carrying out the objects of this Act, according to its true intent and purpose, and, in particular, but without limiting the generality of the foregoing, may make regulations:

(a) prescribing the terms and conditions under which war supplies may be made available to any of the United Nations;

(b) prescribing the procedure to be followed by the Board in carrying out its duties under this Act;

(c) prescribing rules to determine the value of war supplies.

Loan authorized; 1931, c. 27

7. (1) The Governor in Council may, in addition to the sums now remaining unborrowed and negotiable of the loans authorized by Parliament by any Act heretofore passed, raise by way of loan, under the provisions of *The Consolidated Revenue and Audit Act, 1931*, by the issue and sale or pledge of securities of Canada in such form, for such separate sums, at such rate of interest and upon such other terms and conditions as the Governor in Council may approve, such sum or sums of money, not exceeding in the aggregate the sum of one thousand million dollars ($1,000,000,000) as may be required for the purposes of this Act.

Charge upon Consolidated Revenue Fund

(2) The principal raised by way of loan under this Act and the interest thereon shall be a charge upon and payable out of the Consolidated Revenue Fund.

Annual Report to Parliament; Proviso

8. As soon as practicable after the close of each fiscal year, the Board shall prepare and lay before Parliament a report of operations under this Act: Provided that such report shall not contain any information the disclosure of which would, in the opinion of the Governor in Council, be prejudicial to the security of Canada or of any other United Nation.

AN ACT TO AMEND THE WAR APPROPRIATION (UNITED NATIONS MUTUAL AID) ACT, 1943, AND FOR GRANTING TO HIS MAJESTY AID FOR THE PURPOSES OF THE SAID ACT.

(Assented to 23rd June, 1944.)

His Majesty, by and with the advice and consent of the Senate and House of Commons of Canada, enacts as follows:—

1. This Act may be cited as *The War Appropriation (United Nations Mutual Aid) Act, 1944*.

2. Paragraph (*d*) of section two of *The War Appropriation (United Nations Mutual Aid) Act, 1943*, chapter seventeen of the statutes of 1943–44, is amended by deleting the word "and" at the end of subparagraph (iv) thereof, inserting the word "and" after subparagraph (v) and adding the following subparagraph thereto:—

"(vi) commodities, services and equipment required by the United Nations Relief and Rehabilitation Administration."

3. Subsection one of section three of the said Act is repealed and the following substituted therefor:—

"3. (1) There shall be a Board to be called the Canadian Mutual Aid Board consisting of the Minister of Munitions and Supply, the Minister of National Defence, the Minister of Finance, the Minister of Agriculture, the Minister of Justice, and the Minister of Trade and Commerce acting as a committee of the King's Privy Council for Canada, which shall be charged with the administration of this Act."

4. Section four of the said Act is repealed and the following substituted therefor:—

"4. (1) The Board may on behalf of His Majesty, in accordance with the strategic needs of the war or to facilitate the securing of a just and enduring peace, contribute, exchange, deliver, transfer title to or possession of or otherwise make available war supplies to any of the United Nations other than Canada or to the United Nations Relief and Rehabilitation Administration and for that purpose or as incidental thereto may cause to be purchased or otherwise acquired or procured war supplies in Canada through the agency of the Minister of Munitions and Supply or any other agency of His Majesty and, out of monies appropriated for the purpose, may provide or make available the funds required to pay expenditures incurred in carrying out the purposes described herein.

(2) It shall be good and sufficient consideration for making war supplies available under subsection one of this section that the said war supplies are to be used in the joint and effective prosecution of the war or the securing of a just and enduring peace, but no war supplies shall be so made available to any of the United Nations except upon terms and conditions approved by the Governor in Council or by regulations, and the Governor in Council may require, in respect of specific classes of supplies or any specific transfer of supplies under subsection one of this section, such payment or repayment in kind or property or such reciprocal action or provision of supplies or such other direct or indirect benefit as the Governor in Council deems appropriate."

5. In addition to any other sums appropriated therefor, there may be

paid out of the Consolidated Revenue Fund, for the purposes of *The War Appropriation (United Nations Mutual Aid) Act, 1943*, a sum or sums not exceeding eight hundred million dollars ($800,000,000) exclusive of any sums paid for war supplies for which payment shall be made in cash by the United Nations Relief and Rehabilitation Administration or any of the United Nations to which such supplies shall be made available under the said Act.

6. (1) The Governor in Council may, in addition to the sums now remaining unborrowed and negotiable of the loans authorized by Parliament by any Act heretofore passed, raise by way of loan, under the provisions of *The Consolidated Revenue and Audit Act, 1931*, by the issue and sale or pledge of securities of Canada in such form, for such separate sums, at such rate of interest and upon such other terms and conditions as the Governor in Council may approve, such sum or sums of money not exceeding in the aggregate the sum of eight hundred million dollars ($800,000,000) as may be required for the purposes of *The War Appropriation (United Nations Mutual Aid) Act, 1943*.

(2) The principal raised by way of loan under this Act and the interest thereon shall be a charge upon and payable out of the Consolidated Revenue Fund.

AGREEMENT BETWEEN THE GOVERNMENTS OF CANADA AND THE UNITED KINGDOM ON THE PRINCIPLES APPLYING TO THE PROVISION BY CANADA OF CANADIAN WAR SUPPLIES TO THE UNITED KINGDOM UNDER THE WAR APPROPRIATION (UNITED NATIONS MUTUAL AID) ACT OF CANADA 1943

Signed at Ottawa, February 11, 1944

Whereas Canada and the United Kingdom are associated in the present war, and

Whereas it is desirable that war supplies should be distributed among the United Nations in accordance with strategic needs of the war and in such manner as to contribute most effectively to the winning of the war and the establishment of peace, and

Whereas it is expedient that the conditions upon which such war supplies are made available by one United Nation to another should not be such as to burden post-war commerce, or lead to the imposition of trade restrictions or otherwise prejudice a just and enduring peace, and

Whereas the Governments of Canada and the United Kingdom are mutually desirous of concluding an agreement in regard to the conditions upon which Canadian war supplies will be made available to the United Kingdom,

The Undersigned, being duly authorized by their respective Governments for the purpose, have agreed as follows:—

Article I

The Government of Canada will make available under the War Appropriation (United Nations Mutual Aid) Act of Canada, 1943, to the Government of the United Kingdom such war supplies as the Government of Canada shall authorize from time to time to be provided.

Article II

The Government of the United Kingdom will continue to contribute to the defence of Canada and the strengthening thereof and will provide such articles, services, facilities or information as it may be in a position to supply and as may from time to time be determined by common agreement in the light of the development of the war.

Article III

The Government of the United Kingdom will, in support of any applications to the Government of Canada for the provision of war supplies under this agreement, furnish the Government of Canada with such relevant information as the Government of Canada may require for the purpose of deciding upon the applications and for executing the purposes of this agreement.

Article IV

The Government of the United Kingdom agrees to use any war supplies delivered to it under this agreement in the joint and effective prosecution of the war.

Article V

The Government of the United Kingdom will not without the consent of the Government of Canada sell to any other Government or to persons in other countries war supplies delivered to it under this agreement.

Article VI

The Government of Canada will not require the Government of the United Kingdom to re-deliver to the Government of Canada any war supplies delivered under this agreement except as specifically provided in Articles VII and VIII and subject to any special agreement which may be concluded in the circumstances contemplated in Article IX.

Article VII

Title to any cargo ships delivered under this agreement will remain with the Government of Canada and the ships shall be chartered to the Government of the United Kingdom on terms providing for their re-delivery.

Article VIII

Upon the cessation of hostilities in any major theatre of war, any war supplies which have been transferred to the Government of the United Kingdom under this agreement and are still in Canada or in ocean transit shall revert to Canadian ownership, except those supplies destined for a theatre of war in which hostilities have not ceased or supplies made available for relief purposes or such other supplies as the Government of Canada may specify.

Article IX

The Government of Canada reserves the right to request:

(a) the delivery, after the cessation of hostilities in any theatre of war, for relief and rehabilitation purposes, to another United Nation or to an international organization, of automotive equipment supplied under this agreement;

(*b*) the transfer to Canadian forces serving outside Canada after the cessation of hostilities of vehicles, aircraft, ordnance or military equipment supplied under this agreement to the Government of the United Kingdom if such war supplies are required for the use of such Canadian forces and are not required by the Government of the United Kingdom for military operations; and

(*c*) the return to Canada after the war, if required in Canada for Canadian purposes, of aircraft and automotive equipment supplied under this agreement which may still be serviceable, due regard being had to the degree of wastage likely to have been suffered by these articles, provided that when the identity of such Canadian equipment has been lost as a result of pooling arrangements or for other reasons, the Government of the United Kingdom may substitute equipment of a similar type.

The Government of the United Kingdom agrees to use its best endeavours to meet any such requests on such reasonable terms and conditions as shall be settled in consultation with the Government of Canada.

Article X

The Governments of Canada and the United Kingdom re-affirm their desire to promote mutually advantageous economic relations between their countries and throughout the world. They declare that their guiding purposes include the adoption of measures designed to promote employment, the production and consumption of goods, and the expansion of commerce through appropriate international agreements on commercial policy, with the object of contributing to the attainment of all the economic objectives set forth in the Declaration of August 14th, 1941, known as the Atlantic Charter.

Article XI

This agreement will take effect as from this day's date. It shall apply to war supplies furnished to the Government of the United Kingdom by the Government of Canada under the authority of the War Appropriation (United Nations Mutual Aid) Act of Canada, 1943, or substituted Act, including supplies furnished under the said Act before the conclusion of this agreement. It shall continue in force until a date to be agreed upon by the two Governments.

Dated at Ottawa, this eleventh day of February, nineteen hundred and forty-four.

Signed for and on behalf of the Government of Canada

W. L. MACKENZIE KING.

C. D. HOWE.

Signed for and on behalf of the Government of the United Kingdom

MALCOLM MACDONALD.

APPENDIX VII

The Lend-Lease and Mutual Aid Settlement

The 'Settlement for Lend-Lease, Reciprocal Aid, Surplus War Property and Claims' was effected by a joint statement appended to the 'Financial Agreement between The Governments of the United States and the United Kingdom' dated 6th December 1945 (Cmd. 6708), which was signed by the Hon. Fred M. Vinson, Secretary of the United States Treasury, and for the Government of the United Kingdom by the British Ambassador, Lord Halifax. The settlement was worked out in detail in 'Specific Agreements' concluded in March 1946 which are contained in Cmd. 6778, March 1946. See also Cmd. 7471, July 1948. For the discussion on the settlement see above, Chapter IX, section vi, p. 477.

THE LEND-LEASE AND MUTUAL AID SETTLEMENT

Joint Statement regarding Settlement for Lend-Lease, Reciprocal Aid, Surplus War Property and Claims

1. The Governments of the United States and the United Kingdom have reached an understanding for the settlement of Lend-Lease and Reciprocal Aid, for the acquisition of United States Army and Navy surplus property, and the United States interest in installations, located in the United Kingdom, and for the final settlement of the financial claims of each government against the other arising out of the conduct of the war. Specific agreements necessary to implement these understandings, setting forth the terms in detail, and consistent herewith, are in the course of preparation and will shortly be completed.

2. This settlement for Lend-Lease and Reciprocal Aid will be complete and final. In arriving at this settlement both governments have taken full cognizance of the benefits already received by them in the defeat of their common enemies. They have also taken full cognizance of the general obligations assumed by them in Article VII of the Mutual Aid Agreement of 23rd February, 1942, and the understandings agreed upon this day with regard to commercial policy. Pursuant to this settlement, both governments will continue to discuss arrangements for agreed action for the attainment of the economic objectives referred to in Article VII of the Mutual Aid Agreement. The Governments expect in these discussions to reach specific conclusions at an early date with respect to urgent problems such as those in the field of telecommunications and civil aviation. In the light of all the foregoing, both governments agree that no further benefits will be sought as consideration for Lend-Lease and Reciprocal Aid.

3. The net sum due from the United Kingdom to the United States for the settlement of Lend-Lease and Reciprocal Aid, for the acquisition of surplus property, and the United States interest in installations, located in the United Kingdom, and for the settlement of claims shall be $650,000,000 subject to the accounting adjustment referred to below. This amount consists of

(a) a net sum of $118,000,000 representing the difference between the amount of the services and supplies furnished or to be furnished by each government to the other government after V-J day through Lend-Lease and Reciprocal Aid channels, less the net sum due to the United Kingdom under the claims settlement, and

(b) a net sum of $532,000,000 for all other Lend-Lease and Reciprocal Aid items, and for surplus property, and the United States interest in installations, located in the United Kingdom and owned by the United States Government.

The actual amounts due to the respective governments for items included in (a) above other than claims will, however, be ascertained by accounting in due course, and the total sum of $650,000,000 will be adjusted for any difference between the sum of $118,000,000 mentioned above, and the actual sum found to be due. All new transactions between the two governments after 31st December, 1945, will be settled by cash payment.

4. The total liability found to be due to the Government of the United States will be discharged on the same terms as those specified in the Financial Agreement concluded this day for the discharge of the credit provided therein.

5. In addition to the financial payments referred to above, the two governments have agreed upon the following:—

(a) appropriate non-discriminatory treatment will be extended to United States nationals in the use and disposition of installations in which there is a United States interest;

(b) appropriate settlements for the Lend-Lease interest in installations other than in the United Kingdom and the colonial dependencies will be made on disposal of the installations;

(c) the United States reserves its right of recapture of any Lend-Lease articles held by United Kingdom armed forces, but the United States has indicated that it does not intend to exercise generally this right of recapture;

(d) disposals for military use to forces other than the United Kingdom armed forces of Lend-Lease articles held by the United Kingdom armed forces at V-J day, and disposals for civilian use other than in the United Kingdom and the colonial dependencies of such Lend-Lease articles, will be made only with the consent of the United States Government, and any net proceeds will be paid to the United States Government. The United Kingdom Government agrees that except to a very limited extent it will not release for civilian use in, or export from, the United Kingdom and colonial dependencies, Lend-Lease articles held by the United Kingdom armed forces;

(e) the Government of the United Kingdom will use its best endeavours to prevent the export to the United States of any surplus property transferred in accordance with this understanding.

6. The Government of the United Kingdom agrees that, when requested by the Government of the United States from time to time prior to 31st December, 1951, it will transfer, in cash, pounds sterling to an aggregate

dollar value not in excess of $50,000,000 at the exchange rates prevailing at the times of transfer, to be credited against the dollar payments due to the Government of the United States as principal under this settlement. The Government of the United States will use these pounds sterling exclusively to acquire land or to acquire or construct buildings in the United Kingdom and the colonial dependencies for the use of the Government of the United States, and for carrying out educational programmes in accordance with agreements to be concluded between the two governments.

7. The arrangements set out in this statement are without prejudice to any settlements concerning Lend-Lease and Reciprocal Aid which may be negotiated between the Government of the United States and the Governments of Australia, New Zealand, the Union of South Africa, and India.

APPENDIX VIII

The War Claims Settlement between Canada and the United Kingdom

The War Claims Settlement between the United Kingdom and Canada was concluded on 6th March 1946 following negotiations at Ottawa between the two Governments. The text is printed in Cmd. 6904, September 1946: 'Financial Agreement and Agreement on the Settlement of War Claims between the Governments of the United Kingdom and of Canada', 6th March 1946. The Financial Agreement provided for a Canadian credit to the United Kingdom in the transitional post-war period. See Chapter XI (pp. 482–88) on the post-war settlement with Canada.

AGREEMENT ON THE SETTLEMENT OF WAR CLAIMS BETWEEN THE GOVERNMENT OF THE UNITED KINGDOM AND THE GOVERNMENT OF CANADA

The Government of the United Kingdom and the Government of Canada, in order to arrive at a prompt and final settlement of all outstanding accounts between them arising out of the war, agree as follows:

ARTICLE 1

The Government of the United Kingdom will pay to the Government of Canada the sum of $150,000,000 and thereupon each of the two Governments will, with the exceptions noted below, cancel all claims against the other which arose on or after September 3, 1939, and prior to March 1, 1946, in respect of supplies, services, facilities and accommodation delivered or furnished during that period, whether such claims are known or unknown.

ARTICLE 2

The two Governments agree that such payment and cancellation shall be in full settlement of all such claims and neither Government will raise or pursue any such claims against the other.

ARTICLE 3

The settlement covered by this Agreement includes without limitation thereto—

(a) All claims of the Government of Canada in respect of the construction for the Admiralty of ships which were in the course of construction on September 1, 1945, and which were to be completed by agreement between the two Governments;

(b) All claims arising out of the operations of the Inspection Board of the United Kingdom and Canada and in this case the period covered by the settlement shall extend to March 31, 1946, the Government of Canada taking over all the assets and liabilities of that Board as of that date;

524

(c) All claims of the Government of the United Kingdom arising out of the operation by the Department of Munitions and Supply of Canada of joint production projects and all claims relating to the period before March 1, 1946, arising from past or future re-negotiation of contracts or the retroactive adjustment of prices paid by or charged to the Government of the United Kingdom in Canada;

(d) All claims between the two Governments arising from the sharing of profits or losses before March 1, 1946, under contracts or arrangements made before that date and where projects covered by profit or loss sharing agreements continue in operation beyond that date, shares of profits or losses accruing on and after that date shall not be affected by this Agreement except in the case of the Inspection Board covered in paragraph (b) above;

(e) All claims between the two Governments arising from the disposal in the United Kingdom of surplus war assets of the Government of Canada, or from the disposal in Canada of surplus war assets of the Government of the United Kingdom, provided that this Agreement shall not prejudice the right of either Government to remove any of its surplus war assets from the country of the other, either for its own use or for transfer to others; and

(f) All claims of the Government of Canada in respect of the costs incurred by it under contracts entered into before March 1, 1946, for the manufacture of locomotives and rolling stock in Canada for the Government of India, without prejudice to the right of the Government of the United Kingdom to recover the amount of such claims from the Government of India.

Article 4

(i) The balance in the United Kingdom Suspense Account held by the Bank of Canada on February 28, 1946, shall be paid to the Government of the United Kingdom.

(ii) The balance in the United Kingdom Cash Receipts Account held by the Receiver General of Canada on February 28, 1946, shall be paid to the Government of Canada without prejudice to the right of the Government of the United Kingdom to claim reimbursement from third countries in respect of payments made on their behalf out of the United Kingdom Cash Receipts Account.

Article 5

The settlement covered by this Agreement shall not include the following—

(a) The loan to the Government of the United Kingdom under the War Appropriation (United Kingdom Financing) Act, 1942, which is covered by another agreement;

(b) The amount of $425,000,000 owing by the Government of the United Kingdom to the Government of Canada with respect to the British Commonwealth Air Training Plan, which is covered by another agreement;

(c) Claims of the two Governments arising out of the sharing of military relief expenditures which are to be dealt with in accordance with the procedures already established or to be established;

(d) Claims arising out of established procedures under which periodical settlements are made in regard to payment of pensions and war service gratuities, reimbursement of expenditures for salaries, pay and allowances, travelling and living expenses of personnel on an individual basis, the transfer of personal funds of prisoners of war and other similar payments of a routine nature;

(e) Claims arising out of the settlement of accounts between postal administrations;

(f) Balances held by departments of either Government on behalf of and to the order of departments of the other Government.

ARTICLE 6

Each Government agrees to repay to the other amounts paid since February 28, 1946, in respect of claims cancelled under this Agreement.

ARTICLE 7

The two Governments will consult together, through their appropriate departments and representatives, concerning the interpretation and implementation of this Agreement.

In witness whereof the undersigned, being duly authorized thereto by their respective Governments, have signed this Agreement.

Signed in duplicate at Ottawa this 6th day of March, 1946.

For the Government of Canada:

J. L. ILSLEY,

Minister of Finance.

For the Government of the United Kingdom:

MALCOLM MACDONALD,

High Commissioner for the United Kingdom.

APPENDIX IX

The United Kingdom Balance of Payments in World War II

The following statement and tables, prepared by the Treasury in February 1951, were received after the text of this book was completed. They are based on more complete data than were available when Chapters VII and XI were written and carry the analysis further than any of the statistical papers published during the latter part of the war and immediately after it.

THE UNITED KINGDOM BALANCE OF PAYMENTS IN WORLD WAR II

1. In the attached tables are assembled the basic facts about the development of the United Kingdom (and sterling area) external financial position in World War II, which for this purpose is taken as running from September 1939 to December 1945.

2. Complete accounts of this kind were not collected during World War II. There are good records of dollar incomings and outgoings, and good records of our relations with Canada. There are good records, likewise, of relations with some individual non-sterling countries. All this steadily improved from 1940 onwards, although it never reached the clarity of definition and comprehensiveness which has been developed since. The data about relationships with other sterling area countries are more fragmentary. Material on Lend-Lease and Reciprocal Aid is very complex and much more research would be needed before it could be broken down in detail with any certitude.

3. In these tables, an attempt has been made to express the balance of payments in a manner which includes free deliveries under Lend-Lease and Reciprocal Aid alongside cash transactions; in other words, this seeks to cover the whole of the international transfers to and from the United Kingdom, and not simply those which were paid for in cash. In the summary, Table I, a division is made between 'War' transactions—munitions transfers and inter-governmental payments for war supplies and services—and 'Civil' transactions. It is impossible to draw a hard-and-fast line between the two, and some items have no doubt been included in one which, on a precise definition, should be in the other. Nevertheless, the distinction is of some significance.

4. It would no doubt be possible to improve these figures if substantially more research work was done. Additional research might establish details more firmly. But it must be recognised that in any event there are huge gaps in the records, especially in the early years of the war, and it would be impossible by any expenditure of effort to provide estimates which could be regarded as being even as reliable as our returns for post-war years. On the other hand, there is no reason to suppose that research

would lead to significant alterations of the general picture as presented in these tables, and we would regard the tables as being reasonably adequate for historical purposes and for drawing the conclusions about the past which guide policy in the future.

16th February 1951.

UNITED KINGDOM BALANCE OF PAYMENTS 1939–45

I. SUMMARY

£000 million

	Total	U.S.A.	Canada	R.S.A.[a] (excl. Egypt and Palestine)	Other
CURRENT DEFICIT					
'War' Transactions					
Munitions	5·4	4·1	1·3	0·0	0·0
Other Government payments	3·6	0·0	0·0	2·3	1·3
Total war expenditure .	9·0	4·1	1·3	2·3	1·3
Reciprocal aid . . .	2·1	1·3	—	—	0·8
Government receipts . .	1·8	0·0	0·7	0·7	0·4
Deficit	5·1	2·8	0·6	1·6	0·1
'Civil' Transactions					
Food imports . . .	2·8	0·8	0·6	1·0	0·4
Raw materials . . .	2·1	0·6	0·3	0·7	0·5
Other imports (incl. ships and oil)	1·9	1·8	0·0	0·1	—
Shipping (net) . . .	0·6	0·7	0·1	−0·2	0·0
Other invisibles (net) . .	−0·5	−0·2	−0·2	−0·2	0·1
United Kingdom exports .	−2·0	−0·2	−0·2	−1·1	−0·5
Deficit	4·9	3·5	0·6	0·3	0·5
DEFICIT 'WAR' AND 'CIVIL' .	10·0	6·3	1·2	1·9	0·6
MEANS OF FINANCING					
Gifts to United Kingdom .	7·5	6·7	0·8	—	—
Gifts by United Kingdom .	−2·1	−1·3	—	—	−0·8
Sale of investments . .	1·1	0·2	0·3	0·6	0·0
Accumulation of liabilities .	3·5	0·2	0·2	2·2	0·9
Change in reserves (gain, −) .	−0·1	−0·1	—	—	—
Requisitioning of balances of gold and dollars . .	0·1	0·1	—	—	—
Inter-regional transactions and errors and omissions . .	—	0·5	−0·1	−0·9	0·5
	10·0	6·3	1·2	1·9	0·6

[a] R.S.A. = Rest of the Sterling Area, i.e. the Sterling Area except for the United Kingdom.

II. UNITED KINGDOM GENERAL BALANCE OF PAYMENTS

£000 million

	Sept.–Dec. 1939	1940	1941	1942	1943	1944	1945	Total
Current Account Debits								
Imports (including *all* supplies of munitions)								
Munitions	0·1	0·2	0·5	0·8	1·4	1·7	0·7	5·4
Food, drink and tobacco . .	0·1	0·4	0·4	0·4	0·4	0·6	0·5	2·8
Raw materials and semi-manufactures	0·1	0·3	0·3	0·3	0·4	0·4	0·3	2·1
Other (including ships) . .	0·0	0·1	0·1	0·3	0·5	0·5	0·4	1·9
Total . . .	0·3	1·0	1·3	1·8	2·7	3·2	1·9	12·2
Shipping (cash + lend-lease) .	0·0	0·1	0·2	0·2	0·2	0·3	0·1	1·1
Government overseas expenditure (excl. munitions) . . .	0·0	0·4	0·4	0·6	0·7	0·7	0·8	3·6
Total debits . .	0·3	1·5	1·9	2·6	3·6	4·2	2·8	16·9
Credits								
Exports (cash) . . .	0·1	0·4	0·4	0·3	0·2	0·2	0·4	2·0
Reciprocal aid (inc. services) .	—	—	—	0·1	0·7	0·8	0·5	2·1
Other Governments' expenditure in United Kingdom . .	0·0	0·1	0·1	0·2	0·4	0·6	0·4	1·8
Shipping (cash) . . .	0·0	0·1	0·1	0·1	0·1	0·1	0·0	0·5
Other (net) and errors and omissions	0·0	0·1	0·2	0·2	0·1	0·0	−0·1	0·5
Total credits . .	0·1	0·7	0·8	0·9	1·5	1·7	1·2	6·9
Deficit on current account + errors and omissions (= disinvestment and financing)	0·2	0·8	1·1	1·7	2·1	2·5	1·6	10·0
Disinvestment and financing account								
Grants, etc.: *From* United States	—	—	0·3	1·0	2·0	2·4	1·0	6·7
Canada .	—	—	—	0·2	0·1	0·2	0·3	0·8
To(−) United States	—	—	—	−0·1	−0·4	−0·5	−0·3	−1·3
Other .	—	—	—	—	−0·3	−0·3	−0·2	−0·8
Sales of securities, etc. . .	0·0	0·2	0·3	0·2	0·2	0·1	0·1	1·1
Increase in liabilities (£ and $) .	0·1	0·2	0·6	0·5	0·7	0·7	0·7	3·5
Decrease in reserves . .	0·0	0·4	−0·1	−0·1	−0·2	−0·1	0·0	−0·1
Requisitioned gold and dollars .	0·1	0·0	—	—	—	—	—	0·1
Total disinvestment and financing .	0·2	0·8	1·1	1·7	2·1	2·5	1·6	10·0

Note. To some extent the pricing of lend-lease goods was too high, for purposes of comparing economic efforts—though not for the construction of a hypothetical wartime balance of payments. This applied mainly to munitions, where the figure of 5·4, above, might be reduced to 3·9 if a more "appropriate" exchange rate was used; and to shipbuilding, reducing "other imports" from 2·0 to 1·8. See R. G. D. Allen's article in the journal of the *Royal Statistical Society*, 1946, op. cit., Table 11. The total of Grants from U.S. would thus be 5·0 instead of 6·7.

III. STERLING AREA BALANCE IN
UNITED STATES DOLLARS (GROSS)

$000 million

Current Account with U.S.A.	Sept. 1939– Dec. 1940	1941	1942	1943	1944	1945	Total
Debits							
U.K.: Imports(*a*)							
Cash: Munitions	0·6	1·2	0·6	0·1	0·1	0·0	2·6
Food, drink and tobacco . .	0·2	0·0	0·0	0·1	0·1	0·2	0·6
Raw materials . . .	0·4	0·1	0·0	0·0	0·0	0·0	0·5
Other	0·9	0·2	0·1	0·0	0·1	0·5	1·8
Lend-lease:							
Munitions	—	0·2	1·8	4·4	5·6	1·8	13·8
Food	—	0·3	0·5	0·6	0·8	0·3	2·5
Raw materials . . .	—	0·1	0·4	0·6	0·6	0·3	2·0
Other	—	0·2	0·7	1·8	1·7	1·2	5·6
Total imports . .	2·1	2·3	4·1	7·6	9·0	4·3	29·4
Other debits	0·7	0·6	1·1	1·2	1·4	1·1	6·1
Total U.K. . . .	2·8	2·9	5·2	8·8	10·4	5·4	35·5
R.S.A. Payments and Lend-lease supplies	0·5	0·7	1·0	1·3	1·3	1·2	6·0
Total debits . . .	3·3	3·6	6·2	10·1	11·7	6·6	41·5
Credits							
U.K.: Exports	0·2	0·1	0·1	0·1	0·1	0·1	0·7
Reciprocal aid . . .	—	—	0·3	1·5	1·9	1·3	5·0
Other credits (incl. errors and omissions) . . .	0·6	0·6	0·7	0·8	0·9	0·9	4·5
Total U.K. . . .	0·8	0·7	1·1	2·4	2·9	2·3	10·2
R.S.A. Receipts and reciprocal aid .	0·7	0·8	0·7	1·1	1·4	1·3	6·0
Total credits . .	1·5	1·5	1·8	3·5	4·3	3·6	16·2
Sterling Area deficit on current account with U.S.A.	1·8	2·1	4·4	6·6	7·4	3·0	25·3
Capital items entering gold and dollar deficit	0·8	0·0	0·0	−0·1	0·0	0·2	0·9
Total deficit with U.S.A. . .	2·6	2·1	4·4	6·5	7·4	3·2	26·2
Gold and dollar payments to Canada .	0·2	—	0·0	0·2	0·1	0·1	0·6
Other countries . . .	0·5	0·2	0·1	0·2	0·5	0·3	1·8
New gold, and gold and dollar dis-hoarding(−)	−1·4(*d*)	−0·6	−0·4	−0·4	−0·3	−0·4	−3·5
Total net gold and dollar deficit(*b*) .	1·9	1·7	4·1	6·5	7·7	3·2	25·1
Financing of deficit(*b*)							
Sales of securities, etc. . . .	0·3	0·3	0·0	0·1	0·0	0·1	0·8
Loans(*c*)	—	0·4	0·0	—	—	0·6	1·0
Decrease in gross gold and U.S. $ reserves(*c*)	1·6	−0·1	−0·4	−0·8	−0·6	0·0	−0·3
Lend-lease: U.K. (and Colonies) .	—	1·1	4·2	8·1	9·8	3·8	27·0
R.S.A.	—	0·0	0·6	0·9	1·0	0·6	3·1
Reciprocal aid: U.K. . . .	—	—	−0·3	−1·5	−1·9	−1·3	−5·0
R.S.A. . . .	—	—	—	−0·3	−0·6	−0·6	−1·5
Total financing . .	1·9	1·7	4·1	6·5	7·7	3·2	25·1

(*a*) Including *all* Lend-Lease supplies attributable to U.K. (not only imports).
(*b*) N.B. that sales of securities etc.—apart from collateral—are regarded as *financing* items.
(*c*) Belgian 1941–43 gold loan excluded in this table.
(*d*) Includes −0·2 for change in private dollar balances, and −0·4 (possibly too low) for gold windfalls.

IV. STERLING AREA BALANCE WITH CANADA

	Sept. 1939 Dec. 1940	1941	1942	1943	1944	1945	Total	Total
	£ million							$000 million
Debits								
U.K. Imports, etc.								
Munitions(a) .	70	130	210	260	330	290	1,290	5·2
Food, etc. . .	70	70	70	90	110	130	540	2·2
Raw materials .	50	60	40	40	40	40	270	1·1
Other . :	—	10	10	10	0	0	30	0·1
Total . . .	190	270	330	400	480	460	2,130	8·6
Other payments .	30	40	50	60	50	50	280	1·1
Total U.K. .	220	310	380	460	530	510	2,410	9·7
R.S.A. Payments . .	30	50	70	50	60	80	340	1·4
Total debits .	250	360	450	510	590	590	2,750	11·1
Credits								
U.K. Exports . .	40	30	30	20	20	20	160	0·7
Canadian expenditure in U.K. (etc.) . .	—	20	40	210(c)	250	160	680	2·6
Other receipts (incl. errors and omissions) .	50	50	70	70	70	60	370	1·5
Total U.K. .	90	100	140	300	340	240	1,210	4·8
R.S.A. Receipts . .	20	30	20	20	20	30	140	0·6
Total credits .	110	130	160	320	360	270	1,350	5·4
Sterling Area deficit on current account . . .	140	230	290	190	230	320	1,400	5·7
Financing of deficit								
Sales of securities, etc. .	60	60	80	20	20	20	260	1·1
Gold and U.S. $ payments . . .	60	—	10	40	20	20	150	0·6
Decrease in Canadian $ holdings . . .	0	0	0	0	−20	10	−10	0·0
Increase in U.K. sterling liabilities . . .	20	170	−180	10	0	0	20	0·1
Loans . . .	—	—	160	0	−10	−10	140	0·5
Grants, etc.								
To U.K.(b) . .	—	—	220	120	200	260	800	3·2
R.S.A. . . .	—	—	—	0	20	20	40	0·2
	140	230	290	190	230	320	1,400	5·7

(a) Including (1940–42) factory construction.
(b) Including Canadian Contribution (1942), Mutual Aid, Section 3 Advances (later written off), etc.
(c) Including purchase of war factories in Canada and other special transactions, 100.

V. UNITED KINGDOM BALANCE OF PAYMENTS WITH REST OF STERLING AREA (EXCLUDING EGYPT, SUDAN, PALESTINE AND TRANSJORDAN)

£ million

	Sept. 1939– Dec. 1940	1941	1942	1943	1944	1945	Total
Debits							
Imports: Food, drink and tobacco . . .	210	150	150	130	150	160	950
Raw materials . .	160	110	100	100	120	90	680
Other . . .	30	20	20	20	20	20	130
Total . . .	400	280	270	250	290	270	1,760
Overseas war expenditure .	100	200	360	470	500	650	2,280
Total payments . . .	500	480	630	720	790	920	4,040
Credits							
Exports	280	200	170	120	150	190	1,110
Other Governments' expenditure in U.K.	50	80	120	140	150	130	670
Other (net)	120	80	50	40	40	60	390
	450	360	340	300	340	380	2,170
Deficit on current account . .	50	120	290	420	450	540	1,870
Disinvestment and financing							
Sales of assets . . .	50	120	130	140	60	60	560
Increase in liabilities . .	230	130	340	440	490	520	2,150
Purchases of gold (−) . .	−190	−140	− 90	−110	− 90	− 90	−710
Net U.S. $ surplus of R.S.A. (−)	− 50	− 30	− 50	−120	−120	− 30	−400
Net Canadian $ deficit of R.S.A.	10	20	50	30	20	30	160
Total identified disinvestment and financing	50	100	380	380	360	490	1,760
Errors and omissions; non-$ inter-area transfers, private capital movements, etc. . . .	—	20	− 90	40	90	50	110

Index

INDEX

(The suffix letter 'n' denotes a footnote)

S.O. Code No. : 63/111/3/14*.